Meeting the Ethical Challenges of Leadership

Sixth Edition

To my students

Meeting the Ethical Challenges of Leadership

Casting Light or Shadow

Sixth Edition

Craig E. Johnson
George Fox University

Los Angeles | London | New Delhi
Singapore | Washington DC | Melbourne

FOR INFORMATION:

SAGE Publications, Inc.
2455 Teller Road
Thousand Oaks, California 91320
E-mail: order@sagepub.com

SAGE Publications Ltd.
1 Oliver's Yard
55 City Road
London EC1Y 1SP
United Kingdom

SAGE Publications India Pvt. Ltd.
B 1/I 1 Mohan Cooperative Industrial Area
Mathura Road, New Delhi 110 044
India

SAGE Publications Asia-Pacific Pte. Ltd.
3 Church Street
#10-04 Samsung Hub
Singapore 049483

Acquisitions Editor: Maggie Stanley
Development Editor: Abbie Rickard
eLearning Editor: Katie Ancheta
Editorial Assistant: Neda Dallal
Production Editor: Olivia Weber-Stenis
Copy Editor: Erin Livingston
Typesetter: C&M Digitals (P) Ltd.
Proofreader: Ellen Howard
Indexer: Diggs Publication Services
Cover Designer: Candice Harman
Marketing Manager: Ashlee Blunk

Printed in the United States of America.

ISBN 978-1-5063-2163-9

This book is printed on acid-free paper.

Certified Chain of Custody
Promoting Sustainable Forestry
www.sfiprogram.org
SFI-01268

SFI label applies to text stock

19 20 21 10 9 8 7 6 5 4 3 2

Brief Contents

Detailed Contents

Preface

You have chosen an excellent time to study ethical leadership. Interest in the topic is greater than ever, generating a constant stream of new books, articles, and research studies as well as the creation of new leadership ethics units and courses. We are learning much more about the factors that make up ethical (and unethical) leadership, how leaders make moral choices, how leaders create ethical groups and organizations, how leaders can behave more ethically in a global society, and so on. You have a rapidly growing body of knowledge to draw from in your efforts to become a more ethical leader and follower.

This edition of *Meeting the Ethical Challenges of Leadership* incorporates the latest developments in the field but, like previous versions, is guided by seven principles. First, there are few topics as important as leadership ethics. To highlight that fact, I've adopted Parker Palmer's metaphor of light and shadow as the book's central metaphor. Palmer reminds us that leaders have the power to do significant benefit or substantial harm. In extreme cases, leaders literally make the difference between life and death for their followers.

Second, we need to recognize the reality of bad leadership. Understanding why and how leaders cast shadows can help us prevent destructive behaviors and promote positive leadership. At the same time, we can also learn a great deal from the example of good leaders. Models of ethical and unethical leadership are found throughout the text.

Third, there are important ethical demands associated with the leadership role. Those who want to serve as leaders have a responsibility to exercise their authority on behalf of others. There are also ethical challenges associated with the follower role.

Fourth, the study of leadership ethics must draw from a wide variety of academic disciplines and traditions. Philosophers have been interested in the moral behavior of leaders for centuries. In the modern era, they have been joined by social scientists, resulting in significant advances in our understanding of moral and immoral leadership. As a consequence, material for this text is drawn not only from philosophy but also from political science, psychology, social psychology, neuroscience, management, business ethics, communication, education, sociology, and other fields. This multidisciplinary approach introduces readers to (1) how moral decisions are made (what scholars describe as the descriptive perspective on ethics) and (2) how to lead in a moral manner (the prescriptive or normative perspective).

Fifth, both theory and practice are essential to learning. I try to balance presentation of important concepts and research findings with opportunities for application through self-assessments, case analyses, and exploration exercises.

Sixth, texts should be readable. My objective is to write in an informal, accessible style. I don't hesitate to bring in my own experiences and, in some cases, my biases in the hope of engaging readers and sparking discussion and disagreement.

Seventh, improvement is the bottom line. The ultimate goal of teaching and writing about ethics is to produce more ethical leaders. I believe that ethical development is part of leadership (and followership) development. Leaders and followers can develop their ability to make and carry through on their moral decisions, just as they develop their other competencies. *Meeting the Ethical Challenges of Leadership* is designed to help students build their ethical expertise through theoretical understanding, skill development, case and film analysis, group and class discussions, personal assessment and reflection, research projects, and writing assignments.

KEY FEATURES

Examples and Case Studies

Whatever their specific contexts, leaders face similar kinds of ethical choices. For that reason, I draw examples from a wide variety of settings: business, medicine, sports, law enforcement, education, government, nonprofit organizations, and the military. Cases continue to play an important role in this edition. Discussion probes at the end of each case encourage readers to reflect on key ethics issues and concepts and to apply what they have learned from that chapter to these narratives.

Leadership Ethics at the Movies

Each of these short summaries introduces a feature film or documentary (new to this edition) that illustrates principles related to the chapter discussion. This feature is designed to encourage students to (1) identify the important ethical principles portrayed in the film, (2) analyze and evaluate how the characters respond to moral dilemmas, and (3) draw ethical implications and applications from the movie. I provide discussion questions for each film to get you started.

Self-Assessments

The self-assessments are designed to help readers measure their performance with respect to important behaviors, skills, or concepts discussed in the chapters. Two self-assessments are found at the end of each chapter.

Focus on Follower Ethics

This feature addresses the ethical challenges facing followers. Followers are critical to the success of any enterprise. The "Focus on Follower Ethics" box in each chapter helps students recognize and master the ethical demands of the follower role.

Implications and Applications

This section, found immediately after the body of each chapter, reviews key ideas and their ramifications for readers.

For Further Exploration, Challenge, and Self-Assessment

This feature encourages interaction with chapter content. Activities include brainstorming exercises, small-group discussions, conversational dyads, debates, self-analysis, personal reflection, and application and research projects.

WHAT'S NEW TO THIS EDITION?

The most significant addition is a new chapter on exercising ethical influence. Leadership is the exercise of influence, and moral considerations should guide leaders' selection of influence tactics. Chapter 7 introduces the ethical issues surrounding four sets of important leader influence tools: compliance gaining, the communication of expectations (the Pygmalion Effect), argumentation, and negotiation. The chapter concludes with a look at leader resistance to persuasion.

Along with the additional chapter, there is new/revised/expanded coverage of the following:

- Leader hypocrisy
- Leader personality disorders
- Moral identity
- Duty orientation
- Developing leadership virtues
- Values
- Personal mission statements
- Story and character development
- Administrative evil
- Ethical followership
- Decision-making formats
- Intelligent disobedience
- Ethics of virtual teams
- Corporate citizenship
- Corporate governance
- Ethical socialization
- Common morality
- Crisis preparation
- Organizational resilience
- Extreme leadership

Most of the case studies from previous editions have been replaced. Some of the new cases in this edition involve Malala Yousafzai, Team Foxcatcher, Bill Cosby, Turing Pharmaceutical, Volkswagen, retired Duke track coach Al Buehler, the Flint Michigan water crisis, Subway's Jared Fogle, the Ashley Madison website, the National Football League concussion epidemic, Scotland's HBOS bank, Amazon, The Container Store, Apple and Foxconn, the Ebola epidemic, New Orleans hurricane recovery, and explorer Ernest Shackleton. Cases based on real-life events, held over from the fifth edition, have been updated. Other fictional cases have been added. There are new self-assessments related to narcissism, apology, altruism, duty orientation, argumentation, negotiation, class project social loafing, moral foundations theory, and corporate Samaritans.

ANCILLARIES

Instructor Teaching Site

A password-protected instructor's manual is available at **study.sagepub.com/johnsonme cl6e** to help instructors plan and teach their courses. These resources have been designed to help instructors make the classes as practical and interesting as possible for students:

- **Overview for the instructor** offers the author's insights on how to use this book most effectively in a course on leadership ethics.
- **Chapter tests** offer a variety of questions to assist with assessment of student learning.
- **PowerPoint slides** capture key concepts and terms for each chapter for use in lectures and review.
- **Leadership ethics sample course syllabus** provides a model for structuring a course.
- **Leadership seminar sample syllabus** is an additional course option for a seminar format.
- **Teaching strategies** offer ideas and insights into various approaches to teaching and learning.
- **Assignments and projects** provide unique and highly creative activities for meaningful involvement in learning.
- **SAGE journal articles** give access to full journal articles that instructors can assign and use as further teaching tools in class.
- **Case notes** provide an essential reference and teaching tool for using the case studies in the book.

Student Study Site

An open-access student study site can be found at **study.sagepub.com/johnsonmecl6e.** The site offers **SAGE journal articles**, with access to recent, relevant, full-text articles from SAGE's leading research journals. Each article supports and expands on the concepts presented in the book. This feature also provides discussion questions to focus and guide student interpretation.

Acknowledgments

Colleagues and students provided practical and emotional support during the writing of this edition, just as they did for earlier versions. Kristina Findley and Michelle and Paul Shelton contributed ancillary materials. Students enrolled in my leadership seminar, doctoral ethics seminar, business ethics, and leadership communication classes shaped this and earlier editions by responding to chapter content, exercises, and cases. I am particularly grateful to instructors who adopted the first five editions of *Meeting the Ethical Challenges of Leadership*, which made this sixth edition possible. I also want to thank readers, both faculty and students, who have e-mailed me with comments and corrections. I've had the opportunity to meet some of you at International Leadership Association conferences, where you introduced yourselves and offered encouragement and feedback. Five reviewers provided insightful responses that guided my revisions for this edition. Editor Maggie Stanley ably picked up where her predecessors at SAGE left off, assisted by the rest of the SAGE staff. Finally, I want to once again thank my wife, Mary, who continues to encourage my writing efforts, though it often means less time together.

SAGE gratefully acknowledges the contributions of the following reviewers: Cheryl L. Evans, University of Central Oklahoma; Rita Fields, Madonna University; Carolyn J. Thompson, University of Missouri–Kansas City; and LaVonne Williams-Fedynich, Texas A&M University–Kingsville.

Introduction

LEADERS: THE BAD NEWS AND THE GOOD NEWS

When it comes to leaders, there is both bad news and good news. The bad news is that wherever we turn—business, military, politics, medicine, education, or religion—we find leaders toppled by ethical scandals. Nearly all have sacrificed their positions of leadership and their reputations. Many face civil lawsuits, criminal charges, and jail time. The costs can be even greater for followers. Consider, for example, the following:

- Seventy-eight senior executives from J.P. Morgan, Goldman Sachs, Merrill Lynch, Deutsche Bank, Citigroup, Wells Fargo, and other banks have been charged with concealing risks and lying to investors, which contributed to the world financial crisis of 2007–2008. Millions lost their jobs and homes during the global recession.

- Executives at air bag manufacturer Takata refused to acknowledge that the company's air bags could explode, sending metal shrapnel into drivers and passengers. At least six people were killed, and 100 were injured; nearly 35 million vehicles were recalled.

- Riots broke out in Ferguson, Baltimore, Chicago, Minneapolis, and other American cities after police were accused of the unjustified killings of black suspects.

- Owners and managers of a Massachusetts pharmacy allegedly failed to sterilize a pain drug shipped to hospitals and other health care providers, triggering a meningitis outbreak. Two company executives face murder charges.

- The Islamic terrorist group Boko Haram has driven 1.5 million people from their homes in Nigeria through killings and kidnappings. The militants force kidnapped girls, such as the nearly 300 abducted from the Chibok school, to convert to Islam and to marry Boko Haram soldiers. Some become fighters themselves.

- Executives at Mitsubishi admitted to overstating the fuel economy ratings of hundreds of thousands of the company's cars.

- Officials at Swiss food giant Nestle acknowledged that the seafood it buys from Thailand is caught and processed by slave laborers.

- Fans around the world were disillusioned when South African runner Oscar Pistorius, the first double amputee to participate in the Olympics and a champion of the disabled, was convicted of murdering his girlfriend.

- Former Detroit Mayor Kwame Kilpatrick was jailed for taking $9.6 million in kickbacks for steering city contracts to a friend and using nonprofit funds to pay for personal expenses. His corrupt administration helped push the city into bankruptcy.
- A West Virginia coal mine explosion took the lives of 29 miners after officials at Massey Energy failed to follow basic safety procedures. The company's founder was convicted of lying to safety authorities.
- Coaches and administrators at Baylor University ignored or downplayed sexual assault allegations against football players who were later convicted of rape. Instead of reporting the accusations as required by law, officials discouraged victims from filing reports, leaving them in continued danger from their assailants.

The misery caused by unethical leaders drives home an important point: Ethics is at the heart of leadership.[1] When we assume the benefits of leadership, we also assume ethical burdens. I believe that as leaders, we must make every effort to act in such a way as to benefit rather than damage others, to cast light instead of shadow. Doing so will significantly reduce the likelihood that we will join the future ranks of fallen leaders.

Fortunately, we can also find plenty of examples of leaders who brighten the lives of those around them. That's the good news. Consider these examples:

- When health authorities were slow to respond to the Ebola crisis in West Africa, local residents and international volunteers stepped in to care for the sick. They were honored as *Time* magazine's 2014 People of the Year.
- Former president Jimmy Carter, in his 90s, continues to work with Habitat for Humanity and his humanitarian Carter Center, even after a brain cancer diagnosis.
- Ordinary citizens of New Orleans spearheaded restoration of the city after Hurricane Katrina, the largest natural disaster in United States history.
- The 2015 winners of the CNN Hero Award are involved in helping others through a variety of community efforts ranging from providing free medical care to the homeless in Pittsburgh to harvesting rainwater in India to offering support to single mothers stricken with cancer in Arizona.
- Myanmar's Daw Aung San Suu Kyi, after decades under house arrest, is now assisting with the country's transition from military rule to a democracy.
- Managers and employees at the Fukushima Daiichi Nuclear Power Plant in Japan risked massive radiation exposure to prevent a meltdown following a tsunami that severely damaged the facility.

- Two teachers were hailed as heroes during a theater shooting in Louisiana. The first teacher jumped in front of the second to shield her from bullets and was wounded. The second teacher, though shot in the leg, was able to crawl to a fire alarm and pull it to summon help.
- Pope Francis has inspired millions of Catholics and non-Catholics alike through his humble lifestyle and compassion for the world's poor.

You should find this book helpful if you are a leader or an aspiring leader who (1) acknowledges that there are ethical consequences associated with the leadership role, (2) wants to exert positive influence over others, (3) seeks to make more informed ethical choices and to follow through on your decisions, and (4) desires to foster ethical behavior in others. You will also find useful insights if you are a follower who wants to behave ethically and bring out the best in your leaders.

There is no guarantee that after reading this book, you will act in a more ethical fashion in every situation. Nor can you be sure that others will reach the same conclusions as you do about what is the best answer to an ethical dilemma or that you will succeed in improving the ethical climate of your group or organization. Nevertheless, you can increase your ethical competence and encourage others to do the same. This book is dedicated to that end.

DEFINING TERMS

Because this is a book about leadership ethics, we need to clarify what both of these terms mean. *Leadership* is the exercise of influence in a group context.[2] Want to know who the leaders are? Look for the people having the greatest impact on the group or organization. Leaders are change agents engaged in furthering the needs, wants, and goals of leaders and followers alike. They are found wherever humans associate with one another, whether in social movements, sports teams, task forces, nonprofit agencies, state legislatures, military units, or corporations.

No definition of leadership is complete without distinguishing between *leading* and *following*. Generally, leaders get the most press. The newfound success of a college football team is a case in point. The head coach gets most of the credit for changing a losing team into a winner, but the turnaround is really the result of the efforts of many followers. Assistant coaches work with offensive and defensive lines, quarterbacks, and kicking teams; trainers tend to injuries; academic tutors keep players in school; athletic department staff members solicit contributions for training facilities; and sports information personnel draw attention to the team's accomplishments.

In truth, leaders and followers function collaboratively, working together toward shared objectives. They are relational partners who play complementary roles.[3] Whereas leaders exert a greater degree of influence and take more responsibility for the overall direction of the group, followers are more involved in implementing plans and doing the work. During the course of a day or week, we typically shift between leader and follower roles—heading up a project team at work, for example, while taking the position of follower as a student in a night class. As a result, we need to know how to behave ethically as both leaders and followers.

Moving from a follower role to a leadership role brings with it a shift in expectations. Important leader functions include establishing direction, organizing, coordinating activities and resources, motivating, and managing conflicts. Important follower functions include carrying out important group and organizational tasks (engineering, social work, teaching, accounting), generating new ideas about how to get jobs done, working in teams, and providing feedback.[4]

Viewing leadership as a role should put to rest the notion that leaders are born, not made. The fact that nearly all of us will function as leaders at some point if we haven't already done so means that leadership is not limited to those with the proper genetic background, income level, or education. Ordinary people emerged as leaders during the shooting that seriously injured Arizona congresswoman Gabby Giffords and killed six others, for instance. An intern on the congresswoman's staff applied pressure to Giffords's head wound, saving her life. One member of the crowd prevented the killer from reloading his weapon by grabbing a loaded magazine he had dropped and another clubbed the shooter in the back of his head with a folding chair. One of the wounded, a seventy-four-year-old army colonel, tackled the gunman, and he and other bystanders subdued him. A doctor and nurse shopping at the Safeway where the attack occurred provided treatment for victims.

Leadership should not be confused with position, although leaders often occupy positions of authority. Those designated as leaders, such as a disillusioned manager nearing retirement, don't always exert a great deal of influence. On the other hand, those without the benefit of a title on the organizational chart can have a significant impact. Angela Merkel was a quiet East German scientist who went on to become Chancellor of the reunited Germany. Under her direction, the country has taken the lead in addressing Europe's Syrian refugee crisis. Erin Brockovich was a poor single mother in California without legal training who helped victims of chemical poisoning reach a multimillion-dollar legal settlement with Pacific Gas and Electric. Mohamed Bouazizi was a Tunisian fruit vendor who burned himself alive to protest political oppression and lack of economic opportunity. His dramatic act launched the Arab Spring, a popular uprising that toppled several dictatorships in the Middle East. (See Case Study 0.1 at the end of this introduction for another example of an unlikely leader.)

Human leadership differs in important ways from the pattern of dominance and submission that characterizes animal societies. The dominant female hyena or male chimpanzee rules over the pack or troop through pure physical strength. Each maintains authority until some stronger rival (often seeking mates) comes along. Unlike other animals, which seem to be driven largely by instinct, humans consciously choose how they want to influence others. We can rely on persuasion, rewards, punishments, emotional appeals, rules, and a host of other means to get our way. Freedom of choice makes ethical considerations an important part of any discussion of leadership. The term *ethics* refers to judgments about whether human behavior is right or wrong. We may be repulsed by the idea that a male lion will kill the offspring of the previous dominant male when he takes control of the pride. Yet we cannot label his actions as unethical because he is driven by a genetic imperative to start his own bloodline. We can and do condemn the actions of leaders who decide to lie, belittle followers, and enrich themselves at the expense of the less fortunate.

Some philosophers distinguish between *ethics,* which they define as the systematic study of the principles of right and wrong behavior, and *morals,* which they describe as specific standards of right and wrong ("Thou shall not steal"; "Do unto others as they would do unto you"). Just as many scholars appear to use these terms interchangeably. I will follow the latter course.

The practice of *ethical leadership* is a two-part process involving personal moral behavior and moral influence.[5] Ethical leaders earn that label when they act morally as they carry out their duties and shape the ethical contexts of their groups, organizations, and societies. Both components are essential. Leaders must demonstrate such character traits as justice, humility, optimism, courage, and compassion; make wise choices; and master the ethical challenges of their roles. In addition, they are responsible for the ethical behavior of others. (Complete Self-Assessment 0.1 to determine how well your leader fills each of these roles.) These dual responsibilities intertwine. As we'll see later in the book, leaders act as role models for the rest of the organization. How followers behave depends in large part on the example set by leaders. Conversely, leaders become products of their own creations. Ethical climates promote the moral development of leaders as well as that of followers, fostering their character and improving their ability to make and follow through on ethical choices. Ethical organizational environments are marked by integrity, justice, trust, a concern for how goals are achieved, and a sense of social responsibility. They also have safeguards that keep both leaders and followers from engaging in destructive behaviors.

There is a widespread misconception that ethics and effectiveness are incompatible. Many believe that in order to be effective, leaders have to sacrifice their ethical standards. They are convinced of the truth of the old adage "Nice guys (or gals) finish last." However, investigators report that ethical leaders are frequently more, not less, effective than their unethical colleagues; for example:[6]

- Ethical leaders are rated as more promotable and effective.

- Those working for ethical leaders are more satisfied and are more committed to their organizations and their managers. They work harder, are more willing to report problems to management, and are more productive.

- Members of work groups led by moral leaders are less likely to engage in theft, sabotage, cheating, and other deviant behaviors. In addition, they are less likely to engage in workplace incivility—putting others down, making demeaning remarks, excluding others, and so on.

- Ethical leadership enhances organizational trust levels, fostering perceptions that the organization is competent, open, concerned for employees, and reliable. Such trust leads to improved organizational performance and greater profitability.

- Ethical chief executive officers (CEOs) encourage their companies to engage in socially responsible behavior.

- Employees who consider their leaders to be moral persons and moral managers also believe that their organizations are effective.

- Ethical leadership is linked to follower creativity and innovation.
- Ethical leadership fosters an ethical organizational climate, which, in turn, increases job satisfaction and commitment to the organization.
- Ethical leadership can have a positive impact beyond the workplace. Spouses of employees working for ethical leaders report higher family satisfaction.
- Followers in both Western and non-Western cultures want leaders of high character who respect the rights and the dignity of others.

In sum, while unethical leaders can prosper, a growing body of evidence suggests that if you strive to be an ethical leader, you are more likely to be a successful one as well.

OVERVIEW OF THE BOOK

Part I of this book, "The Shadow Side of Leadership," examines the important topic of leadership's dark side. Chapter 1 outlines common shadows cast by leaders: abuse of power and privilege, mismanagement of information, misplaced and broken loyalties, inconsistency, and irresponsibility. Chapter 2 explores the reasons leaders often cause more harm than good and then outlines strategies for stepping out of the shadows and into the light.

After identifying the factors that cause us to cast shadows as leaders, the discussion turns to mastering them. To do so, we will need to look inward. Part II, "Looking Inward," focuses on the inner dimension of leadership. Chapter 3 examines the role of character development in overcoming our internal enemies and faulty motivations, and Chapter 4 explores the nature of evil, forgiveness, apology, and spirituality.

Part III, "Ethical Standards and Strategies," addresses moral decision making and provides the theory and tactics we need to develop our ethical expertise. Chapter 5 surveys a wide range of ethical perspectives that can help us set moral priorities, while Chapter 6 describes the process of ethical decision making as well as formats that we can use to make better moral choices and follow through on our decisions. Chapter 7 (new to this edition) looks at how to choose ethical influence tactics. Chapter 8 introduces theories specifically developed to guide the ethical behavior of leaders.

Part IV, "Shaping Ethical Contexts," looks at ways in which leaders can shed light in a variety of situations. Chapter 9 examines ethical group decision making. Chapter 10 describes the creation of ethical organizational climates. Chapter 11 highlights the challenges of ethical diversity. Chapter 12 provides an overview of ethical leadership in crisis situations.

Expect to learn new terminology along with key principles, decision-making formats, and important elements of the ethical context. This information is drawn from a number of different fields of study—philosophy, communication, theology, history, psychology, neuroscience, sociology, political science, and organizational behavior—because we need insights from many different disciplines if we are to step out of the shadows. You can anticipate reading about and then practicing a variety of skills, ranging from information gathering to listening and conflict management.

With these preliminaries out of the way, let's begin with Chapter 1, which takes a closer look at some of the ethical hurdles faced by leaders.

Case Study 0.1

A GIRL TAKES ON THE TALIBAN (AND WORLD LEADERS)

One of the world's most powerful advocates for children's education is also one of the youngest. Malala Yousafzai began her career as an activist in 2008, at age 11, in the remote Swat Valley of Pakistan. After the Taliban began attacking girls' schools in her region, she gave a radio interview in which she declared, "How dare the Taliban take away my basic right to education?"[1] The next year, she began blogging for the BBC, describing what it was like to live under Taliban rule. Malala wrote under an assumed name but her identity was revealed, making her a target for the Taliban. Despite the risk, she continued to speak out about the right of girls and women. Malala and her father, an educator and anti-Taliban activist, received death threats from the militant group. On October 12, 2012, a Taliban gunman boarded the bus she was taking home from school and shot her in the left side of the head. (Two other girls were also injured.) Yousafzai was transferred to a Birmingham, England, hospital after initially receiving treatment in a Pakistani military facility. The young advocate suffered no permanent brain damage, though part of her skull had to be removed to relieve brain swelling. She still suffers partial paralysis on the left side of her face as well as loss of some hearing in her left ear.

The Taliban's attempt to silence Malala had the opposite result. More people than ever were drawn to her cause. Citizens from around the world expressed their support for her during her recovery. She gave a speech to the United Nations (UN) on her 16th birthday and became the youngest winner of the Nobel Peace Prize, at age 17, in 2014. (She shared the prize with Indian children's rights champion Kailash Satyarthi.) Yousafzai and her father created the Malala Fund, which promotes twelve years of free education for all the world's children, particularly girls. (An estimated 63 million children, over 5 million in Pakistan, don't receive an education, and millions of others learn in substandard conditions.) In one project, the Malala Fund covered the costs of opening up a school for 200 Syrian girl refugees.

Malala does not hesitate to take on world leaders in her fight for universal education. She faults the UN for seeking to provide only an elementary and middle school education to children. She told UN members to make twelve years of schooling their goal: "Your dreams were too small. Now it is time that you dream bigger."[2] Malala notes that just an eight-day halt to military spending would pay for "12 years of free, quality education to every child on the planet."[3] When she visited the White House, she told President Obama to stop drone warfare and to invest in education instead. She criticized the president of Nigeria for not doing enough to rescue schoolgirls kidnapped by Boko Haram.

Due to Taliban death threats, Malala and her family will not be able to return to their homeland from Britain in the foreseeable future. Tragically, she is not the only Pakistani child to be shot by the Taliban. Taliban gunmen murdered 140 teachers and children, most of them boys between the ages of 12 and 16, at a school in the city of Peshawar. In other attacks, the militant group used bombs to blow up girls on a school playground and on a school bus.

(Continued)

(Continued)

Discussion Probes

1. How do you account for the fact that a girl from rural Pakistan became a leading spokesperson for worldwide childhood education?

2. Can you think of any other examples of leaders, like Malala, who overcame humble circumstances and significant barriers to become leaders?

3. What gives Malala Yousafzai the courage to speak boldly to world leaders?

4. Is Malala more effective as an advocate for children's education because she is young?

5. Is Malala's goal of universal 12-year education too ambitious?

Notes

1. Yousafzai, M., & Lamb, C. (2013). *I am Malala: The girl who stood up for education and was shot by the Taliban*. New York, NY: Back Bay Books, p. 142.

2. Kristof, N. (2015, September 26). Malala Yousafzai's fight continues. *The New York Times*, Op-Ed.

3. Malala Yousafzai biography. (2015, December 9). *Biography.com*.

Sources

Baker, A. (2013, December 19). Runner-up: Malala Yousafzai, the fighter. *Time.com*
Boone, J. (2015, December 15). Peshawar school attack: One year on 'the country is changed completely.' *The Guardian*.
Kellaway, K. (2015, October 15). Malala Yousafzai: 'I want to become prime minister of my country.' *The Guardian*.

SELF-ASSESSMENT 0.1

Ethical Leadership Scale

Instructions: In responding to the following items, think about your chief executive officer (CEO) or top leader at work. Indicate your level of agreement with the statements in the next section by circling your responses.

1 = strongly disagree

2 = disagree

3 = neutral

4 = agree

5 = strongly agree

My organization's CEO/top leader

1. listens to what employees have to say.

   1   2   3   4   5

2. disciplines employees who violate ethical standards.

   1   2   3   4   5

3. conducts his or her personal life in an ethical manner.

   1   2   3   4   5

4. has the best interests of employees in mind.

   1   2   3   4   5

5. makes fair and balanced decisions.

   1   2   3   4   5

6. can be trusted.

   1   2   3   4   5

7. discusses business ethics or values with employees.

   1   2   3   4   5

8. sets an example of how to do things the right way in terms of ethics.

   1   2   3   4   5

9. defines success not just by results but also by the way that they are obtained.

   1   2   3   4   5

10. asks, "What is the right thing to do?" when making decisions.

    1   2   3   4   5

Scoring: Add up your responses to the 10 items. Total score can range from 10 to 50. The higher the score, the more ethical you believe your leader to be.

Source: Brown, M. E., Trevino, L. K., & Harrison, D. A. (2005). Ethical leadership: A social learning perspective for construct development and testing. *Organizational Behavior and Human Decision Processes, 97,* 117–134. Used by permission.

NOTES

1. See Ciulla, J. B. (2004). Leadership ethics: Mapping the territory. In J. B. Ciulla (Ed.), *Ethics, the heart of leadership* (2nd ed., pp. 3–24). Westport, CT: Praeger.
2. Bass, B. M. (1990). *Bass and Stogdill's handbook of leadership* (3rd ed.). New York, NY: Free Press.
3. Hollander, E. P. (1992). The essential interdependence of leadership and followership. *Current Directions in Psychological Science, 1,* 71–75; Kellerman, B. (2008). *Followership: How followers are creating change and changing leaders.* Boston, MA: Harvard Business School Press.

4. Johnson, C. E., & Hackman, M. Z. (1997). *Rediscovering the power of followership in the leadership communication text.* Paper presented at the annual convention of the National Communication Association, Chicago, Illinois.

5. Brown, M. E., & Trevino, L. K. (2006). Ethical leadership: A review and future directions. *Leadership Quarterly, 17,* 595–616.

6. Brown, M. E., & Trevino, L. K. (2006). Socialized charismatic leadership, values congruence, and deviance in work groups. *Journal of Applied Psychology, 91,* 954–962; Brown, M. E., Trevino, L. K., & Harrison, D. A. (2005). Ethical leadership: A social learning perspective for construct development and testing. *Organizational Behavior and Human Decision Processes, 97,* 117–134; Davis, A. L., & Rothstein, H. R. (2006). The effects of the perceived behavioral integrity of managers on employee attitudes: A meta-analysis. *Journal of Business Ethics, 67,* 407–419; Eisenbeiss, S. A., van Knippenberg, D., & Fahrbach, C. M. (2015). Doing well by doing good? Analyzing the relationship between CEO ethical leadership and firm performance. *Journal of Business Ethics, 128,* 635–651; Johnson, C. E., Shelton, P. M., & Yates, L. (2012). Nice guys (and gals) finish first: Ethical leadership and organizational trust, satisfaction, and effectiveness. *International Leadership Journal, 4*(1), 3–19; Khuntia, R., & Suar, D. (2004). A scale to assess ethical leadership of Indian and public sector managers. *Journal of Business Ethics, 49,* 13–26; Liao, Y., Liu, X-Y., Kwan, H., & Jinsong, L. (2015). Work–family effects of ethical leadership. *Journal of Business Ethics, 128,* 535–545; Neubert, M. J., Carlson, D. S., Kacmar, K. M., Roberts, J. A., & Chonko, L. B. (2009). The virtuous influence of ethical leadership behavior: Evidence from the field. *Journal of Business Ethics, 90,* 157–170; Ng, T. W. H., & Feldman, D. C. (2014). Ethical leadership: Meta-analytic evidence of criterion-related and incremental validity. *Journal of Applied Psychology, 100,* 948–965; Resick, C. J., Hanges, P. J., Dickson, M. W., & Mitchelson, J. K. (2006). A cross-cultural examination of the endorsement of ethical leadership. *Journal of Business Ethics, 63,* 345–359; Rubin, R. S., Dierdorff, E. C., & Brown, M. E. (2010). Do ethical leaders get ahead? Exploring ethical leadership and promotability. *Business Ethics Quarterly, 20,* 215–236; Taylor, S. G., & Pattie, M. W. (2014). When does ethical leadership affect workplace incivility? The moderating role of follower personality. *Business Ethics Quarterly, 24,* 595–616; Wu, L-Z., Kwan, H. K., Hong-kit, F., Chiu, R. K., & He, X. (2015). CEO ethical leadership and corporate social responsibility: A moderated mediation model. *Journal of Business Ethics, 130,* 819–831; Yidong, T., & Xinxin, L. (2013). How ethical leadership influences employees' innovative work behavior: A perspective of intrinsic motivation. *Journal of Business Ethics, 116,* 441–455.

PART I

The Shadow Side of Leadership

The Leader's Light or Shadow

1

We know where light is coming from by looking at the shadows.

—HUMANITIES SCHOLAR PAUL WOODRUFF

WHAT'S AHEAD

This chapter introduces the dark (bad, toxic) side of leadership as the first step in promoting good or ethical leadership. The metaphor of light and shadow dramatizes the differences between moral and immoral leaders. Leaders have the power to illuminate the lives of followers or to cover them in darkness. They cast light when they master ethical challenges of leadership. They cast shadows when they (1) abuse power, (2) hoard privileges, (3) mismanage information, (4) act inconsistently, (5) misplace or betray loyalties, and (6) fail to assume responsibilities.

A DRAMATIC DIFFERENCE/THE DARK SIDE OF LEADERSHIP

In an influential essay titled "Leading from Within," educational writer and consultant Parker Palmer introduces a powerful metaphor to dramatize the distinction between ethical and unethical leadership. According to Palmer, the difference between moral and immoral leaders is as sharp as the contrast between light and darkness, between heaven and hell:

> A leader is a person who has an unusual degree of power to create the conditions under which other people must live and move and have their being, conditions that can be either as illuminating as heaven or as shadowy as hell. A leader must take special responsibility for what's going on inside his or her own self, inside his or her consciousness, lest the act of leadership create more harm than good.[1]

For most of us, *leadership* has a positive connotation. We have been fortunate enough to benefit from the guidance of teachers or coaches, for example, or we admire noteworthy historical leaders. As we saw in the introduction, ethical leaders brighten the lives of those around them significantly by building trust, commitment, and satisfaction; by reducing negative behavior; and by increasing individual and collective performance. However, Palmer urges us to pay more attention to the shadow side of leadership. Political figures, parents, clergy, and business executives have the potential to cast as much shadow as they do light. Refusing to face the dark side of leadership makes abuse more likely. All too often, leaders "do not even know they are making a choice, let alone how to reflect on the process of choosing."[2]

Other scholars have joined Palmer in focusing on the dark or negative dimension of leadership. Claremont Graduate University professor Jean Lipman-Blumen uses the term *toxic leaders* to describe those who engage in destructive behaviors and who exhibit dysfunctional personal characteristics.[3] These behaviors and qualities (summarized in Table 1.1) cause significant harm to followers and organizations.

Harvard professor Barbara Kellerman believes that limiting our understanding of leadership solely to good leadership ignores the reality that a great many leaders engage in destructive behaviors.[4] Overlooking that fact, Kellerman says, undermines our attempts to promote good leadership:

> I take it as a given that we promote good leadership not by ignoring bad leadership, nor by presuming that it is immutable, but rather by attacking it as we would a disease that is always pernicious and sometimes deadly.[5]

According to Kellerman, bad leaders can be ineffective, unethical, or ineffective and unethical. She identifies seven types of bad leaders:

Incompetent. These leaders don't have the motivation or the ability to sustain effective action. They may lack emotional or academic intelligence, for example, or be careless, distracted, or sloppy. Some cannot function under stress, and their communication and decisions suffer as a result. Former Defense Secretary Donald Rumsfeld failed as leader of the invasion of Iraq. He didn't understand the political situation and that the war wasn't over when American troops entered Baghdad. He was unable to generate an effective strategy for waging an extended campaign against highly motivated insurgents.

Rigid. Rigid leaders may be competent, but they are unyielding, unable to accept new ideas, new information, or changing conditions. Thabo Mbeki is one such leader. After becoming president of South Africa in 1999, he insisted that HIV does not cause AIDS and withheld antiretroviral drugs from HIV-positive pregnant women. These medications would have dramatically cut the transmission of the disease to their babies.

Intemperate. Intemperate leaders lack self-control and are enabled by followers who don't want to intervene or can't. The political career of Toronto mayor Rob Ford demonstrates intemperate leadership in action. Ford admitted to using illegal drugs, sometimes while drunk, and was photographed using crack cocaine. Despite calls for his resignation, he stood for reelection until cancer forced him to withdraw from the race. He ran instead for his old district seat and won by a large margin.

Callous. The callous leader is uncaring or unkind, ignoring or downplaying the needs, wants, and wishes of followers. Former hotel magnate Leona Helmsley personifies the

TABLE 1.1

The Behaviors and Personal Characteristics of Toxic Leaders

Destructive Behaviors	Toxic Qualities
Leaving followers worse off	Lack of integrity
Violating human rights	Insatiable ambition
Feeding followers' illusions; creating dependence	Enormous egos
Playing to the basest fears and needs of followers	Arrogance
Stifling criticism; enforcing compliance	Amorality (inability to discern right from wrong)
Misleading followers	Avarice (greed)
Subverting ethical organizational structures and processes	Reckless disregard for the costs of their actions
Engaging in unethical, illegal, and criminal acts	Cowardice (refusal to make tough choices)
Building totalitarian regimes	Failure to understand problems
Failing to nurture followers, including successors	Incompetence in key leadership situations
Setting constituents against one another	
Encouraging followers to hate or destroy others	
Identifying scapegoats	
Making themselves indispensable	
Ignoring or promoting incompetence, cronyism, and corruption	

Source: Adapted from Lipman-Blumen, J. (2005). *The allure of toxic leaders: Why we follow destructive bosses and corrupt politicians—and how we can survive them.* Oxford, England: Oxford University Press, pp. 19–23.

callous leader. She earned the title "the Queen of Mean" by screaming at employees and firing them for minor infractions such as having dirty fingernails. Helmsley later served time in prison for tax evasion. (She once quipped, "Only the little people pay taxes.")

Corrupt. These leaders and (at least some of their followers) lie, cheat, and steal. They put self-interest ahead of the public interest. The top officers of FIFA, the governing body of world soccer, are exemplars of this type of leader. Most of the group's leaders are targets of a corruption probe. They are accused of taking bribes from cities hoping to host the World Cup as well as from broadcasters and athletic apparel companies.

Insular. The insular leader draws a clear boundary between the welfare of his or her immediate group or organization and outsiders. Former U.S. President Bill Clinton behaved in an insular manner when he didn't intervene in the Rwandan genocide that took the lives of 800,000 to 1 million people in 1994. He later traveled to Africa to apologize for failing to act even though he had reliable information describing how thousands of Tutsis were being hacked to death by their Hutu neighbors.

Evil. Evil leaders commit atrocities, using their power to inflict severe physical or psychological harm. Abu Bakr al-Baghdadi is one example of an evil leader. He heads ISIS, the Middle Eastern terrorist group known for beheading male captives and turning female captives into sex slaves for Islamic State in Iraq and Syria (ISIS) soldiers. Al-Baghdadi told his followers that Muslim believers have the right to enslave all nonbelievers.

Lipman-Blumen and Kellerman developed their typologies based on case studies of prominent leaders. Now investigators are shifting the focus to ordinary leaders. In one project, two researchers at Bond University in Australia (along with a colleague from the United States) asked employees to explain why they would label someone as a bad leader, describe how a bad leader made them feel, and describe the impact bad leaders had on them and the organization as a whole.[6] Respondents reported that bad leaders are incompetent (they are unable to use technology, for example, and can't work with subordinates or plan strategy) and unethical (they demonstrate poor ethics as well as poor personal and interpersonal behavior). Such leaders made respondents angry and frustrated while lowering their self-esteem. Individual and collective performance suffered as a result. Those working under bad leaders reported feeling more stress at home. They had trouble sleeping, for instance, and felt fatigued. Negative emotions toward their leaders consumed their thoughts and hurt their family relationships. According to the survey, bad leaders often go unpunished; instead, many are promoted or rewarded.

Using information generated by this study, the researchers developed a tool to measure destructive organizational leadership. They discovered that demonstrating just a couple of bad behaviors was enough to label a leader as destructive, even though he or she might also have lots of positive qualities. The Bond scholars identified seven clusters of destructive leader behaviors:[7]

> *Cluster 1:* This type of leader makes poor decisions (often based on inadequate information), lies and engages in other unethical behavior, cannot deal with new technology, and typically fails to prioritize and delegate.

> *Cluster 2:* This type of leader lacks critical skills. She or he is unable to negotiate or persuade and cannot develop or motivate subordinates.

Cluster 3: This type of leader makes good decisions and has the necessary leadership skills but is overly controlling and micromanages followers.

Cluster 4: This type of leader can't deal with conflict but plays favorites and behaves inconsistently.

Cluster 5: This type of leader isn't all that bad but isn't all that good either. Leaders in this category don't seek information from others, don't change their minds, and don't do a good job of coordinating followers.

Cluster 6: This type of leader isolates the group from the rest of the organization.

Cluster 7: This type of leader creates a situation of "significant misery and despair." Leaders in this group are brutal and bullying, frequently lying and engaging in other unethical behavior.

Ståle Einarsen and his Norwegian colleagues offer an alternative classification of bad leadership based on its negative effects either on the organization or on followers. Destructive leaders can be antiorganization, antisubordinates, or both.[8] *Tyrannical leaders* reach organizational goals while abusing followers. *Supportive-disloyal leaders* care for the welfare of subordinates at the expense of organizational goals. They may tolerate loafing or stealing, for example. *Derailed leaders* act against the interests of both subordinates and the organization. As they bully, manipulate, deceive, and harass followers, they may also be stealing from the organization, engaging in fraudulent activities, and doing less than expected. *Laissez-faire leaders* engage in passive and indirect negative behavior. They occupy leadership positions but don't exercise leadership, therefore hurting followers and their organizations. *Constructive leaders,* on the other hand, care about subordinates and help the organization achieve its goals while using resources wisely. Einarsen and his fellow researchers found a high rate of bad leadership in Norwegian organizations, with 61% of respondents reporting that their immediate supervisors engaged in ongoing destructive behavior over the past six months. Laissez-faire behavior was by far most common form of bad leadership, followed by supportive-disloyal leadership, derailed leadership, and tyrannical leadership.[9] (Turn to Self-Assessment 1.1 at the end of this chapter to determine whether your leader engages in destructive leadership behavior.)

Evidence that bad leaders can cause significant damage continues to grow. In an analysis of the results of 57 studies, investigators found that destructive leader behavior is linked to a wide range of negative outcomes.[10] Those serving under destructive leaders have negative attitudes toward their superiors, resist their leaders' influence attempts, and engage more frequently in counterproductive work behaviors. In addition, these followers have negative attitudes toward their jobs and their organizations. Their personal well-being also suffers as they experience negative emotions and stress.

In sum, Palmer was right to emphasize the importance of the shadow side of leadership. Followers from around the world have lots of firsthand experience with bad leaders and report that such leaders cause significant damage. It apparently takes only a few destructive behaviors to overcome a leader's positive qualities. In addition, the shadows cast by destructive leaders extend beyond the workplace; the home lives of followers are damaged as well.

THE LEADER'S SHADOWS

When we function as leaders, we take on a unique set of ethical burdens in addition to a set of expectations and tasks. These involve issues of power, privilege, information, consistency, loyalty, and responsibility. How we handle the challenges of leadership determines whether we cause more harm than good or, to return to Palmer's metaphor, whether we cast light or shadow. Unless we're careful, we're likely to cast one or more of the shadows described in this section. (For a list of the ethical challenges faced by those in the follower role, see "Focus on Follower Ethics: The Ethical Challenges of Followership.")

The Shadow of Power

Power is the foundation for influence attempts. The more power we have, the more likely others are to comply with our wishes. Power comes from a variety of sources. One typology, for example, divides power into two categories: hard and soft.[11] *Hard power* uses inducements (bonuses, raises) and threats (arrests, firings) to get people to go along. *Soft power* is based on attracting others rather than forcing them or inducing them to comply. Leaders use soft power when they set a worthy example, create an inspiring vision, and build positive relationships with subordinates. Typically, those without formal authority rely more heavily on soft power, but even those in formal leadership positions, such as military officers, try to attract followers by acting as role models and emphasizing the group's mission. Effective leaders combine hard and soft power into *smart power* to achieve their goals. For instance, a manager may try to persuade an employee to follow a new policy while at the same time outlining the penalties the subordinate will face if he or she does not comply.

The most popular power classification system identifies five power bases.[12] *Coercive power* is based on penalties or punishments such as physical force, salary reductions, student suspensions, or embargoes against national enemies. *Reward power* depends on being able to deliver something of value to others, whether tangible (bonuses, health insurance, grades) or intangible (praise, trust, cooperation). *Legitimate power* resides in the position, not the person. Supervisors, judges, police officers, drill sergeants, instructors, and parents have the right to control our behavior within certain limits. A boss can require us to carry out certain tasks at work, for example; but in most cases, he or she has no say in what we do in our free time. In contrast to legitimate power, *expert power* is based on the characteristics of the individual regardless of that person's official position. Knowledge, skills, education, and certification all build expert power. *Referent (role model) power* rests on the admiration one person has for another. We're more likely to do favors for a supervisor we admire or to buy a product promoted by our favorite sports hero.

Leaders typically draw on more than one power source. The manager who is appointed to lead a task force is granted legitimate power that enables her to reward or punish. Yet in order to be successful, she'll have to demonstrate her knowledge of the topic, skillfully direct the group process, and earn the respect of task force members through hard work and commitment to the group. ("Leadership Ethics at the Movies: *Selma*" describes one leader who skillfully uses his power, and the power used by his opponents, to achieve a worthy objective.)

Focus on Follower Ethics

THE ETHICAL CHALLENGES OF FOLLOWERSHIP

Followers, like leaders, face their own set of ethical challenges. Followers walk on the dark side when they fail to meet the moral responsibilities of their roles. Important ethical challenges confronted by followers include those described below.

The Challenge of Obligation. Followers contribute to a shadowy atmosphere when they fail to fulfill their minimal responsibilities by coming to work late, taking extended breaks, not carrying out assignments, undermining the authority of their leaders, stealing supplies, and so on. However, they can also contribute to an unethical climate by taking on too many obligations. Employees forced to work mandatory overtime and salaried staff at many technology and consulting firms work 70–80 hours a week, leaving little time for family and personal interests. They experience stress and burnout, and their family relationships suffer.

Followers also have ethical duties to outsiders. Carpenters and other tradespeople involved in home construction have an obligation to buyers to build high-quality houses and to meet deadlines, for example. Government employees owe it to taxpayers to spend their money wisely by working hard while keeping expenses down.

These questions can help us sort out the obligations we owe as followers:

- Am I doing all I reasonably can to carry out my tasks and further the mission of my organization? What more could I do?
- Am I fulfilling my obligations to outsiders (clients, neighbors, community, customers)? Are there any additional steps I should take?

- Am I giving back to the group or organization as much as I am taking from it?
- Am I carrying my fair share of the workload?
- Am I serving the needs of my leaders?
- Am I earning the salary and benefits I receive?
- Can I fulfill my organizational obligations and, at the same time, maintain a healthy personal life and productive relationships? If not, what can I do to bring my work and personal life into balance?

The Challenge of Obedience. Groups and organizations couldn't function if members refused to obey orders or adhere to policies, even the ones they don't like. As a result, followers have an ethical duty to obey. However, blindly following authority can drive followers to engage in illegal and immoral activities that they would never participate in on their own. Obeying orders is no excuse for unethical behavior. Therefore, deciding when to disobey is critical. To make this determination, consider the following factors: Does this order appear to call for unethical behavior? Would I engage in this course of action if I weren't ordered to? What are the potential consequences for others, and for myself, if these directions are followed? Does obedience threaten the mission and health of the organization as a whole? What steps should I take if I decide to disobey?

The Challenge of Cynicism. There is a difference between healthy skepticism, which prevents followers from being exploited, and unhealthy cynicism, which undermines individual and group performance. Followers darken the atmosphere when they become organizational cynics. That's because cynicism destroys commitment and undermines trust. Collective performance suffers as a result. Few give their best effort when they are disillusioned with the group. Cynical employees feel less identification with and commitment to their employers while being more resistant to change; they are less likely to go beyond their job duties to help their colleagues and their organizations. The greater the degree of cynicism, the more effort is directed toward attacking the organization at the expense of completing the task at hand.

The Challenge of Dissent. Expressing disagreement is an important ethical duty of followership. Followers should take issue with policies and procedures that are inefficient, harmful, or costly and with leaders who harm others or put the organization at risk. Doing so serves the mission of the organization while protecting the rights of its members and the larger community. Although followers contribute to a shadowy environment when they fail to speak up, they can go too far by generating a constant stream of complaints. Ethical followers know when to speak up (not every issue is worth contesting) and when to wait until a more important issue comes along. They must also determine whether the problem is significant enough to justify going outside the organization (becoming a whistle-blower) if leaders don't respond.

The Challenge of Bad News. Delivering bad news is risky business. Followers who tell their bosses that the project is over budget, that sales are down, or that the software doesn't work as promised may be verbally abused, demoted, or fired. Organizations and leaders pay a high price when followers hide or cover up bad news, deny responsibility, or shift blame. Leaders can't correct problems they don't know exist. Failure to address serious deficiencies such as accounting fraud, cost overruns, and product contamination can destroy an organization. Leaders who don't get feedback about their ineffective habits—micromanaging, poor listening skills, indecisiveness—can't address those behaviors. When leaders deny accountability and shift blame, this undermines trust and diverts people's focus from solving problems to defending themselves.

To avoid contributing to a shadowy environment, followers must deliver bad news and accept responsibility for their actions. They also need to pay close attention to how they deliver bad tidings, selecting the right time, place, and message channel. Significant problems should be brought to the leader's attention immediately, when he or she is most receptive, and delivered face-to-face whenever possible, not through e-mail, faxes, and other, less personal channels.

Source: Adapted from Johnson, C. E. (2015). *Organizational ethics: A practical approach* (3rd ed.). Thousand Oaks, CA: SAGE, Ch. 9.

Additional Sources

Bedian, A. G. (2007). Even if the tower is "ivory," it isn't "white": Understanding the consequences of faculty cynicism. *Academy of Management Learning and Education, 6,* 9–32.

Dean, J. W., Brandes, P., & Dharwadkar, R. (1998). Organizational cynicism. *Academy of Management Review, 23,* 341–352.

Hajdin, M. (2005). Employee loyalty: An examination. *Journal of Business Ethics, 59,* 259–280.

Roberts, T. P., & Zigarmi, D. (2014). The impact of dispositional cynicism on job-specific affect and work intentions. *International Journal of Psychology, 49,* 381–389.

Roloff, M. E., & Paulson, G. D. (2001). Confronting organizational transgressions. In J. M. Darley, D. M. Messick, & T. R. Tyler (Eds.), *Social influences on ethical behavior in organizations* (pp. 53–68). Mahwah, NJ: Erlbaum.

Schrag, B. (2001). The moral significance of employee loyalty. *Business Ethics Quarterly, 11,* 41–66.

Stanley, D. J., Meyer, J. P., & Topolnytsky, L. (2005). Employee cynicism and resistance to organizational change. *Journal of Business and Psychology, 19,* 429–459.

Leadership Ethics at the Movies

SELMA

Key Cast Members: Davis Oyelowo, Carman Ejogo, Tom Wilkinson, Oprah Winfrey, Andre Holland

Synopsis: In 1965, the American civil rights movement is in full swing. Congress has outlawed segregation, but poll taxes and other restrictions keep blacks from registering to vote. Martin Luther King (played by Oyelowo) organizes a voting rights march from Montgomery to Selma, Alabama. King and his followers face resistance from Alabama governor George Wallace, National Guardsmen, county sheriffs, and President Lyndon Johnson (Wilkinson), who wants King to stop the march. King refuses, insisting instead that Johnson introduce a voting rights bill to Congress. King wins the battle of wills, and the march goes forward with the support of federal authorities.

Johnson then sends Congress voting rights legislation that is passed into law.

Rating: PG-13 for vivid scenes of violence and mature themes

Themes: types of power, use and abuse of power, courage, justice and injustice, vision, shadow of misinformation

Discussion Starters

1. What types of power do the major figures in the film use?

2. How does the abuse of power by King's opponents contribute to his success?

3. How does King appeal to white audiences?

4. What character weaknesses do you note in President Johnson? Do you find anything in his character to admire?

The use of each power type has advantages and disadvantages. For instance, the dispensing of rewards is widely accepted in Western culture but can be counterproductive if the rewards promote the wrong behaviors (see Chapter 10) or go to the wrong people. U.S. workers are more satisfied and productive when their leaders rely on forms of power that are tied to the person (expert and referent) rather than forms of power that are linked to the position (coercive, reward, and legitimate).[13] In addition, positional power is more susceptible to abuse. Coercive tactics have the potential to do the most damage, threatening the dignity as well as the physical and mental health of followers. Leaders, then, have important decisions to make about the types of power they use and when. (Complete Self-Assessment 1.2 to determine the types of power you prefer to use.)

The fact that leadership cannot exist without power makes some Americans uncomfortable. We admire powerful leaders who act decisively, but we can be reluctant to admit that we have and use power. Sadly, our refusal to face up to the reality of power can make us more vulnerable to the shadow side of leadership. Cult leader Jim Jones presided over the suicide–murder of 909 followers in the jungles of Guyana. Perhaps this tragedy could have been avoided if cult members and outside observers had challenged Jones's abuse of power.[14] Conversely, ignoring the topic of power prevents the attainment of worthy objectives, leaving followers in darkness. Consider the case of the community activist who wants to build a new shelter for homeless families. He can't help these families unless he skillfully wields power to enlist the support of local groups, overcome resistance of opponents, raise funds, and secure building permits.

I suspect that we are suspicious of power because we recognize that power has a corrosive effect on those who possess it. We've seen how U.S. President Richard Nixon used the power of his office to order illegal acts against his enemies and how Russian president Vladimir Putin used military force to take over part of the neighboring country of Ukraine. Many corporate leaders have been intoxicated by their power, using their positions to abuse their subordinates. One such boss kept an employee in an all-day meeting even as her mother was dying. Another called the paramedics when an employee had a heart attack and then ordered everyone else to go back to work even as the victim was still lying on the floor. Yet another berated and humiliated a subordinate who suffered an emotional breakdown and had to be hospitalized. His response? "I can't help it if she is overly sensitive."[15]

Unfortunately, abuse of power is an all-too-common fact of life in modern organizations. In Europe, 3%–4% of employees report being the victim of bullying behavior at least once a week and 10%–15% say that they have been the targets of psychological aggression in the past six months.[16] In one U.S. survey, 90% of those responding reported that they had experienced disrespect from a boss at some time during their working careers; 20% said they were currently working for an abusive leader. "Brutal" bosses regularly engage in the following behaviors, some of which will be discussed in more detail later in the chapter:[17]

- *Deceit:* lying and giving false or misleading information
- *Constraint:* restricting followers' activities outside work, such as telling them whom they can befriend, where they can live, with whom they can live, and the civic activities they can participate in
- *Coercion:* making inappropriate or excessive threats for not complying with the leader's directives
- *Selfishness:* blaming subordinates and making them scapegoats
- *Inequity:* supplying unequal benefits or punishments based on favoritism or criteria unrelated to the job
- *Cruelty:* harming subordinates in such illegitimate ways as name-calling or public humiliation
- *Disregard:* ignoring normal standards of politeness; obvious disregard for what is happening in the lives of followers
- *Deification:* creating a master–servant relationship in which bosses can do whatever they want because they feel superior

The cost of the petty tyranny of bad bosses is high. Victims suffer low self-esteem and psychological distress, are less satisfied with their jobs and lives, are less productive, and are more likely to quit. The work unit as a whole is less trusting and cohesive, reducing collective performance.[18] The majority of employees in one study reported spending 10 or more hours every month complaining about abusive and other kinds of bad bosses or listening to the complaints of fellow workers.[19] In addition to complaining, workers respond to tyranny by surrendering their personal beliefs, keeping a low profile, engaging in revenge fantasies, taking indirect revenge (i.e., not supporting the boss at a critical moment), challenging the supervisor directly, or bringing in outsiders (such as the human resources department or the boss's boss) to get help in dealing with the abusive leader.[20]

The greater a leader's power, the greater the potential for abuse. This prompted Britain's Lord Acton to observe that "power corrupts, and absolute power corrupts absolutely." The long shadow cast by absolute power, as in the case of North Korea's Kim Jong-Il (see Chapter 4) and, until recently, the military junta in Burma, can be seen in censorship, repression, torture, imprisonment, murder, and starvation. Businesses and other organizations foster centralization of power through top-down structures that emphasize status differences, loyalty, dependence, fear, and obedience while celebrating "tough" bosses and business practices like hard bargaining and aggressive marketing tactics.[21]

Psychologists offer several explanations for why concentrated power is so dangerous.[22] First, power makes it easier for impulsive, selfish people to pursue their goals without considering the needs of others. They are likely to justify their actions by claiming that their personal rights and interests take priority over obligations to others. Second, those in power protect their positions by attacking those they perceive as threats. Third, powerful leaders are prone to biased judgments.[23] They generally make little attempt to find out how followers think and feel. As a result, they are more likely to hold and act on faulty stereotypes that justify their authority. Powerful people believe that they deserve their high status because powerless people aren't as capable as they are. Fourth, possessing power makes individuals more resistant to feedback from others.

Power deprivation exerts its own brand of corruptive influence.[24] Followers with little power become fixated on what minimal influence they have, becoming cautious, defensive, and critical of others and new ideas. In extreme cases, they may engage in sabotage, such as when one group of fast-food restaurant employees took out their frustrations by spitting and urinating into the drinks they served customers.

To wield power wisely, leaders have to wrestle with all the issues outlined here. They have to consider what types of power they should use and when and for what purposes. They also have to determine how much power to keep and how much to give away. Finally, leaders must recognize and resist the dangers posed by possessing too much power while making sure that followers aren't corrupted by having too little. Fortunately, there is evidence, when it comes to power, that a number of leaders are casting light rather than shadow. They recognize that sharing power prevents power abuses and improves organizational performance. Executives at Zappos, Johnsonville Sausage, Patagonia, Harley-Davidson, McCormick & Company, and other successful organizations have relinquished much of their legitimate, coercive, award, and expert power bases to lower-level leaders. At a great many other companies, self-directed work teams have taken over functions—hiring, scheduling, quality control—that used to be the province of mid- and lower-level managers.

The Shadow of Privilege

Leaders almost always enjoy greater privileges than followers do. The greater the leader's power, generally the greater the rewards he or she receives. Consider the earnings of corporate chief executive officers (CEOs), for example. Top business leaders in the United States are the highest paid in the world. Over the past thirty-five years, the average salary for chief executives of large U.S. firms skyrocketed to $15.2 million (including salary, bonuses, stock, and stock option grants), up an inflation-adjusted 937%.[25] In a recent salary survey, the highest-paid CEOs were David Zaslav of Discovery Communications ($156.1 million), followed by Michael Fries of Liberty Global ($111.9 million) and Mario Gabelli of GAMCO Investors ($88.5 million). A number of CEOs can expect generous payouts even if their companies are taken over. Stephen Wynn of Wynn Resorts is guaranteed $431.9 million, Zaslav $266.8 million, and Yahoo's Marissa Mayer $157.9 million. As the pay of top leaders soared, the paycheck of the average American was left in the dust. Typical U.S. workers now make less, when adjusted for inflation, than did their counterparts in the 1970s. The top 1% of Americans makes approximately 22% of all income, which exceeds the share made by the bottom 50% of the population.

Nonprofit leaders can also abuse the perks that come from their positions of influence. Take the pay of not-for-profit healthcare executives, for example. In one year, the compensation of the top 20 nonprofit hospital CEOs jumped 29.6%, including major increases for Ascension executive Anthony Tersigni (who earned $7.1 million) and Ronald Peterson of the Johns Hopkins Health System (who took home $1.7 million).[26] Greg Mortenson, who founded the Central Asia Institute, which builds schools for girls in Afghanistan and Pakistan, had to repay $1 million to the charity. He purchased luxury items and vacations for himself and his family using Central Asia Institute credit cards. He also billed Central Asia Institute for travel expenses where he was paid up to $30,000 to speak.[27]

Most of us would agree that leaders deserve more rewards than followers do because leaders assume greater risks and responsibilities; many would also agree that some leaders get more than they deserve. Beyond this point, however, our opinions are likely to diverge. Americans are divided over questions such as these: How many additional privileges should leaders have? What should be the relative difference in pay and benefits between workers and top management? How do we close the large gap between the world's haves and the have-nots? We will never reach complete agreement on these issues, but the fact remains that privilege is a significant ethical burden associated with leadership. Leaders must give questions of privilege the same careful consideration as questions of power. The shadow cast by the abuse of privilege can be as long and dark as that cast by the misuse of power. (Turn to Case Study 1.1 for evidence of the dangers of privilege.) Conversely, sharing privilege can cast significant light. Every year, for example, thousands of Americans (often members of religious congregations) leave their comfortable homes to spend their vacations serving in developing nations. There they build schools and homes, dig wells, and provide medical care. Some of the world's richest people, including Warren Buffet, Bill and Melinda Gates, Sheryl Sandburg, Mark Zuckerberg, and Paul Allen, have pledged to give the vast majority of their wealth to philanthropic causes.

The Shadow of Mismanaged Information

Leaders have more access to information than do others in an organization. They are more likely to participate in decision-making processes, network with managers in other units, review personnel files, and formulate long-term plans. Knowledge is a mixed blessing. Leaders must be in the information loop in order to carry out their tasks, but possessing knowledge makes life more complicated. Do they reveal that they are in the know? When should they release information and to whom? How much do they tell? Is it ever right for them to lie?

No wonder leaders are tempted to think ignorance is bliss! If all these challenges weren't enough, leaders face the very real temptation to lie. For instance, government and industry officials denied that the Rocky Flats nuclear facility outside Denver posed a health risk even as the facility continued to release plutonium and toxic chemicals into the air and water.[28] Managers at the Veterans Administration falsified patient access records to disguise the long wait times facing veterans seeking medical treatment.[29] At other times, leaders are eager to hide the truth. The Panama Papers, a massive data leak, revealed that political leaders and wealthy individuals from around the world are secretly sheltering billions in assets in offshore companies.[30] Other leaders don't want to reveal that their judgment might be clouded by conflicts of interest. Executives at the nonprofit Global Energy Balance Network argue that exercise, not diet, is the key to weight loss. However, they failed to mention on their website that the organization is largely funded by Coca Cola, which produces sugary drinks that many experts believe contribute to the obesity epidemic.[31] Three psychiatrists at Harvard medical school advocated for the use of antipsychotic drugs with children while failing to disclose that they had received $4.2 million in payments from the drug industry.[32]

The issues surrounding access to information are broader than deciding whether to lie, to hide the truth, or to tell the truth. Although leaders often decide between lying and truth telling, they are just as likely to be faced with questions related to the release of information. Take the case of a middle manager who has learned about an upcoming merger that will mean layoffs. Her superiors have asked her to keep this information to herself for a couple of weeks until the deal is completed. In the interim, employees may make financial commitments—such as home and car purchases—that they would postpone if they knew that major changes were in the works. Should the manager voluntarily share information about the merger with such employees despite her orders? What happens when a member of her department asks her to confirm or deny the rumor that the company is about to merge? (Turn to Case Study 1.2 to see how leaders at several organizations wrestled with a controversial decision about how much information to release.)

Privacy issues raise additional ethical concerns. E-commerce firms routinely track the activity of Internet surfers, collecting and selling information that will allow marketers to target their advertisements more efficiently. Supermarkets use "courtesy" or "club" cards to track the purchases of shoppers. Children use popular apps for smartphones and tablets to share personal information without their parents' knowledge.[33] Hundreds of thousands of video cameras track our movements at automated teller machines, in parking lots, at stores, and in other public places (and even in not-so-public places, such as high school bathrooms and hospital rooms). Drones now make it possible for law enforcement officials and private citizens to secretly film our homes and backyards from the sky. Our interactions with police officers are likely to be recorded now that body cameras are becoming standard equipment for many police departments.[34]

Employers are also gathering more and more information about employee behavior both on and off the job. Technology allows supervisors to monitor computer keystrokes and computer screens, phone calls, website use, voice mail, and e-mail. According to one survey, at least 66% of U.S. companies track employee Internet use, 45% log key strokes, and 43% track employee e-mails.[35] One digital program tracks every move of every waiter and every order at restaurants. Sociometric Solutions conducts research in the banking, pharmaceutical, health care, and technology industries using sensors embedded in ID badges. These microphones, location sensors, and accelerometers track the communication behaviors of workers—tone of voice, posture, body language, and which employees talk to other employees and for how long. Employers also monitor worker behavior outside the workplace. Employees have been fired for posting offensive comments and pictures on blogs and social networking sites. Employers use personal information on Facebook and other social networking sites to screen out job applicants. In a few cases, companies have asked applicants to provide their social media user names and passwords or to log on to their accounts during job interviews so interviewers can look over their shoulders as they scroll through their sites. Applicants can refuse these requests, but many may not because they fear they won't get hired.

Companies have a right to gather information in order to improve performance and eliminate waste and theft. Organizations are also liable for the inappropriate behavior of members, such as when they send sexist or racist messages using their companies' e-mail systems. Investigators discovered that the restaurant monitoring not only reduced employee theft but increased revenue substantially as staff, knowing they were being observed, encouraged more patrons to order drinks and dessert. Truck sensors enabled UPS to deliver 1.4 million additional packages a day with 1,000 fewer drivers. And monitoring can also lead to better working conditions. Bank of America added a 15-minute shared coffee break after a Sociometric Solutions study revealed that employees who took breaks together were more productive and less likely to quit.[36] However, efforts to monitor employee behavior are sometimes done without the knowledge of workers and are inconsistent with organizational values such as trust and community. Invading privacy takes away the right of employees to determine what they reveal about themselves; unwanted intrusion devalues their worth as individuals.[37]

In conclusion, leaders cast shadows not only when they lie but also when they mismanage information and engage in deceptive practices. Unethical leaders

- deny having knowledge that is in their possession,
- hide the truth,
- fail to reveal conflicts of interest,
- withhold information that followers need,
- use information solely for personal benefit,
- violate the privacy rights of followers,
- release information to the wrong people, and
- put followers in ethical binds by preventing them from releasing information that others have a legitimate right to know.

Patterns of deception, whether they take the form of outright lies or the hiding or distortion of information, destroy the trust that binds leaders and followers together. Consider the popularity of conspiracy theories, for example. Many Americans are convinced that the U.S. Air Force is hiding the fact that aliens landed in Roswell, New Mexico. Many also believe that law enforcement officials are deliberately ignoring evidence that John F. Kennedy and Martin Luther King, Jr. were the victims of elaborate assassination plots. More than one-third of Americans polled (and the majority of respondents between the ages of 18 and 29) believe that the George W. Bush administration either planned the attacks on the World Trade Center in 2001 or did nothing after learning in advance of the terrorist plot. These theories may seem illogical, but they flourish in part because government leaders have created a shadow atmosphere through deceit. It wasn't until after the first Gulf War that we learned that our "smart bombs" weren't really so smart and missed their targets. The president and other cabinet officials overstated the danger posed by Saddam Hussein in order to rally support for the second Gulf War.

University of California, Davis history professor Kathryn Olmsted argues that many Americans believe that the government is out to get them in large part because government officials have previously engaged in secret conspiracies.[38] In 1962, for example, the Joint Chiefs of Staff cooked up a plan to get citizens to support a war on Fidel Castro's Cuba by sending a drone plane painted to look like a passenger airliner over the island to be shot down. Fortunately, this plot (dubbed "Operation Northwoods") never went into effect. However, many others were implemented. According to Olmsted,

> By the height of the Cold War, government agents had consorted with mobsters to kill a foreign leader, dropped hallucinogenic drugs into the drinks of unsuspecting Americans in random bars, and considered launching fake terrorist attacks on Americans in the United States. Public officials had denied potentially life-saving treatment to African American men in medical experiments, sold arms to terrorists in return for American hostages, and faked documents to frame past presidents for crimes they had not committed. . . . Later, as industrious congressmen and journalists revealed these actual conspiracies by the government, many Americans came to believe that the most outrageous conspiracy theories about the government could be plausible.[39]

Leaders must also consider ethical issues related to the image they hope to project to followers. In order to earn their positions and to achieve their objectives, leaders carefully manage the impressions they make on others. Impression management can be compared to a performance on a stage.[40] Leader-actors carefully manage everything from the setting to their words and nonverbal behaviors in order to have the desired effects on their follower audiences. For example, presidential staffers make sure that the chief executive is framed by visual images (Mount Rushmore, the Oval Office) that reinforce his (or her) messages and presidential standing. Like politicians, leaders in charge of such high-risk activities as mountain climbing and whitewater kayaking also work hard to project the desired impressions. In order to appear confident and competent, they stand up straight, look others in the eye, and use an authoritative tone of voice.

Impression management is integral to effective leadership because followers have images of ideal leaders called *prototypes*.[41] We expect that the mountain climbing guide will be confident (otherwise, we would cancel the trip!), that the small-group leader will be active in group discussions, and that the military leader will stay calm under fire. The closer the person is to the ideal, the more likely it is that we will select that person as leader and accept her or his influence. Nonetheless, some people (including a number of students) find the concept of impression management ethically troubling. They particularly value integrity and see such role-playing as insincere because a leader may have to disguise his or her true feelings in order to be successful.

There is no doubt that impression management can be used to reach immoral ends. Disgraced financier Bernie Madoff, for example, convinced investors that he was a financial genius even as he was stealing their money in a gigantic fraud scheme. Careerists who are skilled at promoting themselves at the expense of others are all too common.[42] It would be impossible to eliminate this form of influence, however. For one thing, others form impressions of us whether we are conscious of that fact or not. They judge our personality and values by what we wear, for instance, even if we don't give much thought to what we put on in the morning. Most of us use impression management to convey our identities accurately, not to conceal them or to manipulate others.

When considering the morality of impression management, we need to consider its end products. Ethical impression managers meet group wants and needs, not just the needs of the leaders. They spur followers toward highly moral ends. These leaders use impression management to convey accurate information, to build positive interpersonal relationships, and to facilitate good decisions. Unethical impression managers produce the opposite effects, subverting group wishes and lowering purpose and aspiration. These leaders use dysfunctional impression management to send deceptive messages, to undermine relationships, and to distort information, which leads to poor conclusions and decisions.[43]

The Shadow of Inconsistency

Leaders deal with a variety of constituencies, each with its own set of abilities, needs, and interests. In addition, they like some followers better than others. Leader–member exchange (LMX) theory is based on the notion that a leader develops a closer relationship with one group of followers than with others.[44] Members of the "in-group" become the leader's advisers, assistants, and lieutenants. High levels of trust, mutual influence, and support characterize their exchanges with the leader. Members of the "out-group" are expected to carry out the basic requirements of their jobs. Their communication with the leader is not as trusting and supportive. Not surprisingly, members of in-groups are more satisfied and productive than members of out-groups. For that reason, LMX theorists encourage leaders to develop close relationships with as many of their followers as possible.

Situational variables also complicate leader–follower interactions. Guidelines that work in ordinary times may break down under stressful conditions. A professor may state in a syllabus that five absences will result in a student's flunking the class, for instance. However, she may have to loosen that standard if a flu epidemic strikes the campus.

Diverse followers, varying levels of relationships, and elements of the situation make consistency an ethical burden of leadership. Should we, as leaders, treat all followers equally even if some are more skilled and committed or closer to us than others? When should we bend the rules and for whom? Shadows arise when leaders appear to act arbitrarily and unfairly when faced with questions such as these, as in the case of a resident assistant who enforces dormitory rules for some students but ignores infractions committed by friends. Of course, determining whether a leader is casting light or shadow may depend on where you stand as a follower. If you are the star player on your team, you may feel justified taking it easy during practices. If you are less talented, you probably resent the fact that the team's star doesn't have to work as hard as you.

Too often, inconsistency arises between what a leader advocates and how he or she behaves, such as when rabbis and pastors have affairs at the same time they are encouraging members of their congregations to build strong marriages. Employee postings on the website Glassdoor.com reveal that many business leaders fail to live up to the values they espouse. Ross Stores made the list of worst companies to work for (based on Glassdoor ratings) even though the company "makes it an 'everyday priority' to treat its associates with respect." Employees complained about their extremely low salaries and heavy workloads even as the company's profits increased dramatically. Dillard department store CEO William Dillard III urges his managers to bring out what is unique to each employee, but Glassdoor reviewers complained that top management doesn't seem to care about what goes on at lower levels of the company.[45]

In recent years, a number of prominent figures seem to have taken inconsistency to a new level. Former Speaker of the House Dennis Hastert advocated for stronger punishment for sex crimes and sexual abuse of children while paying hush money to a man he molested when working as a high school wrestling coach. Josh Duggar of the reality show *19 and Counting* (which promoted religious values) and employee of the conservative Family Research Council confessed to molesting girls when he was a teen, being addicted to pornography, and cheating on his wife.[46] (Turn to Case Study 1.3 to see yet another example of a celebrity whose private behavior failed to match his public persona.)

Issues of inconsistency can also arise in a leader's relationships with those outside the immediate group or organization. Misgivings about the current system of financing political elections stem from the fact that large donors can buy access to elected officials and influence their votes. Take the sugar subsidy, for example. Under the federal subsidy program, a small number of mostly wealthy farmers are protected by tariffs on imported sugar and can repay their crop loans with raw sugar, which is then sold at a loss to ethanol producers. Economists estimate that American consumers could save $3.5 billion if the sugar program ended because they could then buy cheaper, imported sugar. In addition, candy makers could add 17,000–20,000 new jobs if sugar prices dropped. However, Congress keeps renewing the subsidy program in large part because sugar producers make generous campaign contributions to representatives from both parties. In 2014, the American Chrystal Sugar Company, for example, donated over $1.3 million to 221 members of Congress.[47]

The Shadow of Misplaced and Broken Loyalties

Leaders must weigh a host of loyalties or duties when making choices. In addition to their duties to employees and stockholders, they must consider their obligations to their families, their local communities, their professions, the larger society, and the environment. Noteworthy leaders put the needs of the larger community above selfish interests. For example, outdoor clothing manufacturer Timberland receives praise for its commitment to community service and social responsibility. Company leaders pay employees for volunteer service, partner with community groups, and support nonprofit organizations through the sale of selected products. In contrast, those leaders who appear to put their own interests first are worthy of condemnation.

Loyalties can be broken as well as misplaced. If anything, we heap more scorn on those who betray our trust than on those who misplace their loyalties. Many of history's villains are traitors: Judas Iscariot, Benedict Arnold, Vidkun Quisling (he sold out his fellow Norwegians to the Nazis), and Tokyo Rose, a U.S. citizen who broadcast to American troops on behalf of the Japanese during World War II. More recent examples of leaders who violated the trust of followers include Enron CEO Kenneth Lay, who assured workers that the firm was in good shape even as it was headed toward collapse, and the leaders of Lehman Brothers, who told investors that the firm was strong even as it was struggling to raise money to stave off bankruptcy during the financial crisis.[48]

Employees are often victimized by corporate betrayal motivated by the bottom line. Individuals commonly develop deep loyalties to their coworkers and to their employers. As a consequence, they may do more than is required in their job descriptions, turn down attractive job offers from other employers, and decide to invest their savings in company stock.[49] Unfortunately, companies and their leaders often fail to respond in kind. During economic downturns, they are quick to slash salaries and benefits and to lay off even the most loyal workers. Even if business is good, they don't hesitate to merge with other firms, eliminating positions, or to shut down domestic plants and research facilities in order to move their operations overseas, where labor costs are lower. Organizational leaders admit that their organizations aren't as loyal as they used to be. One survey of senior level North American managers found that only 13% believe that their organizations are more loyal than they were five years ago.[50] It's no wonder that leaders who stick by their workers shine so brightly. One such leader is Bob Moore, who turned over ownership of his Red Mill Natural Foods company to his employees on his 81st birthday. Another is oilman Jeffrey Hildebrand. He carried through on his promise to give bonuses to his 1,400 Hilcorp employees even though oil prices plummeted. Each worker received $100,000 when the firm doubled oil production.[51]

As egregious as corporate examples of betrayal appear, they pale in comparison to cases where adults take advantage of children. Catholic priests in Massachusetts, Oregon, New Mexico, Brazil, Ireland, Germany, and elsewhere used their positions as respected spiritual authorities to gain access to young parishioners for sexual gratification.[52] Church leaders, bishops, and cardinals failed to stop the abusers. In far too many instances, they let offending priests continue to minister and to have contact with children. Often, church officials transferred pedophile priests without warning their new congregations about these men's troubled pasts. Officials at Pennsylvania State University turned a blind eye to evidence that assistant football coach Jerry Sandusky was abusing young boys. In another example involving the betrayal of children, two Pennsylvania juvenile court judges sentenced undeserving young offenders to for-profit detention centers in return for cash payments.

The fact that I've placed the loyalty shadow after such concerns as power and privilege is not intended to diminish its importance. Philosopher George Fletcher argues that we define ourselves through our loyalties to families, sports franchises, companies, and other groups and organizations.[53] Fellow philosopher Josiah Royce contends that loyalty to the right cause produces admirable character traits like justice, wisdom, and compassion.[54] Loyalty is a significant burden placed on leaders. In fact, well-placed loyalty can make a significant moral statement. Such was the case with Pee Wee Reese. The Brooklyn Dodger never wavered in his loyalty to Jackie Robinson, the first black player in baseball's major leagues. In front of one especially hostile crowd in Cincinnati, Ohio, Reese put his arm around Robinson's shoulders in a display of support.[55]

Pay particular attention to the shadow of loyalty as you analyze the feature films highlighted in the "Leadership Ethics at the Movies" boxes in each chapter. In many of these movies, leaders struggle with where to place their loyalties and how to honor the trust others have placed in them.

The Shadow of Irresponsibility

Earlier, we observed that breadth of responsibility is one of the factors distinguishing between the role of leader and that of follower. Followers are largely responsible for their own actions or, in the case of a self-directed work team, for those of their peers. This is not the case for leaders. They are held accountable for the performance of entire departments or other units. However, determining the extent of a leader's responsibility is far from easy. Can we blame a college coach for the misdeeds of team members during the off-season or for the excesses of the university's athletic booster club? Are clothing executives responsible for the actions of their overseas contractors who force workers to labor in sweatshops? Do employers owe employees a minimum wage level, a certain degree of job security, and safe working conditions? If military officers are punished for following unethical orders, should those who issue those orders receive the same or harsher penalties?

Leaders act irresponsibly when they fail to make reasonable efforts to prevent misdeeds on the part of their followers, ignore or deny ethical problems, don't shoulder responsibility for the consequences of their directives, or deny their duties to followers. We don't hold coaches responsible for everything their players do. Nonetheless, we want them to encourage their athletes to obey the law and to punish any misbehavior. Most of us expect Gap, Nike, Sears, Walmart, and Banana Republic to make every effort to treat their overseas labor force fairly, convinced that the companies owe their workers (even the ones employed by subcontractors) decent wages and working conditions. When a company's employees break the law or make mistakes, we want the CEO to take accountability. That was the case at J.P. Morgan Chase when a London trader lost more than $3 billion in risky trades. CEO Jamie Dimon first called the crisis a "tempest in a teapot," a statement that drew heavy criticism from financial analysts. Only later did he take responsibility, saying, "I am absolutely responsible. The buck stops with me."[56]

Many corporate scandals demonstrate what can happen when boards of directors fail to live up to their responsibilities. Far too many boards in the past functioned only as rubber stamps. Made up largely of friends of the CEO and those doing business with the firm, they were quick to approve executive pay increases and other management proposals. Some board members appeared interested only in collecting their fees and made little effort to understand the operations or finances of the companies they were supposed to be directing. Other members were well-intentioned but lacked expertise. Now federal regulations require that the chair of a corporation's audit committee be a financial expert. The compensation, audit, and nominating committees must be made up of people who have no financial ties to the organization. These requirements should help prevent future abuses, but only if board members take their responsibilities seriously. (I'll have more to say about effective corporate governance in Chapter 10.)

These, then, are some of the common shadows cast by leaders faced with the ethical challenges of leadership. Identifying these shadows raises two important questions: (1) *Why is it that, when faced with the same ethical challenges, some leaders cast light and others cast shadows?* (2) *What steps can we take as leaders to cast more light than shadow?* In the next chapter, we will explore the forces that contribute to the shadow side of leadership and outline ways to meet those challenges.

IMPLICATIONS AND APPLICATIONS

- Understanding the dark (bad, toxic) side of leadership is the first step in promoting good or ethical leadership.

- The contrast between ethical and unethical leadership is as dramatic as the contrast between light and darkness.

- Toxic or bad leaders engage in destructive behaviors. They may be ineffective, unethical, or both. Types of bad leaders include incompetent, rigid, intemperate, callous, corrupt, insular, and evil. Destructive leaders are common and have negative impacts on followers and organizations.

- Certain ethical challenges or dilemmas are inherent in the leadership role. If you choose to become a leader, recognize that you accept ethical burdens along with new tasks, expectations, and rewards.

- Power can have a corrosive effect on values and behavior. You must determine how much power to accumulate, what forms of power to use, and how much power to give to followers.

- If you abuse power, you will generally overlook the needs of followers as you take advantage of the perks that come with your position.

- Leaders have access to more information than do followers. In addition to deciding whether or not to hide or tell the truth, as a leader, you'll have to determine when to reveal what you know and to whom, how to gather and use information, and so on.

- A certain degree of inconsistency is probably inevitable in leadership roles, but you will cast shadows if you are seen as acting arbitrarily and unfairly. You must also attempt to match your behavior with your words and values—to "walk your talk."

- As a leader, you'll have to balance your needs and the needs of your small group or organization with loyalties or duties to broader communities. Expect condemnation if you put narrow, selfish concerns first.

- Leadership brings a broader range of responsibility, but determining the limits of accountability may be difficult. You will cast a shadow if you fail to make a reasonable attempt to prevent abuse or to shoulder the blame, or deny that you have a duty to followers.

- Followers face their own set of ethical challenges. When filling a follower role, you will need to determine the extent of your obligations to the group, decide when to obey or disobey, combat cynicism, offer dissent, and deliver bad news to your leaders.

FOR FURTHER EXPLORATION, CHALLENGE, AND SELF-ASSESSMENT

1. Create an ethics journal. In it, describe the ethical dilemmas you encounter as a leader and as a follower, how you resolve them, how you feel about the outcomes, and what you learn that will transfer to future ethical decisions. You may also want to include your observations about the moral choices made by public figures. Make periodic entries as you continue to read this text.

2. Harvard professor Rosabeth Kanter argues that "powerlessness corrupts and absolute powerlessness corrupts absolutely."[57] Do you agree? What are some of the symptoms of powerlessness?

3. What does your score on the Destructive Leader Behavior Scale (Self-Assessment 1.1) reveal about your leader? How can you use this information to become a more effective follower? As an alternative, reflect on your Personal Power Profile (Self-Assessment 1.2). What do your scores reveal about your attitude toward power and the ethical issues you might face in exercising power? Would you like to change your power profile? How can you do so?

4. What factors do you consider when determining the extent of your loyalty to an individual, a group, or an organization?

5. Debate the following propositions in class:
   - The federal government should set limits on executive compensation.
   - Coaches should be held accountable for the actions of their players in the off-season.
   - Corporate leaders have an obligation to be loyal to their employees.
   - Married politicians and religious figures who have extramarital affairs should be forced to resign.
   - Employers have the right to monitor the behavior of workers when the workers are not on the job.

6. Evaluate the work of a corporate or nonprofit board of directors. Is the board made up largely of outside members? Are the members qualified? Does the board fulfill its leadership responsibilities? Write up your findings.

7. Which shadow are you most likely to cast as a leader? Why? What can you do to cast light instead? Can you think of any other ethical shadows cast by leaders?

8. Write a research paper on the privacy issues surrounding drones and/or police body cameras. Conclude with a set of recommendations on how these issues should be resolved.

9. Look for examples of unethical leadership behavior in the news and classify them according to the six shadows. What patterns do you note? As an alternative, look for examples of ethical leadership. How do these leaders cast light instead of shadow?

10. What is the toughest ethical challenge of being a follower? How do you meet that challenge?

Visit the student study site at **study.sagepub.com/johnsonmecl6e** to access full SAGE journal articles for further research and information on key chapter topics.

Case Study 1.1

THE TRAGEDIES OF TEAM FOXCATCHER

Sometimes great privilege puts leaders at great risk. That was the case for John Du Pont. Du Pont was the great grandson of the founder of the Du Pont Company, the creator of nylon, polyester, Kevlar, Lycra, Teflon and other products. Worth an estimated $200 million, Du Pont grew up in a 40-room mansion modeled on President James Madison's home, set on 400 acres outside of Philadelphia.

Du Pont set his sights on becoming an Olympic champion, first in swimming and then in the five-event pentathlon. When it became obvious that he didn't have world-class talent, he set out to associate with those who did. He brought in top swimmers, wrestlers, and pentathletes to join his Team Foxcatcher (named after his estate), providing training facilities and housing them on his property. He paid the athletes' salaries and covered their expenses when they competed at world events. At the same time, Du Pont gave generously to Villanova University, helping to pay for its basketball arena and swimming facility and funding a new wrestling program. When the Villanova wrestling program folded, he gave to USA Wrestling and became a member of the association's board of directors. Du Pont also donated generously to the local Newtown Square police department. He outfitted every officer with body armor, offered the use of his helicopter, built a shooting range on his estate for the force to use, and allowed some police personnel to live at Foxcatcher Farm.

Mark and Dave Schultz put Team Foxcatcher on the sports map. They were the first brothers to both win Olympic gold medals in wrestling in 1992 and, between them, held several national and international titles. Younger brother Mark took the world championship when wrestling for Du Pont and was featured on the Foxcatcher team poster. However, John Du Pont's increasingly bizarre behavior meant that the team's success was short lived. A loner, he used his money to gain approval, to manipulate others, and to fuel his self-esteem. He paid for competitions where he was guaranteed to win, for example, and held award ceremonies where he was honored. Du Pont insisted that he be called "Coach" even though he had no wrestling credentials. He blatantly violated National Collegiate Athletic Association (NCAA) recruiting rules by flying Villanova wrestling recruits on his private plane and housing them

(Continued)

(Continued)

in expensive hotels. A cocaine user and heavy drinker, his behavior could be friendly at one moment and demeaning the next.

As time went on, John Du Pont's behavior grew darker and darker. He claimed that there were spirits and spies residing in his home and hiding in the treetops. He had the treadmills removed from the training center because he was convinced that their clocks were transporting him back in time. He kicked all African Americans off the team because he determined that black was the color of death. He variously wanted to be called Jesus, the last czar of Russia, and the Dalai Lama. In one incident, he pointed a machine gun at a wrestler and threatened to kill him if he didn't leave the farm.

Fed up with John's manipulative, controlling behavior, Mark Schultz left Team Foxcatcher; but brother Dave, who tried to befriend Du Pont, stayed on. In June 1996, John Du Pont drove to the house on Foxcatcher Farm where Dave and his family were living. As Schultz's wife looked on in horror, John shot Dave three times, killing him. Following the shooting, Du Pont took refuge for 48 hours in his mansion, surrounded by Special Weapons and Tactics (SWAT) teams, until he surrendered. There was little doubt of his guilt; his trial centered on whether or not he was legally insane at the time of the killing. He was convicted of 3rd degree manslaughter (a lesser charge based on the fact that he was apparently a paranoid schizophrenic) and sentenced to 15 to 32 years in prison. After being denied parole in 2009, he died of emphysema in 2010.

Many different people might have prevented Du Pont's downward spiral by challenging his behavior and getting him treatment, but they failed to act because they were dependent on his wealth and influence. Officials at Villanova apparently let him break the rules as long as he paid for the basketball arena and the wrestling program. A security company was happy to bill him for checking his mansion for imaginary listening devices. Newton Square police, who used his shooting range and the body armor he supplied, didn't investigate the report that he brought a gun to practice. (The police department claims that the wrestler didn't file a full report on the incident.) Officials at USA Wrestling debated whether or not to break ties with Du Pont but didn't want to give up the $400,000 he donated annually. The wrestlers were in the most vulnerable position because they had no way to support themselves as they trained between Olympics and world events. They needed proper facilities, world-class sparring partners, and income to compete at the highest levels, all of which Du Pont provided. They failed to intervene on behalf of their benefactor because they feared that they would be kicked off the team. As a consequence, John Du Pont's paranoia went unchecked, and Dave Schultz paid with his life. According crime writer Tim Huddleston, "John's wealth enabled him to buy anything he wanted. It enabled him to set his own rules and vanquish his problems. It also kept him sheltered from everything, including the help he so desperately needed."[1]

Discussion Probes

1. Who is most to blame for failing to stop John Du Pont's downward spiral?

2. Do you blame the members of Team Foxcatcher for staying on even as Du Pont's behavior became more erratic?

3. What are the costs of speaking up to powerful leaders? How do we equip ourselves to do so?

4. Can you think of other leaders whose power and/or wealth put them at great risk?

5. How can colleges and nonprofits ensure that donors don't exert too much influence over their activities?

Note

1. Huddleston, T. (2013). *Wrestling with madness: Jon Eleuthere Du Pont and the Foxcatcher Farm murder*. Absolute Crime Books, p. 75.

Source

Schultz, M. (2014). *Foxcatcher*. New York, NY: Dutton.

Case Study 1.2

KILLERS WITH CAMERAS

Body cameras and social media sites have added a new chilling dimension to murder. Killers can now film their crimes and post them for the world to see. That was the case when a disgruntled former television station employee used a body camera to film his murder of television reporter Alison Parker and cameraman Adam Ward during a live report in Roanoke, Virginia. He then wrote about the shooting on Twitter and uploaded his video to Facebook.

News sources were faced with an ethical dilemma: How much (if any) of the shooter's footage should they show to audiences? ABC News refused to show any of the video, as did CNN. According to ABC anchor George Stephanopoulos, "[It was] Something we wrestled with today: whether to grant the gunman his last wish by playing his video. We will not."[1] CBS News used video from Ward's camera (which was also filming during the attack), though stopping before the actual shooting. CBS news president David Rhodes explained, "Using the material we did, we helped people understand the degree of premeditation behind the attack. If you don't show some of what we showed, you can leave people with the impression that somebody just snapped."[2]

The *New York Daily News* received intense criticism for its decision to use three still photos from the shooter's video under the headline "Shocking slay of reporter, cameraman

(Continued)

(Continued)

EXECUTED." In the first two pictures, a gun is aimed at Parker, interviewing a local chamber of commerce official. In the last frame, Parker displays her shock when seeing the gun's muzzle flash. *Daily News* editors defended their use of the images, saying that the photos were a "definitive part of the story, however disturbing and horrific."[3] According to a spokesperson, the paper's editors believe there should be stronger gun control laws and hoped to bring visibility to the issue "at a time when it is so easy for the public to become inured to such senseless violence."[4] In contrast, *The New York Times* decided not to run the pictures because they were so disturbing, as did the *Boston Globe*, which opted instead to use stills taken from Ward's footage showing Flanagan standing over the cameraman.

Killers are apparently motivated to post videos of their deeds in hopes of drawing attention, as a way to say, "Look at me." In so doing, they stand out from previous mass murderers like the Columbine killers or the Virginia Tech gunman who didn't have the technology to easily film their crimes. As more shooters arm themselves with cameras as well as guns, editors can expect to make more decisions about what horrific images to broadcast or publish.

Discussion Probes

1. Would you watch the video of this or another shooting? Why or why not?

2. Does showing videos filmed by killers encourage others to imitate their behavior?

3. Was using the video of cameraman Ward a better option for media outlets than using the shooter's video?

4. Do you think the *Daily News* was more motivated by principle or by the hope of attracting more readers?

5. Do you support the decision of *Daily News* editors to show the still shots of the shooting on its front page? Why or why not?

6. What ethical principles should editors and other leaders use when deciding what information to release?

Notes

1. Koblin, J. (2015, August 28). Front pages on killings in Virginia spur anger. *The New York Times*, p. A12.

2. Koblin.

3. Koblin.

4. Koblin

Sources

Armitage, C. (2015, August 28). Experts warn against switching on to graphic footage of human tragedy. *Sydney Morning Herald*, p. 2.

Birrell, I. (2015, August 28). Social media and a very modern murder. *The Daily Telegraph*, p. 20.

Blatchford, C. (2015, August 27). For the killers, it's all about: 'Look at me.' *The Star Phoenix,* World, p. D4.

Kludt, T. (2015, August 29). New York Daily News defends showing shocking shooting photos. *CNNMoney*.

Manjoo, F. (2015, August 27). Violence gone viral, in a well-planned social media rollout. *The New York Times*, p. A16.

Shear, M. D., Perez-Pena, R., & Blinder, A. (2015, August 27). Gunman kills 2 on air and posts carnage online. *The New York Times*, p. A1.

Case Study 1.3

PUBLIC MORALIST/PRIVATE SEXUAL PREDATOR

Comedian Bill Cosby is not your ordinary entertainment superstar. He helped break racial barriers as the African American costar of the popular *I Spy* television series of the 1960s. (Some Southern stations refused to carry the program because Cosby had a leading role.) He then went on to write an animated television show based on his creation, Fat Albert, and starred as the patriarch of the African American Huxtable family in *The Cosby Show*. He was also featured in ads for Crest toothpaste and Jell-O. All the while, he continued to tour the country, putting on sold-out comedy performances and producing comedy albums. In addition to his artistic achievements, Cosby earned his master's and doctorate degrees in education from the University of Massachusetts–Amherst. He raised money for his undergraduate alma mater, Temple University, and served on its board of trustees. He received honorary doctorates from a number of colleges and universities.

Cosby used his success, as well as his reputation as a racial pioneer and one of America's favorite television dads, as a platform to speak on moral issues in the African American community. In 2004, he delivered a speech at the National Association for the Advancement of Colored People (NAACP) awards ceremony commemorating the 50th anniversary of the Supreme Court *Brown v. Board of Education* decision, which eliminated separate schools for blacks and whites. In what has subsequently become known as the "Pound Cake Speech," Cosby scolded fellow African Americans both for not taking personal responsibility and for bad parenting:

> These are people going around stealing Coca-Cola. People getting shot in the back of the head over a piece of pound cake! Then we all run out and are outraged: "The cops shouldn't have shot him." What the hell was he doing with the pound cake in his hand? I wanted a piece of pound cake just as bad as anybody else. And I looked at it and I had no money. And something called parenting said if you get caught with it you're going

(Continued)

(Continued)

> to embarrass your mother. Not you're going to get your butt kicked. No.
> You're going to embarrass your mother. You're going to embarrass your
> family.[1]

Cosby also criticized single mothers for having multiple children with different husbands and young black men for wearing backward hats and low-slung pants.

Cosby's Pound Cake Speech marked him as a black conservative and as a moral spokesman. But the address would come back to haunt him. In 2014–2015, over 50 women came forward to accuse the megastar of sexual abuse, most claiming he had drugged and then raped them. The alleged assaults took place over decades; victims were typically young, starstruck women who were excited to meet the comedian and get help with their careers. As the accusations became public, Cosby's defense team tried to keep testimony from an earlier civil sexual abuse trial private. Judge Eduardo Robreno, however, rejected their claim that the comedian was not speaking as a public figure in the earlier court case. In releasing documents to the Associated Press (AP), he cited the Pound Cake Speech and noted, "The stark contrast between Bill Cosby, the public moralist and Bill Cosby, the subject of serious allegations concerning improper (and perhaps criminal) conduct is a matter as to which the AP—and by extension the public—has a significant interest."[2] In the court documents, Cosby admits to securing Quaaludes in order to give them to women he intended to have sex with.

Cosby denies the rape allegations and his legal team has adopted an "attack the accuser" defense strategy. His lawyer asserted it was "ridiculous" and "illogical" for these women to come forward decades after the alleged abuse took place. In court papers, he called one civil suit a "shakedown." There are reports that Cosby's legal advisors leaked negative information about his accusers to the news media. Fear of such aggressive tactics, along with Cosby's power and status, kept women from coming forward when the alleged rapes occurred. According to one accuser, "Who was going to believe me? If he was a regular Joe, I might have done something." Said the brother of another alleged victim, "It was a different time. We all also knew this was a really big guy with a big PR operation and lawyers, and that he could crush us—that he would crush us—and her."[3]

Cosby faces criminal charges for one alleged assault as well as a series of civil suits and a defamation lawsuit based on the character attacks of his legal team. His planned comeback is on hold, likely forever. NBC shelved a new Cosby show featuring the comedian as the patriarch of a large multigenerational family; TV Land stopped showing repeats of *The Cosby Show*. Netflix postponed the debut of a Cosby stand-up comedy special.

Discussion Probes

1. What role did power play in Cosby's sexual misbehavior?

2. How do you account for the great inconsistency between Cosby's public moralizing and his alleged predatory sexual behavior?

3. Can you think of other cases where the public image and private behavior of leaders are in stark contrast?

4. Evaluate the ethics of Cosby's legal strategy. Is it ethical to attack the accuser?

5. Do you refuse to support some entertainers and professional athletes because of their unethical or criminal personal behavior? How do you make this determination?

Notes

1. Blake, M. (2015, July 8). How Bill Cosby's 'Pound Cake' speech backfired on the comedian. *Los Angeles Times*.

2. Blake.

3. Roig-Franzia, M., Higham, S., Farhi, P., & Flaherty, M. P. (2014, November 24). Revealed: The case against Bill Cosby. *The Independent* (UK).

Sources

Alter, C. (2014, November 24). Everything you need to know about the Bill Cosby scandal. *Time*.

Carter, B., Bowley, G., & Manley, L. (2014, November 20). Comeback by Cosby unravels as accounts of rape converge. *The New York Times*, p. A1.

Dillon, N., Niemietz, B., Marcius, C. R., & McShane, L. (2014, November 21). "Act like you're drunk, get your hair wet and put your hand down here." *Daily News*, News, p. 4.

Kole, W. J. (2015, October 15). Tufts University and Goucher College revoke degrees given to Bill Cosby. *HuffPost Entertainment*.

Manley, L., Bowley, G., & Moynihand, C. (2014, December 29). Cosby team's strategy: Hush accusers, insult them, blame the media. *The New York Times*, p. C1.

SELF-ASSESSMENT 1.1

Destructive Leader Behavior Scale

Instructions: Think of a leader, supervisor, or manager you have worked with in the past five years. Rate this individual on each of the following items. A rating of 1 indicates that this person *never* engages in this behavior; a rating of 5 indicates that he or she engages in this behavior *very often*.

1	2	3	4	5
Never				Very Often

1. Avoids addressing important issues
2. Denies subordinates things they are entitled to (e.g., lunch breaks, vacation time)
3. Disciplines subordinates a long time after the rule infraction occurs

4. Discounts feedback or advice from subordinates
5. Fails to defend subordinates from attacks by others
6. Fails to give subordinates credit for jobs requiring a lot of effort
7. Falsely accuses or punishes subordinates for something they were not responsible for
8. Ignores phone calls and/or e-mails
9. Inadequately explains performance reviews
10. Insults or criticizes subordinates in front of others
11. Invades subordinates' privacy
12. Is confrontational when interacting with subordinates
13. Says one thing and does another
14. Shows no clear standards for administering rewards and punishments
15. Accepts financial kickbacks
16. At times, appears to be under the influence of alcohol or recreational drugs while at work
17. Breaks the law while at work
18. Falsifies documents
19. Lets violations of company policy slide
20. Litters the work environment
21. Steals company funds
22. Steals company property and resources
23. Tells people outside the job what a lousy place he or she works for
24. Uses company property for personal use
25. Violates company policy/rules
26. Brings inappropriate sexual material to work (e.g., pornography)
27. Engages in romantic and/or sexual relationships with others from work
28. Hints that sexual favors will result in preferential treatment

Scoring: Possible score ranges from 28 to 140. The higher the score, the greater your leader's destructive behavior. You can also determine the leader's tendency to engage in three types of destructive behavior. Items 1–14 measure subordinate-directed behavior. Items 15–25 measure organization-directed destructive behavior. Items 26–28 measure sexual harassment behaviors.

Source: Thoroughgood, C. N., Tate, B. W., Sawyer, K. B., & Jacobs, R. (2012). Bad to the bone: Empirically defining and measuring destructive leader behavior. *Journal of Leadership & Organizational Studies, 19,* 230-255, p. 241. Used with permission of the publisher.

SELF-ASSESSMENT 1.2

Personal Power Profile

Instructions: Below is a list of statements that describe possible behaviors of leaders in work organizations toward their followers. Read each statement carefully while thinking about *how you prefer to influence others.* Mark the number that most closely represents how you feel.

	Strongly Disagree	Disagree	Neither Agree nor Disagree	Agree	Strongly Agree
I prefer to influence others by					
1. increasing their pay level.	1	2	3	4	5
2. making them feel valued.	1	2	3	4	5
3. giving undesirable job assignments.	1	2	3	4	5
4. making them feel like I approve of them.	1	2	3	4	5
5. making them feel that they have commitments to meet.	1	2	3	4	5
6. making them feel personally accepted.	1	2	3	4	5
7. making them feel important.	1	2	3	4	5
8. giving them good technical suggestions.	1	2	3	4	5
9. making the work difficult for them.	1	2	3	4	5
10. sharing my experience and/or training.	1	2	3	4	5
11. making things unpleasant here.	1	2	3	4	5
12. making work distasteful.	1	2	3	4	5
13. helping them get a pay increase.	1	2	3	4	5

(Continued)

(Continued)

14. making them feel they should satisfy job requirements.	1	2	3	4	5
15. providing them with sound job–related advice.	1	2	3	4	5
16. providing them with special benefits.	1	2	3	4	5
17. helping them get a promotion.	1	2	3	4	5
18. giving them the feeling that they have responsibilities to fulfill.	1	2	3	4	5
19. providing them with needed technical knowledge.	1	2	3	4	5
20. making them recognize that they have tasks to accomplish.	1	2	3	4	5

Scoring: Record your responses to the 20 questions in the corresponding numbered blanks below. Total each column, then divide the result by 4 for each of the five types of influence.

	Reward	Coercive	Legitimate	Referent	Expert
	1	3	5	2	8
	13	9	14	4	10
	16	11	18	6	15
	17	12	20	7	19
Total					
Divide by 4					

Interpretation: A score of 4 or 5 on any of the five dimensions of power indicates that you prefer to influence others by using that particular form of power. A score of 2 or less indicates that you prefer not to employ this particular type of power to influence others. Your power profile is not a simple addition of each of the five sources. Some combinations are more synergistic than the simple sum of their parts. For example, referent power magnifies the impact of other power sources because these other influence attempts are coming from a respected person. Reward power often increases the impact of referent power because people generally tend to like those who can give them things. Some power combinations tend to produce the opposite of synergistic effects. Coercive power, for example, often negates the effects of other types of influence.

Source: Modified version of Hinken, T. R., & Schriesheim, C. A. (1989). Development and application of new scales to measure the French and Raven (1959) bases of social power. *Journal of Applied Psychology, 74,* 561–567. Reprinted with permission.

NOTES

1. Palmer, P. (1996). Leading from within. In L. C. Spears (Ed.), *Insights on leadership: Service, stewardship, spirit, and servant-leadership* (pp. 197–208). New York, NY: John Wiley, p. 200.
2. Palmer, p. 200.
3. Lipman-Blumen, J. (2005). *The allure of toxic leaders: Why we follow destructive bosses and corrupt politicians—and how we can survive them.* Oxford, England: Oxford University Press.
4. Kellerman, B. (2004). *Bad leadership: What it is, how it happens, why it matters.* Boston, MA: Harvard Business School Press; Kellerman, B. (2008). Bad leadership—and ways to avoid it. In J. V. Gallos (Ed.), *Business leadership* (2nd ed., pp. 423–432). San Francisco, CA: Jossey-Bass.
5. Kellerman (2004), p. xvi.
6. Erickson, A., Shaw, J. B., & Agabe, Z. (2007). An empirical investigation of the antecedents, behaviors, and outcomes of bad leadership. *Journal of Leadership Studies, 1,* 26–43.
7. Shaw, J. B., Erickson, A., & Harvey, M. (2011). A method for measuring destructive leadership and identifying types of destructive leaders in organizations. *Leadership Quarterly, 22,* 575–590.
8. Einarsen, S., Aasland, M. S., & Skogstad, A. (2007). Destructive leadership behaviour: A definition and conceptual model. *Leadership Quarterly, 18,* 207–216.
9. Aasland, M. S., Skogstad, A., Notelaers, G., Nielson, M. B., & Einarsen, S. (2010). The prevalence of destructive leadership behavior. *British Journal of Management, 21,* 438–452. For a closely allied approach, see Thoroughgood, C. N., Tate, B. W., Sawyer, K. B., & Jacobs, R. (2012). Bad to the bone: Empirically defining and measuring destructive leader behavior. *Journal of Leadership & Organizational Studies, 19,* 230–255.
10. Schyns, B., & Schilling, J. (2013). How bad are the effects of bad leaders? A meta-analysis of destructive leadership and its outcomes. *Leadership Quarterly, 24,* 138–158.
11. Nye, J. S. (2008). *The powers to lead.* Oxford, England: Oxford University Press.
12. French, R. P., & Raven, B. (1959). The bases of social power. In D. Cartwright (Ed.), *Studies in social power* (pp. 150–167). Ann Arbor: University of Michigan, Institute for Social Research.
13. Hackman, M. Z., & Johnson, C. E. (2013). *Leadership: A communication perspective* (6th ed.). Prospect Heights, IL: Waveland, Ch. 5.
14. Pfeffer, J. (1992, Winter). Understanding power in organizations. *California Management Review, 34,* 29–50.
15. Examples taken from Caudron, S. (1995, September 4). The boss from hell. *Industry Week,* 12–16; Terez, T. (2001, December). You could just spit: Tales of bad bosses. *Workforce,* 24–25.
16. Einarsen, S., Hoel, H., Zaptf, D., & Copper, C. L. (2011). The concept of bullying and harassment at work: The European tradition. In S. Einarsen, H. Hoel, D. Zaptf, & C. L. Cooper (Eds.), *Bullying and harassment in the workplace: Developments in theory, research and practice* (2nd ed., pp. 3–40). Boca Raton, FL: CRC Press.
17. Hornstein, H. A. (1996). *Brutal bosses and their prey.* New York, NY: Riverhead.

18. Ashforth, B. E. (1997). Petty tyranny in organizations: A preliminary examination of antecedents and consequences. *Canadian Journal of Administrative Sciences, 14,* 126–140; Burton, J. P., & Hoobler, J. M. (2006). Subordinate self-esteem and abusive supervision. *Journal of Managerial Science, 3,* 340–355; Tepper, B. J. (2000). Consequences of abusive supervision. *Academy of Management Journal, 43,* 178–190; Tepper, B. J. (2007). Abusive supervision in work organizations: Review, synthesis, and research agenda. *Journal of Management, 33,* 261–289.

19. Bad bosses drain productivity. (2005, November). *Training & Development,* p. 15.

20. For a complete typology of responses to abusive supervisors, see Bies, R. J., & Tripp, T. M. (1998). Two faces of the powerless: Coping with tyranny in organizations. In R. M. Kramer & M. A. Neale (Eds.), *Power and influence in organizations* (pp. 203–219). Thousand Oaks, CA: SAGE.

21. Vega, G., & Comer, D. R. (2005). Bullying and harassment in the workplace. In R. E. Kidwell, Jr. & C. L. Martin (Eds.), *Managing organizational deviance* (pp. 183–203). Thousand Oaks, CA: SAGE.

22. Keltner, D., Langner, C. A., & Allison, M. L. (2006). Power and moral leadership. In D. L. Rhode (Ed.), *Moral leadership: The theory and practice of power, judgment, and policy* (pp. 177–194). San Francisco, CA: Jossey-Bass; Kipnis, D. (1972). Does power corrupt? *Journal of Personality and Social Psychology, 24,* 33–41.

23. Bailon, R. R., Moya, M., & Yzerbyt, V. (2000). Why do superiors attend to negative stereotypic information about their subordinates? Effects of power legitimacy on social perception. *European Journal of Social Psychology, 30,* 651–671; Fiske, S. T. (1993). Controlling other people: The impact of power on stereotyping. *American Psychologist, 48,* 621–628.

24. Smith, P. K., Jostmann, N. B., Galinsky, A. D., & van Dijk, W. W. (2008). Lacking power impairs executive functions. *Psychological Science, 19,* 441–447.

25. Information on income disparities is taken from the following sources: Davis, A., & Mischel, L. (2014, June 12). CEO pay continues to rise as typical workers are paid less. *Economic Policy Institute*; Gelles, D. (2015, May 16). For highest-paid CEOs, the party goes on. *NewYorkTimes.com*; Krantz, M. (2015, December 9). Scram! 5 CEOs can get paid $1.3B to get lost. *USA Today,* p. B2; Upper 1 percent of Americans are rolling in the dough. (December 12, 2012). *The Oregonian,* p. A2.

26. Sandler, M. (2015, August 8). CEO pay soars at top not-for-profits. *Modern Health Care.*

27. Bestselling author owes charity $1M. (2012, April 6). *The Toronto Star,* p. A12.

28. Iversen, K. (2012). *Full body burden: Growing up in the nuclear shadow of Rocky Flats.* New York, NY: Crown.

29. Wagner, D. (2014, June 9). VA scandal audit: 120,000 veterans experience long waits for care. *The Arizona Republic.*

30. Garside, J. (2016, April 3). A world of hidden wealth: Why we are shining a light offshore. *The Guardian*; The Panama Papers: Here's what we know. (2016, April 4). *The New York Times.*

31. O'Connor, A. (2015, August 9). Coca-Cola funds scientists who shift blame for obesity away from bad diets. *The New York Times,* p. A1.

32. Wilson, D. (2009, March 4). Senator asks Pfizer to detail pay to Harvard. *The New York Times,* p. B3.

33. Moses, A. (2012, December 23). Privacy concern as apps share data from kids left to their own devices. *Sunday Age* (Melbourne, Australia), News, p. 3; Pagliery, J. (2014). Apps aimed at children collect a shocking amount of data. *CNN.*

34. Carter, S. (2014, August 3). A battlefield of drones and privacy in your backyard. *Chicago Tribune*; Pearce, M. (2014, September 27). Growing use of police body cameras raises privacy concerns. *Los Angeles Times.*

35. See, for example, the following: Lohr, S. (2014), Unblinking eyes track employees. *The New York Times,* p. A1; Rainey, M. (2012, April/May). Fired before you're hired. *INSIGHT into Diversity,* 18–21; Rosenberg, T. (2011, November 24). An electronic eye on hospital handwashing. *The New York Times,* Opinionator blog; The rise of workplace spying. (2015, July 5). *The Week.*

36. The rise of workplace spying; Lohr.

37. Hubbartt, W. S. (1998). *The new battle over workplace privacy.* New York, NY: AMACOM.

38. Olmsted, K. S. (2009). *Real enemies: Conspiracy theories and American democracy, World War I to 9/11.* Oxford, England: Oxford University Press.

39. Olmsted, pp. 8–9.

40. Brissett, D., & Edgley, C. (1990). The dramaturgical perspective. In D. Brissett & C. Edgley (Eds.), *Life as theater: A dramaturgical sourcebook* (2nd ed., pp. 1–46). New York, NY: Aldine de Gruyter.

41. Brown, D. J., Scott, K. A., & Lewis, H. (2004). Information processing and leadership. In J. Antonakis, A. T. Cianciolo, & R. J. Sternberg (Eds.), *The nature of leadership* (pp. 125–147). Thousand Oaks, CA: SAGE.

42. Bratton, V. K., & Kacmar, K. M. (2004). Extreme careerism: The dark side of impression management. In W. Griffin & K. O'Reilly (Eds.), *The dark side of organizational behavior* (pp. 291–308). San Francisco, CA: Jossey-Bass.

43. Rosenfeld, P., Giacalone, R. A., & Riordan, C. A. (1995). *Impression management in organizations: Theory, measurement, practice.* London, England: Routledge.

44. For more information on LMX theory, see Graen, G. B., & Graen, J. A. (Eds.). (2007). *New multinational network sharing.* Charlotte, NC: Information Age; Graen, G. B., & Uhl-Bien, M. (1998). Relationship-based approach to leadership. Development of leader–member exchange (LMX) theory of leadership over 25 years: Applying a multi-level multi-domain perspective. In F. Dansereau & F. J. Yammarino (Eds.), *Leadership: The multiple-level approaches* (pp. 103–158). Stamford, CT: JAI Press; Schriesheim, C. A., Castor, S. L., & Cogliser, C. C. (1999). Leader–member exchange (LMX) research: A comprehensive review of theory, measurement, and data-analytic practices. *Leadership Quarterly, 10,* 63–114; Vecchio, R. P. (1982). A further test of leadership effects due to between-group variation and in-group variation. *Journal of Applied Psychology, 67,* 200–208.

45. Frolich, T. C., Sauter, M. B., & Stebbins, S. (2015, June 29). The worst companies to work for. *24/7 Wall St/Yahoo Finance.*

46. Bowerman, M. (2015, August 20). Timeline: Duggar sex-abuse scandal. *USA Today Network*; Polman, D. (2015, June 1). Dennis Hastert completes the hypocrisy trifecta. *NewsWorks*;

47. Meyer, J. (2014, June 23). Sugar subsidies are a bitter deal for American consumers. *Economics21.*

48. Berman, D. K. (2008, October 28). The game: Post-Enron crackdown comes up woefully short. *The Wall Street Journal*, p. C2.

49. Caldwell, C. (2011). Duties owed to organizational citizens—ethical insights for today's leader. *Journal of Business Ethics, 102,* 343–356; Elegido, J. M. (2013). Does it make sense to be a loyal employee? *Journal of Business Ethics, 116,* 495–511; Rosanas, J. M., & Velilla, M. (2003). Loyalty and trust as the ethical bases of organizations. *Journal of Business Ethics, 44,* 49–59.

50. Davis, S. (2015, June). Dissed loyalty. *Workforce.com*

51. Helman, C. (2015, December 11). What oil bust? Texas billionaire gives each worker a $100,000 bonus. *Forbes.com*; Tims, D. (2010, February 17). Bob gives Red Mill to workers. *The Oregonian*, pp. A1, A5.

52. Ghosh, B. (2010, March 29). Sins of the fathers. *Time,* 34–37; Pogatchnik, S. (2010, March 14). Abuse scandals hit Catholic Church across Europe. *The Oregonian*, p. A11.

53. Fletcher, G. (1993). *Loyalty: An essay on the morality of relationships.* New York, NY: Oxford University Press.

54. Royce, J. (1920). *The philosophy of loyalty.* New York, NY: Macmillan.

55. Rampersad, A. (1997). *Jackie Robinson.* New York, NY: Alfred A. Knopf.

56. Goldfarb, A. Z. (2012, June 12). JPMorgan CEO Jamie Dimon apologizes for trading losses in Hill testimony. *The Washington Post.*

57. Kanter, R. M. (1979, July–August). Power failure in management circuits. *Harvard Business Review,* 65–75.

2

Stepping Out of the Shadows

Darkness is most likely to get a "hold" when you are safely settled in the good and righteous position, where nothing can assail you. When you are absolutely right is the most dangerous position of all, because, most probably, the devil has already got you by the throat.

—PSYCHOTHERAPIST EDWARD EDINGER

If I only had a little humility, I'd be perfect.

—MEDIA MOGUL TED TURNER

WHAT'S AHEAD

In this chapter, we look at why leaders cast shadows instead of light and how they can master these forces. Shadow casters include (1) unhealthy motivations, (2) personality disorders, (3) faulty thinking caused by mistaken assumptions, (4) failure of moral imagination, (5) moral disengagement, (6) lack of ethical expertise, and (7) contextual (group, organizational, societal) pressures that encourage people to set their personal standards aside. To address these shadow casters, we need to look inward to address our motivations, improve our moral decision making, acquire ethical knowledge and skills, and resist negative situational influences as we create healthy ethical environments. Ethical development, like other forms of leader development, incorporates assessment, challenge, and support. We can track our progress by adopting the skills and strategies used by ethical experts.

Only humans seem to be troubled by the question "Why?" Unlike other creatures, we analyze past events (particularly the painful ones) to determine their causes. The urge to understand and to account for the ethical failures of leaders has taken on added urgency with the continuing string of corporate and political scandals. Observers wonder: Why would bright, talented chief executive officers (CEOs) lie to customers, government regulators, and investors; ignore serious safety problems; make fraudulent loans; and engage in insider trading? Why can't multimillionaire executives be satisfied with what they already have? Why do they feel they need more? Why do politicians lose sight of the fact that they are public servants? How can they urge others to behave ethically at the same time they enrich themselves at taxpayer expense and break the law? (See Box 2.1 for one set of answers to these questions.)

Box 2.1 The Dark Side of Success: The Bathsheba Syndrome

Management professors Dean Ludwig and Clinton Longenecker believe that top managers often become the victims of their own successes, leading even highly moral individuals to abandon their principles. Having achieved their goals after years of service and hard work, these competent, popular, and ethical leaders destroy their careers by engaging in behavior they know is wrong. Ludwig and Longenecker refer to this pattern as the "Bathsheba syndrome," named for the story of King David reported in both the Bible and the Torah. King David, described as a "man after His [God's] own heart" in I Samuel 13:14, expanded the national borders of ancient Israel by vanquishing the country's enemies. Yet, at the height of his powers, he began an affair with Bathsheba. After she got pregnant, he tried to cover up his actions by calling her husband, Uriah, back from the battlefield to sleep with her. When Uriah refused to enjoy the comforts of home while his comrades remained in battle, David sent Uriah back to the front lines to be killed. As Ludwig and Longenecker note, "David's failings as a leader were dramatic even by today's standards and included an affair, the corruption of other leaders, deception, drunkenness, murder, the loss of innocent lives" (p. 265). The fallout from David's immoral behavior was devastating. He lost the child he fathered with Bathsheba; his top military commander, Joab, betrayed him; and one of his sons temporarily drove him from office.

There are four by-products of success that put otherwise ethical leaders in a downward spiral. First, personal and organizational success encourages leaders to become complacent and to lose their strategic focus. They begin to shift their attention to leisure, entertainment, and other self-centered pursuits and fail to provide adequate supervision. David's problems began, for example, when he stayed home instead of going to war with his men. Second, success leads to privileged access to information and people, which the leader uses to fulfill personal desires (like having sex with Bathsheba) instead of serving the organization. Third, success leads to the control of resources, which the leader then uses selfishly. David employed his power to begin the affair, to call Uriah back from the battlefield, and then to order Joab to put Uriah in the thick of the battle and to withdraw, leaving Uriah and his colleagues to be killed. Fourth, control of resources is often tied to an inflated belief in one's ability to control the outcomes of a situation. David was confident that he could cover up his actions, but the prophet Nathan later revealed his sins.

Professors Ludwig and Longenecker offer advice to successful leaders to keep them from becoming victims of the Bathsheba syndrome. Be humble—what happened to David and to other successful leaders can happen to any leader, no matter how smart or skilled. Keep in touch with reality by living a balanced life filled with family, relationships, and interests outside of work. Never be satisfied with current direction and performance. Recognize that privilege and status equip leaders for providing a strategic vision and executing strategy; they are not the reward for past performance or for personal gratification. Assemble a team of ethical managers to provide challenge or support as needed. Finally, recognize that ethical leadership is a component of good leadership. Ethical, effective leaders serve as role models, make wise use of resources, build trust, and make good decisions.

Source: Ludwig, D. C., & Longenecker, C. O. (1993). The Bathsheba syndrome: The ethical failure of successful leaders. *Journal of Business Ethics, 12,* 265–273.

Coming up with an explanation provides a measure of comfort and control. If we can understand *why* something bad has happened (broken relationships, cruelty, betrayal), we may be able to put it behind us and move on. We are also better equipped to prevent something similar from happening again. Such is the case with shadows. If we can identify the reasons for our ethical failures (what I'll call *shadow casters*), we can then step out of the darkness they create.

The first section of this chapter identifies common shadow casters; the second section outlines strategies for meeting these challenges. Keep in mind that human behavior is seldom the product of just one factor. For example, leaders struggling with insecurities are particularly vulnerable to external pressures. Faulty decision making and inexperience often go hand in hand; we're more prone to make poor moral choices when we haven't had much practice. To cast more light and less shadow, we need to address all the factors that undermine ethical performance.

SHADOW CASTERS

Unhealthy Motivations: Internal Enemies or Monsters

Parker Palmer believes that leaders project shadows out of their inner darkness. That's why he urges leaders to pay special attention to their motivations, lest "the act of leadership create more harm than good." Palmer identifies five internal enemies or "monsters" living within leaders that produce unethical behavior.[1] I'll include one additional monster to round out the list.

Monster 1: Insecurity. Leaders often are deeply insecure people who mask their inner doubts through extroversion and by tying their identities to their roles as leaders. Who they are is inextricably bound to what they do. Leaders project their insecurities on others when they use followers to serve their selfish needs.

Monster 2: Battleground mentality. Leaders often use military images when carrying out their tasks, speaking of wins and losses, allies and enemies, and doing battle with the competition. For example, as we'll see in Chapter 10, Amazon's Jeff Bezos is one leader who is ready to declare war on the competition. He is willing to lose millions in order to undercut competitors and capture product categories.[2] Acting competitively becomes a self-fulfilling prophecy; competition begets competitive responses in return. This militaristic approach can be counterproductive. More often than not, cooperation is more productive than competition (see Chapter 9). Instead of pitting departments against each other, for instance, a number of companies use cross-functional project teams and task forces to boost productivity.

Monster 3: Functional atheism. Functional atheism is a leader's belief that she or he has the ultimate responsibility for everything that happens in a group or an organization. As Palmer describes it, "It is the unconscious, unexamined conviction within us that if anything decent is going to happen here, I am the one who needs to make it happen."[3] This shadow destroys both leaders and followers. Symptoms include high stress, broken relationships and families, workaholism, burnout, and mindless activity.

Monster 4: Fear. Fear of chaos drives many leaders to stifle dissent and innovation. They emphasize rules and procedures instead of creativity and consolidate their power instead of sharing it with followers.

Monster 5: Denying death. Our culture as a whole denies the reality of death, and leaders, in particular, don't want to face the fact that projects and programs should die if they are no longer useful. Leaders also deny death through their fear of negative evaluation and public failure. Those who fail should be given an opportunity to learn from their mistakes, not be punished. Only a few executives display the wisdom of IBM founder Thomas Watson. A young executive entered his office after making a $10 million blunder and began the conversation by saying, "I guess you want my resignation." Watson answered, "You can't be serious. We've just spent $10 million educating you!"[4]

Monster 6: Evil. There are lots of other demons lurking in leaders and followers alike—jealousy, envy, rage—but I want to single out evil for special consideration, making it the focus of Chapter 4. Palmer doesn't specifically mention evil as an internal monster, but it is hard to ignore the fact that some people seem driven by a force more powerful than anxiety or fear. Evil may help us answer the question "Why?" when we're confronted with monstrous shadows such as those cast by the Holocaust, the genocides in Serbia and Sudan, and Islamic State in Iraq and Syria (ISIS) terrorist attacks.

A great deal of destructive leadership behavior is driven by self-centeredness, which manifests itself through pride and greed. Self-centered leaders are proud of themselves and their accomplishments. They lack empathy for others and can't see other points of view or learn from followers. They are too important to do "little things" such as making their own coffee or standing in line, so they hire others to handle these tasks for them.[5] Their focus is on defending their turf and maintaining their status instead of on cooperating with other groups to serve the common good. Ego-driven leaders ignore creative ideas and valuable data that come from outside their circles of influence. Goal blockage helps explain the impact of self-centeredness on bad leadership. If self-centered leaders believe that they can't achieve money, status, organizational recognition or other goals, they often respond with deviant and aggressive behavior. They might engage in fraud and embezzlement, for instance, or mistreat followers who appear to be keeping them from reaching their objectives.[6]

Hubris describes the excessive pride of top leaders. The term first appears in Greek mythology to refer to "a sense of overweening pride, a defiance of the gods" which generally ends in death and destruction.[7] The myth of Icarus is the best known of these myths. Icarus's father fashioned a set of artificial wings out of wax and feathers so that he and his son could escape the island where they were being held captive. Icarus ignored his father's warning not to fly to close to the sun. Infatuated with his ability to soar and the adoration of onlookers who mistook him for a god, Icarus rose too high. The wax on his wings melted and he crashed to his death in the sea. Modern hubristic leaders equate themselves with their organizations and resist attempts to step down from power. Former Disney CEO Michael Eisner, for example, had a reputation for arrogance, engaging in nasty court fights with top executives he hired and then fired. He had to be forced to retire, and few mourned his exit.[8]

Greed is another hallmark of self-oriented leaders. They are driven to earn more (no matter how much they are currently paid) and to accumulate additional perks. Greed focuses attention on making the numbers—generating more sales, increasing earnings, boosting the stock price, recruiting more students, collecting more donations. In the process of reaching these financial goals, the few often benefit at the expense of the many, casting the shadow of privilege described in Chapter 1.

The international financial crisis, which stemmed from the collapse of the U.S. housing market, can largely be attributed to greed.[9] Mortgage brokers generated higher commissions and profits by making risky and fraudulent loans. Borrowers often took on too much credit, buying homes or consumer items they couldn't afford. Wall Street banks, eager to make money off of the mortgage market, repackaged mortgages and sold them to investors as "low-risk" products in the United States, Europe, and elsewhere. AIG and other insurers generated revenue by guaranteeing what turned out to be toxic investments. The financial system nearly collapsed when housing prices dropped and consumers defaulted on their loans, putting lenders, investment bankers, investors, and insurers at risk. Economic observers worry that the pattern could repeat itself as the U.S. housing market heats up again with soaring prices and lower down payment requirements.

Personality Disorders

A number of psychologists believe that unethical leadership is the product of destructive personality traits. They identify three closely related traits—narcissism, Machiavellianism, and psychopathy—as the "dark triad" behind the dark side of leadership.[10] (See "Focus on Follower Ethics: The Susceptible Follower" for more information on what motivates subordinates to follow leaders who cast shadows.)

Narcissism has its origins in an ancient Greek fable. In this tale, Narcissus falls in love with the image of himself he sees reflected in a pond. Like their ancient namesake, modern-day narcissists are self-absorbed and self-confident. According to researchers, a certain degree of narcissism is normal and healthy, giving us faith in our own abilities and enabling us to recover from setbacks. The problem comes with high levels of this trait. Extreme narcissists have a grandiose sense of self-importance, believe that they are special, like attention, constantly seek positive feedback, lack empathy, and feel entitled to their power and positions. They also have an unrealistic sense of what they can accomplish.[11]

Moderate narcissism may be positive trait for leaders, at least in the short term. Confident and outgoing, narcissists often as emerge as leaders. They exude confidence, take bold action, and craft inspirational visions for their followers.[12] However, extreme narcissistic leaders engage in a wide range of unethical behaviors. They claim special privileges, demand admiration and obedience, abuse power for their personal ends, fail to acknowledge the contributions of subordinates, claim more than their fair share, lash out in anger, are dishonest, ignore the welfare of others, and have an autocratic leadership style. Narcissists put their groups, organizations, and countries at risk because their dreams and visions are unrealistic and can't be implemented. For example, Napoleon stretched France's resources beyond the breaking point. Jean-Marie Messier, a modern French business leader, followed in Napoleon's footsteps by overextending his financial empire.[13] Messier spent $100 billion trying to build Vivendi—originally a French water and sewage provider—into the largest media and entertainment company in the world

Focus on Follower Ethics

THE SUSCEPTIBLE FOLLOWER

Most researchers interested in studying the impact of destructive leadership concentrate on the traits and behaviors of the leaders. They want to know why these individuals engage in selfish, unethical behavior that undermines the organization and harms others. Focusing solely on the leader, however, can obscure the fact that destructive leadership requires the participation of followers. For example, a medical clinic operator can't overbill insurance companies for treatments without the cooperation of administrative staff, accountants, and (perhaps) nurses and physicians.

One group of scholars argues that we can gain a better understanding of the process of destructive leadership by identifying the factors that make followers susceptible to the influence of destructive superiors. They place susceptible subordinates into two categories: conformers and colluders. Conformers engage in destructive behavior while obeying their leaders. Colluders actively support or contribute to their leaders' destructive missions.

Conformers: Lost souls. Lost souls are needy individuals. They are vulnerable to destructive leaders because they have basic unmet needs (for love and affection, for example), may be experiencing high levels of distress (e.g., flunking out of college, losing a parent), lack a clear sense of self, and have low self-esteem. They comply because they identify with the leader, who offers them a sense of direction, community, and a stronger sense of self and self-esteem.

Conformers: Authoritarians. Authoritarians believe that leaders have a right to demand obedience, and it is their belief in the legitimacy of the leader that triggers their obedience. They reflect an unconditional respect for authority; prefer a simple, well-defined environment; and believe in a just world where people get what they deserve.

Conformers: Bystanders. Bystanders, likely the largest group of susceptible followers, are generally passive and motivated by fear. They let destructive leaders have their way because they think they will be punished if they object. Bystanders generally have negative self-evaluations that convince them that they can't resist, believe that have to submit to whoever is in power, and often see themselves as victims. Highly sensitive to elements of the situation, they remain passive in order to avoid punishment. These individuals are often introverts who lack a courageous, prosocial orientation.

Colluders: Opportunists. Opportunists carry out the destructive directives of their leaders because they believe that they will be rewarded for doing so. Opportunists are ambitious, greedy, and manipulative, lacking in self-control. Rewards—money, status, power—are the key to motivating them to participate in unethical and illegal behaviors.

Colluders: Acolytes. Acolytes are "true believers." They actively partner with the leader because they share the leader's goals and values. They are largely self-motivated. Collaborating with the destructive leader helps them fulfill their personal identities, which have toxic qualities.

Thoroughgood and Padilla apply their model to the child sex abuse scandal at Penn State University. They believe that the university failed

(Continued)

to prevent an assistant coach from abusing young boys because a number of officials conformed to the wishes of powerful football Coach Joe Paterno. Others (including some former football players who served on the Board of Trustees) were devoted acolytes of Paterno and his success.

SOURCES: Thoroughgood, C. N., & Padilla, A. (2013). Destructive leadership and the Penn State scandal: A toxic triangle perspective. *Industrial and Organizational Psychology, 6,* 144-149; Thoroughgood, C. N., Padilla, A., Hunter, S. T., & Tate, B. W. (2012). The susceptible circle: A taxonomy of followers associated with destructive leadership. *Leadership Quarterly, 23,* 897-917.

Additional Sources

Barbuto, J. E. (2000). Influence triggers: A framework for understanding follower compliance. *Leadership Quarterly, 11,* 365-387.

Padilla, A., Hogan, R., & Kaiser, R. B. (2007). The toxic triangle: Destructive leaders, susceptible followers, and conducive environments. *Leadership Quarterly, 18,* 176-194.

by buying phone companies, Internet ventures, cable networks, and Seagram (which owned Universal Studios and Universal Records). His grandiose ambitions outstripped his ability to bring them to fruition. Losses from his collection of mismatched companies mounted, and he was forced out. The result was the greatest financial loss in French corporate history. (Case Study 2.1 describes another leader who demonstrates strong narcissistic tendencies.)

We can expect even more narcissistic leaders in the future if current trends continue. By all indications, narcissism is on the rise. Researchers report, for example, that between 1982 and 2009, narcissism scores among college students increased significantly. (Among business students, finance majors are more narcissistic and less empathetic than accounting and marketing majors.) This "epidemic" of narcissism has been attributed to a range of factors, including permissive parenting, celebrity culture, social media, and materialism.[14]

Machiavellianism, like narcissism, is highly self-centered. Richard Christie and Florence Geis first identified this personality factor in 1970. Christie and Geis named this trait after Italian philosopher Niccolò Machiavelli, who argued in *The Prince* that political leaders should maintain a virtuous public image but use whatever means necessary—ethical or unethical—to achieve their ends.[15] Highly Machiavellian individuals are skilled at manipulating others for their own ends. They have a better grasp of their abilities and reality than narcissists but, like their narcissistic colleagues, engage in lots of self-promotion, are emotionally cold, and are prone to aggressive behavior. Machiavellian leaders often engage in deception because they want to generate positive impressions while they get their way. They may pretend to be concerned about others, for example, or they may assist in a project solely because they want to get in good with the boss. Machiavellians often enjoy a good deal of personal success—organizational advancement, higher salaries—because they are so skilled at manipulation and at disguising their true intentions. Nonetheless, Machiavellian leaders put their groups in danger. They may be less qualified to lead than others who are not as skilled as they in impression management. They are more likely to engage in unethical practices that put the organization at risk because they want to succeed at any cost. If followers suspect that their supervisors are manipulating them, they are less trusting and cooperative, which can make the organization less productive.[16]

Psychopathy makes up the third side of the dark triangle. Psychopaths have a total lack of conscience, which distinguishes them from narcissists and Machiavellians, who are less ruthless and may experience at least some feelings of guilt and remorse for their actions.[17] Psychopaths are attracted to organizations by their desire for power and wealth. Getting to positions of high power is a game to them, and they are prepared to use any tactic to win. Extroverted, energetic, and charming, they find it easy to enter organizations. Once hired, they lie and manipulate others in their single-minded pursuit of power and prestige. As a result of their surface charm, social abilities, and political skill, they often rise to the top of their companies. One study of Australian managers found that the percentage of psychopaths rose at every step up the organizational hierarchy, with the highest percentage found in senior management.[18] Such leaders can undermine the ethical decision-making processes and climate of entire groups. Box 2.2 outlines the negative behaviors of psychopaths as well as the destructive impact they have on followers and organizations.

Faulty Decision Making

Identifying dysfunctional motivations is a good first step in explaining the shadow side of leadership. Yet well-meaning, well-adjusted leaders can also cast shadows, as in the case of Shell UK. In 1995, company officials decided to dispose of the Brent Spar, a large floating oil storage buoy in the North Sea, by sinking it in deep water.[19] This was the least expensive option for disposing of the structure, and the British government signed off on the project. However, Shell and British government leaders failed to give adequate consideration to the environmental impact of their proposal. Greenpeace activists, who were trying to curb the dumping of waste and other contaminants into the world's oceans, argued that deepwater disposal set a bad precedent. They worried that the scuttling the Brent Spar would be the first of many such sinkings, and Greenpeace members twice occupied the Brent Spar in protest. Consumers in continental Europe began boycotting Shell gas stations, and representatives of the Belgian and German governments protested to British officials. Shell withdrew its plan to sink the buoy, and it was towed to Norway instead, where it was cut apart and made part of a quay. Shell later noted that this was a defining event in the company's history, one that made it more sensitive to outside groups and possible environmental issues.

Blame for many ethical miscues can be placed on the way in which decisions are made. Moral reasoning, though focused on issues of right and wrong, has much in common with other forms of decision making. Making a wise ethical choice involves many of the same steps as making other important decisions: identifying the issue, gathering information, deciding on criteria, weighing options, and so on. A breakdown anywhere along the way can derail the process. Problems typically stem from (1) unsound assumptions and (2) failure of moral imagination.

Decision-making experts David Messick and Max Bazerman speculate that many unethical business decisions aren't the products of greed or callousness but stem instead from widespread weaknesses in how people process information and make decisions. In particular, executives have faulty theories about how the world operates, about other people, and about themselves.[20]

Box 2.2 Psychopaths: Behaviors and Outcomes

- Engage in fraud
- Unfairly fire employees
- Claim credit for the work of others
- Use the system to their own advantage
- Increase employee workloads
- Fail to care for the needs of employees
- Exploit employees, creating a disheartened workforce
- Create conflicts between groups, generating chaos
- Bully and humiliate workers
- Lack a sense of corporate social responsibility
- Focus on short-term gain (their wealth and power)

- Disregard the interests of investors
- Increase employee turnover, which drives away skilled, knowledgeable workers
- Damage the environment
- Partner with other psychopaths
- Lower employee job satisfaction
- Increase absenteeism
- Disrupt organizational communication
- Increase the likelihood of corporate failure

Sources: Boddy, C. R. (2006). The dark side of management decisions: Organisational psychopaths. *Management Decision, 44*, 1461-1475; Boddy, C. R. (2011). *Corporate psychopaths: Organisational destroyers.* New York, NY: Palgrave MacMillan.

Theories about How the World Operates

These assumptions have to do with determining the consequences of choices, judging risks, and identifying causes. Executives generally fail to take into account all the implications of their decisions (see Box 2.3). They overlook low-probability events, fail to consider all the affected parties, think they can hide their unethical behavior from the public, and downplay long-range consequences. In determining risk, decision makers generally fail to acknowledge that many events happen by chance or are out of their control. America's involvement in Vietnam, for example, was predicated on the mistaken assumption that the United States could successfully impose its will in the region. Other times, leaders and followers misframe risks, thus minimizing the dangers. For instance, a new drug seems more desirable when it is described as working half of the time rather than as failing half of the time.

The perception of causes is the most important of all our theories about the world because determining responsibility is the first step to assigning blame or praise. In the United States, we're quick to criticize the person when larger systems are at fault. We may criticize salespeople for trying to sell us extended warranties that are generally a waste of money. However, executives should be blamed for requiring their employees to push these products. Messick and Bazerman also point out that we're more likely to blame someone else for acting immorally than for failing to act. We condemn the executive who steals, but we are less critical of the executive who doesn't disclose the fact that another manager is incompetent.

Box 2.3 Decision-Making Biases

THEORIES ABOUT THE WORLD

- Ignoring low-probability events even when they could have serious consequences later
- Limiting the search for stakeholders and thus overlooking the needs of important groups
- Ignoring the possibility that the public will find out about an action
- Discounting the future by putting immediate needs ahead of long-term goals
- Underestimating the impact of a decision on a collective group (e.g., industry, city, profession)
- Acting as if the world is certain instead of unpredictable
- Failing to acknowledge and confront risk
- Framing risk differently than followers
- Blaming people when larger systems are at fault
- Excusing those who fail to act when they should

THEORIES ABOUT OTHER PEOPLE

- Believing that our group is normal and ordinary (good) whereas others are strange and inferior (bad)

- Giving special consideration and aid to members of the in-group
- Judging and evaluating according to group membership (stereotyping)

THEORIES ABOUT OURSELVES

- Rating ourselves more highly than other people
- Underestimating the likelihood that negative things will happen to us, such as divorce, illness, accidents, and addictions
- Believing that we can control random events
- Overestimating our contributions and the contributions of departments and organizations
- Overconfidence, which prevents us from learning more about a situation
- Concluding that the normal rules and obligations don't apply to us

Source: Messick, D. M., & Bazerman, M. H. (1996, Winter). Ethical leadership and the psychology of decision making. *Sloan Management Review, 37*(2), 9–23. See also Bazerman, M. H. (1986). *Management in managerial decision making.* New York, NY: John Wiley.

Theories about Other People

These are our organized beliefs about how *we* differ from *they* (competitors, suppliers, managers, employees, ethnic groups). Such beliefs, which we may not be aware of, influence how we treat other people. Ethnocentrism and stereotyping are particularly damaging.

Ethnocentrism is the tendency to think that our group is better than other groups, that our way of doing things is superior to theirs. We then seek out (socialize with, hire) others who look and act like us. Military leaders often fall into the trap of ethnocentrism when they underestimate the ability of the enemy to resist hardships. For example, commanders have no trouble believing that their own citizens will survive repeated bombings but don't think that civilian populations in other nations can do the same. Such was the case in World War II. The British thought that bombing Berlin would break the spirit of the Germans, forgetting that earlier German air raids on London had failed to drive Britain out of the war. American leaders believed that they could quickly overcome Iraqi resistance in the second Gulf War. Instead, fighting continued for years.

Stereotypes, our beliefs about other groups of people, are closely related to ethnocentrism. These theories (women are weaker than men, the mentally challenged can't do productive work) can produce a host of unethical outcomes, including sexual and racial discrimination. (We'll take a closer look at ethnocentrism and stereotyping in Chapter 11.)

Theories about Ourselves

These faulty theories involve self-perceptions. Leaders need to have a degree of confidence to make tough decisions, but their self-images are often seriously distorted. Executives tend to think that they (and their organizations) are superior, are immune to disasters, and can control events. No matter how fair they want to be, leaders tend to favor themselves when making decisions. Top-level managers argue that they deserve larger offices, more money, and stock options because their divisions contribute more to the success of the organization. Overconfidence is also a problem for decision makers because it seduces them into thinking that they have all the information they need, so they fail to learn more. Even when they do seek additional data, they're likely to interpret new information according to their existing biases.

Unrealistic self-perceptions of all types put leaders at ethical risk. Executives may claim that they have a right to steal company property because they are vital to the success of the corporation. Over time, they may come to believe that they aren't subject to the same rules as everyone else. University of Richmond leadership studies professor Terry Price argues that leader immorality generally stems from such mistaken beliefs.[21] Leaders know right from wrong but often make exceptions for (justify) their own actions. They are convinced that their leadership positions exempt them from following traffic laws or from showing up to meetings on time, for example.

Leaders may justify immoral behavior such as lying or intimidating followers on the grounds that it is the only way to protect the country or to save the company. Unethical leaders may also decide, with the support of followers, that the rules of morality apply only to the immediate group and not to outsiders. Excluding others from moral considerations—from moral membership—justified such unethical practices as slavery and colonization in the past. In recent times, this logic has been used to deny legal protections to suspected terrorists. (Turn to Chapter 4 for an in-depth look at moral exclusion.)

The loftier a leader's position, the greater the chances that he or she will overestimate his or her abilities. Powerful leaders are particularly likely to think they are godlike, believing they are omniscient (all-knowing), omnipotent (all-powerful), and invulnerable (safe from all harm).[22] Top leaders can mistakenly conclude they know everything because they have access to many different sources of information and followers look to them for answers. They believe that they can do whatever they want because they have so much power. Surrounded by entourages of subservient staff members, these same officials are convinced that they will be protected from the consequences of their actions. Former Hewlett-Packard CEO Mark Hurd believed that he could get away with billing the company for unauthorized travel expenses for a female employee who may have been his lover. Former Speaker of the House Dennis Hastert thought he could hide $3.5 million in illegal payments to one of his victims.

Failure of Moral Imagination

According to many ethicists, moral imagination—sensitivity to moral issues and options—is key to ethical behavior and works hand in hand with moral reasoning in the decision-making process.[23] Moral imagination consists of three related components (1) sensitivity to ethical dimensions of the situation, (2) perspective taking (considering other people's point of view), and (3) creation of novel solutions.

Former Merck & Co. CEO Roy Vagelos is one example of a leader with a vivid moral imagination. He proceeded with the development of the drug Mectizan, which treats the parasite that causes river blindness in Africa and South America, even though developing the product would be expensive and there was little hope that patients in poor countries could pay for it.[24] When relief agencies didn't step forward to fund and distribute the drug, Merck developed its own distribution systems in poor nations. Lost income from the drug totaled more than $200 million, but the number of victims (who are filled with globs of worms that cause blindness and death) dropped dramatically. In contrast, National Aeronautics and Space Administration (NASA) engineer Roger Boisjoly, recognized the ethical problem of launching the space shuttle *Challenger* in cold weather in 1985 but failed to generate a creative strategy for preventing the launch. He stopped objecting and deferred to management (normal operating procedure). Boisjoly made no effort to go outside the chain of command to express his concerns to the agency director or to the press. The *Challenger* exploded soon after liftoff, killing all seven astronauts aboard. Failure of moral imagination also contributed to the crash of the space shuttle *Columbia* seventeen years later, as lower-level employees once again failed to go outside the chain of command to express safety concerns.

Moral imagination facilitates ethical reasoning because it helps leaders step away from their typical mental scripts or schemas and to recognize the moral elements of events. Unfortunately, our scripts can leave out the ethical dimension of a situation. Shell officials failed to take into account the ethical considerations of their decision to sink the Brent Spar, for instance. To them, this was a routine business decision, largely based on cost, that would solve an oil industry problem—how to dispose of outdated equipment cheaply. Or consider the case of Ford Motor Company's failure to recall and repair the gas tanks on the Pintos it manufactured between 1970 and 1976. The gas tank on this subcompact was located behind the rear axle. It tended to rupture during any rear-end collision, even at low speed. When this happened, sparks could ignite the fuel, engulfing the car in flames. Fixing the problem would have only cost $11 per vehicle, but Ford refused to act. The firm believed that all small cars were inherently unsafe and that customers weren't interested in safety. Furthermore, Ford managers conducted a cost–benefit analysis and determined that the costs in human life were less than what it would cost the company to repair the problem.

The National Highway Traffic Safety Administration finally forced Ford to recall the Pinto in 1978, but by that time, the damage had been done. The company lost a major lawsuit brought by a burn victim. In a trial involving the deaths of three Indiana teens in a rear-end crash, Ford became the first major corporation to face criminal, not civil, charges for manufacturing faulty products. The automaker was later acquitted, but its image was severely tarnished.

Business professor Dennis Gioia, who served as Ford's recall coordinator from 1973 to 1975, blames moral blindness for the company's failure to act.[25] Ethical considerations were not part of the safety committee's script. The group made decisions about recalls based on the number of incidents and cost–benefit analyses. Because there were only a few reports of gas tank explosions and the expense of fixing all Pinto tanks didn't seem justified, members decided not to act. At no point did Gioia and his colleagues question the morality of putting a dollar value on human life or of allowing customers to die in order to save the company money.

Moral imagination also enhances moral reasoning by encouraging the generation of novel alternatives. Recognizing our typical problem-solving patterns frees us from their power. We are no longer locked into one train of thought but are better able to generate new options. Consider the response of former New York City mayor Michael Bloomberg to the danger of possible violent demonstrations during the 2004 Republican National Convention. Instead of trying to control the movement of protestors and putting more officers on the street (the typical response of mayors), Bloomberg offered peace demonstrators discounts at select hotels, museums, and restaurants during the week of the convention. (Measure your level of moral imagination by completing Self-Assessment 2.1.)

Moral Disengagement

While moral decision making has much in common with other forms of reasoning, it does have unique features. Most important, morality involves determining right and wrong based on personal ethical standards. Normally, we feel guilt, shame, and self-condemnation if we violate our moral code by lying when we believe in truth telling, telling a racist joke when we believe in treating others with dignity, and so on. According to Stanford University social psychologist Albert Bandura, we frequently turn off or deactivate these self-sanctions through the process of moral disengagement. Moral disengagement helps account for the fact that individuals can have a clear sense of right and wrong yet engage in immoral activities. "People do not ordinarily engage in reprehensible conduct," says Bandura, "until they have justified to themselves the rightness of their actions."[26] As a result, they are able to commit unethical behavior with a clear conscience. Using the following mechanisms, they convince themselves that their immoral conduct is moral, minimize their role in causing harm, and devalue the victims of their destructive behavior.[27]

Turning Immoral Conduct into Moral Conduct

Moral justification. Moral justification is a process of self-persuasion. Leaders convince themselves that their harmful behavior is actually moral and beneficial. Team captains justify cheating and dirty play as a way of protecting the team members or team honor. Hiding product defects is defended as a way to keep sales up and thus save the company and jobs.

Euphemistic labeling. Euphemistic language has a sanitizing function, making harmful behavior appear more respectable and reducing personal responsibility. Examples include referring to civilians accidently killed in war as *collateral damage* and using the term *disfellowshipped* to describe those kicked out of some Christian churches. Leaders may also try to exonerate themselves by speaking as if what they did was the product of nameless outside forces. For instance, instead of saying "I laid employees off," they say, "There were layoffs." Or they may use language associated with legitimate enterprises to lend an aura of respectability to illegitimate ones. Members of the Mafia call themselves businessmen instead of criminals, for example, to make their activities appear more acceptable.

Advantageous comparison. Contrast involves comparing unethical or criminal acts with even worse activities, thus making them appear more tolerable. In sports, coaches and players excuse their use of bad language by comparing this offense to more serious violations like fighting with opponents. Defenders of Bill Clinton minimized his sexual affairs by noting that he didn't get the nation into war as did his successor, George W. Bush.

Minimizing Harm

Displacement of responsibility. Individuals are most likely to sanction themselves for bad behavior if they acknowledge their role in causing harm. Therefore, they often put the blame on someone else so as to minimize their responsibility for doing damage to others. Followers may claim that they were following orders when they inflated sales figures, for instance. Leaders often distance themselves from illegal activities by remaining "intentionally uninformed." They don't go looking for evidence of wrongdoing and, if wrongdoing occurs, dismiss these cases as "isolated incidents" caused by followers who didn't understand corporate policies.

Diffusion of responsibility. Diffusing or spreading out responsibility also lessens personal accountability for immoral behavior. In large organizations, division of labor reduces responsibility. For over a decade, employees in many different divisions of General Motors (engineering, customer service, the legal department) knew about a faulty ignition switch on the company's small cars. However, they failed to notify their superiors, to communicate with each other, to reach out to victims, or to offer a fix to the problem. Over a hundred deaths have been linked to the defective switch.[28]

Disregard or distortion of consequences. Hiding suffering is one way to disregard the consequences of harmful actions and reduce the likelihood of self-recrimination. For example, in drone warfare, plane operators cause death and destruction thousands of miles away. Such physical separation makes it easier to kill without remorse. Organizational hierarchies also hide destructive consequences, as executives may not see the outcomes of their choices. They may never visit their oppressive overseas manufacturing facilities, for example. Or if they order layoffs, they may never come face to face with the distraught employees they eliminated from the payroll.

Devaluing Victims

Dehumanization. It is easier to mistreat others if they are seen as less than fully human. In extreme cases, dehumanization leads to rape, genocide, and other acts of atrocity. Viewing outsiders as savages, degenerates, or fiends encourages brutality. Dehumanization can be much more subtle, however. Many societal forces, such as urbanization, mobility, and technology, make it hard to relate to others in personal ways. When people are strangers, they are more likely to be targeted for mild forms of exclusion such as disparaging comments and unfair comparisons.

Attribution of blame. Blaming others is an expedient way to excuse unethical behavior. In a conflict, each party generally blames the other for starting the dispute and each side considers itself faultless. Blaming the victim is also common. If the victim is to blame, then the victimizer is freed from guilt. Some sexual harassers, for instance, excuse their behavior by saying that certain women invite sexual harassment by the way that they dress. Sadly, some victims come to accept the definition put on them by their victimizers.

Moral disengagement is the product of personal and social forces. Society helps determine personal standards (e.g., it is wrong to cheat or to hurt innocent people), but groups and organizations commonly weaken sanctions for violating personal values. As noted above, leaders who engage in unethical acts often declare that such behavior is essential to achieving worthy goals. They help displace responsibility when they order followers to engage in illegal activities. When some group members dehumanize outsiders, others in the group are more likely to do the same. Some followers are more susceptible to moral disengagement than others, including those who are cynical and believe that life is shaped by events outside of their control.[29]

Using scales like the one found in Self-Assessment 2.2, researchers have discovered a strong link between moral disengagement and unethical behavior in a variety of settings.[30] Disengaged children tend to be aggressive and delinquent. Not only are they more likely to bully and to cyberbully, they have less empathy for the victims of bullying. When playing video games, morally disengaged gamers engage more frequently in torture and killing innocent civilians. Morally disengaged high school and college athletes are more prone to antisocial behaviors, such as trying to injure opponents and breaking the rules of the game. At the same time, they are less likely to demonstrate such prosocial behaviors as helping injured opponents or congratulating them for good play. In the work setting, the tendency to morally disengage increases the likelihood of lying, deception, cheating, stealing, computer hacking, favoring the self at the expense of others, damaging company property, using illegal drugs, and making racist remarks. Citizens with a propensity for moral disengagement show higher support for military aggression and harsh punishment for criminals.

Lack of Ethical Expertise

Leaders may unintentionally cast shadows because they lack the necessary knowledge, skills, and experience. Many of us have never followed a formal, step-by-step approach to solving an ethical problem in a group. Or we may not know what ethical perspectives or frameworks can be applied to ethical dilemmas. When you read and respond to Case Study 2.2, for example, you may have a clear opinion about whether or not you would support strict vaccination laws. You may be less clear about the standards you use to reach your conclusion, however. You might use a common ethical guideline ("Public health is more important than individual rights"; "The risks or costs of vaccination programs outweigh the benefits") but not realize that you have done so.

Emotions are critical to ethical decision making and action, as we'll see in Chapter 6. And it is possible to blunder into good ethical choices. Nevertheless, we are far more likely to make wise decisions when we are guided by some widely used ethical principles and standards. These ethical theories help us define the problem, highlight important elements of the situation, force us to think systematically, encourage us to view the problem from a variety of perspectives, and strengthen our resolve to act responsibly.

Lack of expertise undermines our confidence to act ethically—our *ethical efficacy*. Ethical efficacy is the conviction that we have motivation and skills to make an ethical choice and follow through on it. Our level of ethical efficacy has a direct impact on our moral behavior. The lower our sense of ethical efficacy, the less likely we will engage in such ethical behaviors as helping coworkers, confronting abusive supervisors, and trying to improve the ethical climate of our organizations.[31]

Contextual Pressures

Not all shadow casters come from individual forces like unhealthy motivations, faulty decision making, and lack of expertise. Ethical failures are the product of group, organizational, and cultural factors as well. Conformity is a problem for many small groups. Members put a higher priority on group cohesion than on coming up with a well-reasoned choice. They pressure dissenters, shield themselves from negative feedback, keep silent when they disagree, and so on. Alternatively, they may be convinced there is agreement among group members when none exists.[32] Members of these shadowy groups engage in unhealthy communication patterns that generate negative emotions while undermining the reasoning process.

Organizations can also be shadow lands. For instance, car dealerships are known for their deceptive practices, and cell phone retailers have largely earned the same reputation. Although working in such environments makes moral behavior much more difficult, no organization is immune to ethical failure. Some companies focus solely on results without specifying how those results are to be achieved, leaving employees in a moral vacuum. Others reward undesirable behavior or fail to punish those who break the rules. Instead, their leaders punish employees who question actions and policies. Top managers may fire employees who talk about ethical issues so that they can claim ignorance if followers do act unethically. This "don't ask, don't tell" atmosphere forces workers to make ethical choices on their own, without the benefit of interaction. Members of these organizations seldom challenge the questionable decisions of others and assume that everyone supports the immoral acts. (Case Study 2.3 describes how the culture of one organization encouraged a massive fraud.)

Obedience is a particularly strong conformity pressure. Even in highly individualistic cultures like the United States, people appear programmed to follow orders. In one of the most vivid examples of this tendency, psychologist Stanley Milgram asked research subject "teachers" to administer electric shocks to "learners" (who were really confederates and were not hurt) who failed to answer questions correctly. More than 60% of the participants in his 1960s studies were fully obedient. They turned up the power to maximum level at the request of an experimenter dressed in a lab coat, even though the cries and protests of the "learners" grew louder with each increase in voltage. Replications of Milgram's studies forty years later revealed the same pattern, with subjects just as willing to follow the orders of the experimenters.[33] (Turn to "Leadership Ethics at the Movies: *The Imitation Game*" for an example of one leader who resisted conformity pressures.)

Socialization, as we'll see in Chapter 10, can be an important tool for promoting ethical climate. However, this process can also encourage employees to set their personal

Leadership Ethics at the Movies

THE IMITATION GAME

Key Cast Members: Benedict Cumberbatch, Keira Knightley, Matthew Good, Charles Dane

Synopsis: Benedict Cumberbatch plays brilliant British mathematician Alan Turing who joins a secret team assigned to break the Nazi Enigma code during World War II. Through a combination of arrogance and social insensitivity, Turing (who appears to suffer from mild form of autism) soon alienates his supervisor and coworkers. His boss and colleagues want to shut down his efforts to build a code-breaking machine. However, with the help of female mathematician Joan Clarke (played by Keira Knightley), Turing is able to overcome bureaucratic resistance and rally his fellow code breakers. They succeed in breaking the German code using the world's first computer. However, breaking the code is just the first step. British intelligence can't reveal that it has broken the code or the Germans will switch to a new system. Turing's team then develops a statistical program to tell British intelligence how often it can act on decoded information. Their efforts are credited with shortening the war by two years and saving fourteen million lives. Following the war, Turing is prosecuted for being a homosexual and commits suicide. British secrecy laws keep Turing from receiving the credit he deserves until decades after his death.

Rating: PG-13 for mature themes and language

Themes: conformity, obedience, creativity, courage, group problem solving, challenge of misinformation, follower challenges of obedience and dissent, utilitarianism

Discussion Starters

1. How does Turing's lack of social intelligence both help and hinder his efforts as a code breaker?

2. Why do Turing's colleagues rally to his defense?

3. Was British intelligence justified in acting on only some of the decoded information?

4. Was it necessary to keep the Enigma project secret after World War II ended? Why or why not?

---

codes aside. Organizations use orientation sessions, training seminars, mentors, and other means to help new hires identify with the group and absorb the group's culture. Loyalty to and knowledge of the organization are essential. Nonetheless, the socialization process may blind members to the consequences of their actions. For example, leaders at Wal-Mart, who are proud of the company's culture and accomplishments, are often puzzled when neighborhoods oppose their new supercenters and activists criticize the company for low wages and poor treatment of suppliers.[34] Organizations can also deliberately use the socialization process to corrupt new members

Cultural differences, like group and organizational forces, can also encourage leaders to abandon their personal codes of conduct. (We'll examine this topic in more depth in

Chapter 11.) A corporate manager from the United States may be personally opposed to bribery. Her company's ethics code forbids such payments, and so does federal law. However, she may bribe customs officials and government officials in her adopted country if such payments are an integral part of the national culture and appear to be the only way to achieve her company's goals.

So far, our focus has been on how external pressures can undermine the ethical behavior of leaders and followers. However, this picture is incomplete, as we will explore in more depth in the last section of the text. Leaders aren't just the victims of contextual pressures but are the architects of the unethical climates, structures, policies, and procedures that cause groups and organizations to fail in the first place. Corporate scandals are typically the direct result of the actions of leaders who not only engage in immoral behavior but also encourage subordinates to follow their example. They are poor role models, pursue profits at all costs, punish dissenters, reward unethical practices, and so forth. Unethical followers can also encourage unethical behavior in their leaders.

STEPPING OUT OF THE SHADOWS

Now that we've identified the factors that cause us to cast shadows as leaders, we can begin to master them. To do so, we will need to look inward to address our motivations; improve our ethical decision making; acquire ethical knowledge, strategies, and skills; and resist negative contextual influences as we create healthy ethical climates. I hope you will view your ethical development as part of your overall development as a leader. According to researchers at the Center for Creative Leadership (CCL), we can expand our leadership competence, and the skills and knowledge we acquire (including those related to ethics) will make us more effective in a wide variety of leadership situations, ranging from business and professional organizations to neighborhood groups, clubs, and churches.[35] CCL staff members report that leader development is based on assessment, challenge, and support. Successful developmental experiences provide plenty of feedback that lets participants know how they are doing and how others are responding to their leadership strategies. Such feedback can be formal (360-degree feedback, surveys) and informal (feedback from colleagues, observing the reactions of coworkers). Assessment data provoke self-evaluation ("What am I doing well?" "How do I need to improve?") and provide information that aids in self-reflection. Simply put, a leader learns to identify gaps between current performance and where he or she needs to be and then learns how to close those gaps.

The most powerful leadership experiences also stretch or challenge people. As long as people don't feel the need to change, they won't. Difficult and novel experiences, conflict situations, and dealing with loss, failure, and disappointment force leaders outside their comfort zones and give them the opportunity to practice new skills. Each type of challenge teaches a different lesson, so leaders need a variety of experiences. A formal leadership program can reveal a leader's ethical blind spots, for example, and experiencing failure can develop perseverance and resilience.

To make the most of feedback and challenges, leaders need support. Supportive comments ("I appreciate the effort you're making to become a better listener"; "I'm confident that you can handle this new assignment") sustain the leader during the struggle to improve. The most common source of support is other people (family, coworkers, bosses), but developing leaders can also draw on organizational cultures and systems. Supportive organizations believe in continuous learning and staff development, provide funds for training, reward progress, and so on.

All three elements—assessment, challenge, and support—should be part of your plan to increase your ethical competence. You need feedback about how well you handle ethical dilemmas, how others perceive your character, and how your decisions affect followers. You need the challenges and practice that come from moving into new leadership positions. Seek out opportunities to influence others by engaging in service projects, chairing committees, teaching children, or taking on a supervisory role. You also need the support of others to maximize your development. Talk with colleagues about ethical choices at work, draw on the insights of important thinkers, and find groups that will support your efforts to change.

Emeritus Wright State University ethics professor Joseph Petrick argues that we need to develop three broad types of ethical competencies.[36] *Cognitive decision-making competence* encompasses all the skills needed to make responsible ethical choices, including moral awareness, moral understanding, moral reasoning and dialogue, and the resolution of competing arguments and demands. *Affective prebehavioral disposition competence* describes the motivation needed to act on ethical choices. To match our words with our deeds, we need to be morally sensitive, empathetic, courageous, tolerant, and imaginative. *Context management competence* focuses on creating and shaping moral environments. Essential context management skills involve managing formal compliance and ethics systems, overseeing corporate governance, and exercising global citizenship.

Donald Menzel, former president of the American Society of Public Administration, identifies five important moral competencies for those serving in government, which can apply to those in other professions as well.[37] First, as leaders, we should be committed to high standards of personal and professional behavior. Second, we ought to understand relevant ethics codes and laws related to our organizations. Third, we have to demonstrate the ability to engage in ethical reasoning when confronted with moral dilemmas. Fourth, we must identify and then act on important professional values. Fifth, we have to demonstrate our commitment to promoting ethical practices and behaviors in our organizations.

University of Notre Dame psychologists Darcia Narvaez and Daniel Lapsley offer the novice–expert continuum as one way to track our ethical progress.[38] They argue that the more we behave like moral experts, the greater our level of ethical development. Ethical authorities, like experts in other fields, think differently than novices. First, they have a broader variety of schemas to draw from, and they know more about the ethical domain. Their networks of moral knowledge are more developed and connected than those of beginners. Second, they see the world differently than novices. While beginners are often overwhelmed by new data, those with expertise can quickly identify and act on relevant information, such as what ethical principles might apply in a given situation. Third, experts have different skill sets. They are better able than novices to define the moral problem and then match the new dilemma with previous ethical problems they have encountered. "Unlike novices," Narvaez and Lapsley say, "they know *what* information to access, *which* procedures to apply, *how* to apply them, and *when* it is appropriate."[39] As a result, they make faster, better moral decisions.

Narvaez and Lapsley argue that to become an ethical expert, you should learn in a well-structured environment (like a college or university) where correct behaviors are rewarded and where you can interact with mentors and receive feedback and coaching. You will need to master both moral theory and skills (see Box 2.4). You should learn how previous experts have dealt with moral problems and how some choices are better than others. As you gain experience, you'll not only get better at solving ethical problems but also be better able to explain your choices. Finally, you will have to put in the necessary time and focused effort. Ethical mastery takes hours of practice wrestling with moral dilemmas.

Box 2.4 Ethical Skills: A Sampler

Darcia Narvaez developed the following list of ethical skills that should be incorporated into the training offered in ethical education programs. These are also the abilities that we need to develop as leaders and are addressed in this text. Narvaez developed the list after surveying moral exemplars like Martin Luther King, Jr. and virtue theory, as well as scholarship in morality, moral development, positive psychology, and citizenship. Taken together, these skills help us function well in a pluralistic democracy while promoting the health of society as a whole.

ETHICAL SENSITIVITY (RECOGNITION OF ETHICAL PROBLEMS)

Understanding emotional expression

Taking the perspective of others

Connecting to others

Responding to diversity

Controlling social bias

Interpreting situations

Communicating effectively

ETHICAL JUDGMENT (DECISION MAKING)

Understanding ethical problems

Using codes and identifying judgment criteria

Reasoning generally

Reasoning ethically

Understanding consequences

Reflecting on process and outcome

Coping and resilience

ETHICAL FOCUS (MOTIVATION TO ACT ETHICALLY)

Respecting others

Cultivating conscience

Acting responsibly

Helping others

Finding meaning in life

Valuing traditions and institutions

Developing ethical identity and integrity

ETHICAL ACTION (FOLLOWING THROUGH ON MORAL DECISIONS)

Resolving conflicts and problems

Asserting respectfully

Taking initiative as a leader

Implementing decisions

Cultivating courage

Persevering

Working hard

Source: Narvaez, D. (2006). Integrative ethical education. In M. Killen & J. Smetana (Eds.), *Handbook of moral development* (pp. 717–728). Mahwah, NJ: Erlbaum, p. 717. Used with permission of the publisher.

It is important to note that making and implementing ethical decisions takes communication as well as critical thinking skills, as the list in Box 2.4 illustrates. We must be able to articulate our reasoning, convince other leaders of the wisdom of our position, and work with others to put the choice into place. For instance, a manager who wants to eliminate discriminatory hiring practices will have to listen effectively, gather information, formulate and make arguments, appeal to moral principles, and build relationships. Failure to develop these skills will doom the reform effort.

IMPLICATIONS AND APPLICATIONS

- Unethical or immoral behavior is the product of a number of factors, both internal and external. You must address all of these elements if you want to cast light rather than shadow.

- Unhealthy motivations that produce immoral behavior include internal enemies (insecurity, battleground mentality, functional atheism, fear, denying death, evil) and selfishness (pride, hubris, greed).

- The dark triad—narcissism, Machiavellianism, psychopathy—are three personality disorders linked to the dark side of leadership.

- Good leaders can and do make bad ethical decisions because of defective reasoning.

- Beware of faulty assumptions about how the world operates, about other people, and about yourself. These can lead you to underestimate risks and overestimate your abilities and value to your organization. Avoid the temptation to excuse or justify immoral behavior based on your leadership position.

- Exercise your moral imagination: Be sensitive to ethical issues, step outside your normal way of thinking, and come up with creative solutions.

- Be alert to the process of moral disengagement, which involves persuading yourself that immoral conduct is actually moral, minimizing the harm you cause, and devaluing the victims of your destructive actions.

- Leaders may unintentionally cast shadows because they lack the necessary knowledge, skills, and experience.

- Contextual or situational pressures encourage leaders and followers to set aside their personal standards to engage in unethical behavior. Conformity will encourage you to put cohesion above ethical choices. Obedience may override your personal moral code.

- Make your ethical development part of your larger leadership development plan. The three key elements of any development strategy are (1) assessment or feedback that reveals any gaps between current and ideal performance, (2) challenging (difficult, new, demanding) experiences, and (3) support in the form of resources and other people.

- Key ethical competencies involve making responsible ethical decisions, being motivated to follow through on moral choices, and shaping the moral environment.

- To become more of an ethical expert, learn in a well-structured environment, master moral theory and skills, and devote the necessary time and effort to the task of ethical improvement.

FOR FURTHER EXPLORATION, CHALLENGE, AND SELF-ASSESSMENT

1. In a group, identify unhealthy motivations to add to the list provided in this chapter.

2. Are we in the midst of a narcissism epidemic? Are narcissistic leaders a growing danger? Write up your conclusions.

3. Evaluate a well-publicized ethical decision you consider to be faulty. Determine whether mistaken assumptions and/or lack of moral imagination were operating in this situation. Write up your analysis.

4. Complete Self-Assessment 2.2. What do your results reveal about your tendency to excuse your unethical behavior? What steps can you take to avoid this form of faulty reasoning?

5. Rate your ethical development based on your past experience and education. Where would you place yourself on the continuum between novice and expert? What in your background contributes to your rating?

6. Analyze a time when you cast a shadow as a leader. Which of the shadow casters led to your unethical behavior? Write up your analysis.

7. How much responsibility do followers have for supporting destructive leaders? Discuss with a partner.

8. Does your employer pressure you to abandon your personal moral code of ethics? If so, how? What can you do to resist such pressure?

9. Create a plan for becoming more of an ethical expert. Be sure that it incorporates assessment, challenge, and support. Revisit your plan at the end of the course to determine how effective it has been.

STUDENT STUDY SITE

Visit the student study site at **study.sagepub.com/johnsonmecl6e** to access full SAGE journal articles for further research and information on key chapter topics.

Case Study 2.1

THE BAD BOY OF THE PHARMACEUTICAL INDUSTRY

Turing Pharmaceutical founder Martin Shkreli is not likely to win a popularity contest anytime soon. Shkreli set off a firestorm of outrage when his company acquired the rights to a 62-year-old drug, Daraprim, and then raised the price of the medication from $13.50 a pill to $750, an

(Continued)

(Continued)

increase of over 5,000%. HIV patients and women infected during pregnancy (many of them minorities and low income) use the drug to combat a parasite.

Turing Pharmaceutical and Shkreli were blasted in social media for price gouging, and protestors picketed the company's headquarters in Manhattan. Some carried signs with a picture of the CEO and the caption "The Face of Greed." Health officials from the Infectious Diseases Society of America and the HIV Medicine Association sent a joint letter to Turing declaring the price increase "unjustifiable for the medically vulnerable patient population."[1] The United States Senate Special Committee on Aging launched an investigation and presidential candidates from both parties condemned the price hike.

Turing Pharmaceutical isn't the only company to acquire older drugs and then jack up their prices. Rodelis Therapeutics increased the cost of a bottle of a tuberculosis drug from $500 to $10,800. Mylan raised the price of the EpiPen—used for severe allergic reactions—27% a year between 2011 and 2015. Valeant Pharmaceuticals boosted the cost of two heart drugs by hundreds of percent. These price hikes can dramatically increase company profits. Jazz Pharmaceuticals saw revenue from the sleep disorder drug Xyrem increase from $29 million in 2006, when it acquired the medication, to $777.6 million by 2015, based on average price hikes of 29% a year and increased use of the drug.

While Turing Pharmaceutical's business strategy isn't unique, thirty-two-year-old Shkreli quickly became the "bad boy" of the pharmaceutical industry.[2] When criticized, he offered what observers called his "tone-deaf response," which "threw more gasoline on his public relations bonfire."[3] He condemned the Senate investigation, declaring that senators were "trying to make a tempest out of a teacup, and a mountain out of a molehill."[4] He promised a "modest decrease" in the price of Daraprim but didn't specify how much (and later backed off this promise). While he claimed that the company would use the profits from the price hike to develop a better treatment for patients, health care experts disagreed. They wondered why it was necessary to replace an effective, inexpensive drug.

Shkreli's behavior on social media did little to burnish his image. Before he made his account private, the CEO's Twitter feed featured trips to Vegas, the World Wrestling Federation, and fantasies of dating super stars. One tweet read, "Taylor Swift, Katy Perry or [Theranos CEO] Elizabeth Holmes. Who would you date if you were me?"[5] Once he came under attack, he proclaimed that he would troll journalists who "smell liberal" and claimed that he had been swamped with support. He used another Twitter message to yell out his frustration at the picture of him being used in the media: "WILL EVERYONE PLEASE STOP USING THAT UGLY PIC OF ME. I HATE BLOOMBERG FOR TAKING IT—THERE ARE SO MANY BETTER ONES."[6] Shkreli was particularly irate with former presidential candidate Bernie Sanders, who refused a donation from Turing Pharmaceutical. To take revenge, he posted a picture of Sanders riding a unicorn.

Shkreli has a troubled history. Before becoming the "bad boy of pharmaceuticals," Shkreli ran hedge funds and Retrophin, another drug firm.[7] He made millions for himself and his investors but left a trail of lawsuits and accusations in his wake. He had to pay part of a $2.3 million settlement to Lehman Brothers and was sued by two former employees who claimed they didn't get paid.

A former hedge fund executive accused Shkreli of taking over his personal e-mail and Facebook accounts and using social media to harass his family. The board of Retrophin sued its former CEO for using company funds to pay investors in his hedge fund, and the federal government charged him for securities and wire fraud for trying to hide his losses. Shkreli offers his own take on his legal problems. For example, he accuses the former executive of stealing $3 million in profits that should have gone to his hedge fund. He describes the Retrophin lawsuit as "a sad attempt to avoid paying a very large severance amount" and brags, "After being kicked out of my own company, I've built a bigger and better one."[8] His attorney declared that Shkreli was confident he would be cleared of the criminal charges.

Commenting on Shkreli's troubled track record, one of his earliest investors noted that he seems to operate without a moral compass. (This may be due in part to his rapid rise to riches.) According to the investor, "There's nobody there in Martin's life to tell him what the right thing is."[9]

Discussion Probes

1. What shadow casters do you see in Martin Shkreli?
2. Do you think rapid success increases the chances that leaders will victim to shadow casters?
3. How should Shkreli respond to his critics? How should he use social media?
4. Is Turing Pharmaceutical, as well as other companies that follow the same business model, engaged in price gouging or are these firms serving the interests of their investors?
5. Would you invest in Turing Pharmaceutical or other, similar drug companies?
6. Should the federal government regulate drug prices? Why or why not?

Notes

1. Pollack, A. (2015, September 21). Once a neglected treatment, now an expensive specialty drug. *The New York Times*, p. B1.
2. Pollack, A., & Creswell, J. (2015, September 23). The man behind the drug price increase. *The New York Times*, p. B1.
3. Ho, Catherine. (2015, October 11). Working for Turing Pharmaceuticals CEO, "Most hated man in America." *The Washington Post*.
4. Tirrell, M. (2015, November 4). Turing CEO: Senate drug probe is "mountain out of molehill." *CNBC*.
5. Fox, E. J. (2015, September 22). Turing Pharmaceuticals C.E.O.: We'll maybe stop the drug price gouging. *Vanity Fair*.
6. Williams, M. E. (2015, October 20). Don't feed the Shkreli. *Salon.com*
7. Pollack & Creswell.

(Continued)

(Continued)

8. Pollack & Creswell.

9. Pollack & Creswell.

Sources

Cresswell J., Clifford, S., & Pollack, A. (2015, December 18). Drug CEO Martin Shkreli arrested on fraud charges. *The New York Times*, p. A1.

Perrone, M. (2015, November 4). Senate panel summons price-hiking CEO of Turing Pharma. *Associated Press.*

Pollack, A. (2015, October 13). New York Attorney General examining if Turing restricted drug access. *The New York Times*, p. B4.

Pollack, A., & Tavernise, S. (2015, October 18). Big price hikes put spotlight on drugmakers. *The Oregonian*, pp. D1, D2.

Case Study 2.2

THE BATTLE OVER VACCINATIONS

Measles was once the scourge of American school children, infecting 3–4 million kids and adults every year. Best known for causing an itchy head-to-toe red rash, the virus can also produce high fever, seizures, and even death. Development of a measles vaccine dramatically lowered the number of cases. In fact, the immunization effort was so successful that in the year 2000, health authorities declared that measles had been eliminated from the United States.

Unfortunately, the virus launched a comeback. In 2014, the Centers for Disease Control and Prevention reported 644 cases from 27 states. The biggest outbreak started at Disneyland, infecting park workers and visitors who spread the illness to friends, families, and neighbors when they traveled back home. Medical officials blame the resurgence of measles on the anti-immunization movement. According to one pediatric disease specialist, the Disneyland outbreak was "100 percent connected" to the opposition to vaccines. "It wouldn't have happened otherwise—it wouldn't have gone anywhere."[1] Anti-vaxxers believe that risks of immunization outweigh the benefits, so they request exemptions to child vaccination laws. In particular, parents worry that their sons and daughters will contract autism; a fear flamed by a now-discredited British study linking immunization injections to the syndrome. Said one worried mother about the M.M.R. vaccine (measles, mumps, and rubella): "It's the worst shot. Do you want to wake up one morning and the light is gone from her eyes with autism or something?"[2] Anti-vaxxers don't trust medical authorities and suspect that pharmaceutical companies are out to boost their profits by promoting immunization programs. They believe that all parents should have the right to choose whether or not their children receive vaccinations.

In order to prevent outbreaks (to provide "herd immunity"), vaccination rates need to be at 95% and above. A few school districts fall below this percentage because vaccine exemptions tend to cluster in certain areas. In California, for instance, the percentage of unvaccinated kids can run as high as 30%–40% in some wealthy, highly educated school districts outside Los Angeles and San Francisco. Many parents in these districts take an all-natural approach to parenting, which includes serving their children organic foods and keeping them from getting shots.

Disease experts note that the immune systems of infants and young children easily handle the antibodies in the vaccines. They point out that parents who fail to immunize their children are exposing them to needless suffering from a preventable disease. Unvaccinated children also put others in the community at risk. In response, some parents have banned the children of anti-vaxxers from birthday parties and neighborhood get-togethers.

The California legislature responded to the Disney outbreak by passing one of the strongest mandatory vaccination laws in the country, joining West Virginia and Mississippi in banning all exemptions, including those for religious and personal beliefs. Only children whose health would be threatened, such as young patients receiving chemotherapy for cancer, would be allowed to skip the shots. However, legislative proposals to strengthen mandatory vaccination laws in Oregon and Washington were defeated.

Discussion Probe

1. If you were a state legislator, would you support a bill to strengthen mandatory immunization requirements by eliminating personal belief exemptions? Why or why not?

Notes

1. Nagourney, A., & Goodnough, A. (2015, January 22). Measles cases linked to Disneyland, and debate over vaccinations intensifies. *The New York Times*, p. A13.

2. Healy, J., & Paulson, M. (2015, January 31). Vaccine critics turn defensive over measles. *The New York Times*, p. A1.

Sources

Murphy, K. (2014, November 9). The ethics of infection. *The New York Times*, p. SR5.

Perkins, L. (2015, June 30). California governor signs school vaccination law. *NPR*.

Case Study 2.3

VW'S MASSIVE DECEPTION

Between 2008 and 2015, German automaker Volkswagen (VW) installed software in 11 million diesel cars in Europe, South Korea, Canada, and the United States designed to defeat emissions tests. The computer program recognized the difference between the emission test and road conditions and temporarily activated emissions controls. When not being measured, the same vehicles generated up to 40 times the amount of the harmful pollutant nitrogen oxide, which has been linked to lung cancer. The "defeat device" enabled VW cars to pass U.S. emissions tests without the usual loss in fuel economy and engine performance.

A group of professors and students at West Virginia University discovered significant differences between the car's emission results in test and real-life driving conditions in 2013. Officials at Volkswagen initially claimed that the West Virginia findings were inaccurate but later acknowledged the use of the defeat device to environmental regulators in the United States.

VW customers, the public, and government officials wondered how such a massive fraud could continue for so long without being detected. They were skeptical that top executives, who generally have engineering backgrounds, could have been ignorant about a technical device installed on so many of the company's cars and trucks. The scope of the deception suggests that a number of people knew of the defeat device. Said one auto industry observer, "It seems unlikely that just a few key individuals knew about this."[1] Company officials hired an outside law firm to conduct an internal investigation to identify the perpetrators. VW employees (who reportedly were reluctant to come forward) were offered amnesty from punishment if they shared what they knew about the defeat software. Ten senior executives associated with engine and product development were immediately suspended and the number of suspensions may grow as high as 100. Suspicion centered on managers who authorized the installation, engineers who installed the device, and those who knew about the programming but did not share that information with their leaders.

VW's culture made it hard for employees to speak up about the defeat device. Decision making is centralized at company headquarters; frank discussion of problems is discouraged; workers and managers are afraid to speak up. According to the director of a German automotive research group, speaking up is "not the usual thing at Volkswagen if you want to make a career."[2] VW culture has been described as arrogant, insular, isolated, and resistant to change. Engineers are openly disdainful of environmental regulations. Communication within the company is poor, so poor that three Volkswagen board members learned of the defeat device from media reports, not from the company CEO.

Losses from lawsuits, government fines, vehicle recalls, and damaged reputation continue to mount. The company initially set aside $7.3 billion to cover damages but quickly realized that the amount was not enough. (VW could face $18 billion in fines from the U.S. Environmental Protection Agency alone.) Volkswagen may need to cut jobs, and some speculate it might need a German government bailout. To prevent future scandals, VW's leaders promise to decentralize decision making and the firm's new CEO, Matthias Müller, vows to practice a more open management style. However, it remains to be seen if these changes will be enough to prompt managers and workers to speak up when they uncover unethical and illegal behavior.

Discussion Probes

1. Can you think of other examples of where employees knew of corporate misbehavior and kept silent? Why did they fail to speak up?

2. What should be the punishment, if any, for those who knew of the emissions software but didn't report this information?

3. Is offering amnesty an effective strategy for uncovering fraud?

4. What contextual pressures kept employees from speaking up about the emissions program?

5. What additional steps should VW take to change its corporate culture? To encourage employees to share bad news?

6. How much blame for the deception should be placed on top-level VW executives? On the board of directors?

Notes

1. Ivory, D., & Ewing, J. (2015, October 8). In U.S., VW was aware of "possible" problem. *The New York Times*, p. B1.

2. Hakim, D., & Ewing, J. (2015, October 2). In the driver's seat. *The New York Times*, p. B1.

Sources

Alter, A. (2015, November 15). The man who brought down Volkswagen. *Time*, 100–104.

Ewing, J., (2015, October 26). VW investigation focus to include managers who turned a blind eye. *The New York Times*, p. B3.

Ewing, J., & Creswell, J. (2015, November 13). Seeking information, VW offers amnesty to employees. *The New York Times*, p. B1.

Ewing, J., & Mouawad, J. (2015, October 24). 3 directors say VW hid deceit from the board. *The New York Times*, p. A2.

Will a humbled VW now adopt a leadership model of humility? (2015, October 1). *The Christian Science Monitor*, Commentary.

Moral Imagination Scale

The following survey is designed to provide you with feedback on all three components of moral imagination: reproductive, productive, and creative. Respond to each of the following items on a scale of 1 (*strongly disagree*) to 7 (*strongly agree*).

1	2	3	4	5	6	7
Strongly Disagree						Strongly Agree

1. I like to imagine how the consequences of my behavior affect others.
1 2 3 4 5 6 7

2. I anticipate any moral problems that threaten our organization.
1 2 3 4 5 6 7

3. I am not able to imagine similarities and differences between the situation at hand and other situations where I could apply the same rule.*
1 2 3 4 5 6 7

4. I have the ability to recognize which ideas are morally worth pursuing and which are not.
1 2 3 4 5 6 7

5. When I find myself uncertain about how to act in a morally ambiguous situation, I change my understanding of the moral concepts that might be involved.
1 2 3 4 5 6 7

6. I resist any regulations detrimental to the environment, even if I have to risk my current position in the organization.
1 2 3 4 5 6 7

7. I have systematically investigated the factors that may affect the moral decisions of my organization.
1 2 3 4 5 6 7

8. I am careful about condemning past decisions made under entirely different circumstances.
1 2 3 4 5 6 7

9. I accept new regulations of the organization without any justification.*
1 2 3 4 5 6 7

10. In general, when there is a discussion about moral issues, everyone tends to listen to me.
1 2 3 4 5 6 7

11. My moral imagination heightens my ability to perceive morally relevant situations.
1 2 3 4 5 6 7

12. I have the ability to revise my existing moral beliefs so as to adapt to changing conditions.
1 2 3 4 5 6 7

13. My imagination enables me to look at myself from the point of view of another person.
1 2 3 4 5 6 7

14. It would be a waste of time for me to ask the opinion of those who disagree with me when I make a decision.*
1 2 3 4 5 6 7

15. It is difficult for me to bridge the gap between sensory data and intelligent thought.*
1 2 3 4 5 6 7

16. I can put myself in the place of others. 1 2 3 4 5 6 7

17. I do not have enough ability to compare and contrast
    my own culture with that of others.* 1 2 3 4 5 6 7

18. I can create alternative solutions to new moral situations. 1 2 3 4 5 6 7

19. I discipline all my capacities and inclinations
    in order to achieve self-control. 1 2 3 4 5 6 7

20. I do not have moral responsibility for what I imagine
    in terms of affecting others.* 1 2 3 4 5 6 7

21. Once I have generated reasons supporting my belief, I find
    it difficult to generate contradictory reasons.* 1 2 3 4 5 6 7

22. I have trouble understanding others' culture and values.* 1 2 3 4 5 6 7

Scoring: Reverse scoring on items marked with *. Add scores. Possible score range from 24–168.

Source: Adapted from Yurtsever, G. (2006). Measuring moral imagination. *Social Behavior and Personality,* *34,* 205–220.

SELF-ASSESSMENT 2.2

Propensity to Morally Disengage Scale

Instructions: Respond to each item below on a scale of 1 (*strongly disagree*) to 7 (*strongly agree*).

1	2	3	4	5	6	7
Strongly Disagree						Strongly Agree

1. It is okay to spread rumors to defend those you care about.
2. Taking something without the owner's permission is okay as long as you're just borrowing it.
3. Considering the ways people grossly misrepresent themselves, it's hardly a sin to inflate your own credentials a bit.
4. People shouldn't be held accountable for doing questionable things when they were just doing what an authority figure told them to do.
5. People can't be blamed for doing things that are technically wrong when all their friends are doing it too.
6. Taking personal credit for ideas that were not your own is no big deal.
7. Some people have to be treated roughly because they lack feelings that can be hurt.
8. People who get mistreated have usually done something to bring it on themselves.

Scoring: Add up your scores on the eight scale items. Possible total score ranges from 8 to 56. The higher the score, the greater your propensity for or likelihood of participating in the process of moral disengagement.

Source: Moore, C., Detert, J. R., Trevino, L. K., Baker, V. L., & Mayer, D. M. (2012). Why employees do bad things: Moral disengagement and unethical organizational behavior. *Personnel Psychology, 65,* 1–48. Used with permission.

NOTES

1. Palmer, P. (1996). Leading from within. In L. C. Spears (Ed.), *Insights on leadership: Service, stewardship, spirit, and servant-leadership* (pp. 197–208). New York, NY: John Wiley.

2. Stone, B. (2013). *The everything store: Jeff Bezos and the age of Amazon.* New York, NY: Back Bay Books.

3. Palmer, p. 205.

4. Garvin, D. A. (1993, July–August). Building a learning organization. *Harvard Business Review,* 78–91.

5. Nash, L. L. (1990). *Good intentions aside: A manager's guide to resolving ethical problems.* Boston, MA: Harvard Business School Press.

6. Krasikova, D. V., Green, S. G., & LeBreton, J. M. (2013). Destructive leadership: A theoretical review, integration, and future research agenda. *Journal of Management, 39,* 1308–1338.

7. Petit, V., & Bollaert, H. (2012). Flying too close to the sun? Hubris among CEOs and how to prevent it. *Journal of Business Ethics, 108,* 265–283.

8. Pulley, B. (2005, October 17). Last days of the lion king. *Forbes.*

9. Michaelson, A. (2009). *The foreclosure of America: The inside story of the rise and fall of Countrywide Home Loans, the mortgage crisis, and the default of the American dream.* New York, NY: Berkley Books; Wilmers, R. G. (2009, July 27). Where the crisis came from. *The Washington Post,* p. A19.

10. O'Boyle, E. H., Jr., Forsyth, D. R., Banks, G. C., & McDaniel, M. A. (2012). A meta-analysis of the dark triad and work behavior: A social exchange perspective. *Journal of Applied Psychology, 97,* 557–579; Paulus, D. L., & Williams, K. M. (2002). The dark triad of personality: Narcissism, Machiavellianism, and psychopathy. *Journal of Research in Personality, 36,* 556–563.

11. Campbell, W. K., Hoffman, B. J., Campbell, S. M., & Marchisio, G. (2011). Narcissism in organizational contexts. *Human Resource Management Review, 21,* 268–284; Higgs, M. (2009). The good, the bad and the ugly: Leadership and narcissism. *Journal of Change Management, 9,* 165–178; Lubit, R. (2002). The long-term organizational impact of destructively narcissistic managers. *Academy of Management Executive, 18,* 127–183; Maccoby, M. (2003). *The productive narcissist.* New York, NY: Broadway Books; McFarlin, D. B., & Sweeney, P. D. (2010). The corporate reflecting pool: Antecedents and consequences of narcissism in executives. In B. Schyns & T. Hansbrough (Eds.), *When leadership goes wrong: Destructive leadership, mistakes, and ethical failures* (pp. 247–284). Charlotte, NC: Information Age.

12. Brunell, A. B., Gentry, W. A., Campbell, W. K., Hoffman, B. J., Kuhnert, K. W., & DeMarree, K. G. (2008). Leader emergence: The case of the narcissistic leader. *Personality and Social Psychology Bulletin, 34,* 1663–1676; Galvin, B. M., Waldman, D. A., & Balthazard, P. (2010). Visionary communication qualities as mediators of the relationship between narcissism and attributions of leader charisma. *Personnel Psychology, 63,* 509–537; Grijalva, E., & Harms, P. D. (2014). Narcissism: An integrative synthesis and dominance complementarity model. *Academy of Management Perspectives, 28*(2), 108–127; Grijalva, E., Harms, P. D., Newman, D. A., Gaddis, B. H., & Fraley, R. C. (2015). Narcissism and leadership: A meta-analytic review of linear and nonlinear relationships. *Personnel Psychology, 68,* 1–147.

13. Johnson, J., & Orange, M. (2003). *The man who tried to buy the world: Jean-Marie Messier and Vivendi Universal.* New York, NY: Portfolio.

14. Brown, T. A., Sautter, J. A., Littvay, L., Sautter, A. C., & Bearnes, B. (2010). Ethics and personality: Empathy and narcissism as moderators of ethical decision making in business students. *Journal of Education for Business, 85,* 203–208; Twenge, J. M., & Campbell, W. K. (2009). *The narcissism epidemic: Living in the age of entitlement.* New York, NY: Free Press; Twenge, J. M., & Foster, J. D. (2010). Birth cohort increase in narcissistic personality traits among American college students, 1982–2009. *Social Psychological and Personality Science, 1*(1), 99–106.

15. Christie, R., & Geis, F. L. (1970). *Studies in Machiavellianism.* New York, NY: Academic Press.
16. Becker, J. A. H., & O'Hair, H. D. (2007). Machiavellians' motives in organizational citizenship behavior. *Journal of Applied Communication Research, 35,* 246–267; Kessler, S. R., Bandelli, A. C., Spector, P. E., Borman, W. C., Nelson, C. E., & Penney, L. M. (2010). Re-examining Machiavelli: A three-dimensional model of Machiavellianism in the workplace. *Journal of Applied Social Psychology, 40,* 1868–1896.
17. Boddy, C. R. (2006). The dark side of management decisions: Organizational psychopaths. *Management Decision, 44*(10), 1461–1475; Boddy, C. R. (2014). Corporate psychopaths, conflict, employee affective well-being and counterproductive work behavior. *Journal of Business Ethics, 121,* 107–121; Boddy, C. R. (2015). Organisational psychopaths: A ten-year update. *Management Decision, 53,* 2407–2432; Boddy, C. R., Ladyshewsky, R., & Galvin, P. (2010). Leaders without ethics in global business: Corporate psychopaths. *Journal of Public Affairs, 10,* 121–138.
18. Boddy, C. R. (2011). *Corporate psychopaths: Organisational destroyers.* New York, NY: Palgrave McMillan.
19. Jourdan, G. (1998). Indirect causes and effects in policy change: The Brent Spar case. *Public Administration, 76,* 713–770; Zyglidopoulus, S. C. (2002). The social and environmental responsibilities of multinationals: Evidence from the Brent Spar case. *Journal of Business Ethics, 36,* 141–151.
20. Messick, D. M., & Bazerman, M. H. (1996, Winter). Ethical leadership and the psychology of decision making. *Sloan Management Review, 37*(2), 9–23.
21. Price, T. L. (2006). *Understanding ethical failures in leadership.* Cambridge, England: Cambridge University Press. See also De Cremer, D., & van Dijk, E. (2005). When and why leaders put themselves first: Leader behaviour in resource allocations as a function of feeling entitled. *European Journal of Social Psychology, 35,* 553–563.
22. Sternberg, R. J. (2002). Smart people are not stupid, but they sure can be foolish. In R. J. Sternberg (Ed.), *Why smart people can be so stupid* (pp. 232–242). New Haven, CT: Yale University Press.
23. See Caldwell, D. F., & Moberg, D. (2007). An exploratory investigation of the effect of ethical culture in activating moral imagination. *Journal of Business Ethics, 73,* 193–204; Godwin, L. N. (2015). Examining the impact of moral imagination on organizational decision making. *Business & Society, 54,* 254–278; Guroian, V. (1996). Awakening the moral imagination. *Intercollegiate Review, 32,* 3–13; Johnson, M. (1993). *Moral imagination: Implications of cognitive science for ethics.* Chicago, IL: University of Chicago Press; Kekes, J. (1991). Moral imagination, freedom, and the humanities. *American Philosophical Quarterly, 28,* 101–111; Tivnan, E. (1995). *The moral imagination.* New York, NY: Routledge, Chapman, and Hall.
24. Useem, M. (1998). *The leadership moment: Nine stories of triumph and disaster and their lessons for us all.* New York, NY: Times Books; Werhane, P. H. (1999). *Moral imagination and management decision-making.* New York, NY: Oxford University Press.
25. Gioia, D. A. (1992). Pinto fires and personal ethics: A script analysis of missed opportunities. *Journal of Business Ethics, 11,* 379–389.
26. Bandura, A. (2002). Selective moral disengagement in the exercise of moral agency. *Journal of Moral Education, 31,* 101–119, p. 103.
27. Bandura, A. (1999). Moral disengagement in the perpetration of inhumanities. *Personality and Social Psychology Review, 3,* 193–209; Bandura, A., Barbaranelli, C., Caprara, G. V., & Pastoreli, C. (1996). Mechanisms of moral disengagement in the exercise of moral agency. *Journal of Personality and Social Psychology, 71,* 364–374.
28. Korosec, K. (2015, August 24). Ten times more deaths linked to faulty switch than GM first reported. *Fortune.com.*

29. Johnson, C. E. (2014). Why "good" followers go "bad": The power of moral disengagement. *Journal of Leadership Education,* Special Issue, 36–50.

30. Bandura, Barbaranelli, Caprara, & Pastoreli; Barsky, A. (2011). Investigating the effects of moral disengagement and participation on unethical work behavior. *Journal of Business Ethics, 104,* 59–75; Boardley, I. D., & Kavussanu, M. (2007). Development and validation of the Moral Disengagement in Sport Scale. *Journal of Sport & Exercise Psychology, 29,* 608–628; Boardley, I. D., & Kavussanu, M. (2008). The Moral Disengagement in Sport Scale—Short. *Journal of Sports Sciences, 26,* 1507–1517; Hartmann, T. (2012). Moral disengagement during exposure to media violence. In R. Tamborini (Ed.), *Media and the moral mind* (pp. 241–287). Hoboken, NJ; Moore, C., Detert, J. R., Trevino, L. K., Baker, V. L., & Mayer, D. M. (2012). Why employees do bad things: Moral disengagement and unethical organizational behavior. *Personnel Psychology, 65,* 1–48; Obermann, M. L. (2011). Moral disengagement among bystanders to school bullying. *Journal of School Violence, 10,* 239–257; Obermann, M. L. (2011). Moral disengagement in self-reported and peer-nominated school bullying. *Aggressive Behavior, 37,* 133–134; Renati, R., Berrone, C., & Zaneti, M. A. (2012). Morally disengaged and unempathetic: Do cyberbullies fit these definitions? An exploratory study. *Cyberpsychology, Behavior, and Social Networking, 15,* 391–398; Shu, L. L., Gino, F., & Bazerman, M. H. (2009). Dishonest deed, clear conscience: Self-preservation through moral disengagement and motivated forgetting. Harvard Business School Working Paper 09-078.

31. Mitchell, M. S., & Palmer, N. F. (2010). The managerial relevance of ethical efficacy. In M. Schminke (Ed.), *Managerial ethics: Managing the psychology of morality* (pp. 9–108). New York, NY: Routledge.

32. Harvey, J. B. (1988*). The Abilene paradox and other meditations on management.* New York, NY: Simon & Schuster; Janis, I. (1971, November). Groupthink: The problems of conformity. *Psychology Today,* 271–279; Janis, I. (1982). *Groupthink* (2nd ed.). Boston, MA: Houghton Mifflin; Janis, I. (1989). *Crucial decisions: Leadership in policymaking and crisis management.* New York, NY: Free Press; Janis, I., & Mann, L. (1977). *Decision making.* New York, NY: Free Press.

33. Milgram, S. (1965). Some conditions of obedience and disobedience to authority. *Human Relations, 18,* 57–76; Milgram redux. (2008). *The Psychologist, 21,* 748–755; Navarick, D. J. (2009). Reviving the Milgram obedience paradigm in the era of informed consent. *Psychological Record, 59,* 155–170.

34. Fishman, C. (2011). *The Wal-Mart effect.* (Rev. ed.). New York, NY: Penguin Books

35. McCauley, C. D., & Van Velsor, E. (Eds.). (2010). *The Center for Creative Leadership handbook of leadership development* (3rd ed.). San Francisco, CA: Jossey-Bass, p. 4.

36. Petrick, J. A. (2008). Using the business integrity capacity model to advance business ethics education. In D. L. Swanson & D. G. Fisher (Eds.), *Advancing business ethics education* (pp. 103–124). Charlotte, NC: Information Age.

37. Cooper, T. L., & Menzel, D. C. (2013). In pursuit of ethical competence. In T. L. Cooper & D. D. Menzel (Eds.), *Achieving ethical competence for public service leadership* (pp. 3–24). Armonk, NY: M. E. Sharpe; Menzel, D. C. (2010). *Ethics moments in government: Cases and controversies.* Boca Raton, FL: CRC Press.

38. Narvaez, D., & Lapsley, D. K. (2005). The psychological foundations of everyday morality and moral expertise. In D. K. Lapsley & F. C. Power (Eds.), *Character psychology and character education* (pp. 140–165). Notre Dame, IN: University of Notre Dame Press.

39. Narvaez & Lapsley, p. 151.

Looking Inward

The Leader's Character

3

> *The course of any society is largely determined by the quality of its moral leadership.*
>
> **—PSYCHOLOGISTS ANNE COLBY AND WILLIAM DAMON**

> *All human beings seek to live lives not just of pleasure but of purpose, righteousness and virtue.*
>
> **—*NEW YORK TIMES* COLUMNIST DAVID BROOKS**

> *Virtue is better than wealth.*
>
> **—KENYAN PROVERB**

WHAT'S AHEAD

This chapter addresses the inner dimension of leadership ethics. To shed light rather than shadow, we need to develop a strong, ethical character (a well-developed moral identity) made up of positive traits or virtues. We promote our character development directly by addressing individual virtues or indirectly by finding role models, telling and living collective stories, learning from hardship, establishing effective habits, determining a clear sense of direction, and examining our values.

ELEMENTS OF CHARACTER

In football, the best defense is often a good offense. When faced with high-scoring opponents, coaches often design offensive game plans that run as much time as possible off the clock. If they're successful, they can rest their defensive players while keeping the opposing team's offensive unit on the sidelines. By building strong, ethical character, we take a similar proactive approach to dealing with our shadow sides. To keep from projecting our internal enemies and selfishness on others, we need to go on the offensive, replacing or managing our unhealthy motivations through the development of positive leadership traits or qualities called *virtues*.

Interest in virtue ethics, in both Eastern and Western thought, dates back to ancient times. The Chinese philosopher Confucius (551–479 BCE) emphasized that virtues are critical for maintaining relationships and for fulfilling organizational and familial duties.[1] The most important Confucian virtue is benevolence—treating others with respect and promoting their development. Other key Confucian virtues are kindness, trust, honesty, and tolerance. In the West, Greek philosopher Aristotle (383–322 BC) argued that ethical decisions are the product of individual character. In other words, good people—those of high moral character—make good moral choices. Aristotle distinguished between intellectual virtues (prudence and wisdom that provide us with insight) and moral virtues (courage, generosity, justice, wisdom). The exercise of virtues enables us to flourish, to live the best life possible. We are happiest when living well—effectively using our capacities to achieve our purpose as humans.[2]

Despite its longevity, virtue ethics has not always been popular among scholars. They turned instead to the ethical theories we'll address in detail in Chapter 5. Only in recent times have modern philosophers turned back to the virtue approach in significant numbers, attracted in part by its usefulness in everyday life. We must make a lot of ethical decisions on the spot, with no time to apply detailed ethical guidelines or rules.[3] For example, when a follower tells a sexist or racist joke, do we confront the joker? When a fellow student thinks she made a great presentation (but didn't) and asks us for confirmation, do we tell the truth or lie to protect her feelings? When a foreign official approaches us for a bribe, do we pay or not? We will respond in a more ethical manner if our character is marked by integrity, courage, and other virtues.

From a philosophical perspective, virtues have four important features. First, they are not easily developed or discarded but persist over time. Second, virtues shape the way leaders see and behave. Being virtuous makes leaders sensitive to ethical issues and encourages them to act morally. Third, virtues operate largely independent of the situation. A virtue may be expressed in different ways, depending on the context (what is prudent in one situation may not be in the next). Yet virtuous leaders will not abandon their principles to please followers. Fourth, virtues help leaders live better (more satisfying, more fulfilled) lives.[4]

Positive psychologists, like philosophers, are also interested in virtue ethics. Positive psychology is based on the premise that it is better to identify and promote the strengths of individuals instead of repairing their weaknesses (which is the approach of traditional psychologists).[5] Proponents of positive psychology treat virtues as morally valued personality traits. Under this definition, extraversion would not be considered a virtue because, though a personality trait, it is not considered ethically desirable or undesirable. Wisdom, on the other hand, would be considered a virtue because it is widely recognized and honored across cultures. Positive psychologists identify six broad categories of character strengths:[6]

- Wisdom and knowledge—cognitive strengths entailing the acquisition and use of knowledge
- Courage—an emotional strength involving the exercise of will to accomplish goals in the face of opposition, external or internal
- Humanity—an interpersonal strength that involve tending to and befriending others
- Justice—a civic strength underlying healthy community life

- Temperance—a strength protecting against excess
- Transcendence—a strength that forges connections to the larger universe and provides meaning

Some of the virtues identified by philosophers and psychologists appear to have particular significance for leaders. For that reason, I'll discuss these character strengths—courage, temperance, wisdom, justice, optimism, integrity, humility, and compassion—in the pages to follow. In addition to describing each virtue and its importance to leaders, I'll suggest ways to practice that strength in order to develop it.

Courage

Of all the virtues, courage is no doubt the most universally admired.

—*Philosopher André Comte-Sponville*

Courage is being scared to death—and saddling up anyway.

—*Cowboy actor John Wayne*

Courage is overcoming fear in order to do the right thing.[7] Courageous leaders acknowledge the dangers they face and their anxieties. Nonetheless, they move forward despite the risks and costs. The same is true for courageous followers (see "Focus on Follower Ethics: Courageous Followership"). Courage is most often associated with acts of physical bravery and heroism, such as saving a comrade in battle or rescuing a drowning victim. Nevertheless, most courageous acts involve other forms of danger, such as when a school principal faces the wrath of parents for suspending the basketball team's leading scorer before the state tournament or when a manager confronts his boss about unauthorized spending even though he could lose his job for speaking up. Such acts demonstrate moral courage, which involves living out one's personal values even when the price for doing so may be high.[8] One common way in which leaders put moral courage into action is by intervening on behalf of others who are being victimized. For example, the human rights attorney representing jailed dissidents under a repressive regime risks persecution and jail. Courage can also encourage us to endure in the face of hardship, such a physical disability or an economic setback. Ulysses S. Grant demonstrated courageous fortitude as he faced death.[9] To lift his family out of bankruptcy, Grant set out to write his memoirs. However, shortly after starting the project, he was diagnosed with an inoperable throat tumor. Grant refused to rest but continued writing as his condition worsened. Speaking and eating were extremely painful and he constantly coughed and vomited. The former President completed the book nine days before he died. Not only did the two-volume *Personal Memoirs of Ulysses S. Grant* restore the family fortune, but the work was also praised as an important historical record.

People must have courage if they are to function as ethical leaders. Ethical leaders recognize that moral action is risky but continue to model ethical behavior despite the danger. They refuse to set their values aside to go along with the group, to keep silent when customers may be hurt, or to lie to investors. They strive to create ethical environments even when faced with opposition from their superiors and subordinates. They

Focus on Follower Ethics

COURAGEOUS FOLLOWERSHIP

Ira Chaleff, who acts as a management consultant to Congressional offices, government agencies, and companies, believes that courage is the most important virtue for followers. Exhibiting courage is easier for followers if they recognize that their ultimate allegiance is to the purpose and values of the organization, not to the leader. Chaleff outlines five dimensions of courageous followership that equip subordinates to meet the challenges of their role:

The Courage to Assume Responsibility. Followers must be accountable both for themselves and for the organization as a whole. Courageous followers take stock of their skills and attitudes, consider how willing they are to support and challenge their leaders, manage themselves, seek feedback and personal growth, take care of themselves, and care passionately about the organization's goals. They take initiative to change organizational culture by challenging rules and mindsets and by improving processes.

The Courage to Serve. Courageous followers support their leaders through hard, often unglamorous work. This labor takes a variety of forms, such as helping leaders conserve their energies for their most significant tasks, organizing communication to and from leaders, controlling access to leaders, shaping leaders' public images, presenting leaders with options during decision making, preparing for crises, mediating conflicts between leaders, and promoting performance reviews for leaders.

The Courage to Challenge. Inappropriate behavior damages the relationship between leaders and followers and threatens the purpose of the organization. Leaders may break the law, scream at or use demeaning language with employees, display an arrogant attitude, engage in sexual harassment, abuse drugs and alcohol, and misuse funds. Courageous followers need to confront leaders who act in a destructive manner. In some situations, just asking questions about the wisdom of a policy decision is sufficient to bring about change. In more extreme cases, followers may need to disobey unethical orders.

The Courage to Participate in Transformation. Negative behavior, when unchecked, often results in a leader's destruction. Leaders who act destructively may deny that they need to change, or they may attempt to justify their behavior. They may claim that whatever they do for themselves (e.g., embezzling, enriching themselves at the expense of stockholders) ultimately benefits the organization. To succeed in modifying their behavior patterns, leaders must admit they have a problem and acknowledge that they should change. They need to take personal responsibility and visualize the outcomes of the transformation: better health, more productive employees, higher self-esteem, restored relationships. Followers can aid in the process of transformation by drawing attention to what needs to be changed; suggesting resources, including outside facilitators; creating a supportive environment; modeling openness to change and empathy; helping contain abusive behavior; and providing positive reinforcement for positive new behaviors.

The Courage to Leave. When leaders are unwilling to change, courageous followers may take principled action by resigning from the organization.

(Continued)

Departure is justified when a leader's behaviors clash with his or her self-proclaimed values or the values of the group or when the leader degrades or endangers others. Sometimes leaving is not enough. In the event of serious ethical violations, followers must bring the leader's misbehavior to the attention of the public by going to the authorities or the press.

Source: Chaleff, I. (2003). *The courageous follower: Standing up to and for our leaders* (2nd ed.). San Francisco, CA: Berrett-Koehler.

continue to carry out the organization's mission even in the face of dangers and uncertainty. They are also willing blow the whistle—to go outside the organization to bring wrongdoing to the attention of the public and government officials.

Practicing Courage[10]

- Identify times when you did and did not demonstrate courage and what you learned from those experiences.
- Gradually build up your courage by tackling low-level challenges and then moving on to more difficult ones.
- Train in advance for high-threat situations.
- Seek out courageous mentors.
- Don't give up, but put more effort into difficult tasks.

Temperance

> To use things, therefore, and take pleasure in them as far as possible—not, of course, to the point where we are disgusted with them, for there is no pleasure in that—this is the part of a wise man.
>
> —*Dutch philosopher Baruch Spinoza*

Moderation is key to practicing temperance, which is the ability to control emotions and pleasure.[11] The temperate person takes the middle ground between self-disgust/self-denial and self-indulgence. That means enjoying life's pleasures but not being controlled by them—for example, enjoying food without falling into gluttony, drinking but not becoming addicted to alcohol, enjoying sex without becoming trapped by desire. Temperance also means knowing one's limits and living within one's means.

Unfortunately, a great many leaders are intemperate. They are unable to control their anger and rail at subordinates, appear to have an insatiable desire for money and power, and fall victim to their need for pleasure. (See Case Study 3.1 for one example of a sexually intemperate leader.) Intemperate leaders may overreach by trying to know and control all that goes on in their organizations. They also set unrealistically high goals for themselves and their followers and fail to live within their budgets, no matter how inflated their salaries. Professional athletes far too often demonstrate the dangers of intemperance. Many end up broke at the end of their playing careers after spending all their money on expensive cars, mansions, jewelry, homes for friends and family members, luxury clothing, and other items.

Practicing Temperance

- Acknowledge your destructive impulses—anger, impatience, greed, jealousy—and the dangers they pose.
- Be alert to "hot buttons" that can cause you to lose control, such as time pressures, irritating coworkers, and criticism.
- Identify an emotion you would like to restrain or express more effectively. Develop a strategy for doing so.
- Identify your limits (financial, time, pleasure) and live within those constraints.

Wisdom and Prudence (Practical Wisdom)

We judge a person's wisdom by his hope.

—American poet Ralph Waldo Emerson

The goal of human life is to be good. Prudence assists us in getting there.

—Baldwin-Wallace College professors Alan Kolp and Peter Rea

Wisdom draws on knowledge and experience to promote the common good over both the short term and the long term. This virtue is particularly important to leaders, who make decisions that determine the collective fate of their groups and organizations. Wise organizational leaders engage in six practices.[12] First, they are skilled at thinking. They are smart, drawing from a broad base of knowledge to engage in complex decision making. Second, wise leaders demonstrate high emotional capacity. They are empathetic and sensitive, recognizing differences and respecting them. Third, wise leaders are highly collaborative. These individuals work well with others and seek their benefit. Fourth, wise leaders are engaged with their organizations and their worlds. They are proactive, constantly experimenting, forming networks, and adapting to changing circumstances. Fifth, wise leaders are reflective, demonstrating depth. They are keenly aware of their values, needs, and emotions and have a sound sense of self. Sixth, wise leaders are aspiring. Well-intentioned, they pursue principled objectives and hope to make themselves their organizations and their world better places.

Prudence is a form of wisdom that enables individuals to discern or select the best course of action in a given situation.[13] Thomas Aquinas argued that this virtue governs the others, determining when and how the other qualities should be used. For example, prudence reveals what situations call for courage or compassion and helps us determine how to act justly. Foresight and caution are important elements of practical wisdom. Prudent leaders keep in mind the long-term consequences of their choices. As a result, they are cautious, trying not to overextend themselves and their organizations or to take unnecessary risks. Billionaire investor Warren Buffett is one example of a prudent leader.

Buffett, the head of Berkshire Hathaway, sticks to a basic investment strategy, searching for undervalued companies that he can hold for at least ten years. His lifestyle is modest as well (he still lives in the home he bought for $31,500 and earns $100,000 a year). When Buffett and his wife die, 99% of their estate will go to a charitable foundation.

Practicing Wisdom and Prudence

- Be curious and promote curiosity in your followers.
- Ask more questions; give fewer answers.
- Adopt a collaborative leadership style.
- Use case studies to practice making ethical judgments; discuss them with fellow students and colleagues.
- Exercise caution when initiating major organizational changes.
- Base decisions on data.
- Always think long term—consider how your choices and actions will stand the test of time.

Justice

Justice is sweet and musical; but injustice is harsh and discordant.

—Writer Henry David Thoreau

Justice has two components. The first is a sense of obligation to the common good. The second is the fair and equal treatment of others.[14] A just person feels a sense of duty and strives to do his or her part as a member of the team, whether that team is a small group, an organization, or society as a whole. A just person supports equitable rules and laws. In addition, those who are driven by justice believe that all people deserve the same rights, whatever their skills or status.

Although justice is a significant virtue for everyone, regardless of her or his role, it takes on added importance for leaders. To begin, leaders who don't carry out their duties put the group or organization at risk. Furthermore, leaders have a moral obligation to consider the needs and interests of the entire group and to take the needs of the larger community into account. The rules and regulations they implement should be fair and should benefit everyone. In fact, employees often complain about injustice, and their performance suffers when they believe they are being treated unfairly.[15] Leaders also need to guarantee to followers the same rights they enjoy. They should set personal biases aside when making choices by judging others objectively and treating them accordingly. Leaders also have a responsibility to try to correct injustice and inequality caused by others. (You can rate your level of courage, temperance, prudence, and justice by completing Self-Assessment 3.1.)

Practicing Justice

- Look for ways to go above and beyond the minimal requirements of your leader or follower role.

- Set up equitable hiring, promotion, and compensation processes in your organization.

- Make fairness a criterion for every ethical decision you make.

- Consider everyone (both inside and outside the group) who will be impacted by your decisions.

- Work to guarantee the rights of all followers; address inequalities.

Optimism

> Hope is not the conviction that something will turn out well, but the certainty that something makes sense, regardless of how it turns out.
>
> —*Former Czech Republic president Václav Havel*

Optimists expect positive outcomes in the future even if they are currently experiencing disappointments and difficulties.[16] They are more confident than pessimists, who expect that things will turn out poorly. People who are hopeful about the future are more likely to persist in the face of adversity. When faced with stress and defeat, optimists acknowledge the reality of the situation and take steps to improve. Their pessimistic colleagues, on the other hand, try to escape problems through wishful thinking, distractions, and other means.

Optimism is an essential quality for leaders. As we'll see later in the chapter, nearly every leader experiences hardships. Those who learn and grow from these experiences will develop their character and go on to greater challenges. Those who ignore unpleasant realities stunt their ethical growth and may find their careers at an end. At the same time, leaders need to help followers deal constructively with setbacks, encouraging them to persist. Followers are more likely to rally behind optimists who appear confident and outline a positive image or vision of the group's future. Starbucks founder Howard Schultz had to balance realism and optimism when he returned as chief executive officer (CEO) of the company in 2007. Sales and quality were down and the company's share price dropped in half. Schultz made a number of painful cuts in staff and stores but continually shared his faith that the company would rebound stronger than ever. And it did. By 2011, the number of stores had expanded, the stock reached an all-time high, and Schultz was named *Fortune*'s CEO of the year.[17]

Practicing Optimism

- Change your thinking. Rewrite pessimistic thoughts into more optimistic ones. For example, instead of saying "I am a failure," say, "I may have failed this time but I can practice and improve."

- Set realistic goals that you can attain.

- Ask "What can I learn from this experience?" when facing setbacks.

- Limit the amount of time you spend reflecting on your failures.

Integrity

Integrity lies at the very heart of understanding what leadership is.

—Business professors Joseph Badaracco and Richard Ellsworth

Integrity is wholeness or completeness. Leaders possessing this trait are true to themselves, reflecting consistency between what they say publicly and how they think and act privately. They live out their values and keep their promises. In other words, they practice what they preach. They are also honest in their dealings with others.[18]

Nothing undermines a leader's moral authority more quickly than lack of integrity. Followers watch the behavior of leaders closely, and one untrustworthy act can undermine a pattern of credible behavior. Trust is broken, and cynicism spreads. In an organizational setting, common "trust busters" include inconsistent messages and behavior, inconsistent rules and procedures, blaming, dishonesty, secrecy, and unjust rewards.[19] (You can measure the integrity of one of your leaders by completing Self-Assessment 3.2.) Performance suffers when trust is broken. Trust encourages teamwork, cooperation, and risk taking. Those who work in trusting environments are more productive and enjoy better working relationships.[20] (I'll have more to say about trust in Chapter 10.)

Practicing Integrity

- Make the truth a moral imperative; seek to be truthful in all situations.
- Publicly admit your mistakes and encourage others to do the same.
- Imagine yourself as a person of integrity and try to behave in ways that lead to this hoped-for self.
- Foster trust through transparency, consistency, and concern for followers.

Humility

Let us be a little humble; let us think that the truth may not be entirely with us.

—Indian Prime Minister Jawaharlal Nehru

The failure of many celebrity CEOs makes a strong argument for encouraging leaders to be humble. In the 1990s, a number of business leaders, such as Carly Fiorina of Hewlett-Packard, Revlon's Ron Perelman, Disney's Michael Eisner, WorldCom's Bernie Ebbers, and Tyco's Dennis Kozlowski, seemed more like rock stars than corporate executives.[21] These charismatic figures became the public faces of their corporations, appearing on magazine covers and cable television shows and in company commercials. Within a few years, however, most of these celebrity leaders were gone because of scandal (some are still in jail) or poor performance. Quiet leaders who shunned the spotlight replaced them and, in many instances, produced superior results.

Management professors J. Andrew Morris, Celeste Brotheridge, and John Urbanski believe that true humility strikes a balance between having an overly low and having an overly high opinion of the self.[22] It does not consist of low self-esteem, as many people think, or of underestimating one's abilities. Instead, humility is made up of three components. The first of these is self-awareness. A humble leader can objectively assess her or his own strengths and limitations. The second element is openness, which is a product of knowing one's weaknesses. Possessing humility means being open to new ideas and knowledge. The third component is transcendence. Humble leaders acknowledge that there is a power greater than the self. This prevents them from developing an inflated view of their importance while increasing their appreciation for the worth and contributions of others.

Humility has a powerful impact on ethical behavior. Humble leaders are less likely to be corrupted by power, claim excessive privileges, engage in fraud, abuse followers, and pursue selfish goals. They are more willing to serve others instead, putting the needs of followers first while acting as role models. Humility encourages leaders to build supportive relationships with followers that foster collaboration and trust. Because they know their limitations and are open to input, humble leaders are more willing to take advice that can keep them and their organizations out of trouble.

Despite its importance, developing humility may be harder than ever. In the past, leaders were taught to acknowledge their weaknesses and to downplay their accomplishments. For example, the first President Bush consistently took the word "I" out of his speeches. (When he didn't, his mother would call and complain, "George, you're talking about yourself again.")[23] Now, we live in a narcissistic era (see Chapter 1) that promotes selfies, positive self-esteem, self-promotion, and self-disclosure on social media. Turn to Case Study 3.3 for a closer look at fostering character in a self-centered world.

Practicing Humility

- Complete self-assessments that provide you with data about your strengths and weaknesses.
- Acknowledge your character flaws and address them; acknowledge your character strengths and build on them.
- Solicit feedback and ideas from other leaders and followers; act on that input.
- Serve a higher purpose or goal.

Compassion (Kindness, Generosity, Love)

All happiness in the world comes from serving others; all sorrow in the world comes from acting selfishly.

—*Leadership expert Margaret Wheatley*

Compassion and related concepts such as concern, care, kindness, generosity, and love all refer to an orientation that puts others ahead of the self.[24] Those with compassion value others regardless of whether they get anything in return from them. Compassion is an important element of altruism, an ethical perspective addressed in more detail in Chapter 5. An orientation toward others rather than the self separates ethical leaders from their unethical colleagues.[25] Ethical leaders recognize that they serve the purposes of the group. They seek power and exercise influence on behalf of followers. Further, they recognize that they have an obligation to outsiders. Their circle of concern extends beyond their immediate group. In contrast, unethical leaders put their own self-interests first. They are more likely to control and manipulate followers and subvert the goals of the collective while treating outsiders with disdain. In extreme cases, this self-orientation can lead to widespread death and destruction.

Eunice Shriver Kennedy provides an outstanding model of compassionate leadership.[26] Born into the wealthy and powerful Kennedy family, which included her brother John, who became president of the United States, and her brothers Robert and Ted, who became senators, she used her money and political clout on behalf of those with mental limitations. When John Kennedy became president, she convinced him to set up a committee to study developmental disabilities, which led to the creation of the National Institute of Child Health and Human Development. She started a camp for the intellectually disabled at her estate and cofounded the Special Olympics. The first Special Olympics meet had 1,000 contestants. Now, more than 2.5 million athletes in 80 countries take part. Shriver's efforts played a major role in changing public attitudes toward those facing Down syndrome, mental retardation, and other intellectual challenges. They used to be viewed as outcasts and warehoused in mental facilities. Shriver encouraged Americans to see that, with adequate training, those with intellectual limitations could live productive lives and contribute to society. (See Box 3.1 for more information on the development of compassionate leaders.)

Practicing Compassion

- Look for the good in others.
- Imagine how others feel and think (develop empathy).
- Take time to build relationships.
- Get involved in service activities.
- Serve with others to reinforce your commitment to helping.

Forming a Moral Identity

Identifying important leadership virtues is only a start. We then need to embed these qualities into our self-concepts and behavior—to develop what moral psychologists call *moral identity*.[27] Investigators treat moral identity as both a trait and a state. Trait theorists argue that ethical commitments are central to those with strong moral identity. Such individuals define themselves in terms of moral principles and virtues and act consistently regardless of the situation. They are motivated to take moral action because they want to act in harmony with their self-definitions.

For those with a highly developed sense of moral identity, to betray their ethical values is to betray themselves. Martin Luther is as an example of someone who refused to put his standards aside. When called to defend his radical religious beliefs in front of Catholic authorities at the Diet of Worms, Luther declared, "Here I stand; I can do no other." Pope Francis is a contemporary leader with high moral identity. He turns down many papal perks to remain true to his commitment to the poor and to a humble lifestyle. He lives in a modest bungalow instead of the papal apartment, takes his meals with

Box 3.1 The Journey to Humanitarian Leadership

Humanitarian leaders spearhead efforts to feed the homeless, fight sex trafficking, educate street children, bring medical care to poor rural villages, and so on. Researchers Frank LaFasto and Carl Larson wondered why some individuals "take charge of helping people in need" while most of us do not. They conducted interviews with 31 humanitarian leaders ranging from age 16 to 88 from a variety of educational and social backgrounds. The investigators found that, despite their differences, their subjects followed a common path. Seven choice points marked this journey to helping others.

Choice 1: Leveraging Life Experiences. Humanitarian leaders reflect on their life stories. They develop empathy for the needs of others through (1) role models (parents, teachers, religious leaders, friends) and positive values, such as caring for the poor or serving others; (2) a troubling awareness about a societal problem like sex abuse or lack of clean water; or (3) traumatic personal experiences, such as the death of parents or a cancer diagnosis.

Choice 2: Having a Sense of Fairness. Humanitarians are convinced that the world is divided into those who are fortunate and those who are not. The disadvantaged are victims of circumstance and are therefore worthy of help. To make the world fairer, the humanitarian leader believes in providing opportunities for those who have been denied such access by fate.

Choice 3: Believing That We Can Matter. Those out to assist others aren't overwhelmed by the need. Instead, they focus on helping individuals. Meeting the needs of one person is the first step to addressing the broader problem—whether that is poverty, substandard housing, or disease. Humanitarian leaders believe that they have something to offer and know what they can and cannot do to contribute. They try to make the future better for those in need.

Choice 4: Being Open to Opportunity. Compassionate leaders are inclined to say yes to possibilities instead of automatically saying no. They have an external focus. They are attuned to the needs of others, and their impulse is to respond because they have a clear sense of life's direction. Unlike many people, humanitarian leaders align their actions with their convictions.

Choice 5: Taking the First Small Step. Every leader interviewed by LaFasto and Larson reported a pivotal or defining moment when he or she first responded to the impulse to help. Humanitarian leaders don't let the size of the problem discourage them; rather, they do something, no matter how small. While they don't know where their efforts will lead, they still make the commitment to act. Take the case of Ryan Hreljac. Ryan started his humanitarian career as a six-year-old by trying to raise $70 to provide one well for a village in a developing nation. This small step led to the creation of the Ryan's Well Foundation, which has provided sanitation and clean water for three-quarters of a million people around the world.

Choice 6: Persevering. Those who tackle difficult social problems can expect to encounter a great deal of frustration. But they believe in what they are doing and are convinced that reaching their goals is worth the cost. Humanitarian leaders are also adaptable, often turning obstacles into opportunities. If funding sources

(Continued)

(Continued)

dry up, they find new, more stable ones, for example. They maintain their positive focus by taking heart in short-term victories and remaining convinced they can make a difference.

Choice 7: Leading the Way. The passion of humanitarian leaders draws others to their causes. Their enthusiasm, energy, and optimism are contagious. Others join in, and movements are born.

LaFasto and Larson conclude that we all have the potential to become humanitarian leaders. However, to start down the path to socially responsible leadership, we must first answer yes to this question: Do I feel a sense of responsibility for helping others?

Source: LaFasto, F., & Larson, C. (2012). *The humanitarian leader in each of us: Seven choices that shape a socially responsible life.* Thousand Oaks, CA: SAGE.

Cardinals and visitors (taking any available seat), drives a used Renault, often runs his own errands, and makes spontaneous phone calls to ordinary citizens.

State theorists argue that instead of having one unitary self, we have a variety of selves or identities we activate depending on the context.[28] At school, our student self-identity is most important, for example, while our employee identity is more salient at work. These scholars are interested in how elements of the situation prime or activate our moral identity. When our moral identities are activated, we are more concerned about behaving ethically, make better moral choices, engage in more prosocial and fewer antisocial behaviors, and are less likely to excuse our moral failings. Organizations can promote the development of moral identity by (1) providing opportunities to practice virtues, (2) creating positive moral climates where cooperative relationships can flourish, (3) making space for moral discussion and reflection, (4) continuously emphasizing values and mission, and (5) encouraging ongoing involvement in the local community.

Both the trait and state approaches provide important insights into the development of moral identity. Our ultimate goal should be to make moral commitments central to our sense of self, to act in a virtuous manner regardless of the situation. Moral exemplars (see the next section of the chapter) earn this label because of their moral consistency in a variety of settings. At the same time, situational variables play an important role in helping us develop our moral identities. Whatever roles we play, we need opportunities to practice virtues, the encouragement of others, and the support of positive moral climates.

Developing ethical character or moral identity is far from easy, of course. At times, our personal demons will overcome even our best efforts to keep them at bay, and we will fail to live up to our ideals. We're likely to make progress in some areas while lagging in others. We may be courageous yet arrogant, reverent yet pessimistic, optimistic yet unjust. We may be compassionate to family members but cold toward our neighbors. No wonder some prominent leaders reflect both moral strength and weakness. Martin Luther King, Jr., showed great courage and persistence in leading the civil rights movement but engaged in extramarital relationships. Franklin Roosevelt was revered by many of his contemporaries but had a long-standing affair with Lucy Mercer. In fact, Mercer (not Eleanor Roosevelt) was present when he died.

The poor personal behavior of political and business leaders has sparked debate about personal and public morality. One camp argues that the two cannot be separated. Another camp makes a clear distinction between the public arena and private life. According to this second group, we can be disgusted by the private behavior of politicians such as those who engage in extramarital affairs (e.g., Bill Clinton, former New York City mayor Rudy Giuliani, former New York governor Eliot Spitzer) but vote for them anyway based on their performance in office.

I suspect that the truth lies somewhere between these extremes. We should expect contradictions in the character of leaders, not be surprised by them. Private lapses don't always lead to lapses in public judgment. On the other hand, it seems artificial to compartmentalize private and public ethics. Private tendencies can and do cross over into public decisions. Arizona State business ethics professor Marianne Jennings points out that many fallen corporate leaders (e.g., Richard Scrushy [HealthSouth], Dennis Kozlowski [Tyco], Scott Sullivan [WorldCom], Bernie Ebbers [WorldCom]) cheated on their wives or divorced them to marry much younger women.[29] She suggests that executives who are dishonest with the most important people in their lives—their spouses—are likely to be dishonest with others who aren't as significant: suppliers, customers, and stockholders. Furthermore, conducting an affair distracts a leader from his or her duties and provides a poor role model for followers. That's why the Boeing board fired CEO Harry Stonecipher when members discovered that he was having an affair with a high-ranking employee.[30]

In the political arena, Franklin Roosevelt tried to deceive the public as well as his wife and family. He proposed expanding the number of Supreme Court justices from 9 to 15, claiming that the justices were old and overworked. In reality, he was angry with the Court for overturning many New Deal programs and wanted to appoint new justices who would support him. Roosevelt's dishonest attempt to pack the Supreme Court cost him a good deal of his popularity. Bill Clinton's personal moral weaknesses overshadowed many of his political accomplishments and later threatened Hillary Clinton's political career.

CHARACTER BUILDING

In the previous section, I offered some suggestions for fostering individual virtues. These are direct approaches to character development. However, more often than not, virtues develop indirectly, as the byproduct of other activities. In this final section of the chapter, I'll introduce a variety of indirect approaches or factors that encourage the development of leadership virtues. These include identifying role models, hearing stories and living shared stories, learning from hardship, cultivating good habits, creating a personal mission statement, and clarifying values.

Finding Role Models

Character appears to be caught as well as taught. We often learn what it means to be virtuous by observing and imitating exemplary leaders, a process based on the brain's ability to mimic the actions of others and to understand the reasons behind their behaviors. That makes role models crucial to developing high moral character.[31] Eunice Kennedy Shriver is one such role model; William Wilberforce, who led the fight to abolish the British slave trade, is another.

Government ethics expert David Hart argues that it is important to differentiate between different types of moral examples or exemplars.[32] Dramatic acts, such as rescuing a child from danger or saving someone from a burning house, capture our attention. However, if we are to develop worthy character, we need examples of those who demonstrate virtue on a daily basis. Hart distinguishes between *moral episodes* and *moral processes*. Moral episodes are made up of *moral crises* and *moral confrontations*. Moral crises are dangerous, and Hart calls those who respond to them *moral heroes*. Hutus who protected their Tutsi neighbors from slaughter during the Rwandan genocide served as moral heroes, as did Nicholas Winton, who saved Jewish children before World War II broke out. (Read more about Winton in "Leadership Ethics at the Movies: *Nicky's Family*.") Moral confrontations aren't dangerous, but they do involve risk and call for moral champions. Enron's Sherron Watkins acted as a moral champion when she challenged CEO Kenneth Lay about accounting fraud at the company. (Company leaders then explored ways to fire her.)

Moral processes consist of *moral projects* and *moral work*. Moral projects are designed to improve ethical behavior during a limited amount of time and require moral leaders. A moral leader sets out to reduce corruption in government, for example, or to introduce a more effective medical treatment or to improve the working conditions of migrant farm workers. In contrast to a moral project, moral work does not have a beginning or an end but is ongoing. The moral worker strives for ethical consistency throughout life. This moral exemplar might be the motor vehicle department employee who tries to be courteous to everyone who comes to the office or the neighbor who volunteers to coach youth soccer.

Hart argues that the moral worker is the most important category of moral exemplar. He points out that most of life is lived in the daily valleys, not on the heroic mountain peaks. Because character is developed over time through a series of moral choices and actions, we need examples of those who live consistent moral lives. Those who engage in moral work are better able to handle moral crises when they arise. For instance, teachers at Sandy Hook elementary school, who were dedicated to serving children, risked their lives for their charges when a shooter broke into their school in December 2014. The principal and lead teacher ran toward the killer (one was killed, the other wounded). Two teachers died acting as human shields, with their arms wrapped around their students. Other teachers hid children in closets, bathrooms, and offices, comforting them when they could.

Anne Colby and William Damon studied 23 moral workers to determine what we can learn from their lives.[33] They found three common characteristics in their sample:

- *Certainty:* Moral exemplars are sure of what they believe and take responsibility for acting on their convictions.

- *Positivity:* Exemplars take a positive approach to life even in the face of hardship. They enjoy what they do and are optimistic about the future.

- *Unity of self and moral goals:* Exemplars don't distinguish between their personal identity and their ethical convictions. Morality is central to who they are. They believe they have no choice but to help others and consider themselves successful if they are pursuing their mission in life.

What sets exemplars apart from the rest of us is the extent of their engagement in moral issues. We make sure that our children get safely across the street. Moral exemplars, on the other hand, "drop everything not just to see their own children across the street but to feed the poor children of the world, to comfort the dying, to heal the ailing, or to campaign for human rights."[34]

Colby and Damon offer some clues about how we might develop broader moral commitments like the exemplars in their study. They note that moral capacity continues to develop well beyond childhood—some in their sample didn't take on their life's work until their 40s and beyond. Given this fact, we should strive to develop our ethical capacity throughout our lives. The researchers also found that working with others on important ethical tasks or projects fosters moral growth by exposing participants to different points of view and new moral issues. We, too, can benefit by collaborating with others on significant causes, such as working for better children's health care, building affordable housing, or fighting the spread of AIDS. The key is to view these tasks not as burdens but as opportunities to act on what we believe. Adopting a joyful attitude will help us remain optimistic in the face of discouragement.

Leadership Ethics at the Movies

NICKY'S FAMILY

Starring: Nicholas Winton, Joe Schlesinger, rescued children

Synopsis: This docudrama tells the story of Nicholas Winton and those he rescued from almost certain death. In 1938, Winton, a twenty-eight-year-old London stockbroker, traveled to Prague to visit Jews displaced by the Nazi annexation of Czechoslovakian territory. Soon, he found himself aiding desperate Jewish parents wanting to send their children to safety before war broke out. Winton set up a children's rescue organization, raised money, and arranged host families in Britain for 669 children. His motto was "Anything that is not actually impossible can be done." Winton's heroic actions were forgotten for the next fifty years, until his wife uncovered a suitcase in their attic filled with documents from the rescue. She then told the story to British media. Winton

was later reunited with many of his "children" and their families. Winton's adopted children tell of traveling by train to a new land. After the war, many discovered that their biological parents died in Nazi concentration camps.

Rating: Not rated but likely PG for mature themes

Themes: courage, compassion, wisdom, justice, optimism, integrity, humility, moral identity, role models, values

Discussion Starters

1. Why do you think Winton risked his life and career to help strangers?

2. Why did Winton keep his rescue efforts secret?

3. What type of moral exemplar is Winton?

4. Why are so many inspired to follow Winton's example?

Hearing Stories/Living Shared Stories

Fictional stories, whether told through movies, television shows, songs, video games, books, poems, blogs, plays, or YouTube videos, are more than just mere entertainment. Instead, they foster character development in several ways. First, fiction acts like a flight simulator. Pilots train in simulators that provide them with opportunities to practice maneuvers and responses to emergencies without ever leaving the ground. In the same way, fiction gives us opportunities to practice moral reflection and judgment in complex situations before we encounter them in real life. Our brains respond in much the same way to fictional events as they do to events we actually experience.[35]

Second, fiction introduces us to additional moral role models. These fictional exemplars illustrate the vices we want to avoid as well as the virtues we want to develop.

Third, fiction almost always reinforces a positive moral message—virtue is rewarded, antisocial behavior like violence is condemned, and villains are punished.[36] Consider, for example, how justice prevails in such highly popular book and movie franchises as *The Hunger Games*, *Harry Potter*, *The Avengers*, *Star Wars*, and *The Lord of the Rings*. Viewing television programs, where good nearly always triumphs, cultivates the belief that people get what they deserve. As a result, frequent television viewers are more likely to believe in a just world.[37]

Fourth, fiction is highly effective in changing or reinforcing our moral beliefs and attitudes, largely because we aren't aware that it is doing so. The more absorbed we are in the story, the more likely we are to shift our attitudes toward the moral arguments made in the story (e.g., evil people deserve punishment, sex outside of marriage is acceptable if the parties are in love, war is justified).[38] Of course, that fact suggests we choose our stories carefully; we need able to step back from the narrative to evaluate the moral(s) it communicates.

Fifth, fictional narrative helps us understand our possibilities and limits. We can try to deny the reality of death, the fact that we're aging, and that there are factors outside our control. However, stories force us to confront these issues. They also explore common human themes, such as freedom of choice, moral responsibility, conflict between individual and society, conflict between individual conscience and society's rules, and self-understanding.[39]

Sixth, fiction writers help us escape our old ways of thinking and acting. Their best works expand our emotional capacity, enabling us to respond more fully to the needs of others. In one study, for instance, fiction readers scored higher on social awareness and empathy than those reading nonfiction.[40]

The stories told by our communities, like fictional narratives, also play an important role in character development. Virtues are more likely to take root when nurtured by families, schools, governments, and religious bodies. These collectives impart values and encourage self-discipline, caring, and other virtues through the telling of narratives or stories. Shared narratives both explain and persuade. They provide a framework for understanding the world and, at the same time, challenge us to act in specified ways. For example, one of the most remarkable features of the American political system is the orderly transition of power from president to president.[41] George Washington set this precedent by voluntarily stepping down as the country's first leader. His story, told in classrooms, books, and films, helps explain why the current electoral system functions smoothly. Furthermore, modern presidents and presidential candidates follow

Washington's example, as in the case of the 2000 election. Although he garnered more of the popular vote than George W. Bush, Al Gore conceded defeat after the Supreme Court rejected his court challenge.

Stories are lived as well as told. Our moral identity is established in part from living up to the roles we play in the stories we tell. According to virtue ethicist Alasdair MacIntyre, "I can only answer the question 'What am I to do?' if I can answer the prior question, 'Of what story or stories do I find myself a part?'"[42] Worthy narratives bring out the best in us, encouraging us to suppress our inner demons and to cast light instead of shadow. For instance, I am more likely to welcome refugees if I believe that helping strangers is part of the tradition or narrative of my cultural, religious, or national group. If I work for a company known for its integrity, I will more likely tell the truth when promoting the firm's products.

Learning from Hardship

Hardship and suffering also play a role in developing character. The leaders we admire the most are often those who have endured the greatest hardships. Nelson Mandela, Václav Havel, and Aleksandr Solzhenitsyn served extended prison terms, for instance, and Moses endured forty years in exile and forty in the wilderness with his people.

Perhaps no other American leader has faced as much hardship as did Abraham Lincoln. He was defeated in several elections before winning the presidency. Because of death threats, he had to slip into Washington, DC, to take office. He presided over the slaughter of many of his countrymen and women in the Civil War, lost a beloved son, and was ridiculed by Northerners (some in his cabinet) and Southerners alike. However, all these trials seemed to deepen both his commitment to the Union and his spirituality. His second inaugural address is considered to be one of the finest political and theological statements ever produced by a public official.

Trainers at the Center for Creative Leadership (CCL) have identified hardship as one of the factors contributing to leadership development. Leaders develop the fastest when they encounter situations that stretch or challenge them (as we noted in the last chapter). Hardships, along with novelty, difficult goals, and conflict, challenge people. CCL staffers Russ Moxley and Mary Lynn Pulley believe that hardships differ from other challenging experiences because they are unplanned, are experienced in an intensely personal way, and involve loss.[43]

Research conducted by the CCL reveals that leaders experience five common categories of hardship events. Each type of hardship can drive home important lessons.

- *Business mistakes and failures:* Examples of this type of hardship event include losing an important client, failed products and programs, broken relationships, and bankruptcies. These experiences help leaders build stronger working relationships, recognize their limitations, and profit from their mistakes.

- *Career setbacks:* Missed promotions, unsatisfying jobs, demotions, and firings make up this hardship category. Leaders faced with these events lose control over their careers, their sense of self-efficacy or competence, and their professional identity. Career setbacks function as wake-up calls, providing feedback about weaknesses. They encourage leaders to take more responsibility for managing their careers and to identify the type of work that is most meaningful to them.

- *Personal trauma:* Examples of personal trauma include divorce, cancer, death, and difficult children. These experiences, which are a natural part of life, drive home the point that leaders (who are used to being in charge) can't run the world around them. As a result, they may strike a better balance between work and home responsibilities, learn how to accept help from others, and endure in the face of adversity.

- *Problem employees:* Troubled workers include those who steal, defraud, can't perform, or perform well only part of the time. In dealing with problem employees, leaders often lose the illusion that they can turn these people around. They may also learn how important it is to hold followers to consistently high standards and become more skilled at confronting subordinates about problematic behavior.

- *Downsizing:* Downsizing has much in common with career setbacks, but in this type of hardship, leaders lose their jobs through no fault of their own. Downsizing can help leaders develop coping skills and force them to take stock of their lives and careers. Those carrying out the layoffs can also learn from the experience by developing greater empathy for the feelings of followers.

Being exposed to a hardship is no guarantee that you'll learn from the experience. Some ambitious leaders never get over being passed over for a promotion, for instance, and become embittered and cynical. Benefiting from adversity takes what Warren Bennis and Robert Thomas call "adaptive capacity." Bennis and Thomas found that, regardless of generation, effective leaders come through *crucible moments* that have profound impacts on their development.[44] These intense experiences include failures, such as losing an election, but also encompass more positive events, such as climbing a mountain or finding a mentor. They generally fall into three categories. *New territory crucibles,* such as taking an overseas assignment or serving in a new organizational role, put leaders into stretching experiences. *Reversal crucibles* involve loss, defeat, or failure. *Suspension crucibles* involve extended periods of reflection or contemplation, such as between promotions and jobs. The accomplished leaders Bennis and Thomas sampled experienced just as many crises as everyone else but were able to learn important principles and skills from their struggles. This knowledge enabled them to move on to more complex challenges.

Successful leaders see hard times as positive high points of their lives. In contrast, less successful leaders are defeated and discouraged by similar events. To put it another way, effective leaders tell a different story than their ineffective counterparts. They identify hardships as stepping stones, not as insurmountable obstacles. We, too, can enlarge our adaptive capacity by paying close attention to our personal narratives, defining difficult moments in our lives as learning opportunities rather than as permanent obstacles. To see how you can learn from a specific failure, take the following steps:

1. Identify a significant failure from your professional or personal life, and summarize the failure in a sentence (be sure to use the word *failure*).

2. Describe how you felt and thought about the failure immediately after it happened.

3. Move forward in time to identify any positive outcomes that came out of the failure, including skills you acquired, lessons you learned, and any relationships you established.

4. Identify how the failure changed or shaped you as a person, noting any new traits or attitudes you have adopted and whether you are any more mature now than you were before the failure event.[45]

Developing Habits

One of the ways in which we build character is by doing well through our habits. Habits are repeated routines or practices designed to foster virtuous behavior. Examples of good habits include working hard, telling the truth, giving to charity, standing up to peer pressure, and always turning in original work for school assignments. Every time we engage in one of these habits, it leaves a trace or residue. Over time, these residual effects become part of our personality and are integrated into our character. Aristotle sums up the process this way: "Men [and women] become builders by building, and lyre-players by playing the lyre, so too we become just be doing just acts, temperate by doing temperate acts, brave by doing brave acts."[46] Habits also help us become more competent at demonstrating virtues.

Business consultant Stephen Covey developed the most popular list of positive habits. Not only did he author the best-selling book *The Seven Habits of Highly Effective People,* but thousands of businesses, nonprofit groups, and government agencies have participated in workshops offered by the Covey Center for Leadership.[47] In his best seller, Covey argues that effectiveness is based on such character principles as integrity, fairness, service, excellence, and growth. The habits are the tools that enable leaders and followers to develop these characteristics. Covey defines a *habit* as a combination of knowledge (what to do and why to do it), skill (how to do it), and motivation (wanting to do it). Leadership development is an "inside-out" process that starts within the leader and then moves outward to affect others. The seven habits of effective and ethical leaders are as follows:

> *Habit 1: Be proactive.* Proactive leaders realize that they can choose how they respond to events. When faced with career setbacks, they try to grow from these experiences instead of feeling victimized by them. Proactive people also take the initiative by opting to attack problems instead of accepting defeat. Their language reflects their willingness to accept rather than avoid responsibility. A proactive leader makes statements such as "Let's examine our options" and "I can create a strategic plan." A reactive leader, in contrast, makes comments such as "The organization won't go along with that idea," "I'm too old to change," and "That's just who I am."

Habit 2: Begin with the end in mind. This habit is based on the notion that "all things are created twice." First we get a mental picture of what we want to accomplish, and then we follow through on our plans. If we're unhappy with the current direction of our lives, we can generate new mental images and goals, a process Covey calls *rescripting.* Creating personal and organizational mission statements is one way to identify the results we want and thus control the type of life we create. (I'll talk more about how to create a mission statement in the next section.) Covey urges leaders to center their lives on inner principles such as fairness and human dignity rather than on such external factors as family, money, friends, or work. (See Case Study 3.3 to learn more about a coach who kept the end in mind.)

Habit 3: Put first things first. A leader's time should be organized around priorities. Too many leaders spend their days coping with emergencies, mistakenly believing that urgent means important. Meetings, deadlines, and interruptions place immediate demands on their time, but other, less-pressing activities, such as relationship building and planning, are more important in the long run. Effective leaders carve out time for significant activities by identifying their most important roles, selecting their goals, creating schedules that enable them to reach their objectives, and modifying plans when necessary. They also know how to delegate tasks and have the courage to say no to requests that don't fit their priorities.

Habit 4: Think win–win. Those with a win–win perspective take a cooperative approach to communication, convinced that the best solution benefits both parties. The win–win habit is based on these dimensions: character (integrity, maturity, and a belief that the needs of everyone can be met), trusting relationships committed to mutual benefit, performance or partnership agreements that spell out conditions and responsibilities, organizational systems that fairly distribute rewards, and principled negotiation processes in which both sides generate possible solutions and then select the one that works best.

Habit 5: Seek first to understand, then to be understood. Ethical leaders put aside their personal concerns to engage in empathetic listening. They seek to understand, not to evaluate, advise, or interpret. Empathetic listening is an excellent way to build a trusting relationship. Covey uses the metaphor of the emotional bank account to illustrate how trust develops. Principled leaders make deposits in the emotional bank account by showing kindness and courtesy, keeping commitments, paying attention to small details, and seeking to understand. These strong relational reserves help prevent misunderstandings and make it easier to resolve any problems that do arise.

Habit 6: Synergize. Synergy creates a solution that is greater than the sum of its parts and uses right-brain thinking to generate a third, previously undiscovered alternative. Synergistic, creative solutions are generated in trusting relationships—those with full emotional bank accounts—where participants value their differences.

Habit 7: Sharpen the saw. "Sharpening the saw" refers to the continual renewal of the physical, mental, social or emotional, and spiritual dimensions of the self. Healthy leaders care for their bodies through exercise, good nutrition, and stress management. They encourage their mental development by reading good literature and writing thoughtful letters and journal entries. They create meaningful relationships with others and nurture their inner or spiritual values through study or meditation and time in nature. Continual renewal, combined with the use of the first six habits, creates an upward spiral of character improvement.

Developing Personal Mission Statements

Developing a mission statement is the best way to keep the end or destination in mind (Covey's second habit). In recognition of that fact, many management, life, and wellness coaching programs ask participants to create personal mission statements. Jack Groppel, the developer of the Corporate Athlete executive development program, summarizes the role of personal mission statements this way: "A mission statement becomes the North Star for people. It becomes how you make decisions, how you lead, and how you create boundaries."[48] He argues that mission statements are more effective than resolutions ("I want to lose weight"; "I want to get better grades") because they identify the underlying sources of behavior and what individuals find motivating. Consider why you want to lose weight, for example. Losing weight to look better is less motivating than losing weight so you can have enough energy to go on hikes with your significant other or to play team sports with friends.

To get started writing a personal mission statement, consider the following questions used in the Corporate Athlete program:

- How do you want to be remembered?
- How do you want people to describe you?
- Who do you want to be?
- Who or what matters most to you?
- What are your deepest values?
- How would you define success in your life?
- What makes your life really worth living?

If you are looking for examples of leader mission statements, consider these: "To serve as a leader, live a balanced life, and apply ethical principles to make a significant difference" (Denise Morrison, Campbell Soup); "To be a teacher, and to be known for inspiring my students to be more than they thought they could be" (Oprah Winfrey); "To have fun in [my] journey through life and learn from [my] mistakes" (Richard Branson, Virgin Group).[49]

Once you write your mission statement, share it with others (you are more likely to follow through if you do so). Don't be afraid to change your mission statement as you change and grow.

Leadership consultant Juana Bordas offers an alternative method or path for discovering personal leadership purpose based on Native American culture. Native Americans discovered their life purposes while on vision quests. Vision *cairns*, or stone markers, guided members of some tribes. These stone piles served both as directional markers and as reminders that others had passed this way before. Bordas identifies nine cairns or markers for creating personal purpose.[50]

> *Cairn 1: Call your purpose; listen for guidance.* All of us have to be silent in order to listen to our intuition. Periodically, you will need to withdraw from the noise of everyday life and reflect on such questions as "What am I meant to do?" and "How can I best serve?"
>
> *Cairn 2: Find a sacred place.* A sacred place is a quiet place for reflection. It can be officially designated as sacred (e.g., a church or meditation garden) or merely a spot that encourages contemplation, such as a stream, park, or favorite chair.
>
> *Cairn 3: See time as continuous; begin with the child and move with the present.* Our past has a great impact on where we'll head in the future. Patterns of behavior are likely to continue. Bordas suggests that you should examine the impact of your family composition, gender, geography, cultural background, and generational influences. A meaningful purpose will be anchored in the past but will remain responsive to current conditions such as diversity, globalization, and technological change.
>
> *Cairn 4: Identify special skills and talents; accept imperfections.* Take inventory by examining your major activities and jobs and evaluating your strengths. For example, how are your people skills? Technical knowledge? Communication abilities? Consider how you might further develop your aptitudes and abilities. Also take stock of your significant failures. What did they teach you about your limitations? What did you learn from them?
>
> *Cairn 5: Trust your intuition.* Sometimes we need to act on our hunches and emotions. You may decide to turn down a job that doesn't feel right, for instance, in order to accept a position that seems to be a better fit.
>
> *Cairn 6: Open the door when opportunity knocks.* Be ready to respond to opportunities that are out of your control, such as a new job assignment or a request to speak or write. Ask yourself whether this possibility will better prepare you for leadership or fit in with what you're trying to do in life.
>
> *Cairn 7: Find your passion and make it happen.* Passion energizes us for leadership and gives us stamina. Discover your passion by imagining

the following scenarios: If you won the lottery, what would you continue to do? How would you spend your final six months on Earth? What would sustain you for a hundred more years?

Cairn 8: Write your life story; imagine a great leader. Turn your life into a story that combines elements of reality and fantasy. Imagine yourself as an effective leader and carry your story out into the future. What challenges did you overcome? What dreams did you fulfill? How did you reach your final destination?

Cairn 9: Honor your legacy, one step at a time. Your purpose is not static but will evolve and expand over time. If you're a new leader, you're likely to exert limited influence. That influence will expand as you develop your knowledge and skills. You may manage only a couple of people now, but in a few years, you may be responsible for an entire department or division.

Identifying Values

If a mission statement identifies our final destination, then our values serve as a moral compass to guide us on our journey. Values provide a frame of reference, helping us to set priorities and to distinguish between right and wrong. There are two ways to identify or clarify the values you hold. You can generate a list from scratch or you can rate the values in a list supplied by someone else. If brainstorming a list of important values seems a daunting task, you might try the following exercise developed by James Kouzes and Barry Posner. The "credo memo" asks you to spell out the important values that underlie your philosophy of leadership:

> Imagine that your organization has afforded you the chance to take a six-month sabbatical, all expenses paid. You will be going to a beautiful island where the average temperature is about eighty degrees Fahrenheit during the day. The sun shines in a brilliant sky, with a few wisps of clouds. A gentle breeze cools the island down in the evening, and a light rain clears the air. You wake up in the morning to the smell of tropical flowers.
>
> You may not take any work along on this sabbatical. And you will not be permitted to communicate to anyone at your office or plant—not by letter, phone, fax, e-mail, or other means. There will be just you, a few good books, some music, and your family or a friend.
>
> But before you depart, those with whom you work need to know something. They need to know the principles that you believe should guide their actions in your absence. They need to understand the values and beliefs that you think should steer their decision making and action taking. You are permitted no long reports, however. Just a one-page memorandum.
>
> If given this opportunity, what would you write on your one-page credo memo? Take out one piece of paper and write that memo.[51]

Examples of values that have been included in credo memos include "operate as a team," "listen to one another," "celebrate successes," "seize the initiative," "trust your judgment," and "strive for excellence." These values can be further clarified through dialogue with coworkers. Many discussions in organizations (e.g., how to select subcontractors, when to fire someone, how to balance the needs of various stakeholders) have an underlying value component. Listen for the principles that shape your opinions and the opinions of others.

Working with a list of values can also be useful. Psychologist Gordon Allport identified six major value types. People can be categorized based on how they organize their lives around each of the following value sets.[52] Prototypes are examples of occupations that fit best into a given value orientation.

- *Theoretical:* Theoretical people are intellectuals who seek to discover the truth and pride themselves on being objective and rational. Prototypes: research scientists, engineers
- *Economic:* Usefulness is the most important criterion for those driven by economic values. They are interested in production, marketing, economics, and accumulating wealth. Prototype: small business owners
- *Aesthetic:* Aesthetic thinkers value form and harmony. They enjoy each event as it unfolds, judging the experience based on its symmetry or harmony. Prototypes: artists, architects
- *Social:* Love of others is the highest value for social leaders and followers. These "people persons" view others as ends, not means, and are kind and unselfish. Prototype: social workers
- *Political:* Power drives political people. They want to accumulate and exercise power and enjoy the recognition that comes from being in positions of influence. Prototypes: senators, governors
- *Religious:* Religious thinkers seek unity through understanding and relating to the cosmos as a whole. Prototypes: pastors, rabbis, Muslim clerics

Identifying your primary value orientation is a good way to avoid situations that could cause you ethical discomfort. If you have an economic bent, you will want a job (often in a business setting) where you solve real-life problems. On the other hand, if you love people, you may be uncomfortable working for a business that puts profits first.

Professors Duane Brown and R. Kelly Crace developed a widely used values system called the Life Values Inventory, which you can take online.[53] They outline the following as important values that are key to self-fulfillment and motivation. You can use them to help you reflect on your priorities:

Achievement (challenges, hard work, improvement)

Belonging (acceptance, inclusion)

Concern for the environment (protecting and preserving)

Concern for others (well-being of people)

Creativity (new ideas and creations)

Financial prosperity (making money, buying property)

Health and activity (staying healthy and physically active)

Humility (modesty)

Independence (making own decisions and choosing own direction)

Loyalty to family or group (following traditions and expectations)

Privacy (time alone)

Responsibility (dependability, trustworthiness)

Scientific understanding (employing scientific principles in problem solving)

Spirituality (spiritual beliefs, connection to something greater than the self)

There are two cautions to keep in mind when identifying your values. First, don't put too much importance on materialistic values like wealth, possessions, status, fame, and personal image. Those driven by these external values generally have a lower quality of life. They tend to suffer from depression and anxiety, experience more negative emotions, are more narcissistic, have more physical problems like headaches and backaches, are at a greater risk for drug and alcohol abuse, have more difficulty establishing lasting relationships, and suffer low self-esteem. Materialistic individuals are also more likely to lie and manipulate others while ignoring community and environmental concerns. As employees, they report more burnout and job satisfaction. Instead of seeking wealth and material possessions, focus on intrinsic values that are naturally satisfying and promote psychological well-being. These include values related to self-acceptance/personal growth (choosing what to do, following your curiosity), relatedness/intimacy (expressing love, forming intimate relationships), and community feeling/helpfulness (making other people's lives better, making the world a better place).[54]

Second, values, though critical, have to be translated into action. Consider Enron, for example. The firm had a lofty set of ideals but leaders ignored these values as they engaged in fraud and deception. Further, our greatest struggles come from choosing between two good values. Many corporate leaders value both good customer service and high product quality, but what do they do when reaching one of these goals means sacrificing the other? Pushing to get a product shipped to satisfy a customer may force the manufacturing division into cutting corners in order to meet the deadline. Resolving dilemmas such as these takes more than value clarification; we also need some standards for determining ethical priorities. With that in mind, I will identify ethical decision-making principles in Chapters 5 and 6. But first we need to confront one final shadow caster—evil—in Chapter 4.

IMPLICATIONS AND APPLICATIONS

- Character is integral to effective leadership, often making the difference between success and failure.

- Virtues are positive leadership qualities or traits that help us manage our shadow sides.

- As a leader, seek to develop your courage (overcoming fear in order to do the right thing), temperance (self-control), wisdom (drawing on knowledge and experience to pursue the common good) and prudence (practical wisdom), justice (obligation to the common good, treating others equally and fairly), optimism (expectation of positive outcomes in the future), integrity (wholeness, completeness, consistency), humility (self-awareness, openness, a sense of transcendence), and compassion (kindness, generosity, love).

- Create a moral identity that embeds virtues into your decisions and behavior, making moral commitments central to your self-definition.

- Strive for consistency, but don't be surprised by contradictions in your character or in the character of others. Become more tolerant of yourself and other leaders. At the same time, recognize that a leader's private behavior often influences his or her public decisions.

- Indirect approaches that build character include identifying role models, telling and living out shared stories, learning from hardship, cultivating habits, creating a personal mission statement, and clarifying values.

- Never underestimate the power of a good example. Be on the lookout for real and fictional ethical role models to imitate.

- Fictional stories give you an opportunity to practice moral reflection and judgment while reinforcing positive values. Communal stories encourage you to live up to the role you play in the shared narrative.

- Hardships are an inevitable part of life and leadership. The sense of loss associated with these events can provide important feedback, spur self-inspection, encourage you to develop coping strategies, force you to reorder your priorities, and nurture your compassion. However, to benefit from them, you must see challenges as learning opportunities that prepare you for future leadership responsibilities.

- Positive habits are designed to foster virtuous behavior. Each time we engage in a good habit, it leaves a trace or residue. Over time, these residual effects become integrated into our character. The most popular list of habits includes the following: seek to be proactive, begin with the end in mind, organize around priorities, strive for cooperation, listen for understanding, develop synergistic solutions, and engage in continual self-renewal.

- Having an ultimate destination will encourage you to stay on your ethical track. Develop a personal mission statement that reflects your strengths and passions. Use your values as a moral compass to keep you from losing your way. Avoid values that focus on material possessions and financial success; focus instead on intrinsic values that are naturally satisfying and promote your well-being.

FOR FURTHER EXPLORATION, CHALLENGE, AND SELF-ASSESSMENT

1. Which virtue is most important for leaders? Defend your choice. How can you practice this virtue? Write up your conclusions.

2. Can the private and public morals of leaders be separated? Try to reach a consensus on this question in a group.

3. What steps can you take to develop a more positive outlook about future events?

4. Brainstorm a list of moral exemplars. What does it take to qualify for your list? How would you classify these role models according to the types described in this chapter?

5. Reflect on the ways in which a particular shared narrative has shaped your worldview and behavior. Write up your conclusions.

6. Interview a leader you admire. Determine his or her crucible moment and capacity to learn from that experience. Present your findings to the rest of the class.

7. Rate yourself on each of the seven habits of effective people, and develop a plan for addressing your weaknesses. Explore the habits further through reading and training seminars.

8. Develop a personal mission statement using the guidelines provided in the chapter. As an alternative, collect the personal mission statements of well-known contemporary leaders.

9. Complete the credo memo exercise on page 93 if you haven't already done so. Encourage others in your work group or organization to do the same, and then compare your statements. Use this as an opportunity to engage in a dialogue about values.

STUDENT STUDY SITE

Visit the student study site at **study.sagepub.com/johnsonmecl6e** to access full SAGE journal articles for further research and information on key chapter topics.

Case Study 3.1

A MODERN-DAY LIBERTINE

In France, multiple marriages, multiple affairs, and serial seduction don't usually mean the end of a political or business career. The French are less concerned about the personal lives of powerful people than are citizens in the United States. Particularly in the case of male public figures, affairs and seduction are often seen as signs of strength and virility and thus are admired rather than condemned.

This laissez-faire attitude toward the private sex lives of the political elite may be changing thanks to the excesses of Dominique Strauss-Kahn (known as DSK). A French economist, DSK was head of the International Monetary Fund (IMF) and is credited with playing a major role in

(Continued)

(Continued)

rescuing the world economy during the Global Recession. At one point, he was favored to become France's next president. But he lost his job and his chance of winning the French presidency when he was charged with sexually assaulting a New York hotel maid in 2011. He was cleared of criminal charges in the New York rape case but reached a financial settlement with the victim. Later, he admitted to participating in a series of upscale sex parties in Paris, Washington, and Lille, France, costing around $13,000 each. These events began with formal dinners and ended in orgies. Strauss-Kahn reportedly wanted to have sex with three or four women at each of these parties. To meet his needs and those of other clients, event organizers sometimes hired prostitutes when they couldn't recruit enough other female participants. While prostitution is not a crime in France, employing prostitutes is. DSK was charged with being part of a prostitution ring.

DSK was acquitted after a lengthy trial that subjected French citizens to the lurid details of his sex life, including text messages in which he referred to women as "equipment" and testimony about his rough treatment of sex partners. Strauss-Kahn testified that he had nothing to do with arranging the parties, noting that he generally arrived late. The judge accepted DSK's claim that most of the women were naked and he had no idea who was a prostitute and who was not.

DSK describes himself as a modern-day libertine. Libertinism, which dates back to sixteenth-century Europe, is a philosophy based on the pursuit of "a life without moralistic limits." Its best-known advocate was Giacomo Casanova, who believed that as long as he lived within the law, he should be able to do whatever he wanted. The former IMF chief operated according to the same philosophy, at least when it came to sex, referring to the orgies as "libertinage"—wide-open sexual encounters among willing partners. In a magazine interview, DSK admitted: "I long thought I could lead my life as I wanted. And that includes free behavior between consenting adults. I was too out of step with French society. I was wrong.[1]

While Strauss-Kahn kept the dark side of his sexual proclivities secret, his sexual appetite was public knowledge. He was called the "Great Seducer," the "hot rabbit," and the "frisky Frenchman" before he took over the IMF. His third wife (who has since left him) even argued, "It's important for a man in politics to be able to seduce."[2] At the IMF, he admitted to having an affair with a subordinate.

Entitlement, not lust, may be the best explanation of DSK's libertine behavior. Members of France's elite have long ignored the sexual restrictions put on the middle and lower classes. However, the link between power and sex isn't limited to France. Powerful men and women are more likely than their less powerful counterparts to engage in sexual infidelity, no matter what their nationality. They are more confident and have access to more partners. At the same time, they are less bound by societal rules and have a greater tendency to fail to exercise self-restraint. Commenting on Strauss-Kahn, one political science professor noted:

> For powerful people, it's part of the thrill that they can get things that other people can't get. They are usually surrounded by sycophantic people, and after a while, they come to believe that they have a right to be

surrounded by attractive men and women. There is a sense of entitlement that is a general attribute of power.[3]

DSK paid a high price for his libertine lifestyle. He lost his job and his marriage and faced public humiliation as the sensational details of sexual behavior were revealed to the public. Yet there still may be hope for DSK's political career. According to one poll, 79% of French adults surveyed said that he would make a better president than the current occupant of the office—Francois Hollande.

Discussion Probes

1. Does being a libertine automatically disqualify someone from becoming a good leader?

2. How much should citizens be concerned about the private lives of their political leaders? Are Americans too concerned? Should the French be more concerned?

3. Should DSK be allowed to return to a role in government?

4. What can followers do to prevent their leaders from feeling entitled?

5. What other factors, aside from power, might encourage leaders to believe they are entitled to ignore the rules that apply to everyone else?

Notes

1. Carvajal, D., & de Blume, M. (2012). Strauss-Kahn says sex parties went too far, but lust is not crime. *The New York Times,* p. A1.

2. Gibbs, N. (2011, May). Men behaving badly. What is it about power that makes men crazy? *Time*, pp. 16–30.

3. Politics, power and sex. (2011, May 21). *Belfast Telegraph,* p. 20.

Sources

Bilefsky, D. (2015, February 15). Burlesque tone at trial snarls Strauss–Kahn's effort to restore his image. *The New York Times,* p. A13.

Breeden, A., & Rubin, A. (2015, June 13). French court acquits former I.M.F. chief in case that put his sex life on view. *The New York Times,* p. A5.

Davis, B., & Gauthier-Villars, D. (2008, October 22). IMF chief facing fresh claim of abusing power. *The Australian,* World, p. 12.

Lammers, J., Stoker, J. I., Pollman, M., & Stapel, D. A. (2011). Power increases infidelity among men and women. *Psychological Science, 22,* 1191–1197.

Marnham, P. (2015, June 19). The French know what Dominique Strauss-Kahn gets up to in bed—and they'd still vote for him. *Spectator Blogs.*

Moutet, A. (2011, May 7). "I love women, et alors?" *The Daily Telegraph,* p. A3.

Wolff, L. (2012, October 17). Free to be a sexual predator? *The New York Times,* Op-Ed.

Case Study 3.2

CULTIVATING CHARACTER FROM CROOKED TIMBER

According to *New York Times* commentator David Brooks, too many of us focus on developing the wrong set of virtues. We strive to create résumé virtues—the skills and characteristics that help us excel on the job and appear successful in the eyes of the world. We want to be known as hard working, resilient, tenacious, ambitious, creative, and productive. Brooks argues that we ought to develop our eulogy virtues instead. Eulogy virtues are the ones that get talked about at our funerals—whether we were thoughtful, faithful, kind, and courageous.

Eulogy virtues come from the core of our being and provide us with a sense of meaning. They direct the ways in which we use our resume skills and traits. Developing these deeper qualities is a lifelong process based on the recognition that people are imperfect beings. Brooks declares that we are made from "crooked timber," a phrase he draws from Immanuel Kant's declaration, "Out of the crooked timber of humanity no straight thing was ever made." Character emerges from the moral struggle against our flaws. However, engaging in this struggle takes humility, an increasingly rare virtue in a culture that promotes self-centeredness through such messages as "You are special," "Trust yourself," "Follow your dream," and "Accept no limits."

Brooks describes the lives of several historical figures who recognized that they were crooked timber and spent their lives overcoming their vices in order to develop their character. For example, Francis Perkins gave up a life of privilege to answer the call to improve labor conditions, serving as "The Woman Behind the New Deal." Dwight Eisenhower wrestled with anger and hatred as he projected confidence and cheerfulness as a military commander and President. Philip Randolph fended off sexual and other temptations to remain incorruptible as he founded the railroad porters' union and helped organize the 1963 civil rights march on Washington. Eighteenth-century novelist Mary Ann Eliot overcame anxiety and depression to write a series of novels (*Adam Bede, The Mill on the Floss, Middlemarch*) that illustrate the importance of tolerance for the self and other people. Augustine renounced personal control and ambition in order to experience spiritual insight and gratitude.

Brooks offers a Humility Code that outlines strategies for developing character in a world that he believes makes the self the center of the universe. Some of the provisions of his Humility Code include the following:

- We live for holiness (purpose, virtue) not happiness.
- We may be flawed, but we are wonderfully gifted with the capacity for heroic action.
- Humility is the most important virtue in the struggle against our weaknesses (and pride is the primary vice).
- Vices like fear, lust, and gluttony are short term while character virtues stand the test of time.
- Self-mastery takes help from others—friends, families, role models, traditions, institutions.

- Learn to quiet the self in order to see the world more clearly.

- Organize life around a vocation or calling that serves the community.

- As a leader, push for constant gradual change that recognizes that people are flawed; strike a balance between competing values and goals.

Discussion Probes

1. Do you agree with Brooks that modern Western culture makes the self the center of the universe?

2. What is the value of viewing humans as "crooked timber"? What might be the dangers of this perspective?

3. Is humility the foundation for character development? Why or why not?

4. Which provisions of the Humility Code to you agree with? Take issue with?

5. Can you think of other prominent leaders who struggled to develop their character while wrestling with their weaknesses? How did they cope with their flaws, and what virtues did they develop?

Source

Brooks, D. (2015). *The road to character*. New York, NY: Random House.

Case Study 3.3

STARTING AT THE FINISH LINE

Al Buehler is one of the most influential coaches in the history of U.S. track and field. Buehler coached and taught at Duke University for sixty years, retiring in 2015 at age eighty-four. Over that time, he trained 12 National Collegiate Athletic Association (NCAA) champions, 10 All-Americans, and five Olympians. He served on the U.S. Olympic coaching staff in 1968, 1972, 1984, and 1988 and organized a number of national and international meets, including the first to invite African runners to the United States and a competition with the Soviets at the height of the Cold War. Buehler is a member of the U.S. Track Coaches Association Hall of Fame and recipient of the U. S. Sports Academy's Jackie Robinson Humanitarian Award.

Buehler's character is even more impressive than his accomplishments as a track coach. Known for living out his principles, Buehler invited the team from North Carolina Central University (NCCU), an all-black liberal arts college, to train at Duke in the 1950s. This was several

(Continued)

(Continued)

years before the first African American undergraduates enrolled at Duke and segregation laws were still on the books. He and NCCU coach Dr. LeRoy Walker focused on different events with their combined teams. Buehler refused to participate in any meet that would not accept Walker. When Carlos Rogers and Tommie Smith were booed for protesting racial injustice on the winners stand at the 1968 Mexico City Olympics, Buehler supported the duo, telling them that they had made a genuine statement. He volunteered to drive them to the airport after they had been kicked off the Olympic team. Buehler trained female runner Ellison Goodall Bishop before Duke had a women's team, and she went on to become an All-American. Later, he gave up his men's track scholarships to help implement Title IX, the act aimed at bringing equality to women's sports on college campuses. Every Sunday morning for thirty-five years, Buehler (described by his family as tone deaf) climbed a rickety ladder to play the bells at the church on Duke's campus.

Buehler describes himself as a teacher who happened to specialize in track and field. With that in mind, he focused on the total student, not just on the individual's athletic abilities.

> Basically I am concerned with the overall development of my athletes and students. How high they jump or how fast they run is not nearly as important as what kind of person they turn out to be. I want them to be good husbands, fathers, wives, mothers, sons, daughters, and first-rate citizens.

Buehler used the race metaphor to help prepare his students for life. He asked them to remind themselves why they were doing what they are doing, to remember that they could survive challenges because they have done so before, and to stick to their race plan regardless of what happened. However, Buehler believes that finish lines aren't just endings but also beginnings:

> In my view of life, the finish line is a starting point . . . for dreams, for opening long-closed doors, for challenges, for change. Starting at the finish line also means carrying your principles and values forward beyond the finish line of any race or goal and into how you live your life.

Buehler made a lasting impression on colleagues, athletes, and students. Duke basketball coach Mike Krzyzewski calls him "the best example of a teacher-coach in intercollegiate sports." Carl Lewis, Dave Wottle, Joan Benoit Samuelson, and other Olympic champions describe him as a mentor. When Buehler had a brain tumor removed, he received a constant stream of calls and notes from his former students. Seven-time National Basketball Association (NBA) all-star Grant Hill, who received encouragement from Buehler as a freshman, served as executive producer for a documentary on Buehler's life; and another former student, Amy Unell, served as director. After the documentary aired for the first time, Buehler and Dr. LeRoy Walker received a standing ovation from hundreds of friends, students, and alumni.

Though retired, Buehler's words of wisdom (which he shared with his teams every day) live on:

- If you don't follow your principles, then that's being a phony.

- Take good care of those you love.

- By being true to yourself, you can generate a genuine enthusiasm that will motivate you and inspire those around you.

- Turn your attention on those positive things that enable you to be the best you can be.

- Take responsibility. Only you can determine the course of your life.

- Take action, even when all the odds seem to be against you.

Discussion Probes

1. What virtues does Al Buehler demonstrate? What virtues does he hope to develop in others?

2. What does it mean to you to "start at the finish line?"

3. How does starting at the finish line compare to Covey's second habit: Begin with the end in mind?

4. How does Buehler serve as a moral exemplar?

5. What can we learn from Buehler's example and advice?

Notes

All quotations come from Unell, A. E., & Unell, B. (2012). *Starting at the finish line: Coach Al Buehler's timeless wisdom*. New York, NY: Perigree/Penguin.

Sources

Hill, G., & Unell, A. E. (2010). *Starting at the finish line: The Al Buehler story*. [Documentary]. USA: Story-Tales Productions.

Roth, B. (2015, April 22). After 60 years, a final lap for Al Buehler. *Duke Magazine.*

SELF-ASSESSMENT 3.1

The Leadership Virtues Questionnaire (LVQ)

Instructions: Ask someone else to rate you on the following items, or select one of your leaders and rate that individual. Scale: 1 = not at all, 2 = once in a while, 3 = sometimes, 4 = fairly often, 5 = frequently, if not always. Reverse scoring where indicated. You will generate a score for each individual virtue and a total perceived character score.

1. Does as he/she ought to do in a given situation

2. Does not carefully consider all the information available before making an important decision that impacts others

3. Boldly jumps into a situation without considering the consequences of his/her actions

4. Does not seek out information from a variety of sources so the best decision can be made
5. Considers a problem from all angles and reaches the best decision for all parties involved
6. Would rather risk his/her job than to do something that was unjust
7. May have difficulty standing up for his/her beliefs among friends who do not share the same views
8. Fails to make the morally best decision in a given situation
9. May hesitate to enforce ethical standards when dealing with a close friend
10. Ignores his/her "inner voice" when deciding how to proceed
11. Seems to be overly concerned with his/her personal power
12. Is not overly concerned with his/her own accomplishments
13. Wishes to know everything that is going on in the organization to the extent that he/she micromanages
14. Gives credit to others when credit is due
15. Demonstrates respect for all people
16. May take credit for the accomplishments of others
17. Respects the rights and integrity of others
18. Would make promotion decisions based on a candidate's merit
19. Does not treat others as he/she would like to be treated

Prudence

1. _____
2. _____ (Reverse score)
3. _____ (Reverse)
4. _____ (Reverse)
5. _____
_____ out of 25

Courage (Fortitude)

6. _____
7. _____ (Reverse)
8. _____ (Reverse)
9. _____ (Reverse)
10. _____ (Reverse)
_____ out of 25

Temperance

11. _____ (Reverse)
12. _____
13. _____ (Reverse)
17. _____
_____ out of 15

Justice

14. _____
15. _____
16. _____ (Reverse)
18. _____
19. _____ (Reverse)
_____ out of 30

Total _____ out of 95

Source: Riggio, R. E., Zhu, W., Reina, C., & Maroosis, J. A. (2010). Virtue-based measurement of ethical leadership: The Leadership Virtues Questionnaire. *Consulting Psychology Journal: Practice and Research, 62*(4), 235–250.

Perceived Leader Integrity Scale

Instructions: You can use this scale to measure the integrity of your immediate supervisor or, as an alternative, ask a follower to rate you. The higher the score (maximum 124), the lower the integrity of the leader rated.

The following items concern your immediate supervisor. You should consider your immediate supervisor to be the person who has the most control over your daily work activities. Circle responses to indicate how well each item describes your immediate supervisor. Response choices: 1 = not at all, 2 = somewhat, 3 = very much, 4 = exactly.

1.	Would use my mistakes to attack me personally	1	2	3	4
2.	Always gets even	1	2	3	4
3.	Gives special favors to certain "pet" employees but not to me	1	2	3	4
4.	Would lie to me	1	2	3	4
5.	Would risk me to protect himself or herself in work matters	1	2	3	4
6.	Deliberately fuels conflict among employees	1	2	3	4
7.	Is evil	1	2	3	4
8.	Would use my performance appraisal to criticize me as a person	1	2	3	4
9.	Has it in for me	1	2	3	4
10.	Would allow me to be blamed for his or her mistake	1	2	3	4
11.	Would falsify records if it would help his or her work reputation	1	2	3	4
12.	Lacks high morals	1	2	3	4
13.	Makes fun of my mistakes instead of coaching me as to how to do my job better	1	2	3	4
14.	Would deliberately exaggerate my mistakes to make me look bad when describing my performance to his or her superiors	1	2	3	4
15.	Is vindictive	1	2	3	4
16.	Would blame me for his or her own mistake	1	2	3	4
17.	Avoids coaching me because she or he wants me to fail	1	2	3	4
18.	Would treat me better if I belonged to a different ethnic group	1	2	3	4
19.	Would deliberately distort what I say	1	2	3	4
20.	Deliberately makes employees angry at each other	1	2	3	4
21.	Is a hypocrite	1	2	3	4
22.	Would limit my training opportunities to prevent me from advancing	1	2	3	4
23.	Would blackmail an employee if she or he could get away with it	1	2	3	4

24. Enjoys turning down my requests	1	2	3	4
25. Would make trouble for me if I got on his or her bad side	1	2	3	4
26. Would take credit for my ideas	1	2	3	4
27. Would steal from the organization	1	2	3	4
28. Would risk me to get back at someone else	1	2	3	4
29. Would engage in sabotage against the organization	1	2	3	4
30. Would fire people just because she or he doesn't like them if she or he could get away with it	1	2	3	4
31. Would do things that violate organizational policy and then expect subordinates to cover for him or her	1	2	3	4

Total Score _____

Source: Bartholomew, C. S., & Gustafson, S. B. (1998). Perceived leader integrity scale: An instrument for assessing employee perceptions of leader integrity. *Leadership Quarterly, 9,* 143–144. Used with permission.

NOTES

1. Provis, C. (2010). Virtuous decision making for business ethics. *Journal of Business Ethics, 91,* 3–6; Sim, M. (2007). *Remastering morals with Aristotle and Confucius.* Cambridge, England: Cambridge University Press.

2. Ackerill, J. L. (1981). *Aristotle the philosopher.* Oxford, England: Oxford University Press; Bragues, G. (2006). Seek the good life, not money: The Aristotelian approach to business ethics. *Journal of Business Ethics, 67,* 341–357; Kenny, A. (2004). *Ancient philosophy* (Vol. 1). Oxford, England: Clarenton Press; Shields, C. (2014). *Aristotle* (2nd ed.). New York, NY: Routledge.

3. Johannesen, R. L., Valde, K. S., & Whedbee, K. E. (2008). *Ethics in human communication* (6th ed.). Long Grove, IL: Waveland Press.

4. Annas, J. (2006). Virtue ethics. In D. Copp (Ed.), *The Oxford handbook of ethical theory* (pp. 515–536). Oxford, England: Oxford University Press; Johannesen, R. L. (1991). Virtue ethics, character, and political communication. In R. E. Denton (Ed.), *Ethical dimensions of political communication* (pp. 69–90). New York, NY: Praeger; Timmons, M. (2002). *Moral theory: An introduction.* Lanham, MD: Rowman & Littlefield.

5. Aspinwall, L. G., & Staudinger, U. M. (Eds.). (2002). *A psychology of human strengths: Fundamental questions about future directions for a positive psychology.* Washington, DC: American Psychological Association; Snyder, C. R., & Lopez, S. J. (2005). *Handbook of positive psychology.* Oxford, England: Oxford University Press; Worthington, E. L. Lavelonk, C., Van Tongeren, D. R., Jennings, D. J., Gartener, H. A. L., Davis, D. E., & Hook, J. N. (2014). Virtue in positive psychology. In K. Timpe & C. A. Boyd (Eds.), *Virtues & their vices* (pp. 433–458). Oxford, England: Oxford University Press.

6. Peterson, C., & Seligman, M. E. P. (2004). *Character strengths and virtues: A handbook and classification.* Oxford, England: Oxford University Press.

7. Comte-Sponville, A. (2001). *A small treatise on the great virtues: The uses of philosophy in everyday life.* New York, NY: Metropolitan; Peterson & Seligman.

8. Kidder, R. M. (2005). *Moral courage.* New York, NY: William Morrow; Lopez, S. J., Rasmussen, H. N., Skorupski, W. P., Koetting, K., Petersen, S. E., & Yang, Y. (2010). Folk

conceptualizations of courage. In C. L. S. Pury & S. J. Lopez (Eds.), *The psychology of courage: Modern research on an ancient virtue* (pp. 23–45). Washington, DC: American Psychological Association; Osswald, S., Greitemeyer, T., Fischer, P., & Frey, D. (2010). What is moral courage? Definition, explication, and classification of a complex construct. In C. L. S. Pury & S. J. Lopez (Eds.), *The psychology of courage: Modern research on an ancient virtue* (pp. 149–164). Washington, DC: American Psychological Association.

9. Scarre, G. (2010). *On courage.* London, England: Routledge.

10. Practice strategies for each virtue are largely drawn from sources cited in the chapter as well as from Kilburg, R. R. (2012). *Virtuous leaders: Strategy, character, and influence in the 21st century.* Washington, DC: American Psychological Association; Sosik, J. J. (2006*). Leading with character: Stories of valor and virtue and the principles they teach.* Greenwich, CT: Information Age.

11. Comte-Sponville; Riggio, R. E., Zhu, W., Reina, C., & Maroosis, J. A. (2010). Virtue-based measurement of ethical leadership: The Leadership Virtues Questionnaire. *Consulting Psychology Journal: Practice and Research, 62*(4), 235–250.

12. Intezari, A., & Pauleen, D. J. (2013). Students of wisdom. In W. Kupers & D. J. Pauleen (Eds.), *Handbook of practical wisdom: Leadership, organizational and integral business practice* (pp. 155–174). Burlington, VT: Gower; Kessler, E. H., & Bailey, J. R. (2007). Introduction: Understanding, applying, and developing organizational and managerial wisdom. In E. H. Kessler & J. R. Bailey (Eds.), *Handbook of organizational and managerial wisdom* (pp. xv–xxiv). Thousand Oaks, CA: SAGE.

13. Kolp, A., & Rea, P. (2006). *Leading with integrity: Character-based leadership.* Cincinnati, OH: AtomicDog; Comte-Sponville.

14. Comte-Sponville; Peterson & Seligman; Smith, T. (1999). Justice as a personal virtue. *Social Theory & Practice, 25,* 361–384; Solomon, R. C. (1990). *A passion for justice: Emotions and the origins of the social contract.* Reading, MA: Addison-Wesley.

15. Cohen-Charash, Y., & Spector, P. E. (2001). The role of justice in organizations: A meta-analysis. *Organizational Behavior and Human Decision Processes, 86,* 278–321; Visweswaran, C., & Ones, D. S. (2002). Examining the construct of organizational justice: A meta-analytic evaluation of relations with work attitudes and behaviors. *Journal of Business Ethics, 38,* 193–203.

16. Carver, C. S., & Scheier, M. F. (2005). Optimism. In C. R. Snyder & S. J. Lopez (Eds.), *Handbook of positive psychology* (pp. 231–243). Oxford, England: Oxford University Press.

17. Schultz, H., & Gordon, J. (2011). *Onward: How Starbucks fought for its life without losing its soul.* New York, NY: Rodale.

18. Palanski, M. E., & Yammarino, F. J. (2007). Integrity and leadership: A multi-level conceptual framework. *Leadership Quarterly, 20,* 405–420; Simons, T. L. (2002). Behavioral integrity: The perceived alignment between managers' words and deeds as a research focus. *Organization Science, 13,* 18–35.

19. See Bruhn, J. G. (2001). *Trust and the health of organizations.* New York, NY: Kluwer/Plenum; Elangovan, A. R., & Shapiro, D. L. (1998). Betrayal of trust in organizations. *Academy of Management Review, 23,* 547–566.

20. See Dirks, K. T. (1999). The effects of interpersonal trust on work group performance. *Journal of Applied Psychology, 84,* 445–455; Kramer, R. M., & Tyler, T. R. (Eds.). (1996). *Trust in organizations: Frontiers of theory and research.* Thousand Oaks, CA: SAGE.

21. Crosariol, B. (2005, November 21). The diminishing allure of rock-star executives. *The Globe and Mail,* p. B12; Varachaver, N. (2004, November 15). Glamour! Fame! Org charts! *Fortune,* 76–85.

22. Morris, J. A., Brotheridge, C. M., & Urbanski, J. C. (2005). Bringing humility to leadership: Antecedents and consequences of leader humility. *Human Relations, 58,* 1323–1350. See also Tangney, J. P. (2000). Humility: Theoretical perspectives, empirical findings and directions for future research. *Journal of Social and Clinical Psychology, 19,* 70–82.

23. Brooks, D. (2015). *The road to character*. New York, NY: Random House, p. 262.

24. Peterson & Seligman.

25. Howell, J., & Avolio, B. J. (1992). The ethics of charismatic leadership: Submission or liberation? *Academy of Management Executive, 6*, 43–54.

26. Hodgson, G. (2009, August 12). Eunice Kennedy Shriver; mental health campaigner who founded the Special Olympics. *The Independent,* Obituaries, p. 26; Smith, J. Y. (2009, August 12). The Olympian force behind a revolution. *The Washington Post,* p. A07.

27. Blasi, A. (1984). Moral identity: Its role in moral functioning. In W. M. Kurtines & J. L. Gewirtz (Eds.), *Morality, moral behavior, and moral development* (pp. 128–139). New York, NY: John Wiley; Blasi, A. (2005). Moral character: A psychological approach. In D. K. Lapsley & F. C. Power (Eds.), *Character psychology and character education* (pp. 67–100). Notre Dame, IN: Notre Dame Press; Hardy, S. A., & Carlo, G. (2005). Identity as a source of moral motivation. *Human Development, 48*, 232–256; Lapsley, D. K. (2008). Moral self-identity as the aim of education. In L. P. Nucci & D. Narvaez (Eds.), *Handbook of moral and character education* (pp. 30–52). New York, NY: Routledge.

28. Aquino, K., & Freeman, D. (2009). Moral identity in business situations: A social-cognitive framework for understanding moral functioning. In D. Narvaez & D. K. Lapsley (Eds.), *Personality, identity and character: Explorations in moral psychology* (pp. 375–395). Cambridge, England: Cambridge University Press; Aquino, K., & Reed, A. (2002). The self-importance of moral identity. *Journal of Personality and Social Psychology, 83*, 1423–1440; Reynolds, S. J., & Ceranic, T. L. (2007). The effects of moral judgment and moral identity on moral behavior: An empirical examination of the moral individual. *Journal of Applied Psychology, 92*(6), 1610–1624; Shao, R., Aquino, K., & Freeman, D. (2008). Beyond moral reasoning: A review of moral identity research and its implications for business ethics. *Business Ethics Quarterly, 18*, 513–540; Smith, I. H., Aquino, K., Koleva, S., & Graham, J. (2014). The moral ties that bind . . . even to out-groups: The interactive effect of moral identity and the binding moral foundations. *Psychological Science, 25*, 1554–1562; Weaver, G. R. (2006). Virtue in organizations: Moral identity as a foundation for moral agency. *Organization Studies, 27*, 341–368.

29. Jennings, M. M. (2006). *The seven signs of ethical collapse: How to spot moral meltdowns in companies . . . before it's too late.* New York, NY: St. Martin's Press.

30. Wayne, L. (2005, March 8). Boeing chief is ousted after admitting affair. *The New York Times,* p. A1.

31. Devine, T., Seuk, J. H., & Wilson, A. (2001). *Cultivating heart and character: Educating for life's most essential goals.* Chapel Hill, NC: Character Development; Van Slyke, J. A. (2014). Moral psychology, neuroscience, and virtue. In K. Timpe & C. A. Boyd (Eds.), *Virtues and their vices* (459–479). Oxford, England: Oxford University Press.

32. Hart, D. K. (1992). The moral exemplar in an organizational society. In T. L. Cooper & N. D. Wright (Eds.), *Exemplary public administrators: Character and leadership in government* (pp. 9–29). San Francisco, CA: Jossey-Bass.

33. Colby, A., & Damon, W. (1992). *Some do care: Contemporary lives of moral commitment.* New York, NY: Free Press; Colby, A., & Damon, W. (1995). The development of extraordinary moral commitment. In M. Killen & D. Hart (Eds.), *Morality in everyday life: Developmental perspectives* (pp. 342–369). Cambridge, England: Cambridge University Press.

34. Colby & Damon (1995), p. 363.

35. Oatley, K. (2008). The mind's flight simulator. *Psychologist, 21*, 1030–1032.

36. Gottschall, J. (2012). *The storytelling animal: How stories make us human.* New York, NY: Mariner Books.

37. Appel, M. (2008). Fictional narratives cultivate just-world beliefs. *Journal of Communication, 58*, 62–83.

38. Gottschall.

39. Lisman, C. D. (1996). *The curricular integration of ethics: Theory and practice.* Westport, CT: Praeger.

40. Mar, R. A., Oatley, K., Hirsch, J., de la Paz, J., & Peterson, J. B. (2006). Bookworms versus nerds: Exposure to fiction versus non-fiction, divergent associations with social ability, and the simulation of fictional social worlds. *Journal of Research in Personality, 40,* 694–712.

41. Burns, J. M. (2003). *Transforming leadership: A new pursuit of happiness.* New York, NY: Atlantic Monthly Press, Ch. 5.

42. MacIntyre, A. (1984). *After virtue: A study in moral theory* (2nd ed.). Notre Dame, IN: University of Notre Dame Press, p. 216.

43. Moxley, R. S., & Pulley, M. L. (2004). Hardships. In C. D. McCauley & E. Van Velsor (Eds.), *The Center for Creative Leadership handbook of leadership development* (2nd ed., pp. 183–203). San Francisco, CA: Jossey-Bass.

44. Bennis, W. G., & Thomas, R. J. (2002). *Geeks and geezers: How era, values, and defining moments shape leaders.* Boston, MA: Harvard Business School Press; Thomas, R. J. (2008). *Crucibles of leadership: How to learn from experience to become a great leader.* Boston, MA: Harvard Business Press.

45. Dotlich, D. L., Noel, J. L., & Walker, N. (2008). Learning for leadership: Failure as a second chance. In J. V. Gallos (Ed.), *Business leadership* (2nd ed., pp. 478–485). San Francisco, CA: Jossey-Bass.

46. Aristotle. (1962). *Nichomachean ethics* (M. Ostwald, Trans.; Book II, p. 1.). Indianapolis, IN: Bobbs-Merrill.

47. Covey, S. R. (1989). *The seven habits of highly effective people.* New York, NY: Simon & Schuster.

48. Parker-Pope, T. (2015, January 6). In with the new mission statement. *The New York Times*, p. D4.

49. Vozza, S. (2014, February 25). Personal mission statement of 5 famous CEOs (and why you should write one too). *Fast Company.* Retrieved from http://www.fastcompany.com

50. Bordas, J. (1995). Becoming a servant-leader: The personal development path. In L. Spears (Ed.), *Reflections on leadership* (pp. 149–160). New York, NY: John Wiley.

51. Kouzes, J. M., & Posner, B. Z. (2003). *Credibility: How leaders gain and lose it, why people demand it.* San Francisco, CA: Jossey-Bass, pp. 62–63.

52. Allport, G. (1961). *Pattern and growth in personality.* New York, NY: Holt, Rinehart & Winston; Guth, W. D., & Tagiuri, R. (1965, September–October). Personal values and corporate strategy. *Harvard Business Review,* 123–132.

53. Crace, R. K., & Brown, D. (1992). *The Life Values Inventory.* Minneapolis, MN: National Computer Systems. Available at http://www.lifevalues.org.

54. Kasser, T. (2002). The high price of materialism. Cambridge, MA: Bradford/MIT Press; Kasser, T., Vanssteenkiste, M., & Deckop, J. R. (2006). The ethical problems of a materialistic value orientation for businesses. In J. R. Deckop (Ed.), *Human Resource Management Ethics* (pp. 283–306). Charlotte, NC: Information Age.

4

Combating Evil

The line between good and evil lies in the center of every human heart.

—PSYCHOLOGIST PHILIP ZIMBARDO

Without forgiveness, there is no future.

—SOUTH AFRICAN ARCHBISHOP DESMOND TUTU

WHAT'S AHEAD

In this chapter, we wrestle with the most dangerous of all unhealthy shadow casters: evil. The first section surveys some of the forms or faces of evil. The second section examines the role of forgiveness, both giving and seeking, in breaking cycles of evil. The third section probes the relationship between spirituality and leadership, highlighting how spiritual practices can equip us to deal with evil and to foster more ethical, productive workplaces.

THE FACES OF EVIL

Mass shootings in California, Colorado, South Carolina, Oregon, and other states; the attack on concert goers in Paris; the kidnapping and sexual enslavement of school girls in Nigeria; the murder over one hundred twenty-six thousand people by Mexican drug cartels; suicide bombings and beheadings in the Middle East; human rights violations in North Korea (see Case Study 4.1); and global sex trafficking—all serve as powerful reminders of the existence of evil. While recognizing the presence of evil is an important first step, we can't combat this powerful force until we first understand our opponent. Contemporary Western definitions of evil emphasize its destructiveness.[1] Evil inflicts pain and suffering, deprives innocent people of their humanity, and creates feelings of hopelessness and despair. Evildoers do excessive harm, going well beyond what is needed to achieve their objectives. The ultimate product of evil is death. Evil destroys self-esteem, physical and emotional well-being, relationships, communities, and nations.

We can gain some important insights into the nature of evil by looking at the various forms or faces it displays. In this section, I'll introduce five perspectives on evil. In the next section, I'll talk about how understanding these perspectives can help us better deal with this powerful, destructive force.

Evil as Dreadful Pleasure

University of Maryland political science professor C. Fred Alford defines evil as a combination of dread and pleasure. Alford recruited 60 respondents of a variety of ages and backgrounds to talk about their experiences with evil. He discovered that people experience evil as a deep sense of uneasiness, "the dread of being human, vulnerable, alone in the universe and doomed to die."[2] They do evil when, instead of coming to grips with their inner darkness, they try to get rid of it by making others feel "dreadful." Inflicting this pain is enjoyable. Part of the pleasure comes from their being in charge, of being the victimizers instead of the victims.

Evil can also be a product of chronic boredom.[3] Boredom arises when people lose their sense of meaning and purpose. They no longer enjoy life and try to fill the emptiness they feel inside. Ordinary distractions such as television, movies, surfing the Internet, social media, shopping, and sports don't fill the void, so people turn to evil instead. Evil is an attractive alternative because it engages the full energy and attention of perpetrators. For example, a serial killer has to plan his crimes, locate victims, keep his actions secret, and outsmart law enforcement.

Evil as Exclusion

In moral exclusion, group members draw a mental circle.[4] Those inside the circle (the *moral community* or *scope of justice*) are treated with respect, are considered deserving of sacrifice from other members, and get their fair share of resources. If those within the circle are harmed, other group members come to their rescue. Those outside the circle, on the other hand, are seen as undeserving or expendable. As a result, "harming them appears acceptable, appropriate, or just."[5]

Mild forms of exclusion are part of daily life and include, for example, making sexist comments, applying double standards when judging the behavior of different groups, and making unflattering comparisons to appear superior to others. (Mild exclusion can also include ignoring or allowing such behaviors.) However, moral exclusion can also take extreme forms, resulting in such evils as human rights violations, torture, murder, and genocide. For instance, during World War II, Japanese soldiers viewed the Chinese with contempt. Murdering them was like "squashing a bug or murdering a hog."[6] This mindset allowed Japanese soldiers to rape, torture, and slaughter civilians in the Chinese city of Nanking (now known as Nanjing), killing an estimated 300,000 residents. Prior to prisoner abuse at Abu Ghraib, jailers were told that Iraqi prisoners "are like dogs and if you allow them to believe at any point that they are more than a dog then you've lost control of them."[7] Other examples of evil exclusion include the Russian oppression of Chechen rebels, genocide in Guatemala, Serbian atrocities, attacks on villages in the Darfur region of Sudan, and the killing of Christians and moderate Muslims by Islamic extremist groups.[8] Box 4.1 presents a list of the symptoms of moral exclusion.

Dispute resolution expert Susan Opotow believes that moral exclusion progresses through the following five states or elements, which reinforce one another and can become a vicious cycle that ends in death and destruction.[9]

1. *Conflicts of interest are salient.* Moral exclusion is often set in motion during zero-sum conflicts where one group wins at the expense of the others. As tensions increase, members distance themselves from

Box 4.1 Symptoms of Moral Exclusion

Symptom	Description
Double standards	Having different norms for different groups
Concealing effects of harmful outcomes	Disregarding, ignoring, distorting, or minimizing injurious outcomes that others experience
Reducing moral standards	Asserting that one's harmful behavior is proper while denying one's lesser concern for others
Utilizing euphemisms	Making and sanitizing harmful behavior and outcomes
Biased evaluation of groups	Making unflattering between-group comparisons that bolster one's own group at the expense of others
Condescension and derogation	Regarding others with disdain
Dehumanization	Denying others' rights, entitlements, humanity, and dignity
Fear of contamination	Perceiving contact or alliances with other stakeholders as posing a threat to oneself
Normalization and glorification of violence	Glorifying and normalizing violence as an effective, legitimate, or even sublime form of human behavior while denying the potential of violence to damage people, the environment, relationships, and constructive conflict resolution processes
Victim blaming	Placing blame on those who are harmed
Deindividuation	Believing one's contribution to social problems is undetectable
Diffusing responsibility	Denying personal responsibility for harms by seeing them as the result of collective rather than individual decisions and actions
Displacing responsibility	Identifying others, such as subordinates or supervisors, as responsible for harms inflicted on victims

Source: Opotow, S., Gerson, J., & Woodside, S. (2005). From moral exclusion to moral inclusion: Theory for teaching peace. *Theory into Practice 44*, 303–318, p. 307. Used with permission.

their opponents, focusing on differences based on company, job function, religion, education, hometown, ethnic background, social status, skin color, and other factors. Competition for resources can even set adults against children. Under the Communist regime in Romania, families were forced to have four children when there was little to eat. As a result, survival took priority over the welfare of children, who were seen as competition for food; many children were placed in orphanages. One Romanian cab driver summed up the attitude of many of his countrymen this way: "With so many decent people struggling to get along, why do you bother with the kids? They are not good; they are trash."[10] Only recently have Romanian citizens begun to address the problem of neglected children.

2. *Group categorizations are salient.* The characteristics of competing groups are given negative labels, helping to divide the world into those who deserve empathy and assistance and those who don't. These derogatory labels excuse unfair treatment and negative consequences. In much of Europe, for example, Romanians (often called Gypsies) are described as "lazy," "dirty," and "thieves."[11]

3. *Moral justifications are prominent.* Hurting outsiders is justified and even celebrated as a way to strike a blow against a corrupt enemy. These exclusionary moral claims can be identified by their self-serving nature. They justify doing harm and reinforce moral boundaries by denigrating outsiders. Nazis blamed Jews for causing Germany's defeat in World War I and its subsequent economic collapse. Jews were seen as a threat to the nation's racial purity and Aryan superiority. First, they were excluded from economic, political, and social life, and then, with their humanity denied, they were sent to concentration camps to be gassed.[12]

4. *Unjust procedures are described as expedient.* The damage done by moral exclusion is often disguised because it administered through technical or rational means (see the discussion of evil as bureaucracy below). Unjust procedures often hurt the very people they are supposed to benefit. For example, government bureaucrats in the United States and Australia claimed to be helping native peoples even as they stole their lands and tried to eradicate their cultures.

5. *Harmful outcomes occur.* Exclusion has damaging physical and psychological effects. Members of excluded groups may suffer physical harm like abuse, sickness, and death. At the same time, they suffer from a loss of self-esteem and identity as they internalize the negative judgments of the dominant group. Perpetrators also pay a high price. They have to spend significant energy and resources to deal with conflicts, excuse their behavior, and maintain group boundaries. Excluders also suffer psychologically, as the harm they cause threatens to overshadow any good they do. This was the case under apartheid in South Africa, where Afrikaners could not overcome the stain of racism.

Evil as Deception

Psychiatrist M. Scott Peck identified evil as an extreme form of narcissism or self-absorption.[13] Mentally healthy adults submit themselves to something beyond themselves, like God or love or excellence. Submission to a greater power encourages them to obey their consciences. Evil people, on the other hand, refuse to submit and try to control others instead. They consider themselves above reproach and project their shortcomings, attacking anyone who threatens their self-concepts. Evil individuals are consumed with keeping up appearances. Peck called them "the people of the lie" because they deceive themselves and others in hopes of projecting a righteous image. Peck believed that truly evil people are more likely to live in our neighborhoods than in our jails. They generally hide their true natures and appear to be normal and successful. Inmates, on the other hand, land in prison because they've been morally inconsistent or stupid.

The Columbine killers provide a chilling example of evil as deception. Teens Eric Harris and Dylan Klebold were two highly intelligent, mainstream students from privileged backgrounds who held part-time jobs, bowled regularly, and attended the prom. They were able to deceive school officials, law enforcement authorities, and their parents as they spewed hate on the Internet, assembled explosive devices in a basement, and plotted an assault on their Colorado high school. Armed with bombs, shotguns, napalm, and semiautomatic rifles, the duo killed 14 students and one faculty member, injuring 23 others.[14]

Evil as Bureaucracy

The twentieth century was the bloodiest period in history. An estimated 200 million people died as the direct or indirect result of wars, genocide, and other violence.[15] According to public administration professors Guy Adams and Danny Balfour, the combination of science and technology made the 1900s so destructive.[16] Scientific and technological developments—tanks, airplanes, chemical warfare, nuclear weapons—made killing highly efficient. At the same time, belief in technological progress encouraged government officials to take a rational approach to problems. The integration of these factors produced administrative evil. In administrative evil, organizational members commit heinous crimes while carrying out their daily tasks as "good," "responsible" professionals. Adams and Balfour argue that the true nature of administrative evil is masked or hidden from participants. Hiding evil is easier in the modern organization because, first of all, many people are not comfortable with the term *evil*. The concept is seen as moralistic and outdated; it doesn't fit well into the modern scientific age. Second, large organizations diffuse individual responsibility and compartmentalize work. Individual employees don't feel individually accountable for their acts or realize how their behaviors contribute to evil. Third, professionals focused solely on carrying out their duties find it easier to repackage evil, destructive actions as good, a process called *moral inversion*. In administrative evil, officials are rarely asked to engage in evil; instead, they inflict pain and suffering while fulfilling their job responsibilities, believing that they are serving a worthy cause. Often, the damage is done to what Adams and Balfour call "surplus populations," those groups—ethnic minorities, the poor, immigrants—that are marginalized by society.

The Holocaust provides the most vivid example of administrative evil in action. Extermination camps (designed to eliminate Jews, Gypsies, and other "surplus populations") in Germany would not have been possible without the willing cooperation of thousands of civil servants engaged in such functions as collecting taxes, running municipal governments, and managing the country's social security system. These duties may seem morally neutral, but in carrying them out, public officials condemned millions to death. Government authorities defined who was undesirable and then seized their assets. Administrators managed the ghettos, built concentration camp latrines, and employed slave labor. Even the railway authority did its part. The Gestapo had to pay for each prisoner shipped by rail to the death camps. Railroad officials billed the SS at third-class passenger rates (one way) for adult prisoners, with discounts for children. Guards were charged round-trip fares.

Adams and Balfour believe that administrative evil emerges over time. When wrongdoing first occurs, no one individual sees enough of the big picture to recognize the violation because of compartmentalization and diffusion of responsibility. The longer the wrongdoing goes on, the harder it is to stop as members become more invested in the activity; repeating the behavior legitimizes it. At this point, reversing course takes strong, decisive action. When members finally recognize the evil, their feelings of guilt and shame (and concern for organizational liability) give them a strong incentive to deny the wrongdoing or to engage in moral inversion.

Evil as a Choice

Any discussion of good and evil must consider the role of human choice. Just how much freedom we have is a matter of debate, but a number of scholars argue that we become good or evil through a series of small, incremental decisions. In other words, we never remain neutral but are always moving toward one pole or another. Medieval scholar C. S. Lewis drew on the image of a road to illustrate this point.[17] On a journey, we decide which direction to take every time we come to a fork in the road. We face a similar series of decisions throughout our lives. We can't correct a poor decision by continuing on but must go back to the fork where we went wrong and take the other path.

Psychologist Erich Fromm made the same argument as Lewis. Only those who are very good or very bad do not have a choice; the rest of us do. However, each choice we make reduces our options:

> Each step in life which increases my self-confidence, my integrity, my courage, my conviction also increases my capacity to choose the desirable alternative, until eventually it becomes more difficult to choose the undesirable rather than the desirable action. On the other hand, each act of surrender and cowardice weakens me, opens the path for more acts of surrender, and eventually freedom is lost. Between the extreme when I can no longer do a wrong act and the other extreme when I have lost my freedom to right action, there are innumerable degrees of freedom of choice. In the practice of life, the degree of freedom to choose is different at any given moment. If the degree of freedom to choose the good is great, it needs less effort to choose the good. If it is small, it takes a great effort, help from others, and favorable circumstances.[18]

Fromm uses the story of the Israelites' exodus from ancient Egypt to illustrate what happens when leaders make a series of evil choices. Moses repeatedly asks Pharaoh to let his people go, but the Egyptian ruler turns down every request. Eventually his heart is hardened, and he and his army are destroyed.

Evil as Ordinary

The evil-as-ordinary perspective focuses on the situational factors that cause otherwise ordinary or normal people to become evildoers. Although it may be comforting to think that evildoers must be heartless psychopaths or deranged killers, we know that in many cases, perpetrators look and act a lot like the rest of us. Social philosopher Hannah Arendt pointed this out in her analysis of the trial of Nazi officer Adolf Eichmann in 1961.[19] Eichmann was responsible for the deportation of millions of Jews to concentration and extermination camps. What struck Arendt was how ordinary Eichmann seemed. Half a dozen psychiatrists examined him and certified him as "normal." Arendt used the phrase the "banality of evil" when describing Eichmann to point out that the sources of evil are not mysterious or demonic but commonplace. If that is the case, then any one of us can commit heinous crimes. The Rwandan genocide supports Arendt's thesis. Thousands of ordinary Rwandan Hutus literally went next door or across the street to hack and beat their Tutsi neighbors to death with machetes and other farm implements. Interviews with one group of young killers revealed a chilling routine. They would have a hearty breakfast (running down Tutsis took a lot of energy), meet at the soccer field to get their assignments to kill or loot, march off singing, find and murder victims until the final whistle blew, and then relax with beer and food after a hard day's work.[20]

Philip Zimbardo and other social psychologists have identified a number of situational factors that can turn otherwise "nice" people into torturers and murderers.[21] Zimbardo discovered firsthand the power of the system to promote unethical behavior through his famous Stanford Prison Experiment. In this study, he created a mock prison in the basement of the building housing Stanford University's psychology department and randomly assigned student volunteers to roles as prisoners and guards. It didn't take long for both groups to get caught up in their roles. Soon, the prisoners revolted and the guards retaliated. The jailers strip-searched prisoners, forced them into prolonged exercise, put them into solitary confinement, denied them bathroom privileges (they had to urinate and defecate in their cells), and made them clean toilets by hand. Two prisoners suffered significant emotional trauma and had to be immediately released from the experiment. Zimbardo, who served as the prison warden, also got caught up in the role-play. At one point, he tried to transfer the experiment to an empty cell at the local police station to ensure more security and he got angry when the police refused his request. Zimbardo ended the experiment early after a visitor (who would later become his wife) complained about the disgusting conditions at the "jail." Of the 50 outsiders who visited the mock prison while the experiment was being conducted, she was the only person to object.

Zimbardo went on to analyze the role of situational variables in real-life cases of evil, such as the widespread torture of political opponents in Brazil and prisoner abuse at Iraq's Abu Ghraib prison. According to Zimbardo, ordinary people, such as the military guards at Abu Ghraib, are motivated to do evil when they feel peer pressure to participate in such acts, obey authority, remain anonymous, are given permission to engage in antisocial behavior, and dehumanize others (treat them as less than fully human). Evil is likely to continue when others fail to intervene to stop it.

FACING EVIL

Each of the perspectives just described provides insights into how we as leaders can come to grips with evil. The dreadful pleasure approach highlights both the origins of evil and the attraction of doing evil, forcing us to examine our motivations. We need to ask ourselves, "Am I projecting my insecurities onto others? Am I punishing a subordinate because of her or his poor performance or because exercising coercive power makes me feel strong? Am I making a legitimate request or merely demonstrating that I have the authority to control another person? Am I tempted to harm others just to fill the emptiness I feel inside?"

Evil as exclusion highlights the dangers of putting other groups outside our circle of concern. However, combating moral exclusion is difficult because it often subtle and hard to detect. Further, group members often deny or ignore their exclusionary behavior to protect themselves from guilt or anxiety.[22] Being alert to the symptoms outlined in Box 4.1 is a good place to start. Pay particularly close attention to the language used by group members. Negative labels, critical comments, unfair comparisons, and other verbal strategies narrow the scope of justice. Biased speech also paves the way for more extreme behaviors. Adopting a pluralistic perspective can help leaders deter moral exclusion at each stage of its development.[23] Pluralism acknowledges the legitimacy of a variety of groups. This approach sees conflicts not as win–lose battles but as opportunities to integrate the interests of all parties. Members of pluralistic groups enlarge the definition of the moral community by viewing all persons as worthy of justice. Pluralism encourages group members to be skeptical of self-serving claims and moral justifications for destructive acts, to develop fair procedures for distributing resources, and to support dissenters.

The evil-as-deception viewpoint makes it clear that people aren't always as they seem. On the surface, evil people appear to be successful and well-adjusted. In reality, they exert tremendous energy keeping up appearances. Deceit and defensiveness can serve as warning signs. If we routinely lie to protect our images, refuse constructive feedback, and always blame others, we may be engaged in evil. The same may be true of other leaders and followers who display these behaviors. Peck, like Parker Palmer, believed that to master our inner demons we must first name them. Once we've identified these tendencies, we can begin to deal with them by examining our will. We should determine whether we're willing to submit to a positive force—an ideal, authority—that is greater than we are. Peck urges us to respond to the destructive acts of others with love. Instead of attacking evildoers, we can react with goodness and thereby absorb the power of evil.

The administrative evil perspective introduces a new type of evil, one based on technology and logic. In today's world, evil has increased capacity for destruction. The impacts of evil, once contained by distance and technological limitations, can now extend to the entire world. Further, the face of evil may be masked or hidden from those who participate in it. Combating this form of evil begins with acknowledging that evil exists. Despite recent attempts by some scholars to discount evil, the fact is that evil has been studied for centuries; many different cultures consider evil to be an integral part of human existence.[24] Second, we should periodically step back to look at the big picture. For example, when carrying out our duties, we need to ask, "What is the organization's ultimate goal? Does my role contribute to good or ill? What are the long-term consequences of my actions, beyond short-term effectiveness and efficiency? Am I excusing my bad behavior by calling it justified?" Third, be alert to even small ethical missteps, lest they be repeated and develop into destructive patterns. Fourth, recognize the danger of hiding behind professionalism, which tempts us to set aside our moral standards in order to obey authority. We are ultimately responsible for our decisions. Claiming that we were "just following orders" is no excuse. Finally, remember that the ultimate goal of administrators and managers is protecting the well-being of people, particularly society's most vulnerable members. (See Case Study 4.2 to see how one group of administrators lost sight of this obligation.)

Evil as a choice puts the ethical burden squarely on our shoulders. Group and organizational pressures may contribute to our wrongdoing, but we are the ones who make the decisions to participate in evil acts. Furthermore, the choices we make now will limit our options in the future. Every moral decision, no matter how insignificant it seems at the time, has lasting consequences.

The final perspective, evil as ordinary, is a sobering reminder that we all have the potential to become evildoers. Not only do we as followers need to resist situational influences that can turn us into brutes (see "Focus on Follower Ethics: Resisting Situational Pressures to Do Evil"), but also, as leaders, we should eliminate conditions that promote evil behavior in our subordinates. It is our ethical duty to intervene when we see evil behavior and to reward others who do the same.

MAKING A CASE FOR FORGIVENESS

Breaking the Cycle of Evil

Scott Peck is not alone in arguing that loving acts can overcome evil. A growing number of social scientists believe that forgiving instead of retaliating can prevent or break cycles of evil. In a cycle of evil, aggressive acts provoke retaliation followed by more aggression. When these destructive patterns characterize relations between ethnic groups (e.g., Turks versus Armenians, Serbs versus Croats), they can continue for hundreds of years. Courageous leaders can end retaliatory cycles through dramatic acts of reconciliation, however. As president of Egypt, Anwar Sadat engaged in one such conciliatory gesture when he traveled to Jerusalem to further the peace process with Israel. Pope John Paul II went to the jail cell of his would-be assassin to offer forgiveness. Archbishop Desmond Tutu and Nelson Mandela prevented a bloodbath in South Africa by creating the Truth and Reconciliation Commission. This body, made up of both blacks and whites, investigated crimes committed during the apartheid era and allowed offenders to confess their guilt and ask for pardon. Similar commissions were created after incidents of widespread torture and murder in Argentina, Uruguay, Peru, Guatemala, Rwanda, and elsewhere.

The concept of forgiving evildoers is controversial.[25] Skeptics assert that (1) guilty parties will get off without acknowledging they have done wrong or paying for their crimes, (2) forgiveness is a sign of weakness, (3) forgiveness is impossible in some situations, (4) forgiveness can't be offered until the offender asks for it, and (5) no leader has the right to offer forgiveness on behalf of other victims. Each of these concerns is valid. You will have to decide for yourself whether forgiveness is an appropriate response to evil deeds. However, before you make that determination, I want to describe the forgiveness process and identify some of the benefits that come from extending mercy to others.

Focus on Follower Ethics

RESISTING SITUATIONAL PRESSURES TO DO EVIL: A 10-STEP PROGRAM

Philip Zimbardo offers the following 10-step program designed to help followers resist situational forces that promote evildoing.

"I made a mistake!" Admit your mistakes. (Say "I'm sorry"; "I apologize"; "Forgive me.") Vow to learn from your errors and move on. Don't stay the course if you are engaged in an immoral activity.

"I am mindful." Don't rely on scripts from the past. They can blind you to the tactics of influencers and key elements of the situation. Instead, pay close attention to (be mindful of) the here and now. In addition, think critically. Ask for evidence, imagine future consequences, and reject simple solutions to complex problems. Encourage others to do the same.

"I am responsible." Maintaining personal accountability increases your resistance to conformity pressures. Take charge of your decisions and actions rather than spreading responsibility to your group, coworkers, or military unit. Remember that claiming "everyone else was doing it" is no defense in a court of law.

"I am me, the best I can be." Don't let others take away your individuality, making you anonymous. State your name, credentials, and unique features.

"I respect just authority but rebel against unjust authority." Distinguish between those in authority who deserve your respect and those who are leading others astray or promoting their own interests. Critically evaluate and disobey destructive leaders.

"I want group acceptance but value my independence." Group acceptance is a powerful force but shouldn't overpower your sense of right and wrong. Resist social pressure by stepping out of the group, getting other opinions, and finding new groups more in line with your values.

"I will be more frame vigilant." Frames (words, pictures, slogans, logos) shape our attitudes toward issues and people, often without our being aware of their impact. For example, many politicians use the colors of the flag—red, white, and blue—on their campaign signs and other materials. Be vigilant, noting the way that the frame is designed to shape your thoughts and emotions.

"I will balance my time perspective." Living in the present increases the power of situational influences that promote evil. You are less likely to go along with abusive behavior if you consider the long-term consequences of such actions and remember the values and standards you developed in the past.

"I will not sacrifice personal or civic freedoms for the illusion of security." Reject any offer that involves sacrificing even small freedoms for the promise of future security. Such sacrifices (e.g., loss of privacy, legal protections, and freedom of speech) are immediate and real, but the promised security is often a distant illusion.

"I can oppose unjust systems." Join with others to resist systems that promote evil. Try to bring about change, blow the whistle on corruption, get away from the group or organization, resist groupthink, draw on the resources of outsiders, and so on.

Source: Adapted from Zimbardo, P. G. (2007). *The Lucifer effect: Understanding how good people turn evil.* New York, NY: Random House, pp. 451–456.

The Forgiveness Process

There are many misconceptions about what it means to forgive another person or group of people. According to Robert Enright, professor of educational psychology and president of the International Forgiveness Institute at the University of Wisconsin, forgiveness is *not* the following:[26]

- Forgetting past wrongs to "move on"
- Excusing or condoning bad, damaging behavior
- Reconciling or coming together again (Forgiveness opens the way to reconciliation, but the person being forgiven must change or desire to reconcile.)
- Reducing the severity of offenses
- Offering a legal pardon
- Pretending to forgive in order to wield power over another person
- Ignoring the offender
- Dropping our anger and becoming emotionally neutral

Enright and his colleagues define forgiveness as "a willingness to abandon one's right to resentment, negative judgment, and indifferent behavior toward one who unjustly injured us, while fostering the undeserved qualities of compassion, generosity, and even love toward him or her."[27] This definition recognizes that the wronged party has been unjustly treated (slandered, betrayed, imprisoned); the offended person willingly chooses forgiveness regardless of the offender's response; forgiving involves emotions, thoughts, and behavior; and forgiveness is a process that takes place over time. (To measure your likelihood to forgive others, complete Self-Assessment 4.1.)

Enright and his fellow researchers offer a four-stage model to help people forgive. In the first phase, *uncovering,* a victim may initially deny that a problem exists. However, when the person does acknowledge the hurt, he or she may experience intense feelings of anger, shame, and betrayal. The victim invests a lot of psychic energy in rehashing the offense and comparing his or her condition with that of the offender. Feeling permanently damaged, the person may believe that life is unfair.

During the second phase, *decision,* the injured party recognizes that he or she is paying a high price for dwelling on the injury, considers the possibility of forgiveness, and commits him- or herself to forgiving.

Forgiveness is accomplished in the third stage, *work.* The wronged party tries to understand (not condone) the victimizer's background and motivation. He or she may experience empathy and compassion for the offender. Absorbing pain is the key to this stage. The forgiver decides to endure suffering rather than pass it on, thereby breaking the cycle of evil. Viewed in this light, forgiveness is a gift of mercy to the wrongdoer. In one powerful example of forgiveness, families of some of the black victims of the Charleston South Carolina church shooting declared that that they forgave the white supremacist who gunned their relatives down.[28]

The fourth and final phase, *deepening,* consists of the outcomes of forgiving. A forgiver may find deeper meaning in suffering, realize his or her own need for forgiveness, and come to a greater appreciation for support groups—friends, congregations, classmates. In the end, the person offering forgiveness may develop a new purpose in life and find peace. (See "Leadership Ethics at the Movies: *The Railway Man*" for an example of someone who found peace through offering forgiveness.)

This four-stage model has been used successfully with a variety of audiences: survivors of incest, prison inmates, college students deprived of parental love, those suffering from heart disease, substance abusers, youth at risk for aggressive behavior, and elderly women suffering from depression. In each case, forgivers experienced significant healing. Enright emphasizes that personal benefits should be a by-product, not the motivation, for forgiving. Nonetheless, a growing body of evidence suggests that forgiveness can pay significant psychological, physical, and relational dividends.[29] Those who forgive are released from resentments and experience less depression and anxiety. Overall, they enjoy a higher sense of well-being. By releasing their grudges, forgivers experience better physical health. Reducing anger, hostility, and hopelessness lowers the risk of heart attack and high blood pressure while increasing the body's resistance to disease. Acting mercifully toward transgressors can also help to maintain relationships among friends and family members.

The social scientific study of forgiveness is continuing, and results are extremely encouraging. Forgiving does appear to absorb or defuse evil. If this is the case, then as leaders, we should practice forgiveness when we are treated unjustly by followers, supervisors, peers, or outsiders. At times, however, we will need to go further and follow the examples of Sadat and Mandela by offering forgiveness on behalf of followers in the hope of reconciling with a long-standing enemy.

Donald Shriver uses the metaphor of a cable to explain how warring groups can overcome their mutual hatred and bind together to restore fractured relationships.[30] This cable is made up of four strands. The first strand is *moral truth*. Forgiveness starts with recalling the past and rendering a moral judgment. Both parties need to agree that one or both engaged in behavior that was wrong (see the discussion of political apologies below) and unjust and caused injury. Refusal to admit the truth makes reconciliation impossible. That is why South Africa's Truth and Reconciliation Commission began the process of national healing after the abolition of apartheid by publicly airing black victims' statements and requests for amnesty by white police officers.

The second strand of the cable is *forbearance*—that is, rejecting revenge in favor of restraint. Moral indignation often fuels new crimes as offended parties take their vengeance. Forbearance breaks this pattern and may soften enemies who expect retaliation.

The third strand is *empathy* for the enemies' humanity. Empathy doesn't excuse wrongs but acknowledges that offender and offended share much in common. This recognition opens the way for both sides to live together in peace. Union general Ulysses S. Grant demonstrated how to combine the judgment of wrong with empathy at Appomattox, where Southern troops surrendered to end the U.S. Civil War. On that occasion, Grant wrote the following in his journal. "I felt . . . sad and depressed at the downfall of a foe who had fought so long and valiantly, and had suffered so much for a cause, though that cause was, I believe, one of the worst for which a people ever fought."[31]

The fourth and final strand of the forgiveness cable is *commitment* to restore the broken relationship. Forgivers must be prepared to live and interact with their former enemies. At first, the two parties probably will coexist in a state of mutual toleration.

Later, they may fully reconcile, as the United States and Germany have done since the end of World War II.

In sum, I believe that forgiveness is one of a leader's most powerful weapons in the fight against evil. Or, to return to the central metaphor of this text, forgiving is one of the ways in which leaders cast light rather than shadow. We must face our inner darkness, particularly our resentments and hostilities, in order to offer genuine forgiveness. By forgiving, we short-circuit or break the shadowy, destructive cycles that poison groups, organizations, and societies. Offering forgiveness brightens our lives by reducing our anxiety levels and enhancing our sense of well-being.[32] Requesting forgiveness, as we'll see below, opens the door for reconciliation.

Seeking Forgiveness

Just as we need to offer forgiveness, we need to seek forgiveness. In fact, some observers have called the current era the "Age of Apology." Nearly every week, it seems, a leader offers an apology either for his or her misdeeds or on behalf of the groups he or she leads. Atlanta Archbishop Wilton Gregory apologized for building a $2.2 million mansion with church funds, for example, while cyclist Lance Armstrong confessed to doping during his seven Tour de France victories. Harvard Business School Dean Nitin Nohria said he was "sorry on behalf of the business school" for its poor treatment of female students.

The demand for apologies is likely to increase for several reasons.[33] First, globalization is creating more friction as cultures and values clash; apologies act as a conflict management tool. Second, digital technology reduces the likelihood that misbehavior can be kept secret. Offensive behavior is now broadcast around the world. President George W. Bush and Secretary of Defense Donald Rumsfeld were forced to apologize, for instance, when photographs of prisoner abuse at Abu Ghraib were released. The head of Domino's had to apologize after two North Carolina employees posted YouTube video of themselves engaged in a series of health code violations like putting cheese up their noses and bathing in the restaurant sink. Third, as old regimes crumble, new leaders find that they need to acknowledge the suffering of victims under previous governments. Often, past regimes did not acknowledge their guilt, so the burden falls on incoming officials. As a result, political apologies appear to be increasingly common. Examples include the following:[34]

- British prime minister Tony Blair apologized for his country's inaction during the Irish potato famine of the nineteenth century.
- The Belgian prime minister apologized to Rwandans for not stepping in to prevent the 1994 genocide.
- Germany's chancellor Gerhard Schröder requested forgiveness from the Russian people for the damage done by his nation during World War II.
- U.S. President Bill Clinton expressed regret to Ugandans for African slavery.
- The Natal Law Society apologized for excluding Mohandas K. Gandhi from the practice of law in South Africa.
- The U.S. Senate passed a resolution apologizing for not enacting legislation that would have made lynching a federal crime.

Leadership Ethics at the Movies

THE RAILWAY MAN

Key Cast Members: Colin Firth, Nicole Kidman, Jeremy Irvine, Stellan Skarsgard, Tanroh Ishida, Yutaka Izumihare

Synopsis: Eric Lomax (Firth) is a train enthusiast caught between the past and present. He knows the routes, times, and details of all the trains running in Britain in the early 1980s but continues to flashback to his experience as a prisoner of war in World War II. His Japanese captors beat and tortured him for assembling a radio receiver out of spare parts. The trauma he suffered as a prisoner threatens his marriage to Patti (Kidman). Lomax then decides to confront one of his former captors, translator Takashi Nagase (Ishida). Lomax sets out to exact revenge but decides instead to forgive his former tormenter, who deeply regrets his wartime role. The two develop a close friendship that continues until their deaths. Based on Lomax's autobiography of the same title.

Rating: R for extreme violence and scenes of torture

Themes: evil, forgiveness, repentance, apology, cruelty, courage, compassion, redemption

Discussion Starters

1. Why did Lomax emerge as an informal leader in the prison camp?

2. What virtues did young Lomax demonstrate during his captivity?

3. Did Lomax's fellow veterans help or hinder his recovery from his wartime trauma?

4. How did forgiveness contribute to the healing of both Lomax and Nagase?

- The Oregon state legislature held a public session to revoke and to express regret about an 1849 law that prohibited African Americans from entering Oregon territory.

- British Columbia premier Gordon Campbell apologized to aboriginal peoples for the Canadian province's failure to provide adequate support for their needs.

Businesses and religious groups, too, are have officially apologized for past wrongs. Mitsubishi acknowledged it forced American POWS to work for the company during World War II. J.P. Morgan Chase and Wachovia banks expressed regret for their support of slavery, as did the Southern Baptist convention. The Catholic Church has issued apologies for its inaction during the Holocaust, denigration of women, and other sins and errors.

Apologies are moral acts.[35] In seeking forgiveness, offenders acknowledge that ethical violations have occurred, that a moral or social contract has been broken. Perpetrators accept responsibility for these transgressions and pledge to repair the damage. In apologizing, offenders put themselves in a humble position while helping to restore the dignity of victims and promoting healing. They acknowledge that the victims were indeed wronged and assure them of safety. Apologizing also signals a commitment to the relationship as well as to common values. Victims see the offenders suffer through their expressions of remorse; reparations help to repair the damage. Apologizers develop a sense of integrity and greater self-awareness. By seeking forgiveness, offenders open the door to reconciliation.

Unfortunately, many apologies (*pseudo-apologies* or inauthentic apologies) fail to live up to their moral obligations. The offender, while ostensibly apologizing, refuses to admit guilt, appears insincere, blames others, and so on. For example, when attempting to apologize for doping, Lance Armstrong minimized his offenses. He claimed that the U.S. cycling cheating scheme was limited when compared to the doping program of the East Germans. However, the head of the United States Anti-Doping Agency said that Armstrong's team ran "the most sophisticated, organized and professionalized doping scheme in the history of cycling."[36]

Pseudo-apologies can make a situation worse by further offending victims and trivializing their concerns. The moral or social contract remains broken. Any opportunity for reconciliation is cut off. Inauthentic apologies are frequently vague ("I apologize for whatever I did . . ."), use the passive voice ("Mistakes have been made . . ."), make the offense conditional ("If mistakes were made . . ."), question whether the victim was damaged ("If anyone was hurt . . .), or minimize the damage ("There's really nothing [or very little] to apologize for . . .").[37] Rwandans rejected former United Nations (UN) Secretary General Kofi Annan's apology for failing to intervene in the country's genocide because Annan didn't acknowledge that his inaction as leader contributed to the massacre. Cooking star Paula Deen gave not one but two rambling apologies for her use of racist language that failed to convince sponsors or the media to forgive her. Bernie Madoff offered a courtroom apology during his sentencing for a massive Ponzi scheme. But he only expressed regret for the harm he did to his immediate family, not for the damage he had done to thousands of investors who lost their money.

Apology expert John Kador argues that delivering effective apologies (and avoiding inauthentic apologies) is a critical skill for modern leaders:

> Today's most urgent leadership challenges demand the ability to apologize when you make a mistake. The capacity of leaders to apologize can determine their ability to create the kinds of high-trust organizations required to navigate turbulent times. Apology is a leadership skill. And, like any skill, it can be improved with reflection and practice.[38]

Kador outlines five dimensions of an effective or authentic apology that can help us develop our ability to apologize, whether for our own actions or on behalf of the groups we lead. (You can determine your current apology skill level by completing his quiz found in Self-Assessment 4.2.) We can also use his "5-R" model for evaluating the apologies of others.

Recognition. An authentic apology begins with identifying the specific offenses committed (for example, lying to colleagues, abusing followers, failing to protect the safety of workers). When framing an apology, consider your answers to the following questions:

1. What am I apologizing for?

2. What was the impact of my actions on the victim?

3. What norm or value did I violate?

4. Am I apologizing to the right person?

5. Do I have cause to apologize?

6. Do I have the standing to apologize?

7. Should my apology contain an explanation?

Responsibility. Take personal responsibility for the offenses. Avoid the temptation to blame others, to make excuses, or to defend yourself. Former Oregon U.S. Senator Bob Packwood provided one memorable example of how *not* to take responsibility. Accused of drugging and sexually harassing women, Packwood said, "I'm apologizing for the conduct that it was alleged that I did, and I say I am sorry."[39] Not surprisingly, Packwood was forced to resign from office. (Read Case Study 4.3 to see how one company denied responsibility for the misdeeds of its most famous representative.)

Remorse. "I'm sorry" or "I apologize" or "I regret" should be part of admission of responsibility. These words need to be reinforced with the appropriate nonverbal cues that reflect sadness and remorse. Comedian Steve Harvey drew praise for expressing heartfelt, tearful remorse to Miss Columbia after mistakenly announcing that she was the winner of the Miss Universe pageant.

Restitution. Take concrete steps to aid the victim by, for example, restoring employee benefits or paying restitution for damages. Making amends helps to restore balance to the relationship and signals that you are sincere. It is not always possible to offer tangible restitution. In those cases, offer humility, community service, and other intangible reparations. Football star Michael Vick helped restore his image after being jailed for dog fighting charges by working with the Humane Society of the United States on its anti–dog-fighting campaign.[40]

Repetition. Signal your commitment to not repeat the offensive behavior. This helps the victim overcome her or his reluctance to forgive. As part of his apology for a series of food-borne illnesses at Chipotle, for example, founder Steve Ells vowed to prevent future outbreaks at the restaurant chain by instituting extensive, new, food safety measures.

SPIRITUALITY AND LEADERSHIP

Coming to grips with evil is hard work. We must always be on the lookout for evil in whatever form it takes; continually evaluate our motivations and choices; make a conscious effort to forgive by reshaping our thoughts, emotions, and behaviors; and have the courage to apologize. A great number of leaders turn to spirituality to help equip themselves for these tasks. If spirituality seems to be a strange topic to discuss in a book about leadership ethics, consider the recent explosion of interest in spirituality in the workplace.

More and more academics are studying the link between spiritual values and practices and organizational performance.[41] One interest group in the Academy of Management, for example, focuses on the connection between spirituality and managerial practice and publishes the *Journal of Management, Spirituality & Religion*. A number of other scholarly journals (including the *Journal of Managerial Psychology, Journal of Organizational Change Management, Journal of Management Education, Leadership Quarterly,* and *Journal of Management Inquiry*) have devoted special issues to the topic.

Popular interest in spirituality is also surging. Meditation rooms and reflective gardens are part of many company headquarters. Some organizations sponsor groups for spiritual seekers, hire chaplains, and send employees to business and spirituality workshops. Tom's of Maine, Toro, BioGenex, Interstate Batteries, and Medtronic integrate spiritual values into their organizational cultures. David Whyte, James Autry, and Thomas Chappell are a few of the popular writers who encourage spiritual development at work.

The recent surge of interest in spirituality in the workplace has been fueled in large part by the growing importance of organizations. For better or worse, the corporation has replaced other groups (family, church, social groups) as the dominant institution in society. Work takes up increasing amounts of our time and energy. As a result, we tend to develop more friendships with coworkers and fewer with people outside our workplaces. Many of us want a higher return on this investment of time and energy, seeking meaningful tasks and relationships that serve higher purposes. At the same time, downsizing, restructuring, rapid change, and information overload have generated fear and uncertainty in the workplace, which prompts us to seek stability and to reexamine our lives.[42] Baby boomers, in particular, are reevaluating their priorities, shifting their focus from individual achievement toward purpose and community. For their part, organizations hope to benefit because their members feel a greater sense of connection. Investigators have discovered that spirituality enhances the following:[43]

- Commitment to mission, core values, and ethical standards
- Organizational learning and creativity
- Morale
- Productivity and profitability
- Collaboration and community
- Loyalty
- Willingness to mentor others
- Job effort
- Job satisfaction
- Social support
- Sense of well-being
- Sense of purpose
- Sensitivity to ethical issues

Donde Ashmos Plowman and Dennis Duchon define workplace spirituality as "the recognition that employees have an inner life that nourishes and is nourished by meaningful work that takes place in the context of community."[44] *Inner life* refers to the fact that employees have spiritual needs (their core identity and values) just as they have emotional, physical, and intellectual wants, and they bring the whole person to work. Even industrialist Henry Ford, who only wanted human cogs for his automobile assembly line, noted this fact. "Why is it that I always get the whole person," he complained, "when all I really want is a pair of hands?"[45] *Meaningful work* refers to the fact that workers typically are motivated by more than material rewards. They want their labor to be fulfilling and to serve the needs of society. *Community* refers to the fact that organization members desire connection to others. A sense of belonging fosters the inner life. It should be noted that religion and spirituality overlap but are not identical. Religious institutions encourage and structure spiritual experiences, but spiritual encounters can occur outside formal religious channels.[46]

Interest in spiritual leadership is an offshoot of the larger workplace spirituality movement. Many leaders report that spirituality has played an important role in their character development, giving them the courage to persist in the face of obstacles, remain optimistic, demonstrate compassion, learn from hardship, and clarify their values.[47] Spiritual leadership expert Laura Reave reviewed more than 150 studies and found that leaders who see their work as a calling demonstrate a higher degree of integrity (honesty) and humility, key virtues described in Chapter 3. These character traits, in turn, build trust with followers and foster honest communication.[48] Reave also found that leaders who engage in common spiritual practices are both more ethical and more effective. These behaviors, emphasized in a variety of belief systems, include the following:

- *Demonstrating respect for others' values.* Many spiritual traditions emphasize respect for the individual. Ethical leaders demonstrate their respect for followers by including them in important decisions. By doing so, they empower followers and bring individual, group, and organizational values into alignment. When the values of leaders and followers are aligned, an organization is more likely to enjoy long-term success.

- *Treating others fairly.* Fairness is a natural outcome of viewing others with respect. Employees are very concerned about how fairly they are treated, particularly when it comes to compensation. Followers are more likely to trust leaders who act justly. Subordinates who believe that their supervisors are fair also go beyond their job descriptions to help coworkers.

- *Expressing caring and concern.* Spirituality often takes the form of supportive behavior. Caring leaders typically have more satisfied and productive followers. Concerned leaders are also more likely to build positive relationships that are the key to their personal success. Furthermore, demonstrating care and concern for the community pays dividends. Employees working for firms known for their corporate philanthropy rate their work environments as excellent and ethical, get a greater sense of achievement from their work, and take more pride in their companies.

- *Listening responsively.* Listening and responding to the needs of others is another practice promoted in many spiritual paths. Good listeners are more likely to emerge as group leaders; organizational leaders who demonstrate better listening skills are rated as more effective. Ethical leaders also respond to what they hear by acting on feedback and suggestions.

- *Appreciating the contributions of others.* Most of the world's faith traditions encourage adherents to treat others as creations of a higher power who are worthy of praise. Praise of creation, in turn, becomes an expression of gratitude to God or a higher power. In the workplace, recognizing and praising employee contributions generates goodwill toward the organization, creates a sense of community, and fosters continuing commitment and contribution.

- *Engaging in reflective practice.* Spiritual practice doesn't end with demonstrating fairness, caring, and appreciation to others. It also incorporates individual self-examination or communication with God. Meditation, prayer, journaling, and spiritual reading not only deepen spirituality, but they also pay practical dividends.[49] Leaders who engage in such activities are more effective because they experience less stress, enjoy improved mental and physical health, and develop stronger relationships with others. They are better equipped to rebound from crises and see a greater (transcendent) meaning in even the most stressful circumstances. Self-reflective leaders also manage their emotions more effectively and exercise greater self-discipline.

Tarleton State University (Texas) professor Louis Fry developed the spiritual leadership theory to explain how leaders tap into the desire for meaning and connection to transform organizations.[50] Spiritual leadership begins with the inner life of the leader. Leaders who engage in spiritual practices develop (1) hope and faith in a vision of service to others and (2) a commitment to altruistic love. They then model altruism and develop a vision that helps organization members experience a sense of calling—the belief that life has meaning and makes a difference. This vision builds hope and faith in the future, which encourages employees to put forth their best efforts and to persevere. Spiritually focused leaders also establish cultures based on altruistic love that foster a sense of membership and connection. (I'll have more to say about altruism in Chapter 5.) Leaders and followers enjoy a sense of ethical well-being in which their behavior reflects their inner values. Not only are they more likely to be satisfied, committed, and productive, but the organization as a whole is also changed for the better. Fry reports that spiritual leadership improves sales and financial performance while fostering corporate social responsibility.

The path to individual and organizational spiritual transformation has its ups and downs. After the initial excitement of discovering the benefits of spirituality, individuals and organizations typically hit obstacles—frustration, financial challenges, feelings of emptiness—that demand new spiritual practices and renewed commitment to a greater purpose if growth is to continue.[51] With this in mind, you can use the following values framework to measure the spiritual climate of your workplace and to determine your organization's spiritual progress.[52]

- *Benevolence:* kindness toward others; desire to promote the happiness and prosperity of employees
- *Generativity:* long-term focus; concern about future consequences of actions for this and future generations
- *Humanism*: policies and practices that respect the dignity and worth of every employee; opportunity for personal growth when working toward organizational goals
- *Integrity:* adherence to a code of conduct; honesty; sincerity; candor
- *Justice:* evenhanded treatment of employees; impartiality; unbiased rewards and punishments
- *Mutuality:* feelings of interconnectedness and mutual dependence; employees working together to complete projects and achieve goals
- *Receptivity:* flexible thinking; open-mindedness; willingness to take calculated risks; rewards for creativity
- *Respect:* treatment of employees with esteem and value; demonstration of consideration and concern
- *Responsibility:* independent follow-through on goals despite obstacles; concern with what is right
- *Trust:* confidence in the character and truthfulness of the organization and its representatives by members and outsiders

To this point, our focus has been on the positive benefits of spirituality. However, before ending discussion of the topic, I should note that spiritual leadership has a potential dark side. Noting these pitfalls can keep us from falling victim to them as leaders or followers. To begin, some leaders view spirituality solely as a tool for increasing follower commitment (obedience) and productivity, which increases profits. They lose sight of the fact that spirituality has value in and of itself, helping organizational members find meaning and establish connections. Other leaders try to impose their particular religious and spiritual views on followers. In the worst-case scenario, authoritarian leaders engage in spiritual abuse.[53] They use spirituality to reinforce their power, to seek selfish (often fraudulent) goals, and to foster dependence in followers. Spiritual abuse is a danger in business organizations as well as in religious ones. Common abusive tactics include (1) overemphasizing spiritual authority and forbidding challenges from followers; (2) demanding unquestioning obedience as a sign of follower loyalty, which takes away the right of subordinates to make their own choices; (3) keeping members apart from outsiders and dismissing external critics while at the same time hiding character flaws and unethical practices from the public; (4) insisting on rigid beliefs and behavior while demanding conformity and perfection; (5) suppressing follower dissent through humiliation, deprivation, and other means; and (6) using nearly absolute power to engage in fraud, sexual immorality, and other unethical practices.

IMPLICATIONS AND APPLICATIONS

- Evil takes a variety of forms or faces, including as a sense of dreadful pleasure, as exclusion, as deception, as rational administration, as a series of small but fateful decisions, and as the product of situational forces that convert ordinary people into evildoers. Whatever face it displays, evil is a destructive force that inflicts pain and suffering and ends in death.

- Moral exclusion limits members' willingness to treat outsiders fairly. Combat moral exclusion through pluralism, which encourages team members to broaden their scope of justice to include a wider variety of outside groups.

- Administrative evil is masked or hidden from perpetrators who inflict pain and suffering while carrying out their jobs. Recognize the long-term consequences of carrying out your role; refuse to participate in unethical behavior as part of your professional duties.

- Ultimately, the choice of whether to do or participate in evil is yours.

- Work to eliminate the situational factors—peer pressure, obedience to authority, anonymity, and dehumanization—that turn leaders and followers into evildoers. Intervene to stop evil behavior.

- Forgiveness is one way to defuse or absorb evil. As a leader, you need to seriously consider the role of forgiveness in your relations with followers, peers, supervisors, and outsiders.

- Forgiving does not mean forgetting or condoning evil. Instead, forgivers hold offenders accountable for their actions at the same time they offer mercy. Forgiving takes a conscious act of will, unfolds over time, and replaces hostility and resentment with empathy and compassion.

- Forgiveness breaks cycles of evil and restores relationships. However, you may gain the most from extending mercy. Forgiving can heighten your sense of well-being, give you renewed energy, and improve your health.

- Warring groups can overcome their mutual hatred by facing and judging the past, rejecting revenge in favor of restraint, feeling empathy for their enemies' humanity, and being committed to restoring the broken relationship.

- You will need to seek forgiveness, for yourself or the group you lead, in addition to offering forgiveness. A moral (authentic) apology incorporates recognition of the offense, taking responsibility, expressing remorse, offering restitution, and signaling a commitment to not repeat the offensive behavior. Pseudo-apologies are vague, use the passive voice, make the offense conditional, question whether the victim was damaged, or minimize the danger.

- Spiritual resources can equip you for the demanding work of confronting evil by contributing to your character development.

- Common spiritual practices that can make you more effective and ethical as a leader include (1) demonstrating respect for others' values, (2) treating others fairly, (3) expressing caring and concern, (4) listening responsively, (5) appreciating the contributions of others, and (6) engaging in reflective practice.

- You can foster an ethical organizational climate by acting as a spiritual leader who creates a vision that helps members experience a sense of calling and establishes a culture based on altruistic love.

- Recognize that there is a potential dark side to spiritual leadership. Be careful not to use spirituality solely as a tool to boost productivity, to force your particular beliefs onto followers, or to reinforce your power.

FOR FURTHER EXPLORATION, CHALLENGE, AND SELF-ASSESSMENT

1. Which of the perspectives on evil described in the chapter is most useful to you? How does it help you better understand and prevent evil?

2. Form groups and debate the following proposition: Evil is an outdated concept.

3. Develop your own definition of forgiveness. Does your definition set boundaries that limit when forgiveness can be offered? What right do leaders have to offer or accept forgiveness on behalf of the group?

4. Consider a time when you forgave someone who treated you unjustly. Did you move through the stages identified by Enright and his colleagues? What benefits did you experience? Conversely, describe a time when you asked for and received forgiveness. What process did you go through? How did you and the relationship benefit?

5. Develop your own forgiveness case study based on the life of a leader who prevented or broke a cycle of evil through an act of apology, mercy, or reconciliation.

6. Reflect on your apology skill level based on Self-Assessment 4.2. What does your score reveal? Do you think it accurately reflects your ability to make apologies? What steps can you take to improve?

7. Analyze the apology of a well-known leader and analyze its effectiveness as an ethical statement. Conclude with an overall evaluation and provide suggestions for how the apology could have been improved.

8. What should be the role of spirituality in leadership? Try to reach a consensus on this question in a group.

9. Evaluate the spiritual climate of an organization using the values presented in the chapter. Share your findings with the rest of the class.

STUDENT STUDY SITE

Visit the student study site at **study.sagepub.com/johnsonmecl6e** to access full SAGE journal articles for further research and information on key chapter topics.

Case Study 4.1

CRIMES AGAINST HUMANITY IN THE HERMIT STATE

A United Nations human rights commission recently named North Korea as the most repressive country on earth. The group condemned the North Korean government for

(Continued)

(Continued)

"systemic, widespread, and gross violations of human rights," declaring that the scope of these violations "does not have any parallel in the contemporary world."[1] The UN report said that the abuses were so great that they constituted "crimes against humanity" and recommended that North Korean leaders be referred to the International Criminal Court (ICC) for prosecution[2] Their crimes include

- extermination,
- murder,
- torture,
- enslavement,
- imprisonment,
- rape,
- forced abortions,
- forced disappearances, and
- prolonged starvation.

Until the UN commission's report, discovering the true extent of the country's evil was difficult because North Korea is highly secretive, earning it the label "the Hermit State." Since it was founded in 1948, the Democratic People's Republic of Korea (DPRK) has operated under harsh Stalinist principles, ruled by a family dynasty that demands absolute obedience. Between 1948 and 1987 (under the country's first leader, Kim Il-Sung), as many as 3.5 million people, including American and South Korean soldiers and civilians captured during the Korean War, were murdered or worked until they died. During widespread famine in the 1990s (caused by mismanagement of the food system and the economy), 3%–5% of the population died of hunger. Under current leader Kim Jong-un, hunger continues to threaten the population. A United Nations International Children's Emergency Fund (UNICEF) report estimates that one third of North Korean women and children are malnourished, and in one five-month period, 20,000 people starved to death in one province. The North Korean government could afford to feed its population but spends a huge portion of its budget on the military and feeding the nation's elite.

In the DPRK, human rights violations are the norm. Public executions are held without trials, and suspects are tortured. There are prohibitions against freedom of speech, freedom of religion, freedom of the press, freedom of movement, and freedom of assembly, making the country an "all-encompassing indoctrination machine that takes root from childhood [with the] almost complete denial of the right to freedom of thought."[3] Of particular note is the country's network of secret prison camps. As many as 250,000 citizens, many of them children, are locked in labor camps with no hope of release. There they are literally worked to death—25% don't survive the first year. There are reports of starving prisoners forced to scavenge pieces of corn from excrement in order to survive. And it is easy to be sent to these camps. Folding a newspaper so that the crease falls across a photo of the "Dear Leader" can result in imprisonment, for example. Extended family members are often punished for the missteps of distant relatives. According to law, punishment can extend to three generations of an offender's family. Thus a child can be jailed for the politically incorrect statements of a grandparent. In one case, a son was forced to witness the public execution of his mother and brother.

Few escape from the camps or from the country as a whole. If any citizens do manage to reach neighboring China, DPRK's lone ally, they are returned to North Korea. Female refugees fare the worst. They are often forced into granting sexual favors by Chinese authorities. If they become pregnant, they are coerced into mandatory abortions when they are returned to their homeland.

The Hermit State's isolation has helped spare it from international condemnation. South Korea and the United States have been more concerned with shutting down North Korea's nuclear program than with its human rights abuses. Then, too, North Korea has a powerful ally in China, which wants to protect a fellow Communist state and believes that its neighbor has the right to operate without outside interference. However, pressure on North Korea to change its repressive policies is likely to increase. The UN Commission findings may make it harder for North Korea to find business partners or to receive humanitarian aid. Human rights advocates are calling on South Korea to take a tougher stance on human rights with its northern neighbor. The U.S. Congress plans to pass stronger sanctions against North Korea in response to its nuclear missile tests, measures that could weaken the oppressive regime.

Discussion Probes

1. Can you think of other nations who actively deny human rights and commit crimes against their people?

2. Should the international community provide food aid to North Korea if it is likely to divert the food to the military and to government officials, as it has in the past?

3. What, if anything, can the international community do to stop the abuses in North Korea?

4. Should the United States risk its relationship with China to stop the murder and human rights violations in North Korea?

5. What faces of evil do you see reflected in this case?

Notes

1. Klingner, B. (2014, February 20). U.S. should augment sanctions after North Korean crimes against humanity. *Heritage Foundation*.

2. North Korea committed crimes against humanity, but not genocide: U.N. commission chief. (2015, February 18). *The Japan Times*.

3. Klingner.

(Continued)

(Continued)

Sources

150,000 N. Koreans incarcerated in Soviet-style gulag: Report. (2012, April 11). *Korea Times.*

Dyer, E. (2012, May 2). North Korea continues to brutalize its people and yet we do nothing. *The Telegraph.*

Kim, H-W. (2011, December 19). Genocide and politicide alert: North Korea. *Genocide Watch.*

Park, R. (2012, November 24). Genocide and crimes of humanity ongoing in North Korea. *Forbes.*

Park, R. (2013, July/August). The forgotten genocide: North Korea's prison state. *World Affairs Journal.*

Ramzy, A. (2013, January 24). After successful missile launch, North Korea threatens new nuclear test. *Time.*

Rogers, B. (2013, January 29). North Korea in the dark. *The New York Times,* Op-Ed.

Stein, Y., & Richter, E. D. (2010, Fall). Suspected mass killings—call them democide, politicide, or maybe genocide in North Korea. *Genocide Prevention Now,* no. 4. Retrieved from http://www.genocidepreventionnow.org

Turning a blind eye to North Korea's "hidden gulag." (2012, April 12). *The Washington Post.*

Case Study 4.2

POISONING FLINT, MICHIGAN

Providing clean water should be no problem in Flint, Michigan. After all, the town is only an hour or so away from Lake Huron, the third-largest source of fresh water in the world. Imagine, then, the surprise of Flint residents when they turned on their taps and foul looking, tasting, and smelling water poured out. One day, the liquid would be blue, the next day, green, and the following day, brown or yellow. Citizens began breaking out in rashes after bathing and losing clumps of hair. Some compared the smell of their tap water to the odor of gasoline or the inside of a fish market.

Flint's problems with its water began in 2014, when the city of 100,000, which had previously tapped into Detroit's water system, began drawing water from the Flint River in order to save money as it waited for a new water tunnel to be built. Flint River water contains high levels of chloride; the same chemical found in road salt that corrodes the metal in cars. Water treatment officials failed to add an agent that would prevent the river water from corroding the city's lead pipes and releasing lead into the system. (The estimated cost of treating the water was $80–$100 per day.) General Motors soon stopped using Flint River water to wash automobile parts because doing so corroded them.

Health concerns mounted the longer the city continued using Flint River water. The number of cases of Legionnaires' disease (a serious pneumonia believed linked to the toxic water) spiked, resulting in several deaths. Health researchers discovered high levels of lead in the blood of the city's children. Lead is a neurotoxin that does long-term physical damage.

(There is no safe amount of lead in the human body, according to the Centers for Disease Control and Prevention.) In young children, lead causes behavioral problems and slows cognitive development. The chemical can cause liver and kidney problems in adults.

For 19 months, state and federal officials failed to respond to the water crisis. They acted only after the national press focused on Flint's plight. Governor Rick Snyder apologized, acknowledging that federal, state, and local leaders broke the trust of Flint residents and pledged to take action to correct the problem. He then ordered law enforcement and fire officials to begin delivering bottled water, water filters, and test kits door to door and fired the supervisor of the state's water program. Snyder pledged $28 million to provide bottled water, health care for Flint children, and repairs to the water system. Critics, however, claimed that these actions were too little, too late and called for his resignation. At the same time, the city stopped taking water from the Flint River. But even as these steps were being taken, Flint residents continued to pay some of the highest water bills in the nation for a product that could harm or kill them. (The Michigan legislature agreed to reimburse Flint citizens for a portion of their water bills.)

What went wrong in Flint? Administrative evil may be to blame. Top officials in Michigan believed in a rational approach to public administration. Governor Snyder, a former accountant who had never held office before being elected governor, billed himself as a no-nonsense problem solver with a businesslike approach to running the government. (He ran for office using the slogan "One Tough Nerd.") Once in office, he appointed a series of emergency managers who took control of Flint away from local elected officials. One of the emergency administrators made the decision to use the Flint River water while awaiting the completion of the new water tunnel. Another overruled the city council when it first wanted to return to Detroit's water supply.

Diffused responsibility and compartmentalization were also at work. The State Department of Environmental Quality (DEQ) misinterpreted Environmental Protection Agency (EPA) regulations that required the use of the corrosion treatment, but federal EPA officials who had the authority to force the city to act failed to enforce the law. Instead, EPA managers waited for the city to act, saying at one point, "the ball is in the city's court."[1]

When concerns were raised about Flint's water, state officials were quick to deny the problem. The governor's spokesman assured residents that their concerns were unfounded: "Let me start here—anyone who is concerned about lead in the drinking water in Flint can relax."[2] The DEQ and Department of Community Health went so far as to accuse Flint residents of using their children's health for political gain, claiming "some in Flint are taking the very sensitive issue of children's exposure to lead and trying to turn it into a political football."[3] An EPA water specialist who raised the alarm about lead levels in the water was called a "rogue employee" by his supervisors.

Many in Flint believe that they were ignored because their town is largely black and poor, putting them on the margins of society. (The median income of Flint is half that of the state average, and 40% of residents live below the poverty line.) They are particularly bitter toward the governor. Said one resident: "We're poor. And because we

(Continued)

(Continued)

don't have anybody on our side that has any clout, Snyder didn't care."[4] A number of observers believe that this tragedy would never have taken place in one of the wealthy white communities in Michigan. Then-Presidential candidate Hillary Clinton drove this point home, noting, "What happened in Flint is immoral. The children of Flint are just as precious as the children of any part of America."[5]

Discussion Probes

1. Is this a case of administrative evil in action? Why or why not?

2. Do you think that the residents of Flint were treated differently because they are poor and African American?

3. How much blame should the governor accept for the crisis?

4. Should governors be able to appoint emergency managers who have the power to override the decisions of local elected officials?

5. What steps should the state and federal government take to repair the damage done to Flint and its residents, including children?

Notes

1. Lynch, J. (2016, February 5). DEQ fires worker who supervised Flint's water. *The Detroit News*.

2. Felton, R. (2016, January 16). Flint's water crisis: what went wrong. *The Guardian*.

3. Michigan governor's emails shine light on Flint water crisis. (2016, Feb. 7). *CNN.com*.

4. Sanborn, J. (2016, February 3). The toxic tap. *Time*, 34–39.

5. Alba, M. (2016, Feb. 7). Hillary Clinton: "What happened in Flint is immoral." *NBC News*.

Sources

Bosman, J., & Smith, M. (2016, January 19). Gov. Rick Snyder of Michigan apologizes in Flint water crisis. *The New York Times*.

Fleming, L. N. (2016, January 12). Volunteers deliver water in Flint amid lead crisis. *The Detroit News*.

Fleming, S. J. (2016, February 5). Lee: time to end emergency manager law. *The Detroit News*.

Fonger, R. (2015, October 13). Ex-emergency manager says he's not to blame for Flint River water watch. *MLive.com*.

Michigan governor: Solve Flint water crisis instead of laying blame. (2016, February 5). *Reuters*.

Moore, M. (2016). *10 things they won't tell you about the Flint water tragedy. But I will*. Retrieved from http://michaelmoore.com/10FactsOnFlint/

Spangler, T. (2016, February 5). Second U.S. House panel to hold hearing on Flint water. *Detroit Free Press*.

Case Study 4.3

SUBWAY'S SPOKESMAN NIGHTMARE

For fifteen years, Jared Fogle served as the public face of the Subway sandwich chain, starring in 3,000 commercials. The Indiana native lost 200 pounds by eating Subway sandwiches as a college student. In many of the television ads, he held up his old size-60 jeans to illustrate just how much weight he dropped by making healthy choices at his local Subway store. With Fogle as its front man, Subway doubled its sales to more than $8 billion, becoming the second-largest restaurant chain after McDonalds. (Recently, Starbucks moved into the number-two slot.) A research firm declared that the ads featuring Fogle were "the most effective in the entire U.S. restaurant industry."[1] Fogle was also featured on the company's website (kids could play a game called "Jared's Pants Dance") and the chain planned to launch a new campaign featuring Fogle as a new father taking his wife and preschool children to eat at Subway. As a result of serving as Subway's spokesman, Fogle became a celebrity with an estimated worth of $15 million. He created the Jared Foundation to combat childhood obesity.

The "Subway Guy" secretly used his fame and fortune to hire prostitutes and to secure minors for sex. Twice, he traveled to New York City to have sex with teens at swank hotels. He put the word out that he was looking to bed young girls, saying at one point he "would accept a 16-year-old, but wanted them younger if possible."[2] He began indulging in child pornography with the help of Russell Taylor, a friend he appointed to direct his foundation. Taylor secretly videotaped boys and girls (ages 2–12) visiting his home and shared these images, along with kiddy porn, with Fogle. Fogle pled guilty to child pornography charges and having sex with minors. As part of his plea deal, he agreed to pay $100,000 to each of the victims on Taylor's tape as well to the teens he had sex with in New York City. He received over fifteen years in prison and must register as a sex offender. Investigators report that the Jared Foundation never issued a singe grant, despite promising to provide $2 million to schools and community organizations to lower childhood obesity rates.

After Taylor was arrested on child pornography charges, Subway severed ties with Fogle. Later, when Fogle pled guilty, the company tweeted "Jared Fogle's actions are inexcusable and do not represent our brand's values."[3] The firm denied any knowledge of Fogle's criminal activities, and Fogle told authorities that Subway "didn't know what I was doing."[4] In an effort to further distance itself from Fogle, the chain tweeted, "We no longer have a relationship with Jared and have no further comment."[5]

While Subway may not be legally liable for Fogle's actions, the restaurant chain may have a moral obligation to care for his victims and other victims of child sexual abuse. According to columnist Jonah Sachs of Britain's *Guardian* newspaper, Subway "still has the opportunity to bring out some good from the horror."[6] He urges the company to work with nonprofits to

(Continued)

(Continued)

reduce child sexual abuse: "Yes, there's danger in such a move. Some might see Subway's offer to help as an admission of complicity in Fogle's activity. Others might see the support as a marketing ploy. But it's the right thing to do."[7]

Discussion Probes

1. What is your reaction to Subway's handling of this scandal?

2. Does Subway have any responsibility to Fogle's victims?

3. Should Subway express remorse for Fogle's crimes?

4. Does Subway bear any responsibility for the failure of the Jared Foundation?

5. Should Subway take on childhood sexual abuse as a corporate cause? Would this be seen as an admission of guilt?

6. Are you less likely to eat at Subway because of Fogle's crimes and the firm's response? Why or why not?

Notes

1. Frank, T., Kwiatkowski, M., & Cook, T. (2015, August 23). From obesity to duplicity: Jared's fall to earth. *USA Today.*

2. McShane, L. (2015, August 20). 'The younger the girl, the better.' *Daily News*, p. 4.

3. Sachs, J. (2015, August 27). Subway's silence over the Fogle fiasco leaves a bad taste. *The Guardian.*

4. Sachs.

5. Sachs.

6. Sachs.

7. Sachs.

Sources

Golding, B. (2015, August 20). Underage sex shocker. *The New York Post*, p. 7.

Isidore, D. (2015, November 19). Jared Fogle sentenced to more than 15 years. *CNN Money.*

Malcolm, H., & Whitehouse, K. (2015, August 20). Subway already in trouble before Jared Fogle mess. *USA Today*, p. 1B.

Menon, V. (2015, July 9). Why are companies still buying what celebrities are selling? *The Toronto Star*, p. E1.

Subway planned to rebrand Jared Fogle as family man before FBI raid. (2015, July 9). Thespec.com

Weinstein, S. (2015, August 26). Jared Fogle's childhood obesity charity is a sham. *TVGuide.com*

Williams, A. (2015, August 29). Trust me, I'm skinny. *National Post*, p. WP2.

SELF-ASSESSMENT 4.1

Tendency to Forgive Scale

Instructions: Respond to each of the following items on a scale of 1 (*never*) to 5 (*very often*).

1	2	3	4	5
Never				Very Often

1. I tend to get over it quickly when someone hurts my feelings. _____
2. If someone wrongs me, I think about it a lot afterward. _____
3. I have a tendency to harbor grudges. _____
4. When people wrong me, my approach is just to forgive and forget. _____

Scoring: Reverse your scores on items 2 and 3, and then add up your responses to all four statements. The higher the score (possible scores range from 4 to 28), the more likely you are to forgive others and the less likely you are to bring up offenses from the past.

Source: Brown, R. P. (2003). Measuring individual differences in the tendency to forgive: Construct validity and links with depression. *Personality and Social Psychology Bulletin, 29,* 759–771, p. 770. Published by SAGE Publications on behalf of the Society for Personality and Social Psychology. Inc. Used with permission.

SELF-ASSESSMENT 4.2

Apology Quotient Quiz

Instructions: Consider each of the following ten apologetic statements. For each statement, indicate how likely you would be to say something like this if you had to apologize. For example, if you can imagine yourself apologizing using language similar to that statement, select *likely*. If you decide you would not be comfortable using the statement, select *unlikely*.

1. Believe me, I had no intentions of offending you, but if I did, I'm very sorry.

   ___ unlikely ___ likely

2. I know my carelessness imposed costs on you. I insist that you accept this check as a gesture of my wanting to make things right.

   ___ unlikely ___ likely

3. I know that you feel as bad as I do about what happened, and I'm certain you agree with me about what we need to do to get this behind us.

   ___ unlikely ___ likely

4. I handled things very badly and I'm sorry. I intend to work very hard to earn your trust so that someday it may be possible for you to forgive me.

    ___ unlikely   ___ likely

5. I want to apologize for acting like such a jerk. So, do you accept my apology?

    ___ unlikely   ___ likely

6. I acknowledge that my actions hurt you. I am particularly ashamed that I betrayed you by [name the specific offense here].

    ___ unlikely   ___ likely

7. Yes, I hurt you and I'm sorry, but here's what happened.

    ___ unlikely   ___ likely

8. I'm sorry. I value our friendship and I ask only that in the coming months you allow me to demonstrate that I keep my word.

    ___ unlikely   ___ likely

9. I'm sorry for the inconvenience. My secretary [employee, manager] is normally very reliable.

    ___ unlikely   ___ likely

10. You were right and I was wrong. I behaved very badly that night, and now I'm here to apologize. I'm sorry for losing my temper. I'm sorry for saying the ugly things I said. Most of all, I'm sorry for not coming to you right away.

    ___ unlikely   ___ likely

Scoring: For odd-numbered statements, score 10 points for each item you marked *unlikely* and 0 for each item you marked *likely*. For even-numbered statements, score 10 points for every item you marked *likely* and 0 for each item you marked *unlikely*.

Interpretation:

0–20 *Clueless.* Demonstrates little understanding of apology. Apologies are defensive and begrudging.

30–50 *Novice.* Demonstrates rudimentary understanding of apology. Relationships may have suffered because of poor apologies. Need to develop this skill further to become an effective leader.

60–80 *Accomplished.* Demonstrates effective use of apologies at home, at work, and in leadership roles. Occasionally may offer less effective apologies.

90–100 *Expert.* Demonstrates complete understanding of the elements of apology. Can further refine use of apologies in crisis situations.

Source: Kador, J. (2009). *Effective apology: Mending fences, building bridges, and restoring trust.* Williston, VT: Berrett-Kohler, pp. 25–28. Used with permission.

NOTES

1. Definitions of evil can be found in the following sources: Hallie, P. (1997). *Tales of good and evil, help and harm.* New York, NY: HarperCollins; Katz, F. E. (1993). *Ordinary people and*

extraordinary evil: A report on the beguilings of evil. Albany: State University of New York Press; Kekes, J. (2005). *The roots of evil.* Ithaca, NY: Cornell University Press; Peck, M. S. (1983). *People of the lie: The hope for healing human evil.* New York, NY: Touchstone; Sanford, N., & Comstock, C. (Eds.). (1971). *Sanctions for evil.* San Francisco, CA: Jossey-Bass; Vetelson, A. J. (2005). *Evil and human agency: Understanding collective evildoing.* Cambridge, England: Cambridge University Press. Of course, a host of other definitions are offered by major religions and philosophical systems.

2. Alford, C. F. (1997). *What evil means to us.* Ithaca, NY: Cornell University Press, p. 3.

3. Kekes.

4. Deutsch, M. (1990). Psychological roots of moral exclusion. *Journal of Social Issues, 46*(1), 21–25.

5. Opotow, S. (1990). Moral exclusion and injustice: An introduction. *Journal of Social Issues, 46*(1), 1–20.

6. Chang, I. (1997). *The rape of Nanking: The forgotten holocaust of World War II.* New York, NY: Basic Books, p. 218.

7. Adams, G. B., & Balfour, D. L. (2012). The dynamics of administrative evil in organizations. In C. L. Jurkiewicz (Ed.), *The foundations of organizational evil* (pp. 16–30). Armonk, NY: M.E. Sharpe, p. 28.

8. Opotow, S. (2007). Moral exclusion and torture: The ticking bomb scenario and the slippery ethical slope. *Peace and Conflict: Journal of Peace Psychology, 13,* 457–461.

9. Opotow, S. (1990). Deterring moral exclusion. *Journal of Social Issues, 46*(1), 173–182.

10. Leets, L. (2001). Interrupting the cycle of moral exclusion: A communication contribution to social justice research. *Journal of Applied Social Psychology, 31,* 1859–1891, p. 1863.

11. Tileaga, C. (2006). Representing the "other": A discursive analysis of prejudice and moral exclusion in talk about Romanies. *Journal of Community & Applied Social Psychology, 16,* 19–41.

12. Bar-Tel, D. (1990). Causes and consequences of delegitimization: Models of conflict and ethnocentrism. *Journal of Social Issues, 46*(1), 65–81.

13. Peck.

14. Cullen, D. (2009). *Columbine.* New York, NY: Twelve.

15. Glover, J. (1999). *Humanity: A moral history of the twentieth century.* New Haven, CT: Yale University Press.

16. Adams, G. B. (2011). The problem of administrative evil in a culture of technical rationality. *Public Integrity, 13,* 275–285; Adams, G. B., & Balfour, D. L. (2005). Public-service ethics and administrative evil: Prospects and problems. In H. G. Frederickson & R. K. Ghere (Eds.), *Ethics in public management* (pp. 114–138). Armonk, NY: M.E. Sharpe; Adams, G. B., & Balfour, D. L. (2009). Ethical failings, incompetence, and administrative evil: Lessons from Katrina and Iraq. In R. W. Cox III (Ed.), *Ethics and integrity in public administration: Concepts and cases* (pp. 40–64). Armonk, NY: M. E. Sharpe; Adams, G. B., & Balfour, D. L. (2015). *Unmasking administrative evil* (4th ed.). Armonk, NY: M. E. Sharpe.

17. Lewis, C. S. (1946). *The great divorce.* New York, NY: Macmillan.

18. Fromm, E. (1964). *The heart of man: Its genius for good and evil.* New York, NY: Harper & Row, p. 136.

19. Arendt, H. (1964). *Eichmann in Jerusalem: A report on the banality of evil.* New York, NY: Viking.

20. Hatzfeld, J. (2005). *Machete season: The killers in Rwanda speak* (L. Coverdale, Trans.). New York, NY: Farrar, Straus and Giroux.

21. Zimbardo, P. G. (2005). A situationist perspective on the psychology of evil. In A. G. Miller (Ed.), *The social psychology of good and evil* (pp. 21–50). New York, NY: Guilford; Zimbardo, P. G. (2007). *The Lucifer effect: Understanding how good people turn evil.* New York, NY: Random House. See also Waller, J. (2007). *Becoming evil: How ordinary people commit genocide and mass killing* (2nd ed.). Oxford, England: Oxford University Press.

22. Opotow, S., & Weiss, L. (2000). Denial and the process of moral exclusion in environmental conflict. *Journal of Social Issues, 56,* 475–490.

23. Opotow (1990), Deterring moral exclusion.

24. Adams; Neiman, S. (2002). *Evil in modern thought: An alternative history of philosophy.* Princeton, NJ: Princeton University Press.

25. See Janover, M. (2005). The limits of forgiveness and the ends of politics. *Journal of Intercultural Studies, 26,* 221–235; Murphy, J. G. (2003). *Getting even: Forgiveness and its limits.* Oxford, England: Oxford University Press; Ransley, C., & Spy, T. (Eds.). (2004). *Forgiveness and the healing process: A central therapeutic concern.* New York, NY: Brunner-Routledge.

26. Material on the definition and psychology of forgiveness is taken from the following: Enright, R. D., Freedman, S., & Rique, J. (1998). The psychology of interpersonal forgiveness. In R. D. Enright & J. North (Eds.), *Exploring forgiveness* (pp. 46–62). Madison: University of Wisconsin Press; Enright, R. D., & Gassin, E. A. (1992). Forgiveness: A developmental view. *Journal of Moral Education, 21,* 99–114; Freedman, S., Enright, R. D., & Knutson, J. (2005). A progress report on the process model of forgiveness. In E. L. Worthington, Jr. (Ed.), *Handbook of forgiveness* (pp. 393–406). New York, NY: Routledge; Klatt, J. S., & Enright, R. D. (2011). Initial validation of the unfolding forgiveness process in a natural environment. *Counseling and Values, 56,* 25–42; McCullough, M. E., Pargament, K. I., & Thoresen, C. E. (2000). The psychology of forgiveness: History, conceptual issues, and overview. In M. E. McCullough, K. I. Pargament, & C. E. Thoresen (Eds.), *Forgiveness: Theory, research, and practice* (pp. 1–14). New York, NY: Guilford; Musekura, C. (2010). *An assessment of contemporary models of forgiveness.* New York, NY: Peter Lang; Thomas, G. (2000, January 10). The forgiveness factor. *Christianity Today,* 38–43.

27. Enright, Freedman, & Rique, pp. 46–47.

28. Berman, M. (2015, June 19). "I forgive you." Relatives of Charleston church shooting victims address Dylann Roof. *The Washington Post.*

29. For information on the by-products of forgiveness, see Casarjian, R. (1992). *Forgiveness: A bold choice for a peaceful heart.* New York, NY: Bantam; Enright, R. D. (2012). *The forgiving life.* Washington, DC: American Psychological Association; Enright, Freedman, & Rique; Freedman, Enright, & Knutson; Klatt, J. S., & Enright, R. D. (2009). Investigating the place of forgiveness with in the Positive Youth Development paradigm. *Journal of Moral Education, 38,* 35–52; McCullough, M. E., Sandage, S. J., & Worthington, E. L. (1997). *To forgive is human: How to put your past in the past.* Downers Grove, IL: InterVarsity Press; Thoresen, C. E., Harris, H. S., & Luskin, F. (2000). Forgiveness and health: An unanswered question. In M. E. McCullough, K. I. Pargament, & C. E. Thoresen (Eds.), *Forgiveness: Theory, research, and practice* (pp. 254–280). New York, NY: Guilford; Waltman, M. A., Russell, D. C., Coyle, C. T., Enright, R. D., Holter, A. C., & Swoboda, C. M. (2009). The effects of a forgiveness intervention on patients with coronary artery disease. *Psychology and Health, 24*(1), 11–27; Worthington, E. L., Jr. (2005). Initial questions about the art and science of forgiving. In E. L. Worthington (Ed.), *Handbook of forgiveness* (pp. 1–13). New York, NY: Routledge.

30. Shriver, D. W. (1995). *An ethic for enemies: Forgiveness in politics.* New York, NY: Oxford University Press. See also Wilmot, W. W., & Hocker, J. L. (2001). *Interpersonal conflict* (6th ed.). New York, NY: McGraw-Hill Higher Education, Ch. 1.

31. Shriver, p. 8.

32. Forgiveness also extends to the self. Self-forgiveness acknowledges your dignity and equips you to move forward to restore relationships. See, for example, Holmgren, J. R. (1998). Self-forgiveness and responsible moral agency. *Journal of Value Inquiry, 32,* 75–91; Snow, N. E. (1993). Self-forgiveness. *Journal of Value Inquiry, 27,* 75–80.

33. Kador, J. (2009). *Effective apology: Mending fences, building bridges, and restoring trust.* Williston, VT: Berrett-Koehler; Lazare, A. (2004). *On apology.* Oxford, England: Oxford University Press.

34. Griswold, C. L. (2007). *Forgiveness: A philosophical exploration.* Cambridge, England: Cambridge University Press; Lowenheim, N. (2009). A haunted past: Requesting forgiveness for wrongdoing in international relations. *Review of International Studies, 35,* 531–555; Nobles, M. (2008). *The politics of official apologies.* Cambridge, England: Cambridge University Press; Shriver, D. W. (2001). Forgiveness: A bridge across abysses of revenge. In R. G. Helmick & R. L. Peterson (Eds.), *Forgiveness and reconciliation: Religion, public policy, and conflict transformation* (pp. 151–167). Philadelphia, PA: Templeton Foundation Press.

35. Johnson, C. E., & Shelton, P. M. (2014, October). Ethical leadership in the age of apology. *International Leadership Journal, 6,* 7–29.

36. Macur, J. (2013, January 18). Confession, but continuing to fight. *The New York Times,* p. B11.

37. Lazare.

38. Kador, p. 11.

39. Battistella, E. (2014, May 7). The art of political apology. *Politico.*

40. Michael Vick to work with Humane Society on its campaign against dogfighting. (2009, May 20). *Los Angeles Times.*

41. Oswick, C. (2009). Burgeoning workplace spirituality? A textual analysis of momentum and directions. *Journal of Management, Spirituality & Religion, 6,* 15–25.

42. King, S., Biberman, J., Robbins, L., & Nicol, D. M. (2007). Integrating spirituality into management education in academia and organizations: Origins, a conceptual framework, and current practices. In J. Biberman & M. D. Whitty (Eds.), *At work: Spirituality matters* (pp. 243–256). Scranton, PA: University of Scranton Press.

43. Information on the benefits of workplace spirituality is taken from the following: Craigie, F. C. (1999). The spirit and work: Observations about spirituality and organizational life. *Journal of Psychology and Christianity, 18,* 43–53; Fairholm, G. W. (1996). Spiritual leadership: Fulfilling whole-self needs at work. *Leadership & Organization Development Journal, 17*(5), 11–17; Garcia-Zamor, J. C. (2003). Workplace spirituality and organizational performance. *Public Administration Review, 63,* 355–363; Giacalone, R. A., & Jurkiewicz, C. L. (2003). Right from wrong: The influence of spirituality on perceptions of unethical business activities. *Journal of Business Ethics, 46,* 85–97; Giacalone, R. A., & Jurkiewicz, C. L. (2003). Toward a science of workplace spirituality. In R. A. Giacalone & C. L. Jurkiewicz (Eds.), *Handbook of workplace spirituality and organizational performance* (pp. 3–28). Armonk, NY: M. E. Sharpe; Jurkiewicz, C. L., & Giacalone, R. A. (2004). A values framework for measuring the impact of workplace spirituality on organizational performance. *Journal of Business Ethics, 49,* 129–142; Karakas, F. (2010). Spirituality and performance in organizations: A literature review. *Journal of Business Ethics, 94,* 89–106; Mirvis, P. H. (1997). "Soul work" in organizations. *Organization Science, 8,* 193–206; Rego, A., & Pina e Cunha, M. (2008). Workplace spirituality and organizational commitment: An empirical study. *Journal of Organizational Change Management, 21,* 53–75.

44. Ashmos, D. P., & Duchon, D. (2000). Spirituality at work: A conceptualization and measure. *Journal of Management Inquiry, 9,* 134–145, p. 137; see also Duchon, D., & Plowman, D. A. (2005). Nurturing the spirit at work: Impact on work unit performance. *Leadership Quarterly, 16,* 807–833.

45. Pollard, C. W. (1996). *The soul of the firm.* Grand Rapids, MI: HarperBusiness, p. 25.

46. See Zinnbauer, B. J., & Pargament, K. I. (2005). Religiousness and spirituality. In R. F. Paloutzian & C. L. Park (Eds.), *Handbook of the psychology of religion and spirituality* (pp. 21–42). New York, NY: Guilford.

47. See Judge, W. Q. (1999). *The leader's shadow: Exploring and developing executive character.* Thousand Oaks, CA: SAGE.

48. Reave, L. (2005). Spiritual values and practices related to leadership effectiveness. *Leadership Quarterly, 16,* 655–687.

49. One detailed list of personal and collective spiritual practices can be found in Foster, R. J. (1978). *Celebration of discipline: The path to spiritual growth.* New York, NY: Harper & Row.

50. Fry, L. W. (2003). Toward a theory of spiritual leadership. *Leadership Quarterly, 14,* 693–727; Fry, L. W. (2005). Toward a theory of ethical and spiritual well-being, and corporate social responsibility through spiritual leadership. In R. A. Giacalone, C. L. Jurkiewicz, & C. Dunn (Eds.), *Positive psychology in business ethics and corporate responsibility* (pp. 47–84). Greenwich, CT: Information Age; Fry, L. W. (2008). Spiritual leadership: State-of-the-art and future directions for theory, research, and practice. In J. Biberman & L. Tischler (Eds.), *Spirituality in business: Theory, practice, and future directions* (pp. 106–123). New York, NY: Palgrave Macmillan; Fry, L. W., Vitucci, S., & Cedillo, M. (2005). Spiritual leadership and army transformation: Theory, measurement, and establishing a baseline. *Leadership Quarterly, 16,* 835–862.

51. Benefiel, M. (2005). *Soul at work: Spiritual leadership in organizations.* New York, NY: Seabury Books; Benefiel, M. (2005). The second half of the journey: Spiritual leadership for organizational transformation. *Leadership Quarterly, 16,* 723–747.

52. Jurkiewicz & Giacalone.

53. Boje, D. (2008). Critical theory approaches to spirituality in business. In J. Biberman & L. Tischler (Eds.), *Spirituality in business: Theory, practice, and future directions* (pp. 160–187). New York, NY: Palgrave Macmillan; Tourish, D. (2013). *The dark side of transformational leadership: A critical perspective.* New York, NY: Routledge.

PART III

Ethical Standards and Strategies

5 | General Ethical Perspectives

Leaders are truly effective only when they are motivated by a concern for others.

—BUSINESS PROFESSORS RABINDRA KANUNGO AND MANUEL MENDONCA

WHAT'S AHEAD

This chapter surveys widely used ethical perspectives or systems that leaders can use when making ethical decisions. These approaches include utilitarianism, Kant's categorical imperative, Rawls's justice as fairness, pragmatism, and altruism. For each perspective, I provide a brief description and then offer some suggestions for applying the framework as well as some cautions about doing so.

In Chapter 2, I identified lack of expertise as one reason leaders unintentionally cast shadows. We may lack experience or we may not be aware of the ethical perspectives or frameworks we can apply to ethical dilemmas. The purpose of this chapter is to introduce some widely used systems that leaders can employ when making moral choices. These tools help us identify and clarify problems, force us to think systematically, encourage us to view issues from many different vantage points, and supply us with decision-making guidelines. They play a critical role in the decision-making formats described in the next chapter. I'll introduce each perspective and suggest how it can be applied to ethical decisions. I'll also offer some cautions about the limitations of each approach.

Resist the temptation to select one perspective for decision making while ignoring the others. That would be a mistake. Each offers unique insights. Applying several approaches to the same problem will give you a deeper understanding of the issue, even if the different frameworks lead to different conclusions. You might also find that a particular perspective is more suited to some kinds of ethical dilemmas than to others. Case Study 5.3 is designed as a testing ground for the material in the chapter. After learning about each perspective, apply it to the case. Then come to a final conclusion based on your analysis that incorporates all five approaches.

UTILITARIANISM: DO THE GREATEST GOOD FOR THE GREATEST NUMBER OF PEOPLE

Utilitarianism is based on the premise that ethical choices should be based on their consequences. People probably have always considered the likely outcomes of their decisions when determining what to do. However, this process wasn't formalized and given a name until the eighteenth and nineteenth centuries. English philosophers Jeremy Bentham (1748–1832) and John Stuart Mill (1806–1873) argued that the best decisions generate the most benefits, as compared with their disadvantages, and benefit the largest number of people.[1] In sum, utilitarianism is attempting to do the greatest good for the greatest number of people. Utility can be based on what is best in a specific case (act utilitarianism) or on what is generally best in most contexts (rule utilitarianism). For example, we can decide that telling a specific lie is justified in one situation (to protect someone's reputation) but, as a general rule, believe that lying is wrong because it causes more harm than good.

There are four steps to conducting a utilitarian analysis of an ethical problem.[2] First, clearly identify the action or issue under consideration. Second, specify all those who might be affected by the action (e.g., the organization, the local community, a professional group, society), not just those immediately involved in the situation. Third, determine the likely consequences, both good and bad, for those affected. Fourth, add up the good and the bad consequences. The action is morally right if the benefits outweigh the costs.

Utilitarian analysis can also be used when choosing between two negative alternatives. In these situations, decision makers opt for the least costly option, selecting the lesser of two evils. Such choices are becoming increasingly common as authorities cope with human damage to the environment. Consider, for example, the dispute over whether to close the Chicago Sanitary and Ship Canal, which connects Lake Michigan with the Mississippi River System.[3] Shutting off the canal could prevent the spread of invasive Asian carp into the Great Lakes, thus saving the ecosystem from collapse. However, barge owners who ship gravel, commercial goods, petroleum, and other products argue that the costs of shutting the canal outweigh the potential damage that could come from keeping it open. The courts have ruled that, for now, keeping the canal open is the lesser of the two evils. In the Pacific Northwest, one protected species (the sea lion) is eating thousands of another protected species (salmon) in the Columbia River. Officials have killed some "nuisance" sea lions, determining that this option is least objectionable.[4]

Applications and Cautions

Applications

- Build on your prior experience.
- Carefully examine the outcomes of your decisions.
- Set personal interests aside.
- Recognize when weighing likely consequences is critical.

The notion of weighing outcomes is easy to understand and to apply. Chances are you already use this technique, creating a series of mental balance sheets for all types of decisions, such as determining whether an item, a car, or a vacation package is worth the price; considering a job offer; or evaluating the merits of two political candidates. Take advantage of your experience when weighing the costs and benefits of ethical decisions. Keep your focus on outcomes, which will encourage you to think through your decisions. You'll also be less likely to make rash, unreasoned choices, which is particularly important when it comes to ethical dilemmas. The ultimate goal of evaluating consequences is admirable: to maximize benefits to as many people as possible (not just to yourself). As a result, your personal interests should not be the primary concern when making decisions. Remember, too, that utilitarianism is probably the most defensible approach in some situations. For example, in medical emergencies involving large numbers of injured victims, top priority should go to those who are most likely to survive. It does little good for medical personnel to spend time with terminal patients while other victims who would benefit from treatment die.

Cautions

- Probable consequences are difficult to identify, measure, and evaluate.
- There may be unanticipated outcomes.
- Decision makers may reach different conclusions.
- Be wary of extreme utilitarianism.

Identifying possible consequences can be difficult, particularly for decision makers who represent a variety of constituencies or stakeholders. Take the case of a college president who must decide what academic programs to cut in a budget crisis. Many different groups have a stake in this decision, and each probably will reach a different conclusion about potential costs and benefits. Every department believes that it makes a valuable contribution to the university and serves the mission of the school. Powerful alumni may be alienated by the elimination of their majors. Members of the local community might suffer if the education department is terminated and no longer supplies teachers to area schools or if plays and concerts end because of cutbacks in the theater and music departments. Unanticipated consequences further complicate the choice. If student enrollments increase, the president may have to restore programs that she eliminated earlier. Yet failing to make cuts can put the future of the school in jeopardy.

Even when consequences are clear, you may find that evaluating their relative merits can be daunting. It is hard to compare different kinds of costs and benefits, for example. The construction of a housing development provides new homes but takes farmland out of production. How do we weigh the relative value of urban housing versus family farms? Also, utilitarianism says little about how benefits are to be distributed. Doing the greatest good may mean putting one group at a serious disadvantage so that everyone else will benefit. During World War II, for example, Japanese Americans were warehoused in camps based on the mistaken belief that this would make the nation as a whole safer. Conversely, utilitarian calculations may benefit the few at the expense of the majority. Many who donate funding to medical efforts in developing countries focus their contributions on one disease, such as malaria, hoping to have a major impact on that illness. Such an approach benefits those who suffer from the particular malady but ignores the needs of everyone else suffering from other medical problems, like HIV/AIDS, tuberculosis, cancer, kidney disease, dysentery, and cholera. We also tend to favor ourselves when making decisions. Thus, you are likely to put more weight on consequences that most directly affect you. It's all too easy to confuse the greatest good with your own selfish interests.

Given the difficulty of identifying and evaluating potential costs and benefits, utilitarian decision makers sometimes reach different conclusions when faced with the same dilemma. During its investigation of the San Bernardino terrorist shooting, the Federal Bureau of Investigation (FBI) asked Apple to unlock the iPhone of one of the killers, reasoning that national security concerns outweighed any threat to privacy. Apple objected, arguing that unlocking the phone would give the government and hackers access to information from millions of iPhone owners, which outweighed the benefits of allowing access in this one case.[5]

In its most extreme form, Utilitarianism discounts family, friendship, and community bonds. Australian ethicist Peter Singer uses utilitarian reasoning to argue that the needs of strangers are equal to the needs of those close to us. Imagine, Singer says, that you are walking by a shallow pond and see a drowning child whom you can rescue with little cost or risk to yourself. You ought to wade in and save the toddler. Now imagine that you have been asked to send money to an aid group to save the life of a child in a poor nation. According to Singer, you are just as morally obligated to send the contribution as you are to rescue the drowning child. He urges us to forsake luxuries like movie tickets and music downloads, giving the money to humanitarian aid instead.[6]

You may decide that you agree with Singer's reasoning but should recognize the costs in doing so. (Case Study 5.1 highlights the price paid by individuals who try to live up to Singer's ethical standard.) Giving so much away takes away the freedom to live life the way we choose and may deprive us of the resources we need to take care of ourselves.[7] Very few people are willing to make the sacrifices called for by Singer. Giving to an aid organization doesn't directly convert into saving a life either. (In fact, some aid programs, as we'll see later in the chapter, seem to hurt rather than help recipients.) Most importantly, the majority of us believe that our greatest moral responsibility lies with those who are closest to us—family, friends, neighbors. (The ethic of care described in Box 5.1 explicitly puts the needs of family first.)

KANT'S CATEGORICAL IMPERATIVE: DO WHAT'S RIGHT NO MATTER THE COST

In sharp contrast to the Utilitarians, European philosopher Immanuel Kant (1724–1804) argued that people should do what is morally right no matter the consequences.[8] (The term *categorical* means "without exception.") His approach to moral reasoning is the best-known example of deontological ethics. Deontological ethicists argue that we ought to make choices based on our duty (*deon* is the Greek word for duty). Fulfilling our obligations may run contrary to our personal interests. For example, revealing a product defect to a potential customer might cost us a sale, but is nevertheless the ethical course of action. (Case Study 5.2 describes one group of heroes driven by a sense of duty.)

According to Kant, what is right for one is right for all. We need to ask ourselves one question: Would I want everyone else to make the decision I did? If the answer is yes, the choice is justified. If the answer is no, the decision is wrong. Based on this reasoning, certain behaviors, such as truth telling and helping the poor, are always right. Other acts, such as lying, cheating, and murder, are always wrong. Testing and grading would be impossible if everyone cheated, for example, and cooperation would be impossible if no one could be trusted to tell the truth.

Kant lived well before the advent of the automobile, but violations of his decision-making rule could explain why law enforcement officials have to crack down on motorists who run red lights. So many Americans regularly disobey traffic signals (endangering pedestrians and other drivers) that some communities have installed cameras at intersections to catch violators. Drivers have failed to recognize one simple fact: They may save time by running lights, but they shouldn't do so because the system breaks down when large numbers of people ignore traffic signals.

Kant also emphasized the importance of respecting persons, which has become a key principle in Western moral philosophy.[9] According to Kant, "Act so that you treat humanity, whether in your own person or that of another, always as an end and never as a means only." Although others can help us reach our goals, they should never be considered solely as tools. Instead, we should respect and encourage the capacity of others to think and choose for themselves. Under this standard, it is wrong for companies to expose citizens living near manufacturing facilities to dangerous pollutants without their knowledge or consent. Coercion and violence are immoral because such tactics violate freedom of choice. Failing to assist a neighbor is unethical because ignoring this person's need limits his or her options.

University of Minnesota business professor Norman Bowie argues that following Kantian principles would dramatically change the way that modern organizations operate.[10] To begin, they would respect the inherent dignity of their employees (as well as everyone else who comes into contact with the organization). Instead of laying people off to save money, they might reduce work hours for all workers instead. Retirees and pension holders would continue to receive their promised benefits despite economic downturns. Companies would be transparent by opening their books to employees. From a Kantian perspective, businesses and other organizations function as moral communities in which members have a significant voice in the rules and policies that govern them. They operate like democracies, where members are organizational citizens with rights and duties. Organizational citizens enjoy free speech and privacy rights and receive information on the group's future. Their leaders persuade rather than impose, assisting groups to make wise choices. Managers provide meaningful work, which is another way to treat people as ends and to promote their autonomy. Meaningful work supports the right of employees to make decisions—including moral ones—and provides a living wage.

Applications and Cautions

Applications

- Be duty-bound.
- Always ask yourself if you would want everyone to make the same choice.
- Demonstrate respect for others.

Duty should play a significant role in our ethical deliberations. In fact, the notion that we have a duty to take our ethical responsibilities seriously is a foundational principle of this text. Emphasis on duty encourages persistence and consistent behavior. If you are driven by the conviction that certain behaviors are either right or wrong no matter what the situation, you will be less likely to compromise your personal ethical standards. You are apt to stay the course despite group pressures and opposition and to follow through on your choices. (See "Focus on Follower Ethics: Constructing Ethical Followership" below to see how we can equip ourselves as followers to carry out our ethical duties.)

Kant offers two powerful decision-making tools. First, ask yourself if you would want everyone else to make the same decision. If not, reevaluate your choice before going forward. Second, always respect the dignity of others. Don't use them or violate their rights. Instead, respect the freedom of others to choose for themselves. Share information while avoiding deception, coercion, and violence.

Cautions

- Exceptions exist to nearly every universal law.
- Moral obligations may conflict with one another.
- Ethical guidelines are often demonstrated through unrealistic examples.
- This framework is hard to apply, particularly under stress.

Most attacks on Kant's system of reasoning center on his assertion that there are universal principles that should be followed in every situation. In almost every case, we can think of exceptions. For instance, many of us believe that lying is wrong yet would lie or withhold the truth to save the life of a friend or, in the case of an active school shooter, the lives of classmates and instructors. Countries regularly justify homicide during war. Then, too, moral obligations can conflict. It may be impossible for you to keep promises made to more than one group, for example. Raises promised to employees may have to be set aside so that promised dividends can be paid to stockholders. Or satisfying one duty may mean violating another, as in the case of a whistle-blower who puts truth telling above loyalty to the organization. (See Chapter 6 for more information on ethical dilemmas involving two right values.)

Some contemporary philosophers complain that ethical guidelines like those outlined by Bentham and Kant are applied to extreme situations, not to the types of decisions we typically make. Chances are you won't ever be faced with any of the extraordinary scenarios (e.g., stealing to save a life or lying to the secret police to protect a fugitive) that are often used to illustrate principled decision making.[11] Your dilemmas are likely to be less dramatic. You have to determine whether to confront a coworker about a sexist joke or tell someone the truth at the risk of hurting his or her feelings. You also face time pressures and uncertainty. In a crisis, you don't always have time to carefully weigh consequences or to determine which abstract principle to follow.

JUSTICE AS FAIRNESS: GUARANTEEING EQUAL RIGHTS AND OPPORTUNITIES BEHIND THE VEIL OF IGNORANCE

Many disputes in democratic societies center on questions of justice or fairness. Is it just to give more tax breaks to the rich than to the poor? What is equitable compensation for executives? Should a certain percentage of federal contracts be reserved for minority contractors? Is it fair that Native Americans are granted special fishing rights? Why

Focus on Follower Ethics

CONSTRUCTING ETHICAL FOLLOWERSHIP

How we think about what it means to be a follower has a lot to do with our ethical or unethical behavior as followers. Melissa Carsten, Mary Uhl-Bien, and their colleagues conducted interviews with followers in a variety of industries to determine how they viewed their roles. The investigators discovered that followers define or construct their roles in three ways. *Passive followers* see themselves in a subordinate position. They defer to the leader and focus on carrying out orders. *Active followers* believe it is important to express their opinions and to offer input to their leaders when asked. They may disagree but ultimately remain loyal to the leader. *Proactive followers* don't wait to be asked. They take the initiative, offering unsolicited feedback and advice and challenge their leaders. Proactive followers see themselves as partners (coproducers) with leaders, working with them to reach important organizational goals.

In a subsequent study, Carsten and Uhl-Bien discovered a relationship between follower coproduction beliefs and the willingness to engage in unethical behavior. Those who thought of themselves as active partners with their leaders were less likely to obey the unethical directives of their superiors. Instead, they were more likely to offer constructive resistance by providing alternatives or reasons for noncompliance. Followers who saw themselves as passive and dependent (who had weak coproduction beliefs) were more likely to give in to unlawful or unethical requests, to engage in "crimes of obedience." They shifted or displaced responsibility for their actions to their leaders.

Carsten and Uhl-Bien's research suggests that, in order to stand up to leaders, we need to think of ourselves as their partners. When we challenge our leaders, we encourage them to engage in ethical conduct. We share responsibility for the ethical success or failure of the group whether serving in a leader or follower role.

Sources: Carsten, M. K., & Uhl-Bien, M. (2013). Ethical followership: An examination of followership beliefs and crimes of obedience. *Journal of Leadership & Organizational Studies, 21*, 49–61; Carsten, M. K., Uhl-Bien, M., West, B. J., Patera, J. L., & McGregor, R. (2010). Exploring social constructions of followership: A qualitative study. *Leadership Quarterly, 21*, 543–562.

Additional Sources

Shamir, B. (2007). From passive recipients to active co-producers: Followers' roles in the leadership process. In B. Shamir, R. Pillai, M. C. Bligh, & M. Uhl-Bien (Eds.), *Follower-centered perspectives on leadership* (pp. ix–xxxix). Greenwich CT: Information Age.

Uhl-Bien, M., & Pillai, R. (2007). The romance of leadership and the social construction of followership. In B. Shamir, R. Pillai, M. C. Bligh, & M. Uhl-Bien (Eds.), *Follower-centered perspectives on leadership* (pp. 187–209). Greenwich CT: Information Age.

should young workers have to contribute to the Social Security system when it may not be around when they retire?

In the last third of the twentieth century, Harvard philosopher John Rawls addressed questions such as these in a series of books and articles.[12] He set out to identify principles that would foster cooperation in a society made up of free and equal citizens who, at the same time, must deal with inequalities (e.g., status and economic differences, varying levels of talent and abilities). Rawls rejected utilitarian principles because, as noted earlier, generating the greatest number of benefits for society as a whole can seriously disadvantage certain groups and individuals. Cutting corporate taxes is another case of how utilitarian reasoning can undermine the interests of some groups at the expense of others. This policy may spur a region's overall economic growth, but most of the benefits go to the owners of companies. Other citizens have to pay higher taxes to make up for the lost revenue. Those making minimum wage, who can barely pay for rent and food, are particularly hard-hit. They end up subsidizing wealthy corporate executives and stockholders.

Instead of basing decisions on cost–benefit analyses, Rawls argues, we should follow these principles of justice and build them into our social institutions:

> *Principle 1:* Each person has an equal right to the same basic liberties that are compatible with similar liberties for all.

> *Principle 2:* Social and economic inequalities are to satisfy two conditions: (a) They are to be attached to offices and positions open to all under conditions of fair equality of opportunity. (b) They are to provide the greatest benefit to the least advantaged members of society.

The first principle, the "principle of equal liberty," has priority. It states that certain rights, such as the right to vote, the right to hold property, and freedom of speech, are protected and must be held equal by all persons. Attempts to deny voting rights to minorities would be unethical according to this standard. Principle 2a asserts that everyone should have an equal opportunity to qualify for offices and jobs. Discrimination based on race, gender, or ethnic origin is forbidden. Furthermore, everyone in society ought to have access to the training and education needed to prepare for these roles. Principle 2b, "the difference principle," recognizes that inequalities exist but states that priority should be given to meeting the needs of the poor, immigrants, minorities, and other marginalized groups.

Rawls introduces the "veil of ignorance" to back up his claim that his principles provide a solid foundation for a democratic society such as the United States. Imagine, he says, a group of people who are asked to come up with a set of principles that will govern society. These group members are ignorant of their own characteristics or societal positions. Standing behind this veil of ignorance, these people would choose (a) equal liberty, because they would want the maximum amount of freedom to pursue their interests; (b) equal opportunity, because if they turned out to be the most talented members of society, they would probably land the best jobs and elected offices; and (c) the difference principle, because they would want to be sure they were cared for if they ended up disadvantaged.

Applications and Cautions

Applications

- Follow fairness guidelines.
- Weigh both individual freedom and the good of the community when making decisions.
- Step behind the veil of ignorance when making choices.

As noted in Chapter 1, leaders cast shadows by acting inconsistently. Inconsistent leaders violate commonly held standards of fairness, arbitrarily giving preferential treatment to some followers while denying the same benefits to others who are equally deserving (or more so). Rawls directly addresses the shadow of inconsistency by outlining a set of principles to help us act fairly: Guarantee basic rights to all followers; ensure that followers have equal access to promotion, training, and other benefits; and make special efforts to help followers who have unique needs. (Complete Self-Assessment 5.1 to determine how just your organization is.) Keep in mind the reality of inequalities but strive to balance both individual freedom and the common good. While you want to encourage more talented, skilled, or fortunate followers to pursue their goals, Rawls urges you to make sure the fruits of their labor also benefit their less fortunate neighbors or coworkers.

The veil of ignorance is an important guideline to follow when making moral choices. Whenever possible, try to set aside such considerations as wealth, education, gender, and race. The least advantaged usually benefit when social class differences are excluded from the decision-making process. Our judicial system is one example of an institution that should treat disputants fairly. Unfortunately, economic and racial considerations influence the selection of juries, the determination of guilt and innocence, the lengths of sentences (and where they are served), and nearly every other aspect of the judicial process.

Cautions

- Rawls's principles can only be applied to democratic societies.
- Groups disagree about the meanings of justice and fairness.
- There is lack of consensus about which rights are most important.

Rawls's theory of justice as fairness has come under sharp attack. Rawls himself acknowledged that his model applies only to liberal democratic societies. It cannot work in cultures governed by royal families or religious leaders who are given special powers and privileges denied to everyone else. In addition, the more diverse democratic nations become, the more difficult it is for groups to agree on common values and principles.[13]

Rawls's critics note that definitions of justice and fairness vary widely, a fact that undermines the usefulness of his principles. What seems fair to you often appears grossly unjust to others. Evidence of this fact is found in disputes over college admission criteria. Some assert that admission decisions should favor members of minority groups to redress past discrimination and to enable minorities to achieve equal footing with whites. Others feel that admission standards that take minority status into account are unfair because they deny equal opportunity and ignore legitimate differences in abilities.

Some philosophers point out that there is no guarantee that parties who step behind the veil of ignorance would come up with the same set of principles as Rawls. Rather than emphasize fairness, these people might choose to make decisions based on utilitarian criteria or to emphasize certain rights. For example, libertarians hold that freedom from coercion is the most important human right. Every person should be able to produce and sell as he or she chooses regardless of impact on the poor. Capitalist theorists believe that benefits should be distributed based on the contributions each person makes to the group. They argue that helping out the less advantaged rewards laziness while discouraging productive people from doing their best. Because decision makers may reach different conclusions behind the veil, you may agree with skeptics who contend that Rawls's guidelines lack moral force. You may conclude that other approaches to managing society's inequities are just as valid as the notion of fairness.

PRAGMATISM: ETHICS AS INQUIRY

The approaches discussed so far—utilitarianism, the categorical imperative, and justice as fairness—differ significantly, but all share one characteristic: They are rule-based approaches to resolving ethical dilemmas. Each outlines a set of principles or rules that can be applied to specific situations. In contrast, pragmatism focuses on the *process* of moral decision making. Those taking a pragmatic approach reject the use of abstract principles, believing instead that good ethical choices emerge through the use of inquiry.[14]

Pragmatism was the dominant philosophical movement in the United States from the Civil War through World War II.[15] Charles Peirce (1839–1914) and William James (1842–1910) founded the movement, but it was John Dewey (1859–1952) who emerged as its most prominent spokesperson. Dewey wrote extensively on the topics of education, philosophy, science, and politics over his long career. In recent years, Richard Rorty, Hilary Putnam, and other prominent philosophers and ethicists have returned to the ideas of Dewey for insights into how to approach moral decision making.

Pragmatism gets its name from its focus on using philosophy to solve practical problems.[16] Dewey and other pragmatists believed that the scientific method can be applied to solving human dilemmas. In the scientific method, researchers develop hypotheses, which they then test through experiments. The hypotheses are then modified based on the experimental results. Conclusions are always subject to revision, depending on what the evidence reveals. Taking a pragmatic approach encourages flexibility.

Dewey argued that ethical dilemmas should be approached scientifically as well. Ethical quandaries create a sense of unease or distress, which then prompts us to address the problem. Since we can't conduct an actual physical experiment (as we would when investigating a chemistry problem), we rely on our moral imaginations.[17] Exercising moral imagination involves mentally testing out various courses of action, considering likely outcomes, determining how others might respond, referring to how similar problems have been solved in the past, and so on. Humility and openness to other points of view are key to mental experimentation. We need to admit that our knowledge is limited and welcome new discoveries.[18] According to Dewey, democracy provides the best setting for encouraging this type of experimental thinking and action.

The term *dramatic rehearsal* describes mental imagination in action. In dramatic rehearsal, decision makers conduct a series of imaginary thought experiments to visualize how their decisions could turn out. According to philosopher John McVea, dramatic rehearsal differs in important ways from the calculative, deliberative approach typically used in ethical decision making.[19] Dramatic rehearsal takes into account the emotions of those involved rather than setting feelings aside. Creative solutions emerge through deliberation rather than through the application of rules. Dramatic rehearsal immerses the leader in the specifics of the situation instead of encouraging her or him to rely on rules or guidelines.

While Dewey focused on the process of ethical decision making, he also believed that every ethical decision must be made with an end or value in mind. Ethics needs to answer these questions: "What ends should I strive for?" and "What conduct should I engage in so that I attain these ends?"[20] Dewey believed that each moral decision or habit has an impact on the character of the person making the choice. Making wise choices, then, fosters our character development.[21] Dewey emphasized that individual growth is the ultimate goal of moral decision making. Growth comes from solving problems, which opens up new possibilities for further growth and maturity. In Dewey's words:

> The process of growth, of improvement and progress, rather than the static outcome and result, becomes the significant thing.... The end is no longer a terminus or limit to be reached. It is the active process of transforming the existent situation. Not perfection as a final goal, but the ever-enduring process of perfecting, maturing, refining is the aim in living.... Growth itself is the only moral "end."[22]

Muhammad Yunus, founder of the Grameen Bank of Bangladesh, is an example of a leader who used dramatic rehearsal to address immediate ethical problems. In so doing, he developed his character.[23] In 1972, Yunus returned to his home country of Bangladesh to take up a teaching post after completing his doctorate in economics in the United States. However, the nation's suffering troubled Yunus, and he began to focus on alleviating poverty. He and his students then undertook a series of research projects in order to understand the causes of poverty. They discovered that inability to secure credit kept many from economic security. Rather than turn to charities or the government for help, Yunus developed a creative solution—he started a for-profit bank to lend small amounts to rural villagers. By immersing himself in the plight of poor, he discovered that many village women had skills that they could use in small enterprises if they only had the capital to start their businesses. As a result, many of the bank's loans go to female entrepreneurs.

Later, Yunus promoted the use of cell phones in remote villages. He envisioned that women could start businesses by renting out phones for calls and that the phones would give villagers access to market information. Cell phones would also reduce the isolation of women, which made them vulnerable to abuse.

Because he decided to work on eliminating poverty rather than teaching economics, Yunus ended up pursuing a different career and developing a new set of beliefs and values. Throughout his journey, he always kept the end in view when making decisions:

> I was not trying to become a money lender. I had (originally) no intention of lending money to anyone; all I really wanted was to solve an immediate problem. Even to this day I still view myself, my work and that of my colleagues, as devoted to solving the same immediate problem: the problem of poverty which humiliates and denigrates everything that a human being stands for.[24]

Applications and Cautions

Applications

- Approach ethical problems as you would other dilemmas.
- Immerse yourself in the details of the situation.
- Engage your imagination.
- Acknowledge your limitations.
- Look for creative solutions.
- Embrace your emotions.
- Recognize that your ethical choices shape your character.

Solving ethical problems takes many of same strategies as solving other dilemmas, like determining how to lower costs or increase sales. You must identify options, consider possible outcomes, gather information, experiment, and adjust your conclusions in the light of new information (see Chapter 6). You need to immerse yourself in the details of the situation to gain a better understanding of the challenges you face. In some cases, you may need to choose between imperfect alternatives.

Dramatic rehearsal is a useful tool when facing a moral dilemma. Imagination allows you to experiment with solutions and engage in perspective taking, both of which are essential to ethical problem solving. An experimental approach is particularly important when in a leadership role. You need to acknowledge your limitations—that means continually trying out ideas, recognizing when ideas need to be adjusted in the face of changing conditions, and respecting the input of followers. In other words, develop a "pragmatic temperament" that is flexible and open to change and other points of view. Whenever possible, seek novel solutions. These often emerge during the inquiry process. Rather than rejecting your emotions, embrace them. They can signal that an ethical problem exists and spur you to action. (We'll take a closer look at the role of emotions in ethical decision making in the next chapter.)

Dewey also reminds us that ethical choices aren't isolated events. Ethical choices and the habits they develop have a cumulative impact. Taken together, they determine who we are becoming.

Cautions

- Pragmatism lacks a moral center.
- This approach can lead to undesirable decisions.
- Measuring growth is difficult.

You may be troubled by the fact that pragmatism lacks a "normative core." It offers no guidelines, such as doing the greatest good for the greatest number, for determining right or wrong, or for justifying a choice. Instead, you need to trust that a worthy solution will emerge through the process of inquiry. As some critics note, there is no guarantee that ethical inquiry and experimentation will produce ethical solutions. They point to the example of the Nazis, who engaged in a series of inhuman medical experiments. Doctors euthanized mentally challenged and disabled children, and Josef Mengele carried out gruesome medical experiments at Auschwitz.[25] Then, too, there is confusion about the ultimate goal of pragmatic ethical decision making. Dewey argues that we need to pursue personal growth and development. You will have to define what this lofty but abstract goals mean to you.

ALTRUISM: LOVE YOUR NEIGHBOR

Advocates of altruism argue that love of neighbor is the ultimate ethical standard. Our actions should be designed to help others, whatever the personal cost. The altruistic approach to moral reasoning shares much in common with virtue ethics. Many of the virtues that characterize people of high moral character, such as compassion, hospitality, empathy, and generosity, reflect concern for other people. Clearly, virtuous leaders are other-centered, not self-centered.

Altruism appears to be a universal value, one promoted in cultures in every region of the world. The Dalai Lama urges followers to practice an ethic of compassion, for instance, and benevolence is a central value of Confucianism. Western thought has been greatly influenced by the altruistic emphasis of Judaism and Christianity. The command to love God and to love others as we love ourselves is our most important obligation in Judeo-Christian ethics. Because humans are made in the image of God and God is love, we have an obligation to love others no matter who they are and no matter their relationship to us. Jesus drove home this point in the parable of the Good Samaritan:

> A man was going down from Jerusalem to Jericho when he fell into the hands of robbers. They stripped him of his clothes, beat him, and went away, leaving him half dead. A priest happened to be going down the same road, and when he saw the man, he passed by on the other side. So too, a Levite, when he came to the place and saw him, passed by on the other side. But a Samaritan, as he traveled, came where the man was; and when he saw him, he took pity on him. He went to him and bandaged his wounds, pouring on oil and wine. Then he put the man on his own donkey, took him to an inn, and took care of him. The next day he took out two silver coins and gave them to the innkeeper. "Look after him," he said, "and when I return, I will reimburse you for any extra expense you may have." Which of these three do you think was a neighbor to the man who fell into the hands of robbers? The expert replied, "The one who had mercy on him." Jesus told him, "Go and do likewise." (Luke 10:30–37, New International Version)

Hospice volunteers provide a modern-day example of the unconditional love portrayed in the story of the Good Samaritan. They meet the needs of the dying regardless of their patients' social or religious backgrounds, providing help at significant personal cost without expecting anything in return. (Box 5.1 describes an altruistic ethic based entirely on caring for others.)

Box 5.1 The Ethic of Care

The altruistic ethic of care developed as an alternative to what feminists label as the traditional male-oriented approach to ethics. The utilitarian, categorical imperative and justice-as-fairness approaches emphasize the importance of acting on abstract moral principles, being impartial, and treating others fairly. Carol Gilligan, Nel Noddings, and others initially argued that women take a different approach (have a "different voice") to moral decision making based on caring for others. Instead of expressing concern for people in abstract terms, women care for others through their relationships and tailor their responses to the particular needs of the other individual. Subsequent research revealed that the ethic of care is not exclusive to women. Men as well as women may prefer care to justice.

Philosopher Virginia Held identifies five key components of the care ethic:

1. *Focuses on the importance of noting and meeting the needs of those we are responsible for.* Most people are dependent for much of their existence, including during childhood, during illness, and near the end of life. Morality built on rights and autonomy overlooks this fact. The ethic of care makes concern for others central to human experience and puts the needs of specific individuals—whether a child or an elderly relative—first.

2. *Values emotions.* Sympathy, sensitivity, empathy, and responsiveness are moral emotions that need to be cultivated. This stands in sharp contrast to ethical approaches that urge decision makers to set aside their feelings in order to make rational, impartial determinations. However, emotions need to be carefully monitored and evaluated to make sure they are appropriate. For instance, caregivers caught up in empathy can deny their own needs or end up controlling the recipients of their care.

3. *Specific needs and relationships take priority above universal principles.* The ethic of care rejects the notion of impartiality and believes particular relationships are more important than universal moral principles like rights and freedom. For example, the needs of the immediate family take precedence over the needs of neighbors or of society as a whole. Persons in caring relationships aren't out to promote their personal interests or the interests of humanity; instead, they want to foster ethical relationships with each other. Family and friendships have great moral value in the ethic of care, and caregiving is a critical moral responsibility.

4. *Breaks down the barriers between the public and private spheres.* In the past, men were dominant in the public sphere while relegating women to the private sphere. Men largely made decisions about how to exercise political and economic power while women were marginalized and dependent. The ethic of care argues that the private domain is just as important as the public domain and that problems faced in the private sphere, such as inequality and dependence, also arise in the public sphere.

(Continued)

(Continued)

5. *Views persons as both relational and interdependent.* Each of us starts life depending on others, and we depend on our webs of interpersonal relationships throughout our time on Earth. In the ethic of care, individuals are seen as embedded in particular families, cultures, and historical periods. Being embedded means that we need to take responsibility for others, not merely leave them alone to exercise their individual rights.

Widespread adoption of the ethic of care would significantly change national priorities. Child rearing, education, elder care, and other caring activities would consume a greater proportion of governmental budgets. Societal leaders would ensure that caregivers receive more money, recognition, and status. More men would take on caregiving responsibilities. Organizational leaders would help employees strike a better balance between work and home responsibilities and provide more generous family leave policies. Corporations would devote more attention to addressing societal problems.

Sources: Gilligan, C. (1982). *In a different voice: Psychological theory and women's development.* Cambridge, MA: Harvard University Press; Held, V. (2006). The ethics of care. In D. Copp (Ed.), *The Oxford handbook of ethical theory* (pp. 537–566). Oxford, England: Oxford University Press; Larrabee, M. J. (Ed.). (1993). *An ethic of care: Feminist and interdisciplinary perspectives.* New York, NY: Routledge; Noddings, N. (2003). *Caring: A feminine approach to ethics and moral education.* Berkeley: University of California Press; Tronto, J. C. (1993). *Moral boundaries: A political argument for an ethic of care.* New York, NY: Routledge.

Concern for others promotes healthy social relationships. Society as a whole functions more effectively when people help one another in their daily interactions. Researchers in social psychology, economics, political science, and other fields have discovered that altruistic behavior is more often than not the norm, not the exception.[26] Every day, we help others—by pitching in to help finish a project, shoveling the driveway of an elderly neighbor, listening to a roommate's problems, and so on. ("Leadership Ethics at the Movies: *The Chorus*" presents another example of compassion in action.) Altruism is the driving force behind all kinds of movements and organizations designed to help the less fortunate and to eliminate social problems. Name almost any nonprofit group, ranging from a hospital or medical relief team to a youth club or crisis hotline, and you'll find that it was launched by someone with an altruistic motive. In addition, when we compare good to evil, altruistic acts generally come to mind. Moral heroes and moral champions shine so brightly because they ignore personal risks to battle evil forces.

From this discussion, it's easy to see why altruism is a significant ethical consideration for all types of citizens. (To determine your tendency to engage in altruistic behavior, complete Self-Assessment 5.2.) However, management professors Rabindra Kanungo and Manuel Mendonca believe that concern for others is even more important for leaders than it is for followers.[27] By definition, leaders exercise influence on behalf

Leadership Ethics at the Movies

THE CHORUS

Key Cast Members: Gerald Jugnot, Francois Berleand, Jacque Perrin, Marie Bunel, Jean Baptiste Maunier

Synopsis: After failing as a musician, Clement Mathieu (Jugnot) is hired as a teacher at a French boarding school for troubled boys shortly after the end of World War II. The school's principal (Berleand) runs the school with an iron fist under the motto "Action, reaction." Every infraction is met with severe punishment. Mathieu takes a kinder, gentler approach to discipline, shielding his charges from the wrath of the principal. He rediscovers his love of music and forms a boys' chorus. Mathieu takes special interest in one talented young singer (Maunier) who goes on to become a world-class orchestra conductor. As his final act after being fired from the school, Mathieu adopts a young boy whose parents were killed during the war. In French with English subtitles.

Rating: PG-13 for sexual language and themes and one violent scene

Themes: altruism, the ethic of care, compassion, character, coping with failure, authoritarian leadership, ethical followership, justice, vocation, mentorship

Discussion Starters

1. Does Mathieu strike the right balance between compassion and justice?
2. What virtues does he demonstrate?
3. How does Mathieu respond to failure?
4. How do you define success? According to your definition, was Mathieu successful?

---

of others. They can't understand or articulate the needs of followers unless they focus on the concerns of constituents. To succeed, leaders may have to take risks and forgo personal gain. Leaders intent on benefiting followers will pursue organizational goals, rely on referent and expert power bases, and give power away. Leaders intent on benefiting themselves will focus on personal achievements; rely on legitimate, coercive, and reward power bases; and try to control followers. Kanungo and Mendonca identify four forms of leader altruistic behaviors. *Individual-focused* leader altruistic behaviors include providing training, technical assistance, and mentoring. *Group-focused* leader altruistic behaviors include team building, participative group decision making, and minority advancement programs. *Organizational-focused* leader altruistic attitudes and actions include demonstrating commitment and loyalty, protecting organizational resources, and whistle-blowing. *Societal-focused* leader altruistic behaviors include making contributions to promote social welfare, reducing pollution, ensuring product safety, and maintaining customer satisfaction.[28]

Self-sacrifice is integral to altruistic leadership. In self-sacrifice, leaders postpone or give up personal benefits and share hardships with followers.[29] They may volunteer to do the most unpleasant or risky tasks like leading a military squad into battle, putting off their own salary increases and promotions, or living in poverty alongside those they serve. Self-sacrifice can occur at a specific point in time, as when the chair of Olivetti invested $17 million of his own money to rescue the firm when it was near bankruptcy. Or it can occur over time, as in the case of Ross Perot, president of Electronic Data Systems, who never claimed such privileges as an executive dining room, considering instead that "every employee was a full partner."

Self-sacrificial behavior has a powerful impact on followers.[30] Such behavior motivates subordinates to work together and to make sacrifices of their own. They feel a stronger sense of group identity and perform better on tasks. Self-sacrifice has the greatest influence when it is employed by democratic leaders who are confident in themselves and in the future of their groups and organizations.

Altruism, specifically concern for employees, plays a central role in paternalistic leadership, a leadership style popular in many parts of the world, including Asia, Latin America, Mexico, Turkey, and the Middle East.[31] In benevolent paternalism, leaders act as parental figures who demonstrate concern for the welfare of their workers both on and off the job. They may lend money to their subordinates, attend the weddings of their children, find them housing, and so on. While exploitative paternalists abuse their authority and mistreat followers, benevolent paternalistic leaders set a moral example through selflessness, self-discipline, a strong work ethic, and other positive behaviors. They are genuinely interested in the well-being of their workers who, in turn, treat their supervisors with loyalty and respect.

Applications and Cautions

Applications

- Put the needs of followers before your own needs.
- Act as a role model.
- Use compassion as an important decision-making guideline.

Proponents of altruism make a compelling case for its importance. Compassion for others is critical to the health of society and to leadership. To be an effective leader, you need to be aware of the needs of your followers and be willing to sacrifice on their behalf. You can expect to give up personal benefits and to share hardships faced by your constituents. Put the goals of the group or organization first and empower followers. Practice the altruistic individual-, group-, organizational-, and societal-focused behaviors outlined earlier. By acting selflessly, you inspire others to do the same. Compassion should also be an important consideration in every decision you make. Consider how your choices will affect others; seek solutions that will benefit them.

Cautions

- It is impossible to meet every need.
- The extent of our obligations is unclear.
- Many who profess to love their neighbors fail to act as if they do.
- Altruism takes many different, sometimes conflicting, forms.

You've probably already discovered that love of neighbor is not an easy principle to put into practice. The world's needs far exceed our ability to meet them. How do you decide whom to help and whom to ignore? Then, too, far too many people who claim to follow the Christian ethic fail miserably. They come across as less, not more, caring than those who don't claim to follow this approach. Some of the bitterest wars are religious ones, fought by believers who seemingly ignore the altruistic values of their faiths. There is also disagreement about what constitutes loving behavior. For example, committed religious leaders disagree about the legitimacy of war. Some view military service as an act of love, one designed to defend their families and friends. Others oppose the military, believing that nonviolence is the only way to express compassion for others.

IMPLICATIONS AND APPLICATIONS

- Well-established ethical systems and values can help you make wise moral choices. Whenever possible, employ more than one perspective when faced with an ethical dilemma.

- Two well-meaning leaders can use the same ethical approach and reach different conclusions.

- Utilitarianism weighs the possible costs and benefits of moral choices. According to this approach, you should seek to do the greatest good for the greatest number of people. To conduct a utilitarian analysis, clearly identify the action or issue, specify all who might be affected, determine the likely consequences, and sum up the negative and positive consequences. The action is morally right if the benefits outweigh the costs.

- Kant's categorical imperative urges us to do what's right, no matter the consequences. By this standard, some actions (truth telling, helping others) are always right, while others (lying, cheating, murder) are always wrong. Kant also urges us to treat all people—followers, stakeholders, neighbors—with respect, never using them as tools for reaching our goals.

- The justice-as-fairness approach guarantees the same basic rights and opportunities to everyone in a democratic society. When these basic requirements are met, your responsibility as a leader is to give special consideration to the least advantaged. One way to ensure fairness is by standing behind a veil of ignorance when making choices. Try to set aside such considerations as wealth, education, gender, and race.

- Pragmatism focuses on the process of ethical decision making. Use your imagination to test out options and courses of action. Immerse yourself in the details of the situation and embrace your emotions. Remember that every decision helps to determine up your character.

- Altruism encourages you to put others first, no matter the personal cost. Concern for others is particularly important for leaders who exert influence on behalf of others and requires self-sacrifice. The ethic of care is an altruistic approach to ethics based on meeting the needs of specific individuals. Benevolent paternalistic leadership, which demonstrates concern for employees both on and off the job, is popular in many regions of the world.

FOR FURTHER EXPLORATION, CHALLENGE, AND SELF-ASSESSMENT

1. In a group, generate a list of absolute moral laws or duties that must be obeyed without exception. To make the list, everyone in the group must agree on it. Keep a separate list of the laws or duties that were nominated but failed to receive unanimous support. Present your lists to the rest of the class.

2. Reflect on one of your recent ethical decisions. What ethical system(s) did you follow? Were you satisfied with your choice?

3. Find a partner and generate additional applications and cautions for each of the ethical perspectives presented in this chapter.

4. Given that inequalities will always exist, what is the best way to allocate wealth, education, health care, and other benefits in a democratic society? In organizations? Write up your conclusions.

5. Analyze your response to Self-Assessment 5.1. What does your score reveal about your perception of justice in your organization? How can your organization act more justly? As an alternative, analyze your response to Self-Assessment 5.2. What does your score reveal about your willingness to help others? How can you engage in more altruistic behavior?

6. Debate one or more of the following propositions:

   • The scientific method is the best way to solve ethical problems.

   • To be effective, leaders must practice self-sacrifice.

   • When making ethical choices, compassion is more important than justice.

7. Create your own ethics case based on your personal experience or on current or historical events. Describe the key ethical issues raised in the case and evaluate the characters in the story according to each of the five ethical standards.

8. Apply each of the six perspectives to Case Study 5.3 to determine whether you believe that hacking was a morally justified in this situation. Write up your conclusions.

STUDENT STUDY SITE

Visit the student study site at **study.sagepub.com/johnsonmecl6e** to access full SAGE journal articles for further research and information on key chapter topics.

Case Study 5.1

RADICAL DO-GOODERS

Is it possible to be too concerned for other people? *New Yorker* writer Larissa MacFarquhar asks that question in her book, *Strangers Drowning: Grappling with Impossible Idealism, Drastic Choices, and the Overpowering Urge to Help*. In her book, she profiles people she describes as "radical do-gooders." In order to serve the needy, they move to poverty-stricken countries, give away all of their possessions, gather food from dumpsters so they can contribute more money to the poor, let homeless people live in their houses, donate kidneys to complete strangers, and adopt multiple children with significant disabilities.

The title of MacFarquhar's book comes from a thought experiment that asks, "Should you save your mother from drowning or save two strangers?" Most people would save their mothers. Not so the radical do-gooder who makes the calculation that saving two lives is better than saving one. Extreme altruists don't make a distinction between their families and strangers. MacFarquhar's subjects are willing to sacrifice their loved ones on behalf of large causes. For example, a couple put their children at risk from wild animals and disease to start a leprosarium in an Indian jungle. A missionary risked the life of her son, who had a heart condition, to serve in Mozambique.

MacFarquhar reports that saving others does not always bring happiness. Some of the do-gooders she interviewed experienced joy; others did not. The happy ones take pleasure from the same things the rest of us do, like having a purpose in life, meaningful work, and love. The unhappy ones never lose sight of the misery in the world. They lack the "happy blindness" that allows most of us to at least temporarily ignore the unbearable.

Do-gooders have forced themselves to know, and keep on knowing, that everything they do affects other people and that sometimes (though not always) their joy is purchased with other people's joy. And, remembering that, they open themselves to a sense of unlimited, crushing responsibility.

> Despite feeling an unrelenting burden for others, all of MacFarquhar's interviewees recognized that they had to put limits on how much they could help in order to save themselves. At some point, they had to stop sacrificing for others and realize, for instance, that they couldn't adopt another child, continue to live on the streets, or work without ever taking a break. (pp. 298–299)

MacFarquhar concludes that while radical do-goodism may not always be healthy and can make the rest of feel uneasy, the world is better off because of the presence of these extraordinary altruists: "It may be true that not everyone should be a do-gooder. But it is also true that these strange, hopeful, tough, idealistic, demanding, life-threatening, and relentless people, by their extravagant example, help keep those life-sustaining qualities alive" (p. 301).

(Continued)

(Continued)

Discussion Probes

1. Is it possible to be too concerned for others?

2. Do radical do-gooders make you feel uneasy? Why or why not?

3. What can we learn from the example of radical do-gooders?

4. How should we weigh the needs of strangers against the needs of our family and friends? Would you rescue your mother or two strangers from drowning?

5. How much should we be expected to sacrifice for strangers?

6. How do we determine the limits of our responsibilities to strangers?

Source

MacFarquhar, L. (2015). *Strangers drowning: Grappling with impossible idealism, drastic choices, and the overpowering urge to help*. New York, NY: Penguin Press.

Additional Sources

Brooks, D. (2016, February 5). A question of moral radicalism. *The New York Times*, Op-Ed.

Flesher, A. M. (2003). *Heroes, saints, & ordinary morality*. Washington, DC: Georgetown University Press.

Wilson, D. S. (2015). *Does altruism exist? Culture, genes, and the welfare of others*. New Haven, CT: Yale University Press, Ch. 9.

Case Study 5.2

THE FUKUSHIMA 50

The massive earthquake that struck off the coast of Japan on March 11, 2011, sent a tidal wave over the seawalls protecting the Fukushima Daiichi Nuclear Power Plant. The tsunami knocked out power to the facility, shutting down the cooling systems and leading to explosions in three reactors. Some 160,000 people in the area had to be evacuated because of the dangers of radiation exposure. The facility was close to a total meltdown, which would have meant the release of a massive radioactive cloud, putting Tokyo at risk. As it was, the crisis at Fukushima was the worst nuclear disaster since Chernobyl.

Catastrophe was averted thanks to the heroic actions of plant manager Masao Yoshida and the "Fukushima 50." Yoshida disobeyed orders from headquarters to stop pumping seawater into one of the reactors. The Fukushima 50, including middle-level managers, engineers, technicians, and lower-level workers (many of them temporary employees), stayed on the scene, removing rubble, cleaning up radiation, and restoring electricity. They cleared the way for fire crews to come in and spray water on the remaining reactors to cool them down. One observer describes the scene facing the 50 (in reality, 70–100 individuals) this way:

> What it must be like after a torrent of seawater has ravaged all around, lights are out, radiation is leaking in dangerous amounts, steam valves are pouring out scalding water, intermittent explosions are rending the fabric of the reactor buildings and earthquake aftershocks are convulsing the ground defies description. The hellish scenes painted by 15th-century painter Hieronymus Bosch come to mind.[1]

Engineers from the reactor manufacturer, members of the Japan Self-Defense Forces (charged with dropping water by helicopter on the reactors), and elite firefighters joined the initial 50. They worked around the clock, catching what little sleep they could in crowded conference rooms. The workers were exposed to more radiation in 20–30 minutes than most atomic workers are exposed to in their entire careers. They can expect to suffer from blood disorders and cancers as a result.

Some employees remained on the job out of fear (they worried they would never get another job in the nuclear industry); others were lured by promises of generous bonuses. Most, however, stayed out of a mix of duty, stoicism, and concern for others. The members of the Fukushima 50 shared the dignified stoicism that marked their country's overall response to the crisis. The Japanese term *gaman,* which translates roughly as "perseverance," describes the combination of endurance and self-denial demonstrated by the nation's citizens. Japanese caught in the disaster zone were determined to endure and were willing to sacrifice themselves for others and the community. The young took the elderly to shelters, for example, and neighbors cared for neighbors. Said one man who was delivering food to the poor, "I'm just doing what needs to be done. It's nothing special."[2] Employees at the power plant also demonstrated gaman*.* They recognized that abandoning the plant would cost the lives of their fellow citizens. One engineer volunteered to assist at the plant despite the concerns of his family, believing he had a responsibility to help because he knew how to operate nuclear reactors. He told a reporter, "I'm not leaving this until I'm done. Never."[3]

Sadly, the heroic efforts of the Fukushima 50 have been largely forgotten. The group's members remain anonymous and are afraid to describe what happened during the crisis for fear of being associated with the Tokyo Electric Power Company (TEPCO), the plant operator. Even when the Japanese prime minister publicly thanked several TEPCO employees for their efforts, they refused to be photographed or to give their names. The Japanese public vilified TEPCO for failing to build higher seawalls despite warnings that the plant's defenses were inadequate and for hiding the true magnitude of the radiation danger during the crisis.

(Continued)

(Continued)

Discussion Probes

1. If similar explosions had occurred at a nuclear power plant in another country, do you think the workers there would have stayed on the job? Why or why not?

2. Can you think of other examples of where people risked their lives out of a sense of duty? What explains their actions?

3. In addition to duty, what other ethical principles appeared to motivate the Fukushima 50, those who joined their efforts, and other Japanese citizens?

4. How should Japan and the world honor those who stayed to save the plant?

5. What leadership and followership ethics lessons do you take from this case?

Notes

1. Rowley, A. (2011, March 24). Fukushima fifty: Japan's new heroes. *The Business Times Singapore.*

2. Beech, H., Birmingham, L., Dirkse, T., & Mahr, K. (2011, March 28). How Japan will reawaken. *Time International,* 32–37.

3. The twilight zone. (2011, November 15). *The Economist,* 49–50.

Sources

Come back in 10 years' time. (2011, March 26). *The Economist,* 47–48.

Iwaki, H. T. (2012, October 8). Meet the Fukushima 50? No, you can't. *The Economist.*

Kohler, N., Krolicki, K., Disavano, S., & Fuse, T. (2011, April 2). Wave predicted. *National Post,* p. A25.

McCurry, J. (2013, July 10). Fukushima boss hailed as hero dies. *The Guardian.*

McNeill, D. (2013, March 1). I am one of the Fukushima 50. *Independent.*

Tabuchi, H. (2011, April 11). Less pay, fewer benefits, more radiation; disaster in Japan. *The International Herald Tribune,* p. 6.

Yokota, T., & Yamada, T. (2012, March 12). Disposable heroes. *Newsweek* (International ed.).

Case Study 5.3

A MORAL HACK?

Massive data breaches are becoming more common. In two of the largest breaches, hackers stole credit and debit card information from 40 million Target shoppers and 50–60 million Home Depot customers. Hackers are typically motivated by greed, selling the data to criminals or stealing the identities of victims. In one massive data breach, however, the perpetrators claimed to be motivated by morality, not financial gain.

In 2015 a group called the Impact Team hacked into the social network Ashley Madison. Ashley Madison, with the slogan "Life is short. Have an affair," promotes adultery, claiming to be the "most famous name in infidelity and married dating." The site's parent group, Toronto's Avid Life Media (ALM), also runs websites where older men can meet up with younger women (Established Men) and older women can arrange sexual encounters with younger men (Cougar Life). Initially, the Impact Team threatened to reveal the data of 37 million users from around the globe unless Ashley Madison and Established Men shut down. The hackers described the customers of these sites as "cheating dirtbags who deserve no discretion."[1] They also claimed that Ashley Madison lied to clients who paid $19.00 to delete information from the site, contending that ALM failed to erase all the data as advertised.

When the company refused to close down the two sites, the Impact Team carried out its threat, declaring: "We have explained the fraud, deceit, and stupidity of ALM and their members. Now everyone gets to see their data."[2] In a series of data dumps, the group released user names, e-mail addresses, sexual preferences, height, weight, date of birth, and credit card information. The releases revealed that a number of clients used their government, military, and work e-mail servers to access the service. Leaders appear to be particularly attracted to the site, with capital cities having the top subscription rates. *Fortune 500* executives and congressmen are allegedly clients. Josh Duggar, former star of the reality show *19 and Counting* and former director of the conservative group Family Research Council, has apologized for using the service.

The data dumps had an immediate impact on both clients and the company. Some users apparently received e-mails threatening to out them to their partners unless they paid their blackmailers. Two suicides were linked to the leaks, and marriage counselors predicted an upswing in business as Ashley Madison customers confessed to their spouses. One psychotherapist noted that being listed on the site is hard to explain away because clients must register, create a profile, and search for sex partners. He went on to say, "It's very, very difficult to come back from an affair being uncovered."[3] The hack threatened ALM's plans to go public with an initial stock offering. Media Company president Noel Biderman was forced to resign.

ALM apologized to users and offered a $50,000 reward leading to the arrest of the hackers. The head of the Toronto police team investigating the hack emphasized that the nature of the site was irrelevant: "The fact that some people are offended by this service provided by Ashley Madison cannot deter us and it will not deter us."[4] Under Canadian law, the hackers face a maximum of ten years in prison. They could face life imprisonment if their actions posed a danger to human life.

Other hackers are skeptical that the Impact Team is engaged in moral vigilantism, believing that the group will sell the data. Said one, "They'll profit from this in a big way, especially with the size of this database."[5]

(Continued)

(Continued)

Discussion Probe

1. Was this a moral hack? Why or why not?

Notes

1. Plucinska, J. (2015, July 22). Twenty percent of the Canadian capital's residents are registered on Ashley Madison. *Time.com*.

2. Roberts, P. F. (2015, August 20). The troubling ripple effect of the Ashley Madison data dump. *Christian Science Monitor*.

3. O'Shea, J. (2015, August 21). The leak that could end your marriage. *Irish Independent*, pp. 34, 35.

4. Edmiston, J. (2015, August 24). "This isn't fun and games any more": Toronto police issue stern warning to Ashley Madison hackers. *National Post*.

5. Toh, M. (2015, July 21). Ashley Madison: 'Moral' hacking or old-fashioned stealing? *Christian Science Monitor*.

Sources

Francis, H., Grubb, B., & Biggs, T. (2015, August 24). Cheating site hack has raised ethical questions. *Newcastle Herald* (Australia), p. 20.

Grandoni, D. (2015, July 15). Ashley, a dating website, says hackers may have data on millions. *The New York Times*.

Hern, A. (2015, August 21). Ten questions Ashley Madison needs to answer. *The Guardian*, Technology.

Hopper, T. (2015, August 25). The aftermath of an online hack. *The Star Phoenix* (Saskatoon, Saskatchewan), p. D4.

Kedmey, D. (2015, July 22). Ashley Madison already caved to hackers' demands. *Time.com*.

Shenton, Z. (2015, August 21). Who is Josh Duggar? All you need to know after shamed TV star is exposed in Ashley Madison hack. *Irish Mirror*, Showbiz News.

Victor, D. (2014, August 19). The Ashley Madison data dump, explained. *The New York Times*, Technology.

SELF-ASSESSMENT 5.1

The Organizational Justice Scale

Instructions: Evaluate your employer or another organization of your choice on the following items. Respond to each of the statements on a scale of 1 (*strongly disagree*) to 5 (*strongly agree*).

1. In general, this company (organization) treats its employees (members) fairly.

1	2	3	4	5

2. Generally, employees (members) think of this company (organization) as fair.

    1   2   3   4   5

3. Rewards are allocated fairly in this firm (organization).

    1   2   3   4   5

4. Employees (members) in this firm (organization) are rewarded fairly.

    1   2   3   4   5

5. In this firm (organization), people get the reward or punishment they deserve.

    1   2   3   4   5

6. Supervisors (leaders) in this company (organization) treat employees (members) with dignity and respect.

    1   2   3   4   5

7. Employees (members) can count on being treated with courtesy and respect in this firm (organization).

    1   2   3   4   5

Scoring: Scores can range from 7 to 35. The higher the score, the more just you believe your organization to be. You may want to give this instrument to other organizational members to determine if their perceptions are similar to your own.

Source: Adapted from Trevino, L. K., & Weaver, G. R. (2001). Organizational justice and ethics program "follow through": Influences on employees' harmful and helpful behavior. *Business Ethics Quarterly, 11,* 651–671. Used with permission.

SELF-ASSESSMENT 5.2

The Self Report Altruism Scale

Instructions: Check the category on the right that conforms to the frequency with which you have carried out the following acts. (0 = Never, 5 = Very often.) Scores range from 0–80. The higher the score, the more you believe you engage in altruistic behavior.

	Never	Once	More Than Once	Often	Very Often
1. I have helped push a stranger's car out of the snow.					
2. I have given directions to a stranger.					
3. I have made change for a stranger.					
4. I have given money to a charity.					

	Never	Once	More Than Once	Often	Very Often
5. I have given money to a stranger who needed it (or asked me for it).					
6. I have donated goods or clothes to a charity.					
7. I have done volunteer work for a charity.					
8. I have donated blood.					
9. I have helped carry a stranger's belongings (books, parcels, etc.).					
10. I have delayed an elevator and held the door open for a stranger.					
11. I have allowed someone to go ahead of me in a line (at photocopy machine, in the supermarket).					
12. I have given a stranger a lift in my car.					
13. I have pointed out a clerk's error (in a bank, at the supermarket) in undercharging me for an item.					
14. I have let a neighbor whom I didn't know too well borrow an item of some value to me (e.g., a dish, tools, etc.).					
15. I have bought "charity" Christmas cards deliberately because I knew it was for a good cause.					
16. I have helped a classmate who I did not know that well with a homework assignment when my knowledge was greater than his or hers.					
17. I have, before being asked, voluntarily looked after a neighbor's pets or children without being paid for it.					
18. I have offered to help a handicapped or elderly stranger across a street.					
19. I have offered my seat on a bus or train to a stranger who was standing.					
20. I have helped an acquaintance move households.					

Source: Rushton, J. P., Chrisjohn, R. D., & Fekken, G. C. (1981). The altruistic personality and the self-report altruism scale. *Personality and Individual Differences, 2,* 293–302. Used with permission.

NOTES

1. See the following: Barry, V. (1978). *Personal and social ethics: Moral problems with integrated theory.* Belmont, CA: Wadsworth; Bentham, J. (1948). *An introduction to the principles of morals and legislation.* New York, NY; Hafner; Gorovitz, S. (Ed.). (1971). *Utilitarianism: Text and critical essays.* Indianapolis, IN: Bobbs-Merrill; Timmons, M. (2002). *Moral theory: An introduction.* Lanham, MD: Rowman & Littlefield; Troyer, J. (2003). *The classical utilitarians: Bentham and Mill.* Indianapolis, IN: Hackett; West, H. R. (2004). *An introduction to Mill's utilitarian ethics.* Cambridge, England: Cambridge University Press.

2. De George, R. T. (1995). *Business ethics* (4th ed.). Englewood Cliffs, NJ: Prentice Hall, Ch. 3.

3. Eilperin, J. (2010, February 7). Fight over invasive species turns into fight over lesser of two evils. *The Oregonian,* p. A2.

4. Profile, C. (2015, April 26). Love 'em or hate 'em, sea lions raise concerns on the Columbia. *Oregon Public Broadcasting.*

5. Isaac, M. (2016, February 18). Why Apple is putting up a fight over privacy with the F.B.I. *The New York Times,* p. B4.

6. Singer, P. (1972). Famine, affluence, and morality. *Philosophy and Public Affairs, 1,* 229–243; Singer, P. (2009). *The life you can save: Acting now to end world poverty.* New York, NY: Random House.

7. Schaler, J. A. (Ed.). (2009). *Peter Singer under fire.* Chicago, IL: Open Court/Carus.

8. Christians, C. G., Rotzell, K. B., & Fackler, M. (1999). *Media ethics* (3rd ed.). New York, NY: Longman; Kant, I. (1964). *Groundwork of the metaphysics of morals* (H. J. Ryan, Trans.). New York, NY: Harper & Row; Leslie, L. Z. (2000). *Mass communication ethics: Decision making in postmodern culture.* Boston, MA: Houghton Mifflin; Sucher, S. J. (2008). *The moral leader: Challenges, tools, and insights.* London, England: Routledge; Timmons; Velasquez, M. G. (1992). *Business ethics: Concepts and cases* (3rd ed.). Englewood Cliffs, NJ: Prentice Hall, Ch. 2.

9. Graham, G. (2004). *Eight theories of ethics.* London, England: Routledge, Ch. 6.

10. Bowie, N. E. (2005). Kantian ethical thought. In J. W. Budd & J. G. Scoville (Eds.), *The ethics of human resources and industrial relations* (pp. 61–87). Champaign, IL: Labor and Employment Relations Association.

11. Alderman, H. (1997). By virtue of a virtue. In D. Statman (Ed.), *Virtue ethics* (pp. 145–164). Washington, DC: Georgetown University Press; Meilander, G. (1986). Virtue in contemporary religious thought. In R. J. Neuhaus (Ed.), *Virtue: Public and private* (pp. 7–30). Grand Rapids, MI: Eerdmans.

12. Material on Rawls's theory of justice, including criticism of his approach, is taken from Rawls, J. (1971). *A theory of justice.* Cambridge, MA: Belknap; Rawls, J. (1993). Distributive justice. In T. Donaldson & P. H. Werhane (Eds.), *Ethical issues in business: A philosophical approach* (4th ed., pp. 274–285). Englewood Cliffs, NJ: Prentice Hall; Rawls, J. (2001). *Justice as fairness: A restatement* (E. Kelly, Ed.). Cambridge, MA: Belknap; Velasquez; Warnke, G. (1993). *Justice and interpretation.* Cambridge, England: MIT Press, Ch. 3.

13. Rawls, J. (1993). *Political liberalism.* New York, NY: Columbia University Press.

14. Fesmire, S. (2015). *Dewey.* New York, NY: Routledge; Jacobs, D. C. (2004). A pragmatist approach to integrity in business ethics. *Journal of Management Inquiry, 13,* 215–223.

15. Margolis, J. (2006). Introduction: Pragmatism, retrospective and prospective. In J. R. Shook & J. Margolis (Eds.), *A companion to pragmatism* (pp. 1–9). Malden, MA: Blackwell.

16. Feinstein, M. (2008). John Dewey, inquiry ethics, and democracy. In C. Misak (Ed.), *The Oxford handbook of American philosophy* (pp. 87–109). Oxford, England: Oxford University Press; Nicholson, C. (2013). Education and the pragmatic temperament. In A. Malachowski (Ed.), *The Cambridge companion to pragmatism* (pp. 249–271). Cambridge, England: Cambridge University Press.

17. Alexander, T. M. (1993). John Dewey and the moral imagination: Beyond Putnam and Rorty toward a postmodern ethics. *Transactions of the Charles S. Peirce Society, 29,* 369–400.

18. Weber, E. T. (2011). What experimentalism means in ethics. *Journal of Speculative Philosophy, 25*(1), 98–115.

19. McVea, J. F. (2008). Ethics and pragmatism: John Dewey's deliberative approach. In T. Donaldson & P. H. Werhane (Eds.), *Ethical issues in business: A philosophical approach* (8th ed., pp. 89–100). Upper Saddle River, NJ: Pearson Prentice Hall.

20. Moore, E. C. (1961). *American pragmatism: Peirce, James and Dewey.* Westport CT: Greenwood Press.

21. Carden, S. D. (2006). *Virtue ethics: Dewey and Macintyre.* London, England: Continuum; Pagan, N. O. (2008). Configuring the moral self: Aristotle and Dewey. *Foundations of Science, 13,* 239–250.

22. Dewey, J. (1920). *Reconstruction in philosophy.* New York, NY: Henry Holt, p. 177.

23. Example taken from McVea, J. F. (2007). Constructing good decisions in ethically charged situations: The role of dramatic rehearsal. *Journal of Business Ethics, 70,* 375–390.

24. Yunus, M. (1998, October 31). Banker to the poor. *The Guardian.*

25. Weber.

26. Batson, C. D., Van Lange, P. A. M., Ahmad, N., & Lishner, D. A. (2003). Altruism and helping behavior. In M. A. Hogg & J. Cooper (Eds.), *The SAGE handbook of social psychology* (pp. 279–295). London, England: SAGE; Flescher, A. M., & Worthen, D. L. (2007). *The altruistic species: Scientific, philosophical, and religious perspectives of human benevolence.* Philadelphia, PA: Templeton Foundation Press; Piliavin, J. A., & Chang, H. W. (1990). Altruism: A review of recent theory and research. *American Sociological Review, 16,* 27–65.

27. Kanungo, R. N., & Mendonca, M. (1996). *Ethical dimensions of leadership.* Thousand Oaks, CA: SAGE.

28. Kanungo, R. N., & Conger, J. A. (1990). The quest for altruism in organizations. In S. Srivastra & D. L. Cooperrider (Eds.), *Appreciative management and leadership* (pp. 228–256). San Francisco, CA: Jossey-Bass.

29. Choi, Y., & Mai-Dalton, R. R. (1998). On the leadership function of self-sacrifice. *Leadership Quarterly, 9,* 475–501; Matteson, J. A., & Irving, J. A. (2006). Servant versus self-sacrificial leadership: A behavioral comparison of two follower-oriented leadership theories. *International Journal of Leadership Studies, 2,* 36–51.

30. Choi, Y., & Mai-Dalton, R. R. (1999). The model of followers' responses to self-sacrificial leadership: An empirical test. *Leadership Quarterly, 10,* 397–421; De Cremer, D. (2006). Affective and motivational consequences of leader self-sacrifice: The moderating effect of autocratic leadership. *Leadership Quarterly, 17,* 79–93; De Cremer, D., & van Knippenberg, D. (2004). Leader self-sacrifice and leadership effectiveness: The moderating role of leader self-confidence. *Organizational Behavior and Human Decision Processes, 95,* 140–155.

31. Cheng, M-Y., & Wang, L. (2015). The mediating effect of ethical climate on the relationship between paternalistic leadership and team identification: A team-level analysis in the Chinese context. *Journal of Business Ethics, 129,* 639–654; Erben, G. S., & Guneser, A. B. (2007). The relationship between paternalistic leadership and organizational commitment: Investigating the role of climate regarding ethics. *Journal of Business Ethics, 82,* 955–968; Otken, A. B., & Cenkci, T. (2012). The impact of paternalistic leadership on ethical climate: The moderating role of trust in leader. *Journal of Business Ethics, 108,* 525–536; Pellegrini, E. K., & Scandura, T. A. (2008). Paternalistic leadership: A review and agenda for future research. *Journal of Management, 34,* 566–593.

Ethical Decision Making and Behavior

6

If it ain't got emotion, it ain't got moral swing.

—**NEUROSCIENTIST MARC HAUSER**

As we practice resolving dilemmas, we find ethics to be less a goal than a pathway, less a destination than a trip, less an inoculation than a process.

—**ETHICIST RUSHWORTH KIDDER**

WHAT'S AHEAD

This chapter begins with a look the role of reason and emotion in ethical decision making. It then surveys the components of ethical behavior—moral sensitivity, moral judgment, moral motivation, and moral character—and introduces systematic approaches to ethical problem solving. We'll take a look at four decision-making formats: Kidder's ethical checkpoints, Nash's 12 questions, the Lonergan/Baird method and the Foursquare protocol. After presenting each approach, I'll discuss its relative advantages and disadvantages.

Understanding how we make and follow through on ethical decisions is the first step to making better choices; taking a systematic approach is the second. We'll explore both of these steps in this chapter. After examining the ethical decision-making process, we'll see how guidelines or formats can guide our ethical deliberations.

ETHICAL DECISION MAKING: A DUAL PROCESS APPROACH

For decades, scholars viewed ethical decision making as a cognitive process. Moral psychologists, ethicists, and ethics educators focused on how individuals consciously use logic and reason to solve ethical problems. They assumed that leaders reach their conclusions after careful deliberation. Researchers ignored emotions or treated them with suspicion because feelings could undermine moral reasoning.

In recent years, a growing number of scholars have challenged the cognitive approach to ethical decision making. One critic is psychologist Jonathan Haidt.[1] He argues that we quickly make ethical determinations and then use logic after the fact to justify our choices. Haidt points to *moral dumbfounding* as evidence that moral decision making is the product of intuition, not deliberation. In moral dumbfounding, leaders and followers have strong opinions about right or wrong but can't explain why they feel as they do. For example, when he asked Americans if eating the family dog for dinner was morally wrong, most people felt disgusted but were at a loss to explain why they felt this way.

Haidt calls his approach to ethical decision making the *social intuitionist model* to highlight the role that intuition and social norms play in moral determinations. He argues that automatic processes are the elephant and logic is the rider. In most cases, the elephant goes where it wants to go, though the rider can occasionally steer the pachyderm in a different direction. Our instantaneous intuitions about right and wrong are the product of social forces like our cultural background. For example, dogs are routinely eaten in some societies. In these cultures, which don't treat pets as family members, respondents would approve of eating a dog for dinner. (For more information on cultural differences in core values, see Chapter 11.) Haidt doesn't completely eliminate reason from his model. Other people may challenge our intuitions, introducing new information and arguments that change our initial position. Or we may modify our attitudes based on self-reflection. Other investigators suggest that we engage in automatic responses when reacting to moral violations, like eating the family dog. We employ conscious reasoning when reflecting on complex dilemmas like whether or not to raise the minimum wage.[2]

Researchers in cognitive neuroscience or neuroethics are also challenging the notion that ethical thinking is devoid of emotion.[3] One group of scientists employs the medical case study method. These researchers study individuals with brain damage who engage in antisocial and unethical behavior as a result of their injuries. One early case study involved Phineas Gage, an eighteenth-century railway worker who was injured when a railroad spike went through his skull. Gage retained his reasoning abilities (his IQ was left intact) but lost his emotional capacities. Following the accident, he was unable to keep a job or to make wise decisions due to his emotional deficit. He also demonstrated disrespect for others and a lack of self-control. The same pattern has been found among contemporary patients who suffer damage to the emotional regions of the brain.

Another group of neuroscientists uses neuroimaging to determine which areas of the brain are activated when we are faced with ethical choices. Participants are placed in MRI machines and presented with ethical dilemmas. For instance, they may be asked whether it is okay for a pregnant teen to dump her newborn in a trash can or whether a mother, in order to save the lives of others, should smother her baby to stop its crying. Active brain cells require more oxygen than inactive ones, indicating which parts of the brain are in use when volunteers are responding to moral problems. Neuroimaging studies reveal that ethical decision making is not localized in one portion of the brain but involves several different regions. Ethical thinking activates both cognitive and emotional areas of the brain.

Taking a dual process approach is one way to sort through the relationship between logic and intuition.[4] The dual process perspective is based on the premise that both logic and emotion are essential to making good ethical choices. When faced with a moral dilemma, we need our emotions and intuitions as well as our cognitive abilities. A gut feeling may prompt us to reexamine our initial conclusion, for instance, or reveal aspects of the situation our reason ignored. As neuroscientists have discovered, we can't make good ethical choices without employing our feelings. However, our intuitions and emotions can be wrong. They may be based on mistaken cultural beliefs, for example. Many

Americans used to immediately condemn interracial couples. As time passed, society recognized that this reaction was biased, unfounded, and unjust. Then, too, logic is essential when wrestling with dilemmas that involve competing values or that pit one good option against another (see later in the chapter).[5]

One way to draw on both reason and feeling is to record your initial reaction to an ethical dilemma. When confronted with ethical scenarios like those presented later in the chapter, write down your initial reaction. Then use the decision-making formats and other cognitive tools to test your immediate response. When you're finished, compare your final decision to your initial reaction. Your ultimate conclusion after following a series of steps may be the same as your first judgment. Or you might find that you come to a significantly different decision. (You may also want to test your conclusion to see if it "feels" right.) In any case, you should be more comfortable with your solution because your deliberations were informed both by your experiences, emotions, and intuitions as well as by your conscious reasoning. To assist you in dual processing, I'll be introducing research findings from both the cognitive and intuitionist traditions in the next section of the chapter.

COMPONENTS OF MORAL ACTION

There are a number of models of ethical decision making and action. For example, business ethics educators Charles Powers and David Vogel identify six factors or elements that underlie moral reasoning and behavior that are particularly relevant in organizational settings.[6] The first is *moral imagination,* the recognition that even routine choices and relationships have an ethical dimension. The second is *moral identification and ordering,* which, as the name suggests, refers to the ability to identify important issues, determine priorities, and sort out competing values. The third factor is *moral evaluation,* using analytical skills to evaluate options. The fourth element is *tolerating moral disagreement and ambiguity,* which arises when managers disagree about values and courses of action. The fifth is the ability to *integrate managerial competence with moral competence.* This integration involves anticipating possible ethical dilemmas, leading others in ethical decision making, and making sure any decision becomes part of an organization's systems and procedures. The sixth and final element is a sense of *moral obligation,* which serves as a motivating force to engage in moral judgment and to implement decisions.

James Rest of the University of Minnesota developed what may be the most widely used model of moral behavior. Rest built his four-component model by working backward. He started with the end product—moral action—and then determined the steps that produce such behavior. He concluded that ethical action is the result of four psychological subprocesses: (1) moral sensitivity (recognition), (2) moral judgment, (3) moral focus (motivation), and (4) moral character.[7]

Component 1: Moral Sensitivity (Recognition)

Moral sensitivity (recognizing the presence of an ethical issue) is the first step in ethical decision making because we can't solve a moral problem unless we first know that one exists. A great many moral failures stem from ethical insensitivity. The safety committee at Ford Motor decided not to fix the defective gas tank on the Pinto automobile (see Chapter 2) because members saw no problem with saving money rather than human lives. Toshiba overstated earnings for seven years as managers concentrated on reaching high quarterly goals instead of on maintaining the company's previously high ethical standards.[8] Many students, focused on finishing their degrees, see no problem with cheating. (You can test your ethical sensitivity by completing Self-Assessment 6.1 at the end of the chapter.)

According to Rest, problem recognition requires that we consider how our behavior affects others, identify possible courses of action, and determine the consequences of each potential strategy. Empathy and perspective skills are essential to this component of moral action. If we understand how others might feel or react, we are more sensitive to potential negative effects of our choices and can better predict the likely outcomes of each option.

A number of factors prevent us from recognizing ethical issues. We may not factor ethical considerations into our typical ways of thinking or mental models.[9] We may be reluctant to use moral terminology—*values, justice, right, wrong*—to describe our decisions because we want to avoid controversy or because we believe that keeping silent will make us appear strong and capable.[10] We may even deceive ourselves into thinking that we are acting morally when we are clearly not, a process called *ethical fading*. The moral aspects of a decision fade into the background if we use euphemisms to disguise unethical behavior, numb our consciences through repeated misbehavior, blame others, and claim that only we know the "truth."[11]

Fortunately, we can take steps to enhance our ethical sensitivity (and the sensitivity of our fellow leaders and followers) by doing the following:

- Using active listening and role playing
- Imagining other perspectives
- Stepping back from a situation to determine whether it has moral implications
- Using moral terminology to discuss problems and issues
- Avoiding euphemisms
- Refusing to excuse misbehavior
- Accepting personal responsibility
- Practicing humility and openness to other points of view

In addition to these steps, we can also increase ethical sensitivity by making an issue more salient. The greater the moral intensity of an issue, the more likely it is that decision makers will take note of it and respond ethically.[12] We can build moral intensity by doing the following:

- Illustrating that the situation can cause significant harm or benefit to many people (magnitude of consequences)
- Establishing that there is social consensus or agreement that a behavior is moral or immoral (e.g., legal or illegal, approved or forbidden by a professional association)

- Demonstrating probability of effect, that the act will happen and will cause harm or benefit
- Showing that the consequences will happen soon (temporal immediacy)
- Emphasizing social, psychological, physical, or psychological closeness (proximity) with those affected by our actions
- Proving that one person or a group will greatly suffer due to a decision (concentration of effect)

Finally, paying attention to our emotions can be an important clue that we are faced with an ethical dilemma. Moral emotions are part of our makeup as humans.[13] These feelings are triggered even when we do not have a personal stake in an event. For example, we may feel angry when reading about mistreatment of migrant workers or sympathy when we see a picture of a refugee living in a squalid camp. Moral emotions also encourage us to take action that benefits other people and society as a whole. We might write a letter protesting the poor working conditions of migrant laborers, for instance, or send money to a humanitarian organization working with displaced persons.

Anger, disgust, and contempt are *other-condemning* emotions. They are elicited by unfairness, betrayal, immorality, cruelty, poor performance, and status differences. Anger can motivate us to redress injustices like racism, oppression, and poverty. Disgust encourages us to set up rewards and punishments to deter inappropriate behaviors. Contempt generally causes us to step back from others. Shame, embarrassment, and guilt are *self-conscious emotions* that encourage us to obey the rules and uphold the social order. These feelings are triggered when we violate norms and social conventions, present the wrong image to others, and fail to live up to moral guidelines. Shame and embarrassment can keep us from engaging in further damaging behavior and may drive us to withdraw from social contact. Guilt motivates us to help others and to treat them well.

Sympathy and compassion are *other-suffering emotions.* They are elicited when we perceive suffering or sorrow in our fellow human beings. Such feelings encourage us to comfort, help, and alleviate the pain of others. Gratitude, awe, and elevation are *other-praising (positive) emotions* that open us up to new opportunities and relationships. They are prompted when someone has done something on our behalf, when we run across moral beauty (acts of charity, loyalty, and self-sacrifice, for example), and when we read or hear about moral exemplars (see Chapter 3). Gratitude motivates us to repay others; awe and elevation encourage us to become better persons and to take steps to help others.

In sum, if we experience anger, disgust, guilt, sympathy, or other moral emotions, the chances are good that there is an ethical dimension to the situation that confronts us. We will need to look further to determine if this is indeed the case.

Component 2: Moral Judgment

Once an ethical problem is identified, decision makers select a course of action from the options generated in Component 1. In other words, they make judgments about what is the right or wrong thing to do in this situation.

Moral judgment has generated more research than the other components of Rest's model. Investigators have been particularly interested in (1) cognitive moral development, the process by which people develop their moral reasoning abilities over time, and (2) biases or errors that undermine the decision making process.

Cognitive Moral Development

Harvard psychologist Lawrence Kohlberg argued that individuals progress through a series of moral stages just as they do physical ones.[14] Each stage is more advanced than the one before. Not only do people engage in more complex reasoning as they progress up the stages, but they also become less self-centered and develop broader definitions of morality.

Kohlberg identified three levels of moral development, each divided into two stages. Level I, *preconventional thinking*, is the most primitive and focuses on consequences. This form of moral reasoning is common among children who choose to obey to avoid punishment (Stage 1) or follow the rules in order to meet their interests (Stage 2). Stage 2 thinkers are interested in getting a fair deal: You help me, and I'll help you.

Conventional thinkers (Level II) look to others for guidance when deciding how to act. Stage 3 people want to live up to the expectations of those they respect, such as parents, siblings, and friends, and value concern for others and respect. Stage 4 individuals take a somewhat broader perspective, looking to society as a whole for direction. They believe in following rules at work and the law, for example. Kohlberg found that most adults are Level II thinkers.

Level III, *post-conceptual* or *principled reasoning*, is the most advanced type of ethical thinking. Stage 5 people are guided by utilitarian principles. They are concerned for the needs of the entire group and want to make sure that rules and laws serve the greatest good for the greatest number. Stage 6 people operate according to internalized, universal principles such as justice, equality, and human dignity. These principles consistently guide their behavior and take precedence over the laws of any particular society. According to Kohlberg, fewer than 20% of American adults ever reach Stage 5, and almost no one reaches Stage 6.

Critics take issue with both the philosophical foundation of Kohlberg's model and its reliance on concrete stages of moral development.[15] They contend that Kohlberg based his postconventional stage on Rawls's justice-as-fairness theory and made deontological ethics superior to other ethical approaches. They note that the model applies more to societal issues than to individual ethical decisions. A great many psychologists challenge the notion that people go through a rigid or hard series of moral stages, leaving one stage completely behind before moving to the next. They argue instead that a person can engage in many ways of thinking about a problem, regardless of age.

Rest (who studied under Kohlberg), Darcia Narvaez, and their colleagues responded to the critics by replacing the hard stages with a staircase of developmental schemas.[16] Schemas are networks of knowledge organized around life events. We use schemas when encountering new situations or information. You are able to master information in new classes, for instance, by using strategies you developed in previous courses. According to this "neo-Kohlbergian" approach, decision makers develop more sophisticated moral schemas as they develop. The least sophisticated schema is based on *personal interest*. People at this level are concerned only with what they may gain or lose in an ethical dilemma. No consideration is given to the needs of broader society.

Those who reason at the next level, the *maintaining norms* schema, believe they have a moral obligation to maintain social order. They are concerned with following rules and laws and making sure that regulations apply to everyone. These thinkers believe that there is a clear hierarchy with carefully defined roles (e.g., bosses–subordinates, teachers–students, officers–enlisted personnel). The *postconventional* schema is the most advanced level of moral reasoning. Thinking at this level is not limited to one ethical approach, as Kohlberg argued, but encompasses many different philosophical traditions. Postconventional individuals believe that moral obligations are to be based on shared ideals, should not favor some people at the expense of others, and are open to scrutiny (testing and examination). Such thinkers reason act like moral philosophers, looking behind societal norms to determine whether they serve moral purposes.

Rest developed the Defining Issues Test (DIT) to measure moral development. Subjects taking the DIT (and its successor, the DIT-2) respond to ethical scenarios and then choose statements that best reflect the reasoning they used to come up with their choices. These statements, which correspond to the three levels of moral reasoning, are then scored. In the best-known dilemma, a man's wife is dying of cancer and needs a drug he cannot afford to buy. He must decide whether to steal the drug to save her life.

Hundreds of studies using the DIT reveal that moral reasoning generally increases with age and education.[17] Undergraduate and graduate students benefit from their educational experiences in general and ethical coursework in particular. When education stops, moral development stops. In addition, moral development is a universal concept, crossing cultural boundaries. Principled leaders can boost the moral judgment of a group by encouraging members to adopt more sophisticated ethical schemas.[18]

Models of cognitive development provide important insights into the process of ethical decision making. First, contextual variables play an important role in shaping ethical behavior. Most people look to others as well as to rules and regulations when making ethical determinations. They are more likely to make wise moral judgments if coworkers and supervisors encourage and model ethical behavior. As leaders, we need to build ethical environments. (We'll take a closer look at the formation of ethical groups and organizations in Chapters 9 and 10.) Second, education fosters moral reasoning. Pursuing a bachelor's, master's, or doctoral degree can promote your moral development. As part of your education, focus as much attention as you can on ethics (i.e., take ethics courses, discuss ethical issues in groups and classes, reflect on the ethical challenges you experience in internships). Third, a broader perspective is better. Consider the needs and viewpoints of others outside your immediate group or organization; determine what is good for the local area, the larger society, and the global community. Fourth, moral principles produce superior solutions. The best ethical thinkers base their choices on widely accepted ethical guidelines. Do the same by drawing on important ethical approaches such as utilitarianism, the categorical imperative, altruism, the ethic of care, and justice-as-fairness theory.

Ethical Blind Spots

Harvard professor Max Bazerman and his colleagues believe that unethical choices are often the result of unconscious distortions. These ethical blind spots cause us to participate in or approve of behaviors we would normally condemn. Significant biases include the following:[19]

1. *Overestimating our ethicality.* Studies consistently demonstrate that, when it comes to ethics, we have an inflated opinion of ourselves. We boldly predict, for example, that we will do the right thing when faced with an ethical dilemma. Unfortunately, we

often fall well short of our predictions. This was illustrated by a study of female college students who were asked how they would respond to inappropriate job interview questions like whether they had a boyfriend or whether they think it is appropriate for women to wear a bra to work. Sixty to seventy percent of the participants said they would refuse to answer these questions, challenge the interviewer, or tell him that such queries were inappropriate. However, when a male interviewer actually asked them the offensive questions, none refused to answer. At the end of the session, only a few participants asked the interviewer why he had posed these queries.[20]

Our belief in our inherent goodness may blind us to potential conflicts of interests that can undermine our objectivity and influence our choices. Consider the case of former Vice President Dick Cheney and former Supreme Court Justice Antonin Scalia, for example. The two went duck hunting for a week shortly after the court agreed to hear a case involving Cheney, who was fighting demands that he release documents from the Bush administration's energy task force. Several legal experts said that Scalia should remove himself from the case, since his relationship with the vice president might influence his judgment. In response, Scalia declared: "I do not think my impartiality could reasonably be questioned." Justice Scalia sided with Cheney in the majority decision that allowed the vice president to keep the task force information secret.[21]

2. *Forgiving our own unethical behavior.* Driven by the desire to be moral and behave ethically, we feel a sense of psychological tension called *cognitive dissonance* when we fall short of our ethical standards (i.e., lying when we believe that we are honest). Our "want self" (our desire for status, money, etc.) overcomes our "should self" (who we think we ought to be ethically). To relieve the distress generated when our actions and self-images don't match, we either change our behavior or excuse what we've done. We may convince ourselves that the objectionable behavior was really morally permissible (see the discussion of moral disengagement in Chapter 2). We blame the boss or claim that we were just following orders or that everyone else is doing it. The "everybody is doing it" excuse was used to justify the use of steroids and other performance-enhancing drugs in major league baseball and professional cycling. We may also become "revisionist historians." Using selective recall, we remember events in a way that supports our decisions. We recollect the times we stood up to an unjust boss or told the truth; we forget the times we caved into pressure from a supervisor or lied to make a sale or to get a job.

3. *In-group favoritism.* Doing favors for people we know that share our nationality, neighborhood, religion, social class, or alma mater seems harmless. We may ask our neighbor to hire our son or daughter, for example, or recommend a sorority sister for an overseas program. Trouble comes because when those in power give resources to members of their in-groups, they discriminate against those who are different from them. Caucasian loan officers who relax lending standards for white applicants may end up refusing loans to better-qualified black applicants, therefore hurting the bank's bottom line. In-group favoritism can also prompt us to excuse other's unethical behavior. For example, when basketball players on our team knock opponents to the court, they are "playing hard." When players on the other team knock our team members to the floor, they are "playing dirty." We are particularly willing to forgive shortcomings when we benefit from the choices they have made. Many bank and hedge fund managers funneled money into Bernie Madoff's fraudulent investment fund, the biggest swindle in history,

even though the returns he promised were statistically impossible. They likely ignored the danger signs because they were earning generous fees from Madoff.

4. *Implicit prejudice.* Implicit prejudice is different from visible or explicit forms of prejudice like racism or sexism. Individuals are not generally aware of these biases, which are based on our tendency to associate things that generally go together, like thunder and rain and wealthy people and luxury cars. However, these associations are not always accurate. Thunder doesn't always bring rain and not all high-income individuals drive expensive vehicles. Unconscious biases can undermine ethical decision making. Take hiring decisions, for instance. Personnel managers are likely to exclude qualified applicants if they assume that someone with a physical disability is also mentally challenged or that women can't fill traditionally masculine jobs.

5. *Judging based on outcomes, not the process.* Two leaders can follow the same process when making a decision but we typically judge them differently based on their results. When the decision turns out well, we consider her or him successful. If the outcome is poor, we believe the leader is a failure. Nevertheless, just because a poorly made decision had positive consequences in one case doesn't mean that following the same process will have positive results the next time. In fact, poor decision-making procedures eventually produce bad (unethical) results. Officials at the Peanut Corporation of America repeatedly shipped tainted peanut products. Few, if any, people got sick. However, the last shipment of contaminated products in 2009 eventually caused eight deaths and sickened thousands more.[22] The chief executive officer (CEO) was later sentenced to prison.

Bazerman and his colleagues argue that our good intentions and our determination to act ethically won't be enough to overcome these biases because we aren't aware of them. Instead, we need to acknowledge these blind spots. Admit that that you aren't as ethical and unbiased as you believe, for instance, and that you have a tendency to forgive your ethical misbehavior and that of other group members. Then take steps to combat these ethical distortions. Publicly commit yourself to an ethical course of action ahead of time so your "should" self doesn't get overwhelmed by your "want" self in the heat of the moment. Focus on the moral principles involved in a choice, not on the immediate benefit you might receive. Put yourself in environments that challenge your implicit stereotypes. Include a wider variety of people in the decision-making process; consider a wider variety of job applicants. Audit your organization to determine if it is trapped by in-group biases and eliminate programs that perpetuate the hiring and promotion of those of similar backgrounds. Step behind the veil of ignorance (see Chapter 5) to make more equitable choices. Evaluate the quality of the decision-making process, not the outcome; don't condemn those who make good, quality decisions only to see them turn out badly.

Component 3: Moral Focus (Motivation)

After concluding what course of action is best, decision makers must be focused (motivated to follow through) on their choices. Moral values often conflict with other significant values. For instance, an accountant who wants to blow the whistle on illegal accounting practices at her firm must balance her desire to do the right thing against her desire to keep her job, provide income for her family, and maintain relationships with her fellow workers. She will report the accounting abuses to outside authorities only if moral considerations take precedence over these competing priorities. It's no wonder, then, that there is often a significant gap between knowing and doing, between moral judgment (Component 3) and moral action (Components 3 and 4). Scores on the DIT explain only 20% of the variance in subsequent ethical behavior.[23]

Developing *moral potency* is one way to address the moral thought–action gap.[24] Moral potency is a psychological state or resource made up of moral ownership, moral courage, and moral efficacy. Moral ownership occurs when individuals believe that their teams, organizations, and communities are extensions of themselves. This sense of ownership increases their obligation to behave in an ethical manner. Thus, a project manager who identifies strongly with his team will view status reports as a symbol of his own ethicality. He has a strong motivation to see that such reports are accurate. Moral courage provides the impetus to act despite outside pressures and adversity. Moral efficacy is a leader's belief or confidence that he or she has the ability to carry out the plan of action. For instance, a manager may determine that a high-performing salesperson should be fired for submitting bogus expense reports. Yet, she won't take action if she doesn't think she has the support of top company leaders or if she believes she doesn't have the necessary skills to confront the individual.

As a capability or capacity, moral potency can be developed in ourselves as well as in our followers. (The "Focus on Follower Ethics: Intelligent Disobedience" box provides a closer look at how subordinates can exercise their moral potency.) To foster moral ownership, clarify the ethical responsibilities associated with each organizational role. Identify and commit to professional codes and values while encouraging others to do the same. To develop moral courage, look to courageous leaders as role models and seek to be a courageous role model yourself. (See Chapter 3.) Build in organizational cues that encourage courageous actions. Cadets at U.S. Military Academy at West Point, for instance, must sign an honor code that states they "will not lie, cheat or steal" but also that they will not "tolerate those that do." The second part of the honor code requires cadets to display moral courage if they witness unethical behavior. They are disciplined or removed from the Academy if they fail to do so. To develop moral efficacy, take on increasingly difficult ethical challenges and then debrief them to evaluate your responses. Learn from how others have handled ethical dilemmas. Prepare for ethical challenges through simulations, cases, discussions, and training. The moral efficacy of your followers is directly tied to your moral efficacy as a leader. If you are confident that you can effectively deal with moral problems, your followers will also be confident they can handle such situations.

Psychologists report that self-interest and hypocrisy undermine moral motivation.[25] Sometimes individuals genuinely want to do the right thing, but their integrity is overpowered when they discover that they will have to pay a personal cost for acting in an ethical manner. Others never intend to follow an ethical course of action but engage in *moral hypocrisy* instead. These decision makers "want to appear moral while, if possible, avoiding the cost of actually being moral."[26] In experimental settings, they say that assignments should be distributed fairly but then assign themselves the most desirable tasks while giving less desirable chores to others. Both self-interest and hypocrisy encourage leaders to set their moral principles aside. For example, corporate executives may declare that lower-level employees deserve higher wages. However, whether they really want to help workers or just want to appear as if they do, these executives are not likely to pay employees more if it means that they will earn less as a result.

Rewards play an important role in ethical follow-through. People are prone to give ethical values top priority when rewarded through raises, promotions, public recognition, and other means for doing so. Conversely, moral motivation drops when the reward system reinforces unethical behavior.[27] Unfortunately, misplaced rewards are all too common, as in the case of electronics retailers who reward employees for selling expensive extended warranties on new products. Such warranties are generally a bad deal for consumers.

Emotions also play a part in moral motivation.[28] As noted earlier, sympathy, disgust, guilt, and other moral emotions prompt us to take action. We can use their motivational force to help us punish wrongdoers, address injustice, provide assistance, and so on. Other researchers report that positive emotions such as joy and happiness encourage people to live out their moral choices and to help others. Depression, on the other hand, lowers motivation, and jealousy, rage, and envy contribute to lying, revenge, stealing, and other antisocial behaviors.

You can channel the power of rewards and emotions to increase your moral motivation and the moral motivation of those you lead. Seek out and create ethically rewarding environments. Make sure the reward system of an organization supports ethical behavior before joining it as an employee or a volunteer. Try to reduce the costs of behaving morally by instituting policies and procedures that make it easier to report unethical behavior, combat discrimination, and so forth. Work to align rewards with desired behavior. (We'll take an in-depth look at ethical climate in Chapter 10.) Be concerned about how goals are reached. If all else fails, reward yourself. Take pride in following through on your choices and on living up to your self-image as a person of integrity. Finally, tap into moral emotions. Make a conscious effort to control negative feelings and to put yourself in a positive frame of mind.

Component 4: Moral Character

Executing the plan of action takes character. The positive virtues described in Chapter 3 contribute to ethical follow-through. Courage helps leaders implement their plans despite the risks and costs of doing so while prudence helps them choose the best course of action. Integrity encourages leaders to be true to themselves and their choices. Humility forces leaders to address limitations that might prevent them from taking action. Optimism equips leaders to persist in the face of obstacles and difficulties. Compassion and justice focus the attention of leaders on the needs of others rather than on personal priorities.

In addition to virtues, other personal qualities contribute to moral action.[29] Those with a strong will, as well as confidence in themselves and their abilities, are more likely to persist. The same is true for those with an internal locus of control. Internally oriented people (*internals*) believe that they have control over their lives and can determine what happens to them. Externally oriented people (*externals*) believe that life events are beyond their control and are the product of fate or luck instead. Because they take personal responsibility for their actions, internals are more motivated to do what is right. Externals are more susceptible to situational pressures and therefore less likely to persist in ethical tasks.

Duty orientation is another characteristic linked to moral behavior. Those driven by duty make and act on ethical decisions based largely on their loyalty to the group. They are willing to give up some of their free choice in order to fulfil their obligations.[30]

Focus on Follower Ethics

INTELLIGENT DISOBEDIENCE

Executive coach and consultant Ira Chaleff believes that a great many scandals could be avoided if followers knew when and how to disobey unethical or misguided orders from their leaders. He argues that followers need to learn to practice "intelligent disobedience." The concept of intelligent disobedience comes from guide dog training. Guide dogs for the blind must not only follow the directions of their owners but must also know when to disobey commands that would put both dog and human in harm's way, such as an order to cross the street when a car is coming. Practicing intelligent disobedience is a four-step process: (1) understand the mission, values, and goals of the organization or group; (2) pause and examine any order that seems inconstant with the mission, values, and goals; (3) make a conscious choice to comply or resist the order, offering an alternative when possible; and (4) assume personal accountability for your choice to obey or disobey.

Chaleff notes that, in most cases, obedience is the right option that allows us to benefit from living in communities and organizations. Yet, followers far too often give in to pressure to overstate earnings, falsify student test scores, underreport safety violations, and so on. Some practical suggestions for resisting an unethical order include pausing to gather your thoughts, asking relevant questions, pointing out how the order isn't in the best interest of the leader or the group, and refusing to participate with the leader (and accepting the consequences of doing so). Teachers and supervisors can help children and employees develop refusal skills through discussions, simulations, practice sessions, role-plays, and stories of followers who practiced intelligent disobedience.

The tale of a young nurse provides one dramatic example of intelligent disobedience in action. Her first job out of nursing school was in a hospital emergency room. When a cardiac patient was wheeled in, the emergency room physician ordered her to administer a medication she knew would kill the patient. When she questioned the order, the doctor yelled at her: "You just do it!" The nurse hooked up the IV bag with medication and told the physician it was ready. However, she said she couldn't open valve on the IV bag because it violated her training. He would have to do so himself. Her resistance was enough to prompt the doctor to reconsider the risks and other options. He ordered a different medication and the patient made a complete recovery.

Source: Chaleff, I. (2015). *Intelligent disobedience: Doing right when what you're told to do is wrong.* Oakland, CA: Berrett-Koehler.

Researchers using samples drawn from the U.S. Army, the National Guard, federal employees, and the corporate sector found that a sense of obligation promotes prosocial behaviors while limiting deviant acts. Duty orientation is made up of three dimensions: (1) duty to members, (2) duty to mission, and (3) duty to codes. Duty to members involves supporting and serving the other members of the group, even at cost to the self. Those driven by their obligations to others may mentor a new hire, defend a team member from gossip, donate unused vacation time to an ill coworker, and refuse to share proprietary information with a competitor. Duty to mission means supporting the work and purpose of the group by doing what it takes to see that the group or organization succeeds. This might mean working additional hours or taking on additional responsibilities, for instance. Duty to codes is consistent adherence to rules and norms of the group. Formal codes of ethics (see Chapter 10) lay out rules regarding treatment of others both inside and outside the organization. Norms are the unwritten guidelines that direct behavior. Examples might include "always work your hardest," "admit your mistakes," and "treat all colleagues with respect." Violating formal codes and informal norms brings dishonor to the self and the group. (You can determine your level of duty orientation by completing Self-Assessment 6.2.)

Successful implementation of a decision also requires competence. For instance, modifying the organizational reward system may entail researching, organizing, arguing, networking, and relationship-building skills. These skills are put to maximum use when actors have an in-depth understanding of the organizational context—important policies, the group's history and culture, informal leaders, and so on.

Following the virtue and character-building guidelines presented in Chapter 3 will go a long way to helping you build the virtues you need to put your moral choices into action. Believe that you can have an impact. Otherwise, you are probably not going to carry through when obstacles surface. Develop your skills so that you can better put your moral choice into action and master the context in which you operate. (Turn to Box 6.1 for more suggestions on how to follow through on your ethical choices.) Consider how you might improve your commitment to your group or organization. Finally, practice ethical leadership to encourage followers to develop a duty orientation. Your followers are more likely to feel a sense of obligation if you act as a moral role model, set clear ethical rules and structures, communicate what ethical behaviors are expected, and focus on shared goals.

Box 6.1 Giving Voice to Values

The Giving Voice to Values program is an international effort designed to help participants resist the pressure to set aside their personal standards. Mary Gentile, director of the Giving Voice to Values curriculum, argues that the first step to acting on personal moral standards (developing "moral muscle") is to conduct a thought experiment. Ask, "What if you were going to act on your values—what would you say and do?" (p. xxxv). She then outlines seven pillars or foundational concepts that equip us to act on our ethical choices.

1. *Recognize that certain values are widely shared.* Identifying shared values like courage, compassion, integrity, and wisdom can provide the foundation for resolving values conflicts and for developing shared goals in a variety of cultural settings.

2. *Acknowledge the power of choice.* Most of us can think of a time when we acted on our ethical beliefs or, conversely, failed to do so. Telling the story of both events reveals that we have the power to choose. These narratives help us identify factors that contributed to success in the first case (enablers) and failure in the

(Continued)

(Continued)

second (disablers). Gentile reports that some common enablers include finding allies, gathering information, asking questions, taking incremental steps, and reframing (i.e., redefining ethical misbehavior as a risk, turning competition into a win–win negotiation.)

3. *Treat values conflicts as normal.* Disagreements over ethical choices are common in organizations. If we acknowledge that fact, then we won't be surprised when such disputes arise and will remain calm. We'll also find it easier to appreciate the viewpoint of the other parties instead of vilifying them.

4. *Consider your personal and professional purpose.* Before values conflicts arise, consider the impact you want to have in your job and career. Thinking about why you work and the mission of your organization can provide new arguments to use when voicing values. You'll feel more empowered to speak up, and others may be attracted to your purpose.

5. *Play to personal strengths.* We are more likely to speak up if we know who we are. Acting on values then arises out of our core identity. In addition to identifying your personal purpose, consider the degree of risk you are willing to take, your personal communication style, where your loyalties lie, and your image of yourself. Create a personal narrative or self-story that builds on your strengths and encourages you to act on your convictions.

6. *Find your unique voice.* Expressing values is a learnable skill. There are many different ways to speak out about values in the work setting. Find and develop yours through reflection on your experience, practice (each time you speak up builds moral muscle), and coaching from mentors and peers. When you voice your values as a leader, you encourage your followers to do the same.

7. *Anticipate rationalizations for unethical behavior.* Consider the most likely arguments used to support immoral behavior. Common rationalizations include "Everyone does this; it's standard practice" and "This is not my responsibility; I'm just following orders." Then consider how to best respond. For example, the "everybody is doing it" argument is an exaggeration since (a) not everyone engages in the practice, and (b) if it were standard practice, then there wouldn't be a law against it. The "just following orders" argument reveals that the speaker is uncomfortable with her or his response to the situation and should be open to further discussion.

Source: Gentile, M. C. (2010). *Giving voice to values: How to speak your mind when you know what's right*. New Haven, CT: Yale University Press. For additional information, visit http://www.givingvoicetovalues .com.

DECISION-MAKING FORMATS

Decision-making guidelines or formats can help us make better ethical choices. Taking a systematic approach encourages teams and individuals to carefully define the problem, gather information, apply ethical standards and values, identify and evaluate alternative courses of action, and follow through on their choices. They're also better equipped to defend their decisions. Four ethical decision-making formats are described in the pages to come. I'll provide a balance sheet for each format, outlining its strengths and weaknesses (pros and cons). All four approaches are useful. You may want to use just one or a combination of all of them. The particular format you use is not as important as using a systematic approach to moral reasoning. You can practice these guidelines by applying them to the scenarios described at the end of the chapter.

Kidder's Ethical Checkpoints

Ethicist Rushworth Kidder suggested that nine steps or checkpoints can help bring order to otherwise confusing ethical issues.[31]

1. *Recognize that there is a problem.* This step is critically important because it forces us to acknowledge that there is an issue that deserves our attention and helps us separate moral questions from disagreements about manners and social conventions. For example, being late for a party may be bad manners and violate cultural expectations. However, this act does not translate into a moral problem involving right or wrong. On the other hand, deciding whether to accept a kickback from a supplier is an ethical dilemma.

2. *Determine the actor.* Once we've determined that there is an ethical issue, we then need to decide who is responsible for addressing the problem. I may be concerned that the owner of a local business treats his employees poorly. Nonetheless, unless I work for the company or buy its products, there is little I can do to address this situation.

3. *Gather the relevant facts.* Adequate, accurate, and current information is important for making effective decisions of all kinds, including ethical ones. Details do make a difference. In deciding whether it is just to suspend a student for fighting, for instance, a school principal will want to hear from teachers, classmates, and the offender to determine the seriousness of the offense, the student's reason for fighting, and the outcome of the altercation. The administrator will probably be more lenient if this is the offender's first offense and he was defending himself.

4. *Test for right-versus-wrong issues.* A choice is generally a poor one if it gives you a negative, gut-level reaction (the stench test); would make you uncomfortable if it appeared on the front page of tomorrow's newspaper (the front-page test); or would violate the moral code of someone that you care a lot about (the Mom test). If your decision violates any of these criteria, you had better reconsider.

5. *Test for right-versus-right values.* Many ethical dilemmas pit two core values against each other. Determine whether two good or right values are in conflict with one another in this situation. Right-versus-right value clashes include the following:

- Truth telling versus loyalty to others and institutions. Telling the truth may threaten our allegiance to another person or to an organization, such as when leaders and followers are faced with the decision of whether or not to blow the whistle on organizational misbehavior. Kidder believes that truth versus loyalty is the most common type of conflict involving two deeply held values.
- Personal needs versus the needs of the community. Our desire to serve our immediate group or ourselves can run counter to the needs of the larger group or community.
- Short-term benefits versus long-term negative consequences. Sometimes satisfying the immediate needs of the group (giving a hefty pay raise to employees, for example) can lead to long-term negative consequences (endangering the future of the business).
- Justice versus mercy. Being fair and even-handed may conflict with our desire to show love and compassion.

6. *Apply the ethical standards and perspectives.* Apply the ethical principle that is most relevant and useful to this specific issue. Is it justice as fairness? Utilitarianism? Kant's categorical imperative? Altruism? A combination of perspectives?

7. *Look for a third way.* Sometimes seemingly irreconcilable values can be resolved through compromise or the development of a creative solution. Negotiators often seek a third way to bring competing factions together (see Chapter 7). Such was the case in the deliberations that produced the Camp David peace accord. Egypt demanded that Israel return land on the West Bank seized in the 1967 War. Israel resisted because it wanted a buffer zone to protect its security. The dispute was settled when Egypt pledged that it would not attack Israel again. Assured of safety, the Israelis agreed to return the territory to Egypt.[32]

8. *Make the decision.* At some point, we need to step up and make the decision. This seems a given (after all, the point of the whole process is to reach a conclusion). However, we may be mentally exhausted from wrestling with the problem, get caught up in the act of analysis, or lack the necessary courage to come to a decision. In Kidder's words,

> At this point in the process, there's little to do but decide. That requires moral courage—an attribute essential to leadership and one that, along with reason, distinguishes humanity most

sharply from the animal world. Little wonder, then, that the exercise of ethical decision-making is often seen as the highest fulfillment of the human condition.[33]

9. *Revisit and reflect on the decision.* Learn from your choices. Once you've moved on to other issues, stop and reflect. What lessons emerged from this case that you can apply to future decisions? What ethical issues did it raise?

Balance Sheet

Advantages (Pros)

- Is thorough
- Considers problem ownership
- Emphasizes the importance of getting the facts straight
- Recognizes that dilemmas can involve right–right as well as right–wrong choices
- Encourages the search for creative solutions
- Sees ethical decision making as a learning process

Disadvantages (Cons)

- It is not easy to determine who has the responsibility for solving a problem
- The facts are not always available or there may not be enough time to gather them
- Decisions don't always lead to action

There is a lot to be said for Kidder's approach to ethical decision making. For one thing, he seems to cover all the bases, beginning with defining the issue all the way through to learning from the situation after the dust has settled. He acknowledges that there are problems that we can't do much about and that we need to pay particular attention to gathering as much information as possible. The ethicist recognizes that some decisions involve deciding between two "goods" and leaves the door open for creative solutions. Making a choice can be an act of courage, as Kidder points out, and we can apply lessons learned in one dilemma to future problems.

On the flip side, some of the strengths of Kidder's model can also be seen as weaknesses. As we'll see in Chapter 11, determining responsibility or ownership of a problem is getting harder in an increasingly interdependent world. Who is responsible for poor labor conditions in third world countries, for instance? The manufacturer? The subcontractor? The store that sells the products made in sweatshops? Those who buy the items? Kidder also seems to assume that leaders will have the time to gather necessary information. Unfortunately, in some situations, time is in short supply. Finally, the model seems to equate deciding with doing. As we saw in our earlier discussion of moral action, we can decide on a course of action but not follow through. Kidder is right to say that making ethical choices takes courage. However, it takes even more courage to put the choice into effect.

Nash's 12 Questions

Ethics consultant Laura Nash offers 12 questions that can help businesses and other groups identify the responsibilities involved in making moral choices.[34] She argues that discussions based on these queries can be useful even if the group doesn't reach a conclusion. Managers who answer the questions surface ethical concerns that might otherwise remain hidden, identify common moral problems, clarify gaps between stated values and performance, and explore a variety of alternatives.

1. *Have you defined the problem accurately?* The ethical decision-making process begins with assembling the facts. Determine how many employees will be affected by layoffs, how much the cleanup of toxic materials will cost, or how many people have been injured by faulty products. Finding out the facts can help defuse the emotionalism of some issues (perhaps the damage is not as great as first feared).

2. *How would you define the problem if you stood on the other side of the fence?* Asking how others might feel forces self-examination. From a city government's point of view, constructing a bypass around the town may make good sense by reducing congestion. Farmers might have an entirely different perspective. Building the bypass means taking valuable cropland out of production.

3. *How did this situation occur in the first place?* This question separates the symptoms from the disease. Lying, cheating customers and strained labor relations are generally symptoms of deeper problems. Firing an employee for unethical behavior is a temporary solution. Probe to discover the underlying causes. For example, many dubious accounting practices are the result of pressure to produce high quarterly profits.

4. *To whom and to what do you give your loyalties as a person or group and as a member of the organization?* As we saw in Chapter 1, conflicts of loyalty are hard to sort through. However, wrestling with the problem of ultimate loyalty (Work group? Family? Self? Corporation?) can clarify the values operating in an ethical dilemma.

5. *What is your intention in making this decision?*

6. *How does this intention compare with the likely results?* Questions 5 and 6 probe both the group's intentions and the likely products. Honorable motives don't guarantee positive results. Make sure that the outcomes reflect your motivations.

7. *Whom could your decision or action injure?* Too often, groups consider possible injury only after being sued. Try, in advance, to

determine harmful consequences. What will happen if customers ignore label warnings and spread your pesticide indiscriminately, for example? Will the guns you manufacture end up in the hands of urban gang members? Based on these determinations, you may decide to abandon your plans to make these items or revise the way they are marketed.

8. *Can you engage the affected parties in a discussion of the problem before you make your decision?* Talking to affected parties is one way to make sure that you understand how your actions will influence them. Few of us would want other people to decide what's in our best interest. Yet, we often push forward with projects when we assume we know what's in the best interests of others.

9. *Are you confident that your position will be as valid over a long period of time as it seems now?* Make sure that your choice will stand the test of time. What seem like compelling reasons for a decision may not seem so important months or years later. Consider the U.S. decision to invade Iraq, for instance. American intelligence experts and political leaders tied Saddam Hussein to terrorist groups and claimed that he was hiding weapons of mass destruction. After the invasion, no solid links between Iraqis and international terrorists or weapons of mass destruction were discovered. Our decision to wage this war doesn't appear as justified now as it did in the months leading up to the conflict. Similarly, most Americans supported efforts to oust Libyan dictator Muammar Gaddafi. However, public opinion shifted after an attack on the American embassy in Libya killed the United States ambassador and several others.

10. *Could you disclose, without qualms, your decision or action to your boss, your CEO, the board of directors, your family, or society as a whole?* No ethical decision is too trivial to escape the disclosure test. If you or your group would not want to disclose this action, then you'd better reevaluate your choice.

11. *What is the symbolic potential of your action if understood? Misunderstood?* What you intend may not be what the public perceives (see Questions 5 and 6). If your company is a notorious polluter, contributions to local arts groups may be seen as an attempt to divert attention from your firm's poor environmental record, not as a generous civic gesture.

12. *Under what conditions would you allow exceptions to your stand?* Moral consistency is critical, but is there any basis for making an exception? Dorm rules might require that visiting hours end at midnight on weekdays. Yet, as a resident assistant, is there any time when you would be willing to overlook violations? During finals week? On the evening before classes start? When dorm residents and visitors are working on class projects?

Balance Sheet

Advantages (Pros)

- Highlights the importance of gathering facts
- Encourages perspective taking
- Forecasts results and consequences over time

Disadvantages (Cons)

- Is extremely time-consuming
- May not always reach a conclusion
- Ignores implementation

Like Kidder's ethical checkpoints, Nash's 12 questions highlight the importance of problem identification and information gathering. They go a step further, however, by encouraging us to engage in perspective taking. We need to see the problem from the other party's point of view, consider the possible injury we might cause, invite others to give us feedback, and consider how our actions will be perceived. We also need to envision results and take a long-term perspective, imagining how our decisions will stand the test of time. Stepping back can keep us from making choices we might regret later. For example, the decision to test nuclear weapons on U.S. soil without warning citizens may have seemed justified to officials waging the Cold War. However, now even the federal government admits that these tests were immoral.

I suspect that some groups will be frustrated by the amount of time it takes to answer the 12 questions. Not only is the model detailed, but discussing the problem with affected parties could take a series of meetings over a period of weeks and months. Complex issues such as determining who should clean up river pollution involve a variety of constituencies with very different agendas—government agencies, company representatives, citizens' groups, conservation clubs. Some decision makers may also be put off by the model's ambiguity. Nash admits that experts may define problems differently, that there may be exceptions to the decision, and that groups may use the procedure and never reach a conclusion. Finally, none of the questions use the ethical standards we identified in Chapter 5 or address the problem of implementing the choice once it is made.

The Lonergan/Baird Method

Twentieth-century philosopher Bernard Lonergan (1904–1984) believed all people act like natural scientists, following the same basic pattern of cognitive operations in order to make sense of the world.[35] First, they observe at the physical or *empirical* level (perceive, sense, move, speak). Next, they process this information on an *intellectual* level by asking questions, expressing relationships, developing hypotheses, and coming to an understanding. Then, they put together arguments and come to a judgment on the truthfulness and certainty of the hypotheses or propositions at the *rational* level. Finally, individuals move to the *responsible* level. At this stage, they determine how to act on their conclusions, evaluating various courses of action and then carrying out their decisions.

Ethics expert Catharyn Baird uses Lonergan's model as a framework for making ethical choices, condensing it into the following steps: Be attentive. Be intelligent. Be reasonable. Be responsible. She then develops a set of questions and guidelines for each of Lonergan's four levels.[36]

Step 1: Be attentive—Consider what works and what doesn't.

The first stage sets the parameters of the problem by asking these questions:

- *Who is the ethical actor?* An individual or organization must carry out every ethical decision. (But remember that people and organizations always act on limited knowledge.) Make sure the person or group with the authority to carry out the decision makes the final determination.

- *Who are the stakeholders in the conflict?* All moral decisions have a relational component. Consider all the stakeholders who could be impacted by the choice, including those who have to implement the decision, those directly impacted by the decision, and those whose interests should be protected.

- *What are the facts of the situation?* Be aware of personal biases and try not to prejudge the situation. Describe the situation in neutral language. Set the problem in context, considering such factors as the history of the issue and the relationship between important players.

Step 2. Be intelligent—Sort through the data.

Begin to make sense of the information gathered in Step 1 by considering the following:

- *Is this an ethical question?* Some issues involve conflicts between core values while others are aesthetic (matters of taste) or technical (differing strategies for completing a task or reaching a goal).

- *For the ethical question you identify, what is the very specific issue to be resolved?* Identify which exact values are in conflict in this particular situation. According to Baird, many conflicts in building the common good arise along two axes. The first axis is autonomy versus equality. Those who favor autonomy believe that individuals should have as much freedom as possible to determine how they live—to control their bodies, their labor, and their property. Those valuing equality want to treat everyone fairly. They want to make sure everyone has access to such resources as food, health care, and employment. Baird's other continuum is rationality versus sensibility. Followers who put a priority on rationality know what is expected and follow the rules. They are willing to give up some of their freedom for protection against criminals and terrorists, for example. Those who value sensibility, on the other hand, are flexible, adapting to each new situation. They encourage risk taking and innovation, such as in the creation of new businesses and technologies.

- *Selection of options for action.* Identify courses of action for answering the ethical question. Sometimes the best option is inaction (letting the current policy continue).

Step 3. Be reasonable—Evaluate the options.

Making responsible decisions involves critical evaluation of the options:

- *Follow the analytical rules that bring the best result.* Hone your critical thinking skills. Rigorously examine all assertions and assumptions; make sure that supporting evidence is accurate and relevant. Clearly define your terms. Apply the same critical standards to your own reasoning as you do to the reasoning of others.
- *Evaluate the problem against core principles and values.* Employ ethical perspectives like those described in Chapter 5. Don't just choose your favorite approach but imagine how other perspectives apply.
- *Reasonably apply moral principles and values.* Consider how best to carry out the ethical choice in an ethical manner. (Terminating employees may be necessary but needs to be done with respect, for example.) Employ both the head and the heart, reason and emotion, to make responsible choices. Use imagination to envision an outcome that balances competing interests and values.

Step 4: Be responsible—Act with courage.

To act responsibly, incorporate the following:

- *Correct for bias through ethical maturity.* Ethically mature individuals use reason effectively, nourish relationships, make proper use of power, and strive for integration that models ethical wholeness to others.
- *Attend to the common good.* Consider how your actions will impact the larger community, the global economy, and the environment.
- *Act with courage.* Make the most thoughtful choice possible given the limited information available. Remember, "choosing not to act *is* acting."[37] (The "Leadership Ethics at the Movies: *The Martian*" case describes one team that acted courageously in the face of great danger.)

According to Baird, to become mature ethical agents (ethical experts), we need to engage in continuous improvement based on a constant cycle of behavior and reflection. Mature ethical agents act and then evaluate the results of their decisions. They determine which principles and strategies worked well and which did not. Based on their reflection, they are better equipped to tackle the next moral issue using the four steps described above.

Balance Sheet

Advantages (Pros)

- Is widely used
- Emphasizes the importance of paying attention and gathering data
- Incorporates ethical principles, reason, and emotion
- Recognizes the importance of follow-through

Disadvantages (Cons)

- Overlooks many other types of ethical conflicts
- Is used as a tool rather than as part of an ongoing process

Baird's method has been adopted at a number of colleges and universities that use her Ethics Game © simulation. If your school uses this format, you and your classmates already have a common framework for addressing ethical issues. Lonergan/Baird's emphasis on awareness is particularly noteworthy. All too often, we want to jump to the decision stage. Like good natural scientists, we first need to observe what is going on around us, carefully identifying the important components of the situation. If we don't pay close attention, we will reach flawed conclusions. Then, too, the method incorporates emotion and action, which are missing from Kidder's ethical checkpoints and Nash's 12 questions.

Baird seems to give too much importance to two types of ethical conflicts: autonomy versus equality and rationality versus sensibility. She doesn't address many other common ethical conflicts identified by Kidder and others, such as truth versus loyalty and justice versus mercy. I imagine that most people using her method view it as a tool. Once used, they put it back into their ethical toolboxes. They likely lose sight of the fact that Baird describes ethical decision making as an ongoing process. The goal is continuous improvement and personal ethical development, not just solving particular moral dilemmas.

The Foursquare Protocol

Catholic University law professor and attorney Stephen Goldman offers a decision-making format designed specifically for use in organizational settings. He calls his method a *protocol* because it focuses on the procedures that members use to reach their conclusions.[38] While a general approach, it is designed to help leaders make choices in particular situations involving product safety, conflicts of interests, employee misconduct, and other issues. Codes of ethics lay out general principles about sexual harassment, personal use of company equipment, protecting trade secrets, and other ethical issues. However, those broad guidelines still have to be applied to specific cases. Did an employee's use of a company computer to order Christmas gifts from Amazon violate the code, for instance? Can a salesperson take a client out to an expensive lunch? Can purchasing agents can

Leadership Ethics at the Movies

THE MARTIAN

Key Cast Members: Matt Damon, Jessica Chastain, Chiwetel Ejiofor, Jeff Daniels, Michael Pena, MacKenzie Davis

Synopsis: Astronaut Mark Watney (played by Matt Damon) finds himself alone, a long way from home when his Ares III crew abandons him on Mars. Commander Melissa Lewis (Chastain) and the rest of the mission team believe he is dead. Watney, a botanist, creates a video diary of his efforts to grow potatoes using Martian soil mixed with human waste, to produce water by extracting hydrogen from rocket fuel, and to make his remaining meals last as long as possible. When he reestablishes communication with the National Aeronautics and Space Administration (NASA), the agency's director, Teddy Sanders (Daniels), decides not to notify the Ares crew that Watney is alive lest it distract them from their mission. He also blocks efforts to notify the crew that the quickest way to rescue Watney is to return to Mars using their Hermes spacecraft. He fears that they will opt to turn back, putting their lives at risk. However, the Mars mission director (Ejiofor) leaks the information to the crew. The team decides to return to

rescue their colleague despite the danger and the additional months it will take them to return to Earth. The rescue succeeds but not without a lot of improvisation on the part of Watney and the Ares crew.

Rating: PG-13 for strong language, images of injuries, and brief nudity

Themes: ethical decision making, virtues, utilitarianism, creativity, collaboration, the shadow of misinformation, intelligent disobedience, moral potency, duty orientation

Discussion Starters

1. What virtues does astronaut Watney demonstrate?

2. Was the NASA director justified in withholding information about Watney's survival from the Aries crew?

3. Was it ethical for the mission director to disobey his boss and leak information to the Ares crew?

4. Was the rescue of a single astronaut worth risking the lives of the rest of the crew? Would you feel the same if the mission had failed?

---

accept any gifts from vendors? Goldman believes that the following the protocol ensures that such decisions are reached fairly.

Protocol Element 1: Close description of the situation. (Dig into the facts.)

Ethical decision making begins with digging into the facts. Goldman compares the process to how a physician generates a diagnosis. When determining what is wrong with a patient, the doctor gathers information about the patient's symptoms and relates them to one another to identify the problem. In the same way, we need to get a complete account of the ethical "patient" or problem. Gather data and identify the relevant facts.

Protocol Element 2: Gather accumulated experience in similar situations. (Examine individual reactions to past solutions.)

Doctors rely on their past experience when treating patients; organizational decision makers should do the same. Draw on organizational history or memory. Look to past experiences with similar problems. How did the organization respond to cases of sexual harassment or conflicts of interest in the past, for instance? Explore how other managers have responded to related dilemmas. To be fair, similar cases should treated the same way. Also consider how others will talk about your decision. What has been the organizational conversation about similar choices in the past? What have members described as the right way or the wrong way to handle an ethical issue? In Goldman's words, "If you want to make effective decisions today, you must understand how past responses played out: what worked, what didn't, and what stunk to high heaven."[39] Those conversations should inform your current deliberations. Remember, too, that how you respond to the issue will shape the group's ethical culture going forward. For example, if you excuse those who engage in sexual harassment now, you can expect more cases of harassment in the future.

Protocol Element 3: Recognize the significant distinctions between the current problem and past ones. (Gauge similarities with past situations.)

Identify the important differences between the current situation and past incidents. Some distinctions are insignificant while others are critical. The ability to discern the differences between the unimportant and important differences separates average ethical decision makers from the really good ones. Take two cases of sexual harassment, for instance. Punishment for the offenders should differ depending on the severity of the offense (i.e., sexist jokes vs. pressure to have sex), whether there was retaliation against the victim, and so on.

Protocol Element 4: Situate yourself to decide. (Analyze your decision-making process.)

Once the facts are gathered and sorted, it is time to make the choice. To situate yourself to make the decision, consider three factors. First, what, if any, self-interest do you have in the choice that could compromise your judgment? You might have a financial stake in a course of action, such as when laying off the top salesperson will lower sales figures for your sales department. Or you may be faced with disciplining an employee who is also a friend. Pay attention to how much your personal stake could shape your decision. Second, imagine that you are on the receiving end of your decision, which is likely to be costly to some groups. Consider how you would respond if you were to be laid off, for instance. Third, determine what your moral instincts or intuitions are telling you to do. For instance, are you uneasy about your decision to lay off those with the longest tenure? Do you have a strong sense that protecting the organization's diversity by retaining minority employees is the right thing to do? Try to strike a balance between intuition and reason, neither over- nor underemphasizing either one. Use your instincts to test the choice you make through the application of ethical principles like utilitarianism.

Balance Sheet

Advantages (Pros)

- Highlights the importance of justice and fairness
- Applies broad principles to individual situations
- Situates the decision maker
- Recognizes the influence of self-interest
- Incorporates both intuition and reason

Disadvantages (Cons)

- Undervalues other important ethical values and principles
- Hard to recognize what is relevant and significant and what is not
- Self-interest may still influence our decisions

The Foursquare Protocol rightly recognizes the importance justice and fairness in the organizational context. As I noted in Chapter 1, followers frequently complain about unfair treatment in the workplace. Another advantage of the model is its recognition that many ethical dilemmas in organizations are concerned with how to apply broad policies to specific situations. The particulars of each case are critical to the final determination. Goldman also draws our attention to the dangers of self-interest, the importance of situating ourselves as we decide, and incorporating or balancing both intuition and reason when making choices.

The protocol's justice focus may undervalue other important ethical considerations like care for others. For instance, keeping a poor-performing older employee on the payroll for a few more months, until he or she reaches retirement age, may not appear fair to younger workers but could be justified on the basis of compassion. Goldman emphasizes the importance of focusing on relevant facts but even he acknowledges that, at first, it is hard to determine which information is important. Further, identifying important and unimportant distinctions between ethical situations appears to be function of experience. Many who use his model may not have the background to make these determinations. Finally, acknowledging personal bias is no guarantee that we will keep self-interest from shaping our ethical decisions.

IMPLICATIONS AND APPLICATIONS

- Both logic and emotions are essential to ethical decision making. Draw on both processes when making moral choices. Your initial reaction to an ethical dilemma, based on your emotions, cultural influences, past experiences, and intuitions, can inform the conclusion you reach using a decision-making format.

- Ethical behavior is the product of moral sensitivity, (recognition), moral judgment, moral focus (motivation), and moral character.

- Increase your sensitivity to potential ethical issues through perspective taking, using moral terminology, increasing the moral intensity of issues, and being sensitive to the presence of moral emotions like anger, disgust, guilt, or sympathy.

- Improve your ability to make moral judgments by creating an ethical environment that provides ethical role models and guidelines, continuing your education with a special focus on ethics, considering the needs and perspectives of broader audiences, and basing your decisions on widely accepted moral principles and guidelines.

- Ethical biases or blind spots can cause you to participate in or approve of behaviors you would normally condemn. These errors include overestimating your ethicality, forgiving your unethical behavior, in-group favoritism, implicit prejudice, and judging based on outcomes, not processes. Acknowledging that you could have these blind spots is the first step to overcoming them.

- Increase your moral motivation and that of followers by fostering a sense of loyalty or duty, rewarding ethical choices, responding to moral emotions, and controlling negative feelings.

- Your chances of following through on ethical decisions (moral character) are higher if you (1) develop moral potency (ownership, courage, efficacy), (2) demonstrate virtue, (3) believe you have some control over events in your life, and (4) develop the necessary skills to put your plan into action. Decision-making guidelines can help you make better ethical choices. Possible ethical decision-making formats include Kidder's ethical checkpoints, Nash's 12 questions, the Lonergan/Baird method, and the Foursquare protocol. The particular format you choose is not as important as taking a systematic approach to ethical decision making.

- Whatever format you follow, make every effort to gather in-depth, current, and accurate information.

- Creativity is as vital in making ethical decisions as it is in generating new products and programs. Sometimes you can come up with a "third way" that resolves ethical conflicts.

- Moral dilemmas often involve clashes between two core (good) values. Common right-versus-right dilemmas are truth versus loyalty, short term versus long term, individual versus community, justice versus mercy, autonomy versus equality, and rationality versus sensibility.

- Think of ethical deliberation as an ongoing process. You may go through a sequence of steps and use them again. Return to your decision later to evaluate and learn from it. As soon as one ethical crisis passes, there's likely to be another on the horizon.

- Don't expect perfection. As a leader, make the best choice you can after thorough deliberation but recognize that sometimes, you may have to choose between two flawed alternatives.

FOR FURTHER EXPLORATION, CHALLENGE, AND SELF-ASSESSMENT

1. Analyze your scores on the moral attentiveness test found in Self-Assessment 6.1. On which dimension did you score highest? Lowest? Why? What do you learn from this assessment? How can you improve your sensitivity to the presence of ethical issues?

2. Apply the four-component model to the process you went through when faced with a moral dilemma. How successfully did you complete each stage? What would you do differently next time? Write up your analysis.

3. Develop a plan for improving your moral reasoning as part of your education. How can you take advantage of your college experiences to become more of a postconventional thinker?

4. Evaluate your duty orientation based on your responses to Self-Assessment 6.2. Where do you feel the strongest sense of obligation? The least? How are your scores reflected in your behavior and ethical decisions? Are you comfortable with your scores? If not, how might you raise them?

5. Create an original case study that demonstrates one or more of the ethical blind spots in action.

6. Which of the four decision-making formats do you find most useful? Why?

7. In a group, brainstorm a list of possible ethical dilemmas faced by a college student. How many of these problems involve a clash between two important values (right versus right)? Identify which values are in conflict in each situation.

8. Apply each of the formats to one of the scenarios in Case Study 6.1. First, reach your own conclusion based on your initial reactions without using a format and then discuss the situation in a group. See whether you can reach a consensus. Make note of the important factors dividing or uniting group members. Do you reach different conclusions depending on the system you follow?

9. Use a format from the chapter to analyze an ethical decision facing society (e.g., gay marriage, transgender bathrooms, health care, gun rights, the death penalty). Write up your analysis and conclusions.

STUDENT STUDY SITE

Visit the student study site at **study.sagepub.com/johnsonmecl6e** to access full SAGE journal articles for further research and information on key chapter topics.

Case Study 6.1

ETHICAL SCENARIOS FOR ANALYSIS

SCENARIO A: CLOTHING THE CAMP COUNSELORS

You are a first-year counselor at a camp for needy children, which is subsidized through contributions from individuals and local businesses. Yours is the only camp experience that these disadvantaged kids will ever have. One afternoon, a few hours before the next batch of children is due to arrive, a semi-trailer truck stops by with a donated shipment of new shoes, shirts, and shorts for your campers. Immediately, the other counselors (all of whom have more experience than you do) begin selecting items for personal use. They encourage you to do the same. When questioned, they argue that there is plenty to go around for both kids and counselors and that the clothes are a fringe benefit for underpaid camp staff.

Would you take any shoes or clothing to wear?

Source: Kristina Findley.

SCENARIO B: THE TENURE REVIEW REPORT

You are the chair of the tenure and promotion committee at your small university. Your committee, made up of senior faculty, evaluates the teaching and scholarship of professors and then makes recommendations to the university provost. Committee members take their responsibilities seriously, knowing that peer review—where faculty members evaluate the work of other faculty—plays a critical role in higher education. They feel an obligation to maintain high teaching and research standards. No professor can be tenured (given guaranteed employment) or promoted to a higher rank (associate professor, full professor) without a positive recommendation from your group. Those denied tenure must leave the school at the end of the current school year. Your closest departmental colleague is being reviewed for tenure. (Your families sometimes celebrate holidays together and your children are friends.) He expects that you will offer a positive review and encourage the committee to recommend tenure. Unfortunately, your coworker's teaching evaluations are below average. His scholarship is not strong enough to make up for these shortcomings. You know that your colleague will be devastated by a negative evaluation and will be forced to move to another city to take another position. He will feel betrayed and blame you for the committee's decision, though you are only one voice in the group.

Will you support your colleague's application for tenure?

SCENARIO C: PENALIZING TIMELY PAYMENTS

You are the manager at a regional center that processes credit card payments. Company profits are down because of increased competition from other card issuers that charge lower interest rates. To boost income, the firm raised its penalties for late payments and reduced the length of the billing cycle. These changes were announced to cardholders. However, at the same time, company officials made an unofficial policy change. They instructed you and managers at the other processing centers to apply late penalties when checks arrive right before the due date. In these cases, it will be difficult for cardholders to prove that their payments arrived on time. Some of your colleagues at other processing centers around the country have already begun this practice, knowing that failure to do so could cost them their jobs.

Will you institute this new policy at your processing center?

(Continued)

(Continued)

SCENARIO D: THE WIN–WIN DECISION

You direct the real estate department of a major retail clothing chain. Your primary responsibility is choosing sites for new stores as the company expands. When selecting sites, you use a grading system based on such factors as the average income of area residents, the cost of land, surrounding businesses, and access to local highways and mass transit. Your firm wants to add an outlet in a mid-sized city in a new territory. Your sister owns one of the proposed sites under consideration. When you grade the possible locations, hers is the only one that earns an *A*. The other two sites come in at a *B* and a *C* grade. You decide to recommend your sister's property since it received the highest rating. You do not think you need to notify your supervisors that a relative owns this parcel of land. After all, this appears to be a win–win decision, one that benefits the company and your family. However, you decide to take a couple of days to reflect on your choice before submitting your report.

Should you stay with your initial decision to recommend the property without revealing you are related to the owner?

Source: Adapted from Goldman, S. M. (2008). *Temptations in the office: Ethical choices and legal obligations*. Westport, CT: Praeger, Ch. 5.

SCENARIO E: THE BLOWOUT

You are the coach of a high school girls' basketball team. This is your best season ever, and you are getting ready for the state play-offs. You teach an aggressive brand of basketball that involves playing full-court defense and fast-breaking at every opportunity. As a result, your team scores lots of points. You tell the young women on your squad that they may not always win but that you want them to play hard and to always strive for excellence. Your last game of the regular season is with the worst team in your league, one with many starters who had not played basketball before this year. Not only are they less experienced and talented than your players; they are much shorter as well. Within minutes, the game turns into a rout. By halftime, the score is 50 to 4. Some state high school athletic associations have "mercy rules" that shorten or end lopsided games. Your state does not. This is the last chance your team will have to "tune up" before moving on to much stiffer competition.

In the second half, will you deliberately try to keep the score down by changing how your team plays?

Sources

Brady, E., & Halley, J. (2009, February 24). The blowup over blowouts. *USA Today*, p. 1C.

Coutts, M. (2009, January 27). Would Jesus run up the score? Christian school under fire for winning 100–0. *National Post*, p. A1.

Halley, J. (2009, January 29). Lopsided games are often pointless. *USA Today*, p. 4C.

SCENARIO F: WOULD YOU RUN THESE ADS?

You are the sales manager for a local radio station that has seen a dramatic downturn in ads and revenue as the local economy loses industries and small businesses. One of your biggest advertisers has been MighTY Mortgage. MighTY Mortgage spots feature the company president, Tom Tyler, promising to "save our friends lots of cash." In these commercials, Tyler claims that his company offers the lowest mortgage rates and will pay to have homes appraised.

Two weeks ago, state regulators charged MighTY Mortgage with a variety of unethical and illegal practices. The firm offers no proof that its loan rates are the lowest and charges enough in fees to more than cover the cost of the "free" appraisals. Investigators also found that, in most instances, MighTY failed to properly disclose loan terms to borrowers. The state wants to revoke the company's license, fine Tyler $250,000, and make sure the mortgage lender pays restitution to borrowers. However, final action has not been taken and won't be for several months.

After temporarily pulling his ads, Tom Tyler wants to go back on your station's airwaves with a new set of commercials. The new spots still promise to save listeners lots of money but no longer mention free appraisals. Instead of claiming to offer the lowest interest rate, MighTY Mortgage now says it offers a low interest rate.

Would you broadcast the new commercials for MighTY Mortgage?

Source: Fictional case based on real-life events.

SCENARIO G: THE FERTILITY CLINIC RAFFLE

You are the business manager for a small fertility clinic that helps women conceive through fertility drugs and other procedures. Other small clinics like yours have staged contests to build their mailing lists and to generate publicity, enabling them to compete against larger, better-known fertility centers. Sponsors claim that the contests are successful marketing tools that benefit women who can't afford the treatments, which cost $10,000–$15,000. In one type of contest, women compete for free treatments by submitting essays or videos explaining why they want to have a baby. In another type of contest, winners are selected randomly through raffles. You think that a contest could boost your marketing efforts as well. However, medical ethicists complain that fertility clinic contests take advantage of vulnerable couples and trivialize conception by raffling off the opportunity to have a baby. You realize that, if you hold a raffle, the winner might be a woman who could afford to pay for her treatment.

Would you hold a raffle or some other contest to market your fertility clinic?

Source: Quenqua, D. (2012, October 21). Clinic raffles could make you a winner, and maybe a mother. *The New York Times*, p. A1.

SELF-ASSESSMENT 6.1

Moral Attentiveness

Instructions: Indicate the extent you agree with each of the following statements on a scale of 1 = strongly disagree to 7 = strongly agree.

1. In a typical day, I face several ethical dilemmas.
2. I often have to choose between doing what's right and doing something that's wrong.
3. I regularly face decisions that have significant ethical implications.
4. My life has been filled with one moral predicament after another.
5. Many of the decisions that I make have ethical dimensions to them.
6. I regularly think about the ethical implications of my decisions.
7. I think about the morality of my actions almost every day.
8. I rarely face ethical dilemmas.
9. I frequently encounter ethical situations.
10. I often find myself pondering about ethical issues.
11. I often reflect on the moral aspects of my decisions.
12. I like to think about ethics.

Scoring: Reverse your score on Item 8 and then add up your scores. Items 1–7 measure the extent to which you recognize moral aspects in your everyday experiences. Items 8–12 measure the extent to which you consider and reflect on moral matters. Scores can range from 7 to 49 on items 1–7 and 5 to 35 on items 8–12. Total possible scores for the combined items range from 12 to 84. The higher your scores, the more attentive or sensitive you are to moral issues.

Source: Reynolds, S. J. (2008). Moral attentiveness: Who pays attention to the moral aspects of life? *Journal of Applied Psychology, 93*, 1027–1041. Used with permission of the American Psychological Association.

SELF-ASSESSMENT 6.2

Duty Orientation Scale

Instructions: Think about yourself as a member of a group that is important to you. Rate your level of agreement with each item as it pertains to you as a member.

1 = strongly disagree, 5 = strongly agree

My actions demonstrate that I . . .

1. put the interests of my team ahead of my personal interests.
2. do all that I can to support the organization.
3. am faithful to my team members.

4. am loyal to my leaders and team.

5. accept personal risk or loss in support of the mission/organizational goals.

6. make personal sacrifices to serve the mission/organizational goals.

7. do whatever it takes to not let the mission/organization fail.

8. get the job done under the toughest conditions.

9. do what is right always.

10. demonstrate personal integrity when challenged.

11. will not accept dishonor.

12. set the example for honorable behavior for others.

Scoring: Items 1–4 measure duty to members, Items 4–8 measure duty to mission, and Items 9–12 measure duty to codes. Scores for each dimension range from 4–20. Total scores can range from 12 to 60. The higher your score, the greater your sense of duty or obligation to the group or organization.

Source: Adapted from Hannah, S. T., Jennings, P. L., Bluhm, D., Chunyan Peng, A., & Schaubroeck, J. M. (2014). Duty orientation: Theoretical development and preliminary construct testing. *Organizational Behavior and Human Decision Processes, 123,* 227. Used with permission.

NOTES

1. Haidt, J. (2001). The emotional dog and its rational tail: A social intuitionist approach to moral judgment. *Psychological Review, 108,* 814–834; Haidt, J. (2012). *The righteous mind: Why good people are divided by politics and religion.* New York, NY: Pantheon Books; Lapsley, D. K., & Hill, P. L. (2008). On dual processing and heuristic approaches to moral cognition. *Journal of Moral Education, 37,* 313–332.

2. Salvador, R., & Folger, R. G. (2009). Business ethics and the brain. *Business Ethics Quarterly, 19*(1), 1–31.

3. Boksem, M. A. S., & de Cremer, D. (2009). The neural basis of morality. In D. De Cremer (Ed.), *Psychological perspectives on ethical behavior and decision-making* (pp. 153–166). Charlotte, NC: Information Age; Casebeer, W. D. (2003). Moral cognition and its neural constituents. *Neuroscience, 4,* 841–846; Greene, J. (2005). Cognitive neuroscience and the structure of the moral mind. In P. Carruthers, S. Laurence, & S. Stich (Eds.), *The innate mind: Structure and content* (pp. 338–352). Oxford, England: Oxford University Press; Reynolds, S. J. (2006). A neurocognitive model of the ethical decision-making process: Implications for study and practice. *Journal of Applied Psychology, 91,* 737–748; Tessman, L. (2014). Virtue ethics and moral failure: Lessons from neuroscientific moral psychology. In. M. W. Austin (Ed.), *Virtues in action: New essays in applied virtue ethics* (pp. 171–189). New York, NY: Palgrave Macmillan.

4. Oum, R., & Lieberman, D. (2007). Emotion is cognition: An information-processing view of the mind. In K. D. Vohs, R. F. Baumeister, & G. Lowenstein (Eds.), *Do emotions help or hurt decision making? A hedgefoxian perspective* (pp. 133–154). New York, NY: Russell Sage Foundation; Salvador & Folger.

5. Monin, B., Pizarro, D. A., & Beer, J. S. (2007). Deciding versus reacting: Conceptions of moral judgment and the reason-affect debate. *Review of General Psychology, 11,* 99–111; Monin, B., Pizarro, D. A., & Beer, J. S. (2007). Reason and emotion in moral judgment: Different prototypes lead to different theories. In K. D. Vohs, R. F. Baumeister, & G. Lowenstein (Eds.), *Do emotions help or hurt decision making? A hedgefoxian perspective* (pp. 219–244). New York, NY: Russell Sage Foundation.

6. Powers, C. W., & Vogel, D. (1980). *Ethics in the education of business managers.* Hasting-on-Hudson, NY: Institute of Society, Ethics and the Life Sciences.

7. Rest, J. R. (1986). *Moral development: Advances in research and theory.* New York, NY: Praeger; Rest, J. R. (1993). Research on moral judgment in college students. In A. Garrod (Ed.), *Approaches to moral development* (pp. 201–211). New York, NY: Teachers College Press; Rest, J. R. (1994). Background: Theory and research. In J. R. Rest & D. Narvaez (Eds.), *Moral development in the professions: Psychology and applied ethics* (pp. 1–25). Hillsdale, NJ: Erlbaum.

8. Soble, J. (2015, July 22). Scandal upends Toshiba's lauded reputation. *The New York Times*, p. B3.

9. Werhane, P. H. (1999). *Moral imagination and management decision-making.* New York, NY: Oxford University Press.

10. Bird, F. B. (1996). *The muted conscience: Moral silence and the practice of ethics in business.* Westport, CT: Quorum.

11. Tenbrunsel, A. E., & Messick, D. M. (2004). Ethical fading: The role of self-deception in unethical behavior. *Social Justice Research, 17,* 223–236.

12. Frey, B. F. (2000). The impact of moral intensity on decision making in a business context. *Journal of Business Ethics, 26,* 181–195; Jones, T. M. (1991). Ethical decision making by individuals in organizations: An issue-contingent model. *Academy of Management Review, 15,* 366–395; May, D. R., & Pauli, K. P. (2002). The role of moral intensity in ethical decision-making: A review and investigation of moral recognition, evaluation, and intention. *Business & Society, 41,* 84–117.

13. Haidt, J. (2003). The moral emotions. In R. J. Davidson, K. R. Scherer, & H. H. Goldsmith (Eds.), *Handbook of affective sciences* (pp. 852–870). Oxford, England: Oxford University Press; Moll, J., de Oliveira-Souza, R., Zahn, R., & Grafman, J. (2008). The cognitive neuroscience of moral emotions. In W. Sinnott-Armstrong (Ed.), *Moral psychology: Vol. 3. The neuroscience of morality: Emotion, brain disorders, and development.* Cambridge, MA: MIT Press.

14. Kohlberg, L. A. (1984). *The psychology of moral development: The nature and validity of moral stages* (Vol. 2). San Francisco, CA: Harper & Row; Kohlberg, L. A. (1986). A current statement on some theoretical issues. In S. Modgil & C. Modgil (Eds.), *Lawrence Kohlberg: Consensus and controversy* (pp. 485–546). Philadelphia, PA: Palmer.

15. Rest, J. R., Narvaez, D., Bebeau, M. J., & Thoma, S. J. (1999). *Postconventional moral thinking: A neo-Kohlbergian approach.* Mahwah, NJ: Erlbaum; Trevino, L. K., & Weaver, G. R. (2003). *Managing ethics in business organizations: Social scientific perspectives.* Stanford, CA: Stanford University Press.

16. Rest, Narvaez, Bebeau, & Thoma; Thoma, S. J. (2006). Research on the Defining Issues Test. In M. Killen & J. G. Smetana (Eds.), *Handbook of moral development* (pp. 67–91). Mahwah, NJ: Erlbaum.

17. See the following: Rest (1993); Rest, J. R., & Narvaez, D. (1991). The college experience and moral development. In W. M. Kurtines & J. L. Gewirtz (Eds.), *Handbook of moral behavior and development: Vol. 2. Research* (pp. 229–245). Hillsdale, NJ: Erlbaum; Thoma (2006).

18. Trevino & Weaver.

19. Banaji, M. R., Bazerman, M. H., & Chugh, D. (2003, December). How (un)ethical are you? *Harvard Business Review*, 56–64; Bandura, A. (1999). Moral disengagement in the perpetration of inhumanities. *Personality and Social Psychology Review, 3,* 193–209; Bazerman, M. H., Chugh, D., & Banaji, M. R. (2005, October). When good people (seem to) negotiate in bad faith. *Negotiation, 8,* 3–5; Bazerman, M. H., & Tenbrusel, A. E. (2011). *Blind spots: Why we fail to do what's right and what to do about it.* Princeton, NJ: Princeton University Press; Epley, N., & Dunning, D. (2000). Feeling "holier than thou": Are self-serving assessments produced by errors in self- or social prediction? *Journal of Personality and Social Psychology, 79,* 861–875; Gino, F., Moore, D. A., & Bazerman, M. H. (2008, January). See no evil:

When we overlook other people's unethical behavior. Harvard Business School Working Paper No. 08–045. Available at http://www.people.hbs.edu/mbazerman; Gino, F., Moore, D. A., & Bazerman, M. H. (2009). No harm, no foul: The outcome bias in ethical judgments. Harvard Business School Working Paper 08–080. Available at http://www.people.hbs.edu/mbazerman; Milkman, K. L., Chugh, D., & Bazerman, M. H. (2008). How can decision-making be improved? Harvard Business School Working Paper 08-102. Available at http://www.people.hbs.edu/mbazerman; Shu, L. L., Gino, F., & Bazerman, M. H. (2009). Dishonest deed, clear conscience: Self-preservation through moral disengagement and motivated forgetting. Harvard Business School Working Paper No. 09–078; Tenbrunsel, A. E., Diekman, K. A., Wade-Benzoni, K. A., & Bazerman, M. H. (2009). The ethical mirage: A temporal explanation as to why we aren't as ethical as we think we are. Harvard Business School Working Paper No. 08–012. Available at http://www.people.hbs.edu/mbazerman; Why your negotiating behavior may be ethically challenged—and how to fix it. (2008, April). *Negotiation, 11*(4), 1–5;

20. Woodzicka, J. A., & LaFrance, M. (2001). Real verses imagined gender harassment. *Journal of Social Issues 57*(1), 15–30.

21. Greenhouse, L. (2004, June 25). Justices' ruling postpones resolution of Cheney case. *The New York Times*; Savage, D. G. (2004, January 17). Trip with Cheney puts ethics spotlight on Scalia. *Los Angeles Times.*

22. Harris, G. (2009, February 12). Peanut foods shipped before testing came in. *The New York Times*, p. A24.

23. Rest, Narvaez, Bebeau, & Thoma (1999), p. 101.

24. Hannah, S. T., & Avolio, B. J. (2010). Moral potency: building the capacity for character-based leadership. *Consulting Psychology Journal: Practice and Research, 62,* 291–310.

25. Batson, C. D., & Thompson, E. R. (2001). Why don't moral people act morally? Motivational considerations. *Current Directions in Psychological Science, 10,* 54–57; Batson, C. D., Thompson, E. R., & Chen, H. (2002). Moral hypocrisy: Addressing some alternatives. *Journal of Personality and Social Psychology, 83,* 330–339.

26. Batson & Thompson, p. 54.

27. James, H. S. (2000). Reinforcing ethical decision-making through organizational structure. *Journal of Business Ethics, 28*(1), 43–58; O'Fallon, M. J., & Butterfield, K. D. (2005). A review of the empirical ethical decision-making literature: 1996–2003. *Journal of Business Ethics, 59,* 375–413; Werhane.

28. See the following: Connelly, S., Helton-Fauth, W., & Mumford, M. D. (2004). A managerial in-basket study of the impact of trait emotions on ethical choice. *Journal of Business Ethics, 51,* 245–267; Eisenberg, N. (2000). Emotion, regulation, and moral development. *Annual Review of Psychology, 51,* 665–697; Gaudine, A., & Thorne, L. (2001). Emotion and ethical decision-making in organizations. *Journal of Business Ethics, 31,* 175–187; Griffin, R. W., & O'Leary-Kelly, A. M. (Eds.). (2004). *The dark side of organizational behavior.* San Francisco, CA: Jossey-Bass.

29. O'Fallon & Butterfield; Trevino & Weaver.

30. Hannah, S. T., Jennings, P. L., Bluhm, D., Chunyan Peng, A., & Schaubroeck, J. M. (2014). Duty orientation: Theoretical development and preliminary construct. *Organizational Behavior and Human Decision Processes, 123,* 220–238.

31. Kidder, R. M. (1995). *How good people make tough choices: Resolving the dilemmas of ethical living.* New York, NY: Fireside.

32. Fisher, R., Ury, W., & Patton, B. (2011). *Getting to yes* (Rev. ed.). New York, NY: Penguin.

33. Kidder, p. 186.

34. Nash, L. L. (1989). Ethics without the sermon. In K. R. Andrews (Ed.), *Ethics in practice: Managing the moral corporation* (pp. 243–257). Boston, MA: Harvard Business School Press.

35. Lonergan, B. (1957). *Insight: A study of human understanding.* Toronto, Canada: University of Toronto Press; Lontergran, B. (1973). *Method in theology.* Toronto, Canada: University of Toronto Press.

36. Baird, C. A. (2003). *Every day ethics: Making hard choices in a complex world.* Denver, CO: CB Resources.

37. Baird, p. 138.

38. Goldman, S. M. (2008). *Temptations in the office: Ethical choices and legal obligations.* Westport, CT: Praeger; Goldman, S. M. (2010, August 5). *Loyalty vs. ethics: From the White House to the workplace.* American Management Association. Available at http://www.amanet.org/training.

39. Goldman (2008).

Exercising Ethical Influence

The humblest individual exerts some influence, either for good or evil, upon others.

—HENRY WARD BEECHER, NINETEENTH-CENTURY MINISTER AND ACTIVIST

Managers get the subordinates they expect.

—TEL AVIV UNIVERSITY PROFESSOR EMERITUS DOV EDEN

WHAT'S AHEAD

In this chapter, we'll explore the ethical issues surrounding four sets of influence tools: compliance gaining, the communication of expectations, argumentation, and negotiation. After examining each type of tactic, I'll conclude the chapter with a look at how leaders can resist unethical influence attempts.

ETHICAL ISSUES IN INFLUENCE

Leadership is based on the exercise of influence. Leading means influencing, since leaders must modify the attitudes and behaviors of followers in order to help groups reach their goals. The key for leaders, then, is not *whether* to exercise influence but *how* to do so in an ethical manner. Selecting the appropriate tactic is one of the most important moral choices facing leaders, helping determine whether they brighten or darken the lives of those around them. In this chapter, we'll examine the ethical issues surrounding four sets of influence tools particularly important to leaders: compliance gaining, the communication of expectations, argumentation, and negotiation. We'll conclude with a closer look at how to resist unethical influence attempts.

Compliance Gaining

Compliance-gaining strategies are the verbal tactics that leaders and others use to get their way. They are designed to achieve immediate objectives by convincing targets to go along with requests. Compliance gaining is common in daily life; for example, asking to borrow a roommate's car, convincing a friend to go with you to see a movie, persuading a neighbor to not park in front of your driveway, and enlisting referees for the youth baseball league. (Complete the first item under "For Further Exploration, Challenge, and Self-Assessment" at the end of this chapter to see how often you find yourself in compliance-gaining encounters, either as the persuader or as the target of a request.) Leaders routinely engage compliance gaining as well. Gary Yukl of the State University of New York at Albany and his associates identify the following as common proactive managerial influence tactics used in the organizational setting.[1]

Rational persuasion. Offering factual evidence, explanations, and logical arguments to illustrate that a proposal or request will attain task and organization objectives. Examples include "Customer surveys reveal that the website is hard to navigate and needs to be updated." "Offering more courses on line should increase enrollment."

Apprising. Explaining how compliance with a request will benefit the target (e.g., help a career, make a job more interesting, bring recognition). Examples include "Taking this overseas assignment will put you on the fast track for promotion to international sales manager." "Serving on this committee will give you more visibility around the company."

Inspirational appeals. Generating enthusiasm by appealing to values and ideals; arousing emotions. Examples include "Installing the new emergency communication system will reduce response times and save lives." "Joining our medical research team will put you on the front lines in the fight against the Zika virus and other infectious diseases."

Consultation. Soliciting support by seeking suggestions for improvement; asking for input when planning an activity, strategy, or change. Examples include "How do you think we can retain more students?" "Take a look at this agenda for the stockholders meeting and let me know what you think."

Collaboration. Providing resources and assistance if the target complies with the request. Examples include "I can make the presentation with you." "If you agree to head the project, I will make sure you have no other assignments."

Ingratiation. Generating positive feelings by the use of flattery and praise before or during the request; expressing confidence in the target's ability to fulfill a difficult request. Examples include "Since you know the accounting software much better than I do, you ought to create the financial report." "You should approach the boss with our concerns since she trusts you."

Personal appeals. Appealing to feelings of loyalty and friendship when asking for something. Examples include "Do me a favor and cover the front desk while I am gone." "We've been friends for a long time, so I am counting on you to support my new project."

Exchange. Providing something the target wants in return for compliance; trading favors; promising to reciprocate later or to share the benefits when the job is completed. Examples include "If you support my farm bill, I'll vote for your urban mass transit legislation." "Trade shifts with me now, and I'll trade shifts with you when want to go camping this summer."

Coalition tactics. Enlisting the help of others or the support of coworkers to convince that target to go along with the request. Examples include "The board of directors really likes the expansion proposal." "Your colleague Tom from engineering was one of the first people to get behind this idea."

Legitimating tactics. Claiming the right or authority to make a request; aligning the request with the organization's rules, policies, and traditions. Examples include "The policy manual states I am eligible for two weeks of vacation any time during my first year of employment." "In the past, offices were allocated according to seniority."

Pressure. Demanding, threatening, checking up; persistent reminders. Examples include "If you don't consistently make it to work on time, you'll be fired." "Have you had a chance to review that personnel file yet?"

Consider the power base of the tactic when selecting a compliance strategy. As we noted in Chapter 1, leaders can use hard or soft power. Legitimating and pressure (hard power tactics that are based on coercion and force) are more susceptible to abuse. Rational exchange, inspirational appeals, collaboration and consultation strategies, which rely on attraction and positive relationships, are soft power tactics that pose less danger. (Yukl reports that they are generally more effective as well.) However, the morality of a particular strategy rests on the ends or goals we seek. We may need to use hard power strategies to achieve our ethical goals. Then, too, soft power tactics can be used to support illegitimate requests, such as when executives collaborate with one another to steal from the company.

John Hunter and Franklin Boster's *emotional–ethical threshold* highlights the way in which leaders must balance the cost of using a tactic against the goal they seek.[2] Attempts to gain compliance produce emotional reactions in targets. Prosocial tactics, like rational persuasion, inspirational appeals, collaboration, and consultation, are widely accepted and are more likely to produce positive feelings. Antisocial strategies such as pressure and legitimation, which raise threat levels, are more likely to produce negative feelings. According Hunter and Boster, we must decide just how much negative emotion we are willing to generate in order to get our way. In some situations, the emotional–ethical threshold is high; for example, when asking for a personal favor at work. In these cases, we would probably be unwilling to use a strategy that puts the other person in a bad mood. In other situations, the threshold is low; for example, when safety is at stake or when dealing with destructive behaviors like stealing, aggression, and sexual harassment. We should not hesitate to employ antisocial tactics to end these dangerous, unethical activities, described in more detail in Chapter 10, even if they provoke anger and resentment in targets. (Turn to "Focus on Follower Ethics: Upward Dissent" to see how followers consider the emotional and relational impact of their attempts to exert upward influence.)

Communication of Expectations

The expectations of leaders can have a powerful impact on followers. That's because we tend to live up to the expectations others place on us. Investigators refer to this tendency as *self-fulfilling prophecy* or *the Pygmalion Effect*, after the prince in Greek mythology. Pygmalion created a statue of a beautiful woman, whom he named Galatea. After the

Focus on Follower Ethics

UPWARD DISSENT

Subordinates must exert upward influence to shape the actions, attitudes, and behaviors of their leaders if they are to function as effective, ethical followers. Exerting upward influence is particularly challenging when taking issue with policies, procedures, working conditions, pay, benefits, values, and other factors. Followers lack the power to make the changes themselves so they must express their opposition to those who can. Expressing dissent is risky and could invite retaliation. Then, too, leaders, who have more power, are under no obligation to act on the complaints of subordinates.

Arizona State University professor Jeffrey Kassing studies the ways that workers express dissent to their organizational leaders. He found that employees use five strategies. *Direct-factual appeals* are based on physical evidence, organizational policies and procedures, and personal experience. *Solution presentations* offer ideas for resolving the issue. Solutions can be offered alone or in addition to presenting the facts. *Repetition* describes consistent attempts to draw attention to a problem over an extended period of time. *Circumvention* means taking dissent to someone above the immediate supervisor (the boss's boss or a top executive). *Threatening resignation* is vowing to quit in order to get the management to respond.

Once he identified the five strategies, Kassing then tried to determine which tactics were most successful. According to the employees he surveyed, direct-factual and solution presentations (prosocial strategies) are most effective. Circumvention and repetition are riskier. Threatening resignation poses the most danger and supervisors and organizational members rate this tactic as least competent. Kassing believes that prosocial strategies are most effective because they pose the least threat to the image or "face" of leaders. Circumvention and repetition pose more face threat and can damage the subordinate–supervisor relationship. Threatening resignation does the most relational damage.

Sources: Kassing, J. W. (2002). Speaking up: Identifying employee's upward dissent strategies. *Management Communication Quarterly, 16,* 187–209; Kassing, J. W. (2005). Speaking up competently: A comparison of perceived competence in upward dissent. *Communication Research Reports, 22,* 227–234; Kassing, J. W. (2009). 'In case you didn't hear me the first time': An examination of repetitious upward dissent. *Management Communication Quarterly, 22,* 416–436; Kassing, J. W. (2011). *Dissent in organizations.* Cambridge, England: Polity Press; Kassing, J. W., & Kava, W. (2013). Assessing disagreement expressed to management: Development of the Upward Dissent Scale. *Communication Research Reports, 30,* 46–56.

figure was complete, he fell in love with his creation. The goddess Aphrodite took pity on the dejected prince and brought Galatea to life.

The Pygmalion effect operates in a variety of settings.[3] For example, patients in medical experiments receiving placebos improve because they believe they will get better. Military personnel labeled as having high potential live up to the expectations of their superiors and are more likely to volunteer for dangerous special duty. The high expectations of teachers lead to higher student test and IQ scores as well as to improved performance on cognitive tasks. Clients labeled as "high potential" are less likely to drop out of alcohol treatment programs than those described as "unmotivated." Nursing home residents are less depressed and less likely to be admitted to hospitals when staff members believe these clients will respond more favorably to rehabilitation. Patterns created through expectations tend to persist over time. One long-term study of 500 high school students found that their standardized math test scores in the twelfth grade were influenced, in part, by the expectations their teachers had of their mathematical aptitude in the fourth grade.[4]

Self-fulfilling prophecies have a greater impact on some individuals than others. Disadvantaged groups—those stereotyped as low achievers—tend to benefit most from positive expectations, as do those who lack a clear sense of their abilities or find themselves in a new situation. Men seem to be more influenced by the expectations of their managers than women.[5] Followers who believe that their leaders are trustworthy—competent, benevolent, and act with integrity—are more responsive to their influence attempts.[6] Just as positive expectations can raise performance, negative expectations lower it. This is referred to as the *Golem effect* (*golem* means "dumbbell" in Yiddish).

Expectations are communicated directly and indirectly. Direct methods include expressing confidence in others' ability to complete the task, offering complements, and saying that you expect a good final product. However, self-fulfilling prophecies are more often communicated indirectly because they tend to operate at the subconscious level. Consider, for example, that many leaders believe that they treat all their followers the same way, even when they don't. They don't realize that they are using these four channels to signal high or low expectancies:[7]

1. *Climate*. Climate describes the social and emotional atmosphere leaders create for followers. Leaders act in a friendly, supportive, accepting, and encouraging manner with people they like. They largely do so through nonverbal behaviors that portray warmth and respect while avoiding behaviors that communicate disrespect, coolness, and superiority. Supervisors and instructors signal positive expectations by giving adequate time to employees and students, holding appointments in pleasant surroundings, sitting or standing close to workers or class members, nodding and smiling, making frequent eye contact, and using a warm tone of voice.

2. *Feedback*. Leaders give more frequent positive feedback when they have high expectations of followers, both praising them more often for success and criticizing them less often for failure. In addition, leaders provide more detailed performance feedback to high-expectation followers. Just the opposite occurs with those labeled as poor performers. Organizational supervisors praise their minimal performance more, reinforcing the impression that they expect less from these employees.

3. *Input*. Input refers to the attention and focus given to followers. Superiors give more significant projects and assignments to workers. High expectations create a positive performance spiral.

As employees receive and successfully complete more tasks, they gain self-confidence and the confidence of leaders. These outstanding performers are then given further duties, which they are more likely to complete as well.

4. *Output.* Those tagged as high performers are given more opportunities to speak, to offer their opinions, and to disagree. Leaders pay more attention to these followers when they speak and offer more assistance to them when they're solving problems. In the classroom, teachers call on high achievers more than low achievers, wait less time for low achievers to answer questions, and provide fewer clues and follow-up questions to low achievers.[8]

The Pygmalion effect poses some significant ethical dilemmas, starting with deception. Researchers tell leaders that groups differ in ability even though members have been randomly assigned. This strategy could be used in organizations by telling managers that selected subordinates have more potential when, in reality, there is no evidence to support that claim. Some might argue that this deceit would be justified because the organization would benefit from the superior work of those labeled as high performers. Nevertheless, this would mean lying to these supervisors, which, as in all cases of deception, demonstrates disrespect for others and undermines trust.

Ability grouping is also problematical. Companies routinely fast track some younger employees. Individuals identified as "high potential" then get special training, are assigned to mentors, receive more challenging assignments, and so on. The fortunate few selected for these experiences benefit from the Pygmalion effect while everyone else may suffer from the Golem effect. Those not selected (average or low performers) receive less encouragement and may live down to reduced expectations. Ability grouping in elementary school can be even more damaging because the impact of such labeling is long lasting. Poor readers and test takers grouped together may give up and fall further and further behind, never to catch up.

Communicating high expectations to everyone in the group or organization is an ethical alternative to deception and ability grouping.[9] This approach is more just and encourages everyone to do her or his best. Strategies for improving organization-wide performance should focus on building follower self-efficacy or self-confidence. This can be done by (1) breaking down tasks into manageable segments and providing followers with the time to practice their skills, (2) delivering constructive suggestions about how to improve performance or how to carry out tasks, (3) modeling skills as well as positive thinking and how to deal with failure, and (4) using verbal persuasion ("I know you can do this.") backed with reasons why the follower will succeed ("You have been trained to do this."). In addition to fostering self-efficacy, encourage a learning orientation that emphasizes improvement toward goals. Wanting to learn motivates people to develop their skills and to look for effective task strategies. Mistakes are seen as an opportunity for development. Those who are focused on learning take satisfaction in mastering challenging tasks. (To apply these strategies, turn to Case Study 7.1.)

Even if our organization as a whole doesn't adopt a high-expectations approach, we can still do so as individual leaders. The power of self-fulfilling prophecy puts an ethical burden on us. If followers are to reach their full potential, we need to communicate positive expectations, not negative ones. We should carefully monitor our behavior, particularly subtle cues, to reduce inequities in our treatment of followers. We can also use the *Galatea effect* to insulate ourselves from the negative expectations of those who lead us. The Galatea effect (named after the statue in the Pygmalion myth) refers to the fact that high self-expectation leads to high performance. If we have high expectations for our own performance, we will strive to reach that standard, even when our leaders expect little from us. Meeting and exceeding standards encourages leaders to raise their expectations of us.[10] We can also encourage followers to be their own Galateas.

There is one final ethical issue surrounding self-fulfilling prophecy: Just how high should our expectations be? Setting expectations too low frustrates followers and keeps them from reaching their potential. Setting expectations too high is unrealistic and unjust. Yet, there are times that leaders can convince followers to achieve more than they ever dreamed possible. That was the case with Apple's former chief executive officer (CEO) Steve Jobs. Time after time, he convinced his engineers to meet seemingly impossible deadlines while inventing new technologies. The young company competed successfully with much larger firms because Jobs was able to persuade followers to buy into his vision of the future. Said one employee: "It was a self-fulfilling distortion. You did the impossible, because you didn't realize it was impossible."[11]

Obviously, goals that are realistic for one group of followers will be different for another. However, when setting objectives, remember that specific goals are more effective than vague ones like "Do your best." Goals should be challenging but achievable, and followers should be rewarded for making progress toward objectives. Provide ongoing feedback to clarify expectations and to mark progress toward the goal.[12]

Argumentation

Leaders generally rely on arguments when they want to influence others who take a different side on controversial issues like immigration reform or tax increases. To succeed, they must build a strong case for their positions while at the same time refuting the arguments of those who take alternative positions. Argumentation is important to leaders in every context. In small groups, argumentative members are more likely to emerge as leaders, and groups that argue about ideas generate higher-quality solutions.[13] In organizations, supervisors must defend their own ideas and argue on behalf of subordinates.[14] In public settings, political leaders, public relations specialists, lobbyists, and others debate the merits of lowering taxes, increasing food safety regulations, reducing carbon emissions, and other policies. (Complete Self-Assessment 7.1 to determine how willing you are to argue.)

Ethical argument is based on the recognition of the difference between argumentation and verbal aggression. Argumentation is focused on ideas. Speakers make assertions or claims that they support with evidence and reasons. They present and defend positions with the ultimate goal of reaching the best solution for the group. Verbal aggressiveness, on the other hand, is hostile communication that attacks the self-concepts of others instead of (or in addition to) their stands on the issues. Aggressive tactics include the following:[15]

- Competence attacks ("You're clueless!")
- Character attacks ("You're a liar!")
- Insults

- Teasing
- Ridicule
- Maledictions (statements wishing harm to the other, like "Drop dead.")
- Profanity
- Physical appearance attacks
- Threats
- Nonverbal indicators that express hostility (looks of disgust, clenched fists, rolling eyes, demeaning tone of voice)

Argument is constructive while verbal aggression is destructive. Argument respects the dignity and worth of the other person and produces a number of positive outcomes.[16] Organizational followers give higher ratings to supervisors who are argumentative but not aggressive, and these leaders enjoy higher salaries and career satisfaction. Organizational leaders, in turn, prefer followers who have similar traits, giving argumentative (but not aggressive) subordinates higher performance reviews. In contrast, verbal aggression demeans the other party while generating a host of undesirable effects. Verbal aggressiveness has been linked, for instance, to spousal abuse and family violence and has been found to reduce student learning and instructor credibility. Employees do not like to work for aggressive supervisors who threaten their self-concepts.

Lack of argumentative competence increases the chances that leaders and others will engage in verbal aggression. If participants don't know how to make an argument, they are more likely to fall back on insults, competence attacks, and other unethical tactics (including violence) as they to try to win the dispute. According to argumentation expert Dominic Infante, we can improve our argumentation abilities and thus reduce the likelihood that we will revert to verbal aggression. Infante outlines five skills that collectively make up argumentative competence.[17] After reading about these skills, you can practice them by responding to Case Study 7.2.

Stating the controversy in propositional form. State the problem in the form of a proposition or proposal to clarify what the conflict is about. Framing the argument in the form of a proposal helps identify the sides that people are likely to take on this issue while clarifying where we stand on the issue. We also learn what kind of information we need to gather. Propositions of fact deal with what happened in the past ("Our electronic chip company failed to recognize that consumers were switching from laptops to mobile devices"), the present ("Company revenues are down"), or the future ("Unless the company develops new chips for mobile devices, there will be major reductions in our workforce"). Propositions of value deal with issues of right or wrong: "CEO salaries are way too high." "The country should accept more immigrants from Syria." Propositions of policy deal with proposed courses of action, such as how to reduce gang violence or how to secure more funding for plant expansion. Generally, those making the proposition have the burden to prove that a change is in order.

Inventing arguments. Once the controversy is clearly identified, you need to assemble your arguments. Carefully examine the proposition and develop a case either for or against the proposal. Consider the nature and extent of the problem, who or what is to blame for the situation, possible solutions as well as the best resolution, and the consequences (good and bad) that come from your solution. (Turn to Box 7.1 for additional information on how to assemble arguments.)

Presenting and defending your position. Begin by stating what you want others to accept—the conclusion or claim of your argument. Back up your claim with examples, personal experience, testimonials from others, and statistics. Also, supply reasons or logic for your position. The most common patterns of logic include analogical (drawing similarities between one case and another), causal (one event leads to another), inductive (generalizing from one or a few cases to many), and deductive (moving from a larger category or grouping to a smaller one). You can structure your argument by (1) highlighting the problem and how your solutions will meet the need (problem–solution), (2) comparing the advantages of the proposal against the status quo (comparative advantage), or (3) specifying the criteria for an ideal solution and how your proposal meets those standards (ideal solution). End your presentation with a summary of what you have established. You may need to supplement your position with further evidence and reason if it comes under attack.

Attacking other positions. This argumentative skill identifies the weaknesses in the evidence and reasoning of the other party. However, we also have an ethical obligation to identify the shortcomings of our own arguments in order to eliminate them. Look for the following fallacies of evidence and reasoning in your own position as well as in the positions of others: [18]

Faulty Evidence

- Unreliable and biased sources
- Sources lacking proper knowledge and background
- Inconsistency (disagrees with other sources, source contradicts him- or herself)
- Outdated evidence
- Evidence that appears to support a claim but does not
- Information gathered from secondhand observers
- Uncritical acceptance of statistical data
- Inaccurate or incomplete citation of sources and quotations
- Plagiarism (using the ideas or words of others without proper attribution)

Faulty Reasoning

- Comparing two things that are not alike (false analogy)
- Drawing conclusions based on too few examples or examples that aren't typical of the population as a whole (hasty generalization)
- Believing that the event that happens first always causes the event that happens second (false cause)

- Arguing that complicated problems have only one cause (single cause)
- Assuming without evidence that one event will inevitably lead to a bad result (slippery slope)
- Using the argument to support the argument (begging the question)
- Failing to offer evidence that supports the position (non sequitur)
- Attacking the person instead of the argument (ad hominem)
- Appealing to the crowd or popular opinion (ad populum)
- Resisting change based on past practices (appeal to tradition)
- Attacking a weakened version of an opponent's argument (straw argument)

Managing interpersonal relations. Prevent arguments from deteriorating into verbal aggression. If others aren't as skilled in argument as you, don't humiliate them by showing off your argumentation skills. Save your best efforts for those times you are matched with someone of equal ability. Emphasize equality and what you have in common; demonstrate that you are interested in their viewpoints. Let other participants finish their thoughts instead of interrupting, and deliver your messages in a calm voice at a moderate pace. Infante outlines an argumentative response to those who go on the verbal attack against you: (1) Refute the verbally aggressive claim underlying a personal attack, (2) point out the differences between argumentation and verbal attacks and suggest that the aggressor get back to the argument, (3) do not reciprocate the attack, (4) appeal to reason by pointing out personal attacks are not rational and that the discussion should stay on topic, (5) threaten to leave if the attacks don't cease (and carry through on your threat if necessary).

In addition to distinguishing between argumentation and aggression and developing our argumentative competence, we also need to set some ethical ground rules for argumentation. German philosopher Jürgen Habermas offers one such set of ethical guidelines called *discourse ethics*.[19] Habermas argues that communities—towns, societies, organizations—develop their policies and moral norms by making and refuting claims and assertions. For these community standards to be valid, everyone impacted by a decision has a right to be involved in making that determination, what Habermas calls the Principle of Universalization (Principle U):

> *All* affected can accept the consequences and the side effects its *general* observance can be anticipated to have for the satisfaction of *everyone's* interests (and these consequences are preferred to those of known alternative possibilities for regulation).[20] [Italics added]

According to Principle U, all parties must be free to participate in the discussion without fear of coercion and have roughly the same power to influence each other. Participants should also be prepared to justify their claims and ensure that their statements are logically sound, morally right, and sincerely offered.

Box 7.1 The Toulmin Model

Professor Stephen Toulmin developed one widely used model for developing arguments. In Toulmin's system (which has elements in common with Infante's), the argument begins when an advocate states a conclusion or claim based on fact ("The United States imprisons too many of its citizens"), definition ("Vaping is a form of smoking"), value ("The government owns too much land in the West"), or policy ("Offshore oil drilling should be halted"). Grounds or proof then support the claim. Grounding should be reliable, accurate, of high quality, consistent within itself and with other evidence, and acceptable to the audience. The warrant makes the link from the grounds to the claim. It is the reasoning that justifies that the claim is true. Good warrants appear valid and rational to listeners.

In addition to these three primary elements, Toulmin introduces a secondary triad that can come into play when constructing a unit of argument. Backing is additional evidence that supports the warrant, often providing important background information. To determine if too many Americans are in jail, the audience may need to learn about the history of the prison system in the United States, for example. Qualifiers come into play when arguers need to account for exceptions; they reduce the force of the argument. For example, many abortion opponents argue that abortions should be outlawed *except* in cases of rape or incest. Rebuttals limit claims, showing when they might not be accurate as well as anticipating objections; for instance, "Future offshore oil drilling should be prohibited, *unless* companies have already been granted permits to do so."

Sources: Rybacki, K. C., & Rybacki, D. J. (2004). *Advocacy and opposition: An introduction to argumentation*. Boston, MA: Pearson; Toulmin, S. (1958/2003). *The uses of argument*. London, England: Cambridge University Press.

Discourse ethics may set the bar for argument impossibly high. After all, power and status differences are always present. Nevertheless, keeping this ideal in mind makes moral argument more likely. In a democracy, the presumption is that citizens have a right to set the rules under which they live. Organizations are typically less democratic but even then, leaders can do their part to foster ethical discourse. They can try to locate and involve all those who have a stake in the decision and do their best to ensure that these groups and individuals have a roughly equal voice. They can encourage employees to voice their concerns and resist the temptation to suppress the expression of unpopular ideas. Organizational leaders also have an ethical obligation to encourage sound, truthful evidence and reasoning on the part of all participants.

Negotiation

Negotiation, like argumentation, involves influencing those who actively disagree. However, while the goal of argumentation is to establish the superiority of one position over another, the goal of negotiation is to reach a settlement that satisfies both sides. The negotiation process consists of back-and-forth communication aimed at reaching a joint solution when people are in disagreement.[21] A mix of compatible and incompatible interests marks all negotiations. If the parties didn't share a common goal, they wouldn't negotiate. On the other hand, they must be divided by at least one issue or they wouldn't have to negotiate to reach an agreement. Consider faculty–administration relationships, for instance. Both sides share a common interest in seeing the university survive and prosper as it carries out its mission to educate students. However, faculty members seek higher salaries and benefits and want more colleagues so they can expand their majors and programs. Administrators, for their part, seek to balance the budget. Campus executives have to make sure they can cover not only faculty costs but also pay for other staff, building projects, and other needs. They want to control faculty salaries and hire as few faculty members as possible. Professors and administrators have to negotiate their differences in order to retain faculty while assuring that the school operates within its budget.

Leaders of all kinds engage in negotiation. Project management team leaders negotiate assignments with members. Corporate purchasing agents settle on the price of goods and services with outside suppliers. CEOs and boards negotiate the price of the companies they want to acquire. Legislators haggle over the features of bills in order to pass them. Small-business owners bargain with commercial property companies over lease agreements. Entertainment and sports agents, lawyers, and realtors try to strike the best deals for their clients.

Ethical issues in negotiation generally fall into three categories: the choice of tactics, the distribution of benefits, and the impact of the settlement on those who are not at the bargaining table.[22]

Bargainers have a number of decisions to make about the tactics they will use. Most of these ethical dilemmas involve forms of deceit. Do I declare that I will not go above a certain price when I am prepared to go higher? Do I lie about the facts supporting my position? Do I threaten to pull out of the talks when I don't intend to do so? Do I claim that my supporters won't accept the terms of a settlement that they really would agree to? Do I try to secretly gather information about the other party's position? Do I make commitments that my side is not prepared to keep?

Some argue that deception is okay because both parties know that deceit is to be expected in negotiations. They treat bargaining like a poker game. Just as we expect poker players to hide their cards and bluff about the hands they hold, when we enter negotiations, we should anticipate deceit. However, not everyone understands the "rules" of negotiation. As we'll see, a cooperative negotiator operates under a different set of assumptions than a competitive one. Rules also vary by culture and may not be clear to visitors. Should tourists haggle over the price of bananas at a roadside stand in Honduras, for example? At the very least, deceit shows disrespect for the worth of the other party and thus violates Kant's imperative to treat people as ends not means. Deception reflects self-centeredness, not the other centeredness at the heart of altruism.

David Lax and James Sebenius suggest that we consider the following queries when determining if we should use deceit as a bargaining tactic or tell the truth.[23]

- Will you be comfortable with yourself the next morning? Would you want friends and family to know what you have done? The public?

- Does the tactic conform to the norm of reciprocity—that we treat others like we would like to be treated? How would you feel if the roles were reversed?

- Would you be comfortable counseling someone else to use this strategy?

- If you were to design a negotiation system from scratch, would you allow this strategy? How would you rule on this tactic if you were an outside arbitrator?

- What if everyone used the same method? Would this tactic create a desirable society?

- Are there alternative tactics you can use to avoid lying and deception?

- How can you create value instead of claiming what you think is rightfully yours?

- Does using this tactic further poison the ethical atmosphere for this type of negotiation or in this industry?

In addition to behaving honestly ourselves, we also need to promote honesty in the other party.[24] Seek to reduce the defensiveness that arises out of mutual suspicion by being trustworthy and by being willing to trust. Build a sense of mutual benevolence or concern ("we-ness"). Look for similarities (e.g., family and community ties), socialize with the other party, and hold prenegotiation sessions in neutral locations. Create opportunities for displaying trust by breaking the negotiation process into stages. Demonstrating trust in one step makes it easier to trust in the next stage. Model trustworthiness by keeping your promises, providing information, and standing behind your claims. Place the negotiation in a broader context. Businesses and suppliers generally have long-term relationships. Remind the other party that dishonesty in the current negotiation will impact future negotiations.

The second set of ethical issues in negotiation concerns how the outcomes of the negotiation are distributed. Unequal settlements are condemned as unfair. For example, Wal-Mart has been criticized for squeezing the last penny out of its suppliers. In some cases, Wal-Mart buyers refuse to pay more for products even when they cost more to make.[25] Some vendors have gone out of business as a result. Determining exactly what is fair can be difficult, but making sure all sides benefit is a good start.[26] Also, some of the questions about tactics can be applied to determining fairness as well. Does the settlement violate norms of reciprocity? Would you counsel others to follow the same approach? What if everyone claimed a disproportionate amount of the benefits? What kind of society would that create? Remember, too, that the structure of the bargaining process can be problematic. That's why it is hard for an illegal farm worker to bargain with a fruit grower who can have him deported. Wal-Mart can dictate terms to suppliers because it is so big and accounts for so much of their business. When the bargaining table is so uneven, make additional effort to ensure the process is conducted as fairly as possible.

The third set of ethical issues shifts attention beyond those directly involved in the negotiation. Decisions made by bargainers can have a negative impact on outside groups. For instance, when the local city council agrees to pay much more for garbage removal, all citizens pay the higher rates. Then, too, settlements can adversely impact the environment and future generations. Take the case of landowners who negotiate agreements with oil companies who use fracking to release gas and oil. The property owners may get generous settlements and the firms gain access to the energy they need to generate profits. However, fracking, which involves injecting water deep underground, can contaminate water sources, release radioactive materials from shale, and cause small earthquakes. (Turn to Case Study 7.3 for another example of how negotiated settlements have significant impact on outside parties.) One way to minimize the potential damage of a settlement is to keep the interests of outside stakeholders—current and future—in mind.[27] Consider the legacy you want to leave behind. Would you want to be known and remembered for the terms of this settlement?

Bargainers typically adopt either a distributive or integrative approach to negotiation.[28] Distributive negotiators think in win–lose terms. They assume that they are locked in a battle over a fixed "pie" or value. To them, any gains by one party come at the expense of the other party. Integrative negotiators adopt a win–win approach. They are convinced that the pie can be expanded and that both parties can benefit. They view negotiation as a joint problem-solving session. These contrasting perspectives generate very different behaviors:

Integrative Negotiation	Distributive Negotiation
Open sharing of information	Hidden information
Trade of values interests	Demand of interests
Interest-based discussion	Positional discussion
Mutual goals	Self-goals
Problem solving	Forcing
Explanation	Argument
Relationship building	Relationship sacrificing
Hard on problem	Hard on people

Source: Spangle, M. L., & Isenhart, M. W. (2003). *Negotiation: Communication for diverse settings.* Thousand Oaks, CA: SAGE, p. 15. Used with permission.

Comparing the two approaches reveals that distributive bargainers are more likely to engage in unethical negotiation behavior. They are tempted to deceive, generate unfair settlements, and enter into agreements that have negative consequences for outsiders. (Self-Assessment 7.2 introduces some tough bargaining tactics and asks how willing you might be to use them.) Leaders, then, should adopt an integrative approach whenever possible. Nonetheless, there do appear to be times when the situation calls for a win–lose approach, such as when buying a used car. We also risk being taken advantage of if we come to the table with an integrative approach and the other party is out to get as much as she or he can.

Harvard negotiation experts Roger Fisher, William Ury, and Bruce Patton developed one widely used integrative approach that equips negotiators to take a win–win approach while protecting themselves from being victimized. They call their problem-solving approach *the principled negotiation model*. Here are the four steps of principled negotiation.[29]

1. *Separate the people from the problem.* Make sure you address the human side of negotiation. Try to build a good working relationship from the start. Visualize yourself sitting at the same side of the table as the other person, working together to reach an agreement good for both of you. During the negotiation, address the three types of people problems: perception, emotion, and communication. Don't blame the other party but try to understand his or her perspective. Deal with any misconceptions they have of you. Recognize and address the emotions both sides feel; don't react to emotional outbursts but let the other party let off steam. Actively listen; use "I" language ("I am disappointed with your latest offer") rather than "you" language ("You are trying to take advantage of me"); and think carefully about what you want to say.

2. *Focus on interests, not positions.* A bargaining position is the negotiator's public stance (e.g., "I want a starting salary of $100,000"). An interest, on the other hand, is the reason why the negotiator takes that position. Focusing on positions blinds negotiators to the fact that an interest can be met several ways. In the salary example, the interest of the employee is having enough money to afford housing in an expensive city. This interest could be met with a smaller salary combined with a housing allowance. Or perhaps the company could loan the money for down payment on a house, a loan that is forgiven after several years of employment. Remember that basic human needs like security, well-being, belonging, control over one's life, and recognition can play an important role in negotiations. In talks between the United States and Mexico, for example, the U.S. Secretary of Energy refused to pay a higher price for natural gas, a price negotiated earlier by an oil consortium. The energy secretary (who assumed that the negotiation was about money only) thought that the Mexicans would give in and lower the price because they didn't have another buyer. But the Mexicans also had an interest in being treated with respect. They saw the U.S. action as bullying

their country. Instead of selling the gas, Mexico burned it off.

3. *Invent options for mutual gain.* Having a number of options leads to decisions that are better for both sides. Nevertheless, negotiators often skip this step because they come to premature judgment, look for one single answer, assume that there is one fixed pie, and believe that the other side is responsible for solving their own problems. To overcome these obstacles, bargainers need to separate inventing options from deciding on them, broaden their options, look for mutual gain, and provide other parties with a decision that is easy to accept. Consider the creative solution generated by a man and a woman in a wine shop. They both reached for the last bottle of a particular vintage. Neither was willing to give up the prize. The man wanted the wine because he and his wife drank this particular wine on their first date and they were going to celebrate their first anniversary. The woman, who was a bottle collector, needed this wine bottle for her collection but she didn't drink wine. In the end, they decided to share the cost of the wine. The husband promised to send the bottle to the collector after he and his wife consumed its contents.[30]

4. *Insist on objective criteria.* Don't get into a battle of wills as you approach the final agreement, as one of you will have to back down. One party may force the other into an unsatisfactory solution as a result. Instead, agree on a set of criteria when coming to a settlement. Employ fair standards. This might include referring to the Kelly Blue Book for used car prices, for instance, or the Zillow real estate website for area home values. Use fair procedures (taking turns, turning to an outside expert) as well. One fair procedure is the forced-choice technique. When you were young, your mom or dad may have used this strategy to divide up cakes and pies. In this procedure, one child cuts the pie and the other gets the first choice of which slice to take. Bargainers used the same approach to divide up deep seabed mining sites in the Law of the Sea negotiations. Half of the mining sites were to be mined by private companies from richer nations and the other half by the United Nations (UN) on behalf of poorer countries. The poorer nations worried that the private mining companies, which were more knowledgeable, would keep the best sites to themselves. To break the deadlock, negotiators determined that the private firm would present the UN group with two sites and the UN would then select one. The private company thus had incentive to offer two promising locations since it didn't know which site it would get. (The "Leadership Ethics at the Movies: *Bridge of Spies*" box below describes another real-life, high-stakes negotiation.)

Leadership Ethics at the Movies

BRIDGE OF SPIES

Key cast members: Tom Hanks, Mark Rylance, Amy Ryan, Alan Alda

Synopsis: During the height of the Cold War, New York attorney James Donovan (played by Hanks) is selected by the state bar association to represent captured Russian spy Rudolf Abel (Rylance). Donovan loses the case but convinces the judge to sentence Abel to a long prison sentence instead of death as "insurance" in case Russia captures a U.S. spy. That insurance is needed when American U-2 spy plane pilot Francis Gary Powers is shot down over the Soviet Union. The Central Intelligence Agency (CIA) then approaches Donovan to secretly negotiate an exchange of Abel for Powers in East Germany. While in East Germany, Donovan learns of an American citizen taken captive by the East German government during the construction of the Berlin Wall. He decides, against the wishes of the CIA, to release Abel only if both Powers and the American are returned. To pull off the deal, he must negotiate with both the Russians and the East Germans, who sometimes have competing interests and threaten to pull out of the talks. The exchange takes place at Germany's Glienicke Bridge. Rylance won an Oscar as best supporting actor for his portrayal of Rudolph Abel. Based on historical events.

Rating: PG-13 for some violence and strong language

Themes: distributive and integrative negotiation, dirty tricks, deception, secrecy, courage, compassion, duty

Discussion Starters

1. What dirty tricks did the East Germans and Soviet negotiators employ? Did the Americans use any unethical strategies?

2. Was Donovan justified in lying to his family about his whereabouts during the negotiation?

3. Was it ethical for Donovan to risk the return of Powers in order to secure the release of the other American?

4. What strengths and character traits made Donovan an effective negotiator?

RESISTING INFLUENCE

Up to this point, our focus has been on making ethical use of influence strategies. However, along the way, I noted that as leaders, we must also resist unethical influence attempts. We must be prepared to resist the power of low expectations. When faced with verbal aggression, we need to respond with argumentative competence. When negotiators try to take advantage of us, we should refuse to be victimized. Our groups and organizations suffer if we fail to resist unethical influence. Possible costs include engaging in unethical and illegal (and even deadly) activities, hiring the wrong employees, paying too much for goods and services, giving to unworthy causes, undermining the organization's mission and values, and taking unnecessary risks.

Arizona State social psychologist Robert Cialdini believes that mental shortcuts (what he refers to "automatic, click-whirr responses") leave leaders and others vulnerable to unethical influence.[31] As technology increases the pace of life, it is impossible to carefully evaluate every piece of information that comes to us through Twitter, YouTube, websites, digital books, papers and magazines, cell phones, cable television, streaming video, and other sources. To cope with this flood of data, we frequently make decisions based on a single piece of information instead of considering the entire situation. These mental shortcuts help us deal with information overload and save time. For example, many of us associate price with quality ("If it is expensive, it must be better") and believe that putting something on sale automatically makes it a bargain. Automatic responses produce poor choices if profiteers and others take advantage of the shortcuts to their advantage. Higher price doesn't guarantee quality, for instance, and the item on sale may have been grossly overpriced to begin with, meaning it still isn't a bargain. Recognizing the triggers that activate our click-whirr responses should prompt us to take a critical look at persuasive attempts and to avoid costly missteps. Important triggers include the following.

Reciprocation (Give and Take)

Reciprocation—the obligation to repay others—is a universal norm of human society that encourages cooperation. We feel obligated to respond in kind to the help that we have received from others. The power of reciprocation is long lasting. Following Hurricane Katrina in 2005, the Netherlands provided flood assistance to New Orleans to repay the city for the help it provided to the Dutch after a 1953 flood.

Marketers, salespeople, and public relations professionals are well aware of this standard of human behavior. The Audubon Society, the March of Dimes, and other charities send out free address labels, calendars, and even stamps in hopes that recipients will return the favor by making a donation. Go to warehouse retailer Costco on a weekend and you might be able to eat an entire lunch made up of free samples of cheese, crackers, fruit, sausage, pizza, juice, smoothies, and other foods. Shoppers often respond by buying the items, not because they always taste good but because they feel a sense of obligation. Special interest groups donate to Congressional representatives in hopes they will reciprocate by supporting their legislation.

In another variation of give and take (called *rejection then retreat*), persuaders first make an extreme request and then back off, asking for less. The small request is seen as a concession and, as a result, targets are more likely to comply with it. Also, the follow-up request appears more reasonable than the first one. Cialdini fell victim to this tactic when a Boy Scout approached him to spend $5 on tickets to a circus. He refused. However, when the Scout then asked him to buy $1 candy bars, he agreed, even though he doesn't like chocolate bars. On a more serious note, rejection and retreat may have been behind the Watergate scandal. Nixon's reelection committee agreed to this $250,000 plan by G. Gordon Liddy to break into Democratic party headquarters after first rejecting his earlier proposals for two much more elaborate plans to carry out campaign dirty tricks. One earlier plan would have cost $1 million and the other $500,000. Committee members probably thought the $250,000 Watergate project was a bargain.

The reciprocity norm can lead to disastrous decisions, as the Watergate Scandal demonstrates. It can also produce unwanted debts and trigger unequal exchanges. Concerns about reciprocity are behind attempts to limit political contributions, to limit the size of gifts that buyers can receive from suppliers, and to prevent medical school faculty from working for drug companies.

One way to resist the power of reciprocity is by turning down the initial favor. Don't take free samples at the store, don't accept free trials of Amway products, turn down contributions from controversial donors, don't accept golf outings and lavish dinners from suppliers, and so on. Another strategy is to determine if the offer is genuinely offered. If it is genuine, then reciprocate. If it is a trick, then you are under no obligation to return the favor. Finally, you can turn the tables on unethical influencers. Use the address labels, eat the free cheese and crackers, accept a road atlas, and attend a free financial planning dinner and presentation, but don't give anything in return.

Commitment and Consistency

The second mental shortcut comes out of the desire to appear consistent with previous choices and actions. Consistency reduces the need for careful thought and reduces the likelihood of regret or dissonance after making a decision. Commitments play an important role in consistency. Once we make a commitment, no matter how minor, we want to remain consistent. Using small commitments to leverage bigger ones is called the *foot in the door* strategy. Donors who give small amounts at first are likely to follow up with larger contributions and may even volunteer for the organization. Small sales convert prospects into customers who are likely to make further purchases. Writing down goals increases the likelihood that individuals will follow through and reach those objectives.

Public statements increase the power of commitment. During the Korean War, some American prisoners made pro-communist statements. When their comments were posted around camp or broadcast on the radio, these captives stood by their declarations. Those who want to lose weight or quit smoking are more likely to follow through if they publicly commit to do so. In addition, the greater the effort that goes into the commitment, the more likely that the individual will stay the course. Fraternity hazing rituals demonstrate this principle. During Hell Weeks at some colleges, initiates stand in the snow, suffer beatings, drink until they pass out, are locked in dark rooms, and so on. These hardships increase, not decrease, their loyalty to the group, and they are eager to make next year's pledges undergo the same painful experiences. Finally, when an attitude is internalized through commitment, it is highly resistant to change. The power of internalization was demonstrated in one experiment designed to promote energy saving. Investigators promised Iowa homeowners that if they saved energy, their names would be put in the local newspaper. When the experimenters withdrew the promise of publicity (an external reward), the homeowners actually increased their energy savings because they had internalized the commitment to do so.

The commitment trigger can be used for good ends, such as to increase contributions to charities and to recruit more volunteers. Nonetheless, unscrupulous persuaders often use it to get us to buy unneeded items, to go along with unethical requests, and so on. Cialdini admits that it would be impossible (and undesirable) to eliminate this shortcut from our lives. However, he urges us to avoid dangerous consistency by listening to our stomachs and hearts. If we get a knot in the pit of our stomachs, we need to step back. In these cases, let the exploiter know you are aware of his or her methods. If we feel a momentary doubt about our decision, ask, "Would I make the same choice again?" If not, then don't make the decision in the first place.

Social Proof

In many social situations, we look to others to determine how we should behave, a fact that advertisers seize on to declare that products are "best sellers" or to declare that they are the "fastest-growing" companies. Uncertainty increases the impact of social proof. If we don't know how to interpret the situation, we are more likely to look to others for guidance. This helps account for the so-called bystander effect, where onlookers fail to intervene to help shooting victims or those suffering from strokes or other health emergencies. In many cases, passersby are not sure if the individual is hurt. If others walk on, they assume that there is no emergency and pass by themselves. This is more likely in crowded cities, where citizens are distracted and are less likely to know one another.

Due to the power of social proof, one well-publicized suicide or school shooting is often followed by copycat suicides and mass shootings. Social proof also helps bind members who are often isolated and uncertain of how to act to extremist groups and religious cults.

To resist the social proof trigger, disengage the automatic pilot. Recognize counterfeit evidence of social proof. Actors, for example, give many commercial testimonials, and laugh tracks don't mean a situation comedy is funny. Recognize, too, that there is "pluralistic ignorance" that can lead us to the wrong conclusion. A respected bank in Singapore saw a run on its funds for no particular reason. Why? During a bus strike, a large crowd gathered at a bus stop in front of the bank. Passersby panicked, thinking that that the crowd was there to withdraw funds from a failing bank. Other passersby then got in line to take out funds, and the bank was forced to close in order to avoid a complete crash.

Liking

Most of us recognize that we are more likely to comply with the requests of people we like. This helps explain the success of the Tupperware party, where acquaintances buy from friends and neighbors who host the gatherings. Liking is based on a number of factors, including (1) physical appearance (more attractive people are more likely to get elected, to avoid jail, and to get help), (2) similarity (in dress, hobbies, age, religion, habits, political party), (3) compliments (statements of liking, complements, praise), (4) contact and cooperation (familiarity breeds liking), and (5) association (being linked to positive events, attractive people, and status symbols makes people like us more).

Liking is a powerful force that is almost impossible to resist. Rather than spend energy on resisting, determine instead if the liking is justified. Do you like the persuader more than you should, given the circumstances? If so, then separate the person from the proposal. Focus on the merits of the deal instead.

Authority

Obeying authority allows organizations, communities, and societies to coordinate their activities. However, blind obedience can be disastrous, such as when nurses obey the misguided directives of doctors and soldiers fail to challenge illegal orders. (See the discussion of intelligent disobedience in Chapter 6.) Often, we comply with the appearance of authority, not real authority. We are more likely to obey when persuaders have prestigious titles (MD, Professor, Reverend), are dressed in the cloak of authority (suits, uniforms), and are surrounded by status symbols like fancy jewelry, spacious corner offices, and large houses.

When confronted with an authority figure's influence attempt, ask, "Is this authority truly an expert?" Consider both the person's credentials as well as the relevance of the credentials to the issue at hand. Consider the trustworthiness of the source as well. Even if the expert is truly an expert, she or he may not act in your best interest. A financial planner may put you in a poor investment, for example, if she or he gets a generous commission for selling this particular product.

Scarcity

The scarcity principle is based on the notion that when opportunities are less available, they appear more valuable. Companies take advantage of this shortcut when they declare, for instance, that there are limited seats left on a particular flight or that the mattress sale ends soon. Scarcity gains its power from the fact that things that are tough to get are generally better but also from the fact that we react against restrictions on our freedoms. Gun sales soar when new regulations are proposed (even if there is little chance that they will pass). Censoring sexual content can make it more desirable.

The scarcity principle exerts the most influence when items or information are newly scarce, such as when a government grants rights to traditionally oppressed groups. If these new rights are restricted, the dispossessed are more likely to rebel. Competition amps up the impact of scarcity. Consider, for example, the stampede of customers at retailers during Black Friday sales. Occasionally, individuals are crushed to death as shoppers battle for bargains. Leaders can also find themselves caught up in competition that clouds their judgment. CEOs competing with rivals to buy another firm may offer too much. Sports executives can find themselves paying exorbitant amounts for free agents when they bid against other teams.

Because scarcity muddles our thinking, this trigger is hard to resist. We often find our blood pressure rising when we compete. Yet, this physical reaction should signal us to calm down and proceed with caution. Consider the fact that function, not scarcity, brings value. An item, person, or entity has value because of its usefulness, not because of how scarce it is. Pay only what the item, company, or free agent is worth to you and your organization, regardless of its limited availability.

IMPLICATIONS AND APPLICATIONS

- Selecting the appropriate influence tactic is one of the most important ethical determinations you will make as a leader, shaping whether you brighten or darken the lives of followers.
- Compliance-gaining tactics are direct attempts to get targets to go along with requests. Prosocial strategies (rational persuasion, inspirational appeals, coordination, collaboration) are based on soft power and are more likely to generate positive emotions in receivers. Antisocial tactics (legitimating, pressure) are more threatening

and generate negative feelings. Be cautious about using antisocial tactics, but recognize that the morality of a strategy depends on the ends it serves. Consider your emotional–ethical threshold—how far you are willing to go to generate negative emotions in order to get your way.

- Your expectations as a leader can have a powerful impact on your followers who live up or down to your expectancies. Positive self-fulfilling prophecies (the Pygmalion effect) improve performance. Negative prophecies (the Golem effect) lower performance. You can combat the negative expectations that your leaders have of you by having high expectancies of yourself (the Galatea effect).

- Use direct and indirect methods to communicate positive expectations. Direct means include statements of support and complements. Indirect channels include (1) climate (positive social and emotional atmosphere), (2) feedback (frequent, positive, detailed), (3) input (attention and focus), and (4) output (opportunities to speak, to offer opinions, and to disagree).

- When communicating expectations, avoid deception, ability grouping, and setting unrealistic expectations. Instead, seek to raise the performance of the entire group through building self-efficacy and promoting a learning orientation. Set specific, challenging yet reasonable goals. Provide ongoing feedback and reward progress toward the objectives.

- Argumentation is the key to influencing others who take opposing positions on controversial issues. To engage in moral argument, first recognize the difference between constructive argumentation, which focuses on ideas, and destructive verbal aggression, which attacks the self-concepts of others.

- You are more likely to engage in argument, not verbal aggression, if you develop your argumentative competence. Competent argument is based on five skills: (1) stating the controversy in propositional form, (2) inventing arguments, (3) presenting and defending your position, (4) attacking other positions, and (5) maintaining positive relations with other arguers.

- Setting ethical ground rules can increase the likelihood that participants will engage in moral argument. Try to include those who are impacted by the decision in the discussion, allow all voices to be heard, and monitor the quality and truthfulness of claims, evidence, and logic.

- Negotiation is back-and-forth communication designed to reach a settlement that satisfies both sides when parties share compatible and incompatible interests. Keep in mind the three ethical issues you'll face as a negotiator: choice of tactics, the distribution of benefits, and the impact of the settlement on outsiders.

- Avoid distributive bargaining, a win–lose approach to negotiation that may tempt you to engage in unethical tactics. Take an integrative or win–win approach that promotes ethical behaviors instead.

- Principled negotiation is one integrative approach to negotiation that protects bargainers from being taken advantage of. To engage in principled negotiation, (1) separate the people from the problem; (2) focus on interests, not positions; (3) invent options for mutual gain; and (4) and insist on objective criteria when reaching a settlement.

- As a leader, you will need to resist influence as well as exert influence. Mental shortcuts make us vulnerable to unscrupulous persuaders and can be costly to our groups and organizations. Defend against triggers that generate automatic and sometimes faulty (costly, unethical) compliance: reciprocation (give and take), commitment and consistency, social proof, liking, authority, and scarcity.

FOR FURTHER EXPLORATION, CHALLENGE, AND SELF-ASSESSMENT

1. Keep a compliance log for a day. Record the times that you are the target of compliance messages and the messages you use to get others to comply. Describe the tactics used, whether or not they were effective, reasons for resistance, and your emotional response to messages. Conclude by evaluating the ethics of each tactic based on its power base, objective, and emotional–ethical threshold.

2. What expectations does your leader have of you? How does she or he communicate these expectations? If these expectations are low, how can you counteract their effect and raise the expectancies of your leader? Write up your conclusions.

3. What has been your experience with ability grouping? Is this strategy unethical? Share your thoughts with a partner.

4. Identify forms of faulty evidence and reasoning in a public argument about an ethical issue. Draw from websites, blogs, newspaper editorials, speeches, interviews, debates, congressional hearings, and other sources. Possible topics might include drone warfare, capital punishment, gun control, global warming, and reducing the national debt. Evaluate whether the sources are engaged in ethical argument.

5. Develop an argument based on Case Study 7.2. Join with others who take the same side as you to present and defend your position.

6. Pair off with someone else and compare your scores on Self-Assessment 7.1 or Self-Assessment 7.2. For Self-Assessment 7.1, explain why you both scored as you did, whether you are comfortable with your level of argumentativeness, and how you might raise your score. For Self-Assessment 7.2, explain why each of you thought some tactics were more acceptable than others.

7. Prepare for a negotiation using the steps of the principled negotiation method. How will you separate the people from the problem? How will you identify your interests while acknowledging their interests? What might be some creative win–win options for settlement? What might be objective criteria that could be used to reach a fair agreement?

8. Identify the influence triggers used in the commercials in an hour of television. Are the advertisers making unethical use of these strategies? Does identifying the shortcut increase your resistance to the influence attempt?

STUDENT STUDY SITE

Visit the student study site at **study.sagepub.com/johnsonmecl6e** to access full SAGE journal articles for further research and information on key chapter topics.

Case Study 7.1

GOING DIGITAL

After 125 years, the *South Town Press* is going digital. A large Connecticut-based newspaper chain recently purchased *South Town*, which is the only paper in a medium-sized Alabama city. Soon, *South Town Press* will be converting from traditional daily paper delivery to an online format. Executives at headquarters decided to make this change at all of the chain's papers in response to shifting reading habits. The subscriber base for traditional newspapers is shrinking as more people access their news through phones, tablets, and computers.

Converting to a digital format is a major challenge, particularly for a newspaper with a long history like *South Town Press*. Every aspect of the operation will be impacted, including the news department, advertising, and circulation. The electronic version of the paper will be much shorter, requiring layoffs in the newsroom. At the same time, new technical support staff will be hired.

Joseph "Joe" Pia has been assigned as the new publisher at *South Town Press* to oversee the transition. Joe has a long history in the newspaper business and recently led the move to digital publishing at another of the company's papers in the Midwest. That transition succeeded, but at a high cost. Employees didn't think they could make the change, which slowed the process, and some quit. Salespeople struggled to sell digital ads, and the number of online subscriptions was low at first, though circulation eventually rebounded. Some of the initial digital editions of the paper crashed due to technical problems.

Joe wants to learn from his prior experience to ensure a smoother switch over at *South Town Press*. He believes that *South Town Press* employees have the ability to make the change but, like the staff at his last post, lack confidence in their ability to do so. He also knows that layoffs will initially lower employee morale. Joe takes a couple of days before arriving at *South Town Press* to develop a strategy for the transition. In addition to all the technical details, he gives careful thought to whom he needs to influence and what he wants to communicate to each group and individual. He knows he wants to boost the confidence of the entire staff of 40 while setting a high standard for his leadership team made up of the news editor, information systems manager, circulation manager, and advertising manager. However, he is not sure how he should go about conveying these messages to his staff and team.

Discussion Probes

1. What obstacles does Joe face in communicating high expectations to the entire staff? What advantages does he have?

2. What initial steps should Joe take when arrives at *South Town*?

3. How can the new publisher foster self-efficacy in his entire staff? How can he promote a learning orientation?

4. How can Joe use indirect channels to communicate high expectations to each individual member of his leadership team?

Case Study 7.2

THE PLIGHT OF THE MODERN CHICKEN

Americans eat more chicken than any other type of meat, with producers raising nine billion birds a year. The popularity of chicken is due in large part to its low cost. Through selective breeding, chicken farms raise birds that grow faster and bigger while eating less feed. In the 1920s, the average broiler or meat chicken took four months to reach an average weight of three pounds. Now, it takes less than half that time (48 days) to produce a bird twice that size.

All the focus on rapid growth and size, while good for consumers, has been hard on the chickens. The skeletons of juvenile birds do not develop fast enough to support their body weight. An estimated 15%–30% suffer from leg and joint problems, which makes it impossible for them to walk. As a result, they are forced to lie down and are more susceptible to lesions and other diseases. Their size also makes them prone to heart failure. (Consumers have complained about the tough "woody" taste of some chicken breasts from large birds.) Most meat chickens are slaughtered when young but others are kept to reproduce in breeder flocks. These breeding chickens face an additional health problem. According to a poultry geneticist at Purdue University, "They're so big and heavy, if we let them keep on eating, they couldn't reproduce. So they have to be on a diet, a severe diet, and they're always hungry."[1]

Leaders at the American Society for the Prevention of Cruelty to Animals (ASCPA) and other animal rights groups want poultry companies to abandon the faster-growing breeds and return to slower-growing birds, which currently account for only 2% of meat chickens sold. Slower-growing chickens are in demand in Europe and are popular among U.S. farmers who want to raise the birds by allowing them to roam outdoors. Whole Foods Market, which features organic foods, has announced that it will sell only slower-growing chickens by 2024. Company officials believe that slower-growing birds are healthier and taste better, but they recognize that these chickens will be more expensive to raise. A comparison of a slower-growing breed and the most popular broiler found that the slow-growing chicken consumed 25% more feed.

Officials at the National Chicken Council (NCC), which represents the poultry industry, take issue with the claim that faster-growing birds are unhealthy or suffering, noting their members "have an ethical obligation to make sure that the animals on their farms are well cared for."[2] The NCC has developed a set of welfare guidelines for members based on providing birds with adequate food, water, space, and veterinary care. The organization notes that because fast-growing breeds eat less, less land needs to be set aside to grow chicken feed.

Discussion Probes

1. How would you state this controversy in propositional form? Is your proposition one of fact, value, definition, or policy?

2. Are you for or against the proposition?

(Continued)

(Continued)

3. What evidence would you offer for your position? Where would you look for more information to support your claim?

4. What logic would you use to support your claim?

5. What evidence and logic might the other side use? What objections might they raise to your position?

6. What might be some faulty evidence and reasoning in your argument? In the argument of the other party?

Notes

1. Charles, D. (2016, March 30). Why Whole Foods wants a slower-growing chicken. *National Public Radio*.

2. Animal welfare for broiler chickens. (n.d.). *National Chicken Council*. Retrieved from http://www.nationalchickencouncil.org/industry-issues/animal-welfare-for-broiler-chickens/

Sources

A growing problem: Selective breeding in the chicken industry: The case for slower growth. (2015, November). *ASPCA*. Retrieved from https://www.aspca.org/sites/default/files/chix_white_paper_nov2015_lores.pdf

Bunge, J. (2016, March 17). Whole Foods shifts to slower-growing chickens. *The Wall Street Journal*.

Farm animal welfare: Chickens. (n.d.). *MSPCA Angell*. Retrieved from https://www.mspca.org/animal_protection/farm-animal-welfare-chickens/

Picchi, A. (2016, March 30). 'Woody breast' could bite the chicken business. *CBS News*.

Case Study 7.3

THE HOUSING DEMOLITION DERBY

At first glance, developers make ideal homebuyers. They can pay cash, ensure a quick closing, and almost always outbid individual purchasers. No wonder sellers are often eager to negotiate deals with homebuilders. However, neighbors complain that they pay the long-term costs of these negotiations. In popular urban neighborhoods, developers tear down existing homes and replace them with bigger, more expensive houses. A $300,000 home may be replaced with two $600,000 homes. The new houses completely fill lots that once provided green space and privacy. Those living next door can find themselves living in the perpetual shadow of these McMansions.

Since 2000, Portland, Oregon, has experienced more urban infill than any other of the largest 50 cities in the United States. Developers in Portland target small houses on large lots or homes that aren't well maintained. Many of these homes were constructed in the 1930s or earlier and may have historic value. Knocking them down changes the character of the area. The neighborhood becomes more expensive, driving lower- and middle-class homeowners out in a process called *gentrification*. As one resident caught in the gentrification process put it, "This neighborhood is under attack."[1] Then, too, there is concern about the asbestos, lead-based paint, and other toxic materials that are released during the demolition process. In one six-month period, each demolished house generated 58,558 pounds of landfill waste.

Driven by complaints from neighbors, the city of Portland adopted new rules stipulating that developers won't be issued demolition permits until 35 days after residents are notified. Developers can now receive grants for deconstruction (reusing and recycling). Neighborhood and preservation groups are urging the city to adopt even stronger measures like those in other cities. Vancouver, British Columbia, requires a $15,000 deposit for a demolition permit for pre-1940 residential dwellings or structures considered to have "character." In San Francisco, dwellings over fifty years old have to undergo a Historic Resource Evaluation before demolition approval. Seattle requires builders to meet reuse and recycling requirements.

Portland area developers and real estate brokers assert that urban infill benefits the community by employing construction workers and by providing additional housing to meet the city's housing shortage. This, they believe, keeps homes more affordable overall. Other observers note that some houses scheduled for demolition are poorly made and hard to upgrade. A few dwellings have deteriorated beyond repair. Demolition or deconstruction is the best option in these cases.

Discussion Probes

1. If you were a homeowner approached by a developer, would you refuse to sell based on the concerns of your neighbors?
2. Should neighbors be able to block home demolitions?
3. What responsibility do developers have to established neighborhoods?
4. What benefits do you see in urban infill?
5. Should Portland follow the lead of Vancouver, British Columbia; Seattle; and San Francisco and put additional restrictions on home demolitions? Why or why not?
6. What solutions might benefit sellers, developers, and neighbors?

Note

1. Francis, M. (2015, April 8). Portland's demolition debate lands close to home. *The Oregonian/Oregon Live.*

(Continued)

(Continued)

Sources

Classen, A. (n.d.). Demolition wave rising. *NW Examiner*. Retrieved from http://nwexaminer.com/demolition-wave-rising

Jordan, J. (2015, October 7). Momentum building to reduce demolition waste. *Restore Oregon*.

Seattle Department of Construction and Inspections (2015, January 9). *Seattle permits: Demolition and deconstruction*. Retrieved from http://www.seattle.gov/sdci

Silverman, D. (2013, August 16). *Demolition of dwelling units is strictly regulated by the San Francisco planning code*. Retrieved from http://www.reubenlaw.com/index.php/rj/singleUpdate/new_rules_on_residential_demolitions_and_merger

Spencer-Hartle, B. (2015, October 7). The state of demolitions in Portland. *Restore Oregon*.

The effects of home demolitions. (n.d.). *Portlanders for Effective Zoning*. Retrieved from http://www.fixportlandzoning.com/demolitions.html

SELF-ASSESSMENT 7.1

The Argumentativeness Scale

Instructions: This questionnaire contains statements about arguing controversial issues. Indicate how often each statement is true for you personally by placing the appropriate number in the blank to the left of the statement. Use the following scale:

1 = almost always true

2 = rarely true

3 = occasionally true

4 = often true

5 = almost always true

_____ 1. While in an argument, I worry that the person I am arguing with will form a negative impression of me.

_____ 2. Arguing over controversial issues improves my intelligence.

_____ 3. I enjoy avoiding arguments.

_____ 4. I am energetic and enthusiastic when I argue.

_____ 5. Once I finish an argument, I promise myself that I will not get into another.

_____ 6. Arguing with a person creates more problems for me than it solves.

_____ 7. I have a pleasant, good feeling when I win a point in an argument.

_____ 8. When I finish arguing with someone, I feel nervous and upset.

_____ 9. I enjoy a good argument over a controversial issue.

_____ 10. I get an unpleasant feeling when I realize I am about to get into an argument.

_____ 11. I enjoy defending my point of view on an issue.

_____ 12. I am happy when I keep an argument from happening.

_____ 13. I do not like to miss the opportunity to argue a controversial issue.

_____ 14. I prefer being with people who rarely disagree with me.

_____ 15. I consider an argument an exciting intellectual challenge.

_____ 16. I find myself unable to think of effective points during an argument.

_____ 17. I feel refreshed and satisfied after an argument on a controversial issue.

_____ 18. I have the ability do well in an argument.

_____ 19. I try to avoid getting into arguments.

_____ 20. I feel excitement when I expect that a conversation I am in is leading to an argument.

Scoring:

1. Add your scores on items 2, 4, 7, 9, 11, 13, 15, 17, 18, 20.

(A) Total = _____

2. Add your scores on items 1, 3, 5, 6, 8, 10, 12, 14, 16, 19.

(B) Total = _____

3. Subtract your (B) total from your (A) total.

(C) Total = _____

Score: If the result is any number between 14 and 40, you may have a high motivation to argue. If the result is any number between -4 and 13, you may have a moderate motivation to argue. If the result is any number between -5 and -25, you may have a low motivation to argue.

Source: Infante, D. A., & Rancer, A. S. (1982). A conceptualization and measure of argumentativeness. _Journal of Personality Assessment_, 72–80. Used with permission.

SELF-ASSESSMENT 7.2

Incidents in Negotiation Questionnaire

Instructions: In completing the questionnaire, please try to be as candid as you can about what you think is appropriate and acceptable to do. These are a list of tactics that negotiators sometimes use. You should consider these tactics in the context of a situation in which you will be negotiating for something that is very important to you and your business or other organization. For each tactic, evaluate how appropriate it would be to use this tactic in context specified above, based on the following scale.

1	2	3	4	5	6	7
Not at All Appropriate			Somewhat Appropriate			Very Appropriate

_____ 1. Promise that good things will happen to your opponent if he or she gives you what you want, even if you know that you can't (or won't) deliver these things when the other's cooperation is obtained.

_____ 2. Intentionally misrepresent the nature of negotiations to your opponent in order to strengthen your negotiating arguments or position.

_____ 3. Attempt to get your opponent fired or removed from his or her position so that a new person will take his or her place.

_____ 4. Intentionally misrepresent the nature of negotiations to your constituency (the group you represent) in order to protect delicate discussions that have occurred.

_____ 5. Gain information about an opponent's negotiation position by paying your friends, associates, and contacts to get this information for you.

_____ 6. Make an opening demand that is far greater than what you really hope to settle for.

_____ 7. Convey a false impression that you are in absolutely no hurry to come to a negotiated agreement, thereby putting time pressure on your opponent to concede quickly.

_____ 8. In return for concessions from your opponent now, offer to make future concessions, which you will not follow through on.

_____ 9. Threaten to make your opponent look weak or foolish in front of a boss or others to whom he or she is accountable, even if you know that you won't actually carry out the threat.

_____10. Deny the validity of information that your opponent has that weakens your negotiating position, even though that information is true and valid.

_____ 11. Intentionally misrepresent the progress of negotiations to your constituency in order to make your own position appear stronger.

_____ 12. Talk directly to the people who your opponent reports to or is accountable to and tell them things that will undermine their confidence in your opponent as a negotiator.

_____ 13. Gain information about an opponent's negotiating position by cultivating his or her friendship through expensive gifts, entertaining, or personal favors.

_____ 14. Make an opening demand so high/low that it seriously undermines your opponents' confidence in his or her ability to negotiate a satisfactory settlement.

_____ 15. Guarantee that your constituency will uphold the settlement reached, although you know that they will likely violate the agreement later.

_____ 16. Gain information about an opponent's negotiation position by trying to recruit or hire one of your opponent's teammates (on the condition that the teammate bring confidential information with him or her).

Scoring: Add up your scores for each factor:

Traditional competitive bargaining: Items 6, 7, 14 _____ (range 3–21)

Attacking opponent's network: Items 3, 9, 12 _____ (range 3–21)

False promises: Items 1, 8, 15 _____ (range 3–21)

Misrepresentation: Items 2, 4, 10, 11 _____ (range 4–28)

Inappropriate information gathering: Items 5, 13, 16 _____ (range 3–21)

The higher the score on each factor, the more you approve of its use. North American respondents taking this survey were most likely to use traditional competitive bargaining tactics.

Source: Robinson, R. J., Lewicki, R. J., & Donahue, E. M. (2000). Extending and testing a five factor model of ethical and unethical barging tactics: Introducing the SINS scale. *Journal of Organizational Behavior, 21,* 649–664. Used with permission of the publisher.

Additional Source

Ma, A. (2010). The SINS in business negotiations: Explore the cross-cultural differences in business ethics between Canada and China. *Journal of Business Ethics, 91,* 123–135.

NOTES

1. Yukl, G. (2013). *Leadership in organizations* (8th ed.). Upper Saddle River, NJ: Prentice-Hall; Yukl, G., Falbe, C. M., & Yount, J. (1993). Patterns of influence behaviors for managers. *Group and Organization Management, 18,* 5–28.
2. Hunter, J. E., & Boster F. (1987). A model of compliance-gaining message selection. *Communication Monographs, 54,* 63–84; Wilson, S. R. (2002). *Seeking and resisting compliance: Why people say what they do when trying to influence others.* Thousand Oaks, CA: SAGE.
3. See, for example, Eden, D. (1990). *Pygmalion in management.* Lexington, MA: Lexington Books/D.C. Heath; Eden, D. (1993). Interpersonal expectations in organizations. In P. D. Blank (Ed.), *Interpersonal expectations: Theory, research, and applications* (pp. 154–178). Cambridge, England: Cambridge University Press; Eden, D., & Shami, A. B. (1982). Pygmalion goes to boot camp: Expectancy, leadership, and trainee performance. *Journal of Applied Psychology, 67,* 194–199; Rosenthal, R. (1993). Interpersonal expectations: Some antecedents and some consequences. In P. D. Blank (Ed.), *Interpersonal expectations: Theory, research, and applications* (pp. 3–24). Cambridge, England: Cambridge University Press.
4. Smith, A. E., & Jussim, L. (1999). Do self-fulfilling prophecies accumulate, dissipate, or remain stable over time? *Journal of Personality and Social Psychology, 77,* 548–565.
5. Divir, T., Eden, D., & Bano, J. L. (1995). Self-fulfilling prophecy and gender: Can women be Pygmalion and Galatea? *Journal of Applied Psychology, 80,* 253–270; McNatt, D. B. (2000). Ancient Pygmalion joins contemporary management: A meta-analysis of the result. *Journal of Applied Psychology, 85,* 314–322; White, S. S., & Locke, E. A. (2000). Problems with the Pygmalion effect and some proposed solutions. *Leadership Quarterly, 11,* 389–415.

6. Karakowsky, L., DeGama, N., & McBey, K. (2012). Facilitating the Pygmalion effect: The overlooked role of subordinate perceptions of the leader. *Journal of Occupational and Organizational Psychology 85*, 579–599.

7. Rosenthal.

8. Good, T., & Brophy, J. (1980). *Educational psychology: A realistic approach*. New York, NY: Holt, Rinehart & Winston.

9. White & Locke.

10. Eden, D. (1984). Self-fulfilling prophecy as a management tool: Harnessing Pygmalion. *Academy of Management Review, 9*, 64–73.

11. Isaacson, W. (2011). *Steve Jobs*. New York, NY: Simon & Schuster, p. 119.

12. Locke, E. A., & Latham, G. P. (1990). *A theory of goal setting and task performance*. Englewood Cliffs, NJ: Prentice Hall; Locke, E. A., & Latham, G. P. (Eds.). (2013). *New developments in goal setting and task performance*. New York, NY: Routledge.

13. Limon, M. S., & La France, B. H. (2005). Communication traits and leadership emergence: Examining the impact of argumentativeness, communication apprehension, and verbal aggressiveness in work groups. *Southern Communication Journal, 70*, 123–133; Schultz, B. (1982). Argumentativeness: Its effect in group decision-making and its role in leadership perception. *Communication Quarterly, 3*, 368–375; Schweiger, D. M., Sandberg, W. R., & Rechner, P. (1989). Experiential effects of dialectical inquiry, devil's advocacy, and consensus approaches to strategic decision making. *Academy of Management Journal, 32*, 745–772.

14. Infante, D. A., & Rancer, A. (1996). Argumentativeness and verbal aggressiveness: A review of recent theory and research. In B. Burleson (Ed.), *Communication yearbook 19* (pp. 319–351). Thousand Oaks, CA: SAGE.

15. Rancer, A. S., & Avtgis, T. A. (2006). Argumentative and aggressive communication: Theory, research, and application. Thousand Oaks, CA: SAGE.

16. Infante & Rancer (1996); Rancer & Avtgis (2006).

17. Infante, D. A. (1988). *Arguing constructively*. Prospect Heights, IL: Waveland Press.

18. Inch, E. S., Warnick, B., & Endres, D. (2006). *Critical thinking and communication: The use of reason in argument* (5th ed.). Boston, MA: Pearson.

19. Habermas, J. (1990). *Moral consciousness and communicative action* (C. Lehhardt & S. Weber Nicholsen, Trans.). Cambridge, MA: MIT Press; Leeper, R. V. (1996). Moral objectivity, Jurgen Habermas's discourse ethics, and public relations. *Public Relations Review 22*, 133–150; Meisenbach, R. J. (2006). Habermas's discourse ethics and principle of universalization as a moral framework for organizational communication. *Management Communication Quarterly, 20*, 39–62; Stansbury, J. (2009). Reasoned moral agreement: Applying discourse ethics within organizations. *Business Ethics Quarterly, 19*, 33–56.

20. Habermas, p. 66.

21. Lax, D. A., & Sebenius, J. K. (1986). *The manager as negotiator: Bargaining for cooperation and competitive gain*. New York, NY: The Free Press.

22. Lax, D. A., & Sebenius, J. K. (2004). Three ethical issues in negotiation. In C. Menkel-Meadow & M. Wheeler (Eds.), *What's fair: Ethics for negotiators* (pp. 5–14). San Francisco, CA: Jossey-Bass; Lewicki, R. (1983). Lying and deception. In M. H. Bazerman & R. J. Lewicki (Eds.), *Negotiating in organizations* (pp. 68–90). Beverly Hills, CA: SAGE.

23. Lax & Sebenius (2004).

24. Cramton, P. C., & Dees, J. G. (1993). Promoting honesty in negotiation: An exercise in practical ethics. *Business Ethics Quarterly, 3*, 359–394; Cramton, P. C., & Dees, J. G. (2004). Promoting honesty in negotiation: An exercise in practical ethics. In C. Menkel-Meadow & M. Wheeler (Eds.), *What's fair: Ethics for negotiators* (pp. 108–137). San Francisco, CA: Jossey-Bass.

25. Fishman, C. (2011). *The Wal-Mart effect: How the world's most powerful company really works and how it's transforming the American economy*. (Rev. ed.). New York, NY: Penguin.

26. Wheeler, M. (2004, March). Fair enough: An ethical fitness test quiz for negotiators. *Negotiation*, 3–5.

27. Lax & Sebenius (2004).

28. See, for example, De Dreu, C. K. W., Weingart, L. R., & Kwon, S. (2000). Influence of social motives on integrative negotiation: A meta-analytic review and test of two theories. *Journal of Personality and Social Psychology, 78*, 889–905; Pruitt, D. G. (1983). Achieving integrative agreements. In M. H. Bazerman & R. J. Lewicki (Eds.), *Negotiating in organizations* (pp. 35–50). Beverly Hill, CA: SAGE.

29. Fisher, R., Ury, W., & Patton, B. (2011). *Getting to yes: Negotiating agreement without giving in.* (Rev. ed.). New York, NY: Penguin.

30. Hargie, O., Dickson, D., & Tourish, D. (2004). *Communication skills for effective management.* Houndmills, England: Palgrave Macmillan, pp. 177–178.

31. Cialdini, R. (2009). *Influence: Science and practice.* Boston, MA: Pearson; Rhoads, K. V. L., & Cialdini, R. B. (2002). The business of influence: Principles that lead to success in commercial settings. In J. P. Dillard & M. Pfau (Eds.), *The persuasion handbook* (pp. 513–542). Thousand Oaks, CA: SAGE. See also Pratkanis, A., & Aronson, E. (2001). *Age of propaganda: The everyday use and abuse of persuasion.* New York, NY: Holt.

8

Normative Leadership Theories

The whole point of studying leadership is to answer the question "What is good leadership?"

—PHILOSOPHER AND ETHICIST JOANNE CIULLA

To not be responsible is to not be effective as a leader.

—ARIZONA STATE PROFESSORS DAVID WALDMAN AND BENJAMIN GALVIN

WHAT'S AHEAD

In this chapter, we will look at leadership theories specifically designed to improve the ethical behavior of leaders and followers. These include transformational leadership, servant leadership, authentic leadership, aesthetic leadership, responsible leadership, and Taoism. I'll describe each theory and then make some suggestions for applying it as a leader. I'll also offer some cautions about the limitations of each approach.

Theories are key to the study of any discipline, including leadership. They organize knowledge in a field, explain the relationships between important concepts and variables, and help scholars and practitioners make predictions about what strategies will be effective. Theoretical approaches to leadership generally fall into one of two categories: descriptive and normative. Descriptive theories, as the name implies, describe *how* leaders act. Early researchers at Michigan and Ohio State, for instance, identified two underlying dimensions to leadership styles: task and relationship.[1] They found that some leaders are more focused on the task while others are more focused on building relationships with followers. Normative leadership theories, on the other hand, tell leaders how they *ought* to act. They are explicitly built on moral principles or norms and provide guidelines for promoting ethical leader behavior. Proponents for each normative approach argue that adopting their perspective will enable leaders to function as both moral persons and moral managers. In this chapter, I'll introduce several normative leadership theories that can help you cast more light than shadow.

TRANSFORMATIONAL LEADERSHIP: RAISING THE ETHICAL BAR

Interest in transformational leadership began in 1978 with the publication of the book titled *Leadership* by James MacGregor Burns, a former presidential advisor, political scientist, and historian.[2] Burns contrasted traditional forms of leadership, which he called "transactional," with a more powerful form of leadership he called "transforming." Transactional leaders appeal to lower-level needs of followers—that is, the need for food, shelter, and acceptance. They exchange money, benefits, recognition, and other rewards in return for the obedience and labor of followers; the underlying system remains unchanged. In contrast, transformational leaders speak to higher-level needs, such as esteem, competency, self-fulfillment, and self-actualization. In so doing, they change the very nature of the groups, organizations, or societies they guide. Burns pointed to Franklin Roosevelt and Mahatma Gandhi as examples of leaders who transformed the lives of followers and their cultures as a whole. In a more recent work, *Transforming Leadership*, Burns argued that the greatest task facing transformational leaders is defeating global poverty, which keeps the world's poorest people from meeting their basic needs for food, medicine, education, and shelter.[3]

Moral commitments are at the heart of Burns's definition of transforming leadership. "Such leadership," states Burns, "occurs when one or more persons *engage* with others in such a way that leaders and followers raise one another to higher levels of motivation and morality."[4] Transformational leaders focus on terminal values such as liberty, equality, and justice. These values mobilize and energize followers, create an agenda for action, and appeal to larger audiences.[5] Transforming leaders are driven by duty, the deontological ethical approach described in Chapter 5.[6] They are guided by universal ethical principles, feel a sense of obligation to the group, and treat followers with respect. They are also altruistic, making sacrifices for followers, empowering others, and focusing on shared goals and objectives. Transformational leaders engage in higher-level moral reasoning, demonstrate greater integrity, are more successful at leading organizational ethical turn-arounds, encourage the development of positive ethical climates, institutionalize ethical practices, and foster corporate social responsibility (CSR).[7]

In contrast to transformational leaders, transactional leaders emphasize instrumental values, such as responsibility, fairness, and honesty, which make routine interactions go smoothly. They take a utilitarian approach, judging the morality of actions based on their outcomes. They use their power and position to convince followers to comply so that both they and their subordinates will benefit. More focused on the self, transactional leaders are concerned with protecting their interests rather than in promoting the interests of the group. They are more likely to be controlling than empowering.

In a series of studies, leadership experts Bernard Bass and his colleagues identified the factors that characterize transactional and transformational forms of leadership and demonstrated that transformational leaders can be found in organizations.[8] They discovered that transactional leadership has both active and passive elements. Active transactional leaders engage in *contingent reward* and *management by exception*. They provide rewards and recognition contingent on followers' carrying out their roles and reaching their objectives. After specifying standards and the elements of acceptable performance, active transactional leaders then discipline followers when they fall short. *Passive–avoidant* or *laissez-faire* leaders wait for problems to arise before taking action, or they avoid taking any action at all. These leaders fail to provide goals and standards or to clarify expectations.

According to Bass and Avolio, transformational leadership is characterized by the following:

- *Idealized influence.* Transformational leaders become role models for followers who admire, respect, and trust them. They put followers' needs above their own, and their behavior is consistent with the values and principles of the group.

- *Inspirational motivation.* Transformational leaders motivate by providing meaning and challenge to the tasks of followers. They arouse team spirit, are enthusiastic and optimistic, and help followers develop desirable visions for the future.

- *Intellectual stimulation.* Transformational leaders stimulate innovation and creativity. They do so by encouraging followers to question assumptions, reframe situations, and approach old problems from new perspectives. Transforming leaders don't criticize mistakes but instead solicit solutions from followers.

- *Individualized consideration.* Transformational leaders act as coaches or mentors who foster personal development. They provide learning opportunities and a supportive climate for growth. Their coaching and mentoring are tailored to the individual needs and desires of each follower.

Burns believed that leaders display either transactional or transformational characteristics, but Bass found otherwise. Transforming leadership uses both transactional and transformational elements. Explains Bass, "Many of the great transformational leaders, including Abraham Lincoln, Franklin Delano Roosevelt, and John F. Kennedy, did not shy away from being transactional. They were able to move the nation as well as play petty politics."[9] The transformational leader uses the active elements of the transactional approach (contingent reward and management by exception) along with idealized influence, inspirational motivation, intellectual stimulation, and individualized consideration.[10]

The popularity of the transformational approach probably has more to do with practical considerations than with ethical ones. Evidence continues to mount that transforming leaders are more successful than their transactional counterparts.[11] Their followers are more committed, form stronger bonds with colleagues, work harder, and persist in the face of obstacles. As a result, organizations led by transforming figures often achieve extraordinary results: higher quality, greater profits, improved service, military victories, and better win–loss records. James Kouzes, Barry Posner, Warren Bennis, and Burt Nanus are just some of the popular scholars, consultants, and authors who promote the benefits of transformational leadership.[12]

Burns originally believed that the transforming leader is a moral leader because the ultimate product of transformational leadership is higher ethical standards and performance. However, his definition didn't account for the fact that some leaders can use transformational strategies to reach immoral ends. A leader can act as a role model, provide intellectual stimulation, and be passionate about a cause. Yet the end product of her or his efforts can be evil. Hitler had a clear vision for Germany but left a trail of unprecedented death and destruction.

Acknowledging the difference between ethical and unethical transformational leaders, Bass adopted the terms *authentic* and *pseudo-transformational* to distinguish between the two categories.[13] Authentic transformational leaders are motivated by altruism and marked by integrity. They don't impose ethical norms but allow followers free choice, hoping that constituents will voluntarily commit themselves to moral principles. Followers are viewed as ends in themselves, not as a means to some other end. Pseudo-transformational leaders are self-centered. They manipulate followers in order to reach their personal goals. Envy, greed, anger, and deception mark the groups they lead. Mahatma Gandhi and Martin Luther King, Jr., deserve to be classified as transformational because they promoted universal brotherhood. Islamic State in Iraq and Syria (ISIS) leaders are pseudo-transformational because, although they attract highly committed followers to their vision of an Islamic state, they engage in brutality and reject any other belief system but their own. A list of the products of transformational and pseudo-transformational leadership is found in Box 8.1. You can use this list to determine whether or not the leader described in Case Study 8.1 is transformational.

Applications and Cautions

Applications

- Start small
- Employ the full range of leadership behaviors
- Recognize the universal appeal of transformational leadership

Transformational leadership can seem intimidating at first. Its proponents set a lofty standard—raising the level of morality in an organization or society while transforming its performance. However, you can act as a transformational leader no matter how modest your leadership role. Chances are, you have benefitted from the influence of lower-level transformational leaders. You can probably think of a coach, teacher, shift manager, counselor, pastor, or other figure that had a lasting impact on you and your team. You can exert similar positive influence by engaging in the behaviors that demonstrate idealized influence, inspirational motivation, intellectual stimulation, and individualized consideration. (Complete Self-Assessment 8.1 to determine how likely you are to use transformational strategies.) Keep in mind that transformational leaders also master active transactional tactics. Be prepared to penalize those who fall short of performance standards or break the rules, to reward those who reach their objectives, and so on.

The good news is that you can use transformational behaviors in many contexts, ranging from small, informal groups and military units to large, complex organizations.

Box 8.1 Products of Transformational and Pseudo-transformational Leadership

Transformational Leaders

Raise awareness of moral standards

Highlight important priorities

Increase followers' need for achievement

Foster higher moral maturity in followers

Create a healthy ethical climate (shared values, high ethical standards)

Encourage followers to look beyond self-interests to the common good

Promote cooperation and harmony

Use authentic, consistent means

Use persuasive appeals based on reason

Provide individual coaching and mentoring

Appeal to the ideals of followers

Allow followers freedom of choice

Pseudo-transformational Leaders

Promote special interests at the expense of the common good

Encourage dependency of followers and may privately despise them

Foster competitiveness

Pursue personal goals

Foment greed, envy, hate, and deception

Engage in conflict rather than cooperation

Use inconsistent, irresponsible means

Use persuasive appeals based on emotion and false logic

Keep their distance from followers and expect blind obedience

Seek to become idols for followers

Manipulate followers

Sources: Bass, B. M. (1995). The ethics of transformational leadership. In J. B. Ciulla (Ed.), *Ethics: The heart of leadership* (pp. 169-192). Westport, CT: Praeger; Bass, B. M., & Steidlmeier, P. (1999). Ethics, character, and authentic transformational leadership behavior. *Leadership Quarterly, 10,* 181-217.

Furthermore, transforming leadership appears to be effective in a variety of cultures. Researchers at the Global Leadership and Organizational Behavior Effectiveness (GLOBE) Research Project asked managers in 62 cultures to identify the characteristics of successful leaders. Nine transformational attributes were universally associated with outstanding leadership: motive arouser, foresight, encouraging, communicative, trustworthy, dynamic, positive, confidence builder, and motivational.[14] Other researchers report that transformational leadership enhances follower and organizational performance in a variety of cultural settings, including, for example, Pakistan, India, Egypt, and China.[15]

Cautions

- Equates success with transformation
- Leader centric

- Fosters dependency
- Offers no guarantee against unethical behavior

Unfortunately, many writers and researchers appear more interested in what works than in what is right. To them, transformational leadership equates with successful or effective leadership; leaders are transforming because they achieve extraordinary, tangible results, such as rescuing failing corporations or winning battles. These theorists are less concerned with whether leaders foster higher moral standards or whether transforming tactics serve ethical ends.

It should be noted that transformational theorists have been labeled as *leader-centric* for paying too much attention to leaders while downplaying the contributions of followers. One critic describes the image presented by transformational theorists this way: "The picture is one in which extraordinary leaders exercise a unidirectional influence on more-or-less willing followers, who are presumably little more than empty vessels awaiting a transfusion of insight from their betters."[16] These sceptics have reason for concern. Burns, Bass, and other proponents of transformative leadership argue that leaders play the most important role in determining group morality and performance. Leaders craft the vision, challenge the status quo, and inspire. At times, they may decide to transform the organization in spite of, not because of, followers, as in the case of the chief executive officer (CEO) who overrules his staff in order to bring about change. Critics of transformational leadership argue that followers are just as important to the success of a group as leaders, if not more so. After all, followers do most of the work. Worse yet, transforming leaders can silence dissent and encourage subordinates to sacrifice their legitimate self-interests in order to meet the needs of the group. Or they may encourage their followers to engage in unethical behavior that promotes the organization's success.[17]

So much focus on the leader can create dependency and undermine such values as shared decision making and consensus. Followers won't act independently if they continually look to you for guidance. You may also get an inflated sense of your own importance, tempting you to cast shadows. Bass believed that the distinction between pseudo-transformational and authentic transformational leadership addresses these concerns. Transforming leaders are much less prone to ethical abuses, he asserted, because they put the needs of others first, treat followers with respect, and seek worthy objectives. You'll need to decide for yourself whether transformational theorists have adequately responded to the dangers posed by their perspective. Then, too, recognize that transformational leadership does not make leaders immune to ethical temptations.

SERVANT LEADERSHIP: PUT THE NEEDS OF FOLLOWERS FIRST

Servant leadership has roots in both Western and Eastern thought. Jesus told his disciples that "whoever wants to become great among you must be your servant, and whoever wants to be first must be slave of all" (Mark 10:43–44, New International Version). As we'll see in the final section of this chapter, Chinese philosophers encouraged leaders to be humble valleys. Robert Greenleaf sparked contemporary interest in leaders as servants. Greenleaf, who spent forty years in research, development, and education at

AT&T and twenty-five years as an organizational consultant, coined the term *servant leader* in the 1970s to describe a leadership model that puts the concerns of followers first.[18] Later, he founded a center to promote servant leadership. A number of businesses (The Container Store, AFLAC), nonprofit organizations, and community leadership programs have adopted his model.[19] Margaret Wheatley, Peter Block, Max De Pree, and James Autry have joined Greenleaf in urging leaders to act like servants.

The basic premise of servant leadership is simple yet profound. Leaders should put the needs of followers before their own needs. In fact, what happens in the lives of followers should be the standard by which leaders are judged. According to Greenleaf, when evaluating a leader, we ought to ask, "Do those served grow as persons? Do they, while being served, become healthier, wiser, freer, more autonomous, more likely themselves to become servants?"[20]

By continually reflecting on what would be best for their constituents, servant leaders are less likely to cast shadows by taking advantage of the trust of followers, acting inconsistently, or accumulating money and power. So far, theorists have identified a number of attributes that characterize servant leaders (see Box 8.2). While the lists of attributes vary, five related concepts appear central to servant leadership:

1. **Stewardship**. Being a servant leader means acting on behalf of others.[21] Leaders function as the agents of followers, who entrust them with special duties and opportunities for a limited time. Servant leaders are charged with protecting and nurturing their groups and organizations while making sure that these collectives serve the common good. Stewardship implies accountability for results. However, stewards reach their objectives through collaboration and persuasion rather than through coercion and control.

2. **Obligation**. Servant leaders take their obligations or responsibilities seriously. Max De Pree, former CEO of Herman Miller, a major office furniture manufacturer, offers one list of what leaders owe their followers and institutions.[22]

    - *Assets.* Leaders need to ensure financial stability as well as the relationships and reputation that will ensure future prosperity. Leaders must also provide followers with adequate tools, equipment, and facilities.
    - *A legacy.* When they depart, leaders ought to leave behind people who find meaning, challenge, and joy in their work.
    - *Clear institutional values.* Servant leaders articulate principles that shape both individual and organizational behavior.
    - *Future leadership.* Current leaders are obligated to identify and then develop their successors.
    - *Healthy institutional culture.* Servant leaders are responsible for fostering such organizational characteristics as quality, openness to change, and tolerance of diverse opinions.
    - *Covenants.* Covenants are voluntary agreements that serve as reference points for organization members, providing them

with direction. Leaders and followers who enter into a covenant are bound together in pursuit of a common goal.

- *Maturity.* Followers expect a certain level of maturity from their leaders. Mature leaders have a clear sense of self-worth, belonging, responsibility, accountability, and equality.
- *Rationality.* Leaders supply the reason and understanding that help followers make sense of organizational programs and relationships. A rational environment builds trust, allows followers to reach their full potential, and encourages ongoing organizational learning.
- *Space.* Space is a sense of freedom that allows followers and leaders to be and express themselves. Leaders who create adequate space allow for the giving and receiving of such gifts as new ideas, healing, dignity, and inclusion.
- *Momentum.* Servant leaders help create the feeling that the group is moving forward and achieving its goals. Momentum arises out of a clear vision and strategy supported by productive research, operations, financial, and marketing departments.
- *Effectiveness.* Effectiveness comes from enabling followers to reach their personal and institutional potential. Servant leaders allow followers to assume leadership roles when conditions warrant.
- *Civility and values.* A civilized institution is marked by good manners, respect for others, and service. Wise leaders can distinguish between what is healthy for the organization (dignity of work, hope, simplicity) and what is superficial and unhealthy (consumption, instant gratification, affluence).

3. *Partnership*. Servant leaders view followers as partners, not subordinates. As a consequence, they strive for equity or justice in the distribution of power. Strategies for empowering followers include sharing information, delegating authority to carry out important tasks, and encouraging constituents to develop and exercise their talents. Concern for equity extends to the distribution of rewards as well. For example, both employees and executives receive bonuses when the company does well.

4. *Emotional healing*. Servant leaders help followers and organizations recover from disappointment, trauma, hardship, and broken relationships.[23] They are both empathetic and highly skilled as listeners. They create climates that facilitate the sharing of personal and work-related feelings and issues. Emotional healing restores a sense of wholeness to both individuals and organizations.

5. *Elevating purpose*. In addition to serving followers, servant leaders also serve worthy missions, ideas, and causes. Seeking to fulfill a high moral purpose and understanding the role one plays in

Box 8.2 Servant Leader Attributes

listening	vision	empathy	altruistic calling
empathy	honesty	integrity/honesty	emotional healing
healing	integrity	competence	wisdom
awareness	trust	agreeableness	persuasive mapping
persuasion	service	*(Washington, Sutton,*	organizational
conceptualization	modeling	*& Feild, 2006)*	stewardship
foresight	pioneering	*(Babuto & Wheeler,*	
stewardship	appreciation of others	*2006)*	
commitment to the	empowerment		
growth of people	communication		
building community	credibility		
(Spears, 2004)	competence		
visibility			
interpersonal support	influence		
building community	persuasion		
altruism	listening		
equalitarianism	encouragement		
moral integrity	teaching		
(Reed, Vidaver-Cohen,	delegation		
Colwell, 2011)	*(Russell & Stone, 2002)*		

Sources: Barbuto, J. E., & Wheeler, D. W. (2006). Scale development and construct clarification of servant leadership. *Group & Organization Management, 31,* 300–326; Reed, L. L., Vidaver-Cohen, D., & Colwell, S. R. (2011). A new scale to measure executive servant leadership: Development, analysis, and implications for research. *Journal of Business Ethics, 101,* 415–434; Russell, R. F., & Stone, A. G. (2002). A review of servant leadership attributes: Developing a practical model. *Leadership & Organization Development Journal, 23*(3), 145–157; Spears, L. C. (2004). The understanding and practice of servant leadership. In L. C. Spears & M. Lawrence (Eds.), *Practicing servant leadership: Succeeding through trust, bravery, and forgiveness* (pp. 9–24). San Francisco, CA: Jossey-Bass; Washington, R. R., Sutton, C. D., & Feild, H. S. (2006). Individual differences in servant leadership: The roles of values and personality. *Leadership & Organization Development Journal, 27*(8), 700–716.

the process make work more meaningful to leaders and followers alike. Consider the example of three bricklayers at work in the English countryside. When asked by a traveler to describe what they were doing, the first replied, "I am laying bricks." The second said, "I am feeding my family by laying bricks." The third bricklayer, who had a clearer sense of the purpose for his labor, declared, "Through my work of laying bricks, I am constructing a cathedral, and thereby giving honor and praise to God."

For much of the theory's history, support for servant leadership was anecdotal, consisting largely of lists of servant characteristics and examples of servant leaders. More recently, scholars have begun to subject servant leadership to empirical testing. Servant leadership questionnaires like the one in the Self-Assessment 8.2 have been developed, and researchers are exploring the impact of servant leadership on followers and organizational performance. So far, they have discovered that

- servant leaders help satisfy follower needs and boost their job satisfaction and job performance.
- followers give servant leaders higher character ratings.
- top-level servant leaders encourage lower-level leaders to act as servants.
- servant leadership prompts employees to go beyond their job descriptions to help others.
- those led by servant leaders are less likely to quit and are more committed to their supervisors.
- servant leadership creates an ethical, trusting organizational climate.
- servant leadership can increase sales and profits.
- servant leaders help team members believe in their group's ability to accomplish its tasks.
- servant leadership is accepted across a variety of cultures, though the importance of the dimensions of servant leadership vary between societies.[24]

Applications and Cautions

Applications

- Focus on followers
- Act as a steward
- Cultivate self-awareness
- Pursue elevating purposes

Servant leadership is founded on altruism that, as we saw in Chapter 5, is essential to ethical leadership. You can serve only if you commit yourself to the principle that others should come first. You are far less likely to cast shadows if you approach your leadership roles with one goal in mind: the desire to serve. A great number of ethical abuses stem from leaders acting selfishly. Instead, act out of a sense of stewardship and obligation, promoting the growth of followers and the interests of the larger community. Remember what you "owe" followers. Share, rather than hoard, power, privilege, and information. (See "Leadership Ethics at the Movies: *The Lady*" for an example of a leader who sacrificed a great deal to serve her followers.)

To function as a servant leader, you'll need to cultivate self-awareness. Servant leaders listen to themselves as well as to others, take time for reflection, and recognize the importance of spiritual resources. They are also acutely aware of the importance of pursuing ethical purposes that bring meaning and fulfilment to work. Serving a transcendent goal means that every act of leadership has a moral dimension.

Cautions

- Seems unrealistic
- May not work in every context
- Poses the danger of serving the wrong cause or offering unwise service
- The term *servant* carries a negative connotation

Servant leadership has not met with universal approval. Cynicism is often the first response when this model is presented. "Sounds good in principle," listeners respond, "but it would never work at my company, in my family, at my condominium association meeting, or _____ (fill in the blank)." Like other sceptics, you may have been walked on whenever you tried to be nice to poor performers at work, rebellious teenagers, or nasty neighbors. You may agree with others who equate a servant attitude with passivity.

Skepticism about servant leadership may stem in part from a misunderstanding that equates service with weakness. Servant leaders need to be tough. Sometimes the best way to serve someone is to reprimand or fire that person. Nevertheless, there may be situations in which servant leadership is extremely difficult, if not impossible, to implement, such as in prisons, military boot camps, and emergencies.

Misplaced goals are problems for servant leaders and followers alike. The butler in the novel *The Remains of the Day* by Kazuo Ishiguro illustrates the danger of misspent service. He devotes his entire life to being the perfect servant who meets the needs of his English employer. Sadly, his sacrifice is wasted because the lord of the manor turns out to be a Nazi sympathizer. The desire to serve must be combined with careful reasoning and value clarification. You need to carefully examine who and what you serve, asking yourself questions such as the following: Is this group, individual, or organization worthy of my service? What values am I promoting? What is the product of my service: light or darkness?

You are also charged with giving wise service. Lots of well-intentioned efforts to help others are wasted when leaders fail to do their homework. After the earthquake in Central Asia in 2005, for example, outdoor manufacturers donated high-tech mountaineering tents to victims. Unfortunately, these tents are highly flammable and caught fire from candles, kerosene lanterns, and cooking fires, burning and killing adults and children. After the Haiti earthquake, a group of Idaho church members was jailed after trying to take orphans out of the country—it turns out that the children weren't orphans after all. As we noted in the Chapter 5, some humanitarian efforts are wasted. Worse yet, they can make problems worse and foster dependency in recipients.[25]

Finally, members of some minority groups, particularly African Americans, associate the word *servant* with a history of slavery, oppression, and discrimination. The negative

Leadership Ethics at the Movies

THE LADY

Key Cast Members: Michelle Yeoh, David Thewlis, Jonathan Woodhouse

Synopsis: Aung San Suu Kyi (played by Yeoh) is the daughter of the man who led Burma (Myanmar) to independence in 1947. She was only two years old when her father was murdered. In 1988, Suu Kyi is a married parent of two living in England when she returns to Myanmar to care for her dying mother. Shortly after arriving, she reluctantly agrees to lead the nation's pro-democracy movement protesting against the nation's repressive military regime. The country's generals retaliate by putting her under house arrest for the next fifteen years. In order to ensure that she is not forgotten, Suu's English husband Michael Aris (Thewlis) nominates her for the Nobel Peace Prize. In 1991, she receives the award for serving as "an outstanding example of the power of the powerless." The Lady, as she is known, pays a high personal price for her activism. Her husband and sons cannot visit her. She cannot travel to England when Aris dies of prostate cancer, for fear that she will not be allowed back into Myanmar.

Rating: R for bloody scenes of violence

Themes: servant leadership, self-sacrifice, transformational leadership, authentic leadership, aesthetic leadership, courage

Discussion Starters

1. Why did National League for Democracy officials believe that Aung San Suu Kyi was the only person to lead their party? Do you agree with their reasoning?

2. What skills and traits made Suu Kyi effective when she was thrust into a leadership position?

3. Did Suu Kyi make the right choice in putting the needs of her nation ahead of those of her family?

4. Did receiving the Nobel Prize help protect Suu, as her husband and family had hoped?

connotations surrounding the word may keep you from embracing the idea of servant leadership. You may want to abandon this term and focus instead on related concepts such as altruism and the virtues of concern and compassion.

AUTHENTIC LEADERSHIP: KNOW YOURSELF AND TO YOUR OWN SELF BE TRUE

Ancient Greek and Roman philosophers prized authenticity. "Know thyself" was inscribed on the frieze above the oracle of Delphi and appears in the writings of Cicero and Ovid.[26] Greek thinkers also exhorted listeners "to thine own self be true." Modern scholars have rediscovered the importance of this quality. Proponents of

Authentic Leadership Theory (ALT) identify authenticity as the root construct or principle underlying all forms of positive leadership. The practice of authentic leadership leads to sustainable (long-term) and veritable (ethically sound) organizational performance.[27]

Authenticity has four components: self-awareness, balanced processing, internalized moral perspective, and relational transparency.[28] *Self-awareness* means being conscious of, and trusting in, our motives, desires, feelings, and self-concept. Self-aware people know their strengths and weaknesses, personal traits, and emotional patterns, and they are able to use this knowledge when interacting with others and their environments. *Balanced processing* describes remaining objective when receiving information. Inauthentic processing involves denying, distorting, or ignoring feedback we don't want to acknowledge. We may have to accept the fact that we aren't very good at certain activities (accounting, writing, playing basketball) or that we have problems managing our anger. *Internalized moral perspective* refers to regulating our behavior according to our internal standards and values, not according to what others say. We act in harmony with what we believe and do not change our behavior to please others or to earn rewards or avoid punishment. *Relational transparency* is presenting the authentic self to others, openly expressing true thoughts and feelings appropriate for the situation.

According to Bruce Avolio, Fred Luthans, and their colleagues at the University of Washington, the Gallup Leadership Institute at the University of Nebraska at Lincoln, and elsewhere, authentic leadership has a strong moral component. They make ethics a starting point for their theory, just as Burns did for transforming leadership. This moral element is reflected in their definition of authentic leaders as

> those who are deeply aware of how they think and behave and are perceived by others as being aware of their own and others' values/moral perspectives, knowledge, and strengths; aware of the context in which they operate; and who are confident, hopeful, optimistic, resilient, and of high moral character.[29]

Such leaders acknowledge the ethical responsibilities of their roles, can recognize and evaluate ethical issues, and take moral actions that are thoroughly grounded in their beliefs and values. In order to carry out these tasks, they draw on their courage and resilience—the ability to adapt when confronted with significant risk or adversity.[30] (Turn to Case Study 8.2 for one example of a leader who was able to overcome significant adversity.)

Because authenticity is so critical to positive leadership performance, Avolio, Luthans, and others are interested in how leaders develop this quality. They report that critical incidents called *trigger events* play an important role in the development of the moral component of authentic leadership.[31] These events, like the crucible moments described in Chapter 3, can be positive or negative and promote introspection and reflection. Trigger experiences are often dramatic—facing racial hatred, visiting a third world village—but can also be more mundane, such as reading a significant book. Sometimes a series of small events, like several minor successes or failures, can have a cumulative effect, triggering significant thought. Leaders develop a clearer sense of who they are, including their standards of right and wrong, through these experiences. They build a store of moral knowledge that they can draw on to make better choices when facing future ethical dilemmas.

Authenticity can also be fostered through training and education. For example, trainers and educators can help leaders develop their moral capacity by (1) encouraging them to think about the possible consequences of their leadership decisions, (2) enhancing their perspective taking through discussion and training, (3) exposing them to common moral dilemmas to help them recognize the ethical issues they will face in their jobs, (4) building their belief in their ability to follow through on choices, (5) helping them develop strategies for adapting and coping with new ethical challenges, and (6) pairing them with moral leaders so they can observe authentic behavior firsthand.[32]

Authentic leadership produces a number of positive ethical effects in followers.[33] Followers are likely to emulate the example of authentic leaders who set a high ethical standard. They feel empowered to make ethical choices on their own without the input of the leader and are more likely to act courageously. They align themselves with the values of the organization and become authentic moral agents themselves. Leader authenticity also fosters feelings of self-efficacy (competence), hope, optimism, and resilience in followers, which increases job performance. Authentic followers, for their part, provide feedback that reinforces the authentic behavior of leaders and increases the leaders' self-knowledge. (See "Focus on Follower Ethics: Authentic Followership" for more information on the characteristics of authentic followers.) They also reward their leaders by giving them more latitude to make difficult, unpopular choices. Authentic leadership and followership are more likely to develop in organizational climates that provide the information and other resources that employees need to get their work done, encourage learning, treat members fairly, and set clear goals and performance standards.

Proponents of ALT argue that authenticity pays practical as well as ethical dividends. They cite evidence that authentic leadership is linked to higher follower performance, commitment, satisfaction, and effort.[34] Authentic leaders, particularly because they act with integrity, engender more trust, and trust, in turn, has been linked to higher organizational productivity and performance (see Chapter 10). The positive emotions fostered by leaders also enhance performance. Followers who believe in their abilities are more likely to take initiative and to achieve more, even in the face of difficult circumstances. Feelings of hope and optimism foster willpower. Resiliency enables followers to recover more quickly from setbacks.[35]

ALT has moved into the next stage of development. Most of the initial articles and chapters on authentic leadership offered propositions about ALT that were not supported by empirical research. But now an ALT scale has been developed and tested.[36] Validation of the scale demonstrates that authentic leadership, while sharing features with transformational and servant leadership, is a distinct construct. And authentic leadership is now being tested in other cultural settings, such as Brazil, Australia, India, Iran, and China. So far, the positive effects of authentic leadership appear to generalize across cultures, reducing follower stress and insecurity while increasing job satisfaction, trust, safety, performance, and willingness to blow the whistle on organizational wrongdoing.[37]

Applications and Cautions

Applications

- Recognize the significance of authenticity
- Develop the four components of authenticity
- Foster authenticity in others

Advocates argue persuasively for the importance of authenticity—incorporating values, moral perspectives, virtues, and character in their definition of authentic leadership. Authentic leadership is effective as well as ethical. Authenticity multiplies the impact of leaders and lays the foundation for long-term organizational success. If this is the case, then seek to be an authentic leader. Cultivate the four components of authenticity: develop self-awareness, maintain objectivity when receiving information, rely on internal standards and values, and openly present yourself to others. Consider the trigger events in your life and what they reveal about who you are. (See Item 6 under "For Further Exploration, Challenge, and Self-Assessment" at the end of this chapter.) Foster authenticity in others through your example and the training strategies described earlier.

Cautions

- Some proponents of authentic leadership fall short
- Overstates the significance of authenticity
- Equates authenticity with morality
- Authenticity can be defined as a personal characteristic or as a perception
- Other variables may support or reduce authentic behavior

ALT suffered a serious blow when *The Leadership Quarterly* retracted articles by one of its strongest proponents, Fred Walumbwa. Other researchers found errors in his methodology and were unable to replicate his findings. Arizona State University (where Walumbwa taught prior to moving to Florida International University) conducted its own investigation and criticized him for sloppy research methods, although officials did not believe he had purposely falsified his findings.[38] Nevertheless, the retractions cast doubt on a number of findings related to the positive relationship between leader authenticity and follower performance. Other proponents of authentic leadership have also been accused of behaving in an inauthentic manner. Critics complain that some leaders who hold themselves up as models of authenticity aren't as self-aware, objective, consistent, and moral as they believe themselves to be.[39]

While authenticity is a critical component of ethical leadership, the theory's underlying premise that authenticity is the source of all positive forms of leadership is subject to debate. There may be some other as yet undiscovered source instead. Or there may be multiple sources of ethical leadership. Further, authenticity may be overrated. Stanford business professor Jeffrey Pfeffer points out that leaders frequently act in ways that contradict their feelings in order to carry out their roles. Leaders have to express confidence to attract investors and customers when they feel insecure, give speeches when

Focus on Follower Ethics

AUTHENTIC FOLLOWERSHIP

Authenticity is the mark of ethical followership just as it is for ethical leadership. Authentic leaders and followers encourage transparency, self-awareness, and moral behavior in each other. Together, they build open, healthy relationships and collaborate to achieve worthwhile objectives. Followers have the greatest impact on leaders when they develop psychological ownership, foster trust, and practice transparency.

- *Psychological ownership*: Authentic followers feel like they own the organizations where they work and volunteer. This sense of ownership is based on a sense of belonging ("This is my home"), a sense of identity ("I am a student at _____ University"), a sense of accountability ("I am responsible for this project"), and a sense of efficacy ("I can do this task"). Ownership encourages a variety of ethical behaviors, including (1) meeting the needs of customers when they first come in contact with the firm, (2) taking responsibility for making decisions at lower organizational levels, (3) going beyond what the job requires, and (4) doing whatever it takes to solve problems.

- *Trust*. Authentic followers are vulnerable. They admit their mistakes and encourage their leaders to do the same. For example, when pharmacists admit to near misses (nearly filling the wrong prescription), they prompt their supervisors to take further steps to reduce potential errors. Authentic followers don't take advantage of leaders who admit their mistakes. They also build trust with their leaders by taking on challenges without being asked.

- *Transparency*. Authentic followers say what they mean. By sharing their thoughts, values, and feelings, they help create transparent relationships with their leaders. These relationships are marked by honesty, feedback, and effective communication. Authentic followers also contribute to the creation of transparent organizational climates. In transparent climates, policies and procedures are visible to everyone. Members share important goals and values and put the needs of the group above their own concerns. Because they feel safe, employees reveal problems rather than creating the impression that everything is fine.

Source: Avolio, B. J., & Reichard, R. J. (2008). The rise of authentic followership. In R. E. Riggio, I. Chaleff, & J. Lipman-Blumen (Eds.), *The art of followership: How great followers create great leaders and organizations* (pp. 325–337). San Francisco, CA: Jossey-Bass.

sick, comfort others when they (the leaders) are grieving, and so on. (See the discussion of impression management in Chapter 1.) Pfeffer asserts that inauthentic leadership is far more common (and effective) than authentic leadership.[40]

ALT theorists seem to equate self-awareness with morality. The clearer you are about the self-concept, they claim, the more likely you are to act ethically. Yet the core values of some leaders promote self-seeking, destructive behavior. Then, too, expressing your true self can produce undesirable consequences. Take the case of the boss who fails to temper his criticism of a subordinate. By accurately reflecting what he feels at that moment, he may do lasting damage to the self-concept of his employee. The critical boss believes he is acting authentically; the unfortunate employee and observers probably will conclude that he is callous instead.

Investigations into the effects of authentic leadership have also identified a fundamental tension in the theory. On the one hand, authenticity has been tied to the personal traits described earlier. On the other hand, for authenticity to have a positive influence on organizational behavior, observers must perceive that your behavior is authentic.[41] Authenticity then becomes a product of perception, not of personal beliefs and behaviors. Leaders who hope to be successful must project an authentic image. In other words, *being* authentic is no longer enough. Leaders must also *appear* authentic. This could tempt you to be untrue to yourself. You might fail to act on your values and self-understanding for fear that such behavior could be seen as inauthentic. In addition, inauthentic (pseudo-authentic) leaders could mislead followers by projecting an authentic image.[42] Further research and analysis are needed to resolve this apparent contradiction between the personal and perceptual dimensions of ALT. Further research will also further clarify how other factors, such as personality and self-identity, encourage leaders to act (or to not act) in an authentic manner.

AESTHETIC (BEAUTIFUL) LEADERSHIP

Aesthetic leadership, like authentic leadership, has its roots in classic Greek thought. The word *aesthetic*, or *aisth* in ancient Greek, means "feeling through physical perceptions."[43] Our sensory encounters with people, events, objects, and settings generate emotions. We then construct meanings based on those feelings. Take the case of an unsuccessful job interview, for example. Both individuals see, hear, listen, smell, and touch one another during the meeting. Each then comes away from the encounter with feelings about the appointment and the other party. The interviewer may be disappointed with the applicant and conclude that she or he was not prepared for the session. The frustrated interviewee may go home and complain about how the company representative was cold and distant.

The aesthetic perspective emphasizes the sensory and emotional dimension of organizational life.[44] From this vantage point, organizations serve as stages and leadership is more of an art than a science. Leaders, like artists, make skillful use of dramatic elements (ritual, ceremony, gestures, oratory), design (they transform visions and programs into reality), and orchestration (they bring diverse individuals together to achieve worthy goals).[45] Followers serve as audiences who make aesthetic judgments about leaders and their performances. Successful leaders generate strong positive emotions and attributions. For example, President John F. Kennedy was youthful, energetic, and glamorous. In his speeches, such as the one calling on the United States to put a man on the moon, he appealed to the aspirations of Americans and engaged their imaginations.[46] He is remembered as a highly effective leader, even though he accomplished much less than other, less attractive presidents like Lyndon Johnson and Richard Nixon.

Ethics is integral to aesthetic leadership. For the ancients, aesthetics meant pursuing goals that serve humankind. Aristotle believed that leaders should pursue "human flourishing" and the "good life." Plato (428–348 BC) argued that beauty must serve a good (moral) purpose. Aesthetic and moral judgments overlap. The most ethical course of action is also the most aesthetically pleasing or beautiful.

Contemporary theorists argue that, when it comes to making moral choices, leaders can learn a great deal from artists—musicians, painters, sculptors, actors. Artists incorporate emotion and intuition into their work. As we saw in Chapter 6, these elements also play a critical role in ethical decision making. Investigators identify the following as artistic practices than can enhance moral reasoning.[47]

- *Set aside preconceived notions or ideas.* Drop existing labels and come to the problem with an open mind.
- *Look deeply.* Focus in on what the senses reveal.
- *Take a second look.* Don't be in a hurry to come to a solution but reexamine the issue.
- *Be present in the moment.* Be ready to improvise but, at the same time, anticipate what may come next.
- *Be engaged but detached.* Stay involved in the process but step back when necessary to evaluate reasoning and conclusions.
- *Let the imagination play.* Experiment and ask, "What if?"
- *Take a holistic view.* Look for underlying patterns; recognize that the whole is more than the sum of its parts; include emotion and passion into the decision-making process.
- *Act with courage.* Resist conformity; think differently and accept the consequences for doing so.

British leadership professor Donna Ladkin identifies three components that contribute to a beautiful leadership performance.[48] The first is mastery. An ethical, beautiful leader is competent and possesses the necessary skills and abilities to perform in a given moment. He or she can improvise, applying the correct skills to a particular situation. The second component is coherence. The beautiful, ethical leader is authentic, acting in a way that is consistent with his or her message and purpose. The third component is purpose. The beautiful leader serves the best interests of the community and improves the human condition.

Captain Chesley "Sully" Sullenberger provides one example of a beautiful leadership performance.[49] On January 15, 2009, Sully's plane hit a flock of birds after taking off from New York's La Guardia airport. Sully immediately realized he couldn't reach the nearest landing strip in New Jersey, so he decided to put the aircraft down on the Hudson River. He avoided bridges and nearby high rises while bringing the plane down with its nose up and wings level. Once the plane was on the water, the Captain walked through the cabin twice to make sure everyone was safely off before he left. Not a single life was lost in the incident. Captain Sullenberger's behavior stands in sharp contrast to the ugly behavior of the captain of the Costa Concordia cruise ship. When his cruise liner crashed into the rocks off the Italian coast, Francesco Schettino abandoned ship and headed for shore, leaving many passengers still on board (32 died). Later, the captain denied that he was in charge of the ship at the time of the crash—a claim contradicted by the ship's data recorder.[50]

Applications and Cautions

Applications

- Recognize the physical/sensory dimension of leadership
- View leadership as a performing art
- Make aesthetic judgments
- Decide like an artist

Leadership has a physical or sensory dimension. Followers will make attributions about your motives and effectiveness based on the interactions they have with you. Your behaviors will determine if they think you are honest or dishonest, competent or incompetent, and so on. With this in mind, view leadership as a performing art. Make skillful use of the dramatic elements described above. Put on performances that reflect mastery, coherence, and purpose. To function as an artful leader, you will need to serve high moral purposes and demonstrate practical wisdom, courage, and other virtues.[51] Use beauty as a standard for judging the performances of other artist leaders. When making ethical choices, act like an artist, incorporating the processes described earlier. Set aside preconceived notions, look deeply, let your imagination play, take a holistic view, and so forth. You can practice these behaviors by engaging with paintings, sculpture, concerts, and other works of art. Be intentional when faced with moral dilemmas, concentrating on being fully present in the moment to sense and engage as fully as possible.[52]

Cautions

- Ignores the rational dimension of leadership
- Definitions of beauty vary
- Performances can be dishonest

Resist the temptation to treat leadership as only an art. Leadership is best viewed as both an art *and* a science. Recognizing the aesthetic dimension of leadership doesn't mean that you should reject its rational aspects. To succeed, you will need to understand how organizations operate, make wise choices, engage in strategic planning, and so on. It is also not clear that followers share the same standard of beauty. They may not always agree on what is beautiful (ethical), demonstrating the truth of the old adage, "Beauty is in the eye of the beholder." Viewing leadership as performance can also tempt you to engage in deceit. Leaders can hide their true intentions and manipulate audiences (see the discussion of authentic leadership above). In the early days of Virgin, for example, company founder Richard Branson would use pay phones to call clients. He would then ring the operator and claim that he'd lost his money in the phone. The operator was then required to connect the call and would say to the person answering, "I have Mr. Branson for you." This created the false impression that Branson was important enough to have someone to place his calls.[53]

RESPONSIBLE LEADERSHIP: PROMOTING GLOBAL GOOD THROUGH ETHICAL RELATIONSHIPS

Responsible leadership is an offshoot of global Corporate Social Responsibility. Socially responsible corporations operating in a global economy try to improve social conditions and the environment in addition to making a profit. (I'll have more to say about social responsibility in Chapter 10.) These businesses pay a living wage to workers in developing countries, for example, and adopt environmentally friendly practices like recycling and reducing energy use and pollution. Responding to the claims of stakeholders is an important element of CSR. Stakeholders consist of any group that is affected by the organization's operations. For a multinational corporation, stakeholders include, for example, domestic and foreign governments, nongovernmental organizations (NGOs), suppliers, customers, and employees in locations around the world.

European researchers Nicola Pless and Thomas Maak believe that leaders can help their corporations become a force for global good through exercising responsible leadership.[54] Responsible leaders build ethical relationships with stakeholders. These relationships then create a sense of shared purpose as well as motivation to address social and environmental problems. Maak and Pless define responsible leadership as

> a values-based and principle-driven relationship between leaders and stakeholders who are connected through a shared sense of meaning and purpose through which they raise to higher ethical levels of motivation and commitment for achieving sustainable value creation and responsible change.[55]

Like transformational leadership, responsible leadership elevates the morality of the parties involved. However, responsible leadership incorporates all stakeholder groups affected by the leader and the organization, not just immediate followers. Responsible leaders establish a "web of inclusion" that connects with diverse constituencies. Relationship building can't be done from a position of authority. Instead, responsible leaders must function as equals who bring people together for a common purpose.

Character plays an important role in responsible leadership. Responsible leaders are authentic (see the earlier discussion of ALT) and demonstrate such virtues as honesty, respect, service, and humility. They reflect moral maturity, practice reflection and critical thinking skills, and can generate creative ethical solutions. Drawing from this moral core, responsible leadership then manifests itself in the following roles:[56]

1. *The leader as steward.* Responsible leaders act as guardians of individual and organizational values, maintaining personal and collective integrity while helping the organization act responsibly. They are also custodians, protecting (and hopefully enriching) the values and resources they have been entrusted with. Stewardship incorporates a global perspective and considers the needs of the environment and future generations.

2. *The leader as servant.* Responsible leaders are focused on the needs of followers. They care for them by providing a safe and meaningful work environment, paying fair wages, listening to their concerns, and supporting their development. Responsible leaders also serve the needs of stakeholders through dialogue, by integrating the perspectives of many different groups, and by putting the good of the community above selfish concerns.

3. *The leader as coach.* Responsible leaders develop and support others, motivating diverse individuals and groups to work together to reach a common vision. This requires open communication, conflict management, coping with cultural differences, and providing culturally appropriate feedback. Moral development is an important element of coaching. Ethical leaders help others develop their moral reasoning and reflection skills.

4. *The leader as architect.* Responsible leaders focus on building integrity cultures, which are work environments that help diverse employees engage in meaningful labor; feel respected, included, and recognized; and reach their potential. Responsible leaders also engage in ongoing dialogue with external stakeholders.

5. *The leader as storyteller.* Responsible leaders communicate shared values and meaning through stories. Stories bring to life the organization's vision and values, help create meaning, and assist followers in making sense of the world. By sharing stories, leaders create a corporate identity, foster cooperation, and communicate their visions about their organization's social and environmental responsibilities.

6. *The leader as change agent.* Responsible leaders shape both the process and the product of change. They create a values-based vision, mobilize followers, keep change momentum going, and deal with the anxiety that always surrounds change efforts. In addition, they ensure that change helps create businesses that are founded on core values and sustainable over the long term.

7. *The leader as citizen.* Responsible leaders are just as concerned about the health of the community as they are about the health of their businesses. They recognize that private business and the public sphere are interdependent. Businesses need healthy communities in order to thrive, and healthy communities need the support of thriving businesses.

Responsible leadership has a positive influence on employees as well as on external stakeholders. Employees believe that their work is more meaningful when CSR is central to the organization's mission. They are more attracted to their leaders and, when actively involved in deciding CSR initiatives, are more satisfied, feel a stronger sense of motivation, and are more committed to their organizations. Responsible leadership enhances the ethical climate of the organization while building trust. Higher trust levels then lead to greater organization learning and better performance.[57]

Proponents believe that responsible leaders can be developed through education.[58] The European Foundation for Management Development offers the following guidelines for management education: Graduates should (1) think and act globally, (2) broaden the purpose of the corporation to include accountability to society, and (3) put ethics at the center of all decisions and operations. To accomplish these objectives, education and training programs have to make global responsibility central to the curriculum. Responsibility can also be fostered through real-world experiences. Service learning often increases social awareness and recognition of citizenship responsibilities, whether in students or in professionals. For example, Price Waterhouse pairs with NGOs to address social issues through its Project Ulysses program. Waterhouse employees work with selected nonprofit partners on electricity, sanitation, mental health, and other projects in developing nations. They then return to debrief from their experiences.

Maak and Pless have an ambitious agenda for responsible leadership. They believe that corporate leaders have a duty to act as agents of social change and as "agents of world benefit."[59] Multinational corporations exert greater and greater economic power and enjoy more and more privileges. Therefore, they have a moral obligation to promote social justice by trying to solve political and social problems. Responsible leaders join government and nonprofit leaders in promoting human rights; alleviating poverty and hunger; and fighting HIV/AIDS, malaria, and other illnesses. Such collaboration creates *social capital*—a network of structures, resources, and lasting positive relationships—which can then be used to address other social problems.[60]

Applications and Cautions

Applications

- Develop your sense of social responsibility
- Encourage corporate social responsibility
- Play the role of the responsible leader
- Broaden your focus to outside the organization

Few of us are in a position to lead multinational corporations in the fight against global problems like poverty and substandard housing. Yet, you can do your part to ensure that your organization is socially responsible. Foster your personal sense of responsibility through participation in service learning and service projects. Then act as an informal CSR champion or corporate social entrepreneur by taking steps, in your position, to address social and environmental issues. You might, for example, lead efforts to reduce waste in your department or promote volunteer initiatives.[61] You can act as steward, servant, coach, architect, and storyteller no matter your organizational status. Weave your own web of relationships founded on ethical principles and values. Act out of high character and demonstrate sound moral reasoning, building relationships grounded in trust and integrity. Be concerned about the needs and development of others, both inside and outside the organization. The creation of a more just global society is an ambitious goal, but it is one worth pursuing.

Of the theories discussed in this chapter, only responsible leadership incorporates globalization and external stakeholders. It encourages leaders to work with others to solve difficult problems on every continent. This approach to leadership ethics highlights the fact that you must be concerned about all those who are impacted by your actions, not just your immediate followers.

Cautions

- In the early stages of development
- Overlaps other theories
- Corporations are resistant to an expanded social role
- Liberal bias
- Focuses exclusively on business leadership

Responsible leadership theory is in the early stages of development, which accounts for many of its shortcomings.[62] To this point, only a small group of scholars have explored the implications of responsible leadership, though this number is rapidly growing. Not all agree with the definition of responsible leadership offered by Maak and Pless, arguing instead that responsible leaders can be driven by economic considerations, using CSR to improve the bottom line. Limited empirical evidence has been offered to support the theory's tenets. In fact, conducting research on the theory is a daunting task, since investigators must examine values, decisions, and behaviors at many different levels—individual, organizational, societal, and global. The theorists incorporate elements of authentic leadership, transformational leadership, and servant leadership into their model. How their theory relates to these other approaches needs additional clarification.

You may take issue with Pless and Maak's bold assertion that corporations and their leaders need to be agents of social justice and world benefit. They advocate that businesses take on responsibilities usually associated with governments to address global problems, such as world hunger. Like a great number of observers, you may be uneasy about multinational corporations acting as "quasi-states." Or you might take issue with liberal bias of its advocates. Further, the traditional conception of social responsibility is much more limited than that advocated in responsible leadership. Corporate leaders typically tie their social efforts to their business goals, as in the case of a building supply company supporting a Habitat for Humanity construction project. Then, too, multinational businesses generally target problems related to their operations and locations. For instance, a socially conscious manufacturer will focus on improving living conditions in the communities surrounding its plants. Few corporate leaders appear ready to tackle global issues like the shortage of clean water and widespread poverty, as proponents of responsible leadership urge them to do. (Turn to Case Study 8.3 for one exception).

Continued theoretical development may address what is perhaps the greatest concern about responsible leadership, which is whether this perspective can serve as a general theory of leadership ethics. Maak and Pless developed their theory to foster greater social responsibility in multinational corporations. They specifically address business leaders.

However, you may conclude that the components of responsible leadership would seem to apply to every type of organizational leader. Educators, agency heads, mayors, governors, and others also have to build values-based, principle-driven relationships with diverse stakeholder groups to achieve ethical objectives.

TAOISM: LEAD NATURE'S WAY

Taoism (pronounced "Dowism") is one of the world's oldest philosophies, dating back to ancient China (600–300 BC). The nation had enjoyed peace and prosperity under a series of imperial dynasties but had become a patchwork of warring city-states. Groups of philosophers traveled from one fiefdom to another, offering leaders advice for restoring harmony. The Taoists were one of these "100 Schools of Thought."[63]

The *Tao Te Ching* (usually translated as *The Classic of the Way and Its Power and Virtue*) is Taoism's major text. According to popular tradition, a royal librarian named Lao-Tzu authored this book as he departed China for self-imposed exile. However, most scholars believe that this short volume (5,000 words) is a collection of the teachings of several wise men or sages.[64]

As one of China's traditional philosophies, Taoism continues to shape the values of modern Chinese business leaders. Chinese CEOs report that flexibility and forbearance (important Taoist concepts) are important to their success; lower-level managers take a Taoist approach by acting modestly, giving subordinates autonomy, and encouraging followers to think for themselves.[65] Taoist leadership thinking has also attracted Western audiences. A number of North American scholars and practitioners believe that Taoist principles can help leaders adapt to constant technological and organizational change in the modern workplace.[66]

Understanding the "Way" or *Tao* is the key to understanding Taoist ethical principles. The Tao is the shapeless, nameless force or "nonbeing" that brings all things into existence or being and then sustains them. The Tao takes form in nature and reveals itself through natural principles. These principles then become the standards for ethical behavior. Ethical leaders and followers develop *te*, or character, by acting in harmony with the Tao, not by following rules and commandments. Laws reflect a distrust of human nature and create a new class of citizens—lawbreakers—instead of encouraging right behavior. Efforts to reduce crime, for example, seem to increase it instead:

> Throw away holiness and wisdom,
>
> And people will be a hundred times happier.
>
> Throw away morality and justice,
>
> And people will do the right thing.
>
> Throw away industry and profit, and there won't be any thieves.[67]

"Leave well enough alone" seems to capture the essence of Taoist ethics. Consistent with their hands-off approach, Taoist sages argue that he or she governs best who governs least. Leading is like cooking a small fish: Don't overdo it. The ideal Taoist leader maintains a low profile, leading mostly by example and letting followers take ownership.

> When the Master governs, the people
>
> Are hardly aware that he exists.
>
> Next best is a leader who is loved.
>
> Next, one who is feared.
>
> The worst is one who is despised.
>
> If you don't trust the people,
>
> You make them untrustworthy.
>
> The Master doesn't talk, he acts.
>
> When his work is done,
>
> The people say, "Amazing:
>
> We did it, all by ourselves!"[68]

Taoists rely on images or metaphors drawn from nature and daily life to illustrate the characteristics of model leaders. The first image is that of an uncarved block. An uncarved block of stone or wood is nameless and shapeless, like the Tao itself. Leaders should also be blocklike, avoiding wealth, status, and glory while they leave followers alone.

The second image is the child. Children serve as another reminder that wise leaders don't get caught up in the pursuit of power and privilege but remain humble. Mahatma Gandhi demonstrated childlike character. He dressed simply in clothes he made himself, owned almost nothing, and did not seek political office. Yet he emerged as one of history's most influential leaders.

The third image is water. Water provides an important insight into how leaders ought to influence others by illustrating that there is great strength in weakness. Water cuts through the hardest rock, given enough time. In the same way, the weak often overcome the powerful.[69] Authoritarian governments in Czechoslovakia, Argentina, and Poland were overthrown not by military means but through the efforts of ordinary citizens. Leaders who use soft tactics (listening, empowering, and collaborating) rather than hard ones (such as threats and force) are more likely to overcome resistance to change. Flexibility or pliability is an important attribute of water as well. Water seeks new paths when it meets resistance; leaders should do the same.

The fourth image is the valley. To the Taoists, the universe is made up of two forces: the yin (negative, dark, cool, female, shadows) and the yang (positive, bright, warm, male, sun). Creation operates as it should when these forces are in balance. Although both the yin and the yang are important, Taoists highlight the importance of the yin, or feminine side of leadership, which is represented by the valley metaphor. Leaders should seek to be valleys (which reflect the yin) rather than prominent peaks (which reflect the yang).

The fifth image is the clay pot, which celebrates emptiness by elevating nothing to higher status than something. The most useful part of a pot is the emptiness within. Similarly, the most useful part of a room is the empty space between the walls. Leaders ought to empty themselves, putting aside needless words, superficial thinking, technology, and selfishness. By being empty, leaders can use silence, contemplation, and observation to better understand the workings of the Tao and its ethical principles.

Applications and Cautions

Applications

- Use soft tactics
- Focus on being, not doing
- Temper your use of power and privilege
- Follow nature's example

Taoist thinkers encourage you to be flexible; use soft tactics that facilitate teamwork, such as listening and negotiation. Collaboration is becoming increasingly important in today's workplace as organizations become leaner and flatter. Taoists also emphasize being rather than doing. Act blocklike and childlike to develop your character. Embrace silence and contemplation, cultivate the inner self, reject ambition, and seek to serve rather than to be served.

Taoism cautions against the abuse of power and privilege. The authors of the *Tao Te Ching* reject the use of force except as a last resort. They criticize the feudal lords of their day for living in splendor while their people sink into poverty and starvation. It is difficult to imagine that Taoist sages would approve of the vast difference in pay between American executives and employees, for instance, or give their blessing to politicians who enjoy an extravagant lifestyle at taxpayer expense. In addition, Taoists encourage you to look to nature for insights about leadership. Contemporary authors have begun to follow their lead, identifying leadership lessons that can be drawn from the natural world.[70]

Cautions

- Denies reason
- Rejects codes and laws
- Is ambiguous about many moral issues
- Does not adequately explain evil

There are some serious disadvantages to Taoist ethics. In their attempt to follow nature, Taoists encourage leaders to empty themselves of, among other things, reason. Intuition has its place, but, as we saw in Chapter 6, we need to draw on logic as well. Taoists are rightly skeptical about the effectiveness of moral codes and laws. Nevertheless, laws can change society for the better. For example, civil rights legislation played a significant role in reducing racial discrimination and changing cultural norms. In organizations, reasonable rules, professional guidelines, and codes of conduct can and do play a role in improving ethical climate. (See Chapter 10.)

Although Taoism has much to say about the shadow of power and our relationship to the world around us, you'll find it is silent on many common ethical dilemmas, such as the case of the manager described in Chapter 1 who is asked to keep information about an upcoming merger to herself. What does it mean to follow nature's example when faced with this decision? Perhaps the manager should keep quiet to keep from intruding into the lives of followers. Nonetheless, withholding information would put her in the position of a mountain instead of a valley, giving her an advantage.

Basing moral decision making on conformity to principles manifested in the natural world promotes ethical relativism. The Taoist believes that the ethical action is the one that blends with natural rhythms to produce the desired outcome. In other words, what works is what is right. This approach seems to ignore the fact that what may "work"—generate profits, create pleasure, ensure job security, earn a raise—may be unethical (result in an unsafe product, destroy public trust, exploit workers). Like pragmatism, an ethical perspective I introduced Chapter 5, Taoism seems to lack a moral center. Natural conditions are always changing: Seasons shift; plants and animals grow and die. The flexible leader adapts to shifting circumstances. However, this makes it impossible to come to any definite conclusion about right or wrong. What you determine to be the right moral choice in one context may be wrong in another.

One final concern should be noted: Taoism's firm conviction that humans, in their natural state, will act morally seems to deny the power of evil. My thesis has been that leaders and followers can and do act destructively, driven by their shadow sides.

IMPLICATIONS AND APPLICATIONS

- Seek to be a transforming leader who raises the level of morality in a group or an organization. Transformational leaders speak to higher-level needs and bring about profound changes. They are motivated by duty and altruism and marked by personal integrity. Dimensions of transformational leadership include idealized influence, inspirational motivation, intellectual stimulation, and individualized consideration.

- Putting the needs of followers first reduces the likelihood that you'll cast ethical shadows. Servant leaders are stewards who have significant obligations to both their followers and their institutions, practice partnership, promote healing, and serve worthy purposes.

- Be careful who and what you serve. Make sure your efforts support worthy people and goals and are carefully thought out.

- Authentic leaders have an in-depth knowledge of themselves and act in ways that reflect their core values and beliefs. Authenticity multiplies the effectiveness of leaders and promotes ethical behavior in followers. To function as an authentic leader, you will have to demonstrate self-awareness, balanced processing, internalized moral perspective, and relational transparency.

- Aesthetic leadership emphasizes the sensory and emotional dimensions of organizational life. View leadership as an art and put on beautiful ethical leadership performances that demonstrate mastery, coherence, and moral purpose. Incorporate artistic practices into your ethical decision making by setting aside preconceived notions, looking deeply, and freeing your imagination.

- Responsible leaders build ethical relationships with stakeholders both inside and outside the organization in order to address global problems. In order to act as a responsible leader, you will need to act as a steward, a servant, a coach, an architect, a storyteller, a change agent, and a citizen.

- Taoists argue that nature and elements of everyday life serve as a source of ethical leadership lessons. You can learn from uncarved blocks, children, water, valleys, and clay pots.

FOR FURTHER EXPLORATION, CHALLENGE, AND SELF-ASSESSMENT

1. What additional applications and cautions can you add for each approach described in the chapter? Which perspective do you find most useful? Why?

2. Brainstorm a list of pseudo-transformational and transformational leaders. What factors distinguish between the two types of leader? How do your characteristics compare with those presented in the chapter?

3. Discuss the following propositions in a group: (1) "Sometimes leaders have to be inauthentic in order to fill their roles"; (2) "Business leaders have an ethical duty to address global problems like poverty and hunger"; (3) "Ethical leadership is beautiful leadership."

4. Make a diligent effort to serve your followers for a week. At the end of this period, reflect on your experience. Did focusing on the needs of followers change your behavior? What did you do differently? What would happen if you made this your leadership philosophy? Record your thoughts.

5. Write a case study. Option 1 is to base your case on someone you consider to be an authentic leader. How does this person demonstrate authenticity? What impact has this person had on followers and her or his organization? What can we learn from this leader's example? Option 2 is to base your case on someone you consider to be a responsible leader. How does this individual play the role of a responsible leader? How has his or her business been an agent of global good? What can we learn from this leader's example?

6. Identify the trigger events in your life. How have they contributed to your moral development as a leader?

7. Analyze an instance where you believe that a leader put on a beautiful performance. How did that individual demonstrate mastery, coherence, and purpose?

8. Approach an ethical problem using the artistic practices described in the chapter. After making your decision, reflect on how these strategies shaped your decision-making process and solution.

9. Which image from nature or daily life from Taoism do you find most interesting and helpful? Why? Can you think of additional natural metaphors that would be useful to leaders?

10. Read a popular book on transformational leadership or on a transformational leader. Write a review. Summarize the contents for those who have not read it. Next, evaluate the book. What are its strengths and weaknesses from an ethical point of view? Would you recommend it to others? Why or why not?

STUDENT STUDY SITE

Visit the student study site at **study.sagepub.com/johnsonmecl6e** to access full SAGE journal articles for further research and information on key chapter topics.

Case Study 8.1

A NEW MISSION FOR FERRYPORT COLLEGE

Ferryport College was founded by a group of abolitionists prior to the Civil War. The group wanted to train teachers, clergy, and other professionals for the fight against slavery. After slavery was abolished, Ferryport continued to emphasize social justice, supporting, for example, the early union movement, the Civil Rights Movement, equal opportunities for women, fair trade, and antipoverty initiatives. Social concern is written into the college's mission statement, which states, "Preparing students to improve humanity." Graduation requirements include participation in service projects and internships. In order to promote equality, all faculty members start at the same salary and receive raises based on years of service, not on academic rank. Administrators are paid more than faculty but the difference in compensation is significantly less than at other institutions. Power is shared as well. Administrators consult faculty on all major initiatives and policy changes.

Five years ago, Ferryport faced a crisis. Prospective students didn't seem as interested in social justice; enrollment dropped from 1,500 to 1,100 students. Ferryport lacked a significant endowment fund to make up the loss in tuition revenue in part because its alumni, who gravitate toward low-paying, nonprofit positions, had little money to donate to their alma mater. Major business donors were turned off by Ferryport's support for unions, a raise in the minimum wage, and more government regulation of corporations. Nervous bankers demanded that Ferryport increase its financial reserves from $1 million to $2 million in order to guarantee future loans.

In response to the crisis, the school's board of directors encouraged the president to retire and appointed Gavin Hughes in his place. Hughes had a doctorate in higher education but came to Ferryport from an educational software company. He immediately hired a marketing director who launched a new admissions campaign that highlighted Ferryport's successful sports teams, beautiful campus, and international trips but made no mention of the college's mission or service requirements. In another significant move, he hired a chief financial officer (CFO) from an accounting firm and gave him authority to veto spending, even on academic programs. Hughes then recruited a group of local corporate executives to serve as an informal advisory board to help him operate the college in a "business-like manner." He also increased the number of business people on the Board of Trustees.

President Hughes' moves paid off. The new admissions campaign restored enrollments and the CFO reined in spending. Donations from the local business community increased dramatically, funding the university's reserves, paying for the construction of a badly needed dining hall and sports complex, and increasing the school's endowment. The board of trustees was impressed by the turnaround and granted Hughes and his vice presidents substantial raises. At the same time, the board, at the urging of the president and CFO, decided to delay salary increases for staff and faculty for another year in order to ensure a balanced budget.

Faculty, while grateful for the college's financial stability, expressed concern about the new direction of the school. They could earn substantially more at other colleges and universities but were attracted by Ferryport's social outreach. They worried that the unique culture of Ferryport was being lost in the push to make the college operate like a business. Some complained that money, not mission, now drove the college. Marketing seemed to take priority over the college's traditional values. The president, who was quick to claim personal credit for the college's success, appeared to be consolidating power in his administration, reducing the voice of faculty. Others resented the fact that those from nonacademic backgrounds were making important decisions about academic programs.

Tensions came to a head when President Hughes proposed a new mission statement for Ferryport: "Preparing tomorrow's successful new leaders." No mention was made of social concern, and faculty worried that *success* meant preparing students for lucrative careers rather than preparing them to serve others. At the same time, Hughes proposed a new faculty evaluation system designed to reward high performers. No longer would faculty operate on the same salary scale. Instead, they would be rated on such factors as publications, teaching evaluations, and use of technology in the classroom. Under this pay-for-performance system, raises would depend on how faculty members were rated by administrators.

Upset by the changes, faculty debated whether or not to issue a no-confidence vote in the president. Such a vote is not legally binding; the board of trustees can ignore it. However, President Hughes would find it hard to continue in his position if faculty publicly united in opposition to his leadership.

Discussion Probes

1. Is Hughes a transformational or pseudo-transformational leader?
2. Was it ethical to downplay the college's mission in order to attract more students?
3. Should colleges operate more like businesses?
4. By recruiting business donors, did Hughes sell out the vision and values of the school?
5. Should Ferryport change its vision statement? Why or why not?
6. Is there any way to ensure Ferryport's financial future without further altering its culture? If so, how?
7. If you were a faculty member, would you support a no-confidence vote? If you were on the board of trustees, how would you respond to such a vote?

Case Study 8.2

THE FORENSIC PATHOLOGIST VERSUS THE NATIONAL FOOTBALL LEAGUE

One of the most important moments in U.S. sports history took place not in a stadium, but in a coroner's office. On September 28, 2002, Alleghany County (Pittsburgh) forensic pathologist Dr. Bennet Omalu conducted an autopsy on the body of former Pittsburgh Steeler center Mike Webster. Before his death, football Hall of Famer Webster's life had been in free fall. Depressed, confused, and periodically enraged, the fifty-year-old lost his marriage, family, and business and ended up living under bridges and in his truck. He used superglue to replace his teeth because he couldn't afford to go to the dentist. In constant pain, Webster used a stun gun to knock himself out so he could get to sleep.

Neuropathologist Omalu, born in Nigeria, was one of the few residents of Pittsburgh who wasn't interested in football. He didn't understand the sport and hadn't watched or attended a game. In fact, he was baffled by the city's interest in the Steelers, calling it "part of the American stupidity. You know, in Africa, we believe, yes, the white man is smart but the white man can be foolish."[1] Nonetheless, Omalu had heard news reports about Webster's bizarre behavior and wondered if it was caused by brain damage. Omalu was puzzled during the autopsy when he discovered that the outside of Webster's brain appeared normal. However, driven by curiosity, Omalu received permission to preserve the brain for further analysis. He then took it home to his condo and sent samples out for analysis (which he paid for out of his own pocket). Further examination revealed that the former Steeler's brain was riddled with tiny brown pockets of tau protein. In healthy brains, tau acts like a lubricant. However, when tau congeals into clumps, it acts like sludge, killing healthy brain cells, often in the regions of the brain that control mood, emotions, and higher-level reasoning. Omalu's discovery confirmed what many neurologists had suspected—that football concussions cause permanent brain damage. Omalu named the brain pattern CTE: chronic (long term) traumatic (related to trauma) encephalopathy (referring to damaged brain).

Omalu naively believed that the National Football League (NFL) would welcome his discovery and take steps to reduce the risks to its players. ("I thought they were just gonna come and embrace me and give me a kiss on my cheek."[2]) Instead, the league dismissed his research. Doctors associated with the NFL demanded that he retract the paper publishing his findings, accusing him of fallacious reasoning and being speculative. When the NFL held a summit to address the concussion issue, Omalu was excluded.

The league formed its own concussion study group (headed by a rheumatologist who studies joints, not brains), which asserted that professional football players were somehow immune to brain damage caused by on field collisions and that concussions, if they occurred, were rare. League officials continued to deny that there was any link between concussions and brain damage, pointing to steroid use, genetics, and other factors as causes instead. (Members of Congress and other observers would later point out that these were the same tactics used by Big Tobacco to cover up the dangers of smoking.) Dr. Omalu examined the brain of retired Steeler Terry Long (who killed himself by drinking antifreeze) and former Washington cornerback Andre Waters (who shot himself). Both former players had spiraled down into depression and rage. Once again, the pathologist found the telltale signs of CTE, noting that Waters, who took his life at age forty-five, had the brain of an eighty-five-year-old with early onset Alzheimer's.

NFL commissioner Roger Goodell still refuses to admit a direct link between concussions and diminished brain function (although a top NFL official recently acknowledged one exists). However, the commissioner did oversee a series of rules changes to reduce violent collisions, including lowering the number of kick-off returns and helmet-to-helmet hits. In the past players, begged to return to the game after being concussed for fear of losing their jobs and being seen as "soft." Coaches were all too happy to send them back in. Now, players cannot return until they have been tested by independent doctors and pass concussion protocols. In the meantime, evidence of the dangers of concussions mounts. A Boston University study found symptoms of CTE in 90 out of 94 deceased NFL players. One concussion makes it more likely to suffer another one and concussions have a cumulative effect, resulting in permanent brain damage. Three or more concussions greatly increase the risk. Mild concussions may be as dangerous as serious concussions that daze or knock out players.

Other doctors might have succumbed to the pressure applied by the NFL, the $10 billion industry that operates America's favorite sport. Not so Bennet Omalu. He continues to investigate brain trauma in California where he serves as a county coroner. He established a nonprofit foundation to fund research, cures, and care for people suffering from CTE and other traumatic brain injuries. Omalu views his work as a calling. Deeply spiritual, he believes he speaks on behalf of the dead, giving them a voice. (He talks to bodies during autopsies.) He felt particularly obligated to speak on behalf of Mike Webster:

> Mike Webster spoke to us through the patterns of disease in his tissues. I listened and translated what he said. He said it was not his fault. He said to us that he suffered from the effects of more than twenty thousand blows to his head while he played football. He told us to do something so that younger players who will come after him will not end up like him. He told us to be more compassionate, more understanding, and more patient with his peers who may already be suffering from what he endured.[3]

Omalu has his share of critics, however. Former coworkers considered him overly ambitious and took issue with his $600 tailored suits and his Mercedes Benz automobile. They were offended by his conversations with the dead. (Omalu suspects that the NFL and a number of other researchers dismissed his findings because of his skin color and immigrant status.) Others accuse him of claiming too much credit for his discovery. Most

(Continued)

(Continued)

off-putting is Omalu's lack of social awareness. He doesn't self-censor, saying exactly what he thinks at all times. He doesn't seem to recognize that others aren't as comfortable with autopsies as he. A reporter was shocked to find, for example, that he was keeping preserved brains in tubs in his living room. He offended a group of football players and their families by showing pictures of Webster's autopsy during an information session on the dangers of concussions.

By all indications, the "concussion crisis," sparked in large part by Omalu's 2002 discovery, will continue. A group of former players successfully sued the NFL for $1 billion, and additional lawsuits are on the way. More rules changes may be coming and colleges and high schools are taking concussions seriously. Participation in Pop Warner (youth) football leagues dropped 10% between 2010–2012, the largest decline in the organization's history. Former all-pro quarterback Kurt Warner said he wouldn't want his boys to follow his career path. Mike Ditka, Troy Aikman, Brett Favre, Terry Bradshaw, and other prominent former players said they would not have played had they known what the game would do to their brains.

Discussion Probes

1. Would (or do you) you play football, knowing the risks? Would you let your children play?

2. Are you less likely to watch football, knowing the risk it poses to players?

3. Do you consider Omalu to be a servant leader? An authentic leader?

4. Did Dr. Omalu's status as an outsider—a non-football fan, African immigrant—make it easier to ignore his message?

5. What more should NFL's leaders do in response to the concussion crisis?

Notes

1. Fainaru-Wada, M., & Fainaru, S. (2013). *League of denial*. New York, NY: Three Rivers Press, p. 151.

2. Fainaru-Wada & Fainaru, p. 165.

3. Laskas, J. M. (2015). *Concussion*. New York, NY: Random House, pp. 132–133.

Sources

Armour, N. (2016, March 16). NFL's acknowledgement overdue. *USA Today*, p. 3C

Laskas, J. M. (2009, September 14). Bennet Omalu, concussions, and the NFL: How one doctor changed football forever. *GQ*.

Schwartz, A. (2007, January 18). Expert ties ex-player's suicide to brain damage from football. *The New York Times*, p A1.

Few business leaders take their social responsibilities as seriously as Yvon Chouinard. Chouinard started his career in the 1950s as an elite rock climber, scaling walls at Yosemite and elsewhere. Dissatisfied with available climbing gear, Chouinard began manufacturing pitons—metal stakes hammered into rocks to secure rope—for other climbers and selling them out of the trunk of his car. In 1973, he formed the Patagonia Company to sell shirts, climbing shorts, and other outdoor clothing items.

Chouinard's' love of climbing and the outdoors is reflected in Patagonia's extraordinarily strong environmental commitment. Early on, he declared that his company was an "environmental villain" for making pitons that damaged rock. He then discontinued making pitons (his core business) and began offering aluminum chocks instead. In a few months, the sales of the chocks were soaring. The company donates 1% of its sales (pretax) to environmental causes. Patagonia was the first major company to sell fleeces made out of recycled plastic bottles. When it realized the harm done by traditional cotton farming methods, the firm switched to making items made out organic fibers. Since 1972, the firm has donated $70 million in grants and services to thousands of community-based environmental groups, most with five or fewer staffers.

Company representatives tell prospective customers to only buy what they need. They ran a full-page ad in *The New York Times* headlined, "Don't Buy This Jacket." The ad's text then described the environmental costs of the company's best-selling fleece and asked consumers to think twice before purchasing it or any other product. According to the vice president of global marketing, "We want our customers to do some research and make an educated decision about whether they really need the product, and how to use it. So it's a case of 'Buy less, buy smart.'"[1] Patagonia also offers a free repair service to discourage buyers from tossing their garments, and the company's Worn Wear Wagon travels the country mending Patagonia products. Buyers are asked to sign a pledge to return items they no longer need to company outlets to be recycled, and some of its outlets carry used items. The firm claims that it is able to recycle 100% of its polyester goods, pulling off the buttons and zippers and sending the garments to Asia for remanufacturing. The Footprint Chronicles initiative enables consumers to track all the steps of a product's life cycle on line from raw material though design and manufacture to disposal or remanufacturing to determine its impact on the environment.

Chouinard's environmental vision extends well beyond his company. Patagonia cofounded the Sustainable Apparel Coalition with clothing manufacturers and retailers like Levi-Strauss and Target with the goal of reducing the environmental impact of their businesses. Patagonia's founder seeks "to create a company others companies want to emulate" and

(Continued)

(Continued)

reports that leaders of other businesses have turned to him for advice on how to preserve the environment. Patagonia and other companies are helping to create a national park in Chile, which will be two-thirds the size of Yellowstone.

To ensure that Patagonia's green commitment continues after he is gone, Chouinard was the first company leader to file "benefit corporation" papers in California. The California legislature created this new corporate category for firms that "create material positive impact on society and the environment." (Similar programs can be found in other states.) This law protects companies who want to donate proceeds to social causes from lawsuits brought by shareholders claiming that these policies dilute their stock value. Businesses registered as benefit corporations have to file annual reports outlining the public benefits they provide and have to be evaluated by third parties to determine if they have met those standards. Patagonia can now continue to contribute to environmental causes, even if the company goes public following the death of Chouinard and his wife. After registering his company, the seventy-two-year-old Chouinard said, "My work is over. I feel that we've done what we set out to do. This benefit corporation allows us a way to ensure the values of my company continue."[2]

Patagonia's environmental focus has not hurt its bottom line. Sales went up after the company urged consumers not to buy its products. The firm is experiencing annual double-digit growth, lifting its annual revenues to $570 million. There seems little doubt that Chouinard and Patagonia have created relationships with stakeholders who share their commitment to a greener world.

Discussion Probes

1. How does Yvon Chouinard function as a responsible leader?
2. Can you think of other business executives who also meet the criteria for responsible leadership?
3. Could leaders of publicly held corporations follow Chouinard's example? Should they try to do so?
4. Why did sales increase after Patagonia officials urged consumers to buy less?
5. Does Patagonia put too much emphasis on the environment? Who might be hurt by this commitment?
6. Should all states adopt benefit corporation laws? What are the potential benefits and costs of doing so?

Notes

1. Wright, M. (2011, November 7). Success means telling people to buy less. *The Guardian*.
2. Herdt, T. (2012, January 4). Patagonia first in line to register as a 'benefit corporation.' *Ventura County Star*.

Sources

Archer, M. (2005, October 31). Founder of Patagonia became a businessman accidentally. *USA Today*, Money, p. 5.

Growing the grassroots. (n.d.). Retrieved from http://www.pataonia.com/us

MacKinnon. J. B. (2015, May 21). Patagonia's anti-growth strategy. *The New Yorker*.

Mara, J. (2008, January 17). Patagonia CEO turns retailers green. *Contra Costa Times*.

Martin, J. (2012, May 25). Clothier's products all come in green. *Los Angeles Times*, p. B1.

Ryan, K. (2014, July 31). The bottom line: Patagonia, North Face, and the myth of green consumerism. *Groundswell*.

SELF-ASSESSMENT 8.1

Transformational Leadership Scale

Instructions: Think about a situation in which you either assumed or were given a leadership role. Think about your own behaviors within this context. To what extent does each of the following statement characterize your leadership orientation?

Very little		A moderate amount				Very Much
1	2	3	4	5	6	7

1. Have a clear understanding of where we are going
2. Paint an interesting picture of the future for my group
3. Am always seeking new opportunities for the organization/group
4. Inspire others with my plans for the future
5. Am able to get others to be committed to my dreams
6. Lead by doing, rather than simply by telling
7. Provide a good model for others to follow
8. Lead by example
9. Foster collaboration among group members
10. Encourage employees to be team players
11. Get the group to work together for the same goal
12. Develop a team attitude and spirit among employees
13. Show that I expect a lot from others
14. Insist on only the best performance
15. Will not settle for second best
16. Act without considering the feelings of others
17. Show respect for the personal feelings of others

18. Behave in a manner thoughtful of the personal needs of others
19. Interact with others without considering their personal feelings
20. Challenge others to think about old problems in new ways
21. Ask questions that prompt others to think
22. Stimulate others to rethink the way they do things
23. Have ideas that challenge others to reexamine some of their basic assumptions about work
24. Always give positive feedback when others perform well
25. Give special recognition when others' work is very good
26. Commend others when they do a better-than-average job
27. Personally compliment others when they do outstanding work
28. Frequently do not acknowledge the good performance of others

Scoring: Reverse your scores on questions 16, 19, and 28. There are seven dimension scores to be computed:

> *Articulate vision*—Sum your response to Questions 1–5 and divide by 5.
>
> *Provide appropriate model*—Sum your responses to Questions 6–8 and divide by 3.
>
> *Foster acceptance of goals*—Sum your responses to Questions 9–12 and divide by 4.
>
> *High performance expectations*—Sum your responses to Questions 13–15 and divide by 3.
>
> *Individual support*—Sum your responses to Questions 16–19 and divide by 4.
>
> *Intellectual stimulation*—Sum your responses to Questions 20–23 and divide by 4.
>
> *Transactional leader behaviors*—Sum your responses to Questions 24–28 and divide by 5.

My scores are

> Articulate vision_____
>
> Role model _____
>
> Foster goal acceptance _____
>
> Performance expectations _____
>
> Individual support _____
>
> Intellectual stimulation _____
>
> Transactional leader behavior _____

A score of 6 and greater reflects a strong orientation to engage in each of these behaviors. A score of 2 or less reflects that you are unlikely to engage in each of these behaviors.

Source: Podsakoff, P. M., MacKenzie, S. B., Moorman, R. H., & Fetter, R. (1990). Transformational leader behaviors and their effects on followers' trust in leader, satisfaction, and organizational citizenship behavior. *Leadership Quarterly, 1,* 107–142.

Scale reprinted from Pierce, J. L., & Newstrom, J. W. (2011). *Leaders and the leadership process: Readings, self-assessments and applications* (6th ed.). New York, NY: McGraw-Hook, pp. 369–370. Used with permission.

SELF-ASSESSMENT 8.2

Servant Leadership Questionnaire

Instructions: You can use this questionnaire to rate the servant leadership behaviors of one of your leaders or ask someone else to rate you. Respond to each question on the following scale: 1 = strongly disagree, 2 = somewhat disagree, 3 = somewhat agree, 4 = strongly agree. The scale rates five dimensions of servant leadership, which are described below. Add up the item ratings to come up with the total score for each component.

Add the component scores to come up with a total servant leadership rating (range 24–96).

Response choices: 1 = strongly disagree; 2 = somewhat disagree; 3 = somewhat agree; 4 = strongly agree

1. This person puts my best interests ahead of his/her own.   1   2   3   4
2. This person does everything he/she can do to serve me.   1   2   3   4
3. This person is one I would turn to if I had a personal trauma.   1   2   3   4
4. This person seems alert to what's happening.   1   2   3   4
5. This person offers compelling reasons to get me to do things.   1   2   3   4
6. This person encourages me to dream "big dreams" about the organization.   1   2   3   4
7. This person is good at anticipating the consequences of decisions.   1   2   3   4
8. This person is good at helping me with my emotional issues.   1   2   3   4
9. This person has great awareness of what is going on.   1   2   3   4
10. This person is very persuasive.   1   2   3   4
11. This person believes that the organization needs to play a moral role in society.   1   2   3   4
12. This person is talented at helping me to heal emotionally.   1   2   3   4
13. This person seems in touch with what's happening.   1   2   3   4
14. This person is good at convincing me to do things.   1   2   3   4
15. This person believes that our organization needs to function as a community.   1   2   3   4
16. This person sacrifices his/her own interests to meet my needs.   1   2   3   4
17. This person is one who could help me mend my hard feelings.   1   2   3   4

18. This person is gifted when it comes to persuading me.   1   2   3   4
19. This person is talented at helping me to heal emotionally.   1   2   3   4
20. This person sees the organization for its potential to contribute to society.   1   2   3   4
21. This person encourages me to have a community spirit in the workplace.   1   2   3   4
22. This person goes above and beyond the call of duty to meet my needs.   1   2   3   4
23. This person seems to know what is going to happen.   1   2   3   4
24. This person is preparing the organization to make a positive difference in the future.   1   2   3   4

Scoring:

Altruistic Calling (Having a deep-rooted desire to make a positive difference)

Item 1 _____

Item 2 _____

Item 16 _____

Item 21 _____

Item 22 _____

Total _____ out of 20

Emotional Healing (Fostering spiritual recovery from hardship or trauma)

Item 3 _____

Item 8 _____

Item 12 _____

Item 17 _____

Item 19 _____

Total _____ out of 20

Wisdom (Aware of surroundings and anticipation of consequences)

Item 4 _____

Item 7 _____

Item 9 _____

Item 13 _____

Item 23 _____

Total _____ out of 20

Persuasive Mapping (Using sound reasoning and mental frameworks)

Item 5 _____

Item 6 _____

Item 10 _____

Item 14 _____

Item 18 _____

Total _____ out of 20

Organizational Development (Making a collective, positive contribution to society)

Item 11 _____

Item 15 _____

Item 20 _____

Item 21 _____

Item 24 _____

Total _____ out of 20

Overall score _____ out of 100

Source: Adapted from Barbuto, J. E., & Wheeler, D. W. (2006). Scale development and construct clarification of servant leadership. *Group & Organization Management,* 300–326. Used with permission.

NOTES

1. See, for example, Katz, D., Maccoby, N., Gurin, G., & Floor, L. (1951). *Productivity, supervision, and morale among railroad workers.* Ann Arbor: University of Michigan: Institute for Social Research; Stogdill, R. M., & Coons, A. E. (1957). *Leader behavior: Its description and measurement.* Columbus: Ohio State University, Bureau of Business Research.
2. Burns, J. M. (1978). *Leadership.* New York, NY: Harper & Row.
3. Burns, J. M. (2003). *Transforming leadership: A new pursuit of happiness.* New York, NY: Atlantic Monthly Press.
4. Burns (1978), p. 2.
5. Burns (2003), Ch. 12.
6. Kanungo, R. N. (2001). Ethical values of transactional and transformational leaders. *Canadian Journal of Administrative Sciences, 18,* 257–265.
7. Carlson, D. S., & Perrewe, P. L. (1995). Institutionalization of organizational ethics through transformational leadership. *Journal of Business Ethics, 14,* 829–838; Hood, J. N. (2003). The relationship of leadership style and CEO values to ethical practices in organizations. *Journal of Business Ethics, 43,* 263–273; Puffer, S. M., & McCarthy, D. J. (2008). Ethical turnarounds and transformational leadership: A global imperative for corporate social responsibility. *Thunderbird International Business Review, 50,* 304–314; Toor, S. R., & Ofori, G. (2009). Ethical leadership: Examining the relationships with full range leadership model, employee outcomes, and organizational culture. *Journal of Business Ethics, 90,* 533–547; Turner, N., Barling, J., Epitropaki, O., Butcher, V., & Milner, C. (2002, April). Transformational leadership and moral reasoning. *Journal of Applied Psychology, 87,* 304–311.

8. See the following: Bass, B. M. (1996). *A new paradigm of leadership: An inquiry into transformational leadership*. Alexandria, VA: U.S. Army Research Institute for the Behavioral and Social Sciences; Bass, B. M., Avolio, B. J., Jung, D. I., & Berson, Y. (2003). Predicting unit performance by assessing transformational and transactional leadership. *Journal of Applied Psychology, 88,* 207–218.

9. Bass, B. M. (1990). *Bass & Stogdill's handbook of leadership* (3rd ed.). New York, NY: Free Press, p. 53.

10. See Bass, B. M., & Avolio, B. J. (1993). Transformational leadership: A response to critiques. In M. M. Chemers & R. Ayman (Eds.), *Leadership theory and research: Perspectives and directions* (pp. 49–60). San Diego, CA: Academic Press; Waldman, D. A., Bass, B. M., & Yammarino, F. J. (1990). Adding to contingent-reward behavior: The augmenting effect of charismatic leadership. *Group and Organizational Studies, 15,* 381–394.

11. For evidence of the effectiveness of transformational leadership, see Bass et al. (2003) and the following: Choudhary, A. I., Akhtar, S. A., & Zaheer, A. (2013). Impact of transformational and servant leadership on organizational performance: A comparative analysis. *Journal of Business Ethics, 116,* 433–440; DeGroot, T., Kiker, D. S., & Cross, T. C. (2000). A meta-analysis to review organizational outcomes related to charismatic leadership. *Canadian Journal of Administrative Sciences, 17,* 356–371; Fiol, C. M., Harris, D., & House, R. J. (1999). Charismatic leadership: Strategies for effecting social change. *Leadership Quarterly, 1,* 449–482; Lowe, K. B., & Kroeck, K. G. (1996). Effectiveness correlates of transformational and transactional leadership: A meta-analytic review. *Leadership Quarterly, 7,* 385–425; Pradhan, S., & Pradhan, R. K. (2015). An empirical investigation of relationship among transformational leadership, affective organizational commitment and contextual performance. *Vision, 19,* 227–235; Toor & Ofori.

12. A few examples of popular leadership sources based on a transformational approach include the following: Bennis, W. G., & Nanus, B. (2003). *Leaders: Strategies for taking charge.* New York, NY: Harper Business Essentials; Kotter, J. P. (1990). *A force for change: How leadership differs from management.* New York, NY: Free Press; Kouzes, J. M., & Posner, B. Z. (2012). *The leadership challenge* (5th ed.). San Francisco, CA: Jossey-Bass; Nanus, B. (1992). *Visionary leadership.* San Francisco, CA: Jossey-Bass; Peters, T. (1992). *Liberation management.* New York, NY: Ballantine.

13. Bass, B. M. (1995). The ethics of transformational leadership. In J. Ciulla (Ed.), *Ethics: The heart of leadership* (pp. 169–192). Westport, CT: Praeger.

14. Den Hartog, D. N., House, R. J., Hanges, P. U., Ruiz-Quintanilla, S. A., & Dorfman, P. W. (1999). Culture specific and cross-culturally generalizable implicit leadership theories: Are attributes of charismatic/transformational leadership universally endorsed? *Leadership Quarterly, 10,* 219–257.

15. Choudhary et al.; ElKordy, M. (2013). Transformational leadership and organizational culture as predictors of employees' attitudinal outcomes. *Business Management Dynamics, 3,* 15–26; Pradhan & Pradhan; Sun, W., Xu, A., & Shang, Y. (2014). Transformational leadership, team climate, and team performance within the NPD team: Evidence from China. *Asia Pacific Journal of Management, 31,* 127–147.

16. Tourish, D. (2008). Challenging the transformational agenda: Leadership theory in transition? *Management Communication Quarterly, 21,* 522–528, p. 523.

17. Criticisms of transformational leadership can be found in the following: Kelley, R. (1992). *The power of followership.* New York, NY: Doubleday/Currency; Tourish, D. (2013). *The dark side of transformational leadership: A critical perspective.* New York, NY: Routledge; Tourish, D., & Pinnington, A. (2002). Transformational leadership, corporate cultism and the spirituality paradigm: An unholy trinity in the workplace? *Human Relations, 55*(2), 147–172.

18. Greenleaf, R. K. (1977). *Servant leadership.* New York, NY: Paulist Press.

19. Ruschman, N. L. (2002). Servant-leadership and the best companies to work for in America. In L. C. Spears & M. Lawrence (Eds.), *Focus on leadership: Servant-leadership for the twenty-first century* (pp. 123–139). New York, NY: Wiley; Sendjaya, S., & Sarros, J. C. (2002). Servant leadership: Its origin, development, and application in organizations. *Journal of Leadership and Organization Studies, 9*(2), 57–64; Spears, L. C. (1998). Introduction: Tracing the growing impact of servant-leadership. In L. C. Spears (Ed.), *Insights on leadership* (pp. 1–12). New York, NY: Wiley.

20. Greenleaf, pp. 13–14.

21. Block, P. (1996). *Stewardship: Choosing service over self-interest.* San Francisco, CA: Berrett-Koehler; De Pree, M. (2003). Servant-leadership: Three things necessary. In L. C. Spears & M. Lawrence (Eds.), *Focus on leadership: Servant-leadership for the 21st century* (pp. 89–97). New York, NY: Wiley.

22. De Pree, M. (1989). *Leadership is an art.* New York, NY: Doubleday.

23. Barbuto, J. E., & Wheeler, D. W. (2006). Scale development and construct clarification of servant leadership. *Group & Organization Management, 31*, 300–326; Spears, L. C. (2004). The understanding and practice of servant leadership. In L. C. Spears & M. Lawrence (Eds.), *Practicing servant leadership: Succeeding through trust, bravery, and forgiveness* (pp. 9–24). San Francisco, CA: Jossey-Bass.

24. Barbuto & Wheeler; Ehrhart, M. G. (2004). Leadership and procedural justice climate as antecedents of unit-level organizational citizenship behavior. *Personnel Psychology, 57*, 61–94; Hale, J. R., & Fields, D. (2007). Exploring servant leadership across cultures: A study of followers in Ghana and the USA. *Leadership, 3*(4), 397–417; Jaramillo, F., Grisaffe, D. B., Chonko, L. B., & Roberts, J. A. (2009). Examining the impact of servant leadership on sales force performance. *Journal of Personal Selling & Sales Management, 24*(3), 257–275; Jaramillo, F., Grisaffe, D. B., Chonko, L. B., & Roberts, J. A. (2009). Examining the impact of servant leadership on salesperson's turnover intention. *Journal of Personal Selling & Sales Management, 24*, 351–365; Jones, D. (2012). Does servant leadership lead to greater customer focus and employee satisfaction? *Business Studies Journal, 4*, 21–35; Mayers, D., Bardes, M., & Piccolo, R. F. (2008). Do servant-leaders help satisfy follower needs? An organizational justice perspective. *European Journal of Work and Organizational Psychology, 17*(2), 180–197; Mehta, S., & Pillay, R. (2011). Revisiting servant leadership: An empirical study in Indian context. *The Journal of Contemporary Management Research, 5*(2), 24–41; Melchar, D. E., & Bosco, S. M. (2010). Achieving high organization performance through servant leadership. *The Journal of Business Inquiry, 9*, 74–88; Russell, R. F., & Stone, A. G. (2002). A review of servant leadership attributes: Developing a practical model. *Leadership & Organization Development Journal, 23*(3), 145–157; Schwepker, D. H., & Schultz, R. J. (2015). Influence of the ethical servant leader and ethical climate on customer value enhancing sales performance. *Journal of Personal Selling & Sales Management, 35*, 93–107; Sokoll, S. (2014). Servant leadership and employee commitment to a supervisor. *International Journal of Leadership Studies, 8*, 88–104; Walumbwa, F. O., Hartnell, C. A., & Oke, A. (2010). Servant leadership, procedural justice climate, service climate, employee attitudes, and organizational citizenship behavior: A cross-level investigation. *Journal of Applied Psychology, 95*, 517–529; Washington, R. R., Sutton, C. D., & Feild, H. S. (2006). Individual differences in servant leadership: The roles of values and personality. *Leadership & Organization Development Journal, 27*(8), 700–716.

25. Kennedy, D. (2004). *The dark sides of virtue: Reassessing international humanitarianism.* Princeton, NJ: Princeton University Press.

26. Klenke, K. (2005). The internal theater of the authentic leader: Integrating cognitive, affective, conative and spiritual facets of authentic leadership. In W. L. Gardner, B. J. Avolio, & F. O. Walumbwa (Eds.), *Authentic leadership theory and practice: Origins, effects and development* (pp. 43–81). Amsterdam, The Netherlands: Elsevier.

27. Avolio, B. J., & Gardner, W. L. (2005). Authentic leadership development: Getting to the root of positive forms of leadership. *Leadership Quarterly, 16,* 315–340; Chan, A., Hannah, S. T., & Gardner, W. L. (2005). Veritable authentic leadership: Emergence, functioning, and impacts. In W. L. Gardner, B. J. Avolio, & F. O. Walumbwa (Eds.), *Authentic leadership theory and practice: Origins, effects and development* (pp. 3–41). Amsterdam, The Netherlands: Elsevier.

28. Kernis, M. H. (2003). Toward a conceptualization of optimal self-esteem. *Psychological Inquiry, 14,* 1–26; Walumbwa, F. O., Avolio, B. J., Gardner, W. L., Wernsing, T. S., & Peterson, S. J. (2008). Authentic leadership: Development and validation of a theory-based measure. *Journal of Management, 34*(1), 89–126.

29. Avolio & Gardner, p. 321.

30. Hannah, S. T., Lester, P. B., & Vogelgesang, G. R. (2005). Moral leadership: Explicating the moral component of authentic leadership. In W. L. Gardner, B. J. Avolio, & F. O. Walumbwa (Eds.), *Authentic leadership theory and practice: Origins, effects and development* (pp. 43–81). Amsterdam, The Netherlands: Elsevier; May, D. R., Chan, A. Y. L., Hodges, T. D., & Avolio, B. J. (2003). Developing the moral component of authentic leadership. *Organizational Dynamics, 32,* 247–260.

31. Gardner, W. L., Avolio, B. J., Luthans, F., May, D. R., & Walumbwa, F. O. (2005). "Can you see the real me?" A self-based model of authentic leader and follower development. *Leadership Quarterly, 16,* 343–372.

32. Ilies, R., Morgeson, F. P., & Nahrgang, J. D. (2005). Authentic leadership and eudemonic well-being: Understanding leader–follower outcomes. *Leadership Quarterly, 16,* 373–394; May et al.

33. Avolio, B. J., Gardner, W. L., Walumbwa, F. O., Luthans, F., & May, D. R. (2004). Unlocking the mask: A look at the process by which authentic leaders impact follower attitudes and behaviors. *Leadership Quarterly, 15,* 801–823; Clapp-Smith, R., Vogelgesang, G. R., & Avey, J. B. (2009). Authentic leadership and positive psychological capital: The mediating role of trust at the group level of analysis. *Journal of Leadership & Organizational Studies, 15*(3), 227–240; Gardner et al.; Harvey, P., Martinko, M. J., & Gardner, W. L. (2006). Promoting authentic behavior in organizations: An attributional perspective. *Journal of Leadership and Organizational Studies, 12,* 1–11; Zhu, W., May, D. R., & Avolio, B. J. (2004). The impact of ethical leadership behavior on employee outcomes: The roles of psychological empowerment and authenticity. *Journal of Leadership and Organizational Studies, 11,* 16–26.

34. Leroy, H., Palanski, M. E., & Simons, T. (2012). Authentic leadership and behavioral integrity as drivers of follower commitment and performance. *Journal of Business Ethics, 107,* 255–264; Onorato, M., & Zhu, J. (2014, Winter). An empirical study on the relationships between authentic leadership and organizational trust by industry segment. *SAM Advanced Management Journal,* 26–39; Peus, C., Wesche, J. S., Streicher, B., Braun, S., & Frey, D. (2012). Authentic leadership: An empirical test of its antecedents, consequences, and mediating mechanisms. *Journal of Business Ethics, 107,* 331–348; Wang, H., Sui, Y., Luthans, F., Wang, D., & Wu, Y. (2014). Impact of authentic leadership on performance: Role of followers' positive psychological capital and relational processes. *Journal of Organizational Behavior, 35,* 5–12.

35. Clapp-Smith et al.

36. Walumbwa et al. (2008).

37. Cavazotte, F., Duarte, C., & Gobbo, A. M. (2010). Authentic leader, safe work: The influence of leadership performance. *Brazilian Business Review, 10,* 95–119; Li, F., Yu, K. F., Yang, J., Qi, Z., & Fu, J. H. (2014). Authentic leadership, traditionality, and interactional justice in the Chinese context. *Management and Organization Behavior, 10,* 249–272; Liu, S-M., Liao, J-Q., & Wei, H. (2015). Authentic leadership and whistleblowing: Mediating roles of psychological safety and personal identification. *Journal of Business Ethics, 131,* 107–119; Rahimina, F., & Sharifirad, M. S. (2015). Authentic leadership and employee well-being: The mediating role

of attachment insecurity. *Journal of Business Ethics, 132*, 363–377; Sendjaya, S., Perketi, A., Hartel, C., Hirst, G., & Butarbutar, I. (2016). Are authentic leaders always moral? The role of Machiavellianism in the relationship between authentic leadership and morality. *Journal of Business Ethics, 133*, 125–139.

38. Florida leadership researcher Walumbwa notches sixth retraction. (2015, January 14). *Retraction Watch.*

39. Pfeffer, J. (2015). *Leadership BS: Fixing workplaces and careers one truth at a time.* New York, NY: HarperBusiness.

40. Pfeffer.

41. Clapp-Smith et al.

42. Chan et al.

43. Ladkin, D. (2006). The enchantment of the charismatic leader: Charisma reconsidered as aesthetic encounter. *Leadership, 2*(2), 165–179.

44. Hansen, H., Ropo, A., & Sauer, E. (2007). Aesthetic leadership. *Leadership Quarterly, 18,* 544–560.

45. Duke, D. L. (1986). The aesthetics of leadership. *Educational Administration Quarterly, 22*(1), 7–27.

46. Ladkin (2006); Ladkin, D. (2010). *Rethinking leadership: A new look at old leadership.* Cheltenham, England: Edward Elgar.

47. Elm, D. R. (2014). The artist and the ethicist: Character and process. In D. Koehn & D. Elm (Eds.), *Aesthetics and business ethics* (pp. 53–66). New York, NY: Springer; Ladkin, D. (2011). The art of 'perceiving correctly': What artists can teach us about moral perception. *Tamara: Journal for Critical Organization Inquiry, 9*, 91–101; Taylor S. S., & Elmes, M. B. (2011). Aesthetics and ethics: You can't have one without the other. *Tamara: Journal for Critical Organization Inquiry, 9*, 61–62; Waddock, S. (2014). Wisdom and responsible leadership: Aesthetic sensibility, moral imagination, and systems thinking. In D. Koehn & D. Elm (Eds.), *Aesthetics and business ethics* (pp. 129–147). New York, NY: Springer.

48. Ladkin, D. (2008). Leading beautifully: How mastery congruence and purpose create the aesthetic of embodied leadership practice. *Leadership Quarterly, 19*, 31–41.

49. Haberman, C. (2009, November 29). The story of a landing. *The New York Times,* p. BR15.

50. Squires, N. (2012, July 11). Costa Concordia captain: "I ****** up." *The Telegraph.*

51. Dobson, J. (1999). *The art of management and the aesthetic manager.* Westport, CT: Quorum Books.

52. Abowitz, K. K. (2007). Moral perception though aesthetics: Engaging imaginations in educational ethics. *Journal of Teacher Education, 58*, 287–298; Koehn, D. (2010). Ethics, morality, and art in the classroom: Positive and negative relations. *Journal of Business Ethics Education, 7*, 213–232; Waddock.

53. Ladkin (2008).

54. Maak, T., & Pless, N. M. (2006). Responsible leadership: A relational approach. In T. Maak & N. M. Pless (Eds.), *Responsible leadership* (pp. 33–53). London, England: Routledge; Maak, T., & Pless, N. M. (2006). Responsible leadership in a stakeholder society—A relational perspective. *Journal of Business Ethics, 66,* 99–115; Pless, N. M. (2007). Understanding responsible leadership: Role identity and motivational factors. *Journal of Business Ethics, 74,* 437–456.

55. Maak, T., & Pless, N. M. (2009). Business leaders as citizens of the world. Advancing humanism on a global scale. *Journal of Business Ethics, 88,* 537–550, p. 539.

56. Maak & Pless, Responsible leadership: A relational approach; Pless.

57. Voegtlin, C., Patzer, M., & Scherer, A. G. (2012). Responsible leadership in global business: A new approach to leadership and its multi-level outcomes. *Journal of Business Ethics, 105,* 1–16.

58. Doh, J. P., & Qugley, N. R. (2014). Responsible leadership and stakeholder management: Influence pathways and organizational outcomes. *The Academy of Management Perspectives, 28,*

255–274; Esper, S. C., & Boies, K. (2013). Responsible leadership: A missing link. *Industrial and Organizational Psychology, 6,* 351–354; Maak & Pless, Responsible leadership: A relational approach; Smit, A. (2013). Responsible leadership development through management education: A business ethics perspective. *African Journal of Business Ethics, 7,* 45–51; Voegtlin, Patzer, & Scherer.

59. Pless, N. M., & Maak, T. (2009). Responsible leaders as agents of world benefit: Learnings from "Project Ulysses." *Journal of Business Ethics, 85,* 59–71.

60. Maak, T. (2007). Responsible leadership, stakeholder engagement, and the emergence of social capital. *Journal of Business Ethics, 74,* 329–343.

61. Esper & Boies.

62. For more information on the limitations of responsible leadership and its ongoing development, see Pless, N. M., & Maak, T. (2011). Responsible leadership: Pathways to the future. *Journal of Business Ethics, 98,* 3–13; Waldman, D. A. (2011). Moving forward with the concept of responsible leadership: Three caveats to guide theory and research. *Journal of Business Ethics, 98,* 75–83; Waldman, D. A., & Balven, R. M. (2015). Responsible leadership: Theoretical issues and research directions. *The Academy of Management Perspectives, 1,* 19–29.

63. Material on key components of Taoist thought is adopted from Johnson, C. E. (1997). A leadership journey to the East. *Journal of Leadership Studies, 4*(2), 82–88; Johnson, C. E. (2000). Emerging perspectives in leadership ethics. *Proceedings of the International Leadership Association,* 48–54; Johnson, C. E. (2000). Taoist leadership ethics. *Journal of Leadership Studies, 7,* 82–91.

64. For an alternative perspective on the origins of Taoism, see Kirkland, R. (2002). Self-fulfillment through selflessness: The moral teachings of the Daode Jing. In M. Barnhart (Ed.), *Varieties of ethical reflection: New directions for ethics in a global context* (pp. 21–48). Lanham, MD: Lexington.

65. Cheung, C., & Chan, A. (2005). Philosophical foundations of eminent Hong Kong Chinese CEOs' leadership. *Journal of Business Ethics, 60,* 47–62; Lin, L., Ho, Y., & Wes-Hsin, E. L. (2013). Confucian and Taoist work values: An exploratory study of the Chinese transformational leadership behavior. *Journal of Business Ethics, 113,* 91–103; Ma, L., & Tsui, A. S. (2015). Traditional Chinese philosophies and contemporary leadership. *Leadership Quarterly, 26,* 13–24.

66. See, for example, Autry, J., & Mitchell, S. (1999). *Real power: Business lessons from the Tao Te Ching.* New York, NY: Riverhead; Dreher, D. (1996). *The Tao of personal leadership.* New York, NY: Harper Business; Heider, J. (1992). *The Tao of leadership.* New York, NY: Bantam; Messing, B. (1992). *The Tao of management.* New York, NY: Bantam.

67. Mitchell, S. (Trans.). (1988). *Tao te ching.* New York, NY: Harper Perennial, p. 19.

68. Mitchell, p. 17.

69. Chan, W. (Trans.). (1963). *The way of Lao Tzu.* Indianapolis, IN: Bobbs-Merrill, p. 236.

70. See the following: Kiuchi, T., & Shireman, B. (2002). *What we learned in the rainforest: Business lessons from nature.* San Francisco, CA: Berrett-Koehler; White, B. J., & Prywes, Y. (2007). *The nature of leadership: Reptiles, mammals, and the challenge of becoming a great leader.* New York, NY: AMACOM.

PART IV

Shaping Ethical Contexts

9

Building an Ethical Small Group

Cooperation is the thorough conviction that nobody can get there unless everybody gets there.

—AUTHOR VIRGINIA BURDEN TOWER

Never underestimate a minority.

—BRITISH PRIME MINISTER WINSTON CHURCHILL

WHAT'S AHEAD

This chapter examines ethical leadership in the small-group context. To help create groups that brighten rather than darken the lives of participants, leaders must foster individual ethical accountability among group members, ensure ethical group interaction, avoid moral pitfalls, and establish ethical relationships with other groups.

In his metaphor of the leader's light or shadow, Parker Palmer emphasizes that leaders shape the settings or contexts around them. According to Palmer, leaders are people who have "an unusual degree of power to create the conditions under which other people must live and move and have their being, conditions that can either be as illuminating as heaven or as shadowy as hell."[1] In this final section of the text, I'll describe some of the ways we can create conditions that illuminate the lives of followers in small-group, organizational, global, and crisis settings. Shedding light means both resisting and exerting influence. We must fend off pressures to engage in unethical behavior while actively seeking to create healthier moral environments.

THE LEADER AND THE SMALL GROUP

Leaders spend a great deal of their time in small groups. That's because teams of people do much of the world's work. Groups build roads, craft legislation, enforce laws, raise money, coordinate course schedules, oversee software installations, and so on. See Box 9.1 for a description of the key elements of small groups. Consider, for example, that one fifth of the world's gross domestic project (GDP) or $12 trillion, is spent on temporary projects like advertising campaigns, product launches, and bridge construction.[2] A multitude of other groups oversee ongoing processes like manufacturing, bill processing, and Internet searches. Teams, not individuals, make most important organizational decisions. The higher the leader's organizational position, the more time she or he spends chairing

Box 9.1 Defining the Small Group

In popular usage, the term *group* can refer to everything from several individuals at a bus stop to residents living in the same apartment complex to a crowd at a political rally or concert. However, scholars have a much narrower definition in mind when they study small groups. Several elements set small groups apart:

A common purpose or goal. Several people waiting for a table at a restaurant don't constitute a small group. To be a group, individuals have something they want to accomplish together, such as completing a project for class, choosing a site for a new Walgreens drugstore, or deciding how to reduce homelessness in the city. Having a shared goal and working together leads to sense of belonging or shared identity. Consider, for example, how many groups (Habitat for Humanity volunteers, cancer survivors, dorm floors) display their loyalty by purchasing t-shirts with their team name and slogan.

Interdependence. The success of any individual member depends on everyone doing his or her part. (See the discussion of social loafing later in the chapter.) You may have discovered that, even when you carry through on our responsibilities, your grade goes down when others in your class group don't complete their parts of the project.

Mutual influence. In addition to depending on each other, group members influence each other by giving ideas, listening, agreeing or disagreeing, and so on.

Ongoing communication. In order for a group to exist, members must regularly interact, whether face-to-face or electronically through e-mail, online meetings, videoconferences, and telephone calls. For example, neighbors may live near each other, but they don't constitute a group until they routinely communicate with each other in order to reach a goal like fighting zoning changes.

Specific size. Groups range in size from 3 to 20 people. The addition of the third individual makes a group more complex than a dyad. Group members must manage many relationships, not one. They develop coalitions as well as rules or norms to regulate group behavior. When one member leaves a dyad, it dissolves. However, a group (if large enough) can continue if it loses a member or two. Twenty is typically considered the maximum size for a small group because beyond this number, members can no longer communicate face-to-face.

Small-group communication scholars John Cragan, Chris Kasch, and David Wright summarize the five definitional elements described above in their definition of a small group: "A few people engaged in communication interaction over time, usually in face-to-face and/or computer-mediated environments, who have common goals and norms and have developed a communication pattern for meeting their goals in an interdependent manner."[1]

NOTE

1. Cragan, J. F., Kasch, C. R., & Wright, D. W. (2009). *Communication in small groups: Theory, process, skills* (7th ed.). Boston, MA: Wadsworth.

Source: Adapted from Hackman, M. Z., & Johnson, C. E. (2013). *Leadership: A communication perspective.* Long Grove, IL: Waveland Press, Ch. 7.

or participating in meetings. Top-level executives spend a third of their time working in committees, task forces, and other small-group settings.[3] Leaders also find themselves in charge of groups outside of work, serving as chair of the local Young Men's Christian Association (YMCA) board, for instance, or running the volunteer campaign team for a mayoral candidate.

Chances are, you have discovered for yourself either how bright or how dark group experiences can be. Some of your proudest moments might have taken place in teams. For example, you may have had a life-changing experience working with others on a service project or formed deep friendships on a winning basketball team or done your best work in a group that brought a successful new product to market. At the same time, some of your most painful moments might have come in groups. Your leader may have ignored your input, angry team members may have refused to work together, and the group may have failed to carry its duties or made poor moral choices. Our task as leaders, then, is to help create groups that brighten—not darken—the lives of members and the lives of others they come into contact with. To do so, we must encourage members to take their ethical responsibilities seriously, promote ethical interaction, prevent the group from falling victim to moral pitfalls, and establish ethical relationships with other teams.

FOSTERING INDIVIDUAL ETHICAL ACCOUNTABILITY

A group's success or failure is highly dependent on the behaviors of its individual members. Destructive behavior by just one person can be enough to derail the group process. Every team member has an ethical responsibility to take her or his duties seriously. The job of the leader, then, is to foster ethical accountability, to encourage followers to live up to their moral responsibilities to the rest of the group.

A critical moral duty of group members is to pursue shared goals—to cooperate. Although this might seem like a basic requirement for joining a team, far too many people act selfishly or competitively when working with others. Those pursuing individual goals ignore the needs of teammates. For example, some athletes care more about their own individual statistics, such as points and goals, than about team victories. Competitive individuals seek to advance at the expense of others, such as when the ambitious salesperson hopes to beat out the rest of the sales group to earn the largest bonus. (For a tragic example of a failed attempt at cooperation, see Case Study 9.1.)

Cooperative groups are more productive than those with an individualistic or competitive focus. Cooperative groups[4]

- are more willing to take on difficult tasks and to persist in the face of difficulties;

- retain more information;

- engage in higher-level reasoning and more critical thinking;

- generate more creative ideas, tactics, and solutions;

- transfer more learning from the group to individual members;

- are more positive about the task; and

- spend more time working on tasks.

In addition to being more effective, cooperative groups foster more positive relationships and cohesion between members. This cohesion reduces absenteeism and turnover while producing higher commitment and satisfaction. Members of cooperative groups also enjoy better psychological health (i.e., emotional maturity, autonomy, self-confidence) and learn important social and communication skills.[5] (I'll have more to say about group communication skills later in the chapter.)

As a leader, you can focus attention on shared goals by (1) emphasizing the moral responsibility members have to cooperate with one another, (2) structuring the task so that no one person succeeds unless the group as a whole succeeds, (3) ensuring that all group members are fairly rewarded (don't reward one person for a group achievement, for instance), (4) providing feedback on how well the group and individuals are meeting performance standards, (5) encouraging individuals to help each other complete tasks, and (6) setting aside time for process sessions, where the group reflects on how well it is working together and how it might improve.[6]

Creating a cooperative climate is difficult when group members fail to do their fair share of the work. Social psychologists use the term *social loafing* to describe the fact that individuals often reduce their efforts when placed in groups.[7] Social loafing has been found in teams charged with all kinds of tasks, ranging from shouting and rope pulling to generating ideas, rating poems, writing songs, and evaluating job candidates. Gender, nationality, and age don't seem to have much impact on the rate of social loafing, although women and people from Eastern cultures are less likely to reduce their efforts. (Determine the impact of social loafing on your class project team by completing Self-Assessment 9.1.)

A number of explanations have been offered for social loafing. When people work in a group, they may feel that their efforts will have little impact on the final result. Responsibility for the collective product is shared or diffused throughout the team. It is difficult to identify and evaluate the input of individual participants. The collective effort model, developed by Steven Karau and Kipling Williams, is an attempt to integrate the various explanations for social loafing into one framework. Karau and Williams believe that "individuals will be willing to exert effort on a collective task only to the degree that they expect their efforts to be instrumental in obtaining outcomes that they value personally."[8] According to this definition, the motivation of group members depends on three factors: *expectancy*, or how much a person expects that her or his effort will lead to high group performance; *instrumentality*, the belief that one's personal contribution and the group's collective effort will bring about the desired result; and *valence*, how desirable the outcome is for individual group members.[9] Motivation drops if any of these factors are low. Consider the typical class project group, for example. Team members often slack off because they believe that the group will succeed in completing the project and getting a passing grade even if they do little (low expectancy). Participants may also be convinced that the group won't get an *A* no matter how hard they and others try (low instrumentality). Or some on the team may have other priorities and don't think that doing well on the project is all that important (low valence).

Social loafers take advantage of others in the group and violate norms for fairness or justice. Those being victimized are less likely to cooperate and may slack off for fear of being seen as "suckers." The advantages of being in a small group can be lost because members aren't giving their best effort. Leaders need to take steps to minimize social loafing. According to the collective effort model, they can do so by taking the following steps:

- Evaluating the inputs of individual members
- Keeping the size of work groups small (both face-to-face and virtual)
- Making sure that each person makes a unique and important contribution to the task
- Providing meaningful tasks that are intrinsically interesting and personally involving
- Emphasizing the collective group identity
- Offering performance incentives
- Fostering a sense of belonging

PROMOTING ETHICAL GROUP INTERACTION

Fostering individual accountability is an important first step toward improving a group's ethical performance. However, team members may want to cooperate and work hard but fail to work together effectively. Leaders, then, must also pay close attention to how group members interact during their deliberations. In particular, they need to encourage productive communication patterns that enable members to establish positive bonds and make wise ethical choices. Ethical communication skills and tactics include comprehensive, critical listening; supportive communication; emotional intelligence (EI); productive conflict management; and expression of minority opinion. These behaviors are particularly important in the small-group context, since teams accomplish much of their work through communication. But they are also essential to ethical leadership in the organizational, global, and crisis settings we'll discuss in upcoming chapters. By learning about these patterns in this chapter, you should be better prepared to lead in other contexts as well.

Comprehensive, Critical Listening

We spend much more time listening than speaking in small groups. If you belong to a team with ten members, you can expect to devote approximately 10% of your time to talking and 90% to listening to what others have to say. All listening involves receiving, paying attention to, interpreting, and then remembering messages. However, our motives for listening vary.[10] *Discriminative listening* processes the verbal and nonverbal components of a message. It serves as the foundation for the other forms of listening because we can't accurately process or interpret messages unless we first understand what is being said and how the message is being delivered. 911 operators demonstrate the importance of discriminative listening. They frequently ask anxious callers to repeat details so they can dispatch the right emergency responders to the correct location.

Comprehensive listening is motivated by the need to understand and retain messages. We engage in this type of listening when we attend lectures, receive job instructions, attend oral briefings, or watch the evening weather report. *Therapeutic* or *empathic listening* is aimed at helping the speaker resolve an issue by encouraging him or her to talk about the problem. Those in helping professions such as social work and psychiatry routinely engage in this listening process. All of us act as empathetic listeners, however, when friends and family come to us for help. *Critical listening* leads to evaluation. Critical listeners pay careful attention to message content, logic, language, and other elements of persuasive attempts so that they can identify strengths and weaknesses and render a judgment. *Appreciative listening* is prompted by the desire for relaxation and entertainment. We act as appreciative listeners when we enjoy a song download from iTunes, a live concert, or a play.

Group members engage in all five types of listening during meetings, but comprehensive and critical listening are essential when groups engage in ethical problem solving. Coming up with a high-quality decision is nearly impossible unless group members first understand and remember what others have said. Participants also have to analyze the arguments of other group members critically in order to identify errors, as we saw in our discussion of argumentation in Chapter 7.

There are several barriers to comprehensive, critical listening in the group context. In one-to-one conversations, we know that we must respond to the speaker, so we tend to pay closer attention. In a group, we don't have to carry as much of the conversational load, so we're tempted to lose focus or to talk to the person sitting next to us. The content of the discussion can also make listening difficult. Ethical issues can generate strong emotional reactions because they involve deeply held values and beliefs. The natural tendency is to reject the speaker ("What does he know?" "He's got it all wrong!") and become absorbed in our counterarguments instead of concentrating on the message.[11] Reaching an agreement then becomes more difficult because we don't understand the other person's position but are more committed than ever to our point of view. (The group members described in "Leadership Ethics at the Movies: *Of Gods and Men*" provide one example of effective listening in a highly emotionally charged situation.)

Listening experts Larry Barker, Patrice Johnson, and Kittie Watson make the following suggestions for improving listening performance in a group setting. Our responsibility as leaders is to model these behaviors and encourage other participants to follow our example.[12]

- *Avoid interruptions.* Give the speaker a chance to finish before you respond or ask questions. The speaker may address your concerns before he or she finishes, and you can't properly evaluate a message until you've first understood it.

- *Seek areas of agreement.* Take a positive approach by searching for common ground. What do you and the speaker have in common? Commitment to solving the problem? Similar values and background?

- *Search for meanings and avoid arguing about specific words.* Discussions of terms can keep the group from addressing the real issue. Stay focused on what speakers mean; don't be distracted if they use different terms than you do.

- *Ask questions and request clarification.* When you don't understand, don't be afraid to ask for clarification. Chances are others in the group are also confused and will appreciate more information. However, asking too many questions can give the impression that you're trying to control the speaker.

- *Be patient.* We can process information faster than speakers can deliver it. Use the extra time to reflect on the message instead of focusing on your own reactions or daydreaming.

- *Compensate for attitudinal biases.* All of us have biases based on such factors as personal appearance, age differences, and irritating mannerisms. Among my pet peeves? Men with Elvis hairdos, grown women with little-girl voices, and nearly anyone who clutters his or her speech with "ums" and "uhs." I have to suppress my urge to dismiss these kinds of speakers and concentrate on listening carefully. (Sadly, I don't always succeed.)

- *Listen for principles, concepts, and feelings.* Try to understand how individual facts fit into the bigger picture. Don't overlook nonverbal cues, such as tone of voice and posture, that reveal emotions and, at times, can contradict verbal statements. If a speaker's words and nonverbal behaviors don't seem to match (as in an expression of support uttered with a sigh of resignation), probe further to make sure you clearly understand the person's position.

- *Compensate for emotion-arousing words and ideas.* Certain words and concepts, such as *fundamentalist, socialist, terrorist,* and *fascist,* spark strong emotional responses. We need to overcome our knee-jerk reactions to these labels and strive instead to remain objective.

- *Be flexible.* Acknowledge that others' views may have merit, even though you may not completely agree with them.

- *Listen, even if the message is boring or tough to follow.* Not all messages are exciting and simple to digest, but we need to try to understand them anyway. A boring comment made early in a group discussion may later turn out to be critical to the team's success.

Defensive versus Supportive Communication

Defensiveness is a major threat to accurate listening. When group members feel threatened, they divert their attention from the task to defending themselves. As their anxiety levels increase, they think less about how to solve the problem and more about how they are coming across to others, about winning, and about protecting themselves. Listening suffers because participants distort the messages they receive, misinterpreting the motives, values, and emotions of senders. On the other hand, supportive messages increase accuracy because group members devote more energy to interpreting the content and emotional states of sources. Psychologist Jack Gibb identified six pairs of behaviors, described below, that promote either a defensive or a supportive group atmosphere.[13] Our job as group leader is to engage in supportive communication, which contributes to a positive emotional climate and accurate understanding. At the same time, we need to challenge comments that spark defensive reactions.

Evaluation versus Description. Evaluative messages are judgmental. They can be sent through statements ("What a lousy idea!") or through such nonverbal cues as a sarcastic tone of voice or a raised eyebrow. Those being evaluated are likely to respond by placing blame and making judgments of their own ("Your proposal is no better than mine"). Supportive messages ("I think I see where you're coming from," attentive posture, eye contact) create a more positive environment.

Control versus Problem Orientation. Controlling messages imply that the recipient is inadequate (i.e., uninformed, immature, stubborn, overly emotional) and needs to change. Control, like evaluation, can be communicated both verbally (issuing orders, threats) and nonverbally (stares, threatening body posture). Problem-centered messages reflect a willingness to collaborate, to work together to resolve the issue. Examples of problem-oriented statements include "What do you think we ought to do?" and "I believe we can work this out if we sit down and identify the issues."

Strategy versus Spontaneity. Strategic communicators are seen as manipulators who try to hide their true motivations. They say they want to work with others yet withhold information and appear to be listening when they're not. This false spontaneity angers the rest of the group. On the other hand, behavior that is truly spontaneous and honest reduces defensiveness.

Neutrality versus Empathy. Neutral messages such as "You'll get over it" and "Don't take it so seriously" imply that the listener doesn't care. Empathetic statements, such as "I can see why you would be depressed" and "I'll be thinking about you when you have that appointment with your boss," communicate reassurance and acceptance. Those who receive them enjoy a boost in self-esteem.

Superiority versus Equality. Attempts at one-upmanship generally provoke immediate defensive responses. The comment "I got an *A* in my ethics class" is likely to be met with this kind of reply: "Well, you may have a lot of book learning, but I had to deal with a lot of real-world ethical problems when I worked at the advertising agency." Superiority can be based on a number of factors, including wealth, social class, organizational position, and power. All groups contain members who differ in their social standing and abilities. However, these differences are less disruptive if participants indicate that they want to work with others on an equal basis.

Certainty versus Provisionalism. Dogmatic group members—those who are inflexible and claim to have all the answers—are unwilling to change or consider other points of view. As a consequence, they appear more interested in being right than in solving the problem. Listeners often perceive certainty as a mask for feelings of inferiority. In contrast to dogmatic individuals, provisional discussants signal that they are willing to work with the rest of the team in order to investigate issues and come up with a sound ethical decision.

Emotional Intelligence

Recognizing and managing emotions is essential to maintaining productive, healthy relationships in a group. Consider the negative impact of envy, for instance. Envy arises when people compare themselves to others and fall short. They then experience resentment, hostility, frustration, inferiority, longing, and ill will toward the envied individuals. Envy is common in organizations, which distribute assignments, raises, office space, and other resources unequally among members. However, this feeling may be even more frequent in teams because members know each other well and have more opportunity to engage in comparisons. Those who envy others in the group tend to reduce their efforts (see the earlier discussion of social loafing), are more likely to miss meetings, and are less satisfied with their group experience. The team as a whole is less cohesive and less successful.[14]

Experts assert that groups, like individuals, can learn how to cope with envy and other destructive feelings, as well as foster positive moods, through developing emotional intelligence (EI). They also report that emotionally intelligent groups are more effective and productive.[15] EI consists of (1) awareness and management of personal emotions and (2) recognizing and exerting influence on the emotions of others. Teams with high EI effectively address three levels of emotions: individual, within the team, and between the team and outside groups.[16] At the individual level, they recognize when a member is distracted or defensive. They point out when someone's behavior (e.g., moodiness, tardiness) is disrupting the group and provide extra support for those who need it. At the group level, high-EI teams engage in continual self-evaluation to determine their emotional states. Members speak out when the team is discouraged, for instance, and build an affirmative climate. They develop resources like a common vocabulary and rituals to deal with unhealthy moods. For example, one executive team set 10 minutes aside for a "wailing wall." During these 10 minutes, members could vent their frustrations. They were then ready to tackle the problems they faced.

Raising team EI is an important leadership responsibility, which is accomplished largely through role modeling and establishing norms. As leaders, we must demonstrate our personal EI before we can hope to improve the emotional climate of the group. Effective leaders display emotions that are appropriate to the situation, refrain from hostility, are sensitive to group moods, and take the lead in confronting emotional issues. Confrontation can mean reminding a group member not to criticize new ideas; phoning a member between meetings to talk about his or her rude, dismissive behavior; removing insensitive individuals from the team; calling on quiet members to hear their opinions; or bringing the group together to discuss members' feelings of frustration or discouragement. Modeling such behaviors is critical to establishing healthy emotional norms or habits in the team, like speaking up when the group is discouraged or unproductive and celebrating collective victories. One list of group emotional norms can be found in Box 9.2.

Productive Conflict

In healthy groups, members examine and discuss ideas (solutions, procedures, proposals) in a task-related process that experts call *substantive (constructive) conflict.*[17] Substantive conflicts produce a number of positive outcomes, including these:

- Accurate understanding of the arguments and positions of others in the group
- Higher-level moral reasoning
- Thorough problem analysis
- Improved self-understanding and self-improvement
- Stronger, deeper relationships
- Creativity and change
- Greater motivation to solve the problem
- Improved mastery and retention of information
- Deeper commitment to the outcome of the discussion
- Increased group cohesion and cooperation
- Improved ability to deal with future conflicts
- High-quality solutions that integrate the perspectives of all members

It is important to differentiate between *substantive conflict* and *affective (destructive) conflict*, which is centered on the personal relationships between group members. Those caught in personality-based conflicts find themselves either trying to avoid the problem

Box 9.2 Group Emotional Norms

NORMS THAT CREATE AWARENESS OF EMOTIONS

Interpersonal Understanding

1. Take time away from group tasks to get to know one another.

2. Have a check-in at the beginning of the meeting—that is, ask how everyone is doing.

3. Assume that undesirable behavior takes place for a reason. Find out what that reason is. Ask questions and listen. Avoid negative attributions.

4. Tell your teammates what you're thinking and how you're feeling.

Team Self-Evaluation

1. Schedule time to examine team effectiveness.

2. Create measurable task and process objectives and then measure them.

3. Acknowledge and discuss group moods.

4. Communicate your sense of what is transpiring in the team.

5. Allow members to call a "process check." (For instance, a team member might say, "Process check: Is this the most effective use of our time right now?")

Organizational Understanding

1. Find out the concerns and needs of others in the organization.

2. Consider who can influence the team's ability to accomplish its goals.

3. Discuss the culture and politics in the organization.

4. Ask whether proposed team actions are congruent with the organization's culture and politics.

NORMS THAT HELP REGULATE EMOTIONS

Confronting

1. Set ground rules and use them to point out errant behavior.

2. Call members out on errant behavior.

3. Create playful devices for pointing out such behavior. These often emerge from the group spontaneously. Reinforce them.

Caring

1. Support members: Volunteer to help them if they need it, be flexible, and provide emotional support.

2. Validate members' contributions. Let members know they are valued.

3. Protect members from attack.

4. Respect individuality and differences in perspectives. Listen.

5. Never be derogatory or demeaning.

Creating Resources for Working with Emotions

1. Make time to discuss difficult issues and address the emotions that surround them.

2. Find creative, shorthand ways to acknowledge and express the emotion in the group.

3. Create fun ways to acknowledge and relieve stress and tension.

4. Express acceptance of members' emotions.

Creating an Affirmative Environment

1. Reinforce that the team can meet a challenge. For example, say things like "We can get through this" or "Nothing will stop us."

2. Focus on what you can control.

3. Remind members of the group's important and positive mission.

4. Remind members how the group solved a similar problem before.

5. Focus on problem solving, not blaming.

Building External Relationships

1. Create opportunities for networking and interaction.

2. Ask about the needs of other teams.

3. Provide support for other teams.

4. Invite others to team meetings if they might have a stake in what you are doing.

Source: Adapted from Durskat, V. U., & Wolff, S. B. (2001, March). Building the emotional intelligence of groups. *Harvard Business Review,* 80–90. Used with permission of the publisher.

or, when the conflict can't be ignored, escalating hostilities through name-calling, sarcasm, threats, and verbally aggressive behaviors. (Complete Self-Assessment 9.2 to determine whether your group engages in substantive or affective conflict.) In this poisoned environment, members aren't as committed to the group process, sacrifice in-depth discussion of the problem in order to get done as soon as possible, and distance themselves from the decision. The end result? A decline in reasoning that produces an unpopular, low-quality, and often unethical solution.

Sometimes constructive conflict degenerates into affective conflict.[18] This occurs when disagreement about ideas is seen as an insult or a threat and members display anger because they feel their self-concepts are threatened. Others respond in kind. Members can also become frustrated when task-oriented conflicts seem to drag on and on without resolution. (Turn to Case Study 9.2 for an example of an example of a group caught in an extended conflict.) There are a number of ways that you as a leader can encourage substantive conflict while preventing it from being corrupted into affective conflict. Begin by paying attention to the membership of the group. Form teams made up of people with significantly different backgrounds. Groups concerned with medical ethics, for example, generally include members from both inside the medical profession (nurses, surgeons, hospital administrators) and outside (theologians, ethicists, government officials).

Next, lay down some procedural ground rules—a conflict covenant—before discussion begins. Come up with a list of conflict guideposts as a group: "Absolutely no name-calling or threats." "No idea is a dumb idea." "Direct all critical comments toward the problem, not the person." "You must repeat the message of the previous speaker—to that person's satisfaction—before you can add your comments." Setting such guidelines in particularly in important in virtual teams (see Box 9.3). Highlight the fact that conflict about ideas is an integral part of group discussion and caution against hasty decisions. Encourage individuals to stand firm instead of capitulating. This is also a good time to remind members of the importance of cooperation and emotional intelligence. Groups that emphasize shared goals view conflict as a mutual problem that needs everyone's attention. As a result, team members feel more confident dealing with conflict, and collective performance improves.[19] Teams that demonstrate high levels of EI are also more equipped to manage conflict and therefore perform better. In particular, if members can collectively control their emotions, they listen more closely to opposing ideas and seek the best solution without being upset when their proposals are rejected.[20]

During the discussion, make sure that members follow their conflict covenant and don't engage in conflict avoidance or escalation. Stop to revisit the ground rules when necessary. Use the argumentative competence skills introduced in Chapter 7. Be prepared to support your position. Challenge and analyze the arguments of others as you encourage them to do the same. If members get stuck in a battle of wills, reframe the discussion by asking such questions as "What kind of information would help you change your mind?" "Why shouldn't we pursue other options?" or "What would you do if you were in my position?"[21] You can also ask participants to develop new ways to describe their ideas (in graphs, as numbers, as bulleted lists) and ask them to step back and revisit their initial assumptions in order to find common ground.

After the decision is made, ensure that the team and its members will continue to develop their conflict management skills. Debrief the decision-making process to determine whether the group achieved its goals, work on repairing relationships that might have been bruised during the discussion, and celebrate or remember stories of outstanding conflict management.[22]

Minority Opinion

As we'll see in the next section of the chapter, hearing from members who take issue with the prevailing group opinion is essential if the team is to avoid moral failure. Further, minority dissent can significantly improve group performance.[23] A team with minority members generally comes up with a superior solution, even if the group doesn't change its collective mind. If there is no minority opinion, members focus on one solution. They have little reason to explore the problem in depth, so they disregard novel solutions and quickly converge on one position. Minorities cast doubt on group consensus, stimulating more thought about the dilemma. Members exert more effort because they must resolve the conflict between the majority and minority solutions. They pay closer attention to all aspects of the issue, consider more viewpoints, are more willing to share information, and employ a wider variety of problem-solving strategies. Such divergent thinking produces more creative, higher-quality solutions. When minority dissent is present across a range of groups, the organization as a whole is more innovative. Minorities also block groups from making harmful changes or adopting extreme positions. Responding to the dissenting views of minorities encourages team members to resist conformity in other settings.[24]

Minorities can have an immediate, powerful impact on group opinion under certain conditions. Minorities are most likely to influence the rest of the group when the members are still formulating their positions on an issue, when dissenters can clearly demonstrate the superiority of their stance, and when minorities can frame their positions to fit into the values and beliefs of the group. Well-respected dissenters who consistently advocate for their positions are generally more persuasive. However, more often than not, minority influence is slow and indirect.[25] Majorities initially reject the dissenters' ideas but, over time, forget the source of the arguments and focus instead on the merits of their proposals. This can gradually convert them to the minority viewpoint. At other times, minorities aren't successful at convincing members to go along with them on one issue but shape their opinions on related issues. For example, in one experiment, a minority

Box 9.3 The Ethical Challenges of Virtual Teams

Odds are good that you will find yourself working in a virtual team sometime during your career. Virtual teams are made up of members who work in different geographic locations who coordinate their efforts through electronic communication channels (e-mail, videoconferencing, project management software, groupware). Approximately two thirds of multinational organizations rely on virtual teams to oversee such functions as product development, manufacturing, technical support, customer service, and other functions. Dispersed working groups are becoming more popular as companies expand their international operations and electronic communication tools continue to improve.

Virtual teams pose some special ethical challenges for leaders. Fostering collaboration is harder in dispersed groups. Physical distance often discourages members from committing themselves to the team. They don't have the opportunity to engage in the informal interaction (about children, hobbies, the weather, etc.) that builds trust in face-to-face groups. When they feel less personal connection to other team members, they generate fewer ideas. Anonymity tempts virtual team members to loaf since they can more easily hide their activities (or lack of activity) from other team members.

Conflict appears to be more common in virtual teams. There is a higher likelihood of miscommunication because electronic communication is not as rich as face-to-face interaction. Members lack nonverbal cues to tell, for example, if a speaker is joking or serious. The asynchronous nature of virtual team communication generates problems as well. Members send and receive messages at different times, not simultaneously, as they do when communicating in person. They can get frustrated with delays in return messages and are likely to make negative attributions when others fail to respond in a timely fashion. Participants forget that receivers might not have received the original message or that colleagues in other time zones may be off work. Too much e-mail communication can lead to information overload. Cultural differences can generate significant conflicts in groups made up of members from a variety of countries. For instance, group members from collectivist societies may complain that their North American colleagues aren't cooperative enough or take issue with peer appraisal systems common in individualist cultures. Not only are conflicts more common in virtual teams, physical separation and communication limitations make them harder to resolve.

Group experts make a number of suggestions for addressing the ethical challenges of virtual teams, including the following:

To foster trust and collaboration:

- Start with a face-to-face kickoff meeting.
- Set up channels (such as an electronic bulletin board or a Facebook site) for informal communication.
- Encourage members to share personal information and pictures with other group members.
- Set clear objectives for the group's work.
- Set a standard for responding to e-mail messages, such as within twenty-four hours.
- Remind members that they build trust with other members through successful completion of their tasks and assignments.
- Recognize individual contributions.
- Communicate frequently.

(Continued)

To discourage social loafing:

- Keep the group as small as possible.
- Set clear timelines and hold members to them.
- Regularly monitor the input of individual members.
- Emphasize the importance of each person doing her or his part.

To prevent and manage conflict:

- Use the richest channels whenever possible (videoconferencing instead of e-mail, for instance).
- Outlaw "flaming" and other inappropriate messages.
- Encourage members to recognize the constraints faced by other group members and to be more tolerant when using virtual tools.
- Seek to learn from errors and problems, not to blame.

- Establish a clear procedure for managing conflicts.
- Intervene to mediate conflicts between members.
- Highlight the importance of cultural awareness and tolerance.

Sources: Alnuaimi O. A., Robert Jr., L. P., & Maruping, L. M. (2010). Team size, dispersion, and social loafing in technology-supported teams: A perspective on the theory of moral disengagement. *Journal of Management Information Systems, 27,* 303–230; Chidambaram, L., & Tung, L. L. (2005). Is out of sight, out of mind? An empirical study of social loafing in technology-supported groups. *Information Systems Research, 16,* 149–168; Franz, T. M. (2012). *Group dynamics and team interventions: Understanding and improving team performance.* Hoboken, NJ: Blackwell; Minton-Eversol, T. (2012, July 19). Virtual teams used most by global organizations, survey says. *Society for Human Resource Management*; Rockman, K. W., & Northcraft, G. B. (2006). The ethical implications of virtual interaction. In A. E. Tenbrunsel (Ed.), *Ethics in groups* (pp. 101–123). Oxford, England: Elsevier; Schuman, S. (2010). *The handbook for working with difficult groups: How they are difficult, why they are difficult and what you can do about it.* Chichester, England: Wiley; West, M. A. (2012). *Effective teamwork: Practical lessons from organizational research.* Hoboken, NJ: Wiley.

advocating a position on homosexuals in the military did not change opinions on that topic but did influence attitudes toward gun control, a related subject.[26]

Being in the minority is tough because it runs contrary to our strong desire to be liked and accepted by others. Those who take a minority position are frequently the targets of dislike or disdain. Leaders, then, need to both foster minority opinion and protect dissenters. You can do so by taking these steps:[27]

1. Form groups made up of members who have significantly different backgrounds and perspectives.

2. Encourage participation from all group members.

3. Appoint individuals to argue for an alternative point of view.

4. Develop two options for group members to evaluate based on two different sets of assumptions.

5. Remind members of the importance of minority views.

6. Create a group learning orientation that is more focused on find-
    ing better solutions than on defending one position or another.

7. Offer dissenters your support.

AVOIDING MORAL PITFALLS

Even with positive interaction, moral traps or pitfalls can derail the decision-making process during the course of the group's discussion. As team members communicate, leaders need to help the group steer clear of the following dangers: groupthink, misman-aged or false agreement, and escalating commitment.

Groupthink

Social psychologist Irving Janis believed that cohesion is the greatest obstacle faced by groups charged with making effective, ethical decisions. He developed the label *group-think* to describe groups that put unanimous agreement ahead of reasoned problem solv-ing. Groups suffering from this symptom are both ineffective and unethical.[28] They fail to (a) consider all the alternatives, (b) gather additional information, (c) reexamine a course of action when it's not working, (d) carefully weigh risks, (e) work out contingency plans, or (f) discuss important moral issues. Janis first noted faulty thinking in small groups of ordinary citizens—such as an antismoking support group that decided that quitting was impossible. He captured the attention of fellow scholars and the public through his analysis of major U.S. policy disasters such as the failure to anticipate the attack on Pearl Harbor, the invasion of North Korea, the Bay of Pigs fiasco, and the escalation of the Vietnam War. In each of these incidents, some of the brightest (and presumably most ethically minded) political and military leaders in our nation's history made terrible choices. (Turn to Case Study 9.3 for a recent example of groupthink in action.)

Janis identified the following as symptoms of groupthink. The greater the number of these characteristics displayed by a group, the greater the likelihood that members have made cohesiveness their top priority.

Signs of Overconfidence

- *Illusion of invulnerability.* Members are overly optimistic and prone to take extraordinary risks.

- *Belief in the inherent morality of the group.* Participants ignore the ethical consequences of their actions and decisions.

Signs of Closed-Mindedness

- *Collective rationalization.* Group members invent rationalizations to protect themselves from any feedback that would challenge their operating assumptions.

- *Stereotypes of outside groups.* Group members underestimate the capabilities of other groups (armies, citizens, teams), thinking that people in these groups are weak or stupid.

Signs of Group Pressure

- *Pressure on dissenters.* Dissenters are coerced to go along with the prevailing opinion in the group.
- *Self-censorship.* Individuals keep their doubts about group decisions to themselves.
- *Illusion of unanimity.* Because members keep quiet, the group mistakenly assumes that everyone agrees on a course of action.
- *Self-appointed mind guards.* Certain members take it on themselves to protect the leader and others from dissenting opinions that might disrupt the group's consensus.

The risk of groupthink increases when teams made up of members from similar backgrounds are isolated from contact with other groups. The risks increase still further when group members are under stress (due to recent failure, for instance) and follow a leader who pushes one particular solution. Self-directed work teams (SDWTs), described in more detail in "Focus on Follower Ethics: Self-Leadership in Self-Managed Teams," are particularly vulnerable to groupthink. Members, working under strict time limits, are often isolated and undertrained. They may fail at first, and the need to function as a cohesive unit may blind them to ethical dilemmas.[29]

Irving Janis made several suggestions for reducing groupthink. If you're appointed as the group's leader, avoid expressing a preference for a particular solution. Divide regularly into subgroups and then bring the entire group back together to negotiate differences. Bring in outsiders—experts or colleagues—to challenge the group's ideas. Avoid isolation, keeping in contact with other groups. Role-play the reactions of other groups and organizations to reduce the effects of stereotyping and rationalization. Once the decision has been made, give group members one last chance to express any remaining doubts about the decision. Janis points to the ancient Persians as an example of how to revisit decisions. The Persians made every major decision twice—once while sober and again while under the influence of wine!

A number of investigators have explored the causes and prevention of groupthink.[30] They have discovered that a group is in greatest danger when the leader actively promotes his or her agenda and when it doesn't have any procedures in place (like those described in Chapter 6) for solving problems. With this in mind, solicit ideas from group members. Make sure that the group adopts a decision-making format before discussing an ethical problem.

There are two structured approaches specifically designed to build disagreement or conflict into the decision-making process to reduce the likelihood of groupthink.[31] In the devil's advocate technique, an individual or a subgroup is assigned to criticize the group's decision. The individual's or subgroup's goal is to highlight potential problems with the group's assumptions, logic, evidence, and recommendations. Following the critique, the team gathers additional information and adopts, modifies, or discontinues the proposed course of action. In the dialectic inquiry method, a subgroup or the team as a whole develops a solution. After the group identifies the underlying assumptions of the proposal, selected group members develop a counterproposal based on a different set of assumptions. Advocates of each position present and debate the merits of their

Focus on Follower Ethics

SELF-LEADERSHIP IN SELF-MANAGED TEAMS

An estimated 90% of all U.S. firms employ self-directed work teams (SDWTs) or another form of self-managed groups.[1] An SDWT is made up of 6 to 10 employees from a variety of departments who manage themselves and their tasks. SDWTs operate much like small businesses within the larger organization, overseeing the development of a service or product from start to finish. SDWTs have been credited with improving everything from workplace attendance and morale to productivity and product quality. In SDWTs, individual members have more responsibilities than they do in traditional groups where leaders make the decisions. Those in SDWTs are involved in additional tasks (e.g., staffing, evaluation, scheduling), and they have to develop new knowledge and skills to carry out these duties. Further, the ultimate success of the team now rests with followers, not leaders. In self-directed groups, it is more important than ever that followers meet their ethical obligation to complete their work.

Business experts Christopher Neck and Charles Manz believe that self-leadership is key to living up to our duties as followers. Self-leadership is the process of exercising influence over our thoughts, attitudes, and behaviors and is essential not just to our individual success as followers but to team success as well. According to Neck and Manz,

> Self-leadership is just as important when you are working in a team as when you are working alone. . . . In fact, only by effectively leading yourself as a team member can you help the team lead itself, reach its potential, and thus achieve synergy. (p. 82)

There are three key components to self-leadership. First, we need to lead ourselves to do unattractive but necessary tasks. Altering our immediate worlds and exercising direct control over the self can accomplish this objective. World-altering strategies include (1) using physical reminders and cues (notes, lists, objects) to focus our attention on important tasks; (2) removing negative cues, such as those that are distracting; (3) identifying and increasing positive cues (pleasant settings, music) that encourage us to undertake the work; and (4) associating with other people who reinforce our desirable behavior. Self-control strategies include observing, recording, and analyzing our use of desirable and undesirable behaviors; setting short- and long-term goals; determining our ultimate purpose; rewarding our achievements; and engaging in physical and mental practice to improve performance.

The second component of self-leadership is taking advantage of naturally rewarding activities. Some activities make us feel competent and in control and supply us with a sense of purpose. We don't need external motivation to get us to read a novel, for example, or to play a game of pickup basketball, knit, or paint, if we find these hobbies enjoyable. When we build natural rewards into our endeavors, we are more likely to complete them. For instance, if we enjoy interacting with others, we can make sure that we leave time for informal talk during team meetings. We can also focus on the naturally rewarding aspects of our tasks instead of on the unpleasant aspects. Writing our part of a group paper for class, often perceived as a difficult chore, can be viewed instead as an opportunity to

(Continued)

learn about a new subject and develop knowledge for a future career. In stressful situations, we can engage in emotional self-regulation through exercise, meditation, relaxing music, and other means.

The third component of self-leadership is shaping our psychological worlds or thought self-leadership. Thought self-leadership strategies include visualizing a successful performance (mental imagery); eliminating critical and destructive self-talk, such as "I can't do it"; and challenging unrealistic assumptions. For example, the mental statement "I must succeed at everything, or I'm a failure" is irrational because it sets an impossibly high standard. This destructive thought can be restated as "I can't succeed at everything, but I'm going to try to give my best effort, no matter the task."

Note

1. Appelbaum, S. H., Bethune, M., & Tanenbaum, R. (1999). Downsizing and the emergence of self-managed teams. *Participation and Empowerment: An International Journal, 7,* 109–130.

Source: Neck, C. P., & Manz, C. C. (2012). *Mastering self-leadership: Empowering yourself for personal excellence* (6th ed.). Upper Saddle River, NJ: Prentice Hall.

proposals. The team or outside decision makers determine whether to adopt one position or the other, integrate the plans, or opt for a different solution altogether. Both approaches can take more than one round to complete. For example, a team may decide to submit a second plan for critique or present several counterproposals before reaching a conclusion.

Charles Manz and his colleagues believe that self-managing work teams should replace groupthink with "teamthink."[32] In teamthink, groups encourage divergent views, combining the open expression of concerns and doubts with a healthy respect for their limitations. The teamthink process is an extension of *thought self-leadership*, described above. Like individuals, groups can improve their performance (lead themselves) by adopting constructive thought patterns: visualizing successful performances, eliminating critical and destructive self-talk, and challenging unrealistic assumptions.

Teamthink, like thought self-leadership, is a combination of mental imagery, self-dialogue, and realistic thinking. Members of successful groups use mental imagery to visualize how they will complete a project and jointly establish a common vision ("to provide better job training for the long-term unemployed," "to develop the best new software package for the company"). When talking with each other (self-dialogue), leaders and followers are particularly careful not to put pressure on deviant members; at the same time, they encourage divergent views.

Teamthink members challenge three forms of faulty reasoning that are common to small groups. The first is all-or-nothing thinking. If a risk doesn't seem threatening, too many groups dismiss it and proceed without a backup plan. In contrast, teamthink groups realistically assess the dangers and anticipate possible setbacks. The second common form of faulty group thinking, described earlier, is the assumption that the team is inherently moral. Groups in the grip of this misconception think that anything they do (including lying and sabotaging the work of other groups) is justified. Ethically insensitive, they don't stop to consider the moral implications of their decisions. Teamthink groups avoid this trap, questioning their motivations and raising ethical issues. The third faulty group assumption is the conviction that the task is too difficult, that the obstacles are too great to overcome. Effective, ethical groups instead view obstacles as opportunities and focus their efforts on reaching and implementing decisions.

False Agreement

George Washington University management professor Jerry Harvey offers an alternative to groupthink based on *false agreement*.[33] Harvey believes that blaming group pressure is just an excuse for our individual shortcomings. He calls this the *Gunsmoke myth*. In this myth, the lone Western sheriff (Matt Dillon in the radio and television series) stands down a mob of armed townsfolk out to lynch his prisoner. If group tyranny is really at work, Harvey argues, Dillon stands no chance. After all, he is outnumbered 100 to 1 and could be felled with a single bullet from one rioter. The mob disbands because its members really didn't want to lynch the prisoner in the first place. Harvey contends that falling prey to the *Gunsmoke* myth is immoral because as long as we can blame our peers, we don't have to accept personal responsibility as group members. In reality, we always have a choice as to how to respond.

Professor Harvey introduces the Abilene paradox as an alternative to the *Gunsmoke* myth. He describes a time when his family decided to drive (without air conditioning) 100 miles across the desert from their home in Coleman, Texas, to Abilene to eat dinner. After returning home, family members discovered that no one had really wanted to make the trip. Each agreed to go to Abilene based on the assumption that everyone else in the group was enthusiastic about eating out. Harvey believes that organizations and small groups, like his family, also take needless "trips." An example of the Abilene paradox would be teams who carry out illegal activities that everyone in the group is uneasy about. Five psychological factors account for the paradox:

1. *Action anxiety.* Group members know what should be done but are too anxious to speak up.

2. *Negative fantasies.* Action anxiety is driven in part by the negative fantasies members have about what will happen if they voice their opinions. These fantasies ("I'll be fired or branded as disloyal") serve as an excuse for not attacking the problem.

3. *Real risk.* There are risks to expressing dissent: getting fired, losing income, damaging relationships. However, most of the time, the danger is not as great as we think.

4. *Fear of separation.* Alienation and loneliness constitute the most powerful force behind the paradox. Group members fear being cut off or separated from others. To escape this fate, they cheat, lie, break the law, and so forth.

5. *Psychological reversal of risk and certainty.* Being trapped in the Abilene paradox means confusing fantasy with real risk. This confusion produces a self-fulfilling prophecy. Caught up in the fantasy that something bad may happen, decision makers act in a way that fulfills the fantasy. For instance, group members may support a project with no chances of success because they are afraid they will be fired or demoted if they don't. Ironically, they are likely to be fired or demoted anyway when the flawed project fails.

Breaking out of the paradox begins with diagnosing its symptoms in your group or organization. If the group is headed in the wrong direction, call a meeting where you own up to your true feelings and invite feedback and encourage others to do the same. (Of course, you must confront your fear of being separated from the rest of the group to take this step.) The team may immediately come up with a better approach or engage in extended conflict that generates a more creative solution. You might suffer for your honesty, but you could be rewarded for saying what everyone else was thinking. In any case, you'll feel better about yourself for speaking up.

Escalation of Commitment

One of the consequences of mismanaged agreement is continuing to pursue a failed course of action. Social psychologists refer to this tendency as *escalation of commitment.* Instead of cutting their losses, individuals and groups continue to "throw good money after bad," pouring in more resources. Costs multiply until the moment that the team admits defeat or an outside agency intervenes.[34] Escalation of commitment is a moral trap because it wastes time, money, and effort; threatens the health of the group and the organization; fails to meet important needs; and can even result in significant loss of life. Escalating commitment helps explain why state agencies continue to implement defective software programs, promoters put more money into advertising unpopular music acts, and investors buy additional shares of declining stocks. History is replete with well-publicized examples of this phenomenon, including the automated baggage system at the Denver International Airport (which delayed the opening of the facility and never worked) and the Taurus automated London Stock Exchange system that had to be scrapped. Escalation played a key role in the K2 incident described in Case Study 9.1. Climbers continued to summit even when they should have turned back because they were so close to reaching the top. Many also had corporate sponsors and felt additional pressure to succeed.

Escalation of commitment is driven by a number of factors.[35] The first is *self-enhancement,* or the need to look good. Decision makers are compelled to justify their prior investments, so they reinvest in the original project in order to demonstrate that their initial choice was correct. They deny negative feedback and concentrate on defending past choices instead of focusing on future outcomes as they ought to. Group members find it hard to admit failure publicly because doing so threatens their identity or suggests that they are incompetent. Occasionally, groups escalate in order to show off, as in the case of a company that buys another firm just to demonstrate that it is an important player in the industry.

Sunk costs also drive escalation. It's hard emotionally for group members to give up on previous investments even though such costs cannot influence future outcomes. Imagine, for example, you have two frozen dinners in your freezer, both of which have reached their "use by" date. The dinners are the same except for their price tags. If one cost $3 and the other $5, you will likely choose the more expensive meal for dinner because it seems less wasteful. However, it should make no difference which meal you choose since the dinners are already purchased and your money is spent. Sunk costs help explain why those near the end of a project are more likely to spend additional funds to finish it. In addition, sunk costs can encourage teams to become overly optimistic. The presence of the previous investment tempts decision makers to inflate their estimates of future success. Then, too, decision makers often labor under the illusion of control. They believe that they can control events—business trends, employee behavior, the weather—that are outside their influence.[36]

Risk seeking is a third factor driving escalation. When faced with decisions between two losses, individuals tend to take bigger risks than warranted. They stay the course because they believe that continuing in business or putting more money into the software project will enable them to recoup their losses. They are like the gambler who goes to the horse track and loses $95 of the $100 he intended to bet. When the last race of the day is run, he bets on a long shot, hoping to win back his entire $95. He would be much better off making a safer bet and winning back some of his losses instead. Group interaction can magnify the tendency to take risks because responsibility for the choice is dispersed among group members.

Management professors Mark Keil and Ramiro Montealegre offer insights to leaders who want to help their teams de-escalate from a failed course of action. De-escalation begins with recognizing that there is a problem, followed by reexamining the prior course of action, then searching for alternative courses of action, and finally planning an exit strategy. Keil and Montealegre offer seven steps to help leaders and groups navigate this process:[37]

1. *Don't ignore negative feedback or external pressure.* These are signs that something is amiss. Recognizing these signs early on can greatly reduce escalation costs.

2. *Hire an external auditor.* Bringing in an outside expert or fresh set of eyes can help the group recognize the extent of the problem. A consultant can also recommend action that would be difficult for insiders to suggest.

3. *Don't be afraid to withhold further funding.* Don't provide additional money until more information can be gathered. Withholding funding is a sign to others that something is wrong and also reasserts the leader's control over the project.

4. *Look for opportunities to redefine the problem.* Seek creative solutions and identify additional alternatives. Encourage team members to express their concerns.

5. *Manage impressions.* Help group members to save face by putting the blame on others (if appropriate), by relying on the recommendations of consultants, and by taking the blame yourself.

6. *Prepare your stakeholders.* Warn important stakeholders in the project that you may be shutting it down. Consult with them to get their input.

7. *Deinstitutionalize the project.* Move the project from the core of the firm to the periphery. That might mean, for example, physically relocating the project or de-emphasizing the importance of the project to the group or organization. In the case of the Denver airport baggage system, city officials and the airlines agreed to open the complex without the new system, thus making baggage handling less important to the airport as a whole.

ESTABLISHING ETHICAL RELATIONSHIPS WITH OTHER GROUPS

So far, our focus has been on how leaders can encourage ethical behavior within their groups. Yet, groups rarely operate in isolation. The typical organization is made of subgroups, not individuals, for example. If the organization is to succeed, these teams must coordinate their actions. Leaders must foster ethical interaction between as well as within teams. *Intergroup leadership* is the process of bringing diverse groups together to achieve common goals. Intergroup leadership is becoming increasingly important as organizations decentralize and rely more on teams.[38] In the past, coordinating group activities was the duty of top executives. Now, lower-level leaders must redesign work processes, share information, coordinate patient care and curriculum decisions, develop fund-raising campaigns, and so on.

Competition and conflict are significant barriers to intergroup leadership. Often, the organizational units being asked to work together have been competing for staff, money, office space, and other organizational resources. These groups may also differ in status. Take the case of a business acquisition, for instance. Members of the company being acquired are at a significant disadvantage when compared to their colleagues at the parent firm. They may feel alienated, believing that the dominant group is imposing its policies and values on them. However, group identity is the major obstacle to intergroup leadership. Individuals who define themselves as students, business majors, teachers, accountants, managers, executives, or engineers find it hard to collaborate with those of other identities.

Intergroup leadership expert Todd Pittinsky offers five strategies or pathways to collaboration.[39] Pathway 1 is encouraging intergroup contact. Groups in conflict rarely come into contact with each other, so leaders must bring diverse teams together. Such contact can break down stereotypes and foster liking. Nonetheless, interacting with outsiders does not guarantee that group members will develop positive feelings about their counterparts in other groups. Negative interaction, such as when members of the parent company act in a condescending manner toward members of the acquired firm, can reinforce stereotypes and generate further hostility. Try to lay the groundwork for positive contacts by emphasizing that the teams need to work together to achieve a superordinate or shared objective like instituting a change initiative.

Pathway 2 is managing conflicts over resources by fostering trust. Act in a trustworthy fashion and elicit cooperative behaviors from both groups. Pathway 3 is creating a superordinate identity. Encourage team members to see themselves as part of a larger organization, which helps break down the "us versus them" mentality. Outline a shared vision and continually emphasize the importance of coordination. Politicians in the United States use this tactic when they emphasize that while we have our differences, we are all Americans. Pathway 4 is promoting dual identities. As you highlight shared overarching goals and memberships, encourage subgroups to maintain their distinctive identities. To put it another way, help create *intergroup relational identity*.[40] Effective intergroup leaders help team members recognize that they are part of a larger organization but, at the same time, retain their identities as members of subgroups. Encourage followers to see themselves as members of teams that operate in relationship with other teams. Back up your rhetoric by acting as a boundary spanner.[41] Bridge or span groups by having frequent contact with each team and developing positive relationships with individuals from every group. Be careful not to favor one group over another. Ultimately, your goal is to embody intergroup relational identity because you are seen as leading both teams, not one group or another. Serve as a role model for cooperation.

Pathway 5 is attacking negative attitudes while promoting positive attitudes.[42] As you promote liking through intergroup contact and other means, address negative attitudes. Help followers overcome their dislike of other groups by challenging stereotypes and encouraging them to live up to such values as equality and justice. Pearl Fryar of Bishopville, South Carolina, provides one example of someone who combated a negative stereotype and reduced disliking between racial groups. Whites objected when Fryar, an African American, wanted to move into their neighborhood because they believed black people didn't take care of their yards. Fryar proved them wrong by making his property into a topiary garden filled with plant sculptures. He became the first African American to win the town's Garden of the Month award, and his artistic creations became the centerpiece of a major revitalization effort for his small southern town.

IMPLICATIONS AND APPLICATIONS

- As a leader, you will do much of your work in project and process teams, committees, task forces, boards, and other small groups. Your task is to foster the conditions that brighten, not darken, the lives of group members and result in high performance and ethical choices.

- Because destructive behavior on the part of just one member can derail the group process, encourage participants to take their ethical responsibilities seriously. Foster collaboration by promoting commitment to shared goals; take steps to minimize social loafing.

- Expect to spend most of your time in a group listening rather than speaking. Model effective comprehensive, critical listening behaviors that overcome distractions, biases, and other listening barriers.

- Build a positive, ethical group climate through supportive messages that are descriptive, problem oriented, spontaneous, empathetic, focused on equality, and provisional.

- Model emotional regulation and encourage the development of positive norms that address the needs of individuals, the team, and outside groups.

- To improve problem solving, productivity, and relationships, foster substantive or task-oriented conflict about ideas and opinions. Set ground rules to help the group avoid affective (relational) conflict involving personalities.

- Foster minority opinion in order to promote creative, higher-quality solutions.

- An overemphasis on group cohesion is a significant threat to ethical group behavior. Be alert for the symptoms of groupthink. These include signs of overconfidence (illusion of invulnerability, belief in the inherent morality of the group), signs of closed-mindedness (collective rationalization, stereotypes of outside groups), and signs of group pressure (pressure on dissenters, self-censorship, illusion of unanimity, and self-appointed mind guards).

- The devil's advocate and dialectic inquiry methods are two ways to build in disagreement and reduce the likelihood of groupthink.

- Avoid false agreement or consensus by speaking out if you are concerned about the group's direction.

- Continuing in a failed course of action wastes time and resources. Help your team de-escalate by paying close attention to negative feedback, bringing in outsiders, withholding further funding, redefining the problem, and moving the project to the periphery of the organization.

- As a leader, you will need to help your team establish ethical relationships with other groups. Act as an intergroup leader in order to bring diverse groups together to achieve common goals. Help team members see themselves as part of a larger organization or community while retaining their identities as members of subgroups. Become a boundary spanner; model cooperation.

FOR FURTHER EXPLORATION, CHALLENGE, AND SELF-ASSESSMENT

1. Interview a leader at your school or in another organization to develop a "meeting profile" for this person. Find out how much time this individual spends in meetings during an average week and whether this is typical of other leaders in the same organization. Identify the types of meetings she or he attends and her or his role. Determine whether ethical issues are part of these discussions. As part of your profile, record your reactions. Are you surprised by your findings? Has this assignment changed your understanding of what leaders do?

2. Brainstorm strategies for encouraging commitment to shared goals in a group that you lead or belong to. What steps can you take to implement these strategies?

3. Analyze the impact of social loafing in a project group using Self-Assessment 9.1. What loafing behaviors are particularly destructive? What factors encourage members to reduce their efforts? What can you as a leader do to raise the motivation level of participants?

4. Evaluate a recent ethical decision made by one of your groups. Was it a high-quality decision? Why or why not? What factors contributed to the group's success or failure? How did the leader (you or someone else) shape the outcome for better or worse? How would you evaluate your performance as a leader or team member? Write up your analysis.

5. Develop a plan for becoming a better listener in a group. Implement your plan and then evaluate your progress.

6. Use the self-leadership strategies in "Focus on Follower Ethics: Self-Leadership in Self-Managed Teams" to develop a strategy for carrying out your team responsibilities.

7. Have you ever been part of a group that was victimized by groupthink? If so, which symptoms were present? How did they affect the group's ethical decisions and actions? Does the Abilene paradox (false agreement) offer a better explanation for what happened?

8. Draw from current events to create an escalation of commitment case study. Describe what happened, why the group continued in a failed course of action, and the de-escalation process (if any). Identify what lessons can be learned from this case.

9. With other team members, develop a conflict covenant. Determine how you will enforce this code. Or, as an alternative, complete Self-Assessment 9.2 as a group and develop strategies for engaging in more substantive conflict.

10. Fishbowl discussion: In a fishbowl discussion, one group discusses a problem while the rest of the class looks on and then provides feedback. Assign a group to one of the cases at the end of the chapter. Make sure that each discussant has one or more observers who specifically note his or her behavior. When the discussion is over, observers should meet with their "fish." Then the class as a whole should give its impressions of the overall performance of the team. Draw on the concepts discussed in this chapter when evaluating the work of individual participants and the group.

11. Evaluate your team's relationship with outside groups based on the last section of the chapter.

STUDENT STUDY SITE

Visit the student study site at **study.sagepub.com/johnsonmecl6e** to access full SAGE journal articles for further research and information on key chapter topics.

Case Study 9.1

CHAOS ON K2

K2 has been called the most dangerous mountain in the world. At 28,251 feet, K2 is only slightly shorter than nearby Mt. Everest but is much more difficult to climb. While more than 3,000 have summited Everest, approximately 300 have made it to the top of K2. Among those climbing Everest, 10% die trying, while the death rate on K2 is at 26%. There are several reasons K2 has been nicknamed the "Savage Mountain." Further north than Everest, it is subject to colder and harsher weather conditions. It is also steeper and harder to climb.

During the summer of 2008, climbers jammed into the highest base camp on K2 and prepared to summit. The group was a "virtual UN of expeditions," including teams from the Netherlands, Korea, the United States, Serbia, Australia, and Singapore, along with independent alpinists. Language differences hindered communication. Personality differences and different approaches to climbing generated friction between groups. In one case, for example, a Dutch expedition member shunned an American independent climber because the American didn't bring the right equipment. Tensions increased as weather conditions kept the teams in base camp.

Despite the tensions, team leaders realized that they would need to coordinate their efforts if such a large group were to have any chance at reaching the top. They agreed to send a trail-breaking team out first to pack down snow and set safety lines for those who would come later.

When the weather cleared, twenty-two climbers launched their ascent in the early morning hours of August 1. Trouble began almost immediately. Some tasked with laying down rope didn't show up, and the leader of the trail-breaking team—the only person who had previously summited—fell ill. Members of the first group didn't bring enough line and laid out the rope too soon. As a result, they ran out of line before reaching the most dangerous section of the climb called the Bottleneck, a narrow, steep passage where climbers had to proceed single file. Rope then had to be passed from the bottom to be anchored farther up the slope, delaying the climb. (Later, those who successfully descended failed to mark the way back to camp with flags as they had promised.) A Serbian fell to his death as he started his ascent, and a Pakistani porter died trying to retrieve the body. Soon, climbers were clustered at the bottom of the Bottleneck.

Eighteen climbers managed to make it to the living room–sized summit, which tied the previous single-day K2 record. However, the last climber didn't reach the top until 7:30 p.m. Those who continued ascending past early afternoon put themselves in grave danger. The delay meant they would have to descend in darkness or camp out on the side of the mountain (nicknamed the Death Zone) in temperatures reaching 40 degrees below zero. One climber who summited tried to tell others that it was too late to continue on, but he soon gave up. "As I descended," he said, "everyone stopped to ask me how far it was to the summit. Did I tell people to turn around? No, you can't. There are a lot of people and they are all going up together. It's the majority against you."[1]

As the teams descended, tragedy struck again as a huge ice sheet broke off, sweeping climbers to their deaths. The falling piece of glacier also carried away the ropes that those above the Bottleneck were depending on to lead them to the safety of base camp. Smaller icefalls and avalanches during the night and the next day buried other climbers. Eleven died, making this one of the worst climbing disasters of all time.

Responses to the deadly chaos unfolding on K2 ranged from selfish to heroic. Many focused on their own survival, ignoring the plight of others. Said the head of Dutch team: "They were thinking of using my gas, my rope. Everybody was fighting for himself, and I still do not understand why everybody were leaving each other."[2] The Sherpa climbers, on the other hand, did their best to help. They returned up the mountain from base camp to rescue disoriented climbers. Two Sherpas died while trying to rescue three Koreans tangled in rope. In an amazing feat of mountaineering, one Sherpa tied himself to a colleague who had lost his ice ax. They managed to descend using only one ax between them.

Much of the 2008 K2 disaster can be blamed on natural forces. Icefalls and avalanches claimed the majority of victims. However, human factors played a major role as well. The teams were not able to coordinate their efforts, team members didn't follow through on their responsibilities, and too many climbers fell victim to "summit fever," deciding to continue upward when they should have turned back. Self-centeredness was also a contributing factor. In the past, mountaineering teams viewed their climbs as mutual endeavors and took responsibility for one another. Not so in recent years. As one mountaineering historian noted, modern climbing now is marked by "an ethos stressing individualism and self-preservation."[3]

Ironically, one of the greatest examples of mountaineering selflessness came in a 1954 American summit attempt on K2. When a fellow climber fell ill, his colleagues abandoned their summit attempt and carried him thousands of feet down the mountain, only to see him swept away as they neared safety. A memorial to this climber and others who have died on the mountain still stands. The names of the eleven who died in 2008 were added to this monument.

Discussion Probes

1. Did divisions among the teams doom any attempt to cooperate?

2. Would the teams have been better off climbing on their own?

3. What steps, if any, could the team leaders have taken to foster intergroup identity?

4. Why do you think climbers continued to the top even after they should have turned back?

5. Why are modern climbers apparently more selfish than climbers of the past? What can be done to change the culture of climbing?

6. What leadership and followership ethics lessons do you take from this case?

(Continued)

(Continued)

Notes

1. Viesturs, E., & Roberts, D. (2009). *K2: Life and death on the world's most dangerous mountain.* New York, NY: Broadway, p. 18.

2. Isserman, M. (2008, August 11). The descent of men; a different K2 drama. *The International Herald Tribune,* Opinion, p. 4.

3. Isserman.

Sources

Bowley, G., & Kannapell, A. (2008, August 6). Chaos on the "Mountain that Invites Death." *The New York Times,* p. A1.

Haider, K. (2008, August 5). "Death zone" tragedy. *National Post,* p. A3.

Peterson, S. (2008, August 6). In K2 aftermath, lessons learned. *The Christian Science Monitor.*

Power, M. (2008, November). K2: The killing peak. *Men's Journal.*

Ramesh, R. (2008, August 5). K2 tragedy: Death toll on world's most treacherous mountain reaches 11. *The Guardian,* Home Pages, p. 2.

Taylor, J. (2008, August 5). What makes K2 the most perilous challenge a mountaineer can face? *The Independent,* Comment, p. 30.

Zuckerman, P., & Padoan, A. (2012). *Buried in the sky: The extraordinary story of the Sherpa climbers on K2's deadliest day.* New York, NY: Norton, p. 11.

Case Study 9.2

GETTING THE PROJECT TEAM BACK ON TRACK

Jesse Cruz looked forward to leading his project team in his senior entrepreneurship capstone class. Professor Williams chose Jesse and four other team leaders from among those who applied for the positions. The teams are to create a plan for a new small business. Members may not change teams, though leaders can "fire" one member if that person seriously undermines the group's efforts. At the end of the semester, each group will present its plan to a panel of business alumni who will determine which has the best chance of success and deserves the highest grade.

Jesse's team is made up of seven members (including himself). The group performed well on the first teambuilding exercises and case studies Professor Williams assigned in class. Team members were friendly with one another and willing to share their ideas, though Jesse was concerned that one member, Ralph, seemed to dominate group discussions. That initial good will dissipated quickly when the team sat down to figure out which kind of business it wants to create. Ralph and two other group members (Rose and Isaiah) are pushing to create a plan for a recreational marijuana store. They want to take advantage of the fact that voters in their state recently legalized recreational pot sales. Megan, Joyce, and Bernie have serious doubts about the proposal. They point out that the group would be selling a product banned by their university and still in violation of federal law. They worry that this type of business may be too controversial for the alumni evaluators and would lower the group's grade. Joyce voted against the change in the marijuana law and believes that selling pot is unethical. Megan, Joyce, and Bernie have proposed a variety of alternatives, including a smartphone repair shop and bakery, but can't seem to agree on one option.

Tensions are rising as the group continues to discuss which business to pursue. Jesse's concerns about Ralph have proven to be well founded. He comes across as a know-it-all. He declared on one occasion that those who disagreed with him were "clueless" because they didn't understand how profitable a marijuana business could be. Ralph, Rose, and Isaiah appear more interested in having their way than in listening to their counterparts. They don't seem to recognize how frustrated Megan, Joyce, and Bernie are. In fact, Megan appears to have given up and rarely speaks, checking her cell phone instead. Joyce hasn't helped matters by accusing the marijuana store supporters (whom she referred to as "potheads") of being immoral. Up to this point, Jesse has tried to remain neutral, though he has serious doubts about the marijuana business plan. He has focused on summarizing major points from both sides and encouraging members to listen to one another. He brought donuts to the last meeting in hopes of encouraging a warmer atmosphere.

Jesse realizes that the group is stuck and that the entire project (as well as the semester grade in this senior-level class) is in danger. Even he as team leader doesn't want to come to the group's meetings anymore. While tempted to side with the marijuana business subgroup just to break the deadlock, he recognizes that members of the other subgroup may not complete their parts of the project if this plan is adopted. He needs to determine what to do before the team meets again. Time is running out.

Discussion Probes

1. What has Jesse done right so far as a leader? What mistakes has he made?

2. Should Jesse break the deadlock by supporting the marijuana store proposal? Why or why not?

3. What problems do you note in the interaction between group members?

4. What skills do members need to develop? What procedures or guidelines should they adopt?

5. What steps should Jesse take to foster cooperation and address the unproductive and unethical communication patterns in the group?

6. Should Jesse fire Ralph?

7. What should be Jesse's agenda for the next team meeting?

Case Study 9.3

GROUPTHINK AT THE TOP: THE COLLAPSE OF HBOS

It seemed like a merger made in financial heaven. In 2001, the Halifax Building Society of Britain merged with the Bank of Scotland to form HBOS. The union made a lot of sense. Halifax was a successful retail mortgage lender and Bank of Scotland had experience in corporate lending and treasury investments. Between them, the two well-respected institutions had 450 years of banking experience. Their combined assets of 30 billion pounds made HBOS one of the largest financial institutions in the United Kingdom. Yet, seven years later, HBOS collapsed in one of the biggest bank failures in British history.

The seeds of the bank's destruction were sown shortly after its formation. HBOS executives set out an aggressive growth strategy for HBOS based on increasing loan volume 17% to 20% a year. To reach this target, commercial loan officers had to target smaller, riskier borrowers. Financial regulators warned HBOS of the dangers of making such risky loans, but bank officers ignored their advice. When money loaned far outstripped deposits, the bank had to turn to outside underwriters for funds to make more loans. This made HBOS extremely vulnerable to downturns in the financial markets. When the mortgage crisis began in 2007–2008, many borrowers defaulted and HBOS couldn't raise additional money to cover its losses. The British government forced HBOS to merge with the Lloyds banking group. However, government officials later had to inject 20.5 billion pounds into HBOS to keep it afloat.

A 2013 British Parliamentary review of the bank's collapse was titled "An Accident Waiting to Happen." Investigators condemned the bank's board and top managers, declaring, "The history of HBOS provides a manual of bad banking."[1] Not only was the bank's growth strategy far too ambitious, the firm lacked adequate controls to estimate and control for risk. Loan officers were rewarded for reaching sales targets, not on the quality of their loans. Most of the firm's members had little or no expertise with risk management. Government regulators failed to carry out their responsibilities.

Groupthink also played a significant role in the bank's demise. The top executive team, made up of bank chairman Dennis Stevenson, chief executive officers (CEOs) James Crosby and Andy Hornby, and commercial lending chief Peter Cummings, was supremely confident. In retrospect, their optimism appears delusional. In 2001, the chairman stated that any higher losses from making risky loans would be "more than compensated for by higher product margins."[2] In 2006 and 2007, bank officers boldly proclaimed that the bank was adequately managing its risks and that they were more skilled than their competitors. (This despite the fact that Cummings was the only senior official with significant banking knowledge and experience.) As the global financial crisis loomed and other banks reduced their high-risk loan portfolios, HBOS loaned out even more money. Peter Cummings appeared to mock more prudent lenders, declaring:

The job of banks is to assess risk but in the last 18–24 months that's a job many banks seem to have forgotten. . . . We never forgot. Our decision strength is assessing credit risk and assessing people. We're better at it. . . . Some people look as if they are losing their nerve, beginning to panic even in today's testing property environment, not us.[3]

Top management at HBOS was quick to silence dissenters. Paul Moore, in charge of monitoring the bank's risk, recommended at one board meeting that HBOS reconsider its fast-growth strategy. His warning was ignored. The meeting minutes said instead that risk controls were adequate. When Moore demanded that the minutes be written to reflect his concerns, no changes were made. CEO Crosby fired him instead, replacing him with someone far less qualified. Board members rarely challenged the decisions of the top executive team and didn't engage in much substantive debate during board sessions.

Fallout from the HBOS collapse continues. Both Stevenson and Crosby, who had been knighted, gave up their titles as Lords. They have apologized for their role in the failure. Accounting giant KPMG is being scrutinized for signing off on the bank's financial statements just prior to its collapse. Cummings was forced to pay 500,000 pounds in restitution and was banned from the financial industry. Ten additional officers may be barred from British banking and prevented from serving as company directors in any industry. The Parliamentary committee that reviewed the collapse of HBOS called for a new law making it a criminal offence for bank senior bank staff to engage in "reckless misconduct."

Discussion Probes

1. How can you tell the difference between optimism and delusional optimism?
2. What symptoms of groupthink do you note in the HBOS top management team and board of directors?
3. Do you think top management teams are more vulnerable to groupthink than managers at lower levels of the organization? Why or why not?
4. Should top leaders at HBOS be forced to give up their earnings and pensions?
5. Should bank officials and other corporate leaders be jailed if they act recklessly?
6. Should the accounting firm KPMG be punished for giving HBOS a clean financial bill of health even as it was near collapse?

Notes

1. Parliamentary Commission on Banking Standards. (2013). *An accident waiting to happen: The failure of HBOS*. House of Commons, London, England.
2. McConnell, P. (2014). Reckless endangerment: The failure of HBOS. *Journal of Risk Management in Financial Institutions, 7*, 202–215.
3. McConnell.

(Continued)

(Continued)

Sources

Dale, S. (2012, December 4). Ex-HBOS chief exec Sir James Crosby apologizes for bank failure. *Fundweb.* p. 11.

Hashemi, F. (2016, February 5). Probe into KPMG's audit of failed bank HBOS intensifies. *International Accounting Bulletin.*

Karmali, R. (2015, November 19). HBOS' demise: How it happened. *BBC.*

Not so smart. (2015, November 28). *The Economist.*

Press Association. (2006, January 28). Ex-HBOS bosses face City bans as watchdogs launch bank failure probes. *Daily Mail.* Retrieved from http://www.bankofengland.co.uk/pra/Documents/publications/reports/hbos.pdf

Wallace, T. (2015, November 19). Up to 10 former HBOS executives could be banned over collapse, damning report finds. *The Telegraph.*

SELF-ASSESSMENT 9.1

Class Project Social Loafing Scale

Instructions: To identify the behaviors associated with the impact of social loafing on team performance, respond to the following questions based on your recent experiences with one social loafer in a class project team.

What Did the Social Loafer Do?

(1 = does not describe at all; 2 = describes the least; 3 = does not describe much; 4 = describes somewhat; 5 = describes the most)

1. Member had trouble attending team meetings.
2. Member had trouble paying attention to what was going on in the team.
3. Member was mostly silent during the team meetings.
4. Member engaged in side conversations a lot while the team was working.
5. Member came poorly prepared to the team meetings.
6. Member contributed poorly to the team discussions when present.
7. Member had trouble completing team-related homework.
8. Member mostly declined to take on any work for the team.
9. Member did a poor job of the work she/he was assigned.
10. Member did poor-quality work.
11. Member mostly distracted the team's focus on its goals and objectives.
12. Member did not fully participate in the team's formal presentation.

What Was the Impact of the Social Loafer on Your Team?

Indicate the extent to which you agree or disagree with the following statements about the impact the social loafer had on your team (1 = strongly disagree; 2 = disagree; 3 = neither agree nor disagree; 4 = agree; 5 = strongly agree)

As a result of the social loafing . . .

1. the team took longer than anticipated to complete its tasks.
2. the team meetings lasted longer than expected.
3. the team had fewer good ideas than other teams.
4. team members had to waste their time explaining things to the social loafer.
5. other team members had to do more than their share of work.
6. other team members were frustrated and angry.
7. there was a higher level of stress on the team.
8. other team members had to redo or revise the work done by the social loafer.
9. the work had to be reassigned to other members of the team.
10. the team's final presentation was not as high quality as that of other teams.
11. the team missed deadlines.

Source: Adapted from Jassawalla, A. R., Malshe, A., & Sashittal, H. (2008). Student perceptions of social loafing in undergraduate business classroom teams. *Decision Sciences Journal of Innovative Education, 6,* 423–424. Used with permission.

SELF-ASSESSMENT 9.2

Task/Relationship Conflict Scale

Instructions: The following scale will help you determine if your team is engaged in affective or substantive conflict. Choose a problem-solving group from work or school and answer each of the following questions.

Very Little						A Great Deal
1	2	3	4	5	6	7

1. How much friction is there among members in your group? _____
2. How much are personality conflicts evident in your group? _____
3. How much tension is there among members in your group? _____
4. How much emotional conflict is there among members in your group?_____
5. How often do people in your group disagree about opinions? _____
6. How frequently are there conflicts about ideas in your group? _____
7. How much conflict about the work you do is there in your group? _____
8. To what extent are there differences of opinion in your group? _____

Scoring:

Add up your scores from Questions 1–4 and record the total below. The higher the score, the greater the level of affective conflict in your group. Add up your scores from Questions 5–8 and record the total below. The higher the score, the greater the level of substantive or task conflict in your team.

Affective conflict _____ out of 28   Substantive/task conflict _____ out of 28

Source: Reprinted from Jehn, K. A. (1995, June). A multi-method examination of the benefits and detriments of intragroup conflict. *Administrative Science Quarterly, 40,* 256–282. © Johnson Graduate School of Management, Cornell University.

NOTES

1. Palmer, P. (1996). Leading from within. In L. C. Spears (Ed.), *Insights on leadership: Service, stewardship, spirit, and servant-leadership* (pp. 197–208). New York, NY: John Wiley, p. 200.
2. Statistic retrieved from http://www.pmi.org/certification/what-are-PMI-certifications.aspx
3. Silverman, R. E. (2012, February 4). Where's the boss? Trapped in a meeting. *The Wall Street Journal.*
4. Johnson, D. W., & Johnson, F. P. (2000). *Joining together: Group theory and group skills* (7th ed.). Boston, MA: Allyn & Bacon; Johnson, D. W., & Johnson, R. T. (1989). *Cooperation and competition: Theory and research.* Edina, MN: Interaction; Johnson, D. W., Maruyama, G., Johnson, R., Nelson, D., & Skon, L. (1981). Effects of cooperative, competitive, and individualistic goal structures on achievement: A meta-analysis. *Psychological Bulletin, 82,* 47–62.
5. Johnson, D. W., & Johnson, R. T. (2005). Training for cooperative group work. In M. A. West, D. Tjosvold, & K. G. Smith (Eds.), *The essentials of teamworking: International perspectives* (pp. 131–147). West Sussex, England: John Wiley.
6. Johnson & Johnson (2000); Johnson & Johnson (2005).
7. Amichai-Hamburger, Y. (2003). Understanding social loafing. In A. Sagie, S. Stashevsky, & M. Koslowsky (Eds.), *Misbehaviour and dysfunctional attitudes in organizations* (pp. 79–102). Basingstoke, England: Palgrave Macmillan.
8. Karau, S. J., & Williams, K. D. (2001). Understanding individual motivation in groups: The collective effort model. In M. E. Turner (Ed.), *Groups at work: Theory and research* (pp. 113–141). Mahwah, NJ: Erlbaum, p. 119.
9. Karau, S. J., & Williams, K. D. (1995). Social loafing: Research findings, implications, and future directions. *Current Directions in Psychological Science, 4,* 134–140; Williams, K. D., Harkins, S. G., & Karau, S. J. (2003). Social performance. In M. A. Hogg & J. Cooper (Eds.), *The SAGE handbook of social psychology* (pp. 327–346). London, England: SAGE.
10. Wolvin, A. D., & Coakley, G. C. (1993). A listening taxonomy. In A. D. Wolvin & C. G. Coakley (Eds.), *Perspectives in listening* (pp. 15–22). Norwood, NJ: Ablex.
11. Johnson, J. (1993). Functions and processes of inner speech in listening. In D. Wolvin & C. G. Coakley (Eds.), *Perspectives in listening* (pp. 170–184). Norwood, NJ: Ablex.
12. Barker, L., Johnson, P., & Watson, K. (1991). The role of listening in managing interpersonal and group conflict. In D. Borisoff & M. Purdy (Eds.), *Listening in everyday life: A personal and professional approach* (pp. 139–157). Lanham, MD: University Press of America.
13. Gibb, J. R. (1961). Defensive communication. *Journal of Communication, 11–12,* 141–148. See also Borisoff, D., & Victor, D. A. (1998). *Conflict management: A communication skills approach* (2nd ed.). Boston, MA: Allyn & Bacon, Ch. 2.

14. Duffy, M. K., & Shaw, J. D. (2000). The Salieri syndrome: Consequences of envy in groups. *Small Group Research, 31,* 3–23.

15. Goleman, D., Boyatzis, R., & McKee, A. (2002). The emotional reality of teams. *Journal of Organizational Excellence, 21*(2), 55–65; Gunsel, A., & Acikgoz, A. (2013). The effects of team flexibility and emotional intelligence on software development performance. *Group Decision and Negotiation, 22,* 359–377; Harper, S. R., & White, C. D. (2013). The impact of member emotional intelligence on psychological safety in work teams. *Journal of Behavioral & Applied Management, 15,* 2–10; Prati, L. M., Douglas, C., Ferris, G. R., Ammeter, A. P., & Buckley, M. R. (2003). Emotional intelligence, leadership effectiveness, and team outcomes. *International Journal of Organizational Analysis, 11,* 21–40; Rapisarda, B. A. (2002). The impact of emotional intelligence on work team cohesiveness and performance. *International Journal of Organizational Analysis, 10,* 363–370. Some examples in this section are taken from these sources.

16. Durskat, V. U., & Wolff, S. B. (2001, March). Building the emotional intelligence of groups. *Harvard Business Review,* 80–90.

17. See Amason, A. C. (1996). Distinguishing the effects of functional and dysfunctional conflict on strategic decision making: Resolving a paradox for top management teams. *Academy of Management Journal, 39,* 123–148; Amason, A. C., Thompson, K. R., Hochwarter, W. A., & Harrison, A. W. (1995). Conflict: An important dimension in successful management teams. *Organizational Dynamics, 23,* 20–35; Bell, M. A. (1974). The effects of substantive and affective conflict in problem-solving groups. *Speech Monographs, 41,* 19–23; Bell, M. A. (1979). The effects of substantive and affective verbal conflict on the quality of decisions of small problem-solving groups. *Central States Speech Journal, 3,* 75–82; Johnson, D. W., & Tjosvold, D. (1983). *Productive conflict management.* New York, NY: Irvington.

18. Kotlyar, I., & Karakowsky, L. (2006). Leading conflict? Linkages between leader behaviors and group conflict. *Small Group Research, 37,* 377–403.

19. Alper, S., Tjosvold, D., & Law, K. S. (2000). Conflict management, efficacy, and performance in organizational teams. *Personnel Psychology, 53,* 625–642.

20. Jordan, P. J., & Troth, A. C. (2004). Managing emotions during team problem solving: Emotional intelligence and conflict resolution. *Human Performance, 17,* 195–218.

21. Roberto, M. A. (2005). *Why great leaders don't take yes for an answer.* Upper Saddle River, NJ: Wharton School Publishing

22. Roberto (2005).

23. For summaries of research on minority influence processes, see Crano, W. D., & Seyranian, V. (2009). How minorities prevail: The context/comparison-leniency contract model. *Journal of Social Issues, 65,* 335–363; De Dreu, C. K. W., & Beersma, B. (2001). Minority influence in organizations: Its origins and implications for learning and group performance. In C. K. W. De Dreu & N. K. De Vies (Eds.), *Group consensus and minority influence: Implications for innovation* (pp. 258–283). Malden, MA: Blackwell; Martin, R., & Hewstone, M. (Eds.). (2010). *Minority influence and innovations: Antecedents, processes and consequences* (pp. 365–394). Hoboken, NJ: Psychology Press; Maas, A., & Clark, R. D. (1984). Hidden impact of minorities: Fifteen years of minority influence research. *Psychological Bulletin, 95,* 428–445; Moscovici, S., Mucchi-Faina, A., & Maass, A. (Eds.). (1994). *Minority influence.* Chicago, IL: Nelson-Hall; Moscovici, S., Mugny, G., & Van Avermaet, E. (Eds.). (1985). *Perspectives on minority influence.* Cambridge, England: Cambridge University Press; Nemeth, C. (1994). The value of minority dissent. In S. Moscovici, A. Mucchi-Faina, & A. Maass (Eds.), *Minority influence* (pp. 3–15). Chicago, IL: Nelson-Hall; Nemeth, C., & Chiles, C. (1986). Modeling courage: The role of dissent in fostering independence. *European Journal of Social Psychology, 18,* 275–280.

24. Nemeth, C. (1995). Dissent, group process and creativity: The contribution of minority influence research. In E. Lawler (Ed.), *Advances in group processes* (Vol. 2, pp. 57–75). Greenwich, CT: JAI Press; Nemeth & Chiles.

25. Smith, C. M., & Tindale, R. S. (2009). Direct and indirect minority influence in groups. In R. Martin & M. Hewstone (Eds.), *Minority influence and innovations: Antecedents, processes and consequences* (pp. 263–284). Hoboken, NJ: Psychology Press.

26. Alvaro, E. M., & Crano, W. D. (1997). Indirect minority influence: Evidence for leniency in source evaluation and counterargumentation. *Journal of Personality and Social Psychology, 72,* 949–964.

27. See, for example, De Dreu, C. K. W., & West, M. A. (2001). Minority dissent and team innovation: The importance of participation in decision making. *Journal of Applied Psychology, 86,* 1191–1201; La Pine, J. A. (2005). Adaptation of teams in response to unforeseen change: Effects of goal difficulty and team composition in terms of cognitive ability and goal orientation. *Journal of Applied Psychology, 90,* 1153–1167; Park, G., & DeShon, R. P. (2010). A multilevel model of minority opinion expression and team decision-making effectiveness. *Journal of Applied Psychology, 95,* 824–853; Valacich, J. S., & Schewenk, C. (1995). Devil's advocacy and dialectical inquiry effects on face-to-face and computer-mediated group decision making. *Organizational Behavior and Human Decision Processes, 63,* 158–173.

28. Janis, I. (1971, November). Groupthink: The problems of conformity. *Psychology Today,* 271–279; Janis, I. (1982). *Groupthink* (2nd ed.). Boston, MA: Houghton Mifflin; Janis, I. (1989). *Crucial decisions: Leadership in policymaking and crisis management.* New York, NY: Free Press.

29. Moorhead, G., Neck, C. P., & West, M. S. (1998). The tendency toward defective decision making within self-managing teams: The relevance of groupthink for the 21st century. *Organizational Behavior and Human Decision Processes, 73,* 327–351.

30. See Chen, A., Lawson, R. B., Gordon, L. R., & McIntosh, B. (1996). Groupthink: Deciding with the leader and the devil. *Psychological Record, 46,* 581–590; Esser, J. K. (1998). Alive and well after 25 years: A review of groupthink research. *Organizational Behavior and Human Decision Processes, 73,* 116–141; Flippen, A. R. (1999). Understanding groupthink from a self-regulatory perspective. *Small Group Research, 3,* 139–165; Jones, P. E., & Roelofsma, P. H. M. P. (2000). The potential for social contextual and group biases in team decision-making: Biases, conditions and psychological mechanisms. *Ergonomics, 43,* 1129–1152; Street, M. D. (1997). Groupthink: An examination of theoretical issues, implications, and future research suggestions. *Small Group Research, 28,* 72–93.

31. Cosier, R. A., & Schwenk, C. R. (1990). Agreement and thinking alike: Ingredients for poor decision. *Academy of Management Executive, 4,* 69–74; Schweiger, D. M., Sandberg, W. R., & Rechner, P. (1989). Experiential effects of dialectical inquiry, devil's advocacy, and consensus approaches to strategic decision making. *Academy of Management Journal, 32,* 745–772.

32. Manz, C. C., & Neck, C. P. (1995). Teamthink: Beyond the groupthink syndrome in self-managing work teams. *Journal of Managerial Psychology, 10*(1), 7–15; Manz, C. C., & Sims, H. P. (1989). *Superleadership: Leading others to lead themselves.* Upper Saddle River, NJ: Prentice Hall.

33. Harvey, J. B. (1988). *The Abilene paradox and other meditations on management.* New York, NY: Simon & Schuster. See also Harvey, J. B. (1999). *How come every time I get stabbed in the back my fingerprints are on the knife?* San Francisco, CA: Jossey-Bass.

34. See, for example, Bobocel, D. R., & Meyer, J. P. (1994). Escalating commitment to a failing course of action: Separating the roles of choice and justification. *Journal of Applied Psychology, 79,* 360–363; Edwards, J. C. (2001). Self-fulfilling prophecy and escalating commitment: Fuel for the Waco fire. *Journal of Applied Behavioral Science, 37,* 343–360; McNamara, G., Moon, H., & Bromiley, P. (2002). Banking on commitment: Intended and unintended consequences of an organization's attempt to attenuate escalation of commitment. *Academy of Management Journal, 45,* 443–452; Ross, J., & Staw, B. M. (1993). Organizational escalation and exit: Lessons from the Shoreham Nuclear Plant. *Academy of Management Journal, 36,* 701–732; Staw, B. M. (1981). The escalation of commitment to a course of action. *Academy of Management Review, 6,* 577–587.

35. Drummond, H., & Hodgson, J. (2011). *Escalation in decision-making: Behavioral economics in business.* Burlington, VT: Gower; Sleesman, D. J., Conlon, D. E., McNamara G., & Miles, J. E. (2012). Cleaning up the big muddy: A meta-analytic review of the determinants of escalation of commitment. *Academy of Management Journal, 3,* 541–562.

36. McKenna, F. P. (1993). It won't happen to me: Unrealistic optimism or illusion of control? *British Journal of Psychology, 84,* 39–50.

37. Keil, M., & Montealegre, R. (2000). Cutting your losses: Extricating your organization when a big project goes awry. *Sloan Management Review, 41,* 55–68. See also Drummond & Hodgson; Simonson, I., & Staw, B M. (1992). De-escalation strategies: A comparison of techniques for reducing commitment to losing courses of action. *Journal of Applied Psychology, 77,* 419–426.

38. Ernst, C., & Yip, J. (2009). Boundary-spanning leadership: Tactics to bridge social identity groups in organizations. In T. L. Pittinsky (Ed.), *Crossing the divide: Intergroup leadership in a world of difference* (pp. 87–99). Boston, MA: Harvard Business Press; Pittinsky, T. L., & Simon, S. (2007). Intergroup leadership. *Leadership Quarterly, 18,* 586–605.

39. Ernst & Yip; Pittinsky & Simon.

40. Hogg, M. A., Knippenberg, D., & Rast, D. E. (2012). Intergroup leadership in organizations: Leading across group and organizational boundaries. *Academy of Management Review, 37,* 232–255.

41. Duck, J. M., & Fielding, K. S. (2003). Leaders and their treatment of subgroups: Implications for evaluations of the leader and the superordinate group. *European Journal of Social Psychology, 33,* 387–401; Marrone, J. A. (2010). Team boundary spanning: A multilevel review of past research and proposals for the future. *Journal of Management, 36,* 911–940; Richter, A. W., West, M. A., Van Dick, R., & Dawson, J. F. (2006). Boundary spanners' identification, intergroup contact, and effective intergroup relations. *Academy of Management Journal, 49,* 1252–1269.

42. Pittinsky, T. L. (2010). A two-dimensional model of intergroup leadership: The case of national diversity. *American Psychologist, 65,* 194–200.

Creating an Ethical Organizational Climate

Corruption is a durable and adaptable virus.

—MANAGEMENT PROFESSOR YADONG LUO

Bad ethics is bad business.

—ANONYMOUS

WHAT'S AHEAD

Leaders act as ethics officers for their organizations through the process of social learning and by building positive ethical climates. Healthy ethical climates are marked by recognition of risk, zero tolerance for individual and collective destructive behaviors, justice, integrity (ethical soundness, wholeness, and consistency), trust, concern for process as well as product, structural reinforcement, and organizational citizenship. Important tools for building an ethical organizational climate include core ideology, codes of ethics, socialization, and ethics training.

THE LEADER AS ETHICS OFFICER

In the introduction to this text, I argued that ethics is at the heart of leadership. When we become leaders, we assume the ethical responsibilities that come with that role. Nowhere is this more apparent than in the organizational context. Examine nearly any corporate scandal—Volkswagen's faulty emissions tests, Toshiba's accounting fraud, Goldman Sachs' mortgage and security fraud—and you'll find leaders who engaged in immoral behavior and encouraged their followers to do the same. The same pattern can be found in the nonprofit and governmental sectors (e.g., falsification of patient access records at Veterans Affairs hospitals, misuse of donor funds at the Wounded Warrior Project, lead poisoning in Flint, Michigan). On a more positive note, leaders are largely responsible for creating the organizations we admire for their ethical behavior.

Leaders are the ethics officers of their organizations, casting light or shadow in large part through the example they set.[1] Michael Brown and Linda Trevino draw on social learning theory to explain why and how ethical organizational leaders influence followers.[2] Social learning theory is based on the premise that people learn by observing and then emulating the values, attitudes, and behaviors of people they find legitimate, attractive, and credible. When it comes to ethics, followers look to their leaders as role models and act accordingly. Leaders are generally seen as legitimate, credible, and attractive because they occupy positions of authority with power and status. Ethical leaders build on this foundation. They increase their legitimacy by treating employees fairly and boost their attractiveness by expressing care and concern for followers. They enhance their credibility—particularly perceptions of their trustworthiness—by living up to the values they espouse. Such leaders are open and honest and set clear, high standards that they follow themselves.

Moral leaders make sure that ethics messages aren't drowned out by other messages about tasks and profits. They focus attention on ethics through frequent communication about values, mission, corporate standards, and the importance of ethical behavior. They reinforce follower learning by using rewards and punishments to regulate behavior, which makes it clear which actions are acceptable and which are not.

Trevino, Brown, and their colleagues distinguish between ethical leaders and those who are unethical, hypocritical, or ethically neutral.[3] The *unethical leader* falls short as both a moral person and a moral influence agent. This person casts one or more of the shadows described in Chapter 1 by bullying others, deceiving investors, acting irresponsibly, and so on. At the same time, the unethical leader clearly communicates that ethics don't matter; only results do. "Chainsaw" Al Dunlap was one such leader. As chief executive officer (CEO) of Sunbeam, he drove up the company's stock price by eliminating thousands of jobs while inflating sales figures.

The *hypocritical leader* talks a lot about ethical values but doesn't live up to the rhetoric. As we saw in Chapter 1, former House Speaker Dennis Hastert and Bill Cosby publicly proclaimed moral values while engaging in sexual misconduct.

The *ethically neutral leader* is not clearly seen as either ethical or unethical. This person doesn't send out strong messages about ethics and leaves followers unsure about where he or she stands on moral issues. Ethically neutral leaders appear to be self-centered and focus exclusively on the bottom line. Sandy Weill, former Citigroup CEO, typifies the ethically neutral leader. Weill stayed on the sidelines when it came to ethics, rewarding his managers according to their results. It was during his tenure that star analyst Jack Grubman continued to promote WorldCom and other telecom companies even as they were heading for bankruptcy. From their analysis of the three categories of ethical leadership, Trevino and her colleagues conclude that acting ethically is not enough. Executives must also ensure that employees know that they care (aren't just neutral) about ethics. Otherwise, followers will continue to focus on financial results without concern for ethics. Ethical leaders make ethical considerations a top organizational priority. They create positive ethical climates that promote moral behavior by leaders and followers alike. Identifying the characteristics of healthy ethical climates is the subject of the next section.

ETHICAL CLIMATES

Ethical climate is best understood as part of an organization's culture. From the cultural vantage point, an organization is a tribe. As tribal members gather, they develop their own language, stories, beliefs, assumptions, ceremonies, and power structures. These elements combine to form a unique perspective on the world called the organization's *culture.*[4] How an organization responds to ethical issues is a part of this culture. Every organization faces a special set of ethical challenges, creates its own set of values and norms, develops guidelines for enforcing its ethical standards, honors particular ethical heroes, and so on. Ethical climate, in turn, determines what members believe is right or wrong and shapes their ethical decision making and behavior.

Management professors Bart Victor and John Cullen argue that ethical climates can be classified according to the criteria members use to make moral choices and the groups that members refer to when making ethical determinations.[5] Victor and Cullen identify five primary climate types. *Instrumental* climates follow the principle of ethical egotism. Ethical egotists make decisions based on selfish interests that serve the individual and his or her immediate group and organization. *Caring* climates emphasize concern or care for others. *Law and order* climates are driven by external criteria such as professional codes of conduct. *Rules* climates are governed by the policies, rules, and procedures developed in the organization. *Independence* climates give members wide latitude to make their own decisions. (Complete Self-Assessment 10.1 to determine the ethical climate of your company or organization.)

Leaders would do well to know the particular ethical orientation of their organizations. To begin, each of the five climate types poses unique ethical challenges. Members of instrumental organizations often ignore the needs of others, whereas those driven by a care ethic are tempted to overlook the rules to help out friends and colleagues. Leaders and followers in law and order cultures may be blind to the needs of coworkers because they rely on outside standards for guidance. On the other hand, those who play by organizational rules may be blinded to societal norms. Independence produces the best results when members have the knowledge and skills they need to make good decisions.

Studies using the Victor and Cullen climate types suggest that self-interest poses the greatest threat to ethical performance.[6] Rates of immoral behavior are highest in work units and organizations with instrumental climates, which are more common in for-profit organizations and those directed by authoritarian leaders. Members of these groups are also less committed to their organizations and less satisfied with their jobs. Caring (benevolent) climates promote employee loyalty and contentment. Rules climates discourage ethical misbehavior but don't encourage attachment to the organization. External laws and codes that are internalized into an organization's climate are positively linked with such outcomes as job satisfaction and psychological well-being. Climate has a similar impact on ethical and unethical behavior in a variety of cultural settings, including North America, Europe, Africa, and Asia. (See "Focus on Follower Ethics: Student and Faculty Perceptions of University Ethical Climate" for a closer look at ethical climate in higher education.)

SIGNS OF HEALTHY ETHICAL CLIMATES

There is no one-size-fits-all approach to creating an ethical climate. Rather, we need to identify principles and practices that characterize positive ethical climates. Then we have to adapt these elements to our particular organizational setting. Key markers of highly ethical organizations include recognition of risk, zero tolerance for individual and collective destructive behaviors, justice, integrity, trust, process focus, structural reinforcement, and organizational citizenship.

Focus on Follower Ethics

STUDENT AND FACULTY PERCEPTIONS OF UNIVERSITY ETHICAL CLIMATE

Like other organizations, colleges and universities develop ethical climates. Laura Schulte of the University of Nebraska at Omaha wondered if students and faculty perceive their ethical climates differently. She measured how these followers and leaders rate faculty-to-student, student-to-faculty, and student-to-student interactions and relationships in the college of education (undergraduate) and college of business (graduate) at her university. Schulte developed an ethical climate instrument to measure all three types of interactions. Professors and students responded to such items as "Faculty members go out of their way to help students" and "Students can trust faculty members with confidential information" (faculty to student), "Students act thoughtfully and fairly in the evaluation of professors" and "Students actively participate in class discussions (student to faculty), and "Students feel free to discuss their opinions or beliefs with their peers" and "Students descriptions of their peers' abilities are accurate and fair" (student to student).

In both the undergraduate and graduate samples, faculty rated the quality of faculty-to-student interactions significantly higher than did students. Faculty believed they did a better job of acknowledging outstanding student work, of making exceptions for late work with legitimate excuses, and of being attentive to students during scheduled appointments. But both students and faculty reported that a positive ethical climate is critical for retaining students. Graduate students taking classes with the same group (in a cohort) rated student-to-faculty and student-to-student interactions more favorably than their colleagues in the traditional classroom model.

Professor Schulte and her colleagues believe that the higher power of faculty accounts for their more-optimistic view of ethical climate. The researchers note that perceptions of ethical climate come from the bottom up, not just from the top down. If perceptions of ethical climate came solely from faculty, ethical climate ratings would be significantly higher. How students treat each other and interact with their professors also contributes to the quality of a college's ethical climate. To increase retention, faculty and administrators should create environments that foster cooperation and respect for students.

Sources: Schulte, L. E. (2001). Graduate education faculty and student perceptions of the ethical climate and its importance in the retention of students. *College Student Retention, 3*, 119–136; Schulte, L. E. (2002). A comparison of cohort and non-cohort graduate student perceptions of the ethical climate and its importance in retention. *Journal of College Student Retention, 4*, 29–38; Schulte, L. E., & Carter, A. F. (2004). An assessment of a college of business administration's ethical climate. *The Delta Pi Epsilon Journal, XLVI*, 18–29; Schulte, L. E., Thompson, F., Hayes, K., Noble, J., & Jacobs, E. (2001). Undergraduate faculty and student perceptions of the ethical climate and its importance in retention. *College Student Journal, 35*, 565–576.

Recognition of Risk

Any attempt to foster a positive ethical climate must begin by acknowledging the reality that organizations, like individuals, have their "dark sides." Ethical leaders play a critical role in alerting followers and other leaders to the risks of moral failure. Arizona State University professor Marianne Jennings identifies seven signs that a company may be in ethical danger.[7] Recognizing and responding to these symptoms can help you and your organization avoid disaster.

Sign 1: Pressure to Maintain Numbers

The first sign of ethical trouble is obsession with meeting quantifiable goals. Driven by numbers, companies overstate sales, hide expenses, make bad loans, and ship defective products. Nonprofits also feel the pressure to reach their goal numbers. Universities want to be ranked highly by *U.S. News & World Report* and other publications, so they may lie about graduation and placement rates. Atlanta public school administrators are charged with altering standardized test scores in order to earn performance bonuses. Charities, driven to achieve their fund-raising objectives, may make false claims about how many people they serve.

Sign 2: Fear and Silence

In every moral meltdown, there are indications that something is seriously amiss. For example, employees at Enron circulated a list titled "Top Ten Reasons Enron Restructures So Frequently." Item 7 on the list said, "To keep the outside investment analysts so confused that they will not be able to figure out that we don't know what we're doing." However, few challenge the status quo because those who do so are publicly shamed, demoted, or dismissed. Others don't want to believe that the organization is in trouble; still others are bribed into silence through generous salaries and loan packages.

Sign 3: Young 'Uns and a Bigger-Than-Life CEO

Some CEOs become icons who are adored by the community and the media (although often not by employees). Outsiders are loath to criticize the legendary CEO when everyone else is singing his or her praises. The iconic CEO also surrounds him- or herself with loyal supporters who are often young and inexperienced. For example, CEOs brought in their sons and daughters to help them run American International Group (AIG), Archer Daniels Midland (ADM), and Adelphia, all companies that ran afoul of the law.

Sign 4: Weak Board

The boards of companies on the verge of moral collapse are weak for a variety of reasons. They may have inexperienced members, be made up of friends of the CEO, or be reluctant to reign in a legendary CEO. Members may fail to attend meetings or devote the necessary time to their board roles. Directors at Enron, Tyco, WorldCom, Global Crossing, and other companies failed to stop executives from looting company funds for personal use, making risky investments, lying to investors and regulators, setting up fraudulent accounting schemes, and so forth.

Sign 5: Conflicts of Interest

Conflicts of interest arise when an individual plays two roles and the interests of one role are at odds with those of the other role. Officers of the company are then tempted to profit at the expense of stockholders, employees, and others. That was the case with chief financial officer (CFO) Andrew Fastow of Enron, who made millions from the entities he designed to hide company debt.

Sign 6: Innovation Like No Other

Highly successful companies often believe that they can defy economic and business reality. They might have been the first in a new industry or be headed by an entrepreneurial leader who succeeded against all odds. Their arrogance convinces them that they can continually innovate themselves out of any tight spot. Instead, these groups and their leaders innovate themselves into moral trouble by inventing illegal accounting practices, tax evasion schemes, and faulty business models. The Finova Group grew rapidly by making loans to small businesses and time-share properties turned down by other financial institutions. The firm could charge higher interest, generating greater margins. However, the Finova Group soon had a portfolio full of bad loans. Rather than write these loans off, the company used creative accounting to hide these losses. In some cases, company officers even counted the poor loans as assets.

Sign 7: Goodness in Some Areas Atones for Evil in Others

A good many fallen organizations and leaders try to atone for their sins in one area by doing good in others. Tyco and Dennis Kozlowski, WorldCom and Bernie Ebbers, and Adelphia and John Rigas were all known for their charitable acts: giving to universities and local communities, contributing to disaster relief, encouraging employees to volunteer for service projects, and so on. In the case of endangered organizations, the motive for philanthropy is not serving the common good but soothing the consciences of those involved in fraud, insider trading, accounting tricks, and other misdeeds.

Zero Tolerance for Individual and Collective Destructive Behaviors

Dark-side behaviors are destructive or antisocial actions that deliberately attempt to harm others or the organization.[8] Those who engage in such unethical behaviors are driven to meet their own needs at the expense of coworkers and the group as a whole. Common categories of misbehaviors include incivility, aggression, sexual harassment, and discrimination.

Incivility consists of rude or discourteous actions that disregard others and violate norms for respect.[9] Such actions can be intentional or unintentional. They include leaving a mess for the maintenance staff to pick up, sending a "flaming" e-mail, claiming credit for someone else's work, making fun of a peer, and inadvertently ignoring a team member on the way into the office. Incivility reduces employee job satisfaction, task performance, motivation, loyalty, performance, creativity, and willingness to cooperate.

Aggression refers to consciously trying to hurt others or the organization itself.[10] Aggressive behaviors can take a variety of forms, ranging from refusing to answer e-mails to swearing at coworkers to murder. Such behaviors can be categorized along three dimensions. They can be physical–verbal (destructive words or deeds), active–passive (doing harm by acting or failing to act), or direct–indirect (doing harm directly to the other person or indirectly through an intermediary and attacking something that the target values). Aggression does extensive damage to individuals and organizations. Victims may be hurt; experience more stress, which leads to poor health; become fearful, depressed, or angry; lose the ability to concentrate; and feel less committed to their jobs. Observers of aggressive incidents also experience more anxiety and have a lower sense of well-being and commitment. Performance at the organizational level drops as a product of the aggressive actions of employees. Workplace aggression reduces productivity while increasing absenteeism and turnover. Organizations become the targets of lawsuits and negative publicity.

Sexual harassment is a form of aggression directed largely at women.[11] Quid pro quo harassment occurs when targets are coerced into providing sexual favors in return for keeping their jobs or getting promoted. Hostile work environment harassment exists when job conditions interfere with job performance. Components of hostile working conditions include demeaning comments, suggestive gestures, threats, propositions, bribes, and sexual assault. The work performance of victims declines, and they may quit their jobs. Targets also suffer physically (headaches, sleep loss, nausea, eating disorders) and psychologically (depression, fear, a sense of helplessness).

Discrimination is putting members of selected groups, such as women, minorities, disabled employees, older workers, and homeless people, at a disadvantage. Such negative treatment is generally based on stereotypes and prejudice (e.g., older workers can't learn new skills, Hispanics are lazy). Because of the passage of antidiscrimination laws and changes in societal values, employment discrimination is generally expressed subtly through such behaviors as dismissing the achievements of people of color and women, avoiding members of low-status groups, and hiring and promoting those of similar backgrounds.[12]

Destructive behaviors are all too common in modern organizations. In one study, 20% of the sample reported being the targets of uncivil messages in a given week. In the United States, there were 154,460 incidents of violence resulting in time away from work between 2003–2012 and an average of 700 workplace homicides every year between 1992–2012. One third of women age 18–34 report being victims of sexual harassment at work. The unemployment rate for African Americans is significantly higher than that of Caucasians. The typical black family has only 6% of the wealth of a typical white family, and the typical Latino family has only 8%.[13]

Fortunately, leaders can significantly reduce the rate of destructive behaviors by actively seeking to prevent and control them. Moral leaders do the following:

1. *Create zero-tolerance policies that prohibit antisocial actions.* (We'll take a closer look at codes of ethics later in the chapter.) They insist on employee-to-employee civility, forbid aggression and sexual harassment, and prohibit discrimination. These policies also outlaw other unethical practices like lying to customers or paying kickbacks.

2. *Obey guidelines.* As noted earlier, leaders are powerful role models. Zero-tolerance policies will have little effect if leaders do not follow the rules they set. Ironically, leaders are most likely to violate standards because they believe that they are exceptions to the rules (see the discussion of unhealthy motivations in Chapter 2). Furthermore, because they are in positions of power, leaders are freer to act uncivilly, to bully others, or to offer favors in return for sex.

3. *Constantly monitor for possible violations.* Destructive behavior may be hidden from the view of top leaders. Some managers

are good at "kissing up and kicking down," for example. They act respectfully toward superiors while bullying employees and treating them with disrespect. Ethical leaders actively seek feedback from employees further down the organizational hierarchy. They conduct 360-degree reviews that allow employees to rate their supervisors and provide channels—human relations departments, open-door policies—for reporting misbehaviors. Those who come forward with complaints are protected from retribution.

4. *Move quickly when standards are violated.* Ethical leaders recognize that failing to act sends the wrong message, undermining ethical climate. If left unchecked, incivility escalates into aggression. A culture of aggression forms when abusive members are allowed to act as role models. Victims of sexual harassment won't come forward if they think that their leaders won't respond. Patterns of discrimination perpetuate themselves unless leaders intervene. The U.S. military has been accused of moving slowly to address sexual assaults of both women and men. Officers often discourage victims from reporting sex crimes. Until recently, even if the accused was convicted, the unit's commanding officer could throw out the verdict.[14]

5. *Address the underlying factors that trigger destructive actions.* Moral leaders try to screen out potential employees who have a history of destructive behavior. They also try to eliminate situational elements that produce antisocial action. Important contextual triggers include unpleasant working conditions, job stress, oppressive supervision, perceived injustice (see the discussion below), and extreme competitiveness.[15]

Moral leaders also move quickly to address the destructive actions of groups of employees. In *collective corruption,* two or more individuals cooperate in unethical behavior.[16] They abuse their organizational positions and authority to benefit themselves, their work units, or their organizations. Examples of collective corruption include accounting fraud, price-fixing and bribery, covering up criminal behavior, graft, and nepotism. (A more complete list of corrupt activities is found in Box 10.1.) Observers note that corruption is a slippery slope where the corrupt behaviors of a few individuals can rapidly become part of the organization's culture and ethical climate. First, an individual or group—often encouraged by a leader—decides to engage in an unethical behavior, like bribing a local official to secure a construction contract. If the corrupt decision or act is successful (the bribe leads to a significant profits), then this information is stored in organizational memory and the destructive behavior (bribery) is more likely to be used again in the future. Corruption then becomes the normal routine. Those participating in corrupt activities use a variety of rationalizations to defend their behavior. For instance, they deny that anyone was harmed, claim that they were forced to go along, and appeal to group loyalty to defend their choices. FIFA, the governing

Box 10.1 Categories of Fraud and Misconduct Assessed in KPMG Forensic Survey

KPMG, an accounting and consulting firm, periodically surveys top executives to determine their perceptions of fraud and misconduct in their organizations. KPMG categorizes misbehaviors according to how they affect important groups. The survey assesses the following categories of fraud and misconduct:

COMPROMISING CUSTOMER OR MARKETPLACE TRUST

- Engaging in false or deceptive sales practices
- Submitting false or misleading invoices to customers
- Engaging in anticompetitive practices (e.g., market rigging or "quid pro quo" deals)
- Improperly gathering competitors' confidential information
- Fabricating product quality or safety test results
- Breaching customer or consumer privacy
- Entering into customer contract relationships without proper terms, contracts, or approvals
- Violating contract terms with customers

COMPROMISING SHAREHOLDER OR ORGANIZATIONAL TRUST

- Falsifying or manipulating financial reporting information
- Stealing or misappropriating assets
- Falsifying time and expense reports
- Breaching computer, network, or database controls
- Mishandling confidential or proprietary information

- Violating document retention rules
- Providing inappropriate information to analysts or investors
- Trading securities based on "inside" information
- Engaging in activities that pose a conflict of interest
- Wasting, mismanaging, or abusing the organization's resources

COMPROMISING EMPLOYEE TRUST

- Discriminating against employees
- Engaging in sexual harassment or creating a hostile work environment
- Violating workplace health and safety rules
- Violating employee wage, overtime, or benefit rules
- Breaching employee privacy
- Abusing substances (drugs, alcohol) at work

COMPROMISING SUPPLIER TRUST

- Violating or circumventing supplier selection rules
- Accepting inappropriate gifts or kickbacks from suppliers
- Paying suppliers without accurate invoices or records
- Entering into supplier contracts that lack proper terms, conditions, or approvals
- Violating the intellectual property rights or confidential information of suppliers
- Violating contract or payment terms with suppliers
- Doing business with disreputable suppliers

COMPROMISING PUBLIC OR COMMUNITY TRUST

- Violating environmental standards
- Exposing the public to safety risk
- Making false or misleading claims to the media
- Providing regulators with false or misleading information
- Making improper political contributions to domestic officials
- Making improper payments or bribes to foreign officials
- Doing business with third parties that may be involved in money laundering
- Doing business with third parties prohibited under international trade restrictions and embargoes
- Violating international or human rights

GENERAL

- Violating company values and principles
- Engaging in fraudulent or illegal acts

Source: KPMG Forensic. (2013). *Fraud survey 2013.* Retrieved from https://www.surveys.kpmg.com/aci/fraud_risk.asp. Used with permission.

body of international soccer, is one prominent organization that apparently normalized corruption. A number of top FIFA officials have been arrested on charges of taking bribes. They are accused of accepting money from media outlets, sports equipment companies, and governments in return for granting broadcast and equipment rights and selecting World Cup host countries.

Leaders need to set forth clear ethical expectations and punish offenders before their isolated misbehaviors become part of the organization's memory and operations. If corruption does become part of the group's normal way of doing business, more drastic steps are called for, such as those taken by Siemens Global. For many years, employees at the German engineering firm channeled payments to government officials, primarily in developing countries, to secure contracts. For example, Siemens paid as much as $60 million to produce Argentina's national identity cards and $20 million to build power plants in Israel. When the illegal payment scheme was unearthed in 2006, new CEO Peter Loescher rooted out the corruption by instituting a zero-tolerance policy, removing half the management board, hiring a chief ethics officer, starting an anticorruption training program, and increasing the compliance staff from 86 to 500. The firm, which had to pay $1.6 billion in fines, earned praise from U.S. regulators who cited it as a model for other companies charged with corruption.[17]

Justice

Treating people fairly or justly is another hallmark of an ethical organizational climate.[18] Justice in the workplace takes three forms: distributive, procedural, and interactional. Ethical organizations strive to distribute outcomes like pay, office space, time off, and other organizational resources as fairly as possible. They use fair procedures or policies to make these determinations. Further, moral leaders treat people with dignity and respect and share information about how decisions are made.[19]

Perceptions of justice or injustice have been found to have powerful effects on the attitudes and behaviors of organizational members.[20] Those who believe that their organizations are just are generally more satisfied, committed, trusting, and accepting of authority. They are also more likely to engage in such moral behaviors as helping out other employees and reporting ethical violations to management. In contrast, perceptions of unfair treatment increase such withdrawal behaviors as neglecting job responsibilities, absenteeism, and quitting. Those who believe they have experienced injustice are also more likely to engage in dark-side behaviors like sexual harassment, incivility, and exacting revenge on coworkers or the organization as a whole. In addition, they are less likely to report ethical problems to management. (Turn to Case Study 10.1 for a closer look at companies who have been accused of unjust treatment of some of their employees.)

Strategies for promoting fairness or justice include the following:

- Distribute pay and other benefits according to a well-structured system; explain how pay raises are granted.
- Provide other benefits (training, time off) to employees when they are asked to do more but the budget doesn't allow for raises.
- Offer clear explanations for how resources like budgets and space are distributed; tie decisions to organizational values and purpose.
- Base performance appraisal on job-related criteria; clarify standards and expectations in advance and allow for feedback.
- Involve followers in decision-making processes (grant them a significant voice).
- Allow employees to challenge or appeal job decisions.
- Deal truthfully with organizational members.
- Supply rationales for layoffs and firings; express sincerity, kindness, and remorse.
- Follow through on reports of ethical violations; punish wrongdoers.
- Offer public apologies for injustices and offer compensation to victims of injustice.

Integrity

Integrity is ethical soundness, wholeness, and consistency.[21] All units and organizational levels share a commitment to high moral standards, backing up their ethical talk with their ethical walk. Consistency increases the level of trust, encouraging members and units to be vulnerable to one another.

According to business ethicist Lynn Paine, managers who act with integrity see ethics as a driving force of an enterprise. These leaders recognize that ethical values largely define what an organization is and what it hopes to accomplish. They keep these values in mind when making routine decisions. Their goal? To help constituents learn to govern their own behavior by following these same principles. Paine believes that any effort to improve organizational integrity must include the following elements.[22]

There are sensible, clearly communicated values and commitments. These values and commitments spell out the organization's obligations to external stakeholders (customers, suppliers, neighbors) while appealing to insiders. In highly ethical organizations, members take shared values seriously and don't hesitate to talk about them.

Company leaders are committed to and act on the values. Leaders consistently back the values, use them when making choices, and determine priorities when ethical obligations conflict with one another. For example, former Southwest Airlines president Herb Kelleher put a high value both on the needs of his employees and on customer service. However, it's clear that his workers came first. He didn't hesitate to take their side when customers unfairly criticized them. Such principled leadership was missing at Arthur Andersen, which used to be one of the largest accounting firms in the country. Andersen accountants certified the financial statements of Qwest, Waste Management, Boston Chicken, Global Crossing, WorldCom, and the Baptist Foundation of Arizona, which were all found guilty of accounting fraud. They were reluctant to challenge the accounting practices of clients because they didn't want to lose lucrative consulting contracts with these organizations. Andersen's managing partners dissolved the firm after executives were convicted for obstruction of justice for shredding Enron documents.[23]

The values are part of the routine decision-making process and are factored into every important organizational activity. Ethical considerations shape such activities as planning and goal setting, spending, gathering and sharing information, evaluation, and promotion.

Systems and structures support and reinforce organizational commitments. Systems and structures, such as the organizational chart, how work is processed, budgeting procedures, and product development, serve the organization's values. (I'll have more to say about the relationship between ethics and structure later in the chapter.)

Leaders throughout the organization have the knowledge and skills they need to make ethical decisions. Organizational leaders make ethical choices every day. To demonstrate integrity, they must have the necessary skills, knowledge, and experience. Ethics education and training must be part of their professional development.

Paine and other observers warn us not to confuse integrity with compliance. Ethical compliance strategies are generally responses to outside pressures such as media scrutiny, the U.S. Sentencing Commission guidelines, or the Sarbanes–Oxley Act. Under these federal guidelines, corporate executives can be fined and jailed not only for their ethical misdeeds but also for failing to take reasonable steps to prevent the illegal behavior of employees. Although compliance tactics look good to outsiders, they frequently don't have a lasting impact on ethical climate.[24] Large firms typically have formal ethics strategies in place, including ethics codes and policies, ethics officers, and systems for registering and dealing with ethical concerns and complaints. However, all too often, these programs have minimal influence on company operations. Policies may not be enforced; some complaint hotlines are rarely used; compliance efforts might be underfunded; CEOs may fail to communicate to employees about ethics.[25]

Trust

Ethical organizations are marked by a high degree of trust. Not only do members trust one another, but also, together, they develop a shared or aggregate level of trust that becomes part of the group's culture. *Organizational trust* describes the collective set of positive expectations members hold about the intentions and behaviors of other stakeholders (coworkers, superiors, followers, other departments), which are based on their experiences and interactions as organizational members.[26] These expectations shape how vulnerable individuals and groups are when interacting with one another and with the organization as a whole. For example, a follower who trusts her supervisor is more likely to take the risk of admitting that a project isn't going well. Two team leaders who trust each other are more likely to cooperate to carry out a new change initiative. On the other hand, employees who don't believe that the organization carries through on its commitments aren't likely to put forth their best efforts.

Over the past several decades, trust has moved from the periphery to the center of organizational studies, primarily because it has been linked to so many positive outcomes.[27] Trust binds group members together, fostering collaboration and communication; lowering costs; reducing turnover; encouraging organizational learning, innovation, and work effort; and generating employee satisfaction and commitment. High-trust organizations make higher-quality decisions, operate more efficiently, and are more productive and profitable. They also behave in a more ethical manner. That's because trust involves vulnerability and obligation or duty. Those who trust believe that the other party—individual, group, or organization—will carry through on promises and commitments. They put themselves in a vulnerable position because they are depending on others and will suffer if these parties break their commitments. High-trust organizations fulfill their moral obligations by protecting the rights and interests of members and outsiders.

Collective trust is made up of several factors or dimensions. According to one classification system, members judge an organization to be trustworthy if the group (1) makes good-faith efforts to keep its commitments, (2) is honest when negotiating such commitments, and (3) does not take unfair advantage of members even when provided with the opportunity to do so.[28] Other researchers identify five dimensions of organizational trust: competence, openness, concern, reliability, and identification.[29] *Competence* is the collective perception that leadership—both supervisory and top management—is effective and that the organization can survive. Organizational survival depends on such factors as the ability to create new products rapidly, meet competitive pressures, and find new markets. *Openness* or honesty is the belief that management shares information and is sincere. *Concern* reflects caring and empathy. Concerned leaders (and followers) don't take advantage of the vulnerability of others. *Reliability* describes perceptions of consistent and dependable behavior. Those organizations that match their words and actions generate trust; those that fail to walk the talk undermine trust. *Identification* is the feeling of affiliation and association with the organization. (Determine your work group's degree of trust in another department by completing Self-Assessment 10.2.)

Leaders are key to the development of organizational trust. Moral leaders lay the foundation for collective trust by acting in a trustworthy manner. They demonstrate the character traits described in Chapter 3 (e.g., compassion, humility, courage). They also communicate a clear sense of mission and vision, foster an atmosphere that encourages openness and sharing, are consistent in their behavior, demonstrate caring, follow through on promises and commitments, and so forth. (See Case Study 10.2 for an example of a CEO who has deliberately created a low-trust culture.)

Process Focus (Concern for Means and Ends)

Concern for how an organization achieves its goals is another important indicator of a healthy ethical climate. In far too many organizations, leaders set demanding performance goals but intentionally or unintentionally ignore how these objectives are to be reached. Instead, they pressure employees to produce sales and profits by whatever means possible. Followers then feel powerless and alienated, becoming estranged from the rest of the group. Sociologists use the term *anomie* to refer to this sense of normlessness and unease that results when rules lose their force.[30] Anomie increases the likelihood that group members will engage in illegal activities and reduces their resistance to demands from authority figures who want them to break the law. Loss of confidence in the organization may also encourage alienated employees to retaliate against coworkers and the group as a whole.

Leaders can address the problem of anomie by making sure that goals are achieved through ethical means. False promises cannot be used to land accounts, all debts must be fully disclosed to investors, kickbacks are prohibited, and so on. They can also make a stronger link between means and ends through ethics programs that address all aspects of organizational ethical performance.

Structural Reinforcement

An organization's structure and policies shouldn't undermine the ethical standards of its members. Instead, as I noted in our discussion of integrity, structure should encourage higher ethical performance on the part of both leaders and followers. Four elements of an organization's structure have a particularly strong impact on moral behavior:

1. *Monetary and nonmonetary reward systems.* Organizations often encourage unethical behavior by rewarding it.[31] Consider the case of the software company that paid programmers $20 for each software bug they found and corrected. Soon, programmers were deliberately creating bugs to fix! Another software firm headquartered in Korea gave large incentives to salespeople for making lofty sales targets. This encouraged employees to misrepresent sales by reporting that customers had paid when they had not and by having fellow workers pose as clients. In one nine-month period, 70% of reported sales were fictitious.[32] A visit to the local 10-minute oil change shop provides another case of the impact of misplaced rewards. Some lube and oil franchises pay managers and employees based in part on how many additional services and parts they sell beyond the basic oil change. As a consequence, unscrupulous mechanics persuade car owners to buy unneeded air filters, transmission flushes, and wiper blades. It is not always easy to determine all the consequences of a particular reward system. However, ethical leaders make every effort to ensure that desired moral behaviors are rewarded, not discouraged.

2. *Performance and evaluation processes.* Performance and evaluation processes must reflect the balance between means and ends described earlier, monitoring both

how and *whether* goals are achieved. Ethically insensitive monitoring processes fail to detect illegal and immoral behavior and may actually make such practices more likely. As noted earlier, when poor behavior goes unpunished, followers may assume that leaders condone and expect such actions. Former giant brokerage house Salomon Brothers is a case in point. In the early 1990s, a government securities trader at the firm violated U.S. Treasury Department regulations and confessed to then-CEO John Gutfreund. Gutfreund took no action against the rogue trader, in part because he was a star performer. Failure to swiftly punish this star employee enabled him to continue his illegal behavior and cost Salomon Brothers millions in fines and much of its stock and bond business.[33]

3. *Decision-making rights and responsibilities.* Ethical conduct is more likely when workers are responsible for ethical decisions and have the authority to choose how to respond. Leaders at ethical organizations do all they can to ensure that those closest to the process or problem can communicate their concerns about ethical issues. These managers also empower followers to make and implement their choices. Unfortunately, employees with the most knowledge are often excluded from the decision-making process or lack the power to follow through on their choices. Such was the case in the *Columbia* space shuttle disaster. Lower-level managers were concerned that a piece of foam had damaged the shuttle's protective shield during liftoff. However, higher-ranking National Aeronautics and Space Administration (NASA) officials dismissed their worries. During reentry, superheated gas entered a 6- to 10-inch hole, triggering an explosion that killed seven astronauts.[34]

4. *Corporate governance.* Boards of directors occupy the top of the organizational structure. They select and oversee the managers who run the company or nonprofit while protecting the interests of the stockholders or supporters. Their ethical duties include (1) ensuring that the CEO and senior management operate in an ethical fashion, (2) guaranteeing that top leadership establishes a culture of integrity and compliance, (3) producing accurate financial statements, (4) listening to shareholders, and (5) treating employees and outsiders fairly.[35] Weak boards, as noted earlier, fail to carry out these responsibilities. Effective boards, on the other hand, are made up of independent members who have the expertise as well as the time and energy to devote to their duties. They are actively engaged in the life of the organization by gathering information from employees and lower-level managers, regularly visiting store locations, and so on. Directors on effective boards prevent groupthink by welcoming dissent rather than punishing those who threaten the group's cohesion.[36]

Organizational Citizenship

Concern for those outside the organization is another sign of a healthy ethical climate. Ethical organizations act as good citizens. They acknowledge their obligations to their communities and use their influence to improve society. Organizational citizenship is made of three components. The first is *stakeholder focus*. Organizational citizens recognize that their responsibilities extend to all groups who have an interest or stake in their polices and operations. Stakeholder theorists argue that organizational leaders have an ethical obligation to consider such groups because they have intrinsic value and ought to be treated justly. Reaching out to these parties contributes to the common good of society.[37] Organizational stakeholders might include shareholders, suppliers, competitors, customers, creditors, unions, social activists, governments, local communities, and the general public.[38] Good corporate and organizational citizens seek to be accountable to and to engage with these groups, cooperating with them whenever possible and minimizing the negative impact of organizational activities. When needed, these organizations engage in dialogue with their critics, as Nike did after years of ignoring public outcry about conditions at the factories of its overseas suppliers. The firm invited human rights, labor, and environmental officials to company headquarters to discuss international worker issues.[39]

Corporate social responsibility (CSR) is the second component of organizational citizenship. CSR describes the activities of companies and other organizations aimed at improving the welfare of society.[40] (See the earlier discussion of CSR in Chapter 8.) CSR can take many different forms. Good corporate citizens send volunteers to work on Habitat for Humanity building projects, sponsor food drives, provide free dental clinics in developing countries, set up philanthropic organizations to give money to worthy causes, and so forth. The public increasingly demands that corporations behave responsibly. Seventy-nine percent of Americans believe that businesses should support social causes, for example, and a survey of citizens in 23 countries found that 90% wanted firms to focus on more than profits.[41] Companies that engage in social responsibility efforts frequently benefit, building their reputations while attracting customers. Their employees are loyal, perform better, and are more likely to engage in organizational citizenship behaviors. CSR also makes firms more attractive as potential employers.[42] CSR would be ethically justified even if it didn't pay practical dividends, however. CSR behaviors are altruistic, recognize the dignity of others and promote justice. (Case Study 10.3 describes a leader who runs a profitable business while serving a higher purpose.)

Sustainability or environmental care makes up the third element of organizational citizenship. Sustainable organizations try to protect the environment, doing business in a way that protects future generations.[43] They address environmental problems by taking such steps as capping plant emissions, using recycled components, creating less-toxic products, reducing oil consumption, and buying from environmentally friendly suppliers. They are constantly seeking to improve, as in the case of manufacturers that plan for all the environmental impacts over the life cycle of a product. Patagonia, as we saw in Chapter 8, carefully considers the environmental costs of its garments and tries to mitigate those costs through recycling and reuse. BMW builds cars that are easier to disassemble when they leave the road for good.

Responsible corporate citizens engage in "triple bottom line" accounting. They evaluate their success based not just on financial results but also on their social and environmental performance.[44] Social audits have become "mainstream business practice," with over 90% of the world's 250 largest corporations reporting such information.[45] Starbucks, for example, commissions an annual social responsibility report that indicates whether the company is reaching its social goals.[46] The chain estimates that approximately 96% of its coffee is grown sustainably. At the same time, it supports coffee-growing communities in Africa, South and Central America, and China. Starbucks recently opened its 500th environmentally certified store while reducing water consumption by 23%. Employees can earn free college degrees online through Arizona State University. (More examples of socially responsible corporations can be found in the discussion of core values to follow.)

CLIMATE-BUILDING TOOLS

To build or create ethical organizational climates, leaders rely heavily on four tools: core ideology, codes of ethics, socialization, and ethics training.

Discovering Core Ideology

Management experts James Collins and Jerry Porras use the term *core ideology* to refer to the central identity or character of an organization. The character of outstanding companies remains constant, even as these firms continually learn and adapt. According to Collins and Porras, "Truly great companies understand the difference between what should never change and what should be open for change, between what is genuinely sacred and what is not."[47]

Core values are the first component of core ideology. (See Box 10.2 for some examples.) One way to determine whether a value is sacred to your organization is to ask, "What would happen if we were penalized for holding this standard?" If you can't honestly say that you would keep this value if it cost your group market share or profits, then it shouldn't show up on your final list. To determine core values, Collins and Porras recommend the Mars Group technique. In this approach, participants imagine they have been asked to re-create the very best attributes of their organization (school, business, nonprofit) on another planet. Groups are limited to five to seven people, since space on the rocket ship is scarce. Group members work from personal to organizational values by considering these questions:

- What core values (values that you would hold regardless of whether they were rewarded) do you personally bring to your work?

- What values would you tell your children that you hold at work and that you hope they will hold as working adults?

- If you woke up tomorrow morning with enough money to retire, would you continue to live with those core values? Can you envision them being as valid for you 100 years from now as they are today?

- Would you want to hold these core values even if one or more of them became a competitive disadvantage?

- If you were to start a new organization in a different line of work, what core values would you build into the new organization, regardless of industry?

Groups summarize their conclusions and present them to others in the organization, comparing their values with those of other groups traveling on other spaceships.

Core purpose is the second part of an organization's ideology. *Purpose* is the group's reason for being that reflects the ideals of its members. Here are some examples of corporate purpose/mission statements from some of the largest corporations in four English-speaking nations:[48]

Box 10.2 Core Values

EATON CORPORATION

- Make our customers the focus of everything we do
- Recognize our people as our greatest asset
- Treat each other with respect
- Be fair, honest, and open
- Be considerate of the environment and our communities
- Keep our commitments
- Strive for excellence

LEVI STRAUSS

- Empathy—Walking in other people's shoes
- Originality—Being authentic and innovative
- Integrity—Doing the right thing
- Courage—Standing up for what we believe

AMGEN

- Be science based
- Compete intensely and win
- Create value for patients, staff, and stockholders
- Be ethical
- Trust and respect each other
- Ensure quality
- Work in teams
- Collaborate, communicate, and be accountable

DENNY'S

- Giving our best
- Appreciating others
- A can-do attitude

FIRST HORIZON NATIONAL CORPORATION

- Exceptional teamwork
- Individual accountability
- Absolute determination
- Knowing our customers
- Doing the right thing

CHARLES STEWART MOTT FOUNDATION

- Act honestly, truthfully, and with integrity
- Treat every individual with dignity and respect
- Be responsible, transparent, and accountable
- Benefit communities

Sources: Abrahams, J. (2007). *101 mission statements from top companies.* Berkeley, CA: Ten Speed Press; Kidder, R. M. (2004). Foundation codes of ethics: Why do they matter, what are they, and how are they relevant to philanthropy? *New Decisions for Philanthropic Fundraising, 45,* 75–83.

United States

To provide comprehensive pharmacy solutions that improve productivity and profitability and result in superior patient care and satisfaction. (McKesson)

We are a global family with a proud heritage passionately committed to providing personal mobility for people around the world. (Ford Motor)

Use our pioneering spirit to responsibly deliver energy to the world. (ConocoPhillips)

Australia

To help our customers fulfill their aspirations. (National Australia Bank)

To deliver to customers the right shopping experience each and every time. (Woolworths)

To be the leading international property company. (Lendlease)

Canada

To be the best at helping customers become financially better off. (Bank of Nova Scotia)

To be the world's best gold mining company by finding, acquiring, developing, and producing quality reserves in a safe, profitable, and socially responsible manner. (Barrick Gold Corporation)

To be the world's leading manufacturer of planes and trains. (Bombardier)

Britain

To create value for customers to earn their lifetime loyalty. (Tesco)

Deliver an ever-improving quality shopping experience for our customers with great products at fair prices. (J Sainsbury)

To be the leading systems company, innovating for a safer world. (BAE Systems)

Asking the "Five Whys" is one way to identify organizational purpose. Start with a description of what your organization does and then ask why that activity is important five separate times. Each "Why?" will get you closer to the fundamental mission of your group.

Your organization's purpose statement should inspire members. (Don't make high profits or stock dividends your goal, because these don't motivate people at every level of the organization.) Your purpose should also serve as an organizational anchor. Every other element of your organization—business plans, expansion efforts, buildings, products—will come and go, but your purpose and values will remain. ("Leadership Ethics at the Movies: *Spotlight*" describes one team that remained true to the organizational mission.) Appreciative inquiry (AI) is another effective tool for developing a shared understanding of ethical values. Participants in the AI process set out to discover the organization's positive core and use the group's strengths to guide individual and collective action.[49] AI has been used in a variety of organizational settings, for example, to promote creativity and innovation, facilitate strategic planning, boost quality, and reduce employee turnover as well as to improve ethical performance.

Key Cast Members: Michael Keaton, Mark Ruffalo, Rachel McAdams, Liev Shreiber, John Slatter, Brian d'Arcy, Stanley Tucci

Synopsis: The Boston Globe's Spotlight team is a small group of investigative reporters who take on topics that require months of research before publication. In 2001, a new editor (played by Schreiber) challenges the team, led by Robbie Robinson (Keaton), to investigate the case of Catholic priest John Geoghan. Geoghan sexually abused a number of children but was moved from parish to parish by Cardinal Bernard Law, Archbishop of Boston. The journalists uncover a widespread pattern of abuse and cover-up involving eighty-seven priests. During its investigation, the Spotlight team faces opposition from the Catholic hierarchy as well as from friends and colleagues who support the Church. Archbishop Law resigns after the series appears in print and the worldwide scope of the abusive priest crisis emerges.

Rating: R for sexual content and some sexual language

Themes: mission, values, courage, persistence, leader shadows, corruption, deception

Discussion Starters

1. Why didn't *The Boston Globe* investigate charges of priest sexual abuse earlier?

2. How did the legal system protect abusive priests and the church?

3. What should be the mission and values of journalists? Who do they serve?

4. Who are the heroes of this story?

AI begins by choosing an affirmative topic, based on the assumption that what organizational members study will determine the kind of organizations they create. Asking positive questions ("What are our values?" "What do ethics mean to us?") elicits positive examples and achievements. Once the affirmative topic is selected, AI moves through four stages: discovery, dream, design, and destiny.

The discovery phase identifies the best of what has been and what is. Interviews and brainstorming sessions highlight organizational achievements and important traditions. These could include stories of organizational heroes and how the organization lived up to its commitments during tough times or descriptions of the group's tradition of social responsibility. In the dream phase, participants look to the future to ask, "What might be?" They develop a vision of the organization's ethical future, focusing on the group's ultimate purpose ("What is the world calling us to become?"). The design stage incorporates both the discovery and dream phases by describing exactly how the organization will look and act if it lives up to its values. This ideal organization integrates the positive core elements of the group into the dream created by participants; for instance, a place where everyone can voice his or her concerns about unethical behavior without fear of punishment or a place where commitment to the community takes precedence over short-term profits. In the last stage—destiny—participants collectively commit themselves to building the desired organization. They might design tactics for encouraging dissent, for instance, or develop new community outreach programs.

South African industrial/organizational psychologists Leon van Vuuren and Freddie Crous describe how one university department used AI to develop "an ethical way forward."[50] After identifying core ethical values and experiences during the discovery phase, department members identified key themes during the dream stage. They then put these values in the form of propositions during the design phase. Their important propositions included "We are committed to personal growth and meaningful work," "We respect the uniqueness and contributions of others," and "We act with integrity supported by visible ethical leadership." Departmental members committed themselves to supporting these values, which were formalized in a code of ethics, during the destiny stage.

Codes of Ethics

Codes of ethics are among the most common ethics tools. Companies listed on the New York Stock Exchange and the NASDAQ are required to have them, and under the Sarbanes–Oxley Act, public firms must disclose whether they have such codes for their senior executives.[51] Many government departments, professional associations, social service agencies, and schools have developed codes as well. Nevertheless, formal ethics statements are as controversial as they are popular. Skeptics make these criticisms:[52]

- Codes are too vague to be useful.
- Codes may not be widely distributed or read.
- Most codes are developed as public relations documents designed solely to improve an organization's image.
- Codes don't improve the ethical climate of organizations or produce more ethical behavior.
- Codes often become the final word on the subject of ethics.
- Codes are hard to apply across cultures and in different situations.
- Codes often lack adequate enforcement provisions.
- Codes often fail to spell out which ethical obligations should take priority, or they put the needs of the organization ahead of those of society as a whole.
- Adherence to codes often goes unrewarded.

The experience of Enron highlights the shortcomings of formal ethical statements. Company officials had a "beautifully written" code of ethics that specifically prohibited the off-the-books financial deals that led to its bankruptcy.[53] Unfortunately, these same executives convinced the board of directors to waive this prohibition.

Defenders of ethical codes point to their potential benefits. First, a code describes an organization's ethical stance both to members and to the outside world. Newcomers, in particular, look to the code for guidance about an organization's ethical standards and values. They learn about potential ethical problems they may face in carrying out their duties. Second, a formal ethics statement can improve the group's image while protecting it from lawsuits and further regulation. In the case of wrongdoing, an organization can point to the code as evidence that the unethical behavior is limited to a few individuals and not the policy of the company as a whole. Third, referring to a code can encourage followers and leaders to resist unethical group and organizational pressures. Fourth, a written document can have a direct, positive influence on ethical behavior. Students who sign honor codes, for example, are significantly less likely to plagiarize and cheat on tests.[54] Employees in companies with formal codes of ethics judge themselves, their coworkers, and their leaders to be more ethical than do workers in companies that don't have codes. Members of code organizations believe that their organizations are more supportive of ethical behavior and express a higher level of organizational commitment.[55]

There's no doubt that a code of ethics can be a vague document that has little impact on how members act. A number of organizations use these statements for purposes of image, not integrity. They want to appear concerned about ethical issues while protecting themselves from litigation. Just having a code on file doesn't mean that it will be read or used, as in the case of Enron. Nonetheless, creating an ethical statement can be an important first step on the road to organizational integrity. Although a code doesn't guarantee moral improvement, it is hard to imagine an ethical organization without one. Codes can focus attention on important ethical standards, outline expectations, and help people act more appropriately. They have the most impact when senior executives make them a priority and follow their provisions while rewarding followers who do the same.

Communication ethicists Richard Johannesen, Kathleen Valde, and Karen Whedbee believe that many of the objections to formal codes could be overcome if organizations followed these guidelines:[56]

- Distinguish between ideals and minimum conditions. Identify which parts of the statement are goals to strive for and which are minimal or basic ethical standards.

- Design the code for ordinary circumstances. Members shouldn't have to demonstrate extraordinary courage or make unusual sacrifices in order to follow the code. Ensure that average employees can follow its guidelines.

- Use clear, specific language. Important abstract terms such as *reasonable*, *distort*, and *falsify* should be explained and illustrated.

- Be logically coherent. Prioritize obligations. Which commitments are most important: The client? The public? The employer? The profession?

- Protect the larger community. Don't protect the interests of the organization at the expense of the public. Speak to the needs of outside groups.

- Focus on issues of particular importance to group members. The code should address the group's unique moral issues.

- Stimulate further discussion and modification. Don't file the code away or treat it as the final word on the subject of collective ethics. Use it to spark ethical discussion and modify its provisions when needed.

- Provide guidance for the entire organization and the profession to which it belongs. Spell out the consequences when the business or nonprofit as a whole acts unethically. Who should respond, and how? What role should outside groups (professional associations, accrediting bodies, regulatory agencies) play in responding to the organization's ethical transgressions?

- Outline the moral principles behind the code. Explain *why* an action is right based on ethical standards (deontology, utilitarianism, altruism) like those described in Chapter 5.

- Encourage widespread input. Draw on all constituencies, including management, union members, and professionals, when developing the provisions of the code.

- Back the code with enforcement. Create procedures for interpreting the code and applying sanctions. Ethics offices and officers should set up systems for reporting problems, investigating charges, and reaching conclusions. Possible punishments for ethical transgressions include informal warnings, formal reprimands that are entered into employment files, suspensions without pay, and terminations.

Most codes of ethics address the following:[57]

- *Conflicts of interest.* Conflicts of interest arise when an employee benefits at the expense of the organization or can't exercise independent judgment because of an investment, activity, or association. Even the appearance of a conflict of interest is problematic.

- *Records, funds, and assets.* Organizations must keep accurate records and protect funds and other assets. Such records (including financial statements) must meet state and federal regulations.

- *Information.* In for-profit organizations, employees can be liable if they or even their families reveal confidential information that undermines performance or competitive advantage. In the public sector, codes of ethics encourage employees to share information rather than to withhold it from the public.

- *Outside relationships.* This category addresses contact with customers, suppliers, competitors, contractors, and other outside individuals and organizations and includes prohibitions against bad-mouthing the competition, price-fixing, and the sharing of sensitive information.

- *Employment practices.* This category covers discrimination, sexual harassment, drug use, voluntary activities, and related human resource issues.

- *Other practices.* This category sets policies related to a variety of other topics, including health and safety, the use of technology, the environment, political activities, and the use of organizational assets for personal benefit.

If you're interested in developing or refining a code of ethics, you can use the examples in Box 10.3 as a model.

Ethical Socialization Processes

Socialization describes how individuals make the transition from outsiders to organizational members. During this process, they learn how to perform their individual roles and, at the same time, absorb information about the organization's culture. There are a number of reasons why an organization's socialization efforts can help create a positive ethical climate.[58] Newcomers are generally anxious about how to perform in a new environment. This makes them more open to influence and instruction about ethical behavior. Their values are being formed and, once in place, these principles will shape their behavior for the rest of their organizational careers. When newcomers become established organizational members, they then communicate and model important values and behaviors to the next generations of members.

Socialization occurs in three phases.[59] *Anticipatory socialization* begins before an individual joins a new organization or organizational unit and is shaped by past work experiences, friends, families, and other factors. You probably had expectations about what college would be like well before you completed high school, for example. You then formed impressions of your particular school based its website, talking with alums, and, probably most importantly, speaking with a representative and visiting campus. *Encounter socialization* takes place after newcomers begin their membership. This phase includes formal training and orientation sessions (such as freshmen orientation) designed to integrate newcomers into the organization. Rookies also come under the influence of socializing agents. These include veteran coworkers, supervisors, and mentors. In the college setting, resident assistants, peer advisors, student life staff, upper classmen, and others act as socializing agents. *Metamorphosis socialization* marks the end of the transition to organizational life. At this point, the individual has mastered basic skills and organizational knowledge and is considered a group member. If you are a sophomore or a second-year graduate student, chances are you have entered this phase. (You can evaluate your ethical socialization process as a student or employee by completing Item 11 under "For Further Exploration, Challenge, and Self-Assessment.")

Ethical leaders make the most of the socialization process by clearly describing the organization's values and ethical climate in recruitment materials and during face-to-face interviews. They ask applicants about their ethical experiences and standards. Ethics is a top priority in orientation and training sessions (see the discussion of training below). Managers introduce the group's core ideology and code of ethics, introduce ethics officers and procedures, and so on. Newcomers are placed with socializing agents who reinforce values and standards and are given channels for expressing their concerns about current practices.

Box 10.3 Ethics Codes: A Sampler

CONFLICTS OF INTEREST (CUMMINS INC.)

All of Cummins's employees are expected to use nondiscriminatory practices throughout the supplier selection process. Every employee is expected to avoid any situation in which his or her interests (or those of his or her family) may conflict with the interests of the company. Every employee with a financial interest in any actual or potential supplier or customer must disclose that interest to his or her supervisor immediately and, if applicable, in his or her annual Ethics Certification Statement.

RECORDS, FUNDS, AND ASSETS (PPG INDUSTRIES)

Every individual involved in creating, transmitting, or entering information into PPG's financial records is responsible for doing so accurately, completely, and with appropriate supporting documentation. Compliance with established accounting procedures and controls is necessary at all times. PPG's records, books, and documents must accurately reflect the Company's transactions and provide a full account of the organization's assets, liabilities, revenues, and expenses.

PROTECTING INFORMATION (CITIGROUP)

You must safeguard all personal and confidential information about our clients by ensuring that client information is used only for authorized purposes relating to your job, is only shared with authorized persons and organizations, and is properly and securely maintained.

OUTSIDE RELATIONSHIPS (HEWLETT-PACKARD)

We honor human rights.

- Support and respect the protection of human rights and ensure that our business partners and suppliers do the same.
- Ensure that child labor, prison or forced labor, and physical punishment are never permitted in any operation of HP [Hewett-Packard] or our business partners or suppliers.

EMPLOYMENT PRACTICES (CUMMINS INC.)

Treatment of Each Other at Work

Each employee will treat every other employee, every customer, every vendor, and all others met in the course of work with dignity and respect. Harassment of any type in the workplace will not be tolerated.

OTHER PRACTICES (COCA-COLA)

Personal Political Activity

The Coca-Cola Company encourages personal participation in the political process in a manner consistent with all relevant laws and Company guidelines.

- The Company will not reimburse employees for personal political activity.
- Do not use the Company's reputation or assets, including your time at work, to further your own political activities or interests.

Sources: Center for the Study of Ethics in the Professions at Illinois Institute of Technology. (2013). *Index of codes.* Retrieved from http://ethics.iit.edu/codes; Citigroup, Coca-Cola, Cummins, Eaton, Hewlett-Packard, and PPG corporate websites.

Ethical theorists Blake Ashforth and Vikas Anand argue that, unfortunately, organizational newcomers can be socialized into corrupt activities as well as ethical ones. (See our discussion of contextual pressures in Chapter 2.) These individuals accept unethical and illegal behavior as part of becoming a group member. They can be corrupted through three different avenues: co-optation, incrementalism, and compromise. In *co-optation*, leaders offer rewards that reduce newcomers' discomfort with unethical behavior. Followers may not realize that these incentives are skewing their judgment, making it easier to rationalize destructive behavior. For example, health maintenance organization (HMO) doctors earning cost-reduction bonuses may convince themselves that they are justified in not ordering needed medical tests for patients.

Incrementalism gradually introduces newcomers to unethical practices, leading them up the "ladder of corruption." New members are first persuaded to engage in a practice that is only mildly unethical, such as using private customer information to make additional sales. They then turn to rationalizations offered by peers ("Everybody does it"; "Nobody was really hurt"; "They got what they deserved") to relieve the cognitive dissonance produced by this act. After the initial practice becomes typical, acceptable behavior, individuals are then encouraged to move to increasingly corrupt activities. Eventually, they find themselves engaging in behaviors (e.g., secretly selling private customer information to other companies) they would have rejected when they first joined the organization.

Compromise backs individuals into corruption as they try to solve difficult problems and resolve conflicts. Politicians, for example, make lots of compromises as they try to keep and expand their power. Cutting deals and forming alliances makes it harder for them to maintain their ethical principles. Police detectives also find themselves making compromises. To gather the information they need to solve crimes, they may compromise with informants. First, they overlook minor crimes committed by their sources. Later, they may excuse their informants when they engage in much more serious crimes. Boston Federal Bureau of Investigation (FBI) agent John Connolly fell victim to compromise when he enlisted childhood friend Whitey Bulger as an informant to crack down on the Italian mafia. Bulger, convicted of murdering eleven people, ran his own crime syndicate. Connolly protected Bulger instead of prosecuting him. He gave Bulger information that led to the death of one potential witness and warned the gangster that he was about to be arrested, allowing Bulger to remain free for another sixteen years.

The danger of dysfunctional socialization is greatest when followers join *social cocoons*. A social cocoon is a strong culture that holds values and norms very different from those held by the rest of the organization or society as a whole. New employees who strongly identify with the group tend to compartmentalize their lives, holding one set of values while at work and another outside the job.

Ashforth and Anand believe that recognizing the routes to corruption can equip followers to resist their influence, as can considering the perspective of suppliers, community members, and others outside the group. These investigators encourage organizations to have periodic "introspection days," when organizational members take a careful look at all of their activities and determine the ethical implications of their actions. External facilitators can help employees determine if they are using rationalizations to excuse corrupt behavior.[60]

Ethics Training

Formal ethics training can play an important role in creating and maintaining ethical climates. As noted above, ethics instruction can help promote ethical behavior in newcomers. Training sessions for experienced employees can heighten sensitivity to moral danger signs, reduce destructive behaviors, foster trust, promote organizational integrity, reinforce shared purpose and values, and clarify ethical standards and expectations. Ethics training plays a critical role in helping large organizations meet compliance guidelines set by the U.S. Sentencing Commission. Of course, training efforts do not guarantee that participants will make better moral choices or behave ethically. Nevertheless, effective ethics training can make a positive difference. Effective training does the following:[61]

1. *Focuses on the organization's unique ethical problems.* Every organization faces a unique set of ethical problems and issues. Issues that accountants face (audits, tax advice, financial statements, earnings projections, quarterly earnings statements) are different from those faced by sales professionals (product safety, pricing, product placement, advertising claims), for instance. Introduce examples drawn directly from the organization, industry, and profession. Then equip trainees with the tools they need to address these dilemmas.

2. *Taps into the experiences of participants.* Encourage trainees to reflect on their own values and decision-making strategies as well as important moral moments or episodes in their lives. Solicit their input when selecting issues and cases to discuss. Ask participants to provide dilemmas and insights from their own experiences. They then become instructors, teaching one another. They also receive valuable feedback that enables them to better manage their dilemmas.

3. *Actively engages participants.* Key concepts can be presented in lectures and handouts but you should spend most class time in dyadic, small-group, and large-group discussion, acting as a facilitator. Introduce case studies that raise significant issues and engage the emotions of participants (see the discussion of dual processing in Chapter 6). Ask questions and debate issues. Make sure the training space can be adapted to a variety of teaching strategies. Use online tools to augment—not replace—classroom interaction. Even though Web-based ethics training is becoming increasingly popular because it is cheap and convenient, online-only programs don't appear to be as effective as classroom training. That's because online instruction doesn't facilitate in-depth consideration of complex ethical cases and issues.

4. *Reinforces the organization's ideology and standards.* Training sessions should reinforce other components of the group's ethical climate. Trainers, supervisors, and executives should highlight the group's purpose and core values, tell stories about the

organization's ethical heroes, discuss the code of ethics, provide information about reporting systems, and so on.

5. *Is integrated into the entire curriculum.* Ethics instruction shouldn't be limited only to stand-alone sessions but should be integrated throughout the organizations' training program. For example, discussion of bribery and price-fixing can be integrated into sales instruction. Incorporating ethics in a variety of workshops increases the likelihood that moral concerns will become part of the organization's fabric, helping it to act with integrity.

IMPLICATIONS AND APPLICATIONS

- As a leader, you will serve as an ethics officer of your organization by setting an example for followers and by making sure that ethical messages aren't drowned out by messages about tasks and profits.

- Organizations have varying ethical orientations or ethical climates that affect their ethical decision making and behavior. Climates marked by self-interest are most likely to encourage unethical behavior.

- Be alert to signs that the organization may be headed for moral failure. These include pressure to maintain the numbers; fear and silence; young 'uns and a bigger-than-life CEO; a weak board; conflicts of interest; innovation like no other; and assuming that goodness in some areas atones for evil in others.

- Enforce zero-tolerance policies for individual (incivility, aggression, sexual harassment, discrimination) and collective (fraud, bribery, price-fixing) destructive actions.

- Create perceptions of organizational justice by distributing resources fairly, following equitable processes, and treating others with dignity and respect.

- Build organizational trust—collective perceptions of competence, openness, concern, reliability, and identification—by acting in a trustworthy manner and encouraging others to do the same.

- Recognize that organizational integrity develops through clearly communicated values and commitments, leaders who are committed to these values, application of the values to routine decisions, systems and structures that support organizational commitments, and members who are equipped to make wise ethical choices.

- Don't confuse compliance with integrity. Compliance protects an organization from regulation and public criticism but often has little impact on day-to-day operations. Integrity is at the center of an organization's activities, influencing every type of decision and activity.

- Pay close attention to how your organization achieves its goals. Failure to do so will create anomie and undermine ethical performance.

- Reinforce ethical commitments in your organization through the design of monetary and nonmonetary reward systems, performance and evaluation processes, allocation of decision-making authority, and effective governance.

- Ethical organizations recognize their responsibilities to their communities. They honor their ethical obligations to stakeholder groups, actively work to better society, and seek to operate in an environmentally sustainable fashion.

- Core ideology is essential to any healthy ethical climate. Encourage your organization to identify and communicate its values and purpose.

- Useful codes of ethics can play an important role in shaping ethical climate. Make sure they define and illustrate important terms and address the problems faced by the members of your particular organization. View ethics statements as discussion starters, not as the final word on the topic of organizational morality.

- Socialization processes introduce ethical standards and values to new members and reinforce their importance to organizational veterans. Use the website, brochures, interviews, training, orientation sessions, and socialization agents to promote ethical socialization. Beware of co-optation, incrementalism, and compromise that socialize newcomers into immoral behavior.

- Effective ethics training can promote positive ethical climate if it is adapted to the ethical problems of the organization, taps into the experiences of participants, and actively engages them. Instruction should reinforce other elements of the organization's ethics strategy and be integrated into the entire training program.

FOR FURTHER EXPLORATION, CHALLENGE, AND SELF-ASSESSMENT

1. Select a well-known senior executive and determine whether this person should be classified as ethical, hypocritical, ethically neutral, or unethical. Provide evidence to support your conclusion.

2. Analyze the ethical climate of your organization. In your paper, consider the following questions: How would you classify the organization's ethical orientation based on Self-Assessment 10.1? Overall, would you characterize the climate as positive or negative? Why? What factors shape the moral atmosphere? What role have leaders played in its formation and maintenance? What steps does the organization take to deal with misbehaviors? Does the organization consider both means and ends? How does the group's structure reinforce (or fail to reinforce) espoused values and ethical behavior? What inconsistencies do you note?

3. Discuss each of the following statements in a group or, as an alternative, argue for and against each proposition in a formal debate. Your instructor will set the rules and time limits. Refer to the discussion of argumentation in Chapter 7 for more information on constructing effective arguments.

   - Pro or con: Organizations are less ethical now than they were ten years ago.
   - Pro or con: Formal codes of ethics do more harm than good.
   - Pro or con: Ethical businesses are more profitable over the long term.
   - Pro or con: Organizational values can't be developed; they must be uncovered or discovered instead.
   - Pro or con: An organization's purpose has to be inspirational.

- Pro or con: An organization can change everything except its core values and purpose.
- Pro or con: All business should be actively engaged in CSR.

4. Write a research paper on one form of individual or collective destructive behavior in the workplace. Conclude with suggestions to help leaders curb this type of behavior.

5. Compare and contrast an organization that has a climate of integrity with one that pursues ethical compliance.

6. Describe a time when you experienced anomie in an organization. What factors led to your feelings of powerlessness and alienation? How did anomie influence your behavior? As an alternative, reflect on a time when you felt you were treated unjustly in an organization. What factors led you to believe you were being treated unfairly? How did experiencing injustice influence your behavior?

7. Develop a shared set of values for your class using strategies presented in this chapter.

8. Conduct an analysis of the mission statements of 10 different companies or organizations. Which are most effective? Why?

9. Evaluate an ethical code based on the guidelines presented in this chapter. What are its strengths and weaknesses? How useful would it be to members of the organization? How could the code be improved? What can we learn from this statement?

10. Design an ethics training program for your organization using the guidelines presented in this chapter.

11. Describe your socialization into your school or some other organization from an ethical vantage point. Then evaluate the process. What did the organization do well? What could it have done better? What suggestions would you make to improve the ethical socialization process for future newcomers?

STUDENT STUDY SITE

Visit the student study site at **study.sagepub.com/johnsonmecl6e** to access full SAGE journal articles for further research and information on key chapter topics.

Case Study 10.1

TEMPORARY VISAS/PERMANENT JOB LOSS

Finding employees with specialized technical skills can be difficult for American high-tech firms like Microsoft, Intel, Google, and Apple. Congress created the H-1B visa program to help address this problem. Under the program, American companies can hire foreigners with unique scientific and technology skills as temporary workers. The goal is to supplement the

(Continued)

(Continued)

American workforce, enabling domestic companies to expand. Like a number of other federal initiatives, the H-1B visa program doesn't always function as intended. Infosys, Tata Consulting Services, Accenture, Cognizant, and other large overseas outsourcing firms receive the greatest number of visas. Many foreign workers under contract to these consulting firms don't appear to have specialized technical skills but, rather, do accounting and other office work. Few end up in the high-tech sector, working instead for Disney, Southern California Edison, Northeast Utilities, Toys "R" Us, Fossil, New York Life, Cengage Learning, and other companies. Often, their task is to shadow American employees to learn their jobs so the work can be outsourced, generally to India. When the temporary employees return home, the U.S. workers are laid off. At Toys "R" Us, for example, 70 employees were told that their positions would be transferred to Tata Consultancy Services and were threatened with immediate termination if they didn't cooperate in the "knowledge transfer" program. Those who remained to the end received a severance package. Two hundred and fifty Disney employees were offered a "stay bonus" of 10% of their severance if they stayed 90 days, which did little to ease the pain of having to train their replacements. Said one former worker: "I just couldn't believe they could fly people in to sit at our desks and take over our jobs exactly. It was so humiliating to train somebody else to take over your job. I still can't grasp it."[1]

United States firms defend their decision to hire H-1B temporary workers to replace domestic employees. They argue that doing so is a sound business strategy that results in significant cost savings. (H-1B hires work for 25%–49% less than their U.S. counterparts.) Executives claim that laid-off employees receive generous severance packages (an assertion disputed by some laid-off workers) and that any job losses are more than offset by job gains. Disney, for example, says it created 30,000 jobs over the past decade. Nevertheless, Congress appears ready to revisit the H-1B visa program. Outraged by tales of domestic employees forced to train their foreign replacements, a bipartisan group of Senators has called for revisions in the program. Companies would be required to try harder to hire Americans for open positions and to post job openings on the Labor Department website. The new rules would give more power to the government to investigate fraud and provide added protection for H-1B workers who are totally dependent on the outsourcing firms that employ them.

Discussion Probes

1. Would you agree to train your replacement if you knew your job was going to be outsourced? Why or why not?
2. Is it unjust to force employees to train their replacements? Does doing so take away the dignity of workers?
3. Is using the temporary visa program to outsource jobs unethical or good business? Why?
4. Should Congress end the H-1B temporary visa program?
5. What changes should Congress make in the H-1B program if it continues?

Note

1. Preston, J. (2015, June 4). Pink slips at Disney. But first, training foreign replacements. *The New York Times*, p. A1.

Sources

Editorial Board. (2015, June 15). Workers betrayed by visa loopholes. *The New York Times*, p. A18.

Goel, V. (2014, November 24). Workers in Silicon Valley weigh in on Obama's immigration order. *The New York Times*, p. B3.

Pedicini, S. (2015, October 6). Anti-immigration activists plan Disney protest, call for boycott. *Orlando Sentinel*.

Preston, J. (2015, June 12). Outsourcing companies under scrutiny over visas for technology workers. *The New York Times*, p. A17.

Preston, J. (2015, September 29). Toys 'R' Us brings temporary foreign workers to U.S. to move jobs overseas. *The New York Times*.

Case Study 10.2

LIFE IN THE COMBAT ZONE: WORKING AT AMAZON

You can buy almost anything at Amazon.com. The online retailer, headquartered in Seattle, carries everything from books, DVDs, and video games to cell phones, car parts, medical supplies, and diapers. The company has grown along with its product line. In 2015, the company took in over $100 billion in revenue and passed Wal-Mart in total market value ($250 billion). Founder and CEO Jeff Bezos—who also has significant stake in Google—is now the fifth richest person in the world.

Employees pay a high price for Amazon's success. Blue-collar workers at the company's fulfillment centers are closely monitored. They are tagged with devices that tell them the routes they must travel to pick up items, record how long it takes them to locate each product (and whether they do so quickly enough), and even count their trips to the bathroom. If workers fall behind or spend too much time in the toilet, they are texted warning messages and can be fired. Managers frequently raise packing quotas without warning. All employees are scanned when entering and leaving the centers in order to prevent theft.

In the most notorious case of mistreatment, a number of workers at Amazon's Allentown, Pennsylvania, facility toppled from heat stroke during a summer heat wave. The warehouse had no air conditioning and managers, fearing theft, refused to open doors to increase air circulation. Amazon then hired paramedics and ambulances to stand ready outside the

(Continued)

(Continued)

center to tend to those overcome by the heat. However, those sent home due to the high temperatures were given disciplinary points. (The facility manager claims that she shut down the warehouse three times during the heat wave. Amazon later installed air conditioning.)

Amazon's white-collar workers apparently take their share of abuse as well. Life at headquarters is intense. Bezos fears that Amazon will end up like neighboring Microsoft, which he considers a "country club." To fight off complacency, he pushes his employees hard. Managers put in 80–85 hours a week; working less is considered a weakness. Work–life balance is not a priority, with employees expected to check in via e-mail while on vacation and to participate in extended conference calls on holidays. Those dealing with health issues or caring for family members can expect little sympathy and may be replaced. According to one former Amazon marketer, "Nearly every person I worked with, I saw cry at their desk."[1] Median employee tenure is one year, which ranks the firm among the lowest in the *Fortune 500*. (Company officials claim that this figure is misleading, since many employees have been hired within the past five years due to the firm's rapid growth.)

Amazon can resemble a combat zone. Bezos believes that conflict fosters innovation so he wants executives to tear into the ideas of others. Employees can send praise or criticism about coworkers to management, which encourages colleagues to scheme against those they are competing against in annual performance reviews. In these "rank and yank" sessions, managers debate the ratings of their subordinates. Those with the highest rankings stay; those with the lowest ratings (even good employees) are let go in a process Amazon executives call "Purposeful Darwinism." In a letter to stakeholders, Bezos said, "When I interview people, I tell them, 'You can work long, hard, or smart, but at Amazon, you can't choose two out of three.'"[2]

Encounters with Bezos can leave employees shaken. Volatile and intolerant of mistakes, Bezos has been known to rebuke employees with such declarations as: "Does it surprise you that you don't know the answer to that question?" "Are you lazy or just incompetent?" and "Why are you ruining my life?"[3] He is also ruthless in his dealings with competitors. To become the leading online marketer of diapers, Bezos undersold Diapers.com and then took over the company when it failed. In the "Gazelle Project," Bezos suggested that Amazon attack small publishing houses in the same way that a cheetah attacks a sick gazelle. Technology writer Brad Stone concludes that Bezos and other Amazon executives "have an absolute willingness to torch the landscape around them to emerge the winner."[4]

Some white-collar employees thrive in Amazon's intense environment. They enjoy the challenge and are given plenty of opportunity to innovate, no matter what their role in the company. The drone delivery initiative was the idea of a low-level engineer, for example. Others like the fast pace and pressure, which pushes them beyond what they thought they could achieve. Salaries are competitive and managers receive stock grants. Other companies are often eager to hire those who leave Amazon because of their work ethic. Facebook, for instance, opened a hiring office in Seattle to capture the outflow of Amazon employees. However, some prospective employers are cautious about hiring ex-Amazonians, knowing they can be combative and obsessed with work.

CEO Bezos developed a set of fourteen guidelines or rules, sometimes referred to as *The Amazon Way*, to ensure that the company stays true to its culture. Some of the more notable principles include obsess over the customer (No. 1); take ownership (No. 2); hire and develop the best (No. 5); think big (No. 7); and have a bias for action (No. 8). Employees frequently cite these principles and use them in hiring decisions. Apparently, some Amazonians teach these rules to their kids.

The future looks bright for Amazon. The company is building a series of new office towers that can house 50,000 employees, over three times the number that worked for the company in 2013. It may become the world's first trillion-dollar retailer. However, the company is currently struggling to hire fast enough to keep up with its growth. But Amazon seems in no hurry to change its culture to attract more employees. According to one recruiting video: "You either fit here or you don't. You love it or you don't. There is no middle ground."[5]

Discussion Probes

1. Do you buy products from Amazon? If so, what has been your experience as a customer?

2. Will you continue to purchase from Amazon, knowing its corporate culture?

3. Would you want to work for Amazon? Why or why not?

4. Would Amazon be as successful if it changed its culture to be less driven and combative?

5. Is "Purposeful Darwinism" an ethical approach to hiring and promotion?

6. What ethical danger signs or weaknesses do you see at Amazon?

Notes

1. Kantor, J., & Streitfeld, D. (2015, August 15). Inside Amazon: Wrestling big ideas in a bruising workplace. *The New York Times*.

2. Schwartz, T. (2015, August 21). Why Jeff Bezos should care more for Amazon's employees. *The New York Times.*

3. Stone, B. (2013). *The everything store: Jeff Bezos and the age of Amazon*. New York, NY: Little, Brown, p. 177.

4. Stone, p. 300.

5. Kantor & Streitfeld.

Sources

Head, S. (2014, February 23). Worse than Wal-Mart: Amazon's sick brutality and secret history of ruthlessly intimidating workers. *Salon.com*

Nocera, J. (2015, August 21). Jeff Bezos and the Amazon way. *The New York Times*, Op-Ed.

Rossman, J. (2014). *The Amazon Way: 14 leadership principles behind the world's most disruptive company*. North Charleston, SC: CreateSpace Independent Publishing Platform.

Streitfeld, D. (2011, September 19). Inside Amazon's very hot warehouse. *The New York Times Blogs*.

Case Study 10.3

CONSCIOUS CAPITALISM AT THE CONTAINER STORE

The Container Store is one of America's most admired companies. The retailer, which sells containers and storage units, has been on *Fortune*'s list of "100 Best Companies to Work For" seventeen years in a row. In 2015, the company was also named to the following lists: "Best Workplaces for Camaraderie," "Best Workplaces for Diversity," "Best Workplaces for Women," and "Best Workplaces in Retail." Ninety-three percent of Container Store employees say that they are proud "to tell others I work here." Ninety-two percent believe that management is honest and ethical, and 91% say that the firm is a great place to work.

The company's reputation is largely the product of the philosophy of cofounder, former CEO and current chairman Kip Tindell. Tindell believes in "conscious capitalism," an approach to business based on the belief that companies should serve a higher purpose in addition to making money. (Other companies following this model include Whole Foods Market, Costco, Zappos, and Starbucks.) Conscious leaders want to create caring corporate cultures that promote employee growth while serving stakeholders. For Tindell, this means fostering an "employee-first" mentality: "If you're lucky enough to be somebody's employer, you have a huge moral obligation to make sure they want to get out of bed and come to work in the morning."[1] Tindell summarizes his approach in what he calls his "Foundation Principles." His first principle is: "One great person equals three good persons." Tindall believes that one excellent sales associate is much more productive than three less productive employees. Therefore, the company can afford to pay these individuals well above the industry average. The average Container Stores sales associate makes $48,000 a year and enjoys health care coverage, generous maternity and paternity leave, free snacks, and other perks.

The company provides extensive training for employees based on another Foundation Principle: "Intuition does not come to an unprepared mind." Tindell believes that well-trained employees are better prepared to meet the needs of customers. Full-time employees receive over 263 hours of training in their first year; part-timers receive 177 hours. Continuing employees participate in 31 hours of annual training. (This compares to the retail industry average of eight hours.) The Container Store also reaches out to suppliers through the Foundation Principle, "Fill the other guy's basket to the brim." Tindell seeks to develop a win–win relationship with vendors by helping them develop products, placing orders during slow periods to keep their factories running, paying all invoices on time (or even early), and inviting them to company events. In return, the company gets the opportunity to purchase the most popular products before other companies do, generally at a lower price.

Under Tindell's brand of conscious capitalism, the firm expanded from one store in Dallas in 1978 to 79 locations around the United States. Annual revenue now totals over $790 million. But, when it fell short of sales projections, the company's share price declined dramatically after it went public in 2013. Analysts and critics hoping to raise the stock price urged Tindell to lower wages. Tindell refused to do so, convinced that the company's continued success depends on a well-trained, well-treated sales staff: "A good capitalist will see the value of what we're doing. We would not be as profitable if we did less for our employees and vendors."[2] However, he stepped down as CEO in 2016 when sales continued to lag. (Tindell remains as board chair, and his wife, Sharon, continues as chief merchant and company president.) The Container Store has plans to open additional stores and to increase square footage by 12% a year. Expansion will further raise the profile of the company and may put additional pressure on the firm to abandon some of its principles in order to increase the bottom line.

Discussion Probes

1. Do you agree with Tindell that the company's success is based on treating employees and suppliers well?
2. Can The Container Store continue to resist pressure from stockholders to reduce costs?
3. Should business have a purpose in addition to making money?
4. Are you more likely to shop at The Container Store after learning about its culture?
5. What elements of an ethical climate do you see at The Container Store?

Notes

1. Rohman, J. (n.d.). *With an "employee-first" mentality, everyone wins*. Retrieved from http://www.greatplacetowork.com
2. Berfeld, S. (2015, February 19). Will investors put the lid on The Container Store's generous wages? *Bloomberg Businessweek*.

Sources

The Container Store: An employee-centric retailer. (n.d.). University of New Mexico: Daniels Fund Ethics Initiative. Retrieved from https://danielsethics.mgt.unm.edu/pdf/Container%20Store%20Case.pdf

Koch, J. (2001, March). Thinking outside the box at The Container Store. *Workforce*, 34–38.

Schawbel, D. (2014, October 7). Kip Tindell: How he created an employee-first culture at The Container Store. *Forbes*.

Tindall, K. (2014). *Uncontainable: How passion, commitment and conscious capitalism built a business where everyone thrives*. New York, NY: Grand Central.

Wahba, P. (2016, May 9). Why Container Store's founder is quitting CEO job. *Fortune.com*.

What we stand for. (2016). *The Container Store*. Retrieved from http://sstandfor.continerstore.com

SELF-ASSESSMENT 10.1

Ethical Climate Questionnaire

Instructions: Indicate whether you agree with each of the following statements about your company or organization. Use the scale below and write the number that best represents your answer in the space next to the item.

Completely False	Mostly False	Somewhat False	Somewhat True	Mostly True	Completely True
0	1	2	3	4	5

1. In this company (organization), people are mostly out for themselves. _____

2. The major responsibility for people in this company (organization) is to control costs. _____

3. In this company (organization), people are expected to follow their own personal and moral beliefs. _____

4. People are expected to do anything to further the company's (organization's) interests, regardless of the consequences. _____

5. In this company (organization), people look out for each other's good. _____

6. There is no room for one's personal morals or ethics in this company (organization). _____

7. It is very important to follow strictly the company's (organization's) rules and procedures here. _____

8. Work is considered substandard only when it hurts the company's (organization's) interests. _____

9. Each person in this company (organization) decides for him- or herself what is right and wrong. _____

10. In this company (organization), people protect their own interests above other considerations. _____

11. The most important consideration in this company (organization) is each person's sense of right and wrong. _____

12. The most important concern is the good of all the people in the company (organization). _____

13. The first consideration is whether a decision violates any law. _____

14. People are expected to comply with the law and professional standards over and above other considerations. _____

15. Everyone is expected to stick to company (organization) rules and procedures. _____

16. In this company (organization), our major concern is always what is best for the other person. _____

17. People are concerned with the company's (organization's) interests—to the exclusion of all else. _____

18. Successful people in this company (organization) go by the book. _____

19. The most efficient way is always the right way in this company (organization). _____

20. In this company (organization), people are expected to strictly follow legal or professional standards. _____

21. Our major consideration is what is best for everyone in the company (organization). _____

22. In this company (organization), people are guided by their own personal ethics. _____

23. Successful people in this company (organization) strictly obey the company (organization) policies. _____

24. In this company (organization), the law or ethical code of one's profession is the major consideration. _____

25. In this company (organization), each person is expected, above all, to work efficiently. _____

26. It is expected that you will always do what is right for the customer and public. _____

Scoring:

Caring Climate Score

Add up scores on items 5, 12, 16, 21, 26 = (Range 0–25) _____

Law and Code Climate Score

Add up scores on items 13, 14, 20, 24 = (Range 0–20) _____

Rules Climate Score

Add up scores on items 7, 15, 18, 23 = (Range 0–20) _____

Instrumental Climate Score

Add up scores on items 1, 2, 4, 6, 8, 10, 17, 19, 25 = (Range 0–45) _____

Independence Climate Score

Add up scores on items 3, 9, 11, 22 = (Range 0–20) _____

Sources: Cullen, J. B., Victor, B., & Bronson, J. W. (1993). The Ethical Climate Questionnaire: An assessment of its development and validity. *Psychological Reports, 73,* 667–674; used with permission. See also Victor, B., & Cullen, J. B. (1988). The organizational bases of ethical work climates. *Administrative Science Quarterly, 33,* 101–125.

SELF-ASSESSMENT 10.2

Organizational Trust Inventory

Instructions: Please choose the unit or department about which you can most knowledgeably report the opinions of members of your department or unit.

1. Your department or unit is _____ (enter name of department/unit).

2. The other department or unit about which you are responding is _____ (enter name of department/unit).

To the right of each statement, please write the number (1 = *strongly disagree*; 7 = *strongly agree*) that most closely describes the opinion of members of your department toward the other department. Interpret the blank spaces as referring to the other department about which you are commenting.

1	2	3	4	5	6	7
Strongly Disagree	Disagree	Slightly Disagree	Neither Agree nor Disagree	Slightly Agree	Agree	Strongly Agree

1. We think the people in _____ tell the truth in negotiations. ____

2. We think that _____ meets its negotiated obligations to our department. ____

3. In our opinion, _____ is reliable. ____

4. We think that the people in _____ succeed by stepping on other people. (R) ____

5. We feel that _____ tries to get the upper hand. (R) ____

6. We think that _____ takes advantage of our problems. (R) ____

7. We feel that _____ negotiates with us honestly. ____

8. We feel that _____ will keep its word. ____

9. We think that _____ does not mislead us. ____

10. We feel that _____ tries to get out of its commitments. (R) ____

11. We feel that _____ negotiates joint expectations fairly. ____

12. We feel that _____ takes advantage of people who are vulnerable. (R) ____

Scoring: Reverse item scores where indicated (R) and then add your scores. Total scores can range from 12 to 84. The higher the score, the greater your unit's trust in the members of the other department.

Source: Cummings, L. L., & Bromiley, P. (1996). The Organizational Trust Inventory (OTI): Development and validation. In R. M. Kramer & T. R. Tyler (Eds.), *Trust in organizations: Frontiers of theory and research* (pp. 302–330). Thousand Oaks, CA: SAGE. Used with permission of the authors.

NOTES

1. See, for example, Gottlieb, J. Z., & Sabzgiri, J. (1996). Towards an ethical dimension of decision making in organizations. *Journal of Business Ethics, 15,* 1275–1285; Grojean, M. W., Resick, C. J., Dickson, M. W., & Smith, D. B. (2004). Leaders, values, and organizational climate: Examining leadership strategies for establishing an organizational climate regarding ethics. *Journal of Business Ethics, 55,* 223–241.
2. Brown, M. E., & Trevino, L. K. (2006). Ethical leadership: A review and future directions. *Leadership Quarterly, 17,* 595–616; Brown, M. E., Trevino, L. K., & Harrison, D. A. (2005). Ethical leadership: A social learning perspective for construct development and testing.

Organizational Behavior and Human Decision Processes, 97, 117–134; Trevino, L. K., & Brown, M. E. (2005). The role of leaders in influencing unethical behavior in the workplace. In R. E. Kidwell & C. L. Martin (Eds.), *Managing organizational deviance* (pp. 69–87). Thousand Oaks, CA: SAGE; Trevino, L. K., Brown, M. E., & Pincus, L. (2003). A qualitative investigation of perceived executive ethical leadership: Perceptions from inside and outside the executive suite. *Human Relations, 56,* 5–37; Trevino, L. K., Hartman, L. P., & Brown, M. E. (2000). Moral person and moral manager: How executives develop a reputation for ethical leadership. *California Management Review, 42*(4), 128–133.

3. Trevino et al. (2000); Trevino, L. K., & Nelson, K. A. (2004). *Managing business ethics: Straight talk about how to do it right* (3rd ed.). Hoboken, NJ: John Wiley, Ch. 9.

4. Pacanowsky, M. E., & O'Donnell-Trujillo, N. (1983). Organizational communication as cultural performance. *Communication Monographs, 5,* 126–147.

5. Cullen, J. B., Victor, B., & Bronson, J. W. (1993). The Ethical Climate Questionnaire: An assessment of its development and validity. *Psychological Reports, 73,* 667–674; Victor, B., & Cullen, J. B. (1988). The organizational bases of ethical work climates. *Administrative Science Quarterly, 33,* 101–125; Victor, B., & Cullen, J. B. (1990). A theory and measure of ethical climate in organizations. In W. C. Frederick & L. E. Preston (Eds.), *Business ethics: Research issues and empirical studies* (pp. 77–97). Greenwich, CT: JAI Press.

6. See, for example, Cullen, J. B., Parboteeah, K. P., & Victor, B. (2003). The effects of ethical climates on organizational commitment: A two-study analysis. *Journal of Business Ethics, 46,* 127–141; Fritzsche, D. J. (2000). Ethical climates and the ethical dimension of decision making. *Journal of Business Ethics, 24,* 125–140; Martin, K. D., & Cullen, J. B. (2006). Continuities and extensions of ethical climate theory: A meta-analytic review. *Journal of Business Ethics, 69,* 175–194; Parbotheeah, K. P., Martin, K. D., & Cullen, J. B. (2014). An international perspective on ethical climate. In N. M. Ashkanasy, C. P. M. Wilderom, & M. F. Peterson (Eds.), *The handbook of organizational culture and climate* (2nd ed., pp. 600–617). Los Angeles, CA: SAGE; Peterson, D. K. (2002). The relationship between unethical behavior and the dimensions of the Ethical Climate Questionnaire. *Journal of Business Ethics, 41,* 313–326; Sims, R. L., & Keon, T. L. (1997). Ethical work climate as a factor in the development of person–organization fit. *Journal of Business Ethics, 16,* 1095–1105; Trevino, L. K., Butterfield, K. D., & McCabe, D. L. (1998). The ethical context in organizations: Influences on employee attitudes and behaviors. *Business Ethics Quarterly, 8,* 447–476; Wang, Y-D., & Hseih, J-H. (2012). Toward a better understanding of the link between ethical climate and job satisfaction: A multilevel analysis. *Journal of Business Ethics, 15,* 535–545.

7. Jennings, M. M. (2006). *The seven signs of ethical collapse: How to spot moral meltdowns in companies . . . before it's too late.* New York, NY: St. Martin's Press.

8. Griffin, R. W., & O'Leary-Kelly, A. M. (Eds.). (2004). *The dark side of organizational behavior.* San Francisco, CA: Jossey-Bass; Mumford, M. D., Gessner, T. L., Connelly, M. S., O'Conner, J. A., & Clifton, T. (1993). Leadership and destructive acts: Individual and situational influences. *Leadership Quarterly, 4,* 115–147.

9. Pearson, C. M., & Porath, C. L. (2004). On incivility, its impact and directions for future research. In R. W. Griffin & A. M. O'Leary-Kelly (Eds.), *The dark side of organizational behavior* (pp. 131–158). San Francisco, CA: Jossey-Bass; Pearson, C. M., & Porath, C. L. (2005). On the nature, consequences and remedies of workplace incivility: No time for "nice"? Think again. *Academy of Management Executive, 19,* 7–18; Porath, C. L., & Erez, A. (2007). Does rudeness really matter? The effects of rudeness on task performance and helpfulness. *Academy of Management Journal, 50,* 1181–1197.

10. Buss, A. H. (1961). *The psychology of aggression.* New York, NY: John Wiley.

11. Levy, A. C., & Paludi, M. A. (2002). *Workplace sexual harassment* (2nd ed.). Upper Saddle River, NJ: Prentice Hall.

12. Diboye, R. L., & Halverson, S. K. (2004). Subtle (and not so subtle) discrimination in organizations. In R. W. Griffin & A. M. O'Leary-Kelly (Eds.), *The dark side of organizational behavior* (pp. 404–425). San Francisco, CA: Jossey-Bass.

13. Centers for Disease Control and Prevention. (2014). *Occupational violence*. Retrieved from http://www.cdc.gov/niosh/topics/violence/; Department of Labor. (2016). *Labor force statistics from the current population survey*. Retrieved from http://www.bls.gov/cps/; Shen, H. (2011, July 26). Wealth gap between whites, minorities widens to greatest level in a quarter century. *Huffington Post*; Vaglanos, A. (2015, February 19). 1 in 3 women has been sexually harassed at work, according to survey. *Huffington Post*.

14. Oppel, R. A. (2014, March 3). Military sex assault trial showcases 2 approaches to prosecution. *The New York Times*, p. A12.

15. Baron, R. A. (2004). Workplace aggression and violence: Insights from basic research. In R. W. Griffin & A. M. O'Leary-Kelly (Eds.), *The dark side of organizational behavior* (pp. 23–61). San Francisco, CA: Jossey-Bass.

16. Anand, V., Ashforth, B. E., & Joshi, M. (2004). Business as usual: The acceptance and perpetuation of corruption in organizations. *Academy of Management Executive, 18*, 39–53; Ashforth, B. E., & Anand, V. (2003). The normalization of corruption in organizations. *Research in Organizational Behavior, 25*, 1–52; Darley, J. M. (1996). How organizations socialize individuals into evildoing. In D. M. Messick & A. E. Tenbrunsel (Eds.), *Codes of conduct: Behavioral research into business ethics* (pp. 12–43). New York, NY: Russell Sage Foundation; Luo, Y. (2004). An organizational perspective of corruption. *Management and Organization Review, 1*, 119–154.

17. See, for example, Big victory against global bribery. (2008, December 17). *The Christian Science Monitor*, p. 8; CEO's moral compass steers Siemens. (2010, February 15). *USA Today*, p. 3B; Schubert, S., & Miller, T. C. (2008, December 21). Where bribery was just a line item. *The New York Times*, p. BU1.

18. Cropanzano, R., & Stein, J. H. (2009). Organizational justice and behavioral ethics: Promises and prospects. *Business Ethics Quarterly, 19*, 193–233.

19. Colquitt, J. A., Conlon, D. E., Wesson, M. J., Porter, C. O. L. H., & Yee, N. K. (2001). Justice at the millennium: A meta-analytic review of 25 years of organizational justice research. *Journal of Applied Psychology, 86*, 425–445; Fortin, M. (2008). Perspectives on organizational justice: Concept clarification, social context integration, time and links with morality. *International Journal of Management Reviews, 10*, 93–126; Trevino, L. K., & Weaver, G. R. (2001). Organizational justice and ethics program "follow-through": Influences on employee's harmful and helpful behavior. *Business Ethics Quarterly, 11*, 651–671.

20. Folger, R., & Baron, R. A. (1996). Violence and hostility at work: A model of reactions to perceived injustice. In G. R. VandenBos & E. Q. Bulato (Eds.), *Violence on the job: Identifying risks and developing solutions* (pp. 51–85). Washington, DC: American Psychological Association; Greenberg, J., & Wiethoff, C. (2001). Organization justice as proaction and reaction: Implications for research and application. In R. Cropanzano (Ed.), *Justice in the workplace* (Vol. 2, pp. 271–302). Mahwah, NJ: Erlbaum; Kickul, J. (2001). When organizations break their promises: Employee reactions to unfair processes and treatment. *Journal of Business Ethics, 29*, 289–307; Reb, J., Goldman, B. M., Kray, L. J., & Cropanzano, R. (2006). Different wrongs, different remedies? Reactions to organizational remedies after procedural and interactional injustice. *Personnel Psychology, 59*, 31–64; Trevino & Weaver.

21. A number of authors use the term *integrity* to describe ideal managers and organizations. See Brown, M. T. (2005). *Corporate integrity: Rethinking organizational ethics and leadership.* Cambridge, England: Cambridge University Press; Pearson, G. (1995). *Integrity in organizations: An alternative business ethic.* London, England: McGraw-Hill; Petrick, J. A. (1998). Building organizational integrity and quality with the four Ps: Perspectives, paradigms, processes, and principles. In M. Schminke (Ed.), *Managerial ethics: Moral management of people*

and processes (pp. 115–131). Mahwah, NJ: Erlbaum; Solomon, R. C. (1992). *Ethics and excellence: Cooperation and integrity in business.* New York, NY: Oxford University Press; Srivastva, S. (Ed.). (1988). *Executive integrity.* San Francisco, CA: Jossey-Bass.

22. Paine, L. S. (1996, March–April). Managing for organizational integrity. *Harvard Business Review,* 106–117.

23. Toffler, B. L., & Reingold, J. (2003). *Final accounting: Ambition, greed, and the fall of Arthur Andersen.* New York, NY: Broadway.

24. Andreoli, N., & Lefkowitz, J. (2008). Individual and organizational antecedents of misconduct in organizations. *Journal of Business Ethics, 85,* 309–332; McKendall, M., DeMarr, B., & Jones-Rikkers, C. (2002). Ethical compliance programs and corporate illegality: Testing the assumptions of the corporate sentencing guidelines. *Journal of Business Ethics, 37,* 367–383; Rockness, H., & Rockness, J. (2005). Legislated ethics: From Enron to Sarbanes–Oxley, the impact on corporate America. *Journal of Business Ethics, 57,* 31–54.

25. Weaver, G. R., Trevino, L. K., & Cochran, P. L. (1999). Integrated and decoupled corporate social performance: Management commitments, external pressures, and corporate ethics practices. *Academy of Management Journal, 42,* 539–552; Weber, J., & Wasieleski, D. M. (2013). Corporate ethics and compliance programs: A report, analysis and critiques. *Journal of Business Ethics, 112,* 609–626.

26. Kramer, F. M. (2010). Collective trust within organizations: Conceptual foundations and empirical insights. *Corporate Reputation Review, 13,* 82–97; Shockley-Zalabak, P. S., Ellis, K., & Cesaria, R. (2000). *Measuring organizational trust: A diagnostic survey and international indicator.* San Francisco, CA: International Association of Business Communicators; Shockley-Zalabak, P. S., Ellis, K., & Winograd, G. (2000). Organizational trust: What it means, why it matters. *Organization Development Journal, 18*(4), 35–47.

27. See, for example, Bruhn, J. G. (2001). *Trust and the health of organizations.* New York, NY: Kluwer/Plenum; Dirks, K. T. (1999). The effects of interpersonal trust on work group performance. *Journal of Applied Psychology, 84,* 445–455; Shockley-Zalabak, P. S., Morreale, S. P., & Hackman, M. Z. (2010). *Building the high-trust organization: Strategies for supporting five key dimensions of trust.* San Francisco, CA: Jossey-Bass.

28. Cummings, L. L., & Bromiley, P. (1996). The Organizational Trust Inventory (OTI): Development and validation. In R. M. Kramer & T. R. Tyler (Eds.), *Trust in organizations: Frontiers of theory and research* (pp. 302–329). Thousand Oaks, CA: SAGE.

29. Shockley-Zalabak et al. (2010).

30. Cohen, D. V. (1993). Creating and maintaining ethical work climates: Anomie in the workplace and implications for managing change. *Business Ethics Quarterly, 3,* 343–358.

31. James, H. S. (2000). Reinforcing ethical decision making through organizational structure. *Journal of Business Ethics, 28,* 43–58.

32. Dunn, J., & Schweitzer, M. E. (2005). Why good employees make unethical decisions. In E. W. Kidwell & C. L. Martin (Eds.), *Managing organizational deviance* (pp. 39–60). Thousand Oaks, CA: SAGE.

33. Useem, M. (1998). *The leadership moment: Nine stories of triumph and disaster and their lessons for us all.* New York, NY: Times Books, Ch. 7.

34. Glanz, W. (2003, August 27). NASA ignored dangers to shuttle, panel says. *The Washington Times,* p. A1; Sawyer, K. (2003, August 24). Shuttle's "smoking gun" took time to register. *The Washington Post,* p. A1.

35. Business Roundtable. (2012, March 27). *2012 principles of corporate governance.* Retrieved from http://businessroundtable.org

36. MacAvoy, P. W., & Millstein, I. M. (2003). *The current crisis in corporate governance.* New York, NY: Palgrave Macmillan; Monks, R. G., & Minow, N. (2004). *Corporate governance* (3rd ed.). Malden, MA: Blackwell; Rezaee, A. (2009). *Corporate governance and ethics.* Hoboken, NJ: Wiley.

37. Buchholz, R. A., & Rosenthal, S. B. (2005). Toward a conceptual framework for stakeholder theory. *Journal of Business Ethics, 58,* 137–148; Sims, R. R. (2003). *Ethics and corporate social responsibility: Why giants fall.* Westport, CT: Praeger.

38. Buchholz & Rosenthal; Cooper, S. (2004). *Corporate social performance: A stakeholder approach.* Burlington, VT: Ashgate; Donaldson, T., & Preston, L. E. (1995). The stakeholder theory of the corporation: Concepts, evidence, and implications. *Academy of Management Review, 20,* 65–91; Freeman, R. E., Harrison, J. S., & Wicks, A. C. (2007). *Managing for stakeholders: Survival, reputation, and success.* New Haven, CT: Yale University Press; Goodpaster, K. E. (1991). Business ethics and stakeholder analysis. *Business Ethics Quarterly, 1,* 53–27; Philips, R. (2003). *Stakeholder theory and organizational ethics.* San Francisco, CA: Berrett-Koehler.

39. Zadek, S. (2004, December). The path to corporate responsibility. *Harvard Business Review,* 125–132.

40. Kotler, P., & Lee, N. (2005). *Corporate social responsibility: Doing the most good for your company and your cause.* Hoboken, NJ: John Wiley.

41. Carroll, A. B., & Buchholtz, A. K. (2012). *Business & society: Ethics, sustainability and stakeholder management* (8th ed.). Mason, OH: South-Western Cengage Learning.

42. Aquinas, H., & Glavas, A. (2012). What we know and don't know about corporate social responsibility: A review and research agenda. *Journal of Management, 38,* 932–968.

43. Wheeler, D., Colbert, B., & Freeman, R. E. (2003). Focusing on values: Reconciling corporate social responsibility, sustainability, and a stakeholder approach in a network world. *Journal of General Management, 28,* 1–28.

44. Panchak, P. (2002). Time for a triple bottom line. *Industry Week,* p. 7; Robins, F. (2006). The challenge of TBL: A responsibility to whom? *Business and Society Review, 111,* 1–14.

45. KPMG Forensic. (2013). *Fraud survey 2013.* Retrieved from https://www.surveys.kpmg.com/aci/fraud_risk.asp

46. Information on the Global Responsibility Report can be found on the Starbucks website (see http://www.starbucks.com/responsibility).

47. Collins, J. C., & Porras, J. I. (1996, September–October). Building your company's vision. *Harvard Business Review,* p. 66. See also Collins, J. C. (2001). *Vision framework.* Retrieved from http://www.jimcollins.com/tools/vision-framework.pdf

48. King, D., Case, C. J., & Premo, K. M. (2011). A mission statement analysis comparing the United States and three other English speaking countries. *Academy of Strategic Management Journal, 10,* Special Issue, 21–45.

49. See, for example, Cooperrider, D. L., & Whitney, D. (2005). *Appreciative inquiry: A positive revolution in change.* San Francisco, CA: Berrett-Koehler; Lewis, D., Medland, J., Malone, S., Murphy, M., Reno, K., & Vaccaro, G. (2006). Appreciative leadership: Defining effective leadership methods. *Organization Development Journal, 24*(1), 87–100; Whitney, D., & Trosten-Bloom, A. (2003). *The power of appreciative inquiry: A practical guide to positive change.* San Francisco, CA: Berrett-Koehler.

50. Van Vuuren, L. J., & Crous, F. (2005). Utilising appreciative inquiry (AI) in creating a shared meaning of ethics in organizations. *Journal of Business Ethics, 57,* 399–412.

51. Paine, L. S., Deshpandé, R., Margolis, J. D., & Bettcher, K. E. (2005, December). Up to code: Does your company meet world-class standards? *Harvard Business Review,* 122–133.

52. For more information on the pros and cons of codes of conduct, see Darley, J. M. (2001). The dynamics of authority influence in organizations and the unintended action consequences. In J. M. Darley, D. M. Messick, & T. R. Tyler (Eds.), *Social influences on ethical behavior in organizations* (pp. 37–52). Mahwah, NJ: Erlbaum; Hatcher, T. (2002). *Ethics and HRD: A new approach to leading responsible organizations.* Cambridge, MA: Perseus; Mathews, M. C. (1990). Codes of ethics: Organizational behavior and misbehavior. In W. C. Frederick & L. E. Preston (Eds.), *Business ethics: Research issues and empirical studies* (pp. 99–122). Greenwich, CT: JAI Press; Metzger, M., Dalton, D. R., & Hill, J. W. (1993). The organization

of ethics and the ethics of organizations: The case for expanded organizational ethics audits. *Business Ethics Quarterly, 3,* 27–43; Trevino et al. (1998); Wright, D. K. (1993). Enforcement dilemma: Voluntary nature of public relations codes. *Public Relations Review, 19,* 13–20.

53. Countryman, A. (2001, December 7). Leadership key ingredient in ethics recipe, experts say. *Chicago Tribune,* pp. B1, B6.

54. McCabe, D., & Trevino, L. K. (1993). Academic dishonesty: Honor codes and other contextual influences. *Journal of Higher Education, 64,* 522–569.

55. Adams, J. S., Taschian, A., & Shore, T. H. (2001). Codes of ethics as signals for ethical behavior. *Journal of Business Ethics, 29,* 199–211; Valentine, S., & Barnett, T. (2003). Ethics code awareness, perceived ethical values, and organizational commitment. *Journal of Personal Selling & Sales Management, 23,* 359–367.

56. Johannesen, R. L., Valde, K. S., & Whedbee, K. E. (2008). *Ethics in human communication* (6th ed.). Long Grove, IL: Waveland Press, Ch. 10.

57. Hopen, D. (2002). Guiding corporate behavior: A leadership obligation, not a choice. *Journal for Quality & Participation, 25,* 15–19.

58. Albrecht, T. L., & Bach, B. W. (1997). *Communication in complex organizations: A relational approach.* Fort Worth, TX: Harcourt Brace.

59. Shockley-Zalabak, P. S. (2006). *Fundamentals of organizational communication: Knowledge, sensitivity, skills, values* (6th ed.). Boston, MA: Pearson.

60. Ashforth & Anand.

61. See, for example, Knapp, J. C. (2011). Rethinking ethics training: New approaches to enhance effectiveness. In R. R. Sims & W. I. Sauser (Eds.), *Experiences in teaching business ethics* (pp. 217–230). Charlotte, NC: Information Age; Petrick, J. A. (2008). Using the business integrity capacity model to advance ethics education. In D. L. Swanson & D. G. Fisher (Eds.), *Advancing business ethics education* (pp. 103–124). Charlotte, NC: Information Age; Sauser, W. I. (2011). Beyond the classroom: Business ethics training for professionals. In R. R. Sims & W. I. Sauser (Eds.), *Experiences in teaching business ethics* (pp. 247–261). Charlotte, NC: Information Age; Waples, E. P., Antes, A., Murphy, S. T., Connelly, S., & Mumford, M. D. (2009). A meta-analytic investigation of business ethics instruction. *Journal of Business Ethics, 87,* 133–151; Weber, J. A. (2007). Business ethics training: Insights from learning theory. *Journal of Business Ethics, 70,* 61–85.

Meeting the Ethical Challenges of Leadership in a Global Society

One may also observe in one's travels to distant countries the feelings of recognition and affiliation that link every human being to every other human being.

—ANCIENT GREEK PHILOSOPHER ARISTOTLE

Human beings draw close to one another by their common nature, but habits and customs keep them apart.

—CONFUCIAN SAYING

WHAT'S AHEAD

In this chapter, we examine the moral complexities posed by cultural differences. Ethical global leaders acknowledge the dark side of globalization and recognize the difficulty of making moral choices in cross-cultural settings. To master these challenges, they understand the relationship between cultural values and ethical decisions, address attitudinal obstacles, seek moral common ground, and develop strategies for solving ethical dilemmas in cross-cultural settings.

THE DARK SIDE OF GLOBALIZATION

Globalization may be the most important trend of the twenty-first century. We now live in a global economy shaped by multinational corporations, international travel, the Internet, immigration, and satellite communication systems. Greater cultural diversity is one product of globalization. Not only is there more contact between countries, there is greater cultural diversity within nations. For example, nonwhites account for most of the population growth in the United States, and nineteen of the nation's twenty-five largest counties have majority minority populations. By 2044, whites will be in the minority. In other industrialized nations, many new workers are immigrants. Italy and Germany will need hundreds of thousands of new immigrants each year to maintain their working-age populations to 2050.[1]

Supporters of globalization point to its benefits. Free trade produces new wealth by opening up international markets, they argue. At the same time, the costs of goods and services drop. The greater flow of information and people puts pressure on repressive governments to reform.[2]

Critics of globalization paint a much bleaker picture. They note that global capitalism encourages greed rather than concern for others. Ethical and spiritual values have been overshadowed by the profit motive. Local cultural traditions and the environment are being destroyed in the name of economic growth. The gap between the rich and the poor keeps growing.[3]

Debate over whether the benefits of globalization outweigh its costs is not likely to end anytime soon. This much is clear, however: As leaders, we need to give serious consideration to the dark side of the global society in order to help prevent ethical abuse. With that in mind, let's take a closer look at how leaders cast the shadows outlined in Chapter 1 in a global environment.

The Global Shadow of Power

In the modern world, a leader's power is no longer limited by national boundaries. Increasing interdependence brought about by the integration of markets, communication systems, computers, and financial institutions means that the actions of one leader or nation can have a dramatic impact on the rest of the world. Take the Chinese financial crisis, for instance. When China's leaders revised the nation's financial projections downward and devalued its currency in 2015, stock markets around the world suffered significant declines, resulting in $5 trillion in losses.[4]

Ethical leadership in the multinational context must take into account the potential far-ranging consequences of every choice. Shadows fall when leaders forget this fact. For example, the U.S. government refused for decades to increase mileage requirements for trucks and automobiles, which contributed to global warming. Saudi Arabia's unwillingness to ban terrorist groups contributed to the World Trade Center and Bali bombings. Apple, Intel, and other electronics manufacturers were accused of funding mass rape, murder, and slave labor in the Congo through their purchase of "conflict minerals" mined in the region. Now they must disclose whether they use Congolese titanium, tantalum, tungsten, and gold in their products.[5]

Concentration of power is a by-product of globalization that increases the likelihood of abuse. The United States is a case in point. Critics accuse the world's only superpower of throwing its political and military weight around. Corporations also wield great influence in the global marketplace. Multinational companies have more economic clout than many nations. According to one estimate, 44 of the world's 100 largest economies are corporations.[6]

The Global Shadow of Privilege

As noted earlier, globalization appears to be increasing, not decreasing, the gap between the haves and the have-nots both within and between nations. Oxfam reports that the richest 1% of the world's population owns almost half of the world's wealth; the 85 richest people in the world own as much as the bottom half (3.5 billion people). Seven out of ten people live in nations where economic inequality has increased over the past thirty years.[7] The only good news is that there has been a decline in the number of people in absolute poverty (those earning less than $1.25 a day), largely because of China's economic growth.[8] So far, leaders of wealthy nations have been more interested in promoting the sale of their goods than in opening up their markets to poorer countries. Privileged nations also consume more, which leads to environmental damage in the form of logging, oil drilling, and mineral extraction. This damage has a disproportionate impact on the disadvantaged. Whereas the wealthy can move to cleaner areas, the poor cannot. Instead, poor citizens must deal with the loss of hunting and fishing grounds, clean air, and safe water.

First World Problems and related books and websites humorously highlight the differences between the haves and the have-nots by describing some of the issues faced by those living in the developed world. While those in so-called third world nations have to worry about malnutrition, poverty, disease, and lack of medical care, "First Worlders" are concerned about "problems" such as these:[9]

- Taco Bell doesn't deliver
- Paying for an all-you-can-eat buffet and getting full after consuming only one plate of salad
- Losing the television remote
- Having to use an outdated iPhone 5 as a backup because your iPhone 6 broke
- Finding foam in a "no foam pumpkin-caramel latte"
- Being forced to run outdoors after the treadmill breaks
- Waiting a long time for the hot water in the house to heat up
- Discovering there are no cup holders in the car

Leaders will continue to cast shadows unless they take steps to make globalization more equitable. To do so, they must (a) put the common (international) good above private gain or self- or national interest, (b) create a global economy that recognizes the interconnectedness of all peoples and the importance of sustaining the environment, (c) practice restraint and moderation in the consumption of goods, and (d) seek justice and compassion by helping marginalized groups.[10]

The Global Shadow of Mismanaged Information

Deceit is all too common on the international stage. Nations routinely spy on each other for economic and military purposes and do their best to deceive their enemies. Businesses from industrialized countries frequently take advantage of consumers in economically depressed regions. Take the marketing of infant formula, for instance. Save the Children estimates that the lives of 3,800 babies could be saved every day if they were adequately breast-fed rather than bottle-fed.[11] Breast-fed babies are more resistant to disease and are less likely to sicken and die in impoverished countries where infant formula is frequently diluted or mixed with polluted water. As an added benefit, poor households could then spend their money on other pressing needs. Despite the adoption of the International Code of Marketing of Breastmilk Substitutes in 1981, formula manufacturers continue to engage in a variety of deceptive sales practices, which have drawn the ire of health officials at the World Health Organization and in Bangladesh, Nigeria, Uganda, the Philippines, and other developing nations. These practices include (a) claiming that baby formula is equal to or better than breast-feeding; (b) playing on women's fears that they won't produce enough milk; (c) representing healthy, thriving babies in television ads and on packaging, leaflets, and posters (many women in impoverished nations are particularly vulnerable to these images because they can't read); (d) disguising salespeople as health workers; and (e) gaining medical endorsement by providing free samples to hospitals and gifts to doctors.

In addition to casting shadows through deception, global leaders cast shadows by withholding information. They don't feel as much obligation to share data about safety problems and environmental hazards with foreign nationals as they do with their own citizens. They are guilty of extracting information from poor countries and giving little in return. For example, clinical drug trials in developing countries produce data that go back to company headquarters in Europe or the United States. Weaker countries are given little support in their efforts to develop their own research facilities.[12] (See Scenario B, "Clinical Trials Outsourcing," in Case Study 11.3 for more information on the ethical challenges of conducting medical research in developing nations.)

The Global Shadow of Inconsistency

Economic and social disparities make it hard for leaders of multinational firms and non-profits to act consistently. For instance, what are "fair" wages and working conditions in developing nations? Do workers in these countries deserve to be protected by the same safety standards as employees in industrialized countries? Should drugs that are banned in the United States for their undesirable side effects be sold in countries where their potential health benefits outweigh their risks? Should a multinational corporation follow the stringent pollution regulations of its home country or the lower standards of a host nation? All too often, global leaders answer these questions in ways that cast shadows on disadvantaged world citizens. They pay the bare minimum to workers in developing countries and provide them with less adequate medical care, pay less attention to safety and environmental problems in overseas locations, dump dangerous products they can't sell in their homelands, and so forth. The Ebola epidemic in West Africa (see Chapter 12) provides a vivid demonstration of the shadow of inconsistency in action. Stricken Western workers were airlifted to first-class medical facilities in their homelands while infected African medical personnel remained on site, receiving treatment in rudimentary hospitals and clinics.[13]

The Global Shadow of Misplaced and Broken Loyalties

Traditional loyalties are eroding in an integrated world. In the past, national leaders were expected to meet the needs of their citizens. Now, because their actions affect the lives of residents of other nations, they must consider their duties to people they may never meet. Failure to do so produces shadow in the form of environmental damage, poverty, hunger, and the widening income gap.

Broken loyalties cast shadows in a global society just as they do in individual leader–follower relationships. Many poorer world citizens feel betrayed by the shattered promises of globalization. Trade barriers remain in place, and special interests in wealthy nations continue to receive favored treatment. Economic exploitation adds to this sense of betrayal. Low labor costs drive the investments of many multinational companies. Executives at these firms are continually on the lookout for cheaper labor, so they transfer production to even more economically depressed regions.

The Global Shadow of Irresponsibility

Globalization increases the breadth of leaders' responsibilities because they are accountable for the actions of followers in many different geographic locations. Like local leaders, they can't be blamed for all the misdeeds of their followers. Yet they should be held to the same set of responsibility standards outlined in our discussion of the shadow side of leadership in Chapter 1. In order to cast light instead of shadow, global leaders must do the following:

1. *Make reasonable efforts to prevent followers' misdeeds.* Fostering a consistent, ethical organizational climate in every location can prevent many moral abuses. Integrity and a clear set of guiding values should be as characteristic of branch offices as they are of headquarters. Leaders can establish such climates by (a) clearly stating organizational values, (b) communicating these values to all branches through print and electronic media and training programs, (c) letting business partners know about standards, and (d) translating ethical behavior into performance standards and then evaluating followers based on those criteria.[14]

2. *Acknowledge and address ethical problems wherever they occur.* Geographic and cultural distance makes it easy for global leaders to deny responsibility for the misbehavior of followers. Subcontractors often get the blame for low wages and poor working conditions at foreign manufacturing facilities. More responsible firms acknowledge their duty to adequately supervise the activities of their contractors. In recent years, Apple has come under criticism for working conditions at Foxconn, which manufacturers the iPhone and iPad in China. Read Case Study 11.1 and determine for yourself whether Apple has adequately addressed these issues.

3. *Shoulder responsibility for the consequences of their directives.* Wise global leaders recognize that in trying to do the right thing, they might end up producing some unintended negative consequences. Take well-intentioned efforts to eliminate child labor, for instance. Removing children from the factory floor in developing countries can do significant harm. Poor children are an important source of income for their families. When fired from their manufacturing jobs, they often are forced into prostitution or begging. Levi Strauss realized that eliminating child laborers from its Bangladesh plants could do damage to both the children and their families. After identifying workers under age 14 (the international standard for child labor), company officials asked their contractors to remove these children from the production line while continuing to pay their wages. Levi Strauss covered the kids' school costs—tuition, uniforms, books—and agreed to rehire them when they reached working age.[15]

4. *Admit their duties to followers.* Multinational leaders have obligations to all their followers, regardless of citizenship or ethnic and cultural background, and to the communities where they operate. Following the collapse of Bangladesh's Rana Plaza garment factory, which killed over 1,100 workers and injured 1,800 more, Primark and Loblaw clothing brands created a compensation fund for victims and their families. However, several large retailers, including Sears, JC Penney, Benetton, and Carrefour, refused to participate although they may have had subcontractors producing clothing at the building the day of the collapse.[16]

5. *Hold themselves to the same standards as followers.* Leaders are not above the values, rules, and codes of conduct they impose on their global organizations. While they hold diverse followers to consistent standards, ethical leaders also live up to the same guidelines.

CULTURAL DIFFERENCES AND ETHICAL VALUES

Along with taking stock of the potential moral pitfalls of globalization, leaders need to recognize that cultural diversity makes ethical decision making even harder. Every ethnic group, nation, and religion approaches moral dilemmas from a different perspective. (See Case Study 11.2 for competing responses to the same ethical issue.) What is perfectly acceptable to members of one group may raise serious ethical concerns for another. Understanding the reasons for these differences is an important first step in increasing our ethical competence in cross-cultural encounters.

Defining Culture

The same factors that make up an organization's culture—language, rituals, stories, buildings, beliefs, assumptions, power structures—also form the cultures of communities, ethnic groups, and nations. Cultures are comprehensive, incorporating both the visible (architecture, physical objects, nonverbal behavior) and the invisible (thoughts, attitudes, values). In sum, a culture is "the total way of life of a people, composed of their learned and shared behavior patterns, values, norms, and material objects."[17]

Several features of cultures are worth noting in more detail. These elements include the following:

- *Created.* We often assume that ours is the only way to solve problems. In fact, there are countless ways to deal with the environment, manage interpersonal relationships, produce food, and cope with death. Each cultural group devises its own way of responding to circumstances.

- *Learned.* Elements of culture are passed on from generation to generation and from person to person. Cultural conditioning is both a formal and an informal process that takes place in every context—homes, schools, playgrounds, camps, games. The most crucial aspects of a culture, such as loyalty to country, are constantly reinforced. Patriotism in the United States is promoted through high school civics classes, the singing of the national anthem at sporting events, flags flying on everything from pickup trucks to skyscrapers and giant construction cranes, and Fourth of July and Memorial Day programs.

- *Shared.* The shared nature of culture becomes apparent when we break the rules that are set and enforced by the group. There are negative consequences for violating cultural norms of all types. Punishments vary depending on the severity of the offense. For example, you might receive a cold stare from your professor when your cell phone goes off in class. However, you may face jail time if you break drug laws.

- *Dynamic.* Cultures aren't static but evolve. Over time, the changes can be dramatic, as in the case of gay marriage, which was once banned but now is the law of the land in the United States.

Although each culture has its own set of ethical priorities, researchers have discovered that ethnic groups and nations hold values in common. As a result, cultures can be grouped according to their value orientations. These orientations help explain ethical differences and enable leaders to predict how members of other cultural groups will respond to moral dilemmas. In this section of the chapter, I'll describe two widely used cultural classification systems. I will also introduce a third approach specifically developed to explain moral similarities and differences across cultures. Before we examine the cultural classification systems, however, there are four cautions to keep in mind. First, all categories are gross overgeneralizations. They describe what most people in that culture value. Not all U.S. residents are individualistic, for example, and not all Japanese citizens are collectivists. However, *in general,* more Americans put the individual first, whereas more Japanese emphasize group relations. Second, scholars may categorize the same nation differently and have not studied some regions of the world (such as Africa) as intensively as others (Europe, Asia, and the United States). Third, political and cultural boundaries aren't always identical. For instance, the Basque people live in both France and Spain. Fourth, as noted earlier, cultures are dynamic, so values change. A society may change its ethical priorities over time.

Programmed Value Patterns

Geert Hofstede of the Netherlands conducted an extensive investigation of cultural value patterns.[18] According to Hofstede, important values are "programmed" into members of every culture. He surveyed more than 100,000 IBM employees in 50 countries and three multicountry regions to uncover these value dimensions. He then checked his findings against those of other researchers who studied the same countries. The following four value orientations emerged.

Power Distance

The first category describes the relative importance of power differences. Status differences are universal, but cultures treat them differently. In high power distance cultures

(Philippines, Mexico), inequality is accepted as part of the natural order. Leaders enjoy special privileges and make no attempt to reduce power differentials; however, they are expected to care for the less fortunate. Low power distance cultures (Ireland, New Zealand), in contrast, are uneasy with large gaps in wealth, power, privilege, and status. Superiors tend to downplay these differences and strive for a greater degree of equality.

Individualism versus Collectivism

Hofstede's second value category divides cultures according to their preference for either the individual or the group. Individualistic cultures put the needs and goals of the person and her or his immediate family first. Members of these cultures see themselves as independent actors. In contrast, collectivistic cultures give top priority to the desires of the larger group—extended family, tribe, community. Members of these societies stress connection instead of separateness, putting a high value on their place in the collective. Think back to your decision to attend your current college or university. As a resident of Canada or the United States, you probably asked friends, high school counselors, and family members for advice, but in the end, you made the choice. In a collectivistic society such as Peru or Pakistan, your family or village might well have made this decision for you. There's no guarantee that you would have even gone to college. Families with limited resources can afford to send only one child to school. You might have been expected to go to work to help pay for the education of a brother or sister. (Complete Self-Assessment 11.1 to determine how individualistic or collectivistic you are.)

Masculinity versus Femininity

The third dimension reflects attitudes toward the roles of men and women. Highly masculine cultures such as Venezuela and Italy maintain clearly defined sex roles. Men are expected to be decisive, assertive, dominant, ambitious, and materialistic; women are encouraged to serve. Females are to care for the family, interpersonal relationships, and the weaker members of society. In feminine cultures such as Finland, Denmark, and the Netherlands, the differences between the sexes are blurred. Both men and women can be competitive and caring, assertive and nurturing. These cultures are more likely to stress interdependence, intuition, and concern for others.

Uncertainty Avoidance

This dimension describes the way in which cultures respond to uncertainty. Three indicators measure this orientation: anxiety level, widely held attitudes about rules, and employment stability. Members of high uncertainty avoidance societies (Greece, Portugal) feel anxious about uncertainty and view it as a threat. They believe in written rules and regulations, engage in more rituals, and accept directives from those in authority. In addition, they are less likely to change jobs and view long-term employment as a right. People who live in low uncertainty avoidance cultures (Ireland, Sweden) are more comfortable with uncertainty, viewing ambiguity as a fact of life. They experience lower stress and are more likely to take risks such as starting a new company or accepting a new job in another part of the country. These people are less reliant on written regulations and rituals and are more likely to trust their own judgments instead of obeying authority figures.

Hofstede argues that value patterns have a significant impact on ethical behavior.[19] For example, masculine European countries give little to international development programs but invest heavily in weapons. Feminine European nations do just the opposite. High uncertainty avoidance cultures are prone to prejudice because they follow the credo "What is different is dangerous." Low uncertainty avoidance cultures follow the credo "What is different is curious" and are more tolerant of strangers and new ideas.

Other researchers have joined Hofstede in linking value patterns to ethical attitudes and behavior.[20] They have discovered that members of feminine cultures are more sensitive to the presence of moral issues. Masculine/high power distance/high uncertainty avoidance countries are generally more corrupt, and their citizens are more likely to look to formal codes and policies for ethical guidance. Firms operating in these cultures are generally less attune to the concerns of stakeholders. Consumers from short-term orientation/low power distance/low uncertainty avoidance societies generally punish socially irresponsible firms. National accounting organizations in high individualism/high uncertainty avoidance societies are less likely to adopt ethical standards set by international accounting groups.

Of the four value dimensions, individualism versus collectivism has attracted the most attention. Scholars have used this dimension to explain a variety of cultural differences, including variations in ethical behavior. Management professors Stephen Carroll and Martin Gannon report that individualistic countries prefer universal ethical standards such as Kant's categorical imperative.[21] Collectivistic societies take a more utilitarian approach, seeking to generate the greatest good for in-group members. Citizens of these nations are more sensitive to elements of the situation. Here are examples of how these orientations impact ethical choices:

- *Bribery.* Payoffs tend to be more common in collectivistic nations and may be a way to meet obligations to the community. In some cases, there are laws against the practice, but they take a backseat to history and custom. Individualistic nations view bribery as a form of corruption; payoffs destroy trust and benefit some companies and people at the expense of others.

- *False information.* Individualists are more likely to lie in order to protect their privacy; collectivists are more likely to lie in order to protect the group or family. Those with a collectivistic orientation may promise what they can't deliver in order to reduce tensions between their in-group and outsiders. Individualists condemn this practice as deceptive and therefore unethical.

- *Intellectual property rights.* Whereas individuals own the rights to their creative ideas in individualistic societies, they are expected to share their knowledge in collectivistic nations. Copyright laws are a Western invention based on the belief that individuals should be rewarded for their efforts.

- *Gender equality.* Resistance to gender equality is strongest in collectivistic nations such as Saudi Arabia and Japan. Women are seen as an out-group in these societies. Many men fear that granting women more status—better jobs, leadership positions—would threaten group stability. Individualistic nations are more likely to have laws that promote equal opportunity, although in many of these countries, such as the United States, women hold fewer leadership positions than men and continue to earn less.

Individualism and collectivism are linked to different communication patterns, which also shape the ethical behavior of individuals.[22] Citizens of individualistic societies employ low-context communication in which most of the information in the message is embedded in the message itself. In Northern European countries like Germany and Switzerland, communicators express their thoughts and feelings as clearly as possible; carefully crafted written messages (such as contracts) are critical to doing business. To them, conflict should be faced head-on, which may produce morally questionable outcomes (i.e., damaged relationships, lower group cohesion). Collectivists generally engage in high-context communication where most of the information is contained in the situation or context where the message is delivered. The meaning of a message is shaped in large part by the relationships of the speakers. Speakers in Japan and other high-context cultures communicate indirectly, rarely expressing direct disagreement, for instance. They are more interested in maintaining group harmony than in expressing their true thoughts and feelings and try to avoid direct confrontation. Thus, they are less likely to confront unethical superiors or coworkers or to blow the whistle of organizational misbehavior. They may opt to sacrifice the truth to save face as well as to protect their group.

In addition to shaping our moral choices and communication patterns, both individualism and collectivism create ethical blind spots. Being self- or group-focused can make us particularly susceptible to certain types of ethical abuses. Individualism is linked to high crime rates, narcissism, violence, materialism, suicide, and drug abuse. Collectivism is tied to suppression of individual thought, blind obedience, harsh treatment of outside groups, human rights violations, and wife beating and killing.[23]

Project GLOBE

Project GLOBE (Global Leadership and Organizational Behavior Effectiveness) is an international effort involving 170 researchers who have gathered data from more than 17,000 managers in 62 countries. The researchers hope to better equip global managers by identifying the relationship between cultural values and effective leadership behaviors. Like Hofstede, the GLOBE researchers identify power distance, uncertainty avoidance, gender differentiation (masculinity and femininity), and individualism versus collectivism as important cultural dimensions. However, they extend Hofstede's list by including the following.[24]

In-Group Collectivism

This dimension describes the degree to which societal members take pride in their small groups, families, and organizations. In-group collectivism differs from Hofstede's collectivism dimension, which describes maintaining harmony and cooperation throughout society as a whole. Being a member of a family, a close group, or an employing organization is very important to members of in-group collectivist societies (Iran, India, China), and they have high expectations of other group members. People living in countries that score low on this dimension, such as Denmark, Sweden, and New Zealand, don't have similar expectations of friends and family.

Assertiveness

Assertiveness is the extent to which a culture encourages individuals to be tough, confrontational, and competitive as opposed to modest and tender. Spain and the United States rate high on this dimension; Sweden and New Zealand rate low. Those in highly assertive societies have a take-charge attitude and value competition. They are not particularly sympathetic to the weak and less fortunate. Members of less assertive cultures place more value on empathy, loyalty, and solidarity.

Future Orientation

This is the extent to which a society fosters and reinforces such future-oriented activities as planning and investing (Singapore, Switzerland, the Netherlands) rather than immediate gratification (Russia, Argentina, Poland).

Performance Orientation

This is the degree to which a society encourages and rewards group members for improving performance and demonstrating excellence. In places such as Hong Kong, Singapore, and the United States, training and development are valued, and people take initiative. Citizens prefer the direct communication style described earlier and feel a sense of urgency. In countries such as Russia, Italy, and Argentina, people put loyalty and belonging ahead of performance. They are uncomfortable with feedback and competition and place more weight on someone's family and background than on performance.

Humane Orientation

Humane orientation is the extent to which a culture encourages and honors people for being altruistic, caring, kind, fair, and generous. Support for the weak and vulnerable is particularly high in countries such as Malaysia, Ireland, and the Philippines. People are usually friendly and tolerant and may develop patronage and paternalistic relationships with their leaders. In contrast, power and material possessions motivate people in the former West Germany, Spain, and France. Self-enhancement takes precedence. Individuals are to solve their own problems; children are expected to be independent.

It is clear that differences on these values dimensions can cause some serious ethical conflicts. Those scoring high on in-group collectivism see no problem with hiring friends and family members even when more qualified candidates are available, a fact that will trouble those who believe that members of their in-groups should not expect preferential treatment. (See Scenario A, "The *Raccomandazione*," in Case Study 11.3.) People oriented toward the future will save and invest. They will condemn those who live in the moment and spend all they earn. Competition, direct communication, power, and personal advancement are applauded in assertive, performance-oriented, less-humane groups. These elements are undesirable to people who put more value on harmony, cooperation, family, and concern for others. Those living in assertive, performance-oriented cultures are tempted to engage in unethical activities in order to succeed. The businesses they create are more likely to be focused on shareholders, profits, and results instead of on stakeholders and social responsibility.[25]

Although there is plenty of evidence of ethical diversity in the GLOBE study, there are also signs of common ethical ground. As I noted in Chapter 8, the GLOBE researchers discovered that many of the characteristics associated with transformational leadership—motive arouser, foresight, encouraging, dynamic, motivational, trustworthy, positive, confidence builder, communicative—are admired across cultures (although to varying degrees).[26] In another study, researchers from Florida Atlantic University, the University of Maryland, and Wayne State University analyzed the GLOBE data to determine whether there are aspects of ethical leadership that are important for effective leadership across cultures. Four attributes emerged, although the extent to which each is endorsed and how each is implemented differs across cultures. (See "Focus on Follower Ethics: Ethical Expectations Across Cultures" for a closer look at how the ethical expectations of leaders vary between the United States and several other countries.) Character and integrity (consistency, virtue) were rated as important. So were altruism, collective motivation (putting the interests of the group ahead of personal interests), and encouraging and empowering (helping followers feel competent).[27] Taken together, these dimensions describe positive, people-oriented leadership that respects the rights and dignity of others. The fact that observers from many different cultural backgrounds agree on the attributes of ethical leadership suggests that there are common ethical standards shared by all cultures. We'll take a closer look at those standards later in the chapter.

Moral Foundations

New York University moral psychologist Jonathan Haidt believes that to understand ethical diversity, we first need to understand the psychological systems or foundations of morality. These mental foundations, which are part of our genetic makeup, enable humans to live together successfully in groups. Cultures shape how these systems are used, emphasizing one or more values over the others. Haidt compares these moral intuitions to taste buds. Nearly everyone is born with the same set of taste receptors. But each culture develops its own cuisine, which emphasizes different tastes.

Haidt identified five foundations for our moral intuitions:[28]

1. *Harm/care.* All species are sensitive to suffering in their own offspring, but humans are also sensitive to suffering beyond the family and can feel sympathy for outsiders. Because groups are attuned to cruelty and harm, they generally approve of those who prevent or alleviate suffering and make virtues out of kindness and compassion. However, the other four moral foundations temper the amount of compassion that individuals in different cultures display.

2. *Fairness/reciprocity.* Reciprocity—paying back others—is essential for the formation of alliances between individuals who are not related to each other. All cultures have virtues related to justice and fairness. Yet, while some societies value individual rights and equality, a great many more groups do not.

3. *In-group/loyalty.* Trusting fellow in-group members and distrusting those who belong to other groups have been essential for

Focus on Follower Ethics

ETHICAL EXPECTATIONS ACROSS CULTURES

While followers from different cultures look for similar attributes in their ethical leaders, cultural differences remain. The relative importance of particular ethical leadership qualities varies by country. In one study, Christian Resick and his colleagues asked middle managers in Ireland and the United States to rate the importance of four ethical leadership traits. Respondents in both countries gave equal ratings to (1) altruism (being compassionate and generous), (2) collective (team-oriented) motivation that inspires subordinates to work toward shared goals and to put the needs of the team first, and (3) encouragement that empowers followers to develop self-confidence and self-sufficiency. However, managers in the United States were significantly more likely than their Irish counterparts to rate character/integrity as important. This may be due to in part to differences in collectivism/individualism. In Ireland, which is more collectivist and does business through informal relationships, character and integrity are tied to social networks. In the United States, which is highly individualistic, the character of the leader, who acts largely on his or her own, is more important.

In a second study, Resick and his fellow researchers compared German and U.S. perspectives on ethical leadership. They found that character/integrity, collective motivation, and encouragement were strongly endorsed by managers in each nation, while altruism was rated as less important. As in the Ireland project, U.S. managers placed higher emphasis on character. German subordinates judge integrity based on how the leader treats others, including organizational members and stakeholders; U.S. employees judge the leader based on her or his consistency, honesty, and sincerity. Germans and Americans also differ in how they regulate ethical behavior. Germans prefer self-regulation while Americans rely on codes of ethics and outside regulations like the Sarbanes–Oxley Act.

In a third study, Resick and his team expanded their focus to Asia (China, Hong Kong, and Taiwan). Respondents from the People's Republic of China put the highest value on consideration and respect for others, character, and fairness. Managers from Hong Kong identified character (honesty, trustworthiness), a collective orientation (putting the needs of the organization first), and consideration and respect for others as critical qualities of ethical leaders. Taiwanese managers valued character and accountability (being personally accountable and holding others accountable).

International leaders need to be aware of these subtle differences as they address ethical issues across cultures. For example, the American manager who tries to institute detailed ethical policies in a German subsidiary may communicate that she or he doesn't trust employees. The U.S. manager who demonstrates respect for followers and looks out for their interests is more likely to be seen as an ethical leader. As a result, he or she will be more likely to gain the trust and respect of employees and exercise more influence.

Sources: Keating, M., Martin, G. S., Resick, C. J., & Dickson, M. W. (2007). A comparative study of the endorsement of ethical leadership in Ireland and the United States. *Irish Journal of Management, 28,* 5–30; Martin, G. S., Resick, C. J., Keating, M. A., & Dickson, M. W. (2009). Ethical leadership across cultures: A comparative analysis of German and US perspectives. *Business Ethics: A European Review, 18,* 127–144; Resick, C. J., Hanges, P. J., Dickson, M. W., & Mitchelson, J. K. (2006). A cross-cultural examination of the endorsement of ethical leadership. *Journal of Business Ethics, 63,* 345–359; Resick, C. J., Martin, G. S., Keating, M. A., Dickson, M. W., Kwan, H. K., & Peng, C. (2011). What ethical leadership means to me: Asian, American, and European perspectives. *Journal of Business Ethics, 101,* 435–457.

human survival. As a result, most cultures create virtues out of patriotism, loyalty, and heroism, and some societies (Japan, for instance) put a high value on in-group cohesion. Even when the society as a whole doesn't emphasize loyalty, there are usually sub-groups that do (e.g., the police and the military).

4. *Authority/respect.* Hierarchy is a fact of life in primate as well as human groups. While primates rely on brute strength to assert their dominance, people use such factors as prestige and defer-ence. In many cultures, followers feel respect, awe, and admiration for leaders and expect good leaders to act like wise parents.

5. *Purity/sanctity.* Only humans appear to feel disgust, which helps to protect the body against the transmission of disease through contact with corpses, feces, vomit, and other possible contami-nants. Purity has a social dimension as well. For instance, disgust can be felt for those with deformities or for those of lower social class, such as the untouchables in India. Members of most cul-tural groups disapprove of those individuals who are contami-nated by lust, gluttony, greed, and uncontrolled anger.

Haidt and his colleagues believe that other moral foundations may exist. *Liberty/oppression* has been nominated as the sixth psychological system, for example. Liberty/oppression is based on the degree of freedom people have from external influence to live life as they see fit (negative liberty) as well as access to education, health care, and other systems that allow them to pursue their goals (positive liberty). The origins of this dimension may stem from the need to protect oneself against alpha males who would take advantage of the group.

Cultures differ in the importance they place on the moral foundations. Residents of South Asia, East Asia, and Southeast Asia are more concerned with loyalty and sanctity than members of Western societies. Peoples who have continually faced outside threats and disease are more likely to value the foundations that bind groups together—loyalty, authority, sanctity. The United States and many other Western nations largely focus on reducing harm and promoting autonomy while Muslim societies place a high priority on purity, which is reflected in the segregation of men and women and separation from infidels. (To determine which values are most important to you, complete the Moral Foundations Questionnaire in Self-Assessment 11.2.)

Haidt developed his theory to explain moral differences between cultures but soon discovered that moral foundations can also explain the differences between liberals and conservatives in the United States. Contrasts between these political philosophies fur-ther illustrate how moral foundations shape ethical attitudes. Harm and fairness are more important to liberals, who rate the morality of an action based on whether it hurts or helps others. In contrast, conservatives are more concerned about all five dimensions. The sanctity/purity dimension is the best predictor of liberal and conservative positions on abortion. American liberals, who value autonomy, want to preserve the woman's right to choose while conservatives want to preserve the sanctity of the fetus. Many conservatives oppose illegal immigration based on the conviction that the newcomers are dangerous (purity) and will subvert America (authority), while liberals are pro-immigration based on compassion for the poor (harm) who may be mistreated (fairness). Conservatives demonstrate stronger opposition to flag burning based on in-group (patriotism), authority (subversion), and purity (desecration) values.[29]

Haidt urges leaders to keep all five moral systems in mind when dealing with diverse groups. We need to realize that although purity and authority may not be important to us, they are important to a great proportion of the world's population. We must acknowledge and address these concerns. Unless we are dealing with a highly liberal Western audience, our ethical appeals will be most effective if they speak to loyalty, authority, and purity in addition to care and fairness. Recognizing that strangers have different moral foundations is also an important first step to mutual understanding. The realization that others hold different central moral values reduces feelings of hostility in ethical conflicts. Such hostility is dangerous because it can tempt us to deny others their rights. Instead, we can work with those of different cultures to identify the shared values that make us all human.[30] In the next section, we will take a closer look at principles that can serve as the basis for mutual understanding.

FACING THE CHALLENGES

Understanding the relationship between cultural values and ethical decision making by itself is not enough to meet the ethical challenges posed by globalization and cultural differences. We also need to address attitudinal obstacles to ethical behavior, search for moral common ground with people of other cultures, and identify strategies for making decisions in cross-cultural settings.

Overcoming Attitudinal Obstacles

Prejudice, stereotypes, and ethnocentrism are important attitudinal obstacles to ethical behavior across cultures. *Prejudice* is the prejudgment of out-group members based on prior experiences and beliefs. Prejudice is universal, but the degree of prejudice varies from person to person, ranging from slight bias to extreme prejudice such as that displayed by racist skinheads. Negative prejudgments can be dangerous because they produce discriminatory behavior. For instance, police in many urban areas of the United States believe that African Americans are more likely than members of other groups to commit crimes. As a consequence, officers are more likely to stop and question black citizens, particularly young men, and to use force if they show the slightest sign of resistance.[31] The deaths of unarmed black males at hands of the police led to riots in Ferguson, Missouri, Baltimore, Maryland, and other critics.

Stereotyping is the process of classifying group members according to their perceived similarities while overlooking their individual differences. For example, one persistent stereotype is that Asian Americans have strong technical skills but little managerial aptitude. As a result, some organizations are eager to hire Asian Americans as engineers but are reluctant to put them in managerial roles. Because of perceptual biases, stereotypes are particularly devastating to marginalized groups. The natural tendency is to blame our failures on outside factors and to attribute our success to internal factors. The opposite is true when we evaluate the behavior of low-status groups. When we fall short, we blame other people, bad luck, bad weather, and other external forces. When we succeed, we point to our knowledge, character, skills, motivation, and training. Conversely, when members of marginalized groups fail, it is their laziness, low intelligence, or poor character that is to blame. When they succeed, however, we give the credit to the help they get from others rather than to their individual skills and effort.[32]

Ethnocentrism is the tendency to see the world from our cultural group's point of view. From this vantage point, our customs and values become the standard by which the rest of the world is judged. Our cultural ways seem natural; those of other groups fall short. A certain degree of ethnocentrism is probably inevitable.[33] Ethnocentrism can help a group band together and survive in the face of outside threats. However, ethnocentrism is a significant barrier to cross-cultural communication and problem solving. High levels of ethnocentrism can lead to the following problems:

- Inaccurate attributions about the behavior of those who differ from us (we interpret their behavior from our point of view, not theirs)
- Expressions of disparagement or animosity (ethnic slurs, belittling nicknames)
- Reduced contact with outsiders
- Indifference and insensitivity to the perspectives of members of marginalized groups
- Pressure on other groups to conform to our cultural standards
- Justification for war and violence as a means of expressing cultural dominance

Examples of ethnocentrism abound. For many years, the Bureau of Indian Affairs made assimilation its official policy, forcing Native Americans to send their children to reservation schools, where they were punished for speaking their tribal languages. In other instances, well-meaning people assume that their values and practices are the only right ones. Many early missionaries equated Christianity with Western lifestyles and required converts to dress, live, think, and worship like Europeans or North Americans. The Islamic State in Iraq and Syria (ISIS) uses brutal force to impose its interpretation of the Koran on those living in conquered territories.

Overcoming the barriers described here begins with addressing our attitudes. (Turn to "Leadership Ethics at the Movies: *McFarland USA*" to see how one family dealt with these mental obstacles.) We can reduce our levels of negative prejudice, stereotyping, and ethnocentrism by committing ourselves to mindfulness and dignity and integrity.

In most routine encounters, we tend to operate on autopilot and perform our roles mechanically, without much reflection. When we're engaged in mindless interaction, we're not likely to challenge the ethnocentric assumption that ours is the only way to solve problems. Mindfulness is the opposite of mindlessness. When we're mindful, we pay close attention to our attitudes and behaviors. Three psychological processes take place.[34]

The first is *openness to new categories*. Being mindful makes us more sensitive to differences. Instead of lumping people into broad categories based on age, race, gender, or role, we make finer distinctions within these classifications. We discover that not all student government officers, retirees, engineers, Japanese exchange students, and professors are alike.

The second psychological process involves *openness to new information.* Mindless communication closes us off to new data, and we fail to note the kinds of cultural differences described earlier. We assume that others hold the same ethical values. In mindful communication, we pick up new information as we closely monitor our behavior along with the behavior of others.

The third psychological process is *recognizing the existence of more than one perspective.* Mindlessness results in tunnel vision that ignores potential solutions. Mindfulness, on the other hand, opens our eyes to other possibilities. For example, there can be more than one way to make and implement ethical choices.

Dignity and integrity also ought to characterize all of our interactions with people of other cultures. We maintain our own dignity and integrity by confronting others who engage in prejudicial comments or actions; we maintain the dignity of others by respecting their views. Respect doesn't mean that we have to agree with another's moral stance. But when we disagree, we need to respond in a civil, sensitive manner.

By committing ourselves as leaders to mindful communication, the dignity of others, and personal integrity, we can reduce ethnocentrism and prejudice in the group as a whole. Using morally inclusive language and disputing prejudiced statements, for instance, improves ethical climate because followers will be less likely to attack other groups in our presence. However, if we don't speak out when followers disparage members of out-groups, the practice will continue. We'll share some of the responsibility for creating a hostile atmosphere.

Finding Common Moral Ground

Confronted with a wide range of ethical values and standards, a number of philosophers, business leaders, anthropologists, and others opt for ethical relativism. In ethical relativism, there are no universal moral codes or standards. Each group or society is unique. Therefore, members of one culture can't pass moral judgment on members of another group.

I'll admit that, at first glance, ethical relativism is appealing. It avoids the problem of ethnocentrism while simplifying the decision-making process. We can concentrate on fitting in with the prevailing culture and never have to pass judgment. On closer examination, however, the difficulties of ethical relativism become all too apparent.[35] Without shared standards, there's little hope that the peoples of the world can work together to address global problems. There may be no basis on which to condemn the evil of notorious leaders who are popular in their own countries. Furthermore, the standard of cultural relativism obligates us to follow (or at least not to protest against) abhorrent local practices such as the killing of brides by their in-laws in the rural villages of Pakistan. Without universal rights and wrongs, we have no basis on which to contest such practices.

Cross-cultural research suggests that there might be moral commonalities when making ethical decisions. To determine if there are universal moral principles or a "moral grammar" built into the mental capacities of all humans, investigators use variations of the "trolley problem." In the trolley problem, an out-of-control trolley threatens to kill five people unless immediate action is taken. In one case, the trolley operator is incapacitated

Leadership Ethics at the Movies

McFARLAND, USA

Key cast members: Kevin Costner, Maria Bello, Carlos Pratts, Johnny Ortiz, Ramiro Rodriguez

Synopsis: Failed football coach Jim White finds redemption after he moves to the small central California town of McFarland in the late 1980s. Most of the residents of McFarland are Mexican American farm laborers. Coach White and his family struggle to adapt to the values and customs of their new culture. However, with the guidance of their neighbors, they begin to set down roots in the community. White starts a cross-country team, even though he has no experience as a runner or as a track coach. He has to supply his team members with running shoes and uniforms and must convince parents to let their boys leave the fields in order to compete. White and his runners overcome these obstacles to win the state championship in their initial year

of competition, the first of nine state titles over a period of fourteen years. Based on a true story.

Rating: PG for mature themes

Themes: ethnocentrism, prejudice, stereotyping, dignity and inclusion, mindfulness, cultural differences, the global shadow of privilege, character, transformational leadership

Discussion Starters

1. What character traits and attitudes enabled Jim White and his family to adapt to a different cultural setting?

2. What examples of ethnocentrism, prejudice, and stereotyping do you see in the film?

3. How was Coach White transformed through his experience coaching the cross-country team?

and a passenger has to decide whether or not to throw a switch, diverting the vehicle to safety on a sidetrack (and saving the five passengers) but killing a pedestrian who happens to be standing on the rails. In the other case, someone standing by the tracks must decide whether or not to intervene directly by throwing another bystander into the path of the trolley to slow it down and save the five passengers.

One group of researchers collected responses to the trolley problem from 30,000 subjects in 120 countries.[36] There was widespread agreement across all national, religious, and education groups. By a significant margin, participants said they would throw the switch to save the trolley passengers but not throw someone onto the tracks to accomplish the same goal. Respondents reported that throwing a switch is an impersonal act, and they saw the death of the pedestrian as an unfortunate consequence. On the other hand, throwing a bystander onto the track is a deliberate, highly personal act that makes the victim a means to an end.

The trolley problem may be hypothetical, but it has parallels in real life. The American Medical Association (AMA) believes that hastening death by withholding treatment is more acceptable than hastening death through a drug overdose. The medical group permits passive euthanasia for terminally ill patients (which is similar to throwing the trolley switch). However, the AMA opposes active euthanasia (which raises the same concerns as throwing a bystander onto the trolley track).

Research into the neurological basis of moral judgments is in the initial stages (see the discussion of dual processing in Chapter 6) but suggests that, when it comes to ethics, there might some cultural unity to go along with cultural diversity. Common morality and cosmopolitanism are two approaches to uncovering ethical commonalities.

Common Morality

Former Dartmouth philosophy professor Bernard Gert believed that we can identify the elements that make up the moral grammar common to all people.[37] These components arise out of the human experience, particularly the universal recognition that people are vulnerable and can be harmed by others. This *common morality* forms a system that rational people intuitively support because it both protects them and the people they care about. Immoral actions have negative consequences, causing suffering in the form of pain, loss of freedom and pleasure, disability, and death. Moral rules are designed to lessen these harms.

Citizens refer to universal principles when defending their choices. They frequently break these guidelines but, when they do, they must provide justification for their actions. However, sharing a common morality doesn't eliminate disagreement about ethical issues. "Although all rational people will agree on the answers to most moral questions," said Gert, "they need not agree on the answers to all of them."[38] Disagreements center, first of all, on whom is protected by the moral code. Some ethicists believe that animals deserve the same moral protections as people, for instance. Second, decision makers also disagree about how to rank the relative worth of harms and benefits. For example, legislators differ over whether the benefit of increased national security is worth the loss of privacy and freedom of movement that results from stricter security measures. Third, estimates of the harmful and beneficial consequences of a violation vary between decision makers. Take the case of lying to a friend to protect her or his feelings. Some would argue that the costs of this deception are far outweighed by the benefit to the friend. Others would say that lying in this instance hurts the friend by providing inaccurate feedback and reflects poor character on the part of the liar. Finally, there can be conflict over whether or not an action, such as honoring a patient's request to be taken off of life support, is immoral and needs justification.

Gert argued that the following ten rules account for all types of actions that are either forbidden or required. As noted above, every intentional violation of one of these rules demands that the violator provide a reason for his or action. Common justifications include the need to kill in war, to lie to protect the organization, to imprison criminals to protect society, to inflict pain to punish immoral behavior, and to break the law to serve a higher cause. The first five rules described below outlaw basic harms and the last five prohibit actions that could cause these harms.

> *Rule 1: "Do not kill."* This guideline prevents the most serious of harms—the permanent loss of consciousness.

> *Rule 2: "Do not cause pain."* Everyone wants to avoid pain, whether physical or mental.

Rule 3: "Do not disable." ("Do not deprive of ability.") It is possible to disable someone physically (amputations, blinding), mentally (fostering addictions, creating phobias), and volitionally (restricting movement).

Rule 4: "Do not deprive of freedom." This rule extends beyond physical imprisonment. It also includes job discrimination, which denies employment opportunities to certain groups, and stealing, which limits the options of victims. In addition, the dictum addresses "freedom from being acted upon." Individuals have the right to avoid unwanted sexual touching and invasions of privacy, for instance.

Rule 5: "Do not deprive of pleasure." Pleasure takes a variety of forms, such as sleep, sexual satisfaction, and beauty. Depriving others of their rest, sexual enjoyment (through female circumcision, for example), or beauty (by destroying artworks or architecture) are violations of this standard.

Rule 6: "Do not deceive." Lying is only one way to deceive. Other forms of deception include withholding needed information, spreading false rumors, and fostering faulty assumptions.

Rule 7: "Keep your promises." This rule covers both formal promises like labor contracts as well as informal promises made to other individuals. Often, there are legal consequences for violating formal promises, such as when a company breaks the terms of a contract with a vendor.

Rule 8: "Do not cheat." Cheating involves acting unfairly in a way that gives the cheater an advantage. Common examples of cheating include plagiarizing on academic papers, bribing a foreign official to get a building contract, tinkering with a scale, and, as we saw in Chapter 2, cheating on auto emissions tests.

Rule 9: "Obey the law." With some exceptions (i.e., segregation statutes), laws generally keep society functioning smoothly. They stop violations of the first five rules, which prevent harm.

Rule 10. "Do your duty." This rule covers those who play particular roles in society—doctors, lawyers, financial advisors, professors. They must carry out the duties associated with their positions (treating the sick, representing clients, providing objective financial advice, presenting course content) or face condemnation. Rule 10 also applies to duties that arise from particular situations. We expect individuals to help others in need if they are in close proximity and can do so.

Cosmopolitanism

Cosmopolitanism is another attempt to develop a universal ethic. Cosmopolitans believe that that since we live in a global society, we should consider ourselves citizens of the world (cosmopolitans) rather than of one particular nation-state. This approach acts as an "ethics of strangers" in a world where we increasingly interact with those outside our cultural group.[39]

Cosmopolitanism has a long history in Western philosophy, stretching back to the ancient Greco-Roman Stoic philosophers, such as Diogenes, Cicero, Seneca, Marcus Aurelius, who saw the world as one united city made up of individuals who were related to one another. Immanuel Kant proposed the creation of an international legal authority to regulate relations between nations. He encouraged hospitality toward foreigners. Modern moral cosmopolitanism is based on three elements. The first is *individualism*. According to ethicist Thomas Pogge, "The ultimate units of concern are human beings, or persons—rather than, say, family lines, tribes, ethnic cultural, or religious communities, nations, or states."[40] The second component is *universality*. We should be equally concerned about every human being, no matter who they are and where they live. The third component is *generality*, the belief that everyone in the world should make persons their primary concern, extending their obligations to those outside their immediate group.

Driven by these three convictions, cosmopolitans take a humanistic or altruistic approach to globalization, believing that every human being has dignity and value, regardless of their location, status, or background. They have a strong sense of global justice and work to ensure human rights. Their duty to care (see Chapter 5) extends to the "distant needy"—the less privileged who are often found in the world's developing nations. Cosmopolitans act on that concern by providing assistance to others around the world. In particular, cosmopolitans argue that affluent businesses and nations have a responsibility to give to less fortunate people and nations.

Additional evidence of ethical common ground comes from universal codes of ethics, which have enabled members of the world community to punish crimes against humanity and to create international regulatory bodies. Responsible multinational corporations such as The Body Shop, Nike, and Starbucks adhere to widely held moral principles as they conduct business in a variety of cultural settings. Three particularly noteworthy codes are the United Nations Declaration of Human Rights, the Global Business Standards Codex, and the Caux Principles.

United Nations Declaration of Human Rights

Following World War II, a conflict fought in large part to protect human freedoms, the United Nations adopted the Universal Declaration of Human Rights. According to this document, human rights are granted to individuals based solely on their status as persons or, to put it another way, "We are all entitled to human rights simply on the basis that we are human beings."[41] These rights protect the inherent dignity of every person regardless of race, ethnic background, place of residence, age, income, physical ability, or social status. Some of the key rights spelled out in the Universal Declaration include the following:[42]

> *Article 4.* No one shall be held in slavery or servitude; slavery and the slave trade shall be prohibited in all their forms.

> *Article 5.* No one shall be subjected to torture or to cruel, inhuman, or degrading treatment or punishment.

> *Article 9.* No one shall be subjected to arbitrary arrest, detention, or exile.

> *Article 13.* Everyone has the right to freedom of movement and residence.

Article 19. Everyone has the right to freedom of thought, conscience, and religion.

Article 25. Everyone has the right to a standard of living adequate for the health and well-being of himself [or herself] and of his [or her] family.

Article 26. Everyone has a right to an education.

More recently, the United Nations launched the Global Compact to encourage multinational corporations to honor human rights, labor rights, and the environment while at the same time fighting corruption. The Compact has more than 8,600 business and nonbusiness members from more than 130 countries. Business participants undergo an annual certification process to measure how well they are adhering to 10 universal principles (e.g., avoiding human rights abuse, eliminating child labor, working against extortion and bribery). They work with nongovernmental organizations (NGOs) and other groups to tackle societal and environmental problems.[43]

The Global Business Standards Codex

Harvard business professor Lynn Paine and her colleagues argue that world-class corporations base their codes of ethics on a set of eight universal, overarching ethical principles.[44] Paine's group compiled these guidelines after surveying a variety of global and corporate codes of conduct and government regulations. The researchers offer their Global Business Standards Codex as a benchmark for those who want to conform to universal standards of corporate conduct.

1. *Fiduciary principle.* Act on behalf of the company and its investors. Be diligent and loyal in carrying out the firm's business. As a trustee, be candid (open and honest).

2. *Property principle.* Respect and protect property and the rights of its owners. Don't steal or misuse company assets, including information, funds, and equipment. Avoid waste and take care of property entrusted to you.

3. *Reliability principle.* Honor all commitments. Keep promises and follow through on agreements, even when they are not in the form of legally binding contracts.

4. *Transparency principle.* Do business in a truthful manner. Avoid deceptive acts and practices and keep accurate records. Release information that should be shared in a timely fashion but maintain confidentiality and privacy as necessary.

5. *Dignity principle.* Respect the dignity of all who come in contact with the corporation, including employees, suppliers, customers, and the public. Protect their health, privacy, and rights. Avoid coercion. Promote human development instead by providing learning and development opportunities.

6. *Fairness principle.* Deal fairly with everyone. Engage in fair competition, provide just compensation to employees, and be even-handed in dealings with suppliers and corporate partners. Practice nondiscrimination in both employment and contracting.

7. *Citizenship principle.* Act as a responsible member of the community by (a) obeying the law, (b) protecting the public good (not engaging in corruption, protecting the environment), (c) cooperating with public authorities, (d) avoiding improper involvement in politics, and (e) contributing to the community (e.g., economic and social development, giving to charitable causes).

8. *Responsiveness principle.* Engage with outsiders (neighborhood groups, activists, customers) that may have concerns about the company's activities. Work with other groups to better society while not usurping the government's role in protecting the public interest.

The Caux Principles

The Caux Round Table is made up of business executives from the United States, Japan, and Europe who meet periodically in Caux, Switzerland. Round Table members hope to set a world standard by which to judge business behavior. Their principles are based on twin ethical ideals. The first is the Japanese concept of *kyosei*, which refers to living and working together for the common good. The second is the Western notion of human dignity, the sacredness and value of each person as an end rather than as a means to someone else's end.[45]

> *Principle 1. The responsibilities of corporations: Beyond shareholders toward stakeholders.* Corporations have a responsibility to improve the lives of everyone they come in contact with, starting with employees, shareholders, and suppliers and then extending out to local, national, regional, and global communities.

> *Principle 2. The economic and social impact of corporations: Toward innovation, justice, and world community.* Companies in foreign countries should not only create jobs and wealth but also foster better social conditions—education, welfare, and human rights. Corporations have an obligation to enrich the world community through innovation, the wise use of resources, and fair competition.

> *Principle 3. Corporate behavior: Beyond the letter of law toward a spirit of trust.* Businesses ought to promote honesty, transparency, integrity, and keeping promises. These behaviors make it easier to conduct international business and to support a global economy.

> *Principle 4. Respect for rules: Beyond trade friction toward cooperation.* Leaders of international firms must respect both international and local laws in order to reduce trade wars and to promote the free flow of goods and services.

Principle 5. Support for multilateral trade: Beyond isolation toward world community. Firms should support international trading systems and agreements and eliminate domestic measures that undermine free trade.

Principle 6. Respect for the environment: Beyond protection toward enhancement. A corporation ought to protect and, if possible, improve the physical environment through sustainable development and cutting back on the wasteful use of natural resources.

Principle 7. Avoidance of illicit operations: Beyond profit toward peace. Global business leaders must ensure that their organizations aren't involved in such forbidden activities as bribery, money laundering, support of terrorism, drug trafficking, and organized crime.

After spelling out general principles, the Caux accord applies them to important stakeholder groups. Leaders following these standards hope to (a) treat customers and employees with dignity, (b) honor the trust of investors, (c) create relationships with suppliers based on mutual trust, (d) engage in just behavior with competitors, and (e) work for reform and human rights in host communities. The Caux Round Table has also developed principles to guide NGOs. Integrity—remaining faithful to the group's mission to serve the common good—should be the fundamental operating principle for NGOs. Starting from this foundation of integrity, these organizations should serve the public benefit, operate transparently, practice open governance, remain independent, respect the law, demonstrate care, and be accountable.[46]

Making Ethical Choices in Culturally Diverse Settings

The universal principles described above play an important role when we are faced with making ethical decisions involving more than one culture. According to business ethicists Thomas Donaldson and Thomas Dunfee, we need to hold fast to global principles while we take local values into account.[47] Their integrative social contracts theory (ISCT) provides one set of guidelines for balancing respect for ethical diversity with adherence to universal ethical standards.

ISCT is based on the idea of social contracts—agreements that spell out the duties of institutions, communities, and societies. The theory is integrative because it incorporates two kinds of contracts: macrosocial and microsocial. *Macrosocial* contracts are broader and lay the foundation for how people interact with one another. The requirement that the government protect its citizens and the belief that employers should respect the rights of workers are examples of ideal contracts. *Microsocial* contracts govern the relationships between the members of specific groups (local towns, regions, nations, companies, professions). These contracts are revealed by the norms of the group. For example, those who participate in auctions must adhere to the norms of the auction community, which include revealing whether participants have the means to back up their bids and not interfering with others who are making bids. Community contracts are considered authentic or binding if members of the group have a voice in the creation of the norms, if members can exit the group if they disagree with prevailing norms, and if the norms are widely recognized and practiced by group members. Under these standards, prohibitions against free speech in countries ruled by repressive regimes would not be authentic because citizens had no say in creating these rules and can't leave the community if they want to do so.

Local communities have a great deal of latitude or *moral free space* to create their own rules, and these norms should be respected whenever possible. An Indonesian manager participating in an Australian real estate auction should obey Australian auction norms, for instance. However, universal principles such as those described in the previous section (what Donaldson and Dunfee call *hypernorms*) take priority when global principles clash with community standards. Exploitation of workers through excessive hours, low pay, imprisonment, and sexual abuse might be the norm in some developing countries. But such practices should be rejected because they violate hypernorms that urge us to respect the dignity of other human beings and treat them fairly and humanely.

To make decisions following ISCT guidelines, follow these steps:

1. Identify all relevant stakeholders or communities.

2. Determine whether these communities are legitimate. (Do they allow voice and exit by members?)

3. Identify authentic norms (those that are widely known and shared).

4. Determine whether the norms are legitimate (do not conflict with hypernorms).

5. Resolve any conflicts between legitimate norms. (If both sets of norms do not conflict with universal standards, go with the option that is dominant—the one accepted by the larger community.)

University of Louisiana professors J. Brooke Hamilton, Stephen Knouse, and Vanessa Hill (HKH) offer another set of guidelines for making choices in ethically diverse contexts. They provide six questions specifically designed to help managers at multinational enterprises (MNEs) make moral choices when corporate values conflict with business practices in the host country.[48] The questions described below, which make up the HKH model, are designed to serve as a discussion/decision guide, not as a rigid set of steps. Managers don't have to come to a definite answer to one question before moving to another. They may return to earlier questions later and answer them differently.

1. *What is the questionable practice (QP) in this situation?*
   - In the initial stage of the HKH decision-making format, managers determine that the norms of the MNE clash with the norms of the local culture. At this point, the disparity is labeled as *questionable* because it may involve cultural differences rather than ethical issues. The key is to come to a clear understanding of the nature of the conflict.

2. *Does the QP violate any laws that are enforced?*
   - If the QP violates laws of the home country (the U.S. Foreign Corrupt Practices Act, for example, or European Union prohibitions against bribery) or the host country, it should be discontinued.

3. *Is the QP simply a cultural difference, or is it also a potential ethics problem?*
   - A QP reflects a cultural difference if it "does not cause harm and appears to be that culture's legitimate way of achieving some worthwhile business or social outcome."[49] It rises to the level of a potential ethical issue if it creates harm or violates a universal global principle like treating people with respect and practicing the Golden Rule.

4. *Does the QP violate the firm's core values or code of conduct, an industry-wide or international code to which the firm subscribes, or a firmly established hypernorm?*
   - How managers answer this question will be determined by whether they believe that their companies are driven solely by the desire to comply with the law or whether they believe their firms are committed to ethical integrity instead (see Chapter 10). Compliance-driven firms are more likely to conform to local rules because they are primarily interested in following the law; survival is the core value. Integrity-driven firms have a higher standard. Managers at these firms judge local practices based on whether they conform to important corporate values (customer service, treating employees fairly) and such international guidelines as the Caux Principles and the Global Business Standards Codex.

5. *Does the firm have leverage (something of value to offer) in the host country that allows the firm to follow its own practices rather than the QP?*
   - Only managers at integrity-driven companies will ask this question, as managers at compliance-oriented firms will go along with local practices. If the firm can offer significant benefits like jobs, cash, training, and new technology, it can better resist the pressure to engage in unethical activity and can negotiate a way to adapt to local customs without violating its core values. For instance, a large Western oil firm that values equal treatment of both genders may be able to leverage its power in a traditionalist Middle Eastern country to promote women to positions of organizational authority.

6. *Will market practices in the host country improve if the firm follows its own practices rather than the QP in the host country marketplace?*
   - A company without leverage will have to conform to customs of the home country or exit the market. However, if the

firm has such leverage, it has an obligation to try to improve conditions in the countries in which it operates. Modeling respect for individuals, honest business practices, and concern for the environment can encourage local firms and other MNEs to do the same and result in better living and working conditions and a healthier economy.

You can practice your ability to make cross-cultural ethical choices by applying the steps of the ISCT and HKH models to the diversity scenarios in Case Study 11.3.

IMPLICATIONS AND APPLICATIONS

- Acknowledging the dark side of globalization reduces the likelihood of ethical abuse on the world stage. As a leader in a global environment, you must take additional care to avoid casting shadows of power, privilege, mismanaged information, inconsistency, misplaced and broken loyalties, and irresponsibility.

- Cultural differences make ethical decisions more difficult. Nevertheless, resist the temptation to revert to your old ways of thinking or to blindly follow local customs. Try instead to expand your capacity to act ethically in multicultural situations.

- Understanding the relationship between cultural differences and ethical values can help you predict how members of another group will respond to moral questions.

- Two popular cultural value classification systems are Hofstede's programmed values (power distance, individualism versus collectivism, masculinity versus femininity, uncertainty avoidance) and the GLOBE cultural dimensions, which include Hofstede's categories along with in-group collectivism, assertiveness, future orientation, performance orientation, and humane orientation. Be alert to the ethical blind spots created by your cultural values.

- All humans seem concerned about care, fairness, loyalty, respect for authority, and purity. But cultures differ in the relative importance they put on each of these moral foundations, which leads to ethical conflicts. Keep all five psychological or moral systems in mind when dealing with diverse groups.

- To expand your capacity to act ethically in a global society, address attitudinal obstacles and look for common moral ground.

- Prejudice, stereotypes, and ethnocentrism are barriers to diversity and lead to moral abuses. You can avoid casting shadows if you commit yourself to mindfulness and human dignity and integrity.

- Common morality and cosmopolitanism are two attempts to identify universal moral standards. Common morality is founded on the premise that we want to protect both ourselves and those we care about. Cosmopolitanism acts as an ethics of strangers that encourages us to see ourselves as citizens of the world.

- Evidence for common ethical ground can be found in United Nations Declaration of Human Rights and two business codes—the Global Business Codex and the Caux Principles.

- To make ethical decisions in cross-cultural settings, take both local values and global principles into account. Follow community norms except when they conflict with universal moral standards. As a business leader, make the most of your company's leverage in another country to improve local conditions.

FOR FURTHER EXPLORATION, CHALLENGE, AND SELF-ASSESSMENT

1. Complete Self-Assessment 11.1. How individualistic or collectivistic are you and why? How does your orientation shape your behavior and ethical decision making?

2. Complete Self-Assessment 11.2. How do your core values influence your perspective on ethical issues? (Supply examples.) How you can use this information to reach a common understanding with others of different political or cultural backgrounds? Write up your reflections.

3. Form groups and debate the following proposition: Globalization has done more harm than good.

4. Pair off and brainstorm a list of the advantages and disadvantages of ethical diversity. What conclusions do you draw from your list?

5. Using the Internet, compare press coverage of an international ethical issue from a variety of countries. How does the coverage differ and why? Write up your findings.

6. Rate yourself on one or both of the cultural classification systems described in this chapter. Create a value profile of your community, organization, or university. How well do you fit in?

7. Write a response to the following: Is there a common morality that peoples of all nations can share? Which of the global approaches described in the chapter best reflects these shared standards and values? If you were to create your own declaration of global ethics, what would you put on it?

STUDENT STUDY SITE

Visit the student study site at **study.sagepub.com/johnsonmecl6e** to access full SAGE journal articles for further research and information on key chapter topics.

Case Study 11.1

BEING WORKED TO DEATH?

If you own an Apple iPhone, chances are that China's Foxconn Technology manufactured it. The company's 1.2 million workers produced the iPhone 5 and currently assemble the iPhone 6.

(Continued)

(Continued)

In addition to making phones and tablets for Apple, the firm manufactures products for Samsung, Microsoft, IBM, Hewlett Packard, Amazon, Dell, and Sony.

Despite its size, few Westerners had heard of Foxconn until eighteen of its employees attempted suicide in 2010 by jumping out of factory and company dormitory windows.[1] Apple customers wondered whether their devices had cost the lives of workers; Western and Chinese media outlets began to press Foxconn and Apple leaders for answers as to why so many employees were taking their own lives.

Foxconn founder Terry Gou and other executives noted that the rate of "self-killing" at the company was close to China's average. They defended the company's labor conditions, pointing to the fact that workers are provided with food, dormitories, coffee shops, and swimming pools in a clean, campus-like setting. Indeed, Foxconn facilities appear far superior to those at many other Chinese manufacturing plants where, at least in the past, workers had to find their own food and places to sleep. Gou vowed to "leave no stone unturned" as the company tried to find a way to reduce the number of suicides. Large safety nets were strung around all company buildings to catch any future jumpers. The company also introduced suicide prevention centers and raised wages. Officials at Apple said they were "disturbed and deeply saddened" by the deaths. Apple then hired an outside organization, the Fair Labor Association, to audit Foxconn working conditions. Chief executive officer (CEO) Tim Cook traveled to the Foxconn's Zhengzhou, China factory to investigate and commissioned a team of suicide prevention experts to make recommendations to Foxconn's leaders.

Unfortunately, worker suicides continued. In 2012, a group of workers threatened to jump off the roof of a Wuhan factory after their bosses refused to provide promised severance pay. In 2013, three workers took their lives over a three-week period. In 2014, there were at least six suicides.

Union groups, human rights activists and investigative reporters blame the ongoing suicides on the military-like atmosphere at Foxconn plants. The story of seventeen-year-old Tian Yu illustrates the harsh conditions at Foxconn facilities. Yu jumped from a Foxconn factory window. She survived her fall but is paralyzed for life. Here is a description of her typical work day prior to her suicide attempt:

> Yu's job was inspecting screens to ensure they weren't scratched. She woke at 6:30 a.m., attended an unpaid meeting at 7:20 a.m. and started work 20 minutes later. Lunch was at 11 a.m. and she usually skipped dinner to work until 7:40 p.m.—a 12-hour day. Technicians from the engineering department time monitored every task and, if workers can meet the quotas, the targets are increased. Anyone unable to meet their hourly quota is not allowed to rest. Conversation in the workshop was forbidden.[2]

Mandatory overtime greatly increases the pressure on workers. One undercover reporter investigating working conditions at Foxconn had to work eighteen days in a row even though he repeatedly asked for time off. Another reporter, whose longest shift was 16 hours, described the fatigue he felt: "Every time I got back to the dormitories, I wouldn't want to move. Even if I was hungry, I wouldn't want to get up to eat. I just wanted to lie down and rest."[3] Exhausted employees rarely have the time or energy to enjoy the swimming pools or coffee shops provided by their employer. Instead, they return to dorm rooms filled with strangers selected to live together by Foxconn management.

The Fair Labor Association reports that Foxconn workers are putting in less overtime. However, it is hard to imagine that the relentless demands on employees will ease unless Apple bears more of the cost of improving labor conditions. Apple executives could provide more funding to improve working conditions and/or offer more generous contract terms. And the company could afford to make these concessions. While Foxconn profit margins declined (as low as 1.7%), Apple's profit margins soared to as high as 44%, making Apple one of the richest companies in the world. According to CBS money columnist Margaret Heffernan, Apple stockholders are increasing their wealth at the expense of Foxconn employees.

> You don't have to be an economist to appreciate that this is fundamentally a redistribution of wealth, from the productivity of Foxconn workers to the shareholders. What that means is that the employees of Foxconn don't just make our phones; they also fund our portfolios.[4]

Discussion Probes

1. If you own an iPhone, are you bothered by working conditions at Foxconn plants? Do you worry that the production of your phone might have contributed to a death of a worker?

2. How much blame, if any, for worker suicides should go to CEO Gou and Foxconn? To the leaders of Apple?

3. Is Foxconn being unfairly scrutinized, given that its facilities and treatment of workers may be better than at other manufacturing firms in China? Is Apple being unfairly singled out for criticism, given that a number of other electronics firms also have contracts with Foxconn?

4. Has Apple taken enough responsibility for the treatment of those who manufacture its projects?

5. Should Apple accept lower profits to help those who work for its subcontractors? As an Apple stockholder, would you be willing to accept a lower stock price if the company did so?

6. What global shadows are cast in this case?

Notes

1. Estimates on the number of deaths vary between news sources. Getting accurate information from Foxconn on employee suicides is difficult.

(Continued)

(Continued)

2. Heffernan, M. (2013, August 7). What happened after the Foxconn suicides. *CBS News*.

3. Bilton, R. (2014, December 18). Apple 'failing to protect Chinese factory workers." *BBC Panorama*.

4. Heffernan.

Sources

Adams, S. (2012, September 12). Apple's new Foxconn embarrassment. *Forbes*.

Barboza, D. (2010, May 27). Deaths shake a titan in China. *The New York Times*, p. B1.

Barboza, D., & Duhigg, C. (2012, September 11). China plant again faces labor issue on iPhones. *The New York Times,* p. B1.

Chakrabortty, A. (2013, August 5). The woman who nearly died making your iPad. *Guardian*.

Goel, V. (2013, May 17). Foxconn audit finds a workweek still too long. *The New York Times*, p. B7.

Johnson, J. (2011, February 28). 1 million workers. 90 million phones. 17 suicides. Who's to blame? *Wired*.

McCarthy, K. (2015, August 7). Another death in Apple's 'Mordor'—its Foxconn Chinese assembly plant. *The Register*.

Xi, Y. (2015, February 5). Union official links Foxconn deaths to excessive overtime. *LaborNotes*.

Xian, Z. (2015, February 3). Foxconn's long hours causing workers' deaths: Union. *ChinaDaily.com.cn*

Young, N. (2011, February 16). Apple's new chief visits Chinese factory to hang nets after workplace suicides. *DailyMail.com*

Case Study 11.2

THE DENTIST AS LION KILLER

Walter Palmer is not your ordinary dentist. Instead of playing golf to relax, Palmer kills large game animals using only a bow and arrow. His trophies include an elk, a bear, a leopard, a bison, and, most recently, one of the world's most famous lions.

Palmer paid $55,000 to hunt a lion in Zimbabwe. According to reports, Palmer's Zimbabwean guides lured a large black-mane male out of a national park (where it was protected) onto private land by tying a dead animal to the side of a vehicle. Palmer then shot the lion with his bow, but it survived. After two days of tracking, a professional hunter finished the kill. Palmer took the head and skin, leaving the rest of the carcass to rot.

Word soon spread that Palmer had killed Cecil, an iconic lion who was a favorite of park visitors and locals. Cecil was part of an ongoing lion study by Oxford university researchers and he was equipped with a GPS collar at the time of his death.

Soon the dentist-hunter became hunted himself. Angry activists took to social media to attack Palmer and to shut down his website. Protestors picketed his dental office in suburban Minneapolis Minnesota and set up a makeshift memorial of plush toys and flowers for Cecil the lion on the doorstep. Vandals wrote "lion killer" on his Florida vacation home. Government officials in Zimbabwe threatened to extradite him to face charges and they jailed his hunter for poaching and the landowner for allowing an illegal hunt on his farm. Palmer—who was forced into hiding for several weeks—apologized for killing Cecil, stating,

> I had no idea that the lion I took was a known, local favorite, was collared and part of a study, until the end of the hunt. I relied on the expertise of my local professional guides to ensure a legal hunt.[1]

Professional hunts are big business in Africa, bringing in badly needed cash—$200 million at last count—to local economies in Namibia, South Africa, Tanzania, Zimbabwe, and elsewhere. (Worries about hurting the hunting business stopped Zimbabwean officials from following through on their threats to charge Palmer.) These trophy hunts are controversial. Some wildlife experts defend them, referring to them as "conservation hunts." They argue that the hunting business provides a financial incentive for protecting wildlife and funds conservation programs. According to one Zimbabwean ecologist, if hunting were banned, locals would poison lions, eliminating them from everywhere but reserves. He concludes: "Even though hunting may seem unpalatable to a lot of people around the world, it is actually very, very necessary."[2]

Animal rights advocates take issue with killing threatened animals in order to save them. In the words of one official at the International Fund for Animal Welfare, "If you pay to take a human life and give to humanitarian causes, it does not make you a humanitarian. And paying money to kill one of the last iconic animals on earth does not make you a conservationist."[3] Hunters sometimes encroach onto protected land to take animals, and hunting fees may not go toward conservation efforts or benefit local black residents.

Zimbabweans are puzzled by all the attention focused on Cecil's death. To them, wildlife is food or a threat. In an op-ed piece appearing in *The New York Times*, Wake Forest doctoral student Goodwell Nzou recounts how lions menaced his village, mauling his uncle and killing a young boy. He was happy when he heard that a lion had been killed, until he learned how many Americans responded: "My excitement was doused when I realized that the lion killer was being painted as the villain. I faced the starkest cultural contradiction I'd experienced during my five years studying in the United States."[4] Nzou and his fellow countrymen wonder why Americans don't pay more attention to the plight of humans. "We Zimbabweans are left shaking our heads," he reports, "wondering why Americans care more about African animals than about African people."[5] And there is plenty of human misery in Zimbabwe. Eighty percent of the population is unemployed, and in 2008, inflation reached 500 billion percent. Zimbabweans' life expectancy is fifty-two years. Out of a population of 15 million, 1.7 million residents between the ages of fifteen and forty-nine are infected with AIDS, and there are a half-million AIDS orphans. One observer summed up conditions in the country this way: "Compared to many of the human residents of Zimbabwe, Cecil the lion had a pretty good life."[6]

The U.S. Fish and Wildlife Service promised an investigation of Palmer's hunt, and officials considered adding the African lion to the list of endangered animals. The United Nations

(Continued)

(Continued)

General Assembly passed a resolution addressing illegal hunting and animal trafficking. In the meantime, trophy hunts continue as the populations of lions, elephants, rhinos, and other species continue to shrink.

Discussion Probes

1. Why do you think the death of Cecil the lion sparked so much outrage on social media?

2. Has there been too much concern about this lion and not enough concern for the people of Zimbabwe?

3. Do you think trophy hunts are ethical? Do they help or threaten wildlife conservation?

4. What cultural values are in conflict in this situation? How do you account for the differences between how Westerners and Zimbabweans responded to this event?

5. How can international authorities protect African wildlife while meeting the needs and honoring the values of local residents?

Notes

1. Capecchi, C., & Rogers, K. (2015, July 29). Killer of Cecil the lion finds out that he is a target now, of Internet vigilantism. *The New York Times.*

2. Onishi, N. (2015, August 11). Best way to save Africa's lions? Hunt them, some experts say. *The New York Times*, p. A1.

3. Nzou, G. (2015, August 5). In Zimbabwe, we don't cry for lions. *The New York Times*, p. A19.

4. Nzou.

5. Phillip, A. (2015, May 21). Texas hunter who paid $350,000 to kill an endangered rhino has bagged his prey. *The Washington Post.*

6. Porubcansky, M. (2015, July 30). Cecil the lion had a better life than most people in Zimbabwe. *MinnPost.*

Sources

Dzirutwe, M. (2015, July 30). "What lion?" Zimbabweans ask, amid global Cecil circus. *Reuters.*

Izadi, E., & Ohiheiser, A. (2015, July 29). As anger escalates over lion's death, Zimbabwean men appear in court. *Washington Post.*

Mutsaka, F. (2015, September 7). Why would Zimbabwe step back from extraditing Cecil's hunter? *The Christian Science Monitor.*

Perez, C. (2015, August 5). Lion-killing dentist hires ex-cops to protect vacation home. *New York Post.*

Rogers, K. (2015, July 31). U.S. and U.N. respond to killing of lion in Zimbabwe. *The New York Times,* p. A6.

Woods, J. (2015, July 30). Cecil the lion—has the reaction tipped dangerously into overreaction? *The Telegraph.*

Case Study 11.3

ETHICAL DIVERSITY SCENARIOS

SCENARIO A: THE RACCOMANDAZIONE

In Italy, it's not what you know but whom you know that is key to getting a job. A recommendation from the right person (a *raccomandazione*) often gets someone hired, even if the applicant is not the most qualified for the position. The emphasis on connections is blamed for Italy's brain drain, as many outstanding graduates are forced to seek work abroad. You have recently arrived in Italy to manage a small branch office of an international consulting firm. Your best employee asks you to write a letter of recommendation for his daughter who wants a position with one of your major clients. You don't want to offend him, and you recognize the importance that Italians place on their families. At the same time, you don't believe his daughter is any more than an average candidate for this position.

Would you provide the raccomandazione for the employee's daughter?

Source: Associated Press. (2012, September 25). In crisis-hit Europe, nepotism and connection culture stifle youth. *The Daily Star* (Lebanon).

SCENARIO B: CLINICAL TRIALS OUTSOURCING

You are the newly hired research director for a large pharmaceutical company. Like your competitors, your firm is outsourcing clinical drug trials to contract research organizations in such emerging markets as Brazil, Mexico, India, China, and South Africa. Clinical trials involve the use of human subjects to test the effectiveness of new medications. Outsourcing drug tests is becoming increasingly popular. Not only are drug companies having a difficult time finding patients in Western countries, but outsourcing can significantly reduce expenses (clinical trials can account for up to 60% of drug development costs) and the time it takes to get a new drug to market, which can take from nine to twelve years on average.

While lower costs and development times boost profitability and stock prices and speed treatment to patients, relying on contract research organizations greatly increases the chances of ethical abuses. Your company adheres to the World Medical Association's Declaration of Helsinki, which lays out ethical guidelines for medical testing. According to the declaration, subjects must be fully informed of the risks they face when participating in clinical trials. Trial protocols are to be overseen by ethics committees. Every patient who participates in a research project should have access to the most effective treatment identified in the study after it is over. Participants should never be given an ineffective placebo if it leaves them without adequate treatment.

(Continued)

(Continued)

There is evidence that contract research organizations often ignore the Helsinki guidelines. Local review boards, like those in Mexico, are often ineffective, and government regulation is lax. Clinical researchers out to reduce their costs may conduct trials without review, test illegal drugs, and misrepresent the nature of the trials to patients. Some subjects in developing nations don't understand the risks even when the dangers are explained to them or they are so desperate for money that they ignore the risks. The best medications may not be given to subjects. Then, too, distance makes it difficult for drug manufacturers to supervise overseas contractors.

You recognize that while your firm may not be held legally liable for any contract research organization violations, it will be held morally responsible in the court of international opinion.

Will you continue to outsource clinical drug trials to developing nations? If so, what steps might you take to ensure that your contract research organizations will adhere to the Helsinki guidelines?

Source: Abodor, H. (2012). Ethical issues in outsourcing: The case of contract medical research and the global pharmaceutical industry. *Journal of Business Ethics, 105,* 239–255.

SCENARIO C: INTERNATIONAL ADOPTION RESTRICTIONS

For over half a century, more adoptions of foreign children have taken place in the United States than in any other country in the world. In 2010, for example, U.S. parents adopted more than 11,000 children from overseas, followed by the Italians (4,130) and the French (3,504). However, the number of foreign children adopted by American parents declined by 60% between 2004 (the peak year for international adoptions) and 2011. Fewer children have been available for adoption due in large part to The Hague Adoption Convention. This international agreement, which requires signatories to set up a central authority for processing adoptions, is designed to clean up corruption in the adoption process. Take the case of Guatemala. Investigators discovered that adoption paperwork in that nation was frequently forged and that babies were kidnapped from hospitals or stolen from their parents. A number of nations have stopped adoptions as they work to comply with the Adoption Convention. Attitudes toward foreign adoption are also shifting. Improving economic conditions, such as in China, encourage parents to keep their babies. Residents in some provider nations resent international adoption because it signals that they can't take care of their own children. They are supported by United Nations International Children's Emergency Fund (UNICEF), the United Nations children's rights organization, which argues that foreign adoptions should be allowed only in cases where children cannot be properly cared for in their home countries.

As the director of a U.S. adoption agency, you applaud efforts to curb corruption in international adoptions and to promote children's rights. However, you recognize that restrictions are sad news for American parents who believe they can provide education, medical care, and stable homes for needy kids who would otherwise go without. When

Kyrgyzstan halted international adoptions, for example, 2 of 65 children scheduled to come to the United States died in orphanages before their prospective American parents could claim them. Of course, greater restrictions mean that your agency will likely process fewer adoptions.

Would you support efforts to lessen restrictions on international adoptions?

Source: Webley, K. (2013, January 21). The baby deficit. *Time,* 30–39.

SCENARIO D: THE INTERNATIONAL BRANCH CAMPUS

You are the president of a well-known public university in the United States. The royal family of a rich Middle Eastern nation has invited you to establish a branch campus in their country. To get the project off the ground, the king pledged $70 million and promises to build a state-of-the-art facility at the monarchy's expense. Young people in his country are anxious to earn a Western-style education (the world's "gold standard"), providing your school with an additional revenue stream. Your domestic students will get a true global experience by living and studying abroad and the arrangement will raise the profile of the college. You are aware that several international campuses operated by other American universities had to close when they couldn't draw students or lost the support of the host government. While you are confident that your new campus can succeed financially, you are troubled by the ethics of associating your institution, which values academic freedom and free speech, with a repressive regime that imprisons and tortures dissidents and enforces Islamic law. Labor controversies have plagued other Western universities and museums building in the area. Contract laborers, many of them from Asia, often work and live under brutal conditions. Sometimes they don't receive their wages and are beaten and deported when they complain. The nation's rulers assure you that the branch campus will operate in a "free zone" where strict censorship rules will be suspended and academic freedom will be protected. The monarchy also agrees to your demand that an outside organization monitor working conditions during construction of the new campus.

Would you go ahead with plans to build this new branch campus?

Sources: Kaminer, A., & O'Driscoll, S. (2014, May 18). Workers at NYU's Abu Dhabi site faced harsh conditions. *The New York Times;* Pope, J. (2011, October 11). New caution for US universities overseas. *Associated Press;* Schlanger, Z. (2015, January 19). New York University: A case study in what not to do. *NYTimes.com.*

SCENARIO E: THE EXILED PRESIDENT

You are a diplomat in a small Central American country. For years, your home government has pushed for the development of stable democracies in Central America, hoping to end the military coups that once were common in the region. The latest democratically elected

(Continued)

(Continued)

president in your host state came to office with a commitment to the poor. Within weeks of assuming the presidency, he threatened to nationalize the local holdings of several of your home nation's multinational corporations. He condemned your government, and those of several other Western countries, for engaging in "capitalist imperialism." The president's leftist policies angered local business interests, and they soon drove him into exile with the help of the army. Military officers installed a new president who promised to be friendlier toward your nation. However, the new president has yet to set a timeline for holding elections. In the meantime, the exiled president, who still enjoys widespread support among the poor and working classes, wants to return to office. He has asked for help from the international community.

Would you recommend that your government support the deposed president's efforts to return to office? If so, what steps should it take?

SELF-ASSESSMENT 11.1

Individualism/Collectivism Scale

Instructions: This questionnaire will help you assess your individualistic and collectivistic tendencies. Respond by indicating the degree to which the values reflected in each phrase are important to you: 1 = opposed to my values, 2 = not important to me, 3 = somewhat important to me, 4 = important to me, or 5 = very important to me.

_____ 1. Obtaining pleasure or sensuous gratification

_____ 2. Preserving the welfare of others

_____ 3. Being successful by demonstrating my individual competency

_____ 4. Restraining my behavior if it is going to harm others

_____ 5. Being independent in thought and action

_____ 6. Having safety and stability with people with whom I identify

_____ 7. Obtaining status and prestige

_____ 8. Having harmony in my relations with others

_____ 9. Having an exciting and challenging life

_____ 10. Accepting cultural and religious traditions

_____ 11. Being recognized for my individual work

_____ 12. Avoiding the violation of social norms

_____ 13. Leading a comfortable life

_____ 14. Living in a stable society

_____ 15. Being logical in my approach to work

_____ 16. Being polite to others

_____ 17. Being ambitious

_____ 18. Being self-controlled

_____ 19. Being able to choose what I do

_____ 20. Enhancing the welfare of others

Scoring: To find your individualism score, add your responses to the odd-numbered items. To find your collectivism score, add your responses to the even-numbered items. Both scores will range from 10 to 50. The higher your scores, the more individualistic and/or collectivistic you are.

Source: Gudykunst, W. B. (2004). *Bridging differences: Effective intergroup communication* (4th ed.). Thousand Oaks, CA: SAGE. Used with permission.

SELF-ASSESSMENT 11.2

Moral Foundations Questionnaire

Part I Moral Relevance

When you decide whether something is right or wrong, to what extent are the following considerations relevant to your thinking? Please rate each statement using this scale: 0 = not at all relevant, 1 = not very relevant, 2 = slightly relevant, 3 = somewhat relevant, 4 = very relevant, 5 = extremely relevant.

1. Whether or not someone suffered emotionally.
2. Whether or not someone cared for someone weak or vulnerable.
3. Whether or not some people were treated differently from others.
4. Whether or not someone acted unfairly.
5. Whether or not someone's action showed love for his or her country.
6. Whether or not someone did something to betray his or her group.
7. Whether or not someone showed a lack of respect for authority.
8. Whether or not someone conformed to the traditions of society.
9. Whether or not someone violated standards of purity and decency.
10. Whether or not someone did something disgusting.

Part II Moral Judgments

Please read the following sentences and indicate your agreement or disagreement. 0 = strongly disagree, 1 = moderately disagree, 2 = slightly disagree, 3 = slightly agree, 4 = moderately agree, 5 = strongly agree.

11. Compassion for those who are suffering is the most crucial virtue.
12. One of the worst things a person could do is hurt a defenseless animal.

13. When the government makes laws, the number one principle should be ensuring that everyone is treated fairly.

14. Justice is the most important requirement for a society.

15. I am proud of my country's history.

16. People should be loyal to their family members, even when they have done something wrong.

17. Respect for authority is something all children need to learn.

18. Men and women each have different roles to play in society.

19. People should not do things that are disgusting, even if no one is harmed.

20. I would call some acts wrong on the grounds that they are unnatural.

Scoring: Add up the scores on each moral foundation (range 0–20). The higher the score, the more important that foundation is to you.

Care: Items 1, 2, 11, 12 _____

Fairness: Items 3, 4, 13, 14 _____

In-group/Loyalty: Items 5, 6, 15, 16 _____

Authority: Items 7, 8, 17, 18 _____

Purity: Items 9, 10, 19, 20 _____

Source: Graham, J., Nosek, B. A., Haidt, J., Iyer, R., Koleva, S., & Ditto, P. H. (2011). Mapping the moral domain. *Journal of Personality and Social Psychology, 101*, 366–385. Used with permission.

NOTES

1. Frey, W. H. (2014, December 12). New projections point to a majority minority nation in 2044. *Brookings*; Kahn, A. E., & Maxwell, D. J. (2008). Ethics in diversity management leadership. In S. A. Quatro & R. R. Sims (Eds.), *Executive ethics: Ethical dilemmas and challenges for the C-suite* (pp. 247–262). Charlotte, NC: Information Age; Misra. T. (2015, April 9). Where minority populations have become the majority. *Citylab;* Mor Barak, M. E. (2011). *Managing diversity: Toward a globally inclusive workplace* (2nd ed.). Thousand Oaks, CA: SAGE.

2. Dunning, J. H. (2003). Overview. In J. H. Dunning (Ed.), *Making globalization good: The moral challenges of global capitalism* (pp. 11–40). Oxford, England: Oxford University Press; Tavis, T. (2000). The globalization phenomenon and multinational corporate developmental responsibility. In O. F. Williams (Ed.), *Global codes of conduct: An idea whose time has come* (pp. 13–36). Notre Dame, IN: University of Notre Dame Press.

3. Dunning, J. H. (2000). Whither global capitalism? *Global Focus, 12*, 117–136; Muzaffar, C. (2002). Conclusion. In P. F. Knitter & C. Muzaffar (Eds.), *Subverting greed: Religious perspectives on the global economy* (pp. 154–172). Maryknoll, NY: Orbis; Ritzer, G. (2004). *The globalization of nothing.* Thousand Oaks, CA: Pine Forge; Stott, B. R. (2001, January–February). The great divide in the global village. *Foreign Affairs,* 160–177.

4. The great fall of China. (2015, August 29). *The Economist.*

5. Kristof, N. D. (2010, June 27). Death by gadget. *The New York Times,* p. WK11; Wyatt, E. (2012, March 20). Behind the blood money. *The New York Times,* p. B1.

6. Corporate clout 2013: Time for responsible capitalism. (2013). *Global Trends*. Retrieved from http://www.globaltrends.com

7. Shin, L. (2014, January 23). The 85 richest people in the world have as much as the 3.5 billion poorest. *Forbes*. Retrieved from http://www.forbes.com

8. Olinto, P., Beegle, K., Sobrado, C., & Uematsu, H. (2013, October). The state of the poor. *Economic Premise* (The World Bank).

9. Bear, M. (2012). *First World problems.* San Francisco, CA: Weldon Owen; Berbert, K. (2015). 17 unbelievably selfish, yet relatable first world problems. *Elite Daily*. Retrieved from http://elitedaily.com/users/kberbert; Magruder, S. (2015, February 12). Top 100 first world problems list. *Man's Marbles*. Retrieved from http://www.mansmarbles.com/#!Top-100-First-World-Problems-List/

10. Muzaffar.

11. Brady, J. P. (2012). Marketing breast milk substitutes: Problems and perils throughout the world. *Archives of Disease in Children Online.* Retrieved from http://adc.bmj.com; Moorhead, J. (2007, May 15). Milking it. *The Guardian,* p. 8; NAFDAC warns violators of BMS international code. (2007, August 7). *Africa News*; Perlman, L. R., & Roberts, K. (2014). The ethics of state policies restricting access to infant formula and their impact on women's and children's health. In L. Boyd-Judson & P. James (Eds.), *Women's global health: Norms and state policies* (pp. 91–113). Lanham, MD: Lexington Books; Perez, J. (2006, December 4). Yellow pad: What the milk companies don't want you to know. *BusinessWorld,* 1–5; Richter, J. (2001). *Holding corporations accountable: Corporate conduct, international codes and citizen action.* London, England: Zed.

12. Karim, A. (2000, June 23). Globalization, ethics, and AIDS vaccines. *Science,* 21–29.

13. Griffiths, P. D. (2014). Ebola and ethics. *Reviews in Medical Virology, 24,* 363–364.

14. Solomon, C. M. (2001). Put your ethics to a global test. In M. H. Albrecht (Ed.), *International HRM: Managing diversity in the workplace* (pp. 329–335). Oxford, England: Blackwell.

15. Donaldson, T. (1996, September–October). Values in tension: Ethics away from home. *Harvard Business Review,* 48–57.

16. Greenhouse, S. (2013, November 23). U.S. retailers decline to aid factory victims in Bangladesh. *The New York Times,* p. B1.

17. Rogers, E. M., & Steinfatt, T. M. (1999). *Intercultural communication.* Prospect Heights, IL: Waveland, p. 79.

18. Hofstede, G. (1984). *Culture's consequences.* Beverly Hills, CA: SAGE; Hofstede, G., & Hofstede, G. J. (2005). *Cultures and organizations: Software of the mind.* London, England: McGraw-Hill. For a more recent review of Hofstede's cultural dimensions, see Taras, V., Kirkman, B. L., & Steel, P. (2010). Examining the impact of *Culture's consequences*: A three-decade, multilevel, meta-analytic review of Hofstede's cultural value dimensions. *Journal of Applied Psychology, 95,* 405–439.

19. Hofstede, G. (2001). Difference and danger: Cultural profiles of nations and limits to tolerance. In M. H. Albrecht (Ed.), *International HRM: Managing diversity in the workplace* (pp. 9–23). Oxford, England: Blackwell.

20. Chan, A. W. H., & Cheung, H. Y. (2012). Cultural dimensions, ethical sensitivity, and corporate governance. *Journal of Business Ethics, 110,* 45–59; Clements, C. E., Neill, J. D., & Stovall, O. S. (2009). The impact of cultural differences on the convergence of international accounting codes of ethics. *Journal of Business Ethics, 90,* 383–391; Davis, J. H., & Ruhe, J. A. (2003). Perceptions of country corruption: Antecedents and outcomes. *Journal of Business Ethics, 43,* 275–288; Franke, G. R., & Nadler, S. S. (2008). Culture, economic development, and national ethical attitudes. *Journal of Business Research, 61,* 254–264; Husted, B. W. (1999). Wealth, culture and corruption. *Journal of International Business Studies, 30,* 339–359; Vitell, S. J., Nwachukwu, S. L., & Barnes, J. H. (1993). The effects of culture on ethical decision-making:

An application of Hofstede's typology. *Journal of Business Ethics, 12,* 753–760; Williams, G., & Zinkin, J. (2008). The effect of culture on consumers' willingness to punish irresponsible corporate behaviour: Applying Hofstede's typology to the punishment aspect of corporate social responsibility. *Business Ethics: A European Review, 17,* 210–226.

21. Carroll, S. J., & Gannon, M. J. (1997). *Ethical dimensions of management.* Thousand Oaks, CA: SAGE.

22. Hall, E. T. (1976). *Beyond culture.* New York, NY: Random House.

23. Triandis, H. C. (1995). *Individualism and collectivism.* Boulder, CO: Westview Press.

24. Bertsch, A. M. (2012). Validating GLOBE's societal values scales: A test in the U.S.A. *International Journal of Business and Social Science, 3,* 10–23; Chhokar, J. S., Brodbeck, F. C., & House, R. J. (Eds.). (2007). *Culture and leadership across the world: The GLOBE book of in-depth studies of 25 societies.* Mahwah, NJ: Erlbaum; House, R. J., Hanges, P. J., Javidan, M., Dorfman, P. W., & Gupta, V. (Eds.). (2004). *Culture, leadership, and organizations: The GLOBE study of 62 societies.* Thousand Oaks, CA: SAGE; Javidan, M., & House, R. J. (2001). Cultural acumen for the global manager: Lessons from Project GLOBE. *Organizational Dynamics, 29,* 289–305.

25. Quigley, N. R., Sully de Luque, M., & House, R. J. (2005). Responsible leadership and governance in a global context: Insights from the GLOBE study. In J. P. Doh & S. A. Sumpf (Eds.), *Handbook on responsible leadership and governance in global business* (pp. 352–379). Cheltenham, England: Edward Elgar.

26. Den Hartog, D. N., House, R. J., Hanges, P. U., Ruiz-Quintanilla, S. A., & Dorfman, P. W. (1999). Culture-specific and cross-culturally generalizable implicit leadership theories: Are attributes of charismatic/transformational leadership universally endorsed? *Leadership Quarterly, 10,* 219–257.

27. Resick, C. J., Hanges, P. J., Dickson, M. W., & Mitchelson, J. K. (2006). A cross-cultural examination of the endorsement of ethical leadership. *Journal of Business Ethics, 63,* 345–359.

28. Graham, J., Haidt, J., Koleva, S., Motyl, M., Iyer, R., Wojcik, S. P., & Ditto, P. H. (2002). Moral Foundations Theory: The pragmatic validity of moral pluralism. *Advances in Experimental Social Psychology, 47,* 55–130; Haidt, J. (2012). *The righteous mind: Why good people are divided by politics and religion.* New York, NY: Pantheon Books; Haidt, J. (2013). Moral psychology for the twenty-first century. *Journal of Moral Education, 42,* 281–297; Haidt, J., & Bjorklund, F. (2008). Social intuitionists answer six questions about moral psychology. In W. Sinnott-Armstrong (Ed.), *Moral psychology: Vol. 2. The cognitive science of morality: Intuition and diversity* (pp. 182–217). Cambridge: MIT Press; Haidt, J., & Graham, J. (2007). When morality opposes justice: Conservatives have moral intuitions that liberals may not recognize. *Social Justice Research, 20,* 98–116; Jacobs, T. (2009, May). Morals authority. *Miller-McCune,* 47–55.

29. Koleva, S. P., Graham, J., Iyer, R., Ditto, P. H., & Haidt, J. (2012). Tracing the threads: How the five moral concerns (especially purity) help explain culture war attitudes. *Journal of Research in Personality, 46*(2), 184–194.

30. Koleva et al.

31. Drummond, T. (2000, April 3). Coping with the cops. *Time,* 72–73.

32. Brown, R. (1995). *Prejudice: Its social psychology.* Oxford, England: Blackwell; Fiske, S. T. (1998). Stereotyping, prejudice, and discrimination. In D. T. Gilbert, S. T. Fiske, & G. Lindzey (Eds.), *The handbook of social psychology* (Vol. 2, pp. 357–411). Boston, MA: McGraw-Hill.

33. Gudykunst, W. B. (2004). *Bridging differences: Effective intergroup communication* (4th ed.). Thousand Oaks, CA: SAGE; Gudykunst, W. B., & Kim, Y. Y. (1997). *Communicating with strangers: An approach to intercultural communication* (3rd ed.). New York, NY: McGraw-Hill.

34. Langer, E. J. (1989). *Mindfulness.* Reading, MA: Addison-Wesley; Langer, E. J. (1997). *The power of mindful learning.* Reading, MA: Addison-Wesley.

35. Talbot, M. (1999). Against relativism. In J. M. Halstead & T. H. McLaughlin (Eds.), *Education in morality* (pp. 206–217). London, England: Routledge.

36. Hauser, M. D., Young, L., & Cushman, F. (2008). Reviving Rawls's linguistic analogy: Operative principles and the causal structure of moral actions. In W. Sinnott-Armstrong (Ed.), *Moral psychology: Vol. 2. The cognitive science of morality: Intuition and diversity* (pp. 107–144). Cambridge, England: MIT Press.

37. Gert, B. (2004). *Common morality: Deciding what to do*. Oxford, England: Oxford University Press.

38. Gert, p. 5.

39. Appiah, K. A. (2006). *Cosmopolitanism: Ethics in a world of strangers*. New York, NY: Norton; Delanty, G. (2012). Introduction: The emerging field of cosmopolitanism studies. In G. Delanty (Ed.), *International handbook of cosmopolitan studies* (pp. 1–8). Hoboken, NJ: Routledge; Fine, R., & Boon, V. (2007). Introduction: Cosmopolitanism: Between past and future. *European Journal of Social Theory, 10,* 5–16; Hill, L. (2015). Classical Stoicism and the birth of a global ethics: Cosmopolitan duties in a world of local loyalties. *Social Alternatives, 34*(1), 14–18; Maak, T. (2009). The cosmopolitical corporation. *Journal of Business Ethics, 84,* 361–372; Maak, T., & Pless, N. M. (2009). Business leaders as citizens of the world: Advancing humanism on a global scale. *Journal of Business Ethics, 88,* 537–550; Smith, W. (2007). Cosmopolitan citizenship: Virtue, irony and worldliness. *European Journal of Social Theory, 10,* 37–52; Van Hoot, S. (2009). *Cosmopolitanism: A philosophy for global ethics*. Montreal, Quebec, Canada: McGill-Queen's University Press.

40. Pogge, T. (1992). Cosmopolitanism and sovereignty. *Ethics 103*(1), 48–75, p. 48.

41. James, S. A. (2007). *Universal human rights: Origins and development*. New York, NY: LFB Scholarly Publications, p. 2.

42. United Nations. (1948). *The Universal Declaration of Human Rights*. Retrieved from http://www.un.org/en/universal-declaration-human-rights/

43. Rasche, A., & Gilbert, D. U. (2012). Institutionalizing global governance: The role of the United Nations Global Compact. *Business Ethics: A European Review, 21,* 100–114.

44. Paine, L., Deshpandé, R., Margolis, J. D., & Bettcher, K. E. (2005, December). Up to code: Does your company meet world-class standards? *Harvard Business Review,* 122–133.

45. Caux Round Table. (2000). Appendix 26: The Caux Principles. In O. F. Williams (Ed.), *Global codes of conduct: An idea whose time has come* (pp. 384–388). Notre Dame, IN: University of Notre Dame Press.

46. Caux Round Table. (2006). *Principles for non-governmental organizations*. Retrieved from http://www.cauxroundtable.org/index.cfm?&menuid=101

47. Donaldson, T. (2009). Compass and dead reckoning: The dynamic implications of ISCT. *Journal of Business Ethics, 88,* 659–664; Donaldson, T., & Dunfee, T. W. (1994). Toward a unified conception of business ethics: Integrative social contracts theory. *Academy of Management Review, 19,* 252–284; Donaldson, T., & Dunfee T. W. (1999). *Ties that bind: A social contracts approach to business ethics*. Boston, MA: Harvard Business School Press.

48. Hamilton, J. B., Knouse, S. B., & Hill, V. (2009). Google in China: A manager-friendly heuristic model for resolving cross-cultural ethical conflicts. *Journal of Business Ethics, 86,* 143–157. See also Hamilton, J. B., & Knouse, S. B. (2001). Multinational enterprise decision principles for dealing with cross cultural ethical conflicts. *Journal of Business Ethics, 31,* 77–94.

49. Hamilton et al., p. 149.

12

Ethical Crisis Leadership

There is nothing quite like a crisis to test your leadership. It will make you or break you.

—FORMER MEDTRONIC CEO BILL GEORGE

Crisis leadership is more about who you are than what you know.

—CRISIS CONSULTANT BRUCE BLYTHE

WHAT'S AHEAD

This chapter examines ethical leadership in crisis situations. Crises are major unexpected events that pose significant threats to groups and organizations. They pass through three stages: precrisis, crisis event, and postcrisis. Ethical leaders have a series of tasks to carry out during each phase. Six ethical principles and strategies are essential to fulfilling these moral duties: assume broad responsibility, practice transparency, demonstrate care and concern, engage the head as well as the heart, improvise from a strong moral foundation, and build resilience. The chapter concludes with a look at the ethical demands of extreme leadership.

Managing a crisis is the ultimate test of ethical leadership. Bankruptcies, hurricanes, wildfires, tornados, landslides, political scandals, industrial accidents, school shootings, food-borne illnesses, oil spills, fraud, computer data theft, terrorist attacks, and other crisis events bring out the worst or the best in leaders. Decisions must be made quickly under the glare of media scrutiny. Manufacturing plants, office buildings, planes, homes, jobs, and lives may have been lost. Entire organizations, groups, societies, and economic and political systems might be at risk. As we've seen throughout this text, leaders often fail to meet the ethical challenges posed by crises. At Subway, HBOS, Turing Pharmaceutical, and Volkswagen, leaders sparked crises through their unethical behavior. For their part, leaders on K2 ignored widely held moral standards and values in response to the unfolding crisis. On the other hand, we have also seen how other leaders, like Malala Yousafzai and Al Buehler, coped effectively with crisis events. Their values become clearer; their moral commitments become greater.

This chapter introduces the ethical challenges posed by leadership in crisis, building on the foundation laid in earlier chapters. To ethically manage crisis events, you will need to draw on concepts we have discussed previously—values, moral reasoning, normative leadership theories, ethical decision-making formats, ethical communication skills, influence tools, and ethical perspectives, to name a few. However, you will also need to understand the characteristics of crisis as well as the elements of ethical crisis management. The first section of this chapter provides an overview of the nature and stages of crises. It identifies important leadership tasks that must be carried out in each crisis phase. The second section identifies principles and strategies that equip leaders to ethically carry out these responsibilities. The third section highlights the challenges facing ethical leaders in high-risk settings.

CRISIS: AN OVERVIEW

A crisis is any major unanticipated event that poses a significant threat. Such events are rare (making them difficult to prepare for), generate a good deal of uncertainty (their causes and effects are unclear), and are hard to resolve (there is no set formula for determining how to act). Further, decisions about how to deal with a particular crisis must be made rapidly, and those outside the immediate group—customers, clients, suppliers, and neighbors—are also affected.[1]

The stress and anxiety generated by crises makes them particularly hard to manage in an ethical manner. Stress interferes with cognitive abilities. Individuals tend to narrow their focus to just a few perspectives and alternatives. They often perceive the world less accurately and ignore important information. At the organizational level, stress prompts groups to delegate decision-making authority to a small team of top officials, limiting access to diverse viewpoints. Time limits also prevent talking to a variety of stakeholders. All of these factors subvert ethical reasoning and creative problem solving while increasing the likelihood that the needs of some stakeholders will be overlooked.[2]

Investigators divide crises into different types. These types can help leaders better prepare for, and respond to, crisis events. Groups and organizations will be more vulnerable to some types of crises than others. Manufacturers have to be highly concerned about product safety; coastal communities have to be ready for ocean storms. When disaster strikes, the nature of the crisis will also help to determine the course of action. Responding to the disruption of a work stoppage requires one set of strategies, while responding to a computer security breach demands another.

Crisis management experts Matthew Seeger, Timothy Sellnow, and Robert Ulmer identify ten types of crises:[3]

1. *Public perception:* negative stories about the organization's products, personnel, or services; negative rumors, blogs, and websites

2. *Natural disasters:* tornadoes, hurricanes, mudslides, wildfires, blizzards, earthquakes, volcano eruptions

3. *Product or service:* product recalls, food-borne illnesses, concern about products and services generated by the media

4. *Terrorist attacks*: bombings, hijackings, abductions, poisonings

5. *Economic:* cash shortages, bankruptcies, hostile takeovers, accounting scandals

6. *Human resource:* workplace violence, strikes, labor unrest, discrimination, sexual harassment, school and workplace shootings, theft, fraud

7. *Industrial:* mine collapses, nuclear accidents, fires, explosions

8. *Oil and chemical spills*: tanker and railway spills, pipeline and well leaks

9. *Transportation*: train derailments, plane crashes, truck accidents, multivehicle pileups

10. *Outside environment:* collapse of financial systems, rising fuel prices, deregulation, nationalization of private companies, mortgage crisis

Ian Mitroff, former director of the Center for Crisis Management at the University of Southern California, offers an alternative typology based on the intentions of those involved in the crisis event.[4] He notes that there has been a sharp rise in what he labels *abnormal accidents*—deliberate acts that are intentionally designed to disrupt or destroy systems. He contrasts abnormal accidents with *normal accidents,* those unintentional events that cause systems to break down. The Bangkok Thailand shrine bombing, the South Carolina church shootings, kidnappings, and cyberattacks on large corporations and the military would be examples of abnormal accidents. Massive chemical explosions in the port city of Tianjin, China; the collapse of a crane on the Grand Mosque in Saudi Arabia; a fire on a Carnival cruise ship; train derailments; plane crashes; and mining disasters are normal accidents that reflect problems with routine operating procedures. Abnormal accidents are harder to prepare for, but modern organizations have no choice but to plan for them. For instance, since most terrorist acts are aimed at private businesses, not the government, Mitroff argues that businesses have to do their part to respond to terrorist threats. He also points out that even routine crises are becoming harder to deal with in an increasingly complex, interconnected society. Case in point: When United Airlines experienced a short computer glitch, 4,900 domestic and international flights were disrupted, backing up air traffic and delaying thousands of passengers at airports around the world.[5]

The Three Stages of a Crisis

Whatever the type, every crisis passes through three stages: precrisis, crisis event, and postcrisis.[6] In each stage, leaders have a moral obligation to carry out particular tasks or functions. I'll describe these tasks and offer some steps for carrying them out.

Stage 1. Precrisis

Precrisis is the period of normalcy between crisis events. During this, the longest phase, the group or organization typically believes that it understands the risks it faces and can handle any contingency that arises. The temptation to become overconfident grows as the time between crises increases. Funding for backup data sites, disaster drills, training, and other types of crisis preparation may be cut, which increases the likelihood of another crisis.

Complacency isn't the only barrier to crisis prevention. Human biases (decision-making and judgment errors), institutional failures (organizational breakdowns in processing

Box 12.1 Barriers to Crisis Prevention

HUMAN BIASES

- Positive illusions that falsely convince decision makers that a problem doesn't exist or isn't severe enough to require action

- Interpreting events in an egocentric manner that favors the leader and the organization while blaming outsiders

- Discounting the future by ignoring possible long-term costs; refusing to invest resources now to prevent future crises

- Maintaining the dysfunctional status quo by refusing to inflict any harm (such as higher Social Security taxes) that would address a mounting problem (the danger that the Social Security system will become insolvent)

- Failure to recognize problems because they aren't vivid (they are not personally experienced as direct threats)

INSTITUTIONAL FAILURES

- Failure to collect adequate data due to (a) ignoring certain problems and discounting evidence, (b) the presence of conflicting information, and (c) information overload

- Information is not integrated into the organization as a whole because departments operate independently and managers maintain secrecy

- Members lack incentive to take action because they are rewarded for acting selfishly or believe that everyone agrees with current procedures

- Leaders fail to learn from experience or to disseminate lessons learned because information is not recorded or shared or because key organizational members are lost

SPECIAL INTEREST GROUPS

- Impose social burdens—higher taxes, water pollution, high drug prices—in order to benefit themselves

- Blame complex problems on individuals rather than on systems that are at fault

- Oppose reform efforts

Source: Bazerman, M. H., & Watkins, M. D. (2004). *Predictable surprises: The disasters you should have seen coming, and how to prevent them.* Boston, MA: Harvard Business School Press. Reprinted with permission of Waveland Press, Inc. from Hackman, M. Z., & Johnson, C. E. (2013). *Leadership: A communication perspective* (6th ed.). Prospect Heights, IL, p. 413. All rights reserved.

information), and special interest groups (resistance from groups looking out for the interests of their own members) can derail crisis preparedness as well.[7] These factors are summarized in Box 12.1.

Terry Pauchant and Ian Mitroff argue that, in addition to the factors outlined above, misguided ethical assumptions or myths can undermine crisis management. They identify and debunk five unethical beliefs about crisis management:[8]

> *Myth 1: "Crises are inevitable."* Some, but not all, crises are inevitable. But even if some crises (storms and earthquakes) can't be prevented, leaders have an ethical responsibility to do everything they can to prepare for them.

Myth 2: "We lack the basic knowledge to prevent or understand crises." Researchers don't know everything about crisis management. However, they have identified a number of steps leaders can take to prevent crises and to manage them when they occur. When leaders fail to act, the problem is not a lack of knowledge but a lack of will.

Myth 3: "Better technology will prevent future crises." Resolving crises calls for more than technical solutions. Leaders must also communicate effectively, demonstrate flexibility, and think creatively, for example.

A variation of this third myth is the belief that an organization is too large to experience a major crisis. A business clinging to this misconception is really making an unethical statement. In essence, it is saying, "Whenever an organization is so big and powerful that its size will protect it from a major disaster or crisis, then it has no responsibility toward its employees and the surrounding environment and is justified in expressing no concern toward the environment."[9] These same corporations may use formulas to estimate the likelihood and cost of possible disasters. If the formula shows that the risk is low or that the costs of prevention outweigh the costs of disaster, they decide they shouldn't take any action at all, which is unethical. Such was the case with the Love Canal environmental crisis of the late 1970s.[10] Hooker Chemical dumped 21,000 tons of hazardous waste into a canal and conducted a cost-benefit analysis. Officials estimated that cleanup would cost $20 million and treated future residents as potential benefits. Individuals working outside the home were valued based on their modest working-class salaries and on the assumption that their children would earn the same wages. Since the costs of the cleanup apparently outweighed the financial value of neighborhood residents, the company sold the property to the town of Niagara Falls instead of removing the toxic chemicals. An elementary school and homes were built on the site, and residents soon developed blood disorders, kidney and respiratory problems, and other serious health issues. Eventually, the residents were evacuated, and the chemical company and the state of New York were forced to clean up the site at an estimated cost of $137 million. People were sickened and died because, as one resident pointed out, "they decided that we weren't worthy of doing anything."[11]

Myth 4: "Crisis management is inherently detrimental to progress." Risk can never be totally eliminated. Yet some crisis-prone organizations and leaders shouldn't be allowed to engage in dangerous activities without some oversight. Following the financial crisis that began in 2008, for instance, many observers argued that greater restrictions should be placed on the financial industry to prevent future recessions.

Myth 5: "Emotions have no place in crisis management." Emotions have a key role to play in crisis management, as they do in other kinds of ethical decision making (see Chapter 6). Leaders need to see ethics as a conversation, connecting with stakeholders before, during, and after the crisis. They also need to acknowledge the pain and suffering generated by the crisis, which may have been caused by their decisions and actions.

Ethical leaders in the precrisis stage help their groups detect possible trouble and develop strategies for managing crises should they strike. Crisis expert Stephen Fink uses the Greek word *prodromes* (which means "running before") to describe the warning signs that precede a crisis. Ignoring or downplaying these signs generally results in disaster.[12] Tokyo Electric Power Company (TEPCO) had been warned that there was a significant chance that a tsunami would overrun the seawalls at the Fukushima power plant (Chapter 5) and relations between the African American community and Ferguson, Missouri, police were strained long before the shooting of an unarmed black teen touched off days of riots. Prodromes were ignored in both the Boston Marathon bombings and the West, Texas, fertilizer plant explosion, events that occurred during the same week in April 2013. Before the bombings in Boston, Russian officials suspected that one of the alleged bombers had ties to extremist groups and asked the Federal Bureau of Investigation (FBI) to investigate (it discovered no such links). The fertilizer plant in West, Texas, had been fined months earlier for safety violations. Few people in the small town paid much attention to the fact that the plant was located only a few hundred yards from three public schools, an apartment complex, and a nursing home. Fifteen were killed and another 226 injured.[13]

Crisis management experts offer a variety of strategies for recognizing danger signs. To pick up on prodromes, organizations must continually scan the environment, looking outward and inward.[14] In external scanning, organizational leaders survey the broadcast media, websites, YouTube, Twitter, trade journals, and other sources to identify potential dangers. Internal scanning means identifying danger signs coming from those who have an ongoing relationship with the organization, like customers, suppliers, and donors. Surges in product returns and complaints, as well as public criticism and protests, can signal something is amiss.

In addition to environmental scanning, organizations can go looking for trouble. Looking for trouble means actively seeking weaknesses that could prove harmful or fatal to the organization. One commonly used troubleshooting tactic is to brainstorm a list of possible crises. There are a host of possible crises that could strike your college or university, for instance, ranging from floods to campus shootings to student protests to faculty strikes. In a variation on this strategy, develop a "wheel of crises" with the types of crises your company or nonprofit can face.[15] Spin the wheel and wherever it stops, brainstorm all the kinds of possible crises that might occur in that category. Another troubleshooting strategy is to ask members of your organization to play the role of villains and imagine ways to destroy products and processes. (You might also hire outsiders to "spy" on your organization to expose weaknesses.) Yet another tactic is to look to other industries to determine if the dangers they face could pose a threat to your type of organization. One large electronics manufacturer took this approach, imagining itself as part of the food industry. Leaders at this firm thought about how "microbes" and "bugs" might infect their products. They even hired an infectious disease specialist to help prevent such infections. Based on this analysis, executives determined that disgruntled workers could introduce pathogens (computer viruses or faulty parts, for example) into company products. They decided to quarantine suspect shipments until the items were inoculated (repaired). You can determine your crisis readiness and that of your work organization by completing Self-Assessment 12.1.

Not all danger signs are immediately visible. Some emerge from long-term political, social, and ethical trends. These changes sometimes take the form of issues that can threaten an organization. For instance, the trend toward healthy eating led to activist demands that McDonalds retire its advertising icon Ronald McDonald, who is accused of promoting childhood obesity. Chipotle (which faced its own food safety crisis) and other restaurants offering healthier menus have taken market share from McDonalds, forcing the chain to close a number of outlets. Growing recognition of the dangers of concussions, highlighted in the case study at the end of Chapter 8, poses a danger to the business of professional football.

Left unattended, issues can lead to full-blown crises, as in the case of mad cow disease. British officials failed to acknowledge growing evidence that the fatal Creutzfeldt-Jakob (CJD) brain disease could pass from cows to humans who ate contaminated beef.[16] They also underestimated the panic, based on concern about food safety, that resulted when the public found out. The European Union banned beef exports from Britain and two million cattle had to be slaughtered to prevent the spread of the disease. An estimated 100 people died from CJD. In other instances, not recognizing the significance of trends can multiply the damage caused by a crisis. A 2002 ice storm in North and South Carolina caused widespread power outages that lasted for days. During the outages, hundreds of carbon monoxide poisoning cases were reported despite repeated warnings about taking gas and charcoal grills indoors for cooking and heating. Many of these cases were among Latino immigrants who were part of the rapidly growing Spanish-speaking labor force moving into the area. Local utilities didn't recognize the implications of this demographic shift. As a result, the English-only warnings they broadcast failed to reach many of their customers.[17]

Effectively addressing long-term trends requires *issues management*.[18] Issues management begins with identifying emerging issues through the environmental scanning described earlier. Next, determine the significance of each issue and its potential impact, evaluating it on its probability and magnitude. Some issues are not likely to affect your group or organization and, if they do, their effects will be small. Finally, develop strategies for the high-priority issues—those with the highest probability and magnitude. Be proactive whenever possible, taking steps to shape the issue before it becomes a threat or crisis. Proactive steps can turn threats into opportunities. Take the case of restaurants in New York City and in Portland, Oregon, for instance. Many restaurateurs oppose efforts to raise the minimum wage to $15, fearing that increased labor costs will raise food costs and drive customers away. In contrast, a small group of owners sees the minimum wage movement as chance to introduce new compensation systems. They have abolished tips, for example, or asked chefs to also serve diners. These restaurateurs hope to close the pay gap between kitchen workers who don't receive tips and servers who do.

Once weaknesses and potential dangers have been identified, develop a crisis management plan (CMP) to cope with each type of emergency. The CMP should include such details as a list of key members of the public and organizations and how to notify them, members of the crisis management team, contact information for media outlets, and background information on the organization.[19]

Crisis preparation pays off. Crisis-ready organizations are less likely to experience unexpected threats, suffer significantly less damage if such events do strike, and recover much more quickly.[20] In one study, Oxford University researchers compared the stock price of major corporations faced with significant crises.[21] Those firms mishandling crises saw a 7% decline in their stock price after a year. Companies effectively managing crises saw their year-end stock price close an average of 7% higher than before disaster struck. The researchers concluded that it wasn't the amount of damage that made the difference in how the stocks performed. Rather, the key was how management responded when in the media spotlight. Effective response boosted confidence in leadership; ineffective response lowered investor confidence.

Proper crisis preparation can also keep us from abandoning our moral principles. University of Oregon philosopher Naomi Zack notes that, in ordinary times, widely shared moral principles include (1) human life is intrinsically valuable and (2) everyone's life has equal value.[22] Driven by these convictions, we try to preserve and save the lives of everyone we can. No one life is considered more worthy than another. Thus, emergency room doctors treat both the wealthy and the poor. Physicians make every effort to extend life, even of the elderly and the very ill. However, when disaster strikes, responders often don't have enough resources to meet the needs of all victims. They then have to decide who lives and who dies. In medical emergencies this process is called *triage*. Health workers in these situations provide treatment only to those most likely to benefit from treatment or to survive. The lives of all victims are no longer intrinsically worthy or equally valuable. Instead, emergency personnel hope to save as many as possible while excluding others, such as the elderly and those with chronic medical conditions.

Emergency personnel do not have make triage decisions when careful preparation has taken place in advance. Instead, they can rely on the same moral values that guide their decisions during normal times. To adequately prepare for a flu epidemic, for instance, leaders would need to ensure that there are sufficient supplies of vaccine as well as enough hospital beds and ventilators to keep patients alive who contract the disease. Such preparation can be costly. However, according to Zack, crisis preparation is not a luxury to be cut when budgets are tight—it is our ethical duty. "We are morally obligated to plan for disaster," Zack asserts, "because it affects human life and well-being."[23]

Stage 2: Crisis Event

The second stage commences with a "trigger event," like an explosion, a shooting, or bankruptcy, and the recognition that a crisis has occurred. It ends when the crisis is resolved. Realization that a crisis has erupted sparks strong emotions, including surprise, anger, fear, and disbelief. Confusion reigns as group members try to understand what is happening and worry about what will happen to the group and to themselves. At the same time, significant harm is done to people, property, and the larger environment, and the incident garners significant press coverage.

Ethical leaders play a critical role during this stage. They first recognize that a crisis has occurred and persuade others that the group is in grave danger. This is not always an easy task. When tsunamis struck Thailand's beaches in 2004, some 30,000 Swedes were vacationing in the area. A low-ranking official on duty in the Swedish Foreign Ministry recognized the danger to Swedish citizens and alerted her bosses. They, however, did not find the situation alarming. When she persisted in her efforts to warn them, she was reprimanded and called hysterical.[24] (Following the crisis, she was commended for her courage in speaking up.) Case Study 12.1 provides another example of failure to recognize the extent of a crisis, which had tragic consequences.

Once the crisis is recognized, leaders then implement the CMP, mobilize the crisis management team, and focus on damage control. Immediate threats to individuals, property, and the environment take priority. Leaders may need to redeploy staff and such resources as equipment, phone lines, and office space while cooperating with emergency personnel, government officials, neighborhood associations, the media, and other outside groups.

Because the crisis management team is so critical to coping with an active crisis, leaders should pay particular attention to the group's membership. While the exact composition of the team may vary depending on the particular crisis, the typical crisis management team for a large organization consists of the following members:[25]

- Attorney to review messages, reduce legal risk, and specify legal requirements
- Public relations director or coordinator to manage internal and external communication tactics as well as media relations
- Operational managers to coordinate recovery
- Controller or another financial manager with knowledge of financial assets and insurance coverage
- Institutional technology manager to ensure that communication channels are open and to maintain databases
- Regulatory expert to handle coordination with government agencies and to represent the interests of the public
- The chief executive officer (CEO) or a representative from her or his office

One person—typically the CEO—should take primary responsibility as spokesperson in the case of an emergency. This prevents conflicting messages and the spread of misinformation. Contradictory and inaccurate messages were a major problem following the mysterious disappearance of Malaysia Airlines Flight 370 over the Indian Ocean. Malaysian government and airline officials sometimes contradicted each other, as did civilian and military officials. The information they released was often incomplete and inaccurate.[26] An effective spokesperson goes to the scene of the crisis, cooperates with the media, and provides accurate information. Those directly affected by the crisis have particularly important information needs and should take top priority. They not only need to know what happened but also need to learn how to protect themselves. Potential victims of a flu epidemic need to be vaccinated, for example. City residents in the path of a tornado need to be warned to take shelter. Consumers need to learn of contaminated food products. (Turn to Box 12.2 for an example of an effective crisis spokesperson in action.)

Stage 3: Postcrisis

Investigation and analysis take place during the third and final stage. Group members try to determine what went wrong, who was to blame, how to prevent a recurrence of the problem, and so on. This is also a period of recovery during which ethical leaders try to salvage the legitimacy of the group or organization, help group members learn from the crisis experience, and promote healing. The image of an organization generally suffers during a crisis as outsiders blame it for failing to prevent the disaster, causing harm, and not moving quickly enough to help victims. As a consequence, an effective leader must convince the public that the organization has a legitimate reason to exist and can be trusted. The best way to rebuild an organization's image depends a great deal on the particular crisis and the past history of the group. If the organization is not at fault and has a good reputation, simple denial ("We are not at fault") may be sufficient. However, if the organization is to blame (particularly if it has a troubled history), it should admit responsibility, offer compensation to victims, and take corrective action by improving safety procedures, recalling products, and so forth. Not only is this the moral course of action, but attempts to deny truthful accusations typically backfire, further damaging the group's reputation.[27]

The second leadership task in the postcrisis stage is to encourage the group to learn from the experience lest it be repeated again. Organizational crisis learning takes three forms.[28] *Retrospective sense making* looks for causation, determining what members overlooked and identifying faulty assumptions and rationalizations that contributed to the disaster. Such processing broadens the group's base of knowledge and gives it more options for responding in the future. *Reconsidering structure* refers to making major changes in leadership, mission, organizational structure, and policies as a result of the disruption caused by the crisis event. Disaster commissions are sometimes formed to capture learning from crises and to suggest reforms. Following the Twin Towers attack, for example, the 9/11 Commission report led to a major overhaul of the U.S. intelligence system.[29]

Vicarious learning draws from the experiences of other groups and organizations, both good and bad. Some organizations illustrate what *not* to do, while others serve as exemplary role models. Government response to Hurricane Katrina has emerged as a classic example of crisis *mis*management. Local and state officials were slow to order a mandatory evacuation and stranded poorer residents who didn't have cars. The Federal Emergency Management Agency (led by an unqualified manager) waited too long to implement emergency plans, and the president didn't get involved until days had passed. A House congressional committee investigating the disaster concluded that the government's response to Katrina was a "litany of mistakes, misjudgments, lapses, and absurdities."[30] (Turn to Case Study 12.2 for a closer look at how New Orleans has overcome these miscues to recover and renew itself.) There is also much to learn from how BP and the federal government mismanaged the oil spill off the coast of Louisiana. Fortunately, the state and federal response to Hurricane Sandy was much more effective, with a majority of residents expressing approval for the way that government officials intervened.[31]

Box 12.2 Mourner-in-Chief

When disasters like terrorist attacks, storms, and shootings occur, Americans look to their president to express the sorrow of the nation. In these cases, the president becomes the nation's "mourner-in-chief." In 1983, for example, Ronald Reagan expressed the shock of the nation and the world at the downing of a South Korean passenger airliner by a Russian fighter plane. After the shooting of 20 first graders and six adults in Newtown, Connecticut, President Barack Obama offered the following statement at a White House press conference. What made the address particularly powerful was the fact that the president, who normally appeared cool and collected, had to stop during his remarks to wipe away tears.

This afternoon, I spoke with Governor Malloy and FBI Director Mueller. I offered Governor Malloy my condolences on behalf of the nation and made it clear he will have every single resource that he needs to investigate this heinous crime, care for the victims, counsel their families.

We've endured too many of these tragedies in the past few years. And each time I learn the news, I react not as a president, but as anybody else would as a parent. And that was especially true today. I know there's not a parent in America who doesn't feel the same overwhelming grief that I do.

The majority of those who died today were children—beautiful, little kids between the ages of 5 and 10 years old. They had their entire lives ahead of them—birthdays, graduations, weddings,

kids of their own. Among the fallen were also teachers, men and women who devoted their lives to helping our children fulfill their dreams.

So our hearts are broken today for the parents and grandparents, sisters and brothers of these little children, and for the families of the adults who were lost.

Our hearts are broken for the parents of the survivors, as well, for as blessed as they are to have their children home tonight, they know that their children's innocence has been torn away from them too early and there are no words that will ease their pain.

As a country, we have been through this too many times. Whether it is an elementary school in Newtown, or a shopping mall in Oregon, or a temple in Wisconsin, or a movie theater in Aurora, or a street corner in Chicago, these neighborhoods are our neighborhoods and these children are our children. And we're going to have to come together and take meaningful action to prevent more tragedies like this, regardless of the politics.

This evening, Michelle and I will do what I know every parent in America will do, which is hug our children a little tighter, and we'll tell them that we love them, and we'll remind each other how deeply we love one another. But there are families in Connecticut who cannot do that tonight, and they need all of us right now. In the hard days to come, that community needs us to be at our best as Americans, and I will do everything in my power as president to help, because while nothing can fill the space of a lost child or loved one, all of us can extend a hand to those in need, to remind them that we are there for them, that we are praying for them, that the love they felt for those they lost

endures not just in their memories, but also in ours.

May God bless the memory of the victims and, in the words of Scripture, heal the brokenhearted and bind up their wounds.

Source: The White House.

The third leadership task in the postcrisis stage is to promote healing, which helps members move beyond the crisis. Healing begins with explaining what happened. A cause needs to be identified and corrective action taken. Corrective steps might include, for instance, strengthening levees after a hurricane and tightening computer security measures after data have been stolen. Forgetting—replacing feelings of stress, anxiety, and loss with positive emotions like optimism and confidence—is easier when such preventive measures have been put in place. Ethical leaders also shape the memories of what happened by honoring crisis heroes and by marking important anniversaries.

Fostering a sense of renewal that sets aside blame and looks ahead is part of the healing process. The *discourse of renewal* is spontaneous, not carefully planned, and comes directly out of the character and reputation of the leader.[32] Renewal focuses on the future rather than on the past. The discourse of renewal also highlights the opportunities created by the crisis. City officials in Cedar Rapids, Iowa, for example, had a downtown redevelopment plan in place four months after a devastating flood in 2008. Five years after the flood, the town sported a new convention center and hotel, a restored historic theater, and an outdoor amphitheater built on top of a levee.[33] (Box 12.3 summarizes critical competencies for leading in crisis situations.)

COMPONENTS OF ETHICAL CRISIS MANAGEMENT

As we saw in the previous section, ethical leaders have important tasks to carry out in each stage of crisis development. Theorists and researchers have identified six principles and/or strategies that equip them to fulfill these duties. Moral leaders assume broad responsibility, practice transparency, demonstrate care and concern, use their heads as well as their hearts, improvise from a strong moral foundation, and build resilience.

Assume Broad Responsibility

Responsibility is the foundation of ethical crisis leadership.[34] Preventing, managing, and recovering from crises all depend on the willingness of leaders and followers to accept their moral responsibilities. Society grants individuals and organizations significant freedom to make and carry out decisions. Such freedom means that people and groups are accountable for their actions. They have an ethical duty to prevent crises because such events do significant harm. The first step in preventing crises is to behave as a moral

Box 12.3 Crisis Leadership Competencies

To determine the specific skills leaders need to successfully manage crisis situations, Lynn Perry Wooten and Erika Hayes James sampled 20 business crises occurring from 2000 to 2006. Their data set included an Alaska Airlines crash, financial fraud at Tyco, a hepatitis outbreak at Chi-Chi's restaurants, Wal-Mart's response to a gender discrimination lawsuit, and Hurricane Katrina. The researchers found that firms often mishandle one phase of a crisis while responding more effectively to another. They also identified key competencies, described below, that are essential to navigating each crisis phase.

PRECRISIS

- *Sense making.* Sense making answers these questions: How does something become an event? What does the event mean? What should I do relative to the event? The crisis leader then puts the answers to these queries together to develop a plan of action. Making sense of what appear to be unrelated events is also critical to identifying and responding to such warning signs as accident reports, quality problems, and customer complaints.

- *Perspective taking.* Empathy is critical to anticipating and responding to crises. Leaders need to be particularly sensitive to the needs of those who might be hurt by a crisis (victims and victims' families), not just those who are most vocal, like activists and shareholders. This broader perspective can alert leaders to potential dangers and prepare them to act on behalf of stakeholders.

- *Issue selling.* Middle managers, in particular, must be able to convince top management that the organization needs to engage in crisis planning, which is difficult, given the fact that crisis planning is rarely seen as a pressing concern among key decision makers.

- *Organizational agility.* Since crises threaten the organization as a whole, leaders have to bring a variety of departments and units together to prepare for disaster.

- *Creativity.* It takes creativity to design a CMP that identifies a variety of weaknesses, possible scenarios, and effective responses.

CRISIS EVENT

- *Decision making under pressure.* Competent crisis leaders must be able to overcome negative emotions like fear and anxiety as well as time pressures and public scrutiny to make wise choices.

- *Communicating effectively.* During the height of the crisis, leaders are responsible for connecting to a variety of audiences—employees, customers, investors, community leaders, neighbors. They need to provide information, instruction, and assurance while gathering data. They must also express empathy and shape public opinion.

- *Risk taking.* The pressure of a crisis can prompt leaders to fall back on their habits or traditional ways of responding. A crisis, however, often calls for a unique response. For example, the board of Martha Stewart Living Omnimedia was able to shift to a new way of thinking when the company's namesake was jailed for insider trading. The CEO took Martha Stewart off of magazine covers and de-emphasized her connection to other products. Top management also reorganized into executive teams to supervise business units.

POSTCRISIS

- *Promoting organizational resilience.* This competency takes the organization beyond where it was before the crisis struck. When this ability is exercised, individuals and the organization as a whole are able to bounce back from the stress and perform at a higher level.

- *Acting with integrity.* Effective crisis leaders demonstrate personal integrity and make ethical decisions. They act consistently, matching their words and actions. They don't deny responsibility for an industrial accident, for instance, and later admit guilt

to settle a lawsuit. They are able to rebuild public trust by following through on their statements and commitments.

- *Learning orientation.* Any opportunity offered by a crisis is lost unless leaders engage in learning and reflection. Competent crisis leaders learn from their experiences and change the way their organizations operate.

Source: Wooten, L. P., & James, E. H. (2008). Linking crisis management and leadership competencies: The role of human resource development. *Advances in Developing Human Resources, 10,* 352–379.

person. Since a great many crises (fraud, accounting scandals, embezzlement, sexual harassment) are the direct result of the immoral actions of leaders, eliminating these behaviors greatly reduces the group's exposure to scandal. Moral leaders also create healthy ethical organizational climates that have a low risk of moral failure and crisis (see Chapter 10).

In addition to engaging in and fostering ethical behavior, the responsible crisis leader fights against complacency, human biases, institutional weaknesses, special interest groups, and other obstacles to crisis prevention. He or she commits the money and resources needed to identify, prevent, and manage trouble spots. This includes assigning groups to brainstorm potential weaknesses, investing in computer security, holding disaster drills, and creating CMPs. Leaders aren't the only ones who are responsible for crisis prevention, however. This duty extends to everyone who has a role, no matter how small, in anticipating such events. According to crisis prevention expert Robert Allinson, "Anyone who is in any way connected with a potential or actual disaster is responsible for its occurrence."[35]

Sadly, a significant number of organizations still fail to take their crisis prevention responsibilities seriously. A corporate survey revealed that, while the vast majority had CMPs, a significant portion (approximately one fifth) did not.[36]

If a crisis does erupt, leaders are obligated to mitigate the harm they and/or their followers cause to others through, for instance, deceptive advertising, fraud, or industrial accidents. A rapid response is key to fulfilling this ethical duty. Exxon continues to be used as an example of poor crisis management in large part because of its slow response to the grounding of the *Exxon Valdez,* which caused the largest oil spill up to that point in U.S. history. Then-CEO Lawrence Rawl didn't get to the scene of the accident until 10 days after the spill, initial containment efforts were ineffective, and the firm denied at first that it had any responsibility for what happened.[37] More recently, executives at Toyota were slow to respond to sudden acceleration problems in their vehicles, and officials at General Motors waited over a decade to fix an ignition switch problem with its small cars, which led to the deaths of at least 169 people.[38]

When the immediate danger is past, leaders have an obligation to ensure that a similar crisis doesn't happen again and to assure the public of that fact. Their ethical duties include carrying out the postcrisis tasks noted earlier: rebuilding the group's image, helping members learn from the crisis, and promoting healing.

Crises broaden both the scope and the depth of a leader's ethical obligations. In a crisis, the breadth of a leader's responsibility greatly expands. New stakeholder groups are formed, including those who had no previous interest in the organization but are currently threatened as well as members of the general public who learn about the crisis event. Leaders may also need to go to extraordinary lengths (depth) to meet the needs of victims. Take the case of Cantor Fitzgerald, for example. When the terrorist planes hit the World Trade Center in 2001, all of its employees working in the North Tower were killed. CEO Howard Lutnick and his colleagues continue to care for the financial, physical, and emotional needs of surviving family members years after the crisis event. (Turn to "Leadership Ethics at the Movies: *Out of a Clear Blue Sky*" for more information on how Lutnick assumed responsibility for employee families.)

Leadership Ethics at the Movies

OUT OF A CLEAR BLUE SKY

Key Cast Members: Howard and Edie Lutnick, surviving employees and families of Cantor Fitzgerald

Synopsis: Bond trader Cantor Fitzgerald suffered the greatest loss of life in the 9/11 terrorist attacks. All 658 employees at their offices in the Twin Towers died that day. CEO Howard Lutnick, who was taking his son to his first day of school, was spared. He faced the daunting task of saving the company and meeting the needs of survivors while at the same time grieving his brother, a Cantor employee who perished in the collapse of the North Tower. This documentary chronicles the company's attempts to recover and heal over the next ten years. Director Dianne Gardner, whose brother was another Cantor employee who died on September 11th, had access to Lutnick from the first hours following the attack. The CEO had a reputation for being a ruthless businessman but broke down in tears during media interviews. He promised to offer financial compensation to the families of those who died and to pay their health insurance for ten years. Howard appointed his sister Edie to head the Cantor Relief Fund. In the meantime, the firm's few remaining employees struggled to conduct daily business and to make a profit. Lutnick soon came under intense national criticism for failing to deliver quickly on his promises to victims' families. He weathered the storm by meeting with angry relatives and making good on his pledges. Both Howard and Edie found themselves challenged and transformed in ways they never thought possible.

Rating: Not rated but contains video from the tower collapse and intense emotional scenes

Themes: assuming broad responsibility, demonstrating care and compassion, transparency, ethical rationality

Practice Transparency

Like responsibility, transparency is another requirement placed on groups and organizations operating freely in a democratic society. We want governments to reveal the ways they spend our tax dollars, for instance, and require audited financial statements and annual reports from publicly held corporations. Citizens have a right to informed choice. Neighbors ought to learn about the presence of hazardous chemicals at a nearby plant; federal law mandates that colleges provide data on crimes committed on or around their campuses. Failure to disclose information spawns abuses of power and privilege and makes it impossible for individuals to act as informed members of the community.[39] Transparency is key to exercising personal freedom and establishing healthy relationships between individuals, between people and organizations, and between organizations.[40]

Transparency begins with openness. When faced with the challenge of mismanaged information, the transparent leader tells the truth and avoids hiding or distorting information. A transparent group is open about its policies, compensation packages, safety measures, values, spending, positions on political issues, and so on. Leaders regularly share this information through websites, presentations, publications, press releases, and other means. Openness, in turn, is marked by candor and integrity. Ethical leaders are willing to share bad as well as good news, such as when earnings are down and construction plans have to be shelved. Johnson & Johnson's response to the Tylenol poisoning has become a textbook case of crisis management in part because of the firm's honesty. During the product tampering crisis, corporate officials initially denied that there was any potassium cyanide used in the manufacture of Tylenol.[41] Later, when leaders discovered that minute amounts of the chemical were used during testing at some facilities, it immediately released this information to the public. Such candor helped the company recover quickly from this abnormal accident.

Transparency also involves symmetry.[42] Symmetry refers to maintaining balanced relationships with outside groups based on two-way communication. Instead of imposing their will on others, organizations engaged in symmetrical relationships seek to understand and respond to the concerns of stakeholders. They regularly interact with and gather information from customers, vendors, neighbors, activist groups, and others. Even more important, they act on these data, changing their plans as needed. For example, if neighbors strenuously object to the construction of a new product distribution facility, executives may find another location or modify the design of the building to meet the concerns of those living nearby. A study of excellent public relations programs found that the best public relations efforts—those that increase organizational effectiveness and benefit society—are based on symmetrical relationships with stakeholder groups.[43]

Crisis preparedness and trust are two positive by-products of transparency. Openness makes it less likely that leaders will engage in unethical behavior. As ethicist Jeremy Bentham noted, "The more strictly we are watched, the better we behave." Symmetry also serves as an early warning system. Partnerships foster two-way communication that will reveal if customers are having problems with products or services, if activist groups are offended by the organization's environmental practices, and so forth.

Stakeholders and the general public are more prone to trust organizations they perceive as open and give them the benefit of the doubt in crisis situations. As a consequence, these groups suffer less damage to their image and regain their legitimacy more rapidly. For example, Pepsi was the victim of a hoax that started in Seattle: Consumers placed syringes in cans of Diet Pepsi and then complained to the media. The corporation's reputation for safety and quality, as well as its Seattle bottler's work in the community, helped Pepsi weather the crisis and recover quickly.[44]

Maintaining transparency is particularly difficult when a crisis is triggered. First, there are privacy concerns. Victims' families may need to be notified before information can be released to the press. Second, admitting fault can put the organization at a disadvantage in case of a lawsuit. Third, there may be proprietary information about, say, manufacturing processes and recipes, which should not be released to competitors. (Even the leading proponents of corporate transparency agree that businesses have a right to privacy, to security, and to control of certain types of information.)[45] Fourth, uncertainty makes it difficult for an organization to determine what its course of action should be and, as a result, to communicate concrete details to the public. Fifth, being specific may offend some stakeholders who feel that they have been treated unfairly. Sixth, making a commitment to a single course of action too soon may limit the group's ability to deal with the crisis.[46]

Some observers suggest that leaders in a crisis situation use *strategic ambiguity* as an alternative to transparency. In strategic ambiguity, communicators are deliberately vague, which allows them to appeal to multiple audiences.[47] For example, the promise to respond forcefully to a crisis is an abstract statement, which can be interpreted many different ways by stakeholders. It also leaves the door open for the group to choose a variety of possible strategies for managing the crisis event. If challenged, the leader can claim that she or he never made a specific commitment to particular stakeholder groups. Then, too, ambiguous messages are appropriate in early stages of a crisis, when information is scarce and conditions are rapidly changing.[48]

More often than not, however, strategic ambiguity is unethical, used to shift the blame and to confuse stakeholders while providing them with biased and/or incomplete information. This appears to be the case with Jack in the Box.[49] In 1993, children in Washington state were sickened with *E. coli* poisoning after eating hamburgers at the firm's restaurants. Throughout the crisis, Jack in the Box president Robert Nugent made use of ambiguous communication. He emphasized that there was a "potential" link between the illnesses and company food. He pointed to other possible contributors—including a food supplier—to the outbreak and claimed that the firm intended to follow state and federal regulations. (Later, it was revealed that Jack in the Box had failed to adopt Washington's stricter cooking times, which likely would have prevented the outbreak.) The restaurant chain's response was unethical because it (a) favored the needs of internal stakeholders (employees, managers, shareholders) over those of external stakeholders (consumers, regulators) and (b) provided outsiders with incomplete and inaccurate information.

While the amount and type of information to be shared will vary with each crisis, the goal should always be to be as open as possible. Cooperate with the media and government officials, respond quickly to inquiries, provide detailed background information on the crisis, be honest about what happened, release information as soon as it is available, and be more concerned about meeting the needs of victims than about protecting organizational assets (see the discussion of care and concern in the next section). Avoid *stonewalling*, which is uncooperative communication designed to hinder or redirect the flow of information. BP chairman Tony Hayward used stonewalling when testifying before Congress after the Deepwater Horizon oil spill. He repeatedly responded to questions by declaring "The investigations are ongoing"; "I can't answer that question because I'm not a cement engineer," and "I wasn't involved in any of that decision making."[50]

Rhetorician Keith Hearit illustrates how an organization can practice transparency when communicating to stakeholders during a crisis. Hearit believes that, in order to be ethical, the group's explanation of events and response to public criticism must have the right manner and content.[51] *Manner* refers to the form of the communication, which needs to (1) be truthful (disclose relevant information that matches up with the reality of what happened), (2) be sincere (express true regret, reflect the seriousness of the event and its impact, demonstrate commitment to taking corrective action and reconciling with stakeholders), (3) be timely (immediately after the event, in time to help victims deal with the damage), (4) be voluntary (not coerced but driven by moral considerations, seek reconciliation, humble), (5) address all stakeholders (speak to all who were wronged, not just a few groups), and (6) be in the proper context (available to all victims).

The *content* of the message is just as important as the form it takes. The ethical story of events

- clearly acknowledges wrongdoing;
- accepts full responsibility for what happened;
- expresses regret for the offense, the harm done, and failure to carry out responsibilities;
- identifies with the injured parties (both with their suffering and with the damage done to relationships);
- asks for forgiveness;
- seeks reconciliation with injured parties;
- fully discloses information related to the offense;
- offers to carry out appropriate corrective action; and
- offers appropriate compensation.

Demonstrate Care and Concern

Demonstrating concern has practical as well as ethical benefits. Nothing draws more public condemnation than a group that refuses to take responsibility for harming others, as in the case of the *Exxon Valdez,* or appears callous, as when National Aeronautics and Space Administration (NASA) declared that there had been "an apparent malfunction" as millions watched the explosion of the *Challenger* shuttle on television. Victims who have received adequate assistance are less likely to sue the organization later.

When harm occurs, people hold organizations and their leaders responsible even if they didn't mean to hurt others, which is called the *intention effect*.[52] Apparently, the mere existence of harm triggers the impression that the individual or group involved was deliberately out to damage others. Observers also expect corporations to anticipate potential harm—the *foresight effect*. This effect is illustrated by the stiff punishments administered to corporate defendants in civil court cases. Jurors believe that corporations have greater responsibility for harm because they should have greater ability to foresee the consequences of their actions. Jurors also expect a higher level of care from companies based on their greater power, the sense that they have more obligations because they have more resources, and the fact that corporate misdeeds have greater consequences than do those of individuals operating on their own.

Members of the public also judge companies on the way that they respond to natural disasters.[53] Citizens determine the firm's level of benevolent concern by the size and effectiveness of its response. When companies make significant contributions that meet the needs of victims, stakeholders rate them more favorably and consider them to be more ethical. Like the Good Samaritan of the Bible who provided bandages, food, clothing and shelter for the robbery victim lying alongside the road (described in Chapter 5), business Samaritans must not only stop to help but also provide practical assistance. (Self-Assessment 12.2 asks you to evaluate a company's response to a natural disaster.)

While it is in the interest of leaders and organizations to act in a compassionate manner for image and financial reasons as well as to meet the expectations of observers, it is even more important that they do so for ethical reasons. Altruism is particularly relevant to crisis situations. Love of neighbor urges us to meet the needs of those threatened by crisis, no matter who they are. Victims deserve our help because of their status as human beings. Showing concern during a crisis goes well beyond addressing the physical and financial needs of victims. Those harmed by a crisis have significant emotional and spiritual needs, too.[54] They may be overwhelmed with feelings of loss and grief as well as guilt for surviving when others did not. Their sense of security, meaning, and purpose is threatened. Post-traumatic stress disorder, where individuals periodically relive the terror, is common. Of course, victims aren't the only ones to experience many of these reactions. The triggering event, as noted earlier, generates surprise, anger, fear, and disbelief for crisis managers, other group members, and outside observers as well. For instance, mass shootings are traumatic events not only for local residents but also for the country as a whole.

The emotional and spiritual demands of crises mean that ethical leaders need to address the whole person during the crisis and postcrisis stages. They stay in constant communication with group members, calming their fears. They help followers regain their focus and emphasize the importance of community. They arrange for emotional and spiritual counseling and recognize that the whole organization may need to pass through a grieving process. Ethical leaders also recognize that if the group is to heal, they must foster hope while honoring the past.

The ethic of care has been specifically applied to crisis management. The care ethic fosters crisis preparation because those concerned about others are more likely to take their complaints seriously and are therefore more alert to possible signs of trouble. Once they have identified prodromes, they are more likely to give voice to their concerns instead of exiting the organization.[55]

Concern for others can also prompt a group or an organization to go well beyond what the law or fairness requires when responding to a crisis. Consider the case of the San Ysidro, California, McDonald's shooting, for example.[56] On July 18, 1984, a lone gunman out to "hunt humans" shot 40 people at the restaurant (21 died). McDonald's was not at fault and was, in fact, a victim of the attack. But rather than declaring its innocence or decrying the unfairness of headlines blaming it for the carnage, McDonald's followed the "Horwitz Rule." Executive vice president and General Counsel Don Horwitz told management: "I don't want you people to worry or care about the legal implications of what you might say. We are going to do what's right for the survivors and families of the victims, and we'll worry about lawsuits later."[57] (It could have been argued that providing help was evidence that McDonald's was in some way responsible for what happened.) The company then suspended its national advertising campaign out of respect for victims and their families, sent personnel to help with funeral arrangements, paid hospital bills, and flew in relatives to be with their families. Corporate executives sought the counsel of an important local religious leader, attended funerals, demolished the restaurant, and then donated the land to the city.

The steps taken by McDonald's in this instance weren't "fair" and devalued the rights of the firm. After all, the restaurant chain wasn't to blame, and yet its leaders spent millions suspending advertising, creating a fund for families of victims, demolishing the restaurant, donating the land, and so on. Driven by care, corporate officials kept their focus on responsibility to victims and the importance of acknowledging their pain. They listened to the community and worked hard at maintaining connections with local political, community, and religious groups.

Engage the Head as Well as the Heart

Rational thought, problem solving, and other cognitive skills and strategies are important complements to care and compassion in ethical crisis management. Moral leaders respond with their heads as well as their hearts.[58] In particular, they are highly mindful and engage in strategic and ethical rational thinking. (Followers must also engage their heads as well as their hearts—see "Focus on Follower Ethics: Blowing the Whistle: Ethical Tension Points.")

Ethical crisis leaders, in addition to paying heedful attention themselves (see Chapter 11), create *mindful* cultures. University of Michigan business professors Karl Weick and Kathleen Sutcliffe argue that collective mindfulness is the key to creating high-reliability organizations (HROs).[59] HROs (emergency rooms, air traffic control systems, power plants) rarely fail even though they face lots of unexpected events. Attention to minor problems sets HROs apart from their less-reliable counterparts. Unlike crisis-prone organizations that ignore minor deviations until they magnify into a crisis, HROs respond forcefully to the weakest signal that something is wrong.

Weick and Sutcliffe use the deck of an aircraft carrier to illustrate the characteristics of mindful cultures that prevent harmful crises from occurring. One naval crewmember described an aircraft carrier this way:

> Imagine that it's a busy day, and you shrink San Francisco Airport to only one short runway and one ramp and one gate. Make planes take off and land at the same time, at half the present time interval, rock

the runway from side to side, and require that everyone who leaves in the morning returns that same day. Make sure the equipment is so close to the edge of the envelope that it's fragile. Then turn off the radar to avoid detection, impose strict controls on radios, fuel the aircraft in place with their engines running, put an enemy in the air, and scatter live bombs and rockets around. Now, wet the whole thing down with salt water and oil, and man it with 20-year-olds, half of whom have never seen an airplane close up. Oh, and by the way, try not to kill anyone.[60]

Despite the dangers, very few carrier accidents occur because navy leaders encourage five mindful practices. First, carrier crews are *preoccupied with failure*. Every landing is graded, and small problems like a plane in the wrong position are treated as signs that there may be larger issues like poor communication or training. Second, those who work on carriers are *reluctant to simplify*. Each plane is inspected multiple times, and pilots and deck crew communicate responsibilities through hand and voice signals and different-colored uniforms. Third, carrier crews sustain continuous *sensitivity to operations*. Everyone on board is focused on launching and landing aircraft. Officers observe all activities and communicate with each other constantly. Fourth, people on carriers share a *commitment to resilience*. Their knowledge equips them to come up with creative solutions when unexpected events like equipment failures or severe weather occur. Fifth, carrier personnel demonstrate *deference to expertise*. Lower-ranking individuals can overrule their superiors if they have more expertise in, for example, landing damaged planes.

Leaders responding to crises also need to employ *ethical rationality*. Ethical rationality ties together research on business ethics, strategy, and crisis management. *Rationality* is defined as "a firm's ability to make decisions based on comprehensive information and analysis."[61] Rational firms and leaders (which are generally more successful) do a thorough job of scanning the environment and analyzing the information they gather. They are also able to quickly generate lots of alternative solutions and ideas.[62] At the same time, ethics is at the core of their corporate strategy.[63] Such organizations keep the needs of stakeholders in mind and are concerned about building a good society. They make routine choices based on moral principles like utilitarianism and the categorical imperative.

Ethical rationality serves firms well in crisis management. They are less likely to experience crisis events because they continually scan the environment and analyze the data they collect. Leaders are not prone to act selfishly (e.g., lie, ignore stakeholder groups, hurt the environment) because they recognize that all stakeholders have intrinsic value and they are committed to the greater good. When a crisis is triggered, they have more information on hand and can rapidly generate and evaluate alternative courses of action under time pressures. Such firms have a clearer understanding of their stakeholder groups and how they might be affected by crisis events. Further, ethically rational companies (and nonprofits) are more likely to make sound moral choices during a crisis because leaders are in the practice of incorporating ethical principles into routine decision making.

Improvise from a Strong Moral Foundation

Dartmouth professor Paul Argenti interviewed corporate executives whose firms successfully weathered the World Trade Center terrorist attacks. One of the lessons of

Focus on Follower Ethics

BLOWING THE WHISTLE: ETHICAL TENSION POINTS

Deciding to go public with information about organizational misbehavior can cause a crisis. Not only do whistle-blowers put their careers, health, and relationships at risk, they also put their leaders, their coworkers, and the group as a whole in danger. Everyone suffers when the whistle blows. Employees lose their jobs, donations dry up, contracts are canceled, stock prices decline, and so on. Followers must determine whether the benefits of going public (e.g., improving patient safety, protecting the public, eliminating waste and fraud) justify such widespread disruption. To make this determination, ethics professor J. Vernon Jensen argues that potential whistle-blowers must respond to a series of questions or issues that he calls *ethical tension points*. We can use these questions as a guide if we are faced with the choice of going public or keeping silent. Jensen identifies the following as key ethical tension points in whistle-blowing:

- *What is our obligation to the organization?* Do conditions warrant breaking contractual agreements, confidentiality, and loyalty to the group?
- *What are our moral obligations to colleagues in the organization?* How will their lives be affected? How will they respond?

- *What are our ethical obligations to our profession?* Does loyalty to the organization take precedence or do professional standards?
- *Will the act of whistle-blowing adversely affect our families and others close to us?* Is it fair to make them suffer? How much will they be hurt by our actions?
- *What moral obligation do we have to ourselves?* Do the costs of going public outweigh the benefits of integrity and feelings of self-worth that come from doing so?
- *What is our ethical obligation toward the general public?* How will outsiders respond to our message? Do the long-term benefits of speaking out outweigh any short-term costs (fear, anger, uneasiness)?
- *How will my action affect important values such as freedom of expression, truthfulness, courage, justice, cooperativeness, and loyalty?* Will my coming forward strengthen these values or weaken them? What values (friendship, security) will have to take lower priority?

Source: Jensen, J. V. (1996). Ethical tension points in whistleblowing. In J. A. Jaksa & M. S. Pritchard (Eds.), *Responsible communication: Ethical issues in business, industry, and the professions* (pp. 41–51). Cresskill, NJ: Hampton.

9/11, according to Argenti, is that, during a disaster, managers must make quick decisions without guidance.[64] They are more likely to make wise choices if they are prepared. Preparation includes not only training and planning but also instilling corporate values. Employees of several undamaged Starbucks stores near Ground Zero kept their locations open even as the rest of the company's outlets in the United States were closed for the day. They provided free coffee and pastries to hospital staff and rescue workers. Several people were saved when Starbucks workers pulled them inside, rescuing them from collapsing buildings. Leaders and followers at these stores were acting in accordance with one of the eight principles of the Starbucks mission statement, which is "Contribute positively to our communities and our environment." Employees at *The New York Times* and Oppenheimer Funds also drew from their organizations' core ideology to continue to serve readers, customers, and clients.

The ability to ethically improvise is critical in a crisis because no amount of planning and practice can totally equip individuals for the specific challenges they will face during the crisis event. Unethical decisions, such as refusing to take action or responsibility, can cause significant harm and undermine the future of the group or organization. In addition, the crisis forces changes in priorities. Concern for profit must be set aside in favor of damage control and helping victims. The stakeholders who are normally most important (e.g., corporate stockholders and owners) take a backseat to those most directly affected by events.

Successful improvisation requires that employees be empowered to act on their own initiative. They must not only know the moral course of action but also be able to act on their choices, like the Starbucks employees on September 11, 2001. Their decision to distribute free food and drinks cost Starbucks money, but corporate headquarters supported their actions.

Build Resilience

Resilience refers to the collective ability to bounce back from a crisis. While some scholars believe this means returning to the status quo, others argue that resilient groups come out of the crisis stronger than ever before. Those who take a more proactive approach to collective resilience treat it as a capacity that groups can develop.[65] To expand this capacity, leaders foster the resilience of followers at the same time they create resilient organizational cultures. The transformational leadership behaviors described in Chapter 8 are particularly effective at building subordinate resilience.[66] Idealized influence encourages followers to focus on shared values and purpose instead of falling victim to their fears. Inspirational motivation communicates a vision and optimism about the future, which energizes group members. Intellectual stimulation encourages followers to engage in problem solving, critical thinking, and generating alternative perspectives, all of which are critical to responding to emergencies. Individualized consideration builds followers' sense of self-efficacy, which equips them to respond more effectively in a crisis and makes them feel valued. Subordinates who feel valued by their leaders invest more in finding solutions to the threat. Ethical leaders also promote resilient cultures. Resilient organizational cultures are marked by the following:[67]

1. *Psychological safety.* To feel safe, people must be free to ask questions, experiment, and admit mistakes without fear of being seen as ignorant or incompetent. They need to offer critical feedback to others and seek honest feedback. When members feel safe, they take interpersonal risks, which is critical in emergency situations.

2. *Deep social capital.* Deep social capital is built over time on respectful, face-to-face interactions based on honesty and trust.

Social capital fosters the sharing of information and resources in a crisis and builds collaboration. These interactions also set the stage for long-term partnerships after the immediate danger has passed.

3. *Diffused power and accountability*. Resilient organizations disperse influence and accountability instead of being managed top down. Each part of the organization is designed to learn and change. Every member has discretion to make decisions along with the responsibility to reach organizational goals. These elements help organizations respond quickly to changing crisis conditions.

4. *Access to broad resource networks*. Resilient firms develop relationships with suppliers, neighboring businesses, and other groups that they can draw on when faced with a traumatic event.

Communities, like organizations, can develop their resilience. The nonprofit Rockefeller Foundation hopes to equip communities to better prepare and recover from crises by providing 100 cities with funding to hire chief resilience officers (CROs).[68] CROs are charged with developing resilience projects, coordinating stakeholders, eliminating duplication between agencies, and focusing the attention of the public and the government on resilience issues. Each CRO (the first was hired in New Orleans) focuses on the specific challenge facing her or his city. In earthquake-prone Christchurch, New Zealand, for example, the CRO has identified areas (green zones) that are safe to build in. In New York City, the emphasis is on strengthening infrastructure—sewer, water, energy—to better withstand flooding. In Boulder, Colorado, the CRO brings together teams to address drought and fire mitigation. Grant recipients are provided with technical and logistical support, helped with funding strategies, and network with other resilience officers.

THE ETHICAL DEMANDS OF EXTREME LEADERSHIP

While crisis strikes every type of organization, there are some groups that continually operate in crisis environments. First responders, mountain climbers, combat units, Special Weapons and Tactics (SWAT) teams, astronauts, skydivers, search and rescue teams, and others voluntarily place themselves in dangerous settings. Leaders in these contexts put both their physical and mental health at risk to serve their organizations and clients. Failure can result in death.

Extreme settings call for extreme leadership.[69] To care for the needs of their followers, extreme leaders must possess high levels of competence and character. Competence involves not only knowledge of the domain (i.e., combat, firefighting, mountain climbing) but also the ability to make quick ethical choices in constantly changing, ambiguous circumstances. Extreme leaders demonstrate resilience in the face of adversity, modeling coping strategies for group members. Physical stamina helps them overcome obstacles and equips them to make better ethical decisions. (See Case Study 12.3 for an example of a highly effective, ethical extreme leader.)

Character is also critical in life-and-death situations. Extreme leaders demonstrate the following virtues:

- *Courage:* Extreme leaders choose to put themselves in danger and take on more than their fair share of risks. Said one SWAT team leader, "If you put the plan together and you're not comfortable being up there with a foot through the door, then what the hell is up?"[70] They also possesses moral courage, making sure that the team conducts itself in an ethical manner (by not killing unarmed civilians in combat, for example) and questioning orders that put the unit at needless risk.

- *Optimism:* Both optimism and fear are contagious. Successful leaders offer hope that keeps the group going. Ineffective leaders allow their groups to wallow in despair, which saps the will to survive.

- *Integrity/Authenticity:* Followers in high-risk situations want consistent leaders who are transparent about the challenges facing the group. They also demand authenticity (see Chapter 8). When lives are on the line, followers quickly recognize and reject inauthentic leaders who don't live up to their values.

- *Loyalty:* Extreme leaders are intensely loyal to their followers, constantly looking out for their welfare. They may deny themselves rations so that subordinates may eat, for example. At other times, they share in the discomfort of followers. During the war in Afghanistan, the commander of the U.S. 25th Infantry Division military unit demonstrated his willingness to share the discomfort of his troops when he left headquarters on Christmas day and flew to a remote military base. When he arrived, he sent two junior officers back to headquarters to enjoy the holiday. He stayed, spending the day in the back of a truck with soldiers on patrol.

- *Caring:* In order to perform under dangerous conditions, followers must be convinced that their leaders care genuinely care for them. This concern extends to making sure that the needs of followers' families are also met.

- *Humility:* Many extreme leaders—guides, soldiers, police officers—live modestly and don't earn that much more than their followers. They are motivated by their commitment to the group's mission, not wealth. Their humility is particularly apparent when a team member dies. Leaders treat the fallen, no matter how lowly their status or rank, with respect. They recognize that when someone is killed or seriously injured, "the leader has to be small so the focus of the activity can make the decedent or the hospitalized person big."[71]

To date, there is no universal code of ethics for leaders in all types of extreme situations. However, respect for human rights (people's "moral worth") should underlie all decisions of crisis professionals. For military and police forces, this means using lethal force or creating risk for others only when there is no other option (the principle of necessity). Soldiers and law enforcement personnel should use only as much force as needed to accomplish the mission while preserving the rights of those affected by the mission (the principle of proportionality). They shouldn't intentionally harm those who don't pose a threat (the principle of immunity).[72]

Though we may never set out to become crisis professionals, we can learn from their example. When crisis strikes, competence and character make the difference between organizational survival and failure. As leaders, we need to demonstrate our expertise, make rapid moral choices, model resilience, and possess physical stamina. Our character—courage, loyalty, authenticity, compassion, humility—takes on added significance in emergency situations. The fallen should be treated with utmost respect. Concern for the moral worth of others should guide our choices.

IMPLICATIONS AND APPLICATIONS

- A crisis, which is any major unanticipated event that poses a significant threat, will be the ultimate test of your ability to provide ethical leadership.

- Crises can be divided into 10 types: public perception, natural disasters, product or service, terrorist attacks, economic, human resource, industrial, oil and chemical spills, transportation, and outside environment.

- Deliberate attempts to disrupt or destroy systems (abnormal accidents) are on the rise, and you must help your group or organization prepare for them.

- All crises follow a three-stage pattern of development: precrisis, crisis event, and postcrisis.

- Precrisis is the period of normalcy between crisis events. Use this time to identify potential trouble spots, to examine long-term trends that might threaten the group, and to prepare crisis management plans (CMPs).

- The crisis event starts with a trigger event and the recognition that a crisis has occurred. This stage ends when the immediate crisis is resolved. During this phase, your task is to identify the crisis, activate CMPs and teams, appoint a spokesperson, and try to limit the damage.

- Postcrisis is a period of investigation and recovery. Moral leaders try to determine what went wrong and institute corrective measures. They also help the group salvage its reputation, engage in crisis learning, begin the healing process by honoring victims and looking to future opportunities, and fostering resilience (the ability to bounce back from future crises).

- Responsibility is the foundation for ethical crisis leadership. As a leader, you have a duty to try to prevent the harm caused by a crisis, to mitigate the damage caused by your group, to address the needs of all affected stakeholder groups, to take steps to prevent a similar event from happening again, to help the organization learn from the experience, and to foster renewal.

- In an emergency, make transparency your goal. As much as possible, be open with stakeholders and strive to maintain symmetrical relationships with these groups based on two-way communication.

- Altruism (care) should be the driving ethical principle during crisis events. Address the emotional and spiritual concerns of those affected, not just their financial and physical needs. Go beyond what the law and justice require.

- As a leader, you will need to engage the head as well as the heart when responding to crises. Create a mindful culture that closely monitors and corrects even minor problems and deviations. Base decisions on information and analysis as well as on moral values in order to better anticipate and manage crisis events.

- No amount of preparation can prepare you and the rest of your group for every contingency, so you will need to ethically improvise. Successful improvisation draws on the core mission and values of your group or organization.

- Build the collective resilience of your group through transformational leadership behaviors and by fostering a culture marked by psychological safety, diffused power and accountability, deep social capital, and access to broad resource networks.

- Extreme leaders continually operate in high-threat situations. To succeed, they demonstrate competence and character while putting a high value on human life. You can draw from their example when facing crises.

FOR FURTHER EXPLORATION, CHALLENGE, AND SELF-ASSESSMENT

1. Use Self-Assessment 12.1 to determine your readiness level and that of your organization. If possible, distribute the assessment to others in your organization and compare scores.

2. Should all cities have CROs? What tasks should be included in the job description for this position? What skills would it take to fill this position? Write up your conclusions.

3. In a group, brainstorm a list of possible crises that could strike your college or university or work organization. Then select one of these events and outline a crisis management strategy for dealing with this situation. If time permits, assume the role of organizational leaders and conduct a mock press conference, using other members of the class as media representatives. As an alternative, generate a list of long-term trends that could pose a threat to your organization. Develop strategies to proactively address each of the issues raised by these trends.

4. In a research paper, evaluate the crisis response of an organization or city using the ethical standards/strategies described in this chapter. Describe the events and provide an analysis. Include suggestions that would help the organization do a better job of ethical crisis management in the future.

5. React to the following statement: Crises reveal the true character of leaders and their organizations.

6. Create a case study that demonstrates how an organization was able to ethically improvise during a crisis event. Or, as an alternative, create a case study that demonstrates how an organization was able to learn from a crisis event.

7. In a group, come up with a list of guidelines for determining what to reveal and what to keep secret in a crisis.

8. Find a partner and discuss your responses to Self-Assessment 12.2. What role does effectiveness play your judgment of a company's concern? Does the personal involvement of company officials make a difference in this determination?

9. Have you ever been a leader in a life-or-death situation? What ethical challenges did you face and how did you meet these demands? Write up your thoughts.

STUDENT STUDY SITE

Visit the student study site at **study.sagepub.com/johnsonmecl6e** to access full SAGE journal articles for further research and information on key chapter topics.

Case Study 12.1

THE TERROR OF EBOLA

Ebola is a terrifying disease. Victims of the virus suffer from high fever, chills, continuous vomiting and diarrhea, muscle aches, bleeding, severe headaches, rashes, and uncontrollable hiccups. Death rates can range from 25%–90%. The infection puts the body into shock and causes dehydration, low blood pressure, and organ failure. There is no known cure, but patients who receive fluids and other forms of support are much more likely to survive. However, victims may never fully recover, experiencing chronic joint pain and blurred vision for the rest of their lives.

Ebola, first identified in 1976, is transmitted from fruit bats to humans in Africa. It then spreads through contact with the bodily fluids of victims. (This puts medical personnel at particular risk.) Past outbreaks were small and limited to rural areas. That all changed in 2014–2015, when an epidemic in West Africa spread from rural regions to major cities in Liberia, Sierra Leone, and Guinea. According to conservative estimates, 28,000 were infected and more than 11,000 died.

Leaders were slow to respond to the crisis. Government officials initially refused to acknowledge the epidemic and health officers failed to share information with their counterparts in neighboring countries. Local authorities were afraid of declaring a state of emergency for fear of frightening airlines (who might stop flights) and mining companies in this, one of the poorest regions of the world. Some regional medical personnel resisted outside help. Executives at the World Health Organization (WHO) and the Centers for Disease Control underestimated the extent of the epidemic (at one point, prematurely declaring it over). Some nurses, fearing infection, refused to treat Ebola patients.

(Continued)

(Continued)

Early intervention could have contained the spread of Ebola. Instead, the epidemic caught fire. The area's few area hospitals and clinics, which often lacked such basics as hand soap, gloves, and running water, were quickly overwhelmed and the health system collapsed. As world leaders held back, brave volunteers stepped into the breach. *Time* magazine named these Ebola fighters its 2014 Persons of the Year while asking why the global health system was so slow to respond.

> Why, in short, was the battle against Ebola left for month after crucial month to a ragged army of volunteers and near volunteers: doctors who wouldn't quit even as their colleagues fell ill and died; nurses comforting patients while standing in slurries of mud, vomit, and feces; ambulance drivers facing down hostile crowds to transport passengers teeming with the virus; investigators tracing chains of infection through slums hot with disease; workers stoically zipping contagious corpses into body bags in the sun; patients meeting death in lonely isolation to protect others from infection?[1]

Eventually, the WHO., the United States government, and other groups joined local residents, Doctors Without Borders, and other volunteers in the fight against Ebola, setting up a network of clinics. At the same time, regional authorities enforced quarantine and travel restrictions. They created separate graveyards for Ebola victims and banned private burials. The epidemic subsided by the summer of 2015.

Political and cultural factors complicated the battle against Ebola. After years of civil war and unrest in the region, many residents didn't trust their governments. Some believed that the government officials created the epidemic in order to solicit funds from international donors. Authorities raised fear levels by sending inept public health messages, such as that Ebola is an automatic death sentence. Riots broke out Monrovia, the capital city of Liberia, when authorities tried to isolate a crowded neighborhood. Angry mobs threatened medical workers trying to identify victims. In West Africa, families of all religious traditions provide hands-on care to the ill and prepare the bodies of loved ones for burial, which resulted in the infection of relatives until this practice was banned. According to Liberian President Ellen Johnson Sirleaf, "The messages about don't touch the dead, wash your hands, if somebody is sick, leave them—these were all strange things, completely contrary to our tradition and culture."[2] Treatment centers were seen as places where victims went to die surrounded by medical personnel dressed head to toe in protective clothing resembling space suits.

Experts predict that there will be future Ebola epidemics. And the next epidemic could be as devastating as this one. Wealthier nations refuse to increase their contributions to rebuild the health care infrastructure in West Africa. They have also reduced their donations to the WHO. An independent panel concluded that the WHO is unprepared to handle another Ebola or similar epidemic due to budget cuts and reluctance to overrule local government officials.

Until recently, pharmaceutical companies opted not to develop a vaccine for Ebola because they don't profit off of medicines developed for diseases in poor nations. The failure of the world community means that when the terror of Ebola strikes again, it will once again result in thousands of painful and needless deaths.

Discussion Probes

1. Do medical personnel have the responsibility to care for patients no matter the risk in doing so?

2. How do you determine when the need for public health should take precedence over local customs, such as hands-on care for the dead?

3. What is the responsibility of government leaders and citizens in wealthy nations to the health care needs of people in poorer regions?

4. What, if anything, should be done to narrow the gap in medical care between wealthy and poor countries?

5. What can be done to prevent a future Ebola epidemic? To better prepare and respond?

6. How can governments encourage drug companies to develop medications for "unprofitable" diseases like Ebola?

7. What leadership and followership ethics lessons do you take from this case?

Notes

1. Von Drehle, D. (2014, December 22). The ones who answered the call. *Time*, 74.

2. Sack, K., Fink, S., Belluck, P., & Nossiter, A. (2014, December 29). How Ebola roared back. *The New York Times*, p. D1.

Sources

Donovan, G. K. (2014). Ebola, epidemics, and ethics—what we have learned. *Philosophy, Ethics, and Humanities in Medicine*, 9:15. (Online source)

Feldmann, H. (2014, October 9). Ebola—A growing threat? *New England Journal of Medicine, 371*(15), 1375–1377.

Gibbs, N. (2014, December 22). The choice. *Time*, 67–68.

Gimm, G., & Nichols, L. M. (2015, May). Ebola crisis of 2014: Are current strategies enough to meet the long-run challenges ahead? *American Journal of Public Health, 105*(5), E8–E10.

Global health inequity in Ebola treatment is major ethical concern. (2015, January 1). *Medical Ethics Advisor.*

Griffiths, P. D. (2014). Ebola and ethics. *Reviews in Medical Virology, 24*, 363–364.

Markel, H. (2014). Ebola fever and global health responsibilities. *Milbank Quarterly, 92*(4), 633–639.

Onishi, N. (2014, August 20). Clashes erupt as Liberia sets an Ebola quarantine. *The New York Times*, p. A1.

(Continued)

(Continued)

Petesch, C. (2015, August 23). With many Ebola survivors ailing, doctors evaluate situation. *Associated Press.*

Rid, A., & Emanuel, E. J. (2014, October 1). Why should high-income countries help combat Ebola? *Journal of the American Medical Association, 312*(13), 1297–1298.

Sengupta, S. (2015, July 8). Panel calls W.H.O. unfit to handle a crisis like Ebola. *The New York Times*, p. A7.

Single dose Ebola vaccine is safe and effective in monkeys against outbreak strain. (2015, August 6). *NIH News.*

Situation summary. (2015, August 19). *World Health Organization.* Retrieved from http://apps.who.int/gho/data/view.ebola-sitrep.ebola-summary-20150813?lang=en

Case Study 12.2

NEW ORLEANS AS RESILIENCE LAB

Hurricane Katrina was the largest natural disaster in the history of the United States. The 2005 Gulf coast storm displaced a million people, killed 1,800, and caused $188 billion in damage. In New Orleans, the levees failed during the storm surge, sending as much as 20 feet of water into 80% of the city. Residents fled to their roofs and thousands were stranded for days without adequate food, water, or toilet facilities in the Superdome. Television news broadcasts were filled with images of victims wading in putrid water, rooftop rescues, floating bodies (most of them African Americans), and angry citizens waiting for government help.

The New Orleans floodwaters knocked out most of the electrical grid, damaged roads, and ruined thousands of homes and commercial buildings as well as schools, churches, fire stations, and police stations. Residents fled to other cities like Houston and Dallas, dropping the population from 494,000 to 230,000. When the waters subsided, those who wanted to return had nowhere to live and had to decide whether or not to rebuild. (Even homes left standing had to be gutted due to mold and water damage.) One redevelopment official declared, "We have not seen a challenge like this in city rebuilding since World War II."[1]

Judith Rodin, president of the Rockefeller Foundation, calls New Orleans a "resilience lab," one that inspired the Foundation to promote resilience in other cities. By the 10th anniversary of the storm, the city's population returned to over 378,000 and many homes were rebuilt (often with the help of volunteers). Young professionals flocked to the area to work in new technology and bioscience companies and *Forbes* magazine named New Orleans "America's biggest brain magnet." Newcomers can ride to work on a network of bike paths built since the storm. Airport traffic rebounded to surpass pre-Katrina levels, and the tourist industry is booming.

Much of the credit for the city's renaissance goes to ordinary citizens who stepped into leadership roles. Often, they had no leadership training or leadership experience. Yet they succeeded in spite of, not because of, their city, state, and federal governments and the skepticism of the rest of the country. According to journalist and New Orleans resident Roberta Brandes Gratz,

> The people had to overcome endless impediments . . . the inequities of a state buyout program, the inequities of screwed-up regulations, all of which left people wondering what they should do, and then left them with little money to do it.[2]

She drew the title for her book on the city's recovery from a piece of post-Katrina graffiti. One citizen summed up the attitude of many residents toward the rest of the world this way: "We're still here ya bastards."[3]

Examples of grassroots leadership abound. A former Black Panther organized a group called Common Ground, which gutted three thousand homes, businesses, and churches. A white housewife set up a website and resource center to provide rebuilding tips and tools. A weaver exposed corruption and financial wrongdoing in reconstruction programs. Local preservationists fought to save historic buildings from demolition, and environmentalists cut through government red tape to restore coastal areas. A group of New Orleans women lobbied Congress for aid and pressured levee boards to improve flood protection.

The resilience lab has had its share of failures as well as successes. Many ruined houses remain vacant, particularly in black neighborhoods in the Lower Ninth Ward. Most of the new residents flocking to New Orleans are white, lowering the proportion of African Americans in the city from 67% to 60%. Whites generally land the new high-paying jobs while many black residents remain employed in the low-paying tourist industry. Gentrification dramatically increases rents, pushing many lower-income residents out of their neighborhoods. Government officials tore down high-density, low-income housing that survived the storm and replaced it with low-density housing that serves fewer citizens. In addition, many of the problems that plagued the city prior to the storm remain. The poverty rate (27%) is unchanged. Crime and murder rates are high and the police force is demoralized. Graduation rates have improved under a new charter school system, but high-risk students are underserved.

Results from the New Orleans resilience lab demonstrate that crisis recovery can have mixed results. However, there is still much to learn. As Rodin notes, the recovery still has a long way to go. "Ten years isn't long enough. They're still on the journey."[4]

Discussion Probes

1. Do you think the successes of the New Orleans recovery outweigh the failures?

2. How long do you think it will take for the recovery to be complete?

3. What opportunities did Katrina offer the people of New Orleans?

(Continued)

(Continued)

4. When natural disasters strike cities, what can government leaders do to encourage grassroots leaders to stay and rebuild?

5. What, if anything, can be done to ensure that people of all incomes and races share equally in disaster recovery?

Notes

1. Roig-Franzia, M. (2015, August 23). A bittersweet influx. *The Washington Post*, p. A01.

2. Jonsson, P. (2015, August 25). A "new" New Orleans emerges 10 years after hurricane Katrina. *The Christian Science Monitor*.

3. Brandes Gratz, R. (2015). *We're still here ya bastards: How the people of New Orleans rebuilt their city*. New York, NY: Nation Books.

4. Roig-Franzia.

Sources

Associated Press. (2015, August 24). New Orleans rises decade after Katrina but gaps remain. *New Orleans City Business*.

Bucktin, C. (2015, August 16). Hurricane Katrina: Despair of the victims 10 years on. *Daily Mirror*, News, 26–27.

Dart, T. (2015, August 23). New Orleans dares to dream, 10 years after Katrina. *The Observer*, US News.

Jervis, R. (2015, August 23). Nagging divide cuts through New Orleans. *USA Today*, p. 2A.

Jervis, R. (2015, August 24). Post-Katrina New Orleans still the same. *USA Today*, p. 2A.

Rich, N. (2015, August 9). Hurricane's wake. *The New York Times*, p. BR11.

Rivlin, G. (2015). *Katrina: After the flood*. New York, NY: Simon & Schuster.

Robertson, C. (2015, August 30). A decade after Katrina, New Orleans is partying again, and still rebuilding. *The New York Times*, p. A15.

Case Study 12.3

EXTREME LEADERSHIP AT THE BOTTOM OF THE WORLD: EXPLORER ERNEST SHACKLETON

The early twentieth century has been called the Heroic Age of Polar Exploration. Teams of adventurers from Norway and Great Britain competed to see who would be first to reach the South Pole. Antarctic expeditions faced temperatures as low as –100 degrees Fahrenheit and gale force winds up to 200 miles an hour. Britain's Captain Robert Scott tried unsuccessfully to claim Antarctica for the Crown in 1901. Ernest Shackleton, who had accompanied Scott on his first journey, came within 100 miles of the Pole in 1909 but had to turn back to save his party. Scott and his companions died during their second expedition, launched in 1911. Norwegian Roald Amundsen, who set out at the same time as Scott, succeeded in reaching the southernmost point on earth in January 1912.

Undeterred by Amundsen's success, Shackleton decided to launch one last great Polar journey aimed at crossing the entire Antarctic continent. This adventure has been chronicled in a number of books and films, and Shackleton is frequently cited as a role model for contemporary leaders. Author and museum curator Caroline Alexander provides one of the most detailed accounts of the expedition in her book titled *The Endurance: Shackleton's Legendary Antarctic Expedition*. Shackleton and his crew of twenty-seven men set sail on their wooden sailing ship—*The Endurance*—in August 1914, just days before World War I broke out. Soon, the last great Polar journey turned into one of the world's most incredible tales of survival.

The Endurance was trapped by pack ice at the end of January, stranding the party. When the ice melted the following October (springtime in the Southern Hemisphere), it crushed and sank the ship. The crew relocated to ice floes. At the end of April, fifteen months after being marooned, the group abandoned camp on the shrinking ice packs and made it to an uninhabited island in three small dories.

Shackleton and five companions then set out in one of the small boats (only twenty-two feet long) to reach the nearest whaling station on South Georgia Island, 800 miles away. This voyage would later be ranked as one of the greatest sea journeys of all time. The odds were against the small party from the beginning. They were traveling in the dead of winter on one of the roughest oceans in the world. Darkness made navigation nearly impossible and they survived a severe storm, one that sunk a much bigger tanker sailing at the same time in the same waters. The crew overcame these hurdles and, frostbitten and soaked to the skin, reached South Georgia Island. Yet even then, their suffering was far from over. Shackleton and two colleagues had to cross a series of ridges and glaciers before reaching the whaling camp. Alexander describes how the survivors looked when they finally reached help.

> At three in the afternoon, they arrived at the outskirts of Stromness Station. They had traveled for thirty-six hours without rest. Their bearded faces were black with blubber smoke, and their matted hair, clotted with salt, hung almost to their shoulders. Their filthy clothes were in tatters . . . Close to the station they encountered the first humans outside their own party they had set eyes on in nearly eighteen months—two small children, who ran from them in fright. (p. 164)

It would be another four months before Shackleton could reach the rest of his crew stranded on the first island. Amazingly, not one member of the party died during the whole twenty-two-month ordeal.

(Continued)

(Continued)

Many qualities made Shackleton an effective leader. He had great strength and physical stature that enabled him to endure extreme conditions and to deal with rebellious followers. He understood the skills and limitations of each expedition member and made the most of each person's abilities. Shackleton was both accessible and firm. He mixed easily with his men but, at the same time, enforced discipline in a fair, evenhanded manner. Whatever the setting, he quickly established a routine and made every effort to maintain the group's morale, planning song fests, lectures, dog races, and other activities for his men.

Alexander suggests that Shackleton's character was the key to his success. In 1909, Shackleton could have been the first to reach the South Pole but he turned back to save the lives of his companions. As the supply of food dwindled, he made expedition member Frank Wild (who would join him on the *Endurance* voyage) eat one of his (Shackleton's) daily ration of four biscuits. "I do not suppose that anyone else in the world can thoroughly realize how much generosity and sympathy was shown by this," the grateful Wild later wrote. "I DO by GOD I shall never forget it."

Shackleton continued to demonstrate concern and compassion for the needs of his followers on his Trans-Antarctic voyage. When the most unpopular crewmember was laid up with a bad back, the commander let him use his own cabin and brought him tea. He made sure that those of lower rank got the warmest clothes and sleeping bags. During the perilous trip to South Georgia Island, Shackleton kept an eye out for those who were growing weak but never embarrassed anyone by singling him out for special help. If one sailor appeared on the verge of collapse, he made sure that everyone got warm milk or food. Shackleton himself valued optimism above all other virtues. "Optimism," he said, "is true moral courage." Relentless optimism kept him going during the hard times, and he had little patience for those who were anxious about the future.

Alexander sums up the essential quality of Ernest Shackleton's leadership this way:

> At the core of Shackleton's gift for leadership in crisis was an adamantine conviction that quite ordinary individuals were capable of heroic feats if the circumstances required; the weak and the strong could and *must* survive together. The mystique that Shackleton acquired as a leader may partly be attributed to the fact that he elicited from his men strength and endurance they had never imagined they possessed; he ennobled them. (p. 194)

Discussion Probes

1. Generate a list of the virtues demonstrated by Shackleton on the *Endurance* voyage. How does your list compare to the virtues of extreme leaders presented in the chapter?

2. Do dangerous situations like polar exploration and mountain climbing put a premium on some aspects of character that would be less important in other, more routine contexts?

3. How did Shackleton demonstrate resilience? How did he promote resilience in his men?

4. How did Shackleton act as a transformational leader? A servant leader? An authentic leader?

5. What leadership ethics lessons can we draw from the life of Ernest Shackleton?

Sources

Alexander, C. (1999). *The Endurance: Shackleton's legendary Antarctic expedition*. New York, NY: Alfred A. Knopf. (Also available as a PBS Nova documentary film.)

For more information on Shackleton, his expedition, and his model of leadership, see

Giannantonio, C. M., & Hurley-Hanson, A. E. (2013). Extreme leadership: Lessons from Ernest Shackleton and the *Endurance* expedition. In C. M. Giannantonio & A. E. Hurley-Hanson (Eds.), *Extreme leadership: Leaders, teams and situations outside the norm* (pp. 3–14). Cheltenham, England: Edward Elgar.

Morrell, M., Capparell, S., & Shackleton, A. (2001). *Shackleton's way: Leadership lessons from the great Antarctic explorer*. New York, NY: Viking Press.

Perkins, D. N. T. (2000). *Leading at the edge*. New York, NY: AMACOM.

Shackleton, E. (1998). *South: A memoir of the Endurance voyage*. New York, NY: Carroll & Graf.

SELF-ASSESSMENT 12.1

Crisis and/or Disaster Preparedness Scale

This instrument measures how prepared you think you and your organization are for a natural disaster, a terrorist attack, an industrial accident, or another form of crisis. The higher your score (possible scores range from 21 to 84), the higher your level of perceived preparedness.

Instructions: Score each of the following as 1 = strongly disagree, 2 = disagree, 3 = agree, 4 = strongly agree. Reverse scores where indicated.

1. I am very familiar with our building's evacuation plan.   1   2   3   4

2. It would be easy for a potentially threatening nonemployee to gain access to my workplace. (Reverse)   1   2   3   4

3. If my organization suffered a serious crisis, I might lose my job. (Reverse)   1   2   3   4

4. If my organization suffered a serious crisis, I would still get paid until we could reopen.   1   2   3   4

5. My organization has provided each employee with a basic emergency preparedness kit (e.g., flashlight, smoke mask).   1   2   3   4

6. The security at my workplace is adequate.   1   2   3   4

7. If a crisis occurred at my organization, I am familiar with the plan for how family members can get information on the status (e.g., safety) of their relatives.   1   2   3   4

8. In the event of an emergency or a disaster, I am familiar with my organization's plan to continue operations from another location.   1   2   3   4

9. All organization members are required to rehearse portions of our crisis plan (e.g., evacuation).   1   2   3   4

10. If my organization suffered a serious crisis, I would still have my job.   1   2   3   4

11. If my organization suffered a crisis, I would still be covered by my organization's employee benefits (e.g., health insurance).   1   2   3   4

12. Security at my workplace has been significantly increased since September 11, 2001.   1   2   3   4

13. I know where the nearest fire extinguisher is to my desk/workstation.   1   2   3   4

14. If a crisis and evacuation occurred at my organization, I am familiar with our plan on how to communicate with my fellow employees from scattered or emergency locations (e.g., cell phone numbers, websites, e-mail lists).   1   2   3   4

15. Most of our employees are familiar with my organization's crisis/disaster plan.   1   2   3   4

16. As part of our emergency plan, customers and suppliers would be able to contact us for information.   1   2   3   4

17. If my organization suffered a crisis/disaster, I would have the data I need to do my job backed up at a remote site.   1   2   3   4

18. My organization offers to pay to have volunteer employees trained in basic life support techniques (e.g., CPR, first aid).   1   2   3   4

19. My organization has contingency plans in place so our customers would be covered if we suffered a disaster.   1   2   3   4

20. I know where the nearest emergency exits are to my desk/workstation.   1   2   3   4

21. My organization's emergency plan has been coordinated with local agencies (e.g., the fire department, hospitals).   1   2   3   4

Source: Fowler, K. L., Kling, N. D., & Larson, M. D. (2007). Organizational preparedness for coping with a major crisis or disaster. *Business & Society, 46,* 100–101.

SELF-ASSESSMENT 12.2

Corporate Samaritan Scenarios

Instructions: Read the following two scenarios and then rate the corporation's response in each vignette on a scale of 1–7.

Scenario 1

Following a catastrophic natural disaster, a large American corporation donated $2 million in cash to the affected residents. A relief agency reported that the aid provided assistance to a very large number of disaster victims—approximately 80%.

1. How ethical is this company? (1 = not at all; 7 = very much so)
2. How likely would you be to recommend this corporation's products or services to your friends and family? (1= not at all; 7 = very much)
3. How much would you care about the fate of this corporation? (1= not all; 7 = very much)

Scenario 2

Following a catastrophic natural disaster, a large American corporation sent members of its top management team, including the CEO and middle-level managers, to distribute hundreds of goods (around $2 million worth) to the affected residents. A relief agency reported that the aid provided assistance to a very small number of disaster victims—approximately 20%.

1. How ethical is this company? (1= not at all; 7= very much so)
2. How likely would you be to recommend this corporation's products or services to your friends and family? (1= not at all; 7 = very much)
3. How much would you care about the fate of this corporation? (1= not all; 7 = very much)

Scoring: If you are like the majority of students and managers responding to these vignettes, you gave higher ratings to the company in the first scenario than in the second. In the first vignette, the aid was highly effective, though it was delivered in an impersonal manner (high effectiveness/low proximity).

In the second vignette, the aid helped significantly fewer people even though company officials were personally involved in providing the assistance (low effectiveness/high proximity).

Source: Condensed from Jordan, J., Diermeier, D. A., & Galinsky, A. D. (2012). The strategic Samaritan: How effectiveness and proximity affect corporate responses to external crises. *Business Ethics Quarterly 22*(4), 644. Used with permission of the publisher.

NOTES

1. Fearn-Banks, K. (2007). *Crisis communications: A casebook approach* (3rd ed.). Mahwah, NJ: Erlbaum; Pearson, C. M., & Judith, A. C. (1998). Reframing crisis management. *Academy of Management Review, 23*, 59–71.
2. Christensen, S. L., & Kohls, J. (2003). Ethical decision making in times of organizational crises: A framework for analysis. *Business & Society, 42*, 328–358.
3. Coombs, W. T. (1999). *Ongoing crisis communication: Planning, managing, and responding*. Thousand Oaks, CA: SAGE; Seeger, M. W., Sellnow, T. L., & Ulmer, R. R. (2003). *Communication and organizational crisis*. Westport, CT: Praeger.

4. Mitroff, I. I. (2005). *Why some companies emerge stronger and better from a crisis.* New York, NY: AMACOM.

5. For more information on the relationship between complexity and crises, see Perrow, C. (1999). *Normal accidents: Living with high-risk technologies.* Princeton, NJ: Princeton University Press.

6. Seeger et al.

7. Bazerman, M. H., & Watkins, M. D. (2004). *Predictable surprises: The disasters you should have seen coming and how to prevent them.* Boston, MA: Harvard Business School Press.

8. Pauchant, T. C., & Mitroff, I. I. (1992). *Transforming the crisis-prone organization: Preventing individual, organizational, and environmental tragedies.* San Francisco, CA: Jossey-Bass.

9. Pauchant & Mitroff, p. 186.

10. Simola, S. (2010). Anti-corporate anger as a form of care-based moral agency. *Journal of Business Ethics, 94,* 255–269.

11. Livesey, S. M. (2003). Organizing and leading the grassroots: An interview with Lois Gibbs, Love Canal Homeowners Association activist. *Organization, 16,* 448–503.

12. Fink, S. (2002). *Crisis management: Planning for the inevitable.* Lincoln, NE: Backinprint.com.

13. McLaughlin, E. C. (2014, April 22). West, Texas, fertilizer plant blast that killed 15 "preventable," safety board says. *CNN.com*

14. See, for example, Mitroff, I. I., & Anagnos, G. (2001). *Managing crises before they happen: What every executive and manager needs to know about crisis management.* New York, NY: American Management Association; Mitroff, I. I., Pearson, C. M., & Harrington, L. K. (1996). *The essential guide to managing corporate crises: A step-by-step handbook for surviving major catastrophes.* New York, NY: Oxford University Press.

15. Mitroff, I. I., & Alpsaian, M. C. (2003, April). Preparing for evil. *Harvard Business Review,* 109–115.

16. Regester, M., & Larkin, J. (2005). *Risk issues and crisis management: A casebook of best practice* (3rd ed.). London, England: Kogan Page.

17. Dougall, E. (2008, December 12). Issues management. *Institute for Public Relations.* Retrieved from http://www.instituteforpr.org

18. Heath, R. L. (2002). Issues management: Its past, present and future. *Journal of Public Affairs, 2*(4), 209–214.

19. Fearn-Banks.

20. Lee, J., Woeste, J. H., & Heath, R. L. (2007). Getting ready for crises: Strategic excellence. *Public Relations Review, 33,* 334–336.

21. Knight, R. F., & Pretty, D. J. (1996). *The impact of catastrophes on shareholder value.* Oxford, England: Templeton College, University of Oxford.

22. Zack, N. (2009). *Ethics for disaster.* Lanham, MD: Rowman & Littlefield.

23. Zack, p. 29.

24. Daleus, P., & Hansen, D. (2011). Inherent ethical challenges in bureaucratic crisis management: The Swedish experience with the 2004 tsunami disaster. In L. Svedin (Ed.), *Ethics and crisis management* (pp. 21–36). Charlotte, NC: Information Age.

25. Denyer, S. (2014, March 12). Contradictory statements from Malaysia over missing airliner perplex, infuriate. *WashingtonPost.com*

26. Barton, L. (2001). *Crisis in organizations II.* Cincinnati, OH: South-Western.

27. Benoit, W. L. (2004). Image restoration discourse and crisis communication. In D. P. Millar & R. L. Heath (Eds.), *Responding to crisis: A rhetorical approach to crisis communication* (pp. 263–280). Mahwah, NJ: Erlbaum; Coombs, W. T., & Holladay, S. J. (2004). Reasoned action in crisis communication: An attribution theory–based approach to crisis management. In D. P. Millar & R. L. Heath (Eds.), *Responding to crisis: A rhetorical approach to crisis communication* (pp. 95–115). Mahwah, NJ: Erlbaum.

28. Weick, K. E., & Sutcliffe, K. M. (2001). *Managing the unexpected: Assuring high performance in an age of complexity.* San Francisco, CA: Jossey-Bass.

29. Parker, C. F. (2011). The purpose, functions, and ethical dimensions of postcrisis investigations: The case of the 9/11 commission. In L. Svedin (Ed.), *Ethics and crisis management* (pp. 183–198). Charlotte, NC: Information Age.

30. Harris, S., Smallen, J., & Mitchell, C. (2006, February 18). Katrina report spreads blame. *National Journal,* 38; Marek, A. C. (2006, February 27). A post-Katrina public flaying. *U.S. News & World Report,* 62–64.

31. 55% rate government response to Hurricane Sandy positively. (2012, November 12). *Rasmussen Reports.* Retrieved from http://www.rasmussenreports.com

32. Ulmer, R. R., Seeger, M. W., & Sellnow, T. L. (2007). Post-crisis communication and renewal: Expanding the parameters of post-crisis discourse. *Public Relations Review, 33,* 130–134; Ulmer, R. R., Sellnow, T. L., & Seeger, M. W. (2008). Post-crisis communication and renewal: Understanding the potential for positive outcomes in crisis communication. In R. L. Heath & D. H. O'Hair (Eds.), *Handbook of risk and crisis communication* (pp. 302–322). Hoboken, NJ: Routledge.

33. Eligon, J. (2013, July 11). City in Iowa rebuilds from flooding but remains vulnerable. *The New York Times.*

34. Seeger et al.

35. Allinson, R. E. (1993). *Global disasters: Inquiries into management ethics.* New York, NY: Prentice Hall, p. 16.

36. Crisis management and communication. (2012, June). *IR Insight,* Research Report Number 3.

37. Fearn-Banks.

38. Hays, T., & Krisher, T. (2015, September 18). GM agrees to pay $1.5 billion in settlements. *The Oregonian,* pp. G1, G3; Whoriskey, P. (2010, March 19). Toyota resisted government safety findings; automaker followed "game plan," escaped a broad early recall. *The Washington Post,* p. A01.

39. Birkinshaw, P. (2006). Transparency as a human right. In C. Hood & D. Heald (Eds.), *Transparency: The key to better governance?* (pp. 47–57). Oxford, England: Oxford University Press; Sellnow, T. L., & Seeger, M. W. (2013). *Theorizing crisis communication.* Malden, MA: Wiley-Blackwell.

40. Lazarus, H., & McManus, T. (2006). Transparency guru: An interview with Tom McManus. *Journal of Management Development, 25,* 923–936.

41. Fearn-Banks.

42. Christensen, L. T., & Langer, R. (2009). Public relations and the strategic use of transparency: Consistency, hypocrisy, and corporate change. In R. L. Heath, E. L. Toth, & D. Waymer (Eds.), *Rhetorical and critical approaches to public relations II* (pp. 129–153). New York, NY: Routledge.

43. Grunig, J. E. (2001). Two-way symmetrical public relations: Past, present, and future. In R. L. Heath (Ed.), *Handbook of public relations* (pp. 11–30). Thousand Oaks, CA: SAGE; Grunig, L. A., Grunig, J. E., & Dozier, D. M. (2002). *Excellent public relations and effective organizations: A study of communication management in three countries.* Mahwah, NJ: Erlbaum.

44. Fearn-Banks.

45. Lazarus & McManus.

46. Ulmer, R. R., & Sellnow, T. L. (2000). Consistent questions of ambiguity in organizational crisis communication: Jack in the Box as a case study. *Journal of Business Ethics, 25,* 143–155.

47. Eisenberg, E. M. (1984). Ambiguity as strategy in organizational communication. *Communication Monographs, 51,* 227–242; Paul, J., & Strbiak, C. A. (1997). The ethics of strategic ambiguity. *Journal of Business Communication, 34,* 149–159.

48. Kline, S. L., Simunich, B., & Weber, H. (2009). The use of equivocal messages in responding to corporate challenges. *Journal of Applied Communication Research, 37,* 40–58.

49. Ulmer & Sellnow.

50. Smithson, J., & Venette, S. (2013). Stonewalling as an image-defense strategy: A critical examination of BP's response to the Deepwater Horizon explosion. *Communication Studies, 64* (4), 395–410.

51. Hearit, K. M. (2006). *Crisis management by apology: Corporate response to allegations of wrongdoing.* Mahwah, NJ: Erlbaum, Ch. 4.

52. Bauman, D. C. (2011). Evaluating ethical approaches to crisis leadership: Insights from unintentional harm research. *Journal of Business Ethics, 98,* 281–295; Knobe, J. (2006). The concept of intentional action: A case study in the uses of folk psychology. *Philosophical Studies, 130,* 203–231; Knobe, J., & Burra, A. (2006). The folk concepts of intention and intentional action: A cross-cultural study. *Journal of Cognition and Culture, 6,* 113–132.

53. Jordan, J., Diermeier, D. A., & Galinsky, A. D. (2012). The strategic Samaritan: How effectiveness and proximity affect corporate responses to external crises. *Business Ethics Quarterly 22*(4), 621–648.

54. See, for example, Hodgkinson, P. E., & Stewart, M. (1991). *Coping with catastrophe: A handbook of disaster management.* London, England: Routledge; Mitroff.

55. Simola, S. (2005). Concepts of care in organizational crisis prevention. *Journal of Business Ethics, 62,* 341–353.

56. Simola, S. (2003). Ethics of justice and care in corporate crisis management. *Journal of Business Ethics, 46,* 351–361.

57. Starmann, R. G. (1993). Tragedy at McDonald's. In J. A. Gottschalk (Ed.), *Crisis response: Inside stories on managing image under siege* (pp. 309–322). Detroit, MI: Gale Group.

58. Witt, J. L., & Morgan, J. (2002). *Stronger in the broken places: Nine lessons for turning crisis into triumph.* New York, NY: Times Books/Henry Holt.

59. Weick & Sutcliffe. See also Roberts, K. H. (2006). Some characteristics of one type of high reliability organization. In D. Smith & D. Elliott (Eds.), *Key readings in crisis management: Systems and structures for prevention and recovery* (pp. 159–179). London, England: Routledge; Weick, K. E., & Roberts, K. H. (2006). Collective minds in organizations: Heedful interrelating on flight decks. In D. Smith & D. Elliott (Eds.), *Key readings in crisis management: Systems and structures for prevention and recovery* (pp. 343–368). London, England: Routledge.

60. Rochlin, G. I., LaPorte, T. R., & Roberts, K. H. (1987). The self-designing high-reliability organization: Aircraft carrier flight operations at sea. *Naval War College Review, 40*(4), 76–90.

61. Snyder, P., Hall, M., Robertson, J., Jasinski, T., & Miller, J. S. (2006). Ethical rationality: A strategic approach to organizational crisis. *Journal of Business Ethics, 63,* 371–383.

62. Eisenhardt, K. M. (1989). Making fast strategic decisions in high-velocity environments. *Academy of Management Journal, 32,* 543–576.

63. Hosmer, L. T. (1994). Strategic planning as if ethics mattered. *Strategic Management Journal, 15,* 17–34.

64. Argenti, P. (2002, December). Crisis communication: Lessons from 9/11. *Harvard Business Review,* 103–109.

65. Lengnick-Hall, C. A., Beck, T. E., & Lengnick-Hall, M. L. (2011). Developing a capacity for organizational resilience through strategic human resource management. *Human Resource Management Review, 21,* 243–255.

66. Harland, L., Harrison, W., Jones, J. R., & Reiter-Palmon, R. (2005). Leadership behaviors and subordinate resilience. *Journal of Leadership and Organizational Studies, 11,* 1–14; Rajah, R., & Arvey, R. D. (2013). Helping group members develop resilience. In A. J. DuBrin (Ed.), *Handbook of research on crisis leadership in organizations* (pp. 149–173). Cheltenham, England: Edward Elgar.

67. Lengnick-Hall, Beck, & Lengnick-Hall.

68. Karuhanga, J. (2014, December 5). Kigali inducted into world's most "resilient cities." *The New Times* (Kigali); Mccue, M. (2014, July/August). Hiring a hero. *Fast Company, 187,* 50;

McKay, J. (2014, September 12). Chief resilience officers: Coming to your city? *Emergency Management*; Toppo, G. (2013, June 11). At-risk cities ramp up disaster-response planning. *USA Today*; Watts, J. (2014, January 13). Eleven cities to receive funds to increase resiliency. *Bond Buyer, 123*, 34–42.

69. Hannah, S. T., Uhl-Bien, M., Avolio, B. J., & Cavarretta, F. L. (2009). A framework for examining leadership in extreme contexts. *Leadership Quarterly, 20*, 897–919; Kolditz, T. A., & Brazil, D. M. (2005). Authentic leadership in *in extremis* settings: A concept for extraordinary leaders in exceptional situations. In W. L. Gardner, B. J. Avolio, & F. O. Walumbwa (Eds.), *Authentic leadership theory and practice: Origins, effects and development* (pp. 345–356). Amsterdam, The Netherlands: Elsevier, p. 346.

70. Kolditz, T. A. (2005, Fall). The in extremis leader. *Leader to Leader,* 6–18, p. 11.

71. Kolditz, T. A. (2007). *In extremis leadership: Leading as if your life depended on it.* San Francisco, CA: Jossey-Bass. p. 143.

72. Pfaff, C. A., Reich, T., Redman, W., & Hurley, M. (2011). Ethics in dangerous situations. In P. Sweeney, M. D. Matthews, & P. B. Lester (Eds.), *Leadership in dangerous situations: A handbook for the armed forces, emergency, services, and first responders* (pp. 121–138). Annapolis, MD: Naval Institute Press.

EPILOGUE

It's only fair to tell you fellows now that we're not likely to come out of this.

—CAPTAIN JOSHUA JAMES, SPEAKING TO HIS CREW DURING THE HURRICANE OF 1888

Captain Joshua James (1826–1902) is the "patron saint" of the search and rescue unit of the U.S. Coast Guard. James led rescue efforts to save sailors who crashed off the shores of Massachusetts. When word came of a shipwreck, James and his volunteer crew would launch a large rowboat into heavy seas. James would keep an eye out for the stricken vessel as his men rowed, steering with a large wooden rudder. During his career, he never lost a crewman or a shipwrecked person who had been alive when picked up. The captain's finest hour came during a tremendous storm in late November 1888. Over a twenty-four-hour period, James (sixty-two years old at the time) and his men rescued twenty-nine sailors from five ships.

Philip Hallie, who writes about James in his book *Tales of Good and Evil, Help and Harm,* argues that we can understand James's courageous leadership only as an extension of his larger community. James lived in Hull, a tiny, impoverished town on the Massachusetts coast. Most coastal villages of the time profited from shipwrecks. Beachcombers would scavenge everything from the cargo to the sunken ships' timbers and anchors. Unscrupulous people called *mooncussers* would lure boats aground. On dark, moonless nights, they would hang a lantern from a donkey and trick sea captains into sailing onto the rocks.

Unlike their neighbors up and down the coast, the people of Hull tried to stop the carnage. They built shelters for those who washed ashore, cared for the sick and injured, protested against shipping companies and insurers who sent inexperienced captains and crews into danger, and had their lifeboat always at the ready. During the storm of 1888, citizens burned their fences to light the way for Captain James, his crew, and victims alike. According to Hallie,

> Many of the other people of Hull tore up some picket fences near the crest of the hill and built a big fire that lit up the wreck and helped the lifesavers to avoid the flopping, slashing debris around the boat. The loose and broken spars of a ruined ship were one of the main dangers lifesavers had to face. But the sailors on the wrecked ship needed the firelight too. It showed them what the lifesavers were doing, and what they could do to help them. And it gave them hope: It showed them that they were not alone.[1]

The story of Captain James and his fellow villagers is a fitting end to this text. In their actions, they embodied many of the themes introduced earlier: character; values; good versus evil; moral action; altruism; cooperation; transformational, authentic, aesthetic, and servant leadership; social responsibility; ethical crisis leadership; and purpose. The captain, who lost his mother and baby sister in a shipwreck, had one mission in life: saving lives at sea. Following his lead, residents took on nearly insurmountable challenges at great personal cost. They recognized that helpers often need help. By burning their fences, these followers—living in extremely modest conditions—cast a light that literally made the difference between life and death. But like other groups of leaders and followers, they were far from perfect. In the winter hurricane season, the villagers did their best to save lives. In the summer, pickpockets (helped by a corrupt police force) preyed on those who visited the town's resorts. The dark side of Hull shouldn't diminish the astonishing feats of Captain James and his neighbors, however. Hallie calls what James did during the storm of 1888 an example of "moral beauty."

> And moral beauty happens when someone carves out a place for compassion in a largely ruthless universe. It happened in the French village of Le Chambon during the war [World War II], and it happened in and near the American village of Hull during the long lifetime of Joshua James.
>
> It happens, and it fails to happen, in almost every event of people's lives together—in streets, in kitchens, in bedrooms, in workplaces, in wars. But sometimes it happens in a way that engrosses the mind and captivates memory. Sometimes it happens in such a way that the people who make it happen seem to unify the universe around themselves like powerful magnets. Somehow they seem to redeem us all from death-like indifference. They carve a place for caring in the very middle of the quiet and loud storms of uncaring that surround—and eventually kill—us all.[2]

NOTES

1. Hallie, P. (1997). *Tales of good and evil, help and harm.* New York, NY: HarperCollins, p. 146.
2. Hallie, p. 173.

REFERENCES

55% rate government response to Hurricane Sandy positively. (2012, November 12). *Rasmussen Reports.* Retrieved from http://www.rasmussenreports.com

150,000 N. Koreans incarcerated in Soviet-style gulag: Report. (2012, April 11). *Korea Times.*

Aasland, M. S., Skogstad, A., Notelaers, G., Nielson, M. B., & Einarsen, S. (2010). The prevalence of destructive leadership behavior. *British Journal of Management, 21,* 438–452.

Abodor, H. (2012). Ethical issues in outsourcing: The case of contract medical research and the global pharmaceutical industry. *Journal of Business Ethics, 105,* 239–255.

Abowitz, K. K. (2007). Moral perception though aesthetics: Engaging imaginations in educational ethics. *Journal of Teacher Education, 58,* 287–298.

Abrahams, J. (2007). *101 mission statements from top companies.* Berkeley, CA: Ten Speed Press.

Ackerill, J. L. (1981). *Aristotle the philosopher.* Oxford, England: Oxford University Press.

Adams, G. B. (2011). The problem of administrative evil in a culture of technical rationality. *Public Integrity, 13,* 275–285.

Adams, G. B., & Balfour, D. L. (2005). Public-service ethics and administrative evil: Prospects and problems. In H. G. Frederickson

& R. K. Ghere (Eds.), *Ethics in public management* (pp. 114–138). Armonk, NY: M.E. Sharpe.

Adams, G. B., & Balfour, D. L. (2009). Ethical failings, incompetence, and administrative evil: Lessons from Katrina and Iraq. In R. W. Cox III (Ed.), *Ethics and integrity in public administration: Concepts and cases* (pp. 40–64). Armonk, NY: M. E. Sharpe.

Adams, G. B., & Balfour, D. L. (2012). The dynamics of administrative evil in organizations. In C. L. Jurkiewicz (Ed.), *The foundations of organizational evil* (pp. 16–30). Armonk, NY: M.E. Sharpe, p. 28.

Adams, G. B., & Balfour, D. L. (2015). *Unmasking administrative evil* (4th ed.). Armonk, NY: M. E. Sharpe.

Adams, J. S., Taschian, A., & Shore, T. H. (2001). Codes of ethics as signals for ethical behavior. *Journal of Business Ethics, 29,* 199–211.

Adams, S. (2012, September 12). Apple's new Foxconn embarrassment. *Forbes.*

Alba, M. (2016, Feb. 7). Hillary Clinton: 'What happened in Flint is immoral.' *NBC News.*

Albrecht, T. L., & Bach, B. W. (1997). *Communication in complex organizations: A relational approach.* Fort Worth, TX: Harcourt Brace.

Alderman, H. (1997). By virtue of a virtue. In D. Statman (Ed.), *Virtue*

ethics (pp. 145–164). Washington, DC: Georgetown University Press.

Alexander, C. (1999). *The Endurance: Shackleton's legendary Antarctic expedition.* New York, NY: Alfred A. Knopf.

Alexander, T. M. (1993). John Dewey and the moral imagination: Beyond Putnam and Rorty toward a postmodern ethics. *Transactions of the Charles S. Peirce Society, 29,* 369–400.

Alford, C. F. (1997). *What evil means to us.* Ithaca, NY: Cornell University Press.

Allinson, R. E. (1993). *Global disasters: Inquiries into management ethics.* New York, NY: Prentice Hall.

Allport, G. (1961). *Pattern and growth in personality.* New York, NY: Holt, Rinehart & Winston.

Alnuaimi O. A., Robert Jr., L. P., & Maruping, L. M. (2010). Team size, dispersion, and social loafing in technology-supported teams: A perspective on the theory of moral disengagement. *Journal of Management Information Systems, 27,* 303–230.

Alper, S., Tjosvold, D., & Law, K. S. (2000). Conflict management, efficacy, and performance in organizational teams. *Personnel Psychology, 53,* 625–642.

Alter, A. (2015, November 15). The man who brought down Volkswagen. *Time,* 100–104.

Alter, C. (2014, November 24). Everything you need to know about the Bill Cosby scandal. *Time.*

Alvaro, E. M., & Crano, W. D. (1997). Indirect minority influence: Evidence for leniency in source evaluation and counterargumentation. *Journal of Personality and Social Psychology, 72,* 949–964.

Amason, A. C. (1996). Distinguishing the effects of functional and dysfunctional conflict on strategic decision making: Resolving a paradox for top management teams. *Academy of Management Journal, 39,* 123–148.

Amason, A. C., Thompson, K. R., Hochwarter, W. A., & Harrison, A. W. (1995). Conflict: An important dimension in successful management teams. *Organizational Dynamics, 23,* 20–35.

Ames, D. R., Rose, P., & Anderson, C. P. (2006). The NPI-16 as a short measure of narcissism. *Journal of Research in Personality, 40,* 440–450.

Amichai-Hamburger, Y. (2003). Understanding social loafing. In A. Sagie, S. Stashevsky, & M. Koslowsky (Eds.), *Misbehaviour and dysfunctional attitudes in organizations* (pp. 79–102). Basingstoke, England: Palgrave Macmillan.

Anand, V., Ashforth, B. E., & Joshi, M. (2004). Business as usual: The acceptance and perpetuation of corruption in organizations. *Academy of Management Executive, 18,* 39–53.

Andreoli, N., & Lefkowitz, J. (2008). Individual and organizational antecedents of

misconduct in organizations. *Journal of Business Ethics, 85,* 309–332.

Animal welfare for broiler chickens. (n.d.). *National Chicken Council.* Retrieved from http://www.nationalchickencouncil.org/industry-issues/animal-welfare-for-broiler-chickens/

Annas, J. (2006). Virtue ethics. In D. Copp (Ed.), *The Oxford handbook of ethical theory* (pp. 515–536). Oxford, England: Oxford University Press.

Appel, M. (2008). Fictional narratives cultivate just-world beliefs. *Journal of Communication, 58,* 62–83.

Appelbaum, S. H., Bethune, M., & Tanenbaum, R. (1999). Downsizing and the emergence of self-managed teams. *Participation and Empowerment: An International Journal, 7,* 109–130.

Appiah, K. A. (2006). *Cosmopolitanism: Ethics in a world of strangers.* New York, NY: Norton.

Aquinas, H., & Glavas, A. (2012). What we know and don't know about corporate social responsibility. *Journal of Management, 38,* 932–968.

Aquino, K., & Freeman, D. (2009). Moral identity in business situations: A social-cognitive framework for understanding moral functioning. In D. Narvaez & D.K. Lapsley (Eds.), *Personality, identity and character: Explorations in moral psychology* (pp. 375–395). Cambridge, England: Cambridge University Press.

Aquino, K., & Reed, A. (2002). The self-importance of moral identity.

Journal of Personality and Social Psychology, 83, 1423–1440.

Archer, M. (2005, October 31). Founder of Patagonia became a businessman accidentally. *USA Today,* Money, p. 5.

Arendt, H. (1964). *Eichmann in Jerusalem: A report on the banality of evil.* New York, NY: Viking.

Argenti, P. (2002, December). Crisis communication: Lessons from 9/11. *Harvard Business Review,* 103–109.

Aristotle. (1962). *Nichomachean ethics* (M. Ostwald, Trans.). Indianapolis, IN: Bobbs-Merrill.

Armitage, C. (2015, August 28). Experts warn against switching on to graphic footage of human tragedy. *Sydney Morning Herald,* News, p. 2.

Armour, N. (2016, March 16). NFL's acknowledgement overdue. *USA Today,* p. 3C

Ashforth, B. E. (1997). Petty tyranny in organizations: A preliminary examination of antecedents and consequences. *Canadian Journal of Administrative Sciences, 14,* 126–140.

Ashforth, B. E., & Anand, V. (2003). The normalization of corruption in organizations. *Research in Organizational Behavior, 25,* 1–52.

Ashmos, D. P., & Duchon, D. (2000). Spirituality at work: A conceptualization and measure. *Journal of Management Inquiry, 9,* 134–145.

Aspinwall, L. G., & Staudinger, U. M. (Eds.). (2002). *A psychology of human strengths: Fundamental questions about future directions for a positive psychology.* Washington, DC: American Psychological Association.

Associated Press. (2012, September 25). In crisis-hit Europe, nepotism and connection culture stifle youth. *The Daily Star* (Lebanon).

Associated Press. (2015, August 24). New Orleans rises decade after Katrina but gaps remain. *New Orleans City Business.*

Autry, J., & Mitchell, S. (1999). *Real power: Business lessons from the Tao Te Ching.* New York, NY: Riverhead.

Avolio, B. J., & Gardner, W. L. (2005). Authentic leadership development: Getting to the root of positive forms of leadership. *Leadership Quarterly, 16,* 315–340.

Avolio, B. J., Gardner, W. L., Walumbwa, F. O., Luthans, F., & May, D. R. (2004). Unlocking the mask: A look at the process by which authentic leaders impact follower attitudes and behaviors. *Leadership Quarterly, 15,* 801–823.

Avolio, B. J., & Reichard, R. J. (2008). The rise of authentic followership. In R. E. Riggio, I. Chaleff, & J. Lipman-Blumen (Eds.), *The art of followership: How great followers create great leaders and organizations* (pp. 325–337). San Francisco, CA: Jossey-Bass.

Bad bosses drain productivity. (2005, November). *Training & Development,* p. 15.

Bailon, R. R., Moya, M., & Yzerbyt, V. (2000). Why do superiors attend to negative stereotypic information about their subordinates? Effects

of power legitimacy on social perception. *European Journal of Social Psychology, 30,* 651–671.

Baird, C. A. (2003). *Every day ethics: Making hard choices in a complex world.* Denver, CO: CB Resources.

Baker, A. (2013, December 19). Runner-up: Malala Yousafzai, the fighter. *Time.com*

Banaji, M. R., Bazerman, M. H., & Chugh, D. (2003, December). How (un)ethical are you? *Harvard Business Review,* 56–64.

Bandura, A. (1999). Moral disengagement in the perpetration of inhumanities. *Personality and Social Psychology Review, 3,* 193–209.

Bandura, A. (2002). Selective moral disengagement in the exercise of moral agency. *Journal of Moral Education, 31,* 101–119.

Bandura, A., Barbaranelli, C., Caprara, G. V., & Pastoreli, C. (1996). Mechanisms of moral disengagement in the exercise of moral agency. *Journal of Personality and Social Psychology, 71,* 364–374.

Barboza, D. (2010, May 27). Deaths shake a titan in China. *The New York Times,* p. B1.

Barboza, D., & Duhigg, C. (2012, September 11). China plant again faces labor issue on iPhones. *The New York Times,* p. B1.

Barbuto, J. E. (2000). Influence triggers: A framework for understanding follower compliance. *Leadership Quarterly, 11,* 365–387.

Barbuto, J. E., & Wheeler, D. W. (2006). Scale development and construct clarification of servant

leadership. *Group & Organization Management, 31,* 300–326.

Barker, L., Johnson, P., & Watson, K. (1991). The role of listening in managing interpersonal and group conflict. In D. Borisoff & M. Purdy (Eds.), *Listening in everyday life: A personal and professional approach* (pp. 139–157). Lanham, MD: University Press of America.

Baron, R. A. (2004). Workplace aggression and violence: Insights from basic research. In R. W. Griffin & A. M. O'Leary-Kelly (Eds.), *The dark side of organizational behavior* (pp. 23–61). San Francisco, CA: Jossey-Bass.

Barry, V. (1978). *Personal and social ethics: Moral problems with integrated theory.* Belmont, CA: Wadsworth.

Barsky, A. (2011). Investigating the effects of moral disengagement and participation on unethical work behavior. *Journal of Business Ethics, 104,* 59–75.

Bar-Tel, D. (1990). Causes and consequences of delegitimization: Models of conflict and ethnocentrism. *Journal of Social Issues, 46*(1), 65–81.

Bartholomew, C. S., & Gustafson, S. B. (1998). Perceived leader integrity scale: An instrument for assessing employee perceptions of leader integrity. *Leadership Quarterly, 9,* 143–144.

Barton, L. (2001). *Crisis in organizations II.* Cincinnati, OH: South-Western.

Bass, B. M. (1990). *Bass and Stogdill's handbook of leadership* (3rd ed.). New York, NY: Free Press.

Bass, B. M. (1995). The ethics of transformational leadership. In J. B. Ciulla (Ed.), *Ethics, the heart of leadership* (pp. 169–192). Westport, CT: Praeger.

Bass, B. M. (1996). *A new paradigm of leadership: An inquiry into transformational leadership.* Alexandria, VA: U.S. Army Research Institute for the Behavioral and Social Sciences.

Bass, B. M., & Avolio, B. J. (1993). Transformational leadership: A response to critiques. In M. M. Chemers & R. Ayman (Eds.), *Leadership theory and research: Perspectives and directions* (pp. 49–80). San Diego, CA: Academic Press.

Bass, B. M., Avolio, B. J., Jung, D. I., & Berson, Y. (2003). Predicting unit performance by assessing transformational and transactional leadership. *Journal of Applied Psychology, 88,* 207–218.

Bass, B. M., & Steidlmeier, P. (1999). Ethics, character, and authentic transformational leadership behavior. *Leadership Quarterly, 10,* 181–217.

Batson, C. D., & Thompson, E. R. (2001). Why don't moral people act morally? Motivational considerations. *Current Directions in Psychological Science, 10,* 54–57.

Batson, C. D., Thompson, E. R., & Chen, H. (2002). Moral hypocrisy: Addressing some alternatives. *Journal of Personality and Social Psychology, 83,* 330–339.

Batson, C. D., Van Lange, P. A. M., Ahmad, N., & Lishner, D. A. (2003). Altruism and helping behavior. In M. A. Hogg & J.

Cooper (Eds.), *The SAGE handbook of social psychology* (pp. 279–295). London, England: SAGE.

Battistella, E. (2014, May 7). The art of political apology. *Politico.*

Bauman, D. C. (2011). Evaluating ethical approaches to crisis leadership: Insights from unintentional harm research. *Journal of Business Ethics, 98,* 281–295.

Bazerman, M. H. (1986). *Management in managerial decision making.* New York, NY: John Wiley.

Bazerman, M. H., Chugh, D., & Banaji, M. R. (2005, October). When good people (seem to) negotiate in bad faith. *Negotiation, 8,* 3–5.

Bazerman, M. H., & Tenbrunsel, A. E. (2011). *Blind spots: Why we fail to do what's right and what to do about it.* Princeton, NJ: Princeton University Press.

Bazerman, M. H., & Watkins, M. D. (2004). *Predictable surprises: The disasters you should have seen coming and how to prevent them.* Boston, MA: Harvard Business School Press.

Bear, M. (2012). *First world problems.* San Francisco, CA: Weldon Owen.

Becker, J. A. H., & O'Hair, H. D. (2007). Machiavellians' motives in organizational citizenship behavior. *Journal of Applied Communication Research, 35,* 246–267.

Bedian, A. G. (2007). Even if the tower is "ivory," it isn't "white": Understanding the consequences of faculty cynicism. *Academy of Management Learning and Education, 6,* 9–32.

Beech, H., Birmingham, L., Dirkse, T., & Mahr, K. (2011, March 28). How Japan will reawaken. *Time International,* 32–37.

Bell, M. A. (1974). The effects of substantive and affective conflict in problem-solving groups. *Speech Monographs, 41,* 19–23.

Bell, M. A. (1979). The effects of substantive and affective verbal conflict on the quality of decisions of small problem-solving groups. *Central States Speech Journal, 3,* 75–82.

Benefiel, M. (2005). *Soul at work: Spiritual leadership in organizations.* New York, NY: Seabury Books.

Benefiel, M. (2005). The second half of the journey: Spiritual leadership for organizational transformation. *Leadership Quarterly, 16,* 723–747.

Bennis, W. G., & Nanus, B. (2003). *Leaders: Strategies for taking charge.* New York, NY: Harper Business Essentials.

Bennis, W. G., & Thomas, R. J. (2002). *Geeks and geezers: How era, values, and defining moments shape leaders.* Boston, MA: Harvard Business School Press.

Benoit, W. L. (2004). Image restoration discourse and crisis communication. In D. P. Millar & R. L. Heath (Eds.), *Responding to crisis: A rhetorical approach to crisis communication* (pp. 263–280). Mahwah, NJ: Erlbaum.

Bentham, J. (1948). *An introduction to the principles of morals and legislation.* New York, NY: Hafner.

Berbert, K. (2015). 17 unbelievably selfish, yet relatable first world problems. *Elite Daily.* Retrieved from http://elitedaily.com/users/kberbert

Berfeld, S. (2015, February 19). Will investors put the lid on The Container Store's generous wages? *Bloomberg Businessweek*.

Berman, D. K. (2008, October 28). The game: Post-Enron crackdown comes up woefully short. *The Wall Street Journal*, p. C2.

Berman, M. (2015, June 19). "I forgive you." Relatives of Charleston church shooting victims address Dylann Roof. *The Washington Post*.

Bertsch, A. M. (2012). Validating GLOBE's societal values scales: A test in the U.S.A. *International Journal of Business and Social Science*, *3*, 10–23.

Bestselling author owes charity $1M. (2012, April 6). *The Toronto Star*, p. A12.

Bies, R. J., & Tripp, T. M. (1998). Two faces of the powerless: Coping with tyranny in organizations. In R. M. Kramer & M. A Neale (Eds.), *Power and influence in organizations* (pp. 203–219). Thousand Oaks, CA: SAGE.

Big victory against global bribery. (2008, December 17). *The Christian Science Monitor*, p. 8.

Bilefsky, D. (2015, February 15). Burlesque tone at trial snarls Strauss-Kahn's effort to restore his image. *The New York Times*, p. A13.

Bilton, R. (2014, December 18). Apple 'failing to protect Chinese factory workers.' *BBC Panorama*.

Bird, F. B. (1996). *The muted conscience: Moral silence and the practice of ethics in business*. Westport, CT: Quorum.

Birkinshaw, P. (2006). Transparency as a human right. In C. Hood & D. Heald (Eds.), *Transparency: The key to better governance?* (pp. 47–57). Oxford, England: Oxford University Press.

Birrell, I. (2015, August 28). Social media and a very modern murder. *The Daily Telegraph*, p. 20.

Blake, M. (2015, July 8). How Bill Cosby's 'Pound Cake' speech backfired on the comedian. *Los Angeles Times*.

Blasi, A. (1984). Moral identity: Its role in moral functioning. In W. M. Kurtines & J. L. Gewirtz (Eds.), *Morality, moral behavior, and moral development* (pp. 128–139). New York, NY: John Wiley.

Blasi, A. (2005). Moral character: A psychological approach: In D. K. Lapsley & F. C. Power (Eds.), *Character psychology and character education* (pp. 67–100). Notre Dame, IN: Notre Dame Press.

Blatchford, C. (2015, August 27). For the killers, it's all about: 'Look at me.' *The Star Phoenix*, World, p. D4.

Block, P. (1996). *Stewardship: Choosing service over self-interest*. San Francisco, CA: Berrett-Koehler.

Boardley, I. D., & Kavussanu, M. (2007). Development and validation of the Moral Disengagement in Sport Scale. *Journal of Sport & Exercise Psychology*, *29*, 608–628.

Boardley, I. D., & Kavussanu, M. (2008). The Moral Disengagement in Sport Scale—Short. *Journal of Sports Sciences*, *26*, 1507–1517.

Bobocel, D. R., & Meyer, J. P. (1994). Escalating commitment to a failing course of action: Separating the roles of choice and justification. *Journal of Applied Psychology*, *79*, 360–363.

Boddy, C. R. (2006). The dark side of management decisions: Organizational psychopaths. *Management Decision*, *44*(10), 1461–1475.

Boddy, C. R. (2011). *Corporate psychopaths: Organisational destroyers*. New York, NY: Palgrave McMillan.

Boddy, C. R. (2014). Corporate psychopaths, conflict, employee affective well-being and counterproductive work behavior. *Journal of Business Ethics*, *121*, 107–121.

Boddy, C. R. (2015). Organisational psychopaths: A ten-year update. *Management Decision*, *53*, 2407–2432.

Boddy, C. R., Ladyshewsky, R., & Galvin, P. (2010). Leaders without ethics in global business: Corporate psychopaths, *Journal of Public Affairs*, *10*, 121–138.

Boje, D. (2008). Critical theory approaches to spirituality in business. In J. Biberman & L. Tischler (Eds.), *Spirituality in business: Theory, practice, and future directions* (pp. 160–187). New York, NY: Palgrave Macmillan.

Boksem, M. A. S., & De Cremer, D. (2009). The neural basis of morality. In D. De Cremer (Ed.), *Psychological perspectives on ethical behavior and decision-making* (pp. 153–166). Charlotte, NC: Information Age.

Boone, J. (2015, December 15). Peshawar school attack: One year on 'the country is changed completely.' *The Guardian.*

Bordas, J. (1995). Becoming a servant-leader: The personal development path. In L. Spears (Ed.), *Reflections on leadership* (pp. 149–160). New York, NY: John Wiley.

Borisoff, D., & Victor, D. A. (1998). *Conflict management: A communication skills approach* (2nd ed.). Boston, MA: Allyn & Bacon.

Bosman, J., & Smith, M. (2016, January 19). Gov. Rick Snyder of Michigan apologizes in Flint water crisis. *The New York Times.*

Bowerman, M. (2015, August 20). Timeline: Duggar sex-abuse scandal. *USA Today Network.*

Bowie, N. E. (2005). Kantian ethical thought. In J. W. Budd & J. G. Scoville (Eds.), *The ethics of human resources and industrial relations* (pp. 61–87). Champaign, IL: Labor and Employment Relations Association.

Bowley, G., & Kannapell, A. (2008, August 6). Chaos on the "mountain that invites death." *The New York Times,* p. A1.

Brady, E., & Halley, J. (2009, February 24). The blowup over blowouts. *USA Today,* p. 1C.

Brady, J. P. (2012). Marketing breast milk substitutes: Problems and perils throughout the world. *Archives of Disease in Children Online.* Retrieved from http://adc.bmj.com

Bragues, G. (2006). Seek the good life, not money: The Aristotelian

approach to business ethics. *Journal of Business Ethics, 67,* 341–357.

Brandes Gratz, R. (2015). *We're still here ya bastards: How the people of New Orleans rebuilt their city.* New York, NY: Nation Books.

Bratton, V. K., & Kacmar, K. M. (2004). Extreme careerism: The dark side of impression management. In W. Griffin & K. O'Reilly (Eds.), *The dark side of organizational behavior* (pp. 291–308). San Francisco, CA: Jossey-Bass.

Breeden, A., & Rubin, A. (2015, June 13). French court acquits former I.M.F. chief in case that put his sex life on view. *The New York Times,* p. A5.

Brissett, D., & Edgley, C. (1990). The dramaturgical perspective. In D. Brissett & C. Edgley (Eds.), *Life as theater: A dramaturgical sourcebook* (2nd ed., pp. 1–46). New York, NY: Aldine de Gruyter.

Brooks, D. (2015). *The road to character.* New York, NY: Random House.

Brooks, D. (2016, February 5). A question of moral radicalism. *The New York Times,* Op-Ed.

Brown, D. J., Scott, K. A., & Lewis, H. (2004). Information processing and leadership. In J. Antonakis, A. T. Cianciolo, & R. J. Sternberg (Eds.), *The nature of leadership* (pp. 125–147). Thousand Oaks, CA: SAGE.

Brown, M. E., & Trevino, L. K. (2006). Ethical leadership: A review and future directions. *Leadership Quarterly, 17,* 595–616.

Brown, M. E., & Trevino, L. K. (2006). Socialized charismatic

leadership, values congruence, and deviance in work groups. *Journal of Applied Psychology, 91,* 954–962.

Brown, M. E., Trevino, L. K., & Harrison, D. A. (2005). Ethical leadership: A social learning perspective for construct development and testing. *Organizational Behavior and Human Decision Processes, 97,* 117–134.

Brown, M. T. (2005). *Corporate integrity: Rethinking organizational ethics and leadership.* Cambridge, England: Cambridge University Press.

Brown, R. (1995). *Prejudice: Its social psychology.* Oxford, England: Blackwell.

Brown, R. P. (2003). Measuring individual differences in the tendency to forgive: Construct validity and links with depression. *Personality and Social Psychology Bulletin, 29,* 759–771.

Brown, T. A., Sautter, J. A., Littvay, L., Sautter, A. C., & Bearnes, B. (2010). Ethics and personality: Empathy and narcissism as moderators of ethical decision making in business students. *Journal of Education for Business, 85,* 203–208.

Bruhn, J. G. (2001). *Trust and the health of organizations.* New York, NY: Kluwer/Plenum.

Brunell, A. B., Gentry, W. A., Campbell, W. K., Hoffman, B. J., Kuhnert, K. W., & DeMarree, K. G. (2008). Leader emergence: The case of the narcissistic leader. *Personality and Social Psychology Bulletin, 34,* 1663–1676.

Buchholz, R. A., & Rosenthal, S. B. (2005). Toward a conceptual framework for stakeholder theory. *Journal of Business Ethics, 58,* 137–148.

Bucktin, C. (2015, August 16). Hurricane Katrina: Despair of the victims 10 years on. *Daily Mirror,* News, 26–27.

Bunge, J. (2016, March 17). Whole Foods shifts to slower-growing chickens. *The Wall Street Journal.*

Burns, J. M. (1978). *Leadership.* New York, NY: Harper & Row.

Burns, J. M. (2003). *Transforming leadership: A new pursuit of happiness.* New York, NY: Atlantic Monthly Press.

Burton, J. P., & Hoobler, J. M. (2006). Subordinate self-esteem and abusive supervision. *Journal of Managerial Science, 3,* 340–355.

Business Roundtable. (2012, March 27). *2012 principles of corporate governance.* Retrieved from http://businessroundtable.org

Buss, A. H. (1961). *The psychology of aggression.* New York, NY: John Wiley.

Caldwell, C. (2011). Duties owed to organizational citizens—ethical insights for today's leader. *Journal of Business Ethics, 102,* 343–356.

Caldwell, D. F., & Moberg, D. (2007). An exploratory investigation of the effect of ethical culture in activating moral imagination. *Journal of Business Ethics, 73,* 193–204.

Campbell, W. K., Hoffman, B. J., Campbell, S. M., & Marchisio, G. (2011). Narcissism in organizational contexts. *Human Resource Management Review, 21,* 268–284.

Capecchi, C., & Rogers, K. (2015, July 29). Killer of Cecil the lion finds out that he is a target now, of Internet vigilantism. *The New York Times,* p. A11.

Carden, S. D. (2006). *Virtue ethics: Dewey and Macintyre.* London, England: Continuum.

Carlson, D. S., & Perrewe, P. L. (1995). Institutionalization of organizational ethics through transformational leadership. *Journal of Business Ethics, 14,* 829–838.

Carroll, A. B., & Buchholtz, A. K. (2012). *Business and society: Ethics, sustainability, and stakeholder management* (8th ed.). Mason, OH; South-Western Cengage Learning.

Carroll, S. J., & Gannon, M. J. (1997). *Ethical dimensions of management.* Thousand Oaks, CA: SAGE.

Carsten, M. K., & Uhl-Bien, M. (2013). Ethical followership: An examination of followership beliefs and crimes of obedience. *Journal of Leadership & Organizational Studies, 21,* 49–61.

Carsten, M. K., Uhl-Bien, M., West, B. J., Patera, J. L., & McGregor, R. (2010). Exploring social constructions of followership: A qualitative study. *Leadership Quarterly, 21,* 543–562.

Carter, B., Bowley, G., & Manley, L. (2014, November 20). Comeback by Cosby unravels as accounts of rape converge. *The New York Times,* p. A1.

Carter, S. (2014, August 3). A battlefield of drones and privacy in your backyard. *Chicago Tribune.*

Carvajal, D., & de Blume, M. (2012). Strauss-Kahn says sex parties went too far, but lust is not crime. *The New York Times,* p. A1.

Carver, C. S., & Scheier, M. F. (2005). Optimism. In C. R. Snyder & S. J. Lopez (Eds.), *Handbook of positive psychology* (pp. 231–243). Oxford, England: Oxford University Press.

Casarjian, R. (1992). *Forgiveness: A bold choice for a peaceful heart.* New York, NY: Bantam.

Casebeer, W. D. (2003). Moral cognition and its neural constituents. *Neuroscience, 4,* 841–846.

Caudron, S. (1995, September 4). The boss from hell. *Industry Week,* 12–16.

Caux Round Table. (2000). Appendix 26: The Caux principles. In O. F. Williams (Ed.), *Global codes of conduct: An idea whose time has come* (pp. 384–388). Notre Dame, IN: University of Notre Dame Press.

Caux Round Table. (2006). *Principles for non-governmental organizations.* Retrieved from http://www.cauxroundtable.org/index.cfm?&menuid=101

Cavazotte, F., Duarte, C., & Gobbo, A. M. (2010). Authentic leader, safe work: The influence of leadership performance. *Brazilian Business Review, 10,* 95–119.

Center for the Study of Ethics in the Professions at Illinois Institute of Technology. (2013). *Index of codes.* Retrieved from http://ethics.iit.edu/codes

Centers for Disease Control and Prevention. (2014). *Occupational violence.* Retrieved from http://www.cdc.gov/niosh/topics/violence/

CEO's moral compass steers Siemens. (2010, February 15). *USA Today*, p. 3B.

Chakrabortty, A. (2013, August 5). The woman who nearly died making your iPad. *Guardian.*

Chaleff, I. (2003). *The courageous follower: Standing up to and for our leaders* (2nd ed.). San Francisco, CA: Berrett-Koehler.

Chaleff, I. (2015). *Intelligent disobedience: Doing right when what you're told to do is wrong.* Oakland, CA: Berrett-Koehler.

Chan, A., Hannah, S. T., & Gardner, W. L. (2005). Veritable authentic leadership: Emergence, functioning, and impacts. In W. L. Gardner, B. J. Avolio, & F. O. Walumbwa (Eds.), *Authentic leadership theory and practice: Origins, effects and development* (pp. 3–41). Amsterdam, The Netherlands: Elsevier.

Chan, A. W. H., & Cheung, H. Y. (2012). Cultural dimensions, ethical sensitivity, and corporate governance. *Journal of Business Ethics, 110*, 45–59.

Chan, W. (Trans.). (1963). *The way of Lao Tzu.* Indianapolis, IN: Bobbs-Merrill.

Chang, I. (1997). *The rape of Nanking: The forgotten holocaust of World War II.* New York, NY: Basic Books.

Charles, D. (2016, March 30). Why Whole Foods wants a slower-growing chicken. *National Public Radio.*

Chen, A., Lawson, R. B., Gordon, L. R., & McIntosh, B. (1996). Groupthink: Deciding with the leader and the devil. *Psychological Record, 46*, 581–590.

Cheng, M-Y., & Wang, L. (2015). The mediating effect of ethical climate on the relationship between paternalistic leadership and team identification: A team-level analysis in the Chinese context. *Journal of Business Ethics, 129*, 639–654.

Cheung, C., & Chan, A. (2005). Philosophical foundations of eminent Hong Kong Chinese CEOs' leadership. *Journal of Business Ethics, 60*, 47–62.

Chhokar, J. S., Brodbeck, F. C., & House, R. J. (Eds.). (2007). *Culture and leadership across the world: The GLOBE book of in-depth studies of 25 societies.* Mahwah, NJ: Erlbaum.

Chidambaram, L., & Tung, L. L. (2005). Is out of sight, out of mind? An empirical study of social loafing in technology-supported groups. *Information Systems Research, 16*, 149–168.

Choi, Y., & Mai-Dalton, R. R. (1998). On the leadership function of self-sacrifice. *Leadership Quarterly, 9*, 475–501.

Choi, Y., & Mai-Dalton, R. R. (1999). The model of followers' responses to self-sacrificial leadership: An empirical test. *Leadership Quarterly, 10*, 397–421.

Choudhary, A. I., Akhtar, S. A., & Zaheer, A. (2013). Impact of transformational and servant leadership on organizational performance: A comparative analysis. *Journal of Business Ethics, 116*, 433–440.

Christensen, L. T., & Langer, R. (2009). Public relations and the strategic use of transparency: Consistency, hypocrisy, and corporate change. In R. L. Heath, E. L. Toth, & D. Waymer (Eds.), *Rhetorical and critical approaches to public relations II* (pp. 129–153). New York, NY: Routledge.

Christensen, S. L., & Kohls, J. (2003). Ethical decision making in times of organizational crises: A framework for analysis. *Business & Society, 42*, 328–358.

Christians, C. G., Rotzell, K. B., & Fackler, M. (1999). *Media ethics* (3rd ed.). New York, NY: Longman.

Christie, R., & Geis, F. L. (1970). *Studies in Machiavellianism.* New York, NY: Academic Press.

Cialdini, R. (2009). *Influence: Science and practice* (5th ed.). Boston, MA: Pearson.

Ciulla, J. B. (2004). Leadership ethics: Mapping the territory. In J. B. Ciulla (Ed.), *Ethics, the heart of leadership* (2nd ed., pp. 3–24). Westport, CT: Praeger.

Clapp-Smith, R., Vogelgesang, G. R., & Avey, J. B. (2009). Authentic leadership and positive psychological capital: The mediating role of trust at the group level of analysis. *Journal of Leadership & Organizational Studies, 15*, 227–240.

Classen, A. (n.d.). Demolition wave rising. *NW Examiner.* Retrieved from http://nwexaminer.com/demolition-wave-rising

Clements, C. E., Neill, J. D., & Stovall, O. S. (2009). The impact of cultural differences on the convergence of international accounting codes of ethics. *Journal of Business Ethics, 90*, 383–391.

Cohen, D. V. (1993). Creating and maintaining ethical work climates: Anomie in the workplace and implications for managing change. *Business Ethics Quarterly, 3,* 343–358.

Cohen-Charash, Y., & Spector, P. E. (2001). The role of justice in organizations: A meta-analysis. *Organizational Behavior and Human Decision Processes, 86,* 278–321.

Colby, A., & Damon, W. (1992). *Some do care: Contemporary lives of moral commitment.* New York, NY: Free Press.

Colby, A., & Damon, W. (1995). The development of extraordinary moral commitment. In M. Killen & D. Hart (Eds.), *Morality in everyday life: Developmental perspectives* (pp. 342–369). Cambridge, England: Cambridge University Press.

Collins, J. C. (2001). *Vision framework.* Retrieved from http://www.jimcollins.com/tools/vision-framework.pdf

Collins, J. C., & Porras, J. I. (1996, September–October). Building your company's vision. *Harvard Business Review,* 65–77.

Colquitt, J. A., Conlon, D. E., Wesson, M. J., Porter, C. O. L. H., & Yee, N. K. (2001). Justice at the millennium: A meta-analytic review of 25 years of organizational justice research. *Journal of Applied Psychology, 86,* 425–445.

Come back in 10 years' time. (2011, March 26). *The Economist,* 47–48.

Comte-Sponville, A. (2001). *A small treatise on the great virtues: The uses of philosophy in everyday life.* New York, NY: Metropolitan.

Connelly, S., Helton-Fauth, W., & Mumford, M. D. (2004). A managerial in-basket study of the impact of trait emotions on ethical choice. *Journal of Business Ethics, 51,* 245–267.

The Container Store: An employee-centric retailer. (n.d.). University of New Mexico: Daniels Fund Ethics Initiative. Retrieved from https://danielsethics.mgt.unm.edu/pdf/Container%20Store%20Case.pdf

Coombs, W. T. (1999). *Ongoing crisis communication: Planning, managing, and responding.* Thousand Oaks, CA: SAGE.

Coombs, W. T., & Holladay, S. J. (2004). Reasoned action in crisis communication: An attribution theory-based approach to crisis management. In D. P. Millar & R. L. Heath (Eds.), *Responding to crisis: A rhetorical approach to crisis communication* (pp. 95–115). Mahwah, NJ: Erlbaum.

Cooper, S. (2004). *Corporate social performance: A stakeholder approach.* Burlington, VT: Ashgate.

Cooper, T. L., & Menzel, D. C. (2013). In pursuit of ethical competence. In T. L. Cooper & D. D. Menzel (Eds.), *Achieving ethical competence for public service leadership* (pp. 3–24). Armonk, NY: M. E. Sharpe.

Cooperrider, D. L., & Whitney, D. (2005). *Appreciative inquiry: A positive revolution in change.* San Francisco, CA: Berrett-Koehler.

Corporate clout 2013: Time for responsible capitalism. (2013). *Global Trends.* Retrieved from http://www.globaltrends.com

Cosier, R. A., & Schwenk, C. R. (1990). Agreement and thinking

alike: Ingredients for poor decision. *Academy of Management Executive, 4,* 69–74.

Countryman, A. (2001, December 7). Leadership key ingredient in ethics recipe, experts say. *Chicago Tribune,* pp. B1, B6.

Coutts, M. (2009, January 27). Would Jesus run up the score? Christian school under fire for winning 100–0. *National Post,* p. A1.

Covey, S. R. (1989). *The seven habits of highly effective people.* New York, NY: Simon & Schuster.

Crace, R. K., & Brown, D. (1992). *The Life Values Inventory.* Minneapolis, MN: National Computer Systems. Retrieved from http://www.lifevalues.org

Cragan, J. F., Kasch, C. R., & Wright, D. W. (2009). *Communication in small groups: Theory, process, skills* (7th ed.). Boston, MA: Wadsworth.

Craigie, F. C. (1999). The spirit and work: Observations about spirituality and organizational life. *Journal of Psychology and Christianity, 18,* 43–53.

Cramton, P. C., & Dees, J. G. (1993). Promoting honesty in negotiation: An exercise in practical ethics. *Business Ethics Quarterly, 3,* 359–394.

Cramton, P. C., & Dees, J. G. (2004). Promoting honesty in negotiation: An exercise in practical ethics. In C. Menkel-Meadow & M. Wheeler (Eds.), *What's fair: Ethics for negotiators* (pp. 108–137). San Francisco, CA: Jossey-Bass.

Crano, W. D., & Seyranian, V. (2009). How minorities prevail:

The context/comparison-leniency contract model. *Journal of Social Issues, 65,* 335–363.

Cresswell J., Clifford, S., & Pollack, A. (2015, December 18). Drug CEO Martin Shkreli arrested on fraud charges. *The New York Times,* p. A1.

Crisis management and communication. (2012, June). *IR Insight,* Research Report Number 3.

Cropanzano, R., & Stein, J. H. (2009). Organizational justice and behavioral ethics: Promises and prospects. *Business Ethics Quarterly, 19,* 193–233.

Crosariol, B. (2005, November 21). The diminishing allure of rock-star executives. *The Globe and Mail,* p. B12.

Cullen, D. (2009). *Columbine.* New York, NY: Twelve.

Cullen, J. B., Parboteeah, K. P., & Victor, B. (2003). The effects of ethical climates on organizational commitment: A two-study analysis. *Journal of Business Ethics, 46,* 127–141.

Cullen, J. B., Victor, B., & Bronson, J. W. (1993). The Ethical Climate Questionnaire: An assessment of its development and validity. *Psychological Reports, 73,* 667–674.

Cummings, L. L., & Bromiley, P. (1996). The Organizational Trust Inventory (OTI): Development and validation. In R. M. Kramer & T. R. Tyler (Eds.), *Trust in organizations: Frontiers of theory and research* (pp. 302–329). Thousand Oaks, CA: SAGE.

Dale, S. (2012, December 4). Ex-HBOS chief exec Sir James

Crosby apologizes for bank failure. *Fundweb.* p. 11.

Daleus, P., & Hansen, D. (2011). Inherent ethical challenges in bureaucratic crisis management: The Swedish experience with the 2004 tsunami disaster. In L. Svedin (Ed.), *Ethics and crisis management* (pp. 21–36). Charlotte, NC: Information Age.

Darley, J. M. (1996). How organizations socialize individuals into evildoing. In D. M. Messick & A. E. Tenbrunsel (Eds.), *Codes of conduct: Behavioral research into business ethics* (pp. 12–43). New York, NY: Russell Sage Foundation.

Darley, J. M. (2001). The dynamics of authority influence in organizations and the unintended action consequences. In J. M. Darley, D. M. Messick, & T. R. Tyler (Eds.), *Social influences on ethical behavior in organizations* (pp. 37–52). Mahwah, NJ: Erlbaum.

Dart, T. (2015, August 23). New Orleans dares to dream, 10 years after Katrina. *The Observer,* US News.

Davis, A., & Mischel, L. (2014, June 12). CEO pay continues to rise as typical workers are paid less. *Economic Policy Institute.*

Davis, A. L., & Rothstein, H. R. (2006). The effects of the perceived behavioral integrity of managers on employee attitudes: A meta-analysis. *Journal of Business Ethics, 67,* 407–419.

Davis, B., & Gauthier-Villars, D. (2008, October 22). IMF chief facing fresh claim of abusing power. *The Australian,* World, p. 12.

Davis, J. H., & Ruhe, J. A. (2003). Perceptions of country corruption:

Antecedents and outcomes. *Journal of Business Ethics, 43,* 275–288.

Davis, S. (2015, June). Dissed loyalty. *Workforce.com.*

De Cremer, D. (2006). Affective and motivational consequences of leader self-sacrifice: The moderating effect of autocratic leadership. *Leadership Quarterly, 17,* 79–93.

De Cremer, D., & van Dijk, E. (2005). When and why leaders put themselves first: Leader behaviour in resource allocations as a function of feeling entitled. *European Journal of Social Psychology, 35,* 553–563.

De Cremer, D., & van Knippenberg, D. (2004). Leader self-sacrifice and leadership effectiveness: The moderating role of leader self-confidence. *Organizational Behavior and Human Decision Processes, 95,* 140–155.

De Dreu, C. K. W., & Beersma, B. (2001). Minority influence in organizations: Its origins and implications for learning and group performance. In C. K. W. De Dreu & N. K. De Vries (Eds.), *Group consensus and minority influence: Implications for innovation* (pp. 258–283). Malden, MA: Blackwell.

De Dreu, C. K. W., Weingart, L. R., & Kwon, S. (2000). Influence of social motives on integrative negotiation: A meta-analytic review and test of two theories. *Journal of Personality and Social Psychology, 78,* 889–905.

De Dreu, C. K. W., & West, M. A. (2001). Minority dissent and team innovation: The importance of participation in decision making. *Journal of Applied Psychology, 86,* 1191–1201.

De George, R. T. (1995). *Business ethics* (4th ed.). Englewood Cliffs, NJ: Prentice Hall.

De Pree, M. (1989). *Leadership is an art.* New York, NY: Doubleday.

De Pree, M. (2003). Servant-leadership: Three things necessary. In L. C. Spears & M. Lawrence (Eds.), *Focus on leadership: Servant-leadership for the 21st century* (pp. 89–97). New York, NY: John Wiley.

Dean, J. W., Brandes, P., & Dharwadkar, R. (1998). Organizational cynicism. *Academy of Management Review, 23,* 341–352.

DeGroot, T., Kiker, D. S., & Cross, T. C. (2000). A meta-analysis to review organizational outcomes related to charismatic leadership. *Canadian Journal of Administrative Sciences, 17,* 356–371.

Delanty, G. (2012). Introduction: The emerging field of cosmopolitanism studies. In G. Delanty (Ed.), *International handbook of cosmopolitan studies* (pp. 1–8). Hoboken, NJ: Routledge.

Den Hartog, D. N., House, R. J., Hanges, P. U., Ruiz-Quintanilla, S. A., & Dorfman, P. W. (1999). Culture-specific and cross-culturally generalizable implicit leadership theories: Are attributes of charismatic/transformational leadership universally endorsed? *Leadership Quarterly, 10,* 219–257.

Denyer, S. (2014, March 12). Contradictory statements from Malaysia over missing airliner perplex, infuriate. *WashingtonPost.com.*

Department of Labor. (2016). *Labor force statistics from the current population survey.* Retrieved from http://www.bls.gov/cps/

Deutsch, M. (1990). Psychological roots of moral exclusion. *Journal of Social Issues, 46*(1), 21–25.

Devine, T., Seuk, J. H., & Wilson, A. (2001). *Cultivating heart and character: Educating for life's most essential goals.* Chapel Hill, NC: Character Development.

Dewey, J. (1920). *Reconstruction in philosophy.* New York, NY: Henry Holt.

Diboye, R. L., & Halverson, S. K. (2004). Subtle (and not so subtle) discrimination in organizations. In R. W. Griffin & A. M. O'Leary-Kelly (Eds.), *The dark side of organizational behavior* (pp. 404–425). San Francisco, CA: Jossey-Bass.

Dillon, N., Niemietz, B., Marcius, C. R., & McShane, L. (2014, November 21). 'Act like you're drunk, get your hair wet and put your hand down here.' *Daily News,* News, p. 4.

Dirks, K. T. (1999). The effects of interpersonal trust on work group performance. *Journal of Applied Psychology, 84,* 445–455.

Divir, T., Eden, D., & Bano, J. L. (1995). Self-fulfilling prophecy and gender: Can women be Pygmalion and Galatea? *Journal of Applied Psychology, 80,* 253–270.

Dobson, J. (1999). *The art of management and the aesthetic manager.* Westport, CT: Quorum Books.

Doh, J. P., & Qugley, N. R. (2014). Responsible leadership and stakeholder management: Influence pathways and organizational outcomes. *The Academy of Management Perspectives, 28,* 255–274.

Donaldson, T. (1996, September–October). Values in tension: Ethics away from home. *Harvard Business Review,* 48–57.

Donaldson, T. (2009). Compass and dead reckoning: The dynamic implications of ISCT. *Journal of Business Ethics, 88,* 659–664.

Donaldson, T., & Dunfee, T. W. (1994). Toward a unified conception of business ethics: Integrative social contracts theory. *Academy of Management Review, 19,* 252–284.

Donaldson, T., & Dunfee, T. W. (1999). *Ties that bind: A social contracts approach to business ethics.* Boston, MA: Harvard Business School Press.

Donaldson, T., & Preston, L. E. (1995). The stakeholder theory of the corporation: Concepts, evidence, and implications. *Academy of Management Review, 20,* 65–91.

Donovan, G. K. (2014). Ebola, epidemics, and ethics—what we have learned. *Philosophy, Ethics, and Humanities in Medicine,* 9:15. (Online source).

Dotlich, D. L., Noel, J. L., & Walker, N. (2008). Learning for leadership: Failure as a second chance. In J. V. Gallos (Ed.), *Business leadership* (2nd ed., pp.478–485). San Francisco, CA: Jossey-Bass.

Dougall, E. (2008, December 12). Issues management. *Institute for Public Relations.* Retrieved from http://www.instituteforpr.org

Dreher, D. (1996). *The Tao of personal leadership.* New York, NY: HarperBusiness.

Drummond, H., & Hodgson, J. (2011). *Escalation in decision-making: Behavioral economics in business.* Burlington, VT: Gower.

Drummond, T. (2000, April 3). Coping with cops. *Time,* 72–73.

Duchon, D., & Plowman, D. A. (2005). Nurturing the spirit at work: Impact on work unit performance. *Leadership Quarterly, 16,* 807–833.

Duck, J. M., & Fielding, K. S. (2003). Leaders and their treatment of subgroups: Implications for evaluations of the leader and the superordinate group. *European Journal of Social Psychology, 33,* 387–401.

Duffy, M. K., & Shaw, J. D. (2000). The Salieri syndrome: Consequences of envy in groups. *Small Group Research, 31,* 3–23.

Duke, D. L. (1986). The aesthetics of leadership. *Educational Administration Quarterly, 22*(1), 7–27.

Dunn, J., & Schweitzer, M. E. (2005). Why good employees make unethical decisions. In E. W. Kidwell & C. L. Martin (Eds.), *Managing organizational deviance* (pp. 39–60). Thousand Oaks, CA: SAGE.

Dunning, J. H. (2000). Whither global capitalism? *Global Focus, 12,* 117–136.

Dunning, J. H. (2003). Overview. In J. H. Dunning (Ed.), *Making globalization good: The moral challenges of global capitalism*

(pp. 11–40). Oxford, England: Oxford University Press.

Durskat, V. U., & Wolff, S. B. (2001, March). Building the emotional intelligence of groups. *Harvard Business Review,* 80–90.

Dyer, E. (2012, May 2). North Korea continues to brutalize its people and yet we do nothing. *The Telegraph.*

Dzirutwe, M. (2015, July 30). 'What lion?' Zimbabweans ask, amid global Cecil circus. *Reuters.*

Eden, D. (1984). Self-fulfilling prophecy as a management tool: Harnessing Pygmalion. *Academy of Management Review, 9,* 64–73.

Eden, D. (1990). *Pygmalion in management.* Lexington, MA: Lexington Books/D.C. Heath.

Eden, D. (1993). Interpersonal expectations in organizations. In P. D. Blank (Ed.), *Interpersonal expectations: Theory, research, and applications* (pp. 154–178). Cambridge, England: Cambridge University Press.

Eden, D., & Shami, A. B. (1982). Pygmalion goes to boot camp: Expectancy, leadership, and trainee performance. *Journal of Applied Psychology, 67,* 194–199.

Editorial Board. (2015, June 15). Workers betrayed by visa loopholes. *The New York Times,* p. A18.

Edwards, J. C. (2001). Self-fulfilling prophecy and escalating commitment: Fuel for the Waco fire. *Journal of Applied Behavioral Science, 37,* 343–360.

The effects of home demolitions. (n.d.). *Portlanders for Effective*

Zoning. Retrieved from http://www.fixportlandzoning.com/demolitions.html

Ehrhart, M. G. (2004). Leadership and procedural justice climate as antecedents of unit-level organizational citizenship behavior. *Personnel Psychology, 57,* 61–94.

Eilperin, J. (2010, February 7). Fight over invasive species turns into fight over lesser of two evils. *The Oregonian,* p. A2.

Einarsen, S., Aasland, M. S., & Skogstad, A. (2007). Destructive leadership behaviour: A definition and conceptual model. *Leadership Quarterly, 18,* 207–216.

Einarsen, S., Hoel, H., Zaptf, D., & Copper, C. L. (2011). The concept of bullying and harassment at work: The European tradition. In S. Einarsen, H. Hoel, D. Zaptf, & C. L. Cooper (Eds.), *Bullying and harassment in the workplace: Developments in theory, research and practice* (2nd ed., pp. 3–40). Boca Raton, FL: CRC Press.

Eisenbeiss, S. A., van Knippenberg, D., & Fahrbach, C. M. (2015). Doing well by doing good? Analyzing the relationship between CEO ethical leadership and firm performance. *Journal of Business Ethics, 128,* 635–651.

Eisenberg, E. M. (1984). Ambiguity as strategy in organizational communication. *Communication Monographs, 51,* 227–242.

Eisenberg, N. (2000). Emotion, regulation, and moral development. *Annual Review of Psychology, 51,* 665–697.

Eisenhardt, K. M. (1989). Making fast strategic decisions

in high-velocity environments. *Academy of Management Journal, 32,* 543–576.

Elangovan, A. R., & Shapiro, D. L. (1998). Betrayal of trust in organizations. *Academy of Management Review, 23,* 547–566.

Elegido, J. M. (2013). Does it make sense to be a loyal employee? *Journal of Business Ethics, 116,* 495–511.

Eligon, J. (2013, July 11). City in Iowa rebuilds from flooding but remains vulnerable. *The New York Times.*

ElKordy, M. (2013). Transformational leadership and organizational culture as predictors of employees' attitudinal outcomes. *Business Management Dynamics, 3,* 15–26.

Elm, D. R. (2014). The artist and the ethicist: Character and process. In D. Koehn & D. Elm (Eds.), *Aesthetics and business ethics* (pp. 53–66). New York, NY: Springer.

Enright, R. D. (2012). *The forgiving life.* Washington, DC: American Psychological Association.

Enright, R. D., Freedman, S., & Rique, J. (1998). The psychology of interpersonal forgiveness. In R. D. Enright & J. North (Eds.), *Exploring forgiveness* (pp. 46–62). Madison: University of Wisconsin Press.

Enright, R. D., & Gassin, E. A. (1992). Forgiveness: A developmental view. *Journal of Moral Education, 21,* 99–114.

Epley, N., & Dunning, D. (2000). Feeling "holier than thou": Are self-serving assessments produced by errors in self- or social prediction? *Journal of Personality and Social Psychology, 79,* 861–875.

Erben, G. S., & Guneser, A. B. (2007). The relationship between paternalistic leadership and organizational commitment: Investigating the role of climate regarding ethics. *Journal of Business Ethics, 82,* 955–968.

Erickson, A., Shaw, J. B., & Agabe, Z. (2007). An empirical investigation of the antecedents, behaviors, and outcomes of bad leadership. *Journal of Leadership Studies, 1*(3), 26–43.

Ernst, C., & Yip, J. (2009). Boundary-spanning leadership: Tactics to bridge social identity groups in organizations. In T. L. Pittinsky (Ed.), *Crossing the divide: Intergroup leadership in a world of difference* (pp. 87–99). Boston, MA: Harvard Business Press.

Esper, S. C., & Boies, K. (2013). Responsible leadership: A missing link. *Industrial and Organizational Psychology, 6,* 351–354.

Esser, J. K. (1998). Alive and well after 25 years: A review of groupthink research. *Organizational Behavior and Human Decision Processes, 73,* 116–141.

Ewing, J. (2015, October 26). VW investigation focus to include managers who turned a blind eye. *The New York Times,* p. B3.

Ewing, J., & Creswell, J. (2015, November 13). Seeking information, VW offers amnesty to employees. *The New York Times,* p. B1.

Ewing, J., & Mouawad, J. (2015, October 24). 3 directors say VW hid deceit from the board. *The New York Times,* p. A2.

Fainaru-Wada, M., & Fainaru, S. (2013). *League of denial.* New York, NY: Three Rivers Press.

Fairholm, G. W. (1996). Spiritual leadership: Fulfilling whole-self needs at work. *Leadership & Organization Development Journal, 17*(5), 11–17.

Farm animal welfare: Chickens. (n.d.). *MSPCA Angell.* Retrieved from https://www.mspca.org/animal_protection/farm-animal-welfare-chickens/

Fearn-Banks, K. (2007). *Crisis communications: A casebook approach* (3rd ed.). Mahwah, NJ: Erlbaum.

Feinstein, M. (2008). John Dewey, inquiry ethics, and democracy. In C. Misak (Ed.), *The Oxford handbook of American philosophy* (pp. 87–109). Oxford, England: Oxford University Press.

Feldmann, H. (2014, October 9). Ebola—A growing threat? *New England Journal of Medicine, 371*(15), 1375–1377.

Felton, R. (2016, January 16). Flint's water crisis: What went wrong. *The Guardian.*

Fesmire, S. (2015). *Dewey.* New York, NY: Routledge.

Fine, R., & Boon, V. (2007). Introduction: Cosmopolitanism: Between past and future. *European Journal of Social Theory 10,* 5–16.

Fink, S. (2002). *Crisis management: Planning for the inevitable.* Lincoln, NE: Backinprint.com.

Fiol, C. M., Harris, D., & House, R. J. (1999). Charismatic

leadership: Strategies for effecting social change. *Leadership Quarterly, 10,* 449–482.

Fisher, R., Ury, W., & Patton, B. (2011). *Getting to yes* (Rev. ed.). New York, NY: Penguin.

Fishman, C. (2011). *The Wal-Mart effect* (Rev. ed.). New York, NY: Penguin.

Fiske, S. T. (1993). Controlling other people: The impact of power on stereotyping. *American Psychologist, 48,* 621–628.

Fiske, S. T. (1998). Stereotyping, prejudice, and discrimination. In D. T. Gilbert, S. T. Fiske, & G. Lindzey (Eds.), *The handbook of social psychology* (Vol. 2, pp. 357–411). Boston, MA: McGraw-Hill.

Fleming, L. N. (2016, January 12). Volunteers deliver water in Flint amid lead crisis. *The Detroit News.*

Fleming, S. J. (2016, February 5). Lee: Time to end emergency manager law. *The Detroit News.*

Flesher, A. M. (2003). *Heroes, saints, & ordinary morality.* Washington, DC: Georgetown University Press.

Flescher, A. M., & Worthen, D. L. (2007). *The altruistic species: Scientific, philosophical, and religious perspectives of human benevolence.* Philadelphia, PA: Templeton Foundation Press.

Fletcher, G. (1993). *Loyalty: An essay on the morality of relationships.* New York, NY: Oxford University Press.

Flippen, A. R. (1999). Understanding groupthink from a self-regulatory perspective. *Small Group Research, 3,* 139–165.

Florida leadership researcher Walumbwa notches sixth retraction. (2015, January 14). *Retraction Watch.*

Folger, R., & Baron, R. A. (1996). Violence and hostility at work: A model of reactions to perceived injustice. In G. R. VandenBos & E. Q. Bulato (Eds.), *Violence on the job: Identifying risks and developing solutions* (pp. 51–85). Washington, DC: American Psychological Association.

Fonger, R. (2015, October 13). Ex-emergency manager says he's not to blame for Flint River water watch. *MLive.com.*

Fortin, M. (2008). Perspectives on organizational justice: Concept clarification, social context integration, time and links with morality. *International Journal of Management Reviews, 10,* 93–126.

Foster, R. J. (1978). *Celebration of discipline: The path to spiritual growth.* New York, NY: Harper & Row.

Fowler, K. L., Kling, N. D., & Larson, M. D. (2007). Organizational preparedness for coping with a major crisis or disaster. *Business & Society, 46,* 100–101.

Fox, E. J. (2015, September 22). Turing Pharmaceuticals C.E.O.: We'll maybe stop the drug price gouging. *Vanity Fair.*

Francis, H., Grubb, B., & Biggs, T. (2015, August 24). Cheating site hack has raised ethical questions. *Newcastle Herald* (Australia), p. 20.

Francis, M. (2015, April 8). Portland's demolition debate lands close to home. *The Oregonian/ Oregon Live.*

Frank, T., Kwiatkowski, M., & Cook, T. (2015, August 23). From obesity to duplicity: Jared's fall to earth. *USA Today.*

Franke, G. R., & Nadler, S. S. (2008). Culture, economic development, and national ethical attitudes. *Journal of Business Research, 61,* 254–264.

Franz, T. M. (2012). *Group dynamics and team interventions: Understanding and improving team performance.* Hoboken, NJ: Blackwell.

Freedman, S., Enright, R. D., & Knutson, J. (2005). A progress report on the process model of forgiveness. In E. L. Worthington, Jr. (Ed.), *Handbook of forgiveness* (pp. 393–406). New York, NY: Routledge.

Freeman, R. E., Harrison, J. S., & Wicks, A. C. (2007). *Managing for stakeholders: Survival, reputation, and success.* New Haven, CT: Yale University Press.

French, R. P., & Raven, B. (1959). The bases of social power. In D. Cartwright (Ed.), *Studies in social power* (pp. 150–167). Ann Arbor: University of Michigan, Institute for Social Research.

Frey, B. F. (2000). The impact of moral intensity on decision making in a business context. *Journal of Business Ethics, 26,* 181–195.

Frey, W. H. (2014, December 12). New projections point to a majority minority nation in 2044. *Brookings.*

Fritzsche, D. J. (2000). Ethical climates and the ethical dimension of decision making. *Journal of Business Ethics, 24,* 125–140.

Frolich, T. C., Sauter, M. B., & Stebbins, S. (2015, June 29). The worst companies to work for. *24/7 Wall St/Yahoo Finance*.

Fromm, E. (1964). *The heart of man: Its genius for good and evil*. New York, NY: Harper & Row.

Fry, L. W. (2003). Toward a theory of spiritual leadership. *Leadership Quarterly, 14,* 693–727.

Fry, L. W. (2005). Toward a theory of ethical and spiritual well-being, and corporate social responsibility through spiritual leadership. In R. A. Giacalone, C. L. Jurkiewicz, & C. Dunn (Eds.), *Positive psychology in business ethics and corporate responsibility* (pp. 47–84). Greenwich, CT: Information Age.

Fry, L. W. (2008). Spiritual leadership: State-of-the-art and future directions for theory, research, and practice. In J. Biberman & L. Tischler (Eds.), *Spirituality in business: Theory, practice, and future directions* (pp. 106–123). New York, NY: Palgrave Macmillan.

Fry, L. W., Vitucci, S., & Cedillo, M. (2005). Spiritual leadership and army transformation: Theory, measurement, and establishing a baseline. *Leadership Quarterly, 16,* 835–862.

Galvin, B. M., Waldman, D. A., & Balthazard, P. (2010). Visionary communication qualities as mediators of the relationship between narcissism and attributions of leader charisma. *Personnel Psychology, 63,* 509–537.

Garcia-Zamor, J. C. (2003). Workplace spirituality and organizational performance. *Public Administration Review, 63,* 355–363.

Gardner, W. L., Avolio, B. J., Luthans, F., May, D. R., & Walumbwa, F. O. (2005). "Can you see the real me?" A self-based model of authentic leader and follower development. *Leadership Quarterly, 16,* 343–372.

Garside, J. (2016, April 3). A world of hidden wealth: Why we are shining a light offshore. *The Guardian*.

Garvin, D. A. (1993, July–August). Building a learning organization. *Harvard Business Review,* 78–91.

Gaudine, A., & Thorne, L. (2001). Emotion and ethical decision-making in organizations. *Journal of Business Ethics, 31,* 175–187.

Gelles, D. (2015, May 16). For highest-paid CEOS, the party goes on. *NewYorkTimes.com*.

Gentile, M. C. (2010). *Giving voice to values: How to speak your mind when you know what's right*. New Haven, CT: Yale University Press.

Gert, B. (2004). *Common morality: Deciding what to do*. Oxford, England: Oxford University Press.

Ghosh, B. (2010, March 29). Sins of the fathers. *Time,* 34–37.

Giacalone, R. A., & Jurkiewicz, C. L. (2003). Right from wrong: The influence of spirituality on perceptions of unethical business activities. *Journal of Business Ethics, 46,* 85–97.

Giacalone, R. A., & Jurkiewicz, C. L. (2003). Toward a science of workplace spirituality. In R. A. Giacalone & C. L. Jurkiewicz (Eds.), *Handbook of workplace spirituality and organizational performance* (pp. 3–28). Armonk, NY: M. E. Sharpe.

Giannantonio, C. M., & Hurley-Hanson, A. E. (2013). Extreme leadership: Lessons from Ernest Shackleton and the *Endurance* expedition. In C. M. Giannantonio & A. E. Hurley-Hanson (Eds.), *Extreme leadership: Leaders, teams and situations outside the norm* (pp. 3–14). Cheltenham, England: Edward Elgar.

Gibb, J. R. (1961). Defensive communication. *Journal of Communication, 11–12,* 141–148.

Gibbs, N. (2014, December 22). The choice. *Time,* 67–68.

Gilligan, C. (1982). *In a different voice: Psychological theory and women's development*. Cambridge, MA: Harvard University Press.

Gimm, G., & Nichols, L. M. (2015, May). Ebola crisis of 2014: Are current strategies enough to meet the long-run challenges ahead? *American Journal of Public Health, 105*(5), E8–E10.

Gino, F., Moore, D. A., & Bazerman, M. H. (2008, January). See no evil: When we overlook other people's unethical behavior. Harvard Business School Working Paper No. 08-045.

Gino, F., Moore, D. A., & Bazerman, M. H. (2009). No harm, no foul: The outcome bias in ethical judgments. Harvard Business School Working Paper 08-080.

Gioia, D. A. (1992). Pinto fires and personal ethics: A script analysis of missed opportunities. *Journal of Business Ethics, 11,* 379–389.

Glanz, W. (2003, August 27). NASA ignored dangers to shuttle, panel says. *The Washington Times,* p. A1.

Global health inequity in Ebola treatment is major ethical concern. (2015, January 1). *Medical Ethics Advisor.*

Glover, J. (1999). *Humanity: A moral history of the twentieth century.* New Haven, CT: Yale University Press.

Godwin, L. N. (2015). Examining the impact of moral imagination on organizational decision making. *Business & Society, 54,* 254–278.

Goel, V. (2013, May 17). Foxconn audit finds a workweek still too long. *The New York Times,* p. B7.

Goel, V. (2014, November 24). Workers in Silicon Valley weigh in on Obama's immigration order. *The New York Times,* p. B3.

Goldfarb, A. Z. (2012, June 12). JPMorgan CEO Jamie Dimon apologizes for trading losses in Hill testimony. *The Washington Post.*

Golding, B. (2015, August 20). Underage sex shocker. *The New York Post,* p. 7.

Goldman, S. M. (2008). *Temptations in the office: Ethical choices and legal obligations.* Westport, CT: Praeger.

Goldman, S. M. (2010, August 5). *Loyalty vs. ethics: From the White House to the workplace.* American Management Association. Retrieved from http://www.amanet.org/training

Goleman, D., Boyatzis, R., & McKee, A. (2002). The emotional reality of teams. *Journal of Organizational Excellence, 21*(2), 55–65.

Good, T., & Brophy, J. (1980). *Educational psychology: A realistic approach.* New York, NY: Holt, Rinehart & Winston.

Goodpaster, K. E. (1991). Business ethics and stakeholder analysis. *Business Ethics Quarterly, 1,* 53–27.

Gorovitz, S. (Ed.). (1971). *Utilitarianism: Text and critical essays.* Indianapolis, IN: Bobbs-Merrill.

Gottlieb, J. Z., & Sabzgiri, J. (1996). Towards an ethical dimension of decision making in organizations. *Journal of Business Ethics 15,* 1275–1285.

Gottschall, J. (2012). *The storytelling animal: How stories make us human.* New York, NY: Mariner Books.

Graen, G. B., & Graen, J. A. (Eds.). (2007). *New multinational network sharing.* Charlotte, NC: Information Age.

Graen, G. B., & Uhl-Bien, M. (1998). Relationship-based approach to leadership. Development of leader–member exchange (LMX) theory of leadership over 25 years: Applying a multi-level multi-domain perspective. In F. Dansereau & F. J. Yammarino (Eds.), *Leadership: The multiple-level approaches* (pp. 103–158). Stamford, CT: JAI Press.

Graham, G. (2004). *Eight theories of ethics.* London, England: Routledge.

Graham, J., Haidt, J., Koleva, S., Motyl, M., Iyer, R., Wojcik, S. P., & Ditto, P. H. (2002). Moral Foundations Theory: The pragmatic validity of moral pluralism. *Advances in Experimental Social Psychology, 47,* 55–130.

Graham, J., Nosek, B. A., Haidt, J., Iyer, R., Koleva, S., & Ditto, P. H. (2011). Mapping the moral domain. *Journal of Personality and Social Psychology, 101,* 366–385.

Grandoni, D. (2015, July 15). Ashley, a dating website, says hackers may have data on millions. *The New York Times.*

The great fall of China. (2015, August 29). *The Economist.*

Greenberg, J., & Wiethoff, C. (2001). Organization justice as proaction and reaction: Implications for research and application. In R. Cropanzano (Ed.), *Justice in the workplace* (Vol. 2, pp. 271–302). Mahwah, NJ: Erlbaum.

Greene, J. (2005). Cognitive neuroscience and the structure of the moral mind. In P. Carruthers, S. Laurence, & S. Stich (Eds.), *The innate mind: Structure and content* (pp. 338–352). Oxford, England: Oxford University Press.

Greenhouse, L. (2004, June 25). Justices' ruling postpones resolution of Cheney case. *The New York Times.*

Greenhouse, S. (2013, November 23). U.S. retailers decline to aid factory victims in Bangladesh. *The New York Times,* p. B1.

Greenleaf, R. K. (1977). *Servant leadership.* New York, NY: Paulist Press.

Griffin, R. W., & O'Leary-Kelly, A. M. (Eds.). (2004). *The dark side of organizational behavior.* San Francisco, CA: Jossey-Bass.

Griffiths, P. D. (2014). Ebola and ethics. *Reviews in Medical Virology, 24,* 363–364.

Grijalva, E., & Harms, P. D. (2014). Narcissism: An integrative synthesis and dominance complementarity model. *Academy of Management Perspectives, 28*(2), 108–127.

Grijalva, E., Harms, P. D., Newman, D. A., Gaddis, B. H., & Fraley, R. C. (2015). Narcissism and leadership: A meta-analytic review of linear and nonlinear relationships. *Personnel Psychology, 68*, 1–147.

Griswold, C. L. (2007). *Forgiveness: A philosophical exploration.* Cambridge, England: Cambridge University Press.

Grojean, M. W., Resick, C. J., Dickson, M. W., & Smith, D. B. (2004). Leaders, values, and organizational climate: Examining leadership strategies for establishing an organizational climate regarding ethics. *Journal of Business Ethics, 55*, 223–241.

A growing problem: Selective breeding in the chicken industry: The case for slower growth. (2015, November). *ASPCA.* Retrieved from https://www.aspca.org/sites/default/files/chix_white_paper_nov2015_lores.pdf

Growing the grassroots. (n.d.). Retrieved from http://www.pataonia.com/us

Grunig, J. E. (2001). Two-way symmetrical public relations: Past, present, and future. In R. L. Heath (Ed.), *Handbook of public relations* (pp. 11–30). Thousand Oaks, CA: SAGE.

Grunig, L. A., Grunig, J. E., & Dozier, D. M. (2002). *Excellent public relations and effective organizations: A study of communication management in three countries.* Mahwah, NJ: Erlbaum.

Gudykunst, W. B. (2004). *Bridging differences: Effective intergroup communication* (4th ed.). Thousand Oaks, CA: SAGE.

Gudykunst, W. B., & Kim, Y. Y. (1997). *Communicating with strangers: An approach to intercultural communication* (3rd ed.). New York, NY: McGraw-Hill.

Gunsel, A., & Acikgoz, A. (2013). The effects of team flexibility and emotional intelligence on software development performance. *Group Decision and Negotiation, 22*, 359–377.

Guroian, V. (1996). Awakening the moral imagination. *Intercollegiate Review, 32*, 3–13.

Guth, W. D., & Tagiuri, R. (1965, September–October). Personal values and corporate strategy. *Harvard Business Review,* 123–132.

Haberman, C. (2009, November 29). The story of a landing. *The New York Times,* p. BR15.

Habermas, J. (1990). *Moral consciousness and communicative action* (C. Lehhardt & S. Weber Nicholsen, Trans.). Cambridge, MA: MIT Press.

Hackman, M. Z., & Johnson, C. E. (2013). *Leadership: A communication perspective* (6th ed.). Prospect Heights, IL: Waveland.

Haider, K. (2008, August 5). "Death zone" tragedy. *National Post,* p. A3.

Haidt, J. (2001). The emotional dog and its rational tail: A social intuitionist approach to moral judgment. *Psychological Review, 108*, 814–834.

Haidt, J. (2003). The moral emotions. In R. J. Davidson, K. R. Scherer, & H. H. Goldsmith (Eds.), *Handbook of affective sciences* (pp. 852–870). Oxford, England: Oxford University Press.

Haidt, J. (2012). *The righteous mind: Why good people are divided by politics and religion.* New York, NY: Pantheon Books.

Haidt, J. (2013). Moral psychology for the twenty-first century. *Journal of Moral Education, 42*, 281–297.

Haidt, J., & Bjorklund, F. (2008). Social intuitionists answer six questions about moral psychology. In W. Sinnott-Armstrong (Ed.), *Moral psychology: Vol. 2. The cognitive science of morality: Intuition and diversity* (pp. 182–217). Cambridge, England: MIT Press.

Haidt, J., & Graham, J. (2007). When morality opposes justice: Conservatives have moral intuitions that liberals may not recognize. *Social Justice Research, 20*, 98–116.

Hajdin, M. (2005). Employee loyalty: An examination. *Journal of Business Ethics, 59*, 259–280.

Hakim, D., & Ewing, J. (2015, October 2). In the driver's seat. *The New York Times,* p. B1.

Hale, J. R., & Fields, D. (2007). Exploring servant leadership across cultures: A study of followers in Ghana and the USA. *Leadership, 3*, 397–417.

Hall, E. T. (1976). *Beyond culture.* New York, NY: Random House.

Halley, J. (2009, January 29). Lopsided games are often pointless. *USA Today,* p. 4C.

Hallie, P. (1997). *Tales of good and evil, help and harm.* New York, NY: HarperCollins.

Hamilton, J. B., & Knouse, S. B. (2001). Multinational enterprise decision principles for dealing with cross cultural ethical conflicts. *Journal of Business Ethics, 31,* 77–94.

Hamilton, J. B., Knouse, S. B., & Hill, V. (2009). Google in China: A manager-friendly heuristic model for resolving cross-cultural ethical conflicts. *Journal of Business Ethics, 86,* 143–157.

Hannah, S. T., & Avolio, B. J. (2010). Moral potency: Building the capacity for character-based leadership. *Consulting Psychology Journal: Practice and Research, 62,* 291–310.

Hannah, S. T., Jennings, P. L., Bluhm, D., Chunyan Peng, A., & Schaubroeck, J. M. (2014). Duty orientation: Theoretical development and preliminary construct testing. *Organizational Behavior and Human Decision Processes, 123,* 220–238.

Hannah, S. T., Lester, P. B., & Vogelgesang, G. R. (2005). Moral leadership: Explicating the moral component of authentic leadership. In W. L. Gardner, B. J. Avolio, & F. O. Walumbwa (Eds.), *Authentic leadership theory and practice: Origins, effects and development* (pp. 43–81). Amsterdam, The Netherlands: Elsevier.

Hannah, S. T., Uhl-Bien, M., Avolio, B. J., & Cavarretta, F. L. (2009). A framework for examining leadership in extreme contexts. *Leadership Quarterly, 20,* 897–919.

Hansen, H., Ropo, A., & Sauer, E. (2007). Aesthetic leadership. *Leadership Quarterly, 18,* 544–560.

Hardy, S. A., & Carlo, G. (2005). Identity as a source of moral motivation. *Human Development, 48,* 232–256.

Hargie, O., Dickson, D., & Tourish, D. (2004). *Communication skills for effective management.* Houndmills, England: Palgrave Macmillan, pp. 177–178.

Harland, L., Harrison, W., Jones, J. R., & Reiter-Palmon, R. (2005). Leadership behaviors and subordinate resilience. *Journal of Leadership and Organizational Studies, 11,* 1–14.

Harper, S. R., & White, C. D. (2013). The impact of member emotional intelligence on psychological safety in work teams. *Journal of Behavioral & Applied Management, 15,* 2–10.

Harris, G. (2009, February 12). Peanut foods shipped before testing came in. *The New York Times,* p. A24.

Harris, S., Smallen, J., & Mitchell, C. (2006, February 18). Katrina report spreads blame. *National Journal,* 38.

Hart, D. K. (1992). The moral exemplar in an organizational society. In T. L. Cooper & N. D. Wright (Eds.), *Exemplary public administrators: Character and leadership in government* (pp. 9–29). San Francisco, CA: Jossey-Bass.

Hartmann, T. (2012). Moral disengagement during exposure to media violence. In R. Tamborini (Ed.), *Media and the moral mind* (pp. 241–287). Hoboken, NJ.

Harvey, J. B. (1988). *The Abilene paradox and other meditations on management.* New York, NY: Simon & Schuster.

Harvey, J. B. (1999). *How come every time I get stabbed in the back my fingerprints are on the knife?* San Francisco, CA: Jossey-Bass.

Harvey, P., Martinko, M. J., & Gardner, W. L. (2006). Promoting authentic behavior in organizations: An attributional perspective. *Journal of Leadership & Organizational Studies, 12*(3), 1–11.

Hashemi, F. (2016, February 5). Probe into KPMG's audit of failed bank HBOS intensifies. *International Accounting Bulletin.*

Hatcher, T. (2002). *Ethics and HRD: A new approach to leading responsible organizations.* Cambridge, MA: Perseus.

Hatzfeld, J. (2005). *Machete season: The killers in Rwanda speak* (L. Coverdale, Trans.). New York, NY: Farrar, Straus and Giroux.

Hauser, M. D., Young, L., & Cushman, F. (2008). Reviving Rawls's linguistic analogy: Operative principles and the causal structure of moral actions. In W. Sinnott-Armstrong (Ed.), *Moral psychology: Vol. 2. The cognitive science of morality: Intuition and diversity* (pp. 107–144). Cambridge, England: MIT Press.

Hays, T., & Krisher, T. (2015, September 18). GM agrees to pay $1.5 billion in settlements. *The Oregonian,* pp. G1, G3.

Head, S. (2014, February 23). Worse than Wal-Mart: Amazon's sick brutality and secret history of ruthlessly intimidating workers. *Salon.com*

Healy, J., & Paulson, M. (2015, January 31). Vaccine critics turn defensive over measles. *The New York Times,* p. A1.

Hearit, K. M. (2006). *Crisis management by apology: Corporate response to allegations of wrongdoing.* Mahwah, NJ: Erlbaum.

Heath, R. L. (2002). Issues management: Its past, present and future. *Journal of Public Affairs, 2*(4), 209–214.

Heffernan, M. (2013, August 7). What happened after the Foxconn suicides. *CBS News.*

Heider, J. (1992). *The Tao of leadership.* New York, NY: Bantam.

Held, V. (2006). The ethics of care. In D. Copp (Ed.), *The Oxford handbook of ethical theory* (pp. 537–566). Oxford, England: Oxford University Press.

Helman, C. (2015, December 11). What oil bust? Texas billionaire gives each worker a $100,000 bonus. *Forbes.com*

Herdt, T. (2012, January 4). Patagonia first in line to register as a "benefit corporation." *Ventura County Star.*

Hern, A. (2015, August 21). Ten questions Ashley Madison needs to answer. *The Guardian*, Technology.

Higgs, M. (2009). The good, the bad and the ugly: Leadership and narcissism. *Journal of Change Management, 9,* 165–178.

Hill, G., & Unell, A. E. (2010). *Starting at the finish line: The Al Buehler story.* [Documentary]. USA: StoryTales Productions.

Hill, L. (2015). Classical Stoicism and the birth of a global ethics: Cosmopolitan duties in a world of local loyalties. *Social Alternatives, 34*(1), 14–18

Hinken, T. R., & Schriesheim, C. A. (1989). Development and application of new scales to measure the French and Raven (1959) bases of social power. *Journal of Applied Psychology, 74,* 561–567.

Ho, Catherine. (2015, October 11). Working for Turing Pharmaceuticals CEO, 'Most hated man in America.' *The Washington Post.*

Hodgkinson, P. E., & Stewart, M. (1991). *Coping with catastrophe: A handbook of disaster management.* London, England: Routledge.

Hodgson, G. (2009, August 12). Eunice Kennedy Shriver; mental health campaigner who founded the Special Olympics. *The Independent*, Obituaries, p. 26.

Hofstede, G. (1984). *Culture's consequences.* Beverly Hills, CA: SAGE.

Hofstede, G. (2001). Difference and danger: Cultural profiles of nations and limits to tolerance. In M. H. Albrecht (Ed.), *International HRM: Managing diversity in the workplace* (pp. 9–23). Oxford, England: Blackwell.

Hofstede, G., & Hofstede, G. J. (2005). *Cultures and organizations: Software of the mind.* London, England: McGraw-Hill.

Hogg, M. A., Knippenberg, D., & Rast, D. E. (2012). Intergroup leadership in organizations: Leading across group and organizational boundaries. *Academy of Management Review, 37,* 232–255.

Hollander, E. P. (1992). The essential interdependence of leadership and followership. *Current Directions in Psychological Science, 1,* 71–75.

Holmgren, J. R. (1998). Self-forgiveness and responsible moral agency. *Journal of Value Inquiry, 32,* 75–91.

Hood, J. N. (2003). The relationship of leadership style and CEO values to ethical practices in organizations. *Journal of Business Ethics, 43,* 263–273.

Hopen, D. (2002). Guiding corporate behavior: A leadership obligation, not a choice. *Journal for Quality & Participation, 25,* 15–19.

Hopper, T. (2015, August 25). The aftermath of an online hack. *The Star Phoenix* (Saskatoon, Saskatchewan), p. D4.

Hornstein, H. A. (1996). *Brutal bosses and their prey.* New York, NY: Riverhead.

Hosmer, L. T. (1994). Strategic planning as if ethics mattered. *Strategic Management Journal, 15,* 17–34.

House, R. J., Hanges, P. J., Javidan, M., Dorfman, P. W., & Gupta, V. (Eds.). (2004). *Culture, leadership, and organizations: The GLOBE study of 62 societies.* Thousand Oaks, CA: SAGE.

Howell, J., & Avolio, B. J. (1992). The ethics of charismatic leadership: Submission or liberation? *Academy of Management Executive, 6,* 43–54.

Hubbartt, W. S. (1998). *The new battle over workplace privacy.* New York, NY: AMACOM.

Huddleston, T. (2013). *Wrestling with madness: Jon Eleuthere Du Pont and the Foxcatcher Farm murder.* Absolute Crime Books.

Hunter, J. E., & Boster F. (1987). A model of compliance-gaining message selection. *Communication Monographs, 54,* 63–84

Husted, B. W. (1999). Wealth, culture and corruption. *Journal of International Business Studies, 30,* 339–359.

Ilies, R., Morgeson, F. P., & Nahrgang, J. D. (2005). Authentic leadership and eudemonic well-being: Understanding leader–follower outcomes. *Leadership Quarterly, 16,* 373–394.

Inch, E. S., Warnick, B., & Endres, D. (2006). *Critical thinking and communication: The use of reason in argument* (5th ed.). Boston, MA: Pearson.

Infante, D. A. (1988). *Arguing constructively.* Prospect Heights, IL: Waveland.

Infante, D. A., & Rancer, A. S. (1982). A conceptualization and measure of argumentativeness. *Journal of Personality Assessment,* 72–80.

Infante, D. A., & Rancer, A. S. (1996). Argumentativeness and verbal aggressiveness: A review of recent theory and research. In B. Burleson (Ed.), *Communication yearbook 19* (pp. 319–351). Thousand Oaks, CA: SAGE.

Intezari, A., & Pauleen, D. J. (2013). Students of wisdom. In W. Kupers & D. J. Pauleen (Eds.), *Handbook of practical wisdom: Leadership, organizational and integral business practice* (pp. 155–174). Burlington, VT: Gower.

Isaac, M. (2016, February 18). Why Apple is putting up a fight over privacy with the F.B.I. *The New York Times,* p. B4.

Isaacson, W. (2011). *Steve Jobs.* New York, NY: Simon & Schuster.

Isidore, D. (2015, November 19). Jared Fogle sentenced to more than 15 years. *CNN Money.*

Isserman, M. (2008, August 11). The descent of men; a different K2 drama. *The International Herald Tribune,* Opinion, p. 4.

Iversen, K. (2012). *Full body burden: Growing up in the nuclear shadow of Rocky Flats.* New York, NY: Crown.

Ivory, D., & Ewing, J. (2015, October 8). In U.S., VW was aware of 'possible' problem. *The New York Times,* p. B1.

Iwaki, H. T. (2012, October 8). Meet the Fukushima 50? No, you can't. *The Economist.*

Izadi, E., & Ohiheiser, A. (2015, July 29). As anger escalates over lion's death, Zimbabwean men appear in court. *Washington Post.*

Jacobs, D. C. (2004). A pragmatist approach to integrity in business ethics. *Journal of Management Inquiry, 13,* 215–223.

Jacobs, T. (2009, May). Morals authority. *Miller-McCune,* 47–55.

James, H. S. (2000). Reinforcing ethical decision-making through organizational structure. *Journal of Business Ethics, 28,* 43–58.

James, S. A. (2007). *Universal human rights: Origins and development.* New York, NY: LFB Scholarly Publications.

Janis, I. (1971, November). Groupthink: The problems of conformity. *Psychology Today,* 271–279.

Janis, I. (1982). *Groupthink* (2nd ed.). Boston, MA: Houghton Mifflin.

Janis, I. (1989). *Crucial decisions: Leadership in policymaking and crisis management.* New York, NY: Free Press.

Janis, I., & Mann, L. (1977). *Decision making.* New York, NY: Free Press.

Janover, M. (2005). The limits of forgiveness and the ends of politics. *Journal of Intercultural Studies, 26,* 221–235.

Jaramillo, F., Grisaffe, D. B., Chonko, L. B., & Roberts, J. A. (2009). Examining the impact of servant leadership on sales force performance. *Journal of Personal Selling & Sales Management, 29,* 257–275.

Jaramillo, F., Grisaffe, D. B., Chonko, L. B., & Roberts, J. A. (2009). Examining the impact of servant leadership on salesperson's turnover intention. *Journal of Personal Selling & Sales Management, 29,* 351–365.

Jassawalla, A. R., Malshe, A., & Sashittal, H. (2008). Student perceptions of social loafing in undergraduate business classroom teams. *Decision Sciences Journal of Innovative Education, 6,* 423–424.

Javidan, M., & House, R. J. (2001). Cultural acumen for the global manager: Lessons from Project GLOBE. *Organizational Dynamics, 29,* 289–305.

Jehn, K. A. (1995). A multi-method examination of the benefits and detriments of intragroup conflict. *Administrative Science Quarterly, 40,* 256–282.

Jennings, M. M. (2006). *The seven signs of ethical collapse: How to spot moral meltdowns in companies . . . before it's too late.* New York, NY: St. Martin's Press.

Jensen, J. V. (1996). Ethical tension points in whistleblowing. In J. A. Jaksa & M. S. Pritchard (Eds.), *Responsible communication: Ethical issues in business, industry, and the professions* (pp. 41–51). Cresskill, NJ: Hampton.

Jervis, R. (2015, August 23). Nagging divide cuts through New Orleans. *USA Today,* p. 2A.

Jervis, R. (2015, August 24). Post-Katrina New Orleans still the same. *USA Today,* p. 2A.

Johannesen, R. L. (1991). Virtue ethics, character, and political communication. In R. E. Denton (Ed.), *Ethical dimensions of political communication* (pp. 69–90). New York, NY: Praeger.

Johannesen, R. L., Valde, K. S., & Whedbee, K. E. (2008). *Ethics in human communication* (6th ed.). Long Grove, IL: Waveland Press.

Johnson, C. E. (1997). A leadership journey to the East. *Journal of Leadership Studies, 4*(2), 82–88.

Johnson, C. E. (2000). Emerging perspectives in leadership ethics. *Proceedings of the International Leadership Association,* 48–54.

Johnson, C. E. (2000). Taoist leadership ethics. *Journal of Leadership & Organizational Studies, 7*(1), 82–91.

Johnson, C. E. (2014). Why "good" followers go "bad": The power of moral disengagement. *Journal of Leadership Education,* Special Issue, 36–50.

Johnson, C. E. (2015). *Organizational ethics: A practical approach* (3rd ed.). Thousand Oaks, CA: SAGE.

Johnson, C. E., & Hackman, M. Z. (1997). *Rediscovering the power of followership in the leadership communication text.* Paper presented at the annual convention of the National Communication Association, Chicago, Illinois.

Johnson, C. E., & Shelton, P. M. (2014, October). Ethical leadership in the age of apology. *International Leadership Journal, 6,* 7–29.

Johnson, C. E., Shelton, P. M., & Yates, L. (2012). Nice guys (and gals) finish first: Ethical leadership and organizational trust, satisfaction, and effectiveness. *International Leadership Journal, 4*(1), 3–19.

Johnson, D. W., & Johnson, F. P. (2000). *Joining together: Group theory and group skills* (7th ed.). Boston, MA: Allyn & Bacon.

Johnson, D. W., & Johnson, R. T. (1989). *Cooperation and competition: Theory and research.* Edina, MN: Interaction.

Johnson, D. W., & Johnson, R. T. (2005). Training for cooperative group work. In M. A. West, D. Tjosvold, & K. G. Smith (Eds.), *The essentials of teamworking: International perspectives* (pp. 131–147). West Sussex, England: John Wiley.

Johnson, D. W., Maruyama, G., Johnson, R., Nelson, D., & Skon, L. (1981). Effects of cooperative, competitive, and individualistic goal structures on achievement: A meta-analysis. *Psychological Bulletin, 82,* 47–62.

Johnson, D. W., & Tjosvold, D. (1983). *Productive conflict management.* New York, NY: Irvington.

Johnson, J. (1993). Functions and processes of inner speech in listening. In D. Wolvin & C. G. Coakley (Eds.), *Perspectives in listening* (pp. 170–184). Norwood, NJ: Ablex.

Johnson, J. (2011, February 28). 1 million workers. 90 million phones. 17 suicides. Who's to blame? *Wired.*

Johnson, J., & Orange, M. (2003). *The man who tried to buy the world: Jean-Marie Messier and Vivendi Universal.* New York, NY: Portfolio.

Johnson, M. (1993). *Moral imagination: Implications of cognitive science for ethics.* Chicago, IL: University of Chicago Press

Jones, D. (2012). Does servant leadership lead to greater customer focus and employee satisfaction? *Business Studies Journal, 4,* 21–35.

Jones, P. E., & Roelofsma, P. H. M. P. (2000). The potential for social contextual and group biases in team decision-making: Biases, conditions and psychological mechanisms. *Ergonomics, 43,* 1129–1152.

Jones, T. M. (1991). Ethical decision making by individuals in organizations: An issue-contingent model. *Academy of Management Review, 15,* 366–395.

Jonsson, P. (2015, August 25). A 'new' New Orleans emerges

10 years after hurricane Katrina. *The Christian Science Monitor.*

Jordan, J. (2015, October 7). Momentum building to reduce demolition waste. *Restore Oregon.*

Jordan, J., Diermeier, D. A., & Galinsky, A. D. (2012). The strategic Samaritan: How effectiveness and proximity affect corporate responses to external crises. *Business Ethics Quarterly 22*(4), 621–648.

Jordan, P. J., & Troth, A. C. (2004). Managing emotions during team problem solving: Emotional intelligence and conflict resolution. *Human Performance, 17,* 195–218.

Jourdan, G. (1998). Indirect causes and effects in policy change: The Brent Spar case. *Public Administration, 76,* 713–770.

Judge, W. Q. (1999). *The leader's shadow: Exploring and developing executive character.* Thousand Oaks, CA: SAGE.

Jurkiewicz, C. L., & Giacalone, R. A. (2004). A values framework for measuring the impact of workplace spirituality on organizational performance. *Journal of Business Ethics, 49,* 129–142.

Kador, J. (2009). *Effective apology: Mending fences, building bridges, and restoring trust.* Williston, VT: Berret-Kohler.

Kahn, A. E., & Maxwell, D. J. (2008). Ethics in diversity management leadership. In S. A. Quatro & R. R. Sims (Eds.), *Executive ethics: Ethical dilemmas and challenges for the C-suite* (pp. 247–262). Charlotte, NC: Information Age.

Kaminer, A., & O'Driscoll, S. (2014, May 18). Workers at NYU's Abu Dhabi site faced harsh conditions. *The New York Times.*

Kant, I. (1964). *Groundwork of the metaphysics of morals* (H. J. Ryan, Trans.). New York, NY: Harper & Row.

Kanter, R. M. (1979, July–August). Power failure in management circuits. *Harvard Business Review,* 65–75.

Kantor, J., & Streitfeld, D. (2015, August 15). Inside Amazon: Wrestling big ideas in a bruising workplace. *The New York Times.*

Kanungo, R. N. (2001). Ethical values of transactional and transformational leaders. *Canadian Journal of Administrative Sciences, 18,* 257–265.

Kanungo, R. N., & Conger, J. A. (1990). The quest for altruism in organizations. In S. Srivastra & D. L. Cooperrider (Eds.), *Appreciative management and leadership* (pp. 228–256). San Francisco, CA: Jossey-Bass.

Kanungo, R. N., & Mendonca, M. (1996). *Ethical dimensions of leadership.* Thousand Oaks, CA: SAGE.

Karakas, F. (2010). Spirituality and performance in organizations: A literature review. *Journal of Business Ethics, 94,* 89–106.

Karakowsky, L., DeGama, N., & McBey, K. (2012). Facilitating the Pygmalion effect: The overlooked role of subordinate perceptions of the leader. *Journal of Occupational and Organizational Psychology 85,* 579–599.

Karau, S. J., & Williams, K. D. (1995). Social loafing: Research findings, implications, and future directions. *Current Directions in Psychological Science, 4,* 134–140.

Karau, S. J., & Williams, K. D. (2001). Understanding individual motivation in groups: The collective effort model. In M. E. Turner (Ed.), *Groups at work: Theory and research* (pp. 113–141). Mahwah, NJ: Erlbaum.

Karim, A. (2000, June 23). Globalization, ethics, and AIDS vaccines. *Science,* 21–29.

Karmali, R. (2015, November 19). HBOS' demise: How it happened. *BBC.*

Karuhanga, J. (2014, December 5). Kigali inducted into world's most 'resilient cities." *The New Times* (Kigali).

Kasser, T. (2002). *The high price of materialism.* Cambridge, MA: Bradford/MIT Press.

Kasser, T., Vanssteenkiste, M., & Deckop, J. R. (2006). The ethical problems of a materialistic value orientation for businesses. *Human Resource Management Ethics* (pp. 283–306). Charlotte, NC: Information Age Publishing.

Kassing, J. W. (2002). Speaking up: Identifying employee's upward dissent strategies. *Management Communication Quarterly, 16,* 187–209.

Kassing, J. W. (2005). Speaking up competently: A comparison of perceived competence in upward dissent. *Communication Research Reports, 22,* 227–234.

Kassing, J. W. (2009). 'In case you didn't hear me the first time': An examination of repetitious upward dissent. *Management Communication Quarterly, 22,* 416–436.

Kassing, J. W. (2011). *Dissent in organizations.* Cambridge, England: Polity Press.

Kassing, J. W., & Kava, W. (2013). Assessing disagreement expressed to management: Development of the Upward Dissent Scale. *Communication Research Reports, 30,* 46–56.

Katz, D., Maccoby, N., Gurin, G., & Floor, L. (1951). *Productivity, supervision, and morale among railroad workers.* Ann Arbor: University of Michigan, Institute for Social Research

Katz, F. E. (1993). *Ordinary people and extraordinary evil: A report on the beguilings of evil.* Albany: State University of New York Press.

Keating, M., Martin, G. S., Resick, C. J., & Dickson, M. W. (2007). A comparative study of the endorsement of ethical leadership in Ireland and the United States. *Irish Journal of Management, 28,* 5–30.

Kedmey, D. (2015, July 22). Ashley Madison already caved to hackers' demands. *Time.com.*

Keil, M., & Montealegre, R. (2000). Cutting your losses: Extricating your organization when a big project goes awry. *Sloan Management Review, 41,* 55–68.

Kekes, J. (1991). Moral imagination, freedom, and the humanities. *American Philosophical Quarterly, 28,* 101–111.

Kekes, J. (2005). *The roots of evil.* Ithaca, NY: Cornell University Press.

Kellaway, K. (2015, October 15). Malala Yousafzai: 'I want to become prime minister of my country.' *The Guardian.*

Kellerman, B. (2004). *Bad leadership: What it is, how it happens, why it matters.* Boston, MA: Harvard Business School Press.

Kellerman, B. (2008). Bad leadership—and ways to avoid it. In J. V. Gallos (Ed.), *Business leadership* (2nd ed., pp. 423–432). San Francisco, CA: Jossey-Bass.

Kellerman, B. (2008). *Followership: How followers are creating change and changing leaders.* Boston, MA: Harvard Business School Press.

Kelley, R. (1992). *The power of followership.* New York, NY: Doubleday/Currency.

Keltner, D., Langner, C. A., & Allison, M. L. (2006). Power and moral leadership. In D. L. Rhode (Ed.), *Moral leadership: The theory and practice of power, judgment, and policy* (pp. 177–194). San Francisco, CA: Jossey-Bass.

Kennedy, D. (2004). *The dark side of virtue: Reassessing international humanitarianism.* Princeton, NJ: Princeton University Press.

Kenny, A. (2004). *Ancient philosophy* (Vol. 1). Oxford, England: Clarenton Press.

Kernis, M. H. (2003). Toward a conceptualization of optimal self-esteem. *Psychological Inquiry, 14,* 1–26.

Kessler, E. H., & Bailey, J. R. (2007). Introduction: Understanding, applying, and developing organizational and managerial wisdom. In E. H. Kessler & J. R. Bailey (Eds.), *Handbook of organizational and managerial wisdom* (pp. xv–xxiv). Thousand Oaks, CA: SAGE.

Kessler, S. R., Bandelli, A. C., Spector, P. E., Borman, W. C., Nelson, C. E., & Penney, L. M. (2010). Re-examining Machiavelli: A three-dimensional model of Machiavellianism in the workplace. *Journal of Applied Social Psychology, 40,* 1868–1896.

Khuntia, R., & Suar, D. (2004). A scale to assess ethical leadership of Indian and public sector managers. *Journal of Business Ethics, 49,* 13–26.

Kickul, J. (2001). When organizations break their promises: Employee reactions to unfair processes and treatment. *Journal of Business Ethics, 29,* 289–307.

Kidder, R. M. (1995). *How good people make tough choices: Resolving the dilemmas of ethical living.* New York, NY: Fireside.

Kidder, R. M. (2004). Foundation codes of ethics: Why do they matter, what are they, and how are they relevant to philanthropy? *New Decisions for Philanthropic Fundraising, 45,* 75–83.

Kidder, R. M. (2005). *Moral courage.* New York, NY: William Morrow.

Kilburg, R. R. (2012). *Virtuous leaders: Strategy, character, and influence in the 21st century.* Washington, DC: American Psychological Association;

Kim, H-W. (2011, December 19). Genocide and politicide alert: North Korea. *Genocide Watch.*

King, D., Case, C. J., & Premo, K. M. (2011). A mission statement analysis comparing the United States and three other English speaking countries. *Academy of Strategic Management Journal, 10,* Special Issue, 21–45.

King, S., Biberman, J., Robbins, L., & Nicol, D. M. (2007). Integrating spirituality into management education in academia and organizations: Origins, a conceptual framework, and current practices. In J. Biberman & M. D. Whitty (Eds.), *At work: Spirituality matters* (pp. 243–256). Scranton, PA: University of Scranton Press.

Kipnis, D. (1972). Does power corrupt? *Journal of Personality and Social Psychology, 24,* 33–41.

Kirkland, R. (2002). Self-fulfillment through selflessness: The moral teachings of the Daode Jing. In M. Barnhart (Ed.), *Varieties of ethical reflection: New directions for ethics in a global context* (pp. 21–48). Lanham, MD: Lexington Books.

Kiuchi, T., & Shireman, B. (2002). *What we learned in the rainforest: Business lessons from nature.* San Francisco, CA: Berrett-Koehler.

Klatt, J. S., & Enright, R. D. (2009). Investigating the place of forgiveness with in the Positive Youth Development paradigm. *Journal of Moral Education, 38,* 35–52.

Klatt, J. S., & Enright, R. D. (2011). Initial validation of the unfolding forgiveness process in a natural environment. *Counseling and Values, 56,* 25–42.

Klenke, K. (2005). The internal theater of the authentic leader: Integrating cognitive, affective, conative and spiritual facets of authentic leadership. In W. L. Gardner, B. J. Avolio, & F. O. Walumbwa (Eds.), *Authentic leadership theory and practice: Origins, effects and development* (pp. 43–81). Amsterdam, The Netherlands: Elsevier.

Kline, S. L., Simunich, B., & Weber, H. (2009). The use of equivocal messages in responding to corporate challenges. *Journal of Applied Communication Research, 37,* 40–58.

Klingner, B. (2014, February 20). U.S. should augment sanctions after North Korean crimes against humanity. *Heritage Foundation.*

Kludt, T. (2015, August 29). New York Daily News defends showing shocking shooting photos. *CNNMoney.*

Knapp, J. C. (2011). Rethinking ethics training: New approaches to enhance effectiveness. In R. R. Sims & W. I. Sauser (Eds.), *Experiences in teaching business ethics* (pp. 217–230). Charlotte, NC: Information Age.

Knight, R. F., & Pretty, D. J. (1996). *The impact of catastrophes on shareholder value.* Oxford, England: Templeton College, University of Oxford.

Knobe, J. (2006). The concept of intentional action: A case study in the uses of folk psychology. *Philosophical Studies, 130,* 203–231.

Knobe, J., & Burra, A. (2006). The folk concepts of intention and intentional action: A cross-cultural study. *Journal of Cognition and Culture, 6,* 113–132.

Koblin, J. (2015, August 28). Front pages on killings in Virginia spur anger. *The New York Times,* p. A12.

Koch, J. (2001, March). Thinking outside the box at The Container Store. *Workforce,* 34–38.

Koehn, D. (2010). Ethics, morality, and art in the classroom: Positive and negative relations. *Journal of Business Ethics Education, 7,* 213–232.

Kohlberg, L. A. (1984). *The psychology of moral development: The nature and validity of moral stages* (Vol. 2). San Francisco, CA: Harper & Row.

Kohlberg, L. A. (1986). A current statement on some theoretical issues. In S. Modgil & C. Modgil (Eds.), *Lawrence Kohlberg: Consensus and controversy* (pp. 485–546). Philadelphia, PA: Palmer.

Kohler, N., Krolicki, K., Disavano, S., & Fuse, T. (2011, April 2). Wave predicted. *National Post,* p. A25.

Kolditz, T. A. (2005, Fall). The in extremis leader. *Leader to Leader,* 6–18.

Kolditz, T. A. (2007). *In extremis leadership: Leading as if your life depended on it.* San Francisco, CA: Jossey-Bass.

Kolditz, T. A., & Brazil, D. M. (2005). Authentic leadership in in extremis settings: A concept for extraordinary leaders in exceptional situations. In W. L. Gardner, B. J. Avolio, & F. O. Walumbwa (Eds.), *Authentic leadership theory and practice: Origins, effects and development* (pp. 345–356). Amsterdam, The Netherlands: Elsevier.

Kole, W. J. (2015, October 15). Tufts University and Goucher College revoke degrees given to Bill Cosby. *HuffPost Entertainment.*

Koleva, S. P., Graham, J., Iyer, R., Ditto, P. H., & Haidt, J. (2012). Tracing the threads: How the five moral concerns (especially purity) help explain culture war attitudes. *Journal of Research in Personality, 46*(2), 184–194.

Kolp, A., & Rea, P. (2006). *Leading with integrity: Character-based leadership.* Cincinnati, OH: AtomicDog.

Korosec, K. (2015, August 24). Ten times more deaths linked to faulty switch than GM first reported. *Fortune.com.*

Kotler, P., & Lee, N. (2005). *Corporate social responsibility: Doing the most good for your company and your cause.* Hoboken, NJ: John Wiley.

Kotlyar, I., & Karakowsky, L. (2006). Leading conflict? Linkages between leader behaviors and group conflict. *Small Group Research, 37,* 377–403.

Kotter, J. P. (1990). *A force for change: How leadership differs from management.* New York, NY: Free Press.

Kouzes, J. M., & Posner, B. Z. (2003). *Credibility: How leaders gain and lose it, why people demand it.* San Francisco, CA: Jossey-Bass.

Kouzes, J. M., & Posner, B. Z. (2012). *The leadership challenge* (5th ed.). San Francisco, CA: Jossey-Bass.

KPMG. (2013/2015). *The KPMG Survey of Corporate Responsibility: Executive summary.* Retrieved from http://home.kpmg.com

KPMG Forensic. (2013). *Fraud survey 2013.* Retrieved from https://www.surveys.kpmg.com/aci/fraud_risk.asp

Kramer, F. M. (2010). Collective trust within organizations: Conceptual foundations and empirical insights. *Corporate Reputation Review, 13,* 82–97.

Kramer, R. M., & Tyler, T. R. (Eds.). (1996). *Trust in organizations: Frontiers of theory and research.* Thousand Oaks, CA: SAGE.

Krantz, M. (2015, December 9). Scram! 5 CEOs can get paid $1.3B to get lost. *USA Today,* p. B2.

Krasikova, D. V., Green, S. G., & LeBreton, J. M. (2013). Destructive leadership: A theoretical review, integration, and future research agenda. *Journal of Management, 39,* 1308–1338.

Kristof, N. D. (2010, June 27). Death by gadget. *The New York Times,* p. WK11.

Kristof, N. D. (2015, September 26). Malala Yousafzai's fight continues. *The New York Times,* Op-Ed.

Ladkin, D. (2006). The enchantment of the charismatic leader: Charisma reconsidered as aesthetic encounter. *Leadership, 2*(2), 165–179.

Ladkin, D. (2008). Leading beautifully: How mastery congruence and purpose create the aesthetic of embodied leadership practice. *Leadership Quarterly, 19,* 31–41.

Ladkin, D. (2010). *Rethinking leadership: A new look at old leadership questions.* Cheltenham, England: Edward Elgar.

Ladkin, D. (2011). The art of 'perceiving correctly': What artists can teach us about moral perception. *Tamara: Journal for Critical Organization Inquiry, 9,* 91–101

LaFasto, F., & Larson, C. (2012). *The humanitarian leader in each of us: Seven choices that shape a socially responsible life.* Thousand Oaks, CA: SAGE.

Lammers, J., Stoker, J. I., Pollman, M., & Stapel, D. A. (2011). Power increases infidelity among men and women. *Psychological Science, 22,* 1191–1197.

Langer, E. J. (1989). *Mindfulness.* Reading, MA: Addison-Wesley.

Langer, E. J. (1997). *The power of mindful learning.* Reading, MA: Addison-Wesley.

La Pine, J. A. (2005). Adaptation of teams in response to unforeseen change: Effects of goal difficulty and team composition in terms of cognitive ability and goal orientation. *Journal of Applied Psychology, 90,* 1153–1167.

Lapsley, D. K. (2008). Moral self-identity as the aim of education. In L. P. Nucci & D. Narvaez (Eds.), *Handbook of moral and character education* (pp. 30–52). New York, NY: Routledge.

Lapsley, D. K., & Hill, P. L. (2008). On dual processing and heuristic approaches to moral cognition. *Journal of Moral Education, 37,* 313–332.

Larrabee, M. J. (Ed.). (1993). *An ethic of care: Feminist and interdisciplinary perspectives.* New York, NY: Routledge.

Laskas, J. M. (2009, September 14). Bennet Omalu, concussions, and the NFL: How one doctor changed football forever. *GQ.*

Laskas, J. M. (2015). *Concussion.* New York, NY: Random House.

Lax, D. A., & Sebenius, J. K. (1986). *The manager as negotiator: Bargaining for cooperation and competitive gain.* New York, NY: The Free Press.

Lax, D. A., & Sebenius, J. K. (2004). Three ethical issues in negotiation. In C. Menkel-Meadow & M. Wheeler (Eds.), *What's fair: Ethics for negotiators* (pp. 5–14). San Francisco, CA: Jossey-Bass.

Lazare, A. (2004). *On apology.* Oxford, England: Oxford University Press.

Lazarus, H., & McManus, T. (2006). Transparency guru: An interview with Tom McManus. *Journal of Management Development, 25,* 923–936.

Lee, J., Woeste, J. H., & Heath, R. L. (2007). Getting ready for crises: Strategic excellence. *Public Relations Review, 33,* 334–336.

Leeper, R. V. (1996). Moral objectivity, Jurgen Habermas's discourse ethics, and public relations. *Public Relations Review 22,* 133–150

Leets, L. (2001). Interrupting the cycle of moral exclusion: A communication contribution to social justice research. *Journal of Applied Social Psychology, 31,* 1859–1891.

Lengnick-Hall, C. A., Beck, T. E., & Lengnick-Hall, M. L. (2011). Developing a capacity for organizational resilience through strategic human resource management. *Human Resource Management Review, 21,* 243–255.

Leroy, H., Palanski, M. E., & Simons, T. (2012). Authentic leadership and behavioral integrity as drivers of follower commitment and performance. *Journal of Business Ethics, 107,* 255–264.

Leslie, L. Z. (2000). *Mass communication ethics: Decision making in postmodern culture.* Boston, MA: Houghton Mifflin.

Levy, A. C., & Paludi, M. A. (2002). *Workplace sexual harassment* (2nd ed.). Upper Saddle River, NJ: Prentice Hall.

Lewicki, R. (1983). Lying and deception. In M. H. Bazerman & R. J. Lewicki (Eds.), *Negotiating in organizations* (pp. 68–90). Beverly Hills, CA: SAGE.

Lewis, C. S. (1946). *The great divorce.* New York, NY: Macmillan.

Lewis, D., Medland, J., Malone, S., Murphy, M., Reno, K., & Vaccaro, G. (2006). Appreciative leadership: Defining effective leadership methods. *Organization Development Journal, 24*(1), 87–100.

Li, F., Yu, K. F., Yang, J, Qi, Z., & Fu, J. H. (2014). Authentic leadership, traditionality, and interactional justice in the Chinese context. *Management and Organization Behavior, 10,* 249–272.

Liao, Y., Liu, X-Y., Kwan, H., & Jinsong, L. (2015). Work–family effects of ethical leadership. *Journal of Business Ethics, 128,* 535–545.

Limon, M. S., & La France, B. H. (2005). Communication traits and leadership emergence: Examining the impact of argumentativeness, communication apprehension, and verbal aggressiveness in work groups. *Southern Communication Journal, 70,* 123–133.

Lin, L., Ho, Y., & Wes-Hsin, E. L. (2013). Confucian and Taoist work values: An exploratory study of the Chinese transformational leadership behavior. *Journal of Business Ethics, 113,* 91–103.

Lipman-Blumen, J. (2005). *The allure of toxic leaders: Why we follow destructive bosses and corrupt politicians—and how we can survive them.* Oxford, England: Oxford University Press.

Lisman, C. D. (1996). *The curricular integration of ethics: Theory and practice.* Westport, CT: Praeger.

Liu, S-M., Liao, J-Q., & Wei, H. (2015). Authentic leadership and whistleblowing: Mediating roles of psychological safety and personal identification. *Journal of Business Ethics, 131,* 107–119.

Livesey, S. M. (2003). Organizing and leading the grassroots: An interview with Lois Gibbs, Love Canal Homeowners Association activist. *Organization, 16,* 448–503.

Locke, E. A., & Latham, G. P. (1990). *A theory of goal setting and task performance.* Englewood Cliffs, NJ: Prentice Hall.

Locke, E. A., & Latham, G. P. (Eds.). (2013). *New developments in goal setting and task performance.* New York, NY: Routledge.

Lohr, S. (2014), Unblinking eyes track employees. *The New York Times,* p. A1.

Lonergan, B. (1957). *Insight: A study of human understanding.*

Toronto, Canada: University of Toronto Press.

Lonergan, B. (1973). *Method in theology*. Toronto, Canada: University of Toronto Press.

Lopez, S. J., Rasmussen, H. N, Skorupski, W. P., Koetting, K., Petersen, S. E., & Yang, Y. (2010). Folk conceptualizations of courage. In C. L. S. Pury & S. J. Lopez (Eds.), *The psychology of courage: Modern research on an ancient virtue* (pp. 23–45). Washington, DC: American Psychological Association.

Lowe, K. B., & Kroeck, K. G. (1996). Effectiveness correlates of transformational and transactional leadership: A meta-analytic review. *Leadership Quarterly, 7*, 385–425.

Lowenheim, N. (2009). A haunted past: Requesting forgiveness for wrongdoing in international relations. *Review of International Studies, 35*, 531–555.

Lubit, R. (2002). The long-term organizational impact of destructively narcissistic managers. *Academy of Management Executive, 18*, 127–183.

Ludwig, D. C., & Longnecker, C. O. (1993). The Bathsheba syndrome: The ethical failure of successful leaders. *Journal of Business Ethics, 12*, 265–273.

Luo, Y. (2004). An organizational perspective of corruption. *Management and Organization Review, 1*, 119–154.

Lynch, J. (2016, February 5). DEQ fires worker who supervised Flint's water. *The Detroit News*.

Ma, A. (2010). The SINS in business negotiations: Explore the cross-cultural differences in business ethics between Canada and China. *Journal of Business Ethics, 91*, 123–135.

Ma, L., & Tsui, A. S. (2015). Traditional Chinese philosophies and contemporary leadership. *Leadership Quarterly, 26*, 13–24.

Maak, T. (2007). Responsible leadership, stakeholder engagement, and the emergence of social capital. *Journal of Business Ethics, 74*, 329–343.

Maak, T. (2009). The cosmopolitical corporation. *Journal of Business Ethics, 84*, 361–372.

Maak, T., & Pless, N. M. (2006). Responsible leadership: A relational approach. In T. Maak & N. M. Press (Eds.), *Responsible leadership* (pp. 33–53). London, England: Routledge.

Maak, T., & Pless, N. M. (2006). Responsible leadership in a stakeholder society: A relational perspective. *Journal of Business Ethics, 66*, 99–115.

Maak, T., & Pless, N. M. (2009). Business leaders as citizens of the world: Advancing humanism on a global scale. *Journal of Business Ethics, 88*, 537–550.

Maas, A., & Clark, R. D. (1984). Hidden impact of minorities: Fifteen years of minority influence research. *Psychological Bulletin, 95*, 428–445.

MacAvoy, P. W., & Millstein, I. M. (2003). *The current crisis in corporate governance*. New York, NY: Palgrave Macmillan.

Maccoby, M. (2003). *The productive narcissist*. New York, NY: Broadway Books.

MacFarquhar, L. (2015). *Strangers drowning: Grappling with impossible idealism, drastic choices, and the overpowering urge to help*. New York, NY: Penguin Press.

MacIntyre, A. (1984). *After virtue: A study in moral theory* (2nd ed.). Notre Dame, IN: University of Notre Dame Press.

MacKinnon. J. B. (2015, May 21). Patagonia's anti-growth strategy. *The New Yorker*.

Macur, J. (2013, January 18). Confession, but continuing to fight. *The New York Times*, p. B11.

Magruder, S. (2015, February 12). Top 100 first world problems list. *Man's Marbles*. Retrieved from http://www.mansmarbles.com/#!Top-100-First-World-Problems-List/

Malala Yousafzai biography. (2015, December 9). *Biography.com*.

Malcolm, H., & Whitehouse, K. (2015, August 20). Subway already in trouble before Jared Fogle mess. *USA Today*, p. 1B.

Manjoo, F. (2015, August 27). Violence gone viral, in a well-planned social media rollout. *The New York Times*, p. A16.

Manley, L., Bowley, G., & Moynihand, C. (2014, December 29). Cosby team's strategy: Hush accusers, insult them, blame the media. *The New York Times*, p. C1.

Manz, C. C., & Neck, C. P. (1995). Teamthink: Beyond the groupthink syndrome in self-managing work teams. *Journal of Managerial Psychology, 10*(1), 7–15.

Manz, C. C., & Sims, H. P. (1989). *Superleadership: Leading others to lead themselves.* Upper Saddle River, NJ: Prentice Hall.

Mar, R. A., Oatley, K., Hirsch, J., dela Paz, J., & Peterson, J. B. (2006). Bookworms versus nerds: Exposure to fiction versus non-fiction, divergent associations with social ability, and the simulation of fictional social worlds. *Journal of Research in Personality, 40,* 694–712.

Mara, J. (2008, January 17). Patagonia CEO turns retailers green. *Contra Costa Times.*

Marek, A. C. (2006, February 27). A post-Katrina public flaying. *U.S. News & World Report,* 62–64.

Margolis, J. (2006). Introduction: Pragmatism, retrospective and prospective. In J. R. Shook & J. Margolis (Eds.), *A companion to pragmatism* (pp. 1–9). Malden, MA: Blackwell.

Markel, H. (2014). Ebola fever and global health responsibilities. *Milbank Quarterly, 92*(4), 633–639.

Marnham, P. (2015, June 19). The French know that Dominique Strauss-Kahn gets up to in bed—and they'd still vote for him. *Spectator Blogs.*

Marrone, J. A. (2010). Team boundary spanning: A multilevel review of past research and proposals for the future. *Journal of Management, 36,* 911–940.

Martin, G. S., Resick, C. J., Keating, M. A., & Dickson, M. W. (2009). Ethical leadership across cultures: A comparative analysis of German and US perspectives. *Business Ethics: A European Review, 18,* 127–144.

Martin, J. (2012, May 25). Clothier's products all come in green. *Los Angeles Times,* p. B1.

Martin, K. D., & Cullen, J. B. (2006). Continuities and extensions of ethical climate theory: A meta-analytic review. *Journal of Business Ethics, 69,* 175–194.

Martin, R., & Hewstone, M. (Eds.). (2010). *Minority influence and innovations: Antecedents, processes and consequences* (pp. 365–394). Hoboken, NJ: Psychology Press.

Mathews, M. C. (1990). Codes of ethics: Organizational behavior and misbehavior. In W. C. Frederick & L. E. Preston (Eds.), *Business ethics: Research issues and empirical studies* (pp. 99–122). Greenwich, CT: JAI Press.

Matteson, J. A., & Irving, J. A. (2006). Servant versus self-sacrificial leadership: A behavioral comparison of two follower-oriented leadership theories. *International Journal of Leadership Studies, 2,* 36–51.

May, D. R., Chan, A. Y. L., Hodges, T. D., & Avolio, B. J. (2003). Developing the moral component of authentic leadership. *Organizational Dynamics, 32,* 247–260.

May, D. R., & Pauli, K. P. (2002). The role of moral intensity in ethical decision-making: A review and investigation of moral recognition, evaluation, and intention. *Business & Society, 41,* 84–117.

Mayers, D., Bardes, M., & Piccolo, R. F. (2008). Do servant-leaders help satisfy follower needs? An organizational justice perspective. *European Journal of Work and Organizational Psychology, 17,* 180–197.

McCabe, D., & Trevino, L. K. (1993). Academic dishonesty:

Honor codes and other contextual influences. *Journal of Higher Education, 64,* 522–569.

McCarthy, K. (2015, August 7). Another death in Apple's 'Mordor'—its Foxconn Chinese assembly plant. *The Register.*

McCauley, C. D., & Van Velsor, E. (Eds.). (2010). *The Center for Creative Leadership handbook of leadership development* (3rd ed.). San Francisco, CA: Jossey-Bass.

McConnell, P. (2014). Reckless endangerment: The failure of HBOS. *Journal of Risk Management in Financial Institutions, 7,* 202–215.

McCue, M. (2014, July/August). Hiring a hero. *Fast Company, 187,* 50.

McCullough, M. E., Pargament, K. I., & Thoresen, C. E. (2000). The psychology of forgiveness: History, conceptual issues, and overview. In M. E. McCullough, K. I. Pargament, & C. E. Thoresen (Eds.), *Forgiveness: Theory, research, and practice* (pp. 1–14). New York, NY: Guilford.

McCullough, M. E., Sandage, S. J., & Worthington, E. L. (1997). *To forgive is human: How to put your past in the past.* Downers Grove, IL: InterVarsity Press.

McCurry, J. (2013, July 10). Fukushima boss hailed as hero dies. *The Guardian.*

McFarlin, D. B., & Sweeney, P. D. (2010). The corporate reflecting pool: Antecedents and consequences of narcissism in executives. In B. Schyns & T. Hansbrough (Eds.), *When leadership goes wrong: Destructive leadership, mistakes, and ethical failures* (pp. 247–284). Charlotte, NC: Information Age.

McKay, J. (2014, September 12). Chief resilience officers: Coming to your city? *Emergency Management*.

McKendall, M., DeMarr, B., & Jones-Rikkers, C. (2002). Ethical compliance programs and corporate illegality: Testing the assumptions of the corporate sentencing guidelines. *Journal of Business Ethics, 37*, 367–383.

McKenna, F. P. (1993). It won't happen to me: Unrealistic optimism or illusion of control? *British Journal of Psychology, 84*, 39–50.

McLaughlin, E. C. (2014, April 22). West, Texas, fertilizer plant blast that killed 15 'preventable,' safety board says. *CNN.com*.

McNamara, G., Moon, H., & Bromiley, P. (2002). Banking on commitment: Intended and unintended consequences of an organization's attempt to attenuate escalation of commitment. *Academy of Management Journal, 45*, 443–452.

McNatt, D. B. (2000). Ancient Pygmalion joins contemporary management: A meta-analysis of the result. *Journal of Applied Psychology, 85*, 314–322.

McNeill, D. (2013, March 1). I am one of the Fukushima 50. *Independent*.

McShane, L. (2015, August 20). 'The younger the girl, the better.' *Daily News*, p. 4.

McVea, J. F. (2007). Constructing good decisions in ethically charged situations: The role of dramatic rehearsal. *Journal of Business Ethics, 70*, 375–390.

McVea, J. F. (2008). Ethics and pragmatism: John Dewey's deliberative approach. In T. Donaldson & P. H. Werhane (Eds.), *Ethical issues in business: A philosophical approach* (8th ed., pp. 89–100). Upper Saddle River, NJ: Pearson Prentice Hall.

Mehta, S., & Pillay, R. (2011). Revisiting servant leadership: An empirical study in Indian context. *Journal of Contemporary Management Research, 5*(2), 24–41.

Meilander, G. (1986). Virtue in contemporary religious thought. In R. J. Neuhaus (Ed.), *Virtue: Public and private* (pp. 7–30). Grand Rapids, MI: Eerdmans.

Meisenbach, R. J. (2006). Habermas's discourse ethics and principle of universalization as a moral framework for organizational communication. *Management Communication Quarterly, 20*, 39–62.

Melchar, D. E., & Bosco, S. M. (2010). Achieving high organization performance through servant leadership. *Journal of Business Inquiry, 9*, 74–88.

Menon, V. (2015, July 9). Why are companies still buying what celebrities are selling? *The Toronto Star*, p. E1.

Menzel, D. C. (2010). *Ethics moments in government: Cases and controversies*. Boca Raton, FL: CRC Press.

Messick, D. M., & Bazerman, M. H. (1996, Winter). Ethical leadership and the psychology of decision making. *Sloan Management Review, 37*(2), 9–23.

Messing, B. (1992). *The Tao of management*. New York, NY: Bantam.

Metzger, M., Dalton, D. R., & Hill, J. W. (1993). The organization of ethics and the ethics of organizations: The case for expanded organizational ethics audits. *Business Ethics Quarterly, 3*, 27–43.

Meyer, J. (2014, June 23). Sugar subsidies are a bitter deal for American consumers. *Economics21*.

Michael Vick to work with Humane Society on its campaign against dogfighting. (2009, May 20). *Los Angeles Times*.

Michaelson, A. (2009). *The foreclosure of America: The inside story of the rise and fall of Countrywide Home Loans, the mortgage crisis, and the default of the American dream*. New York, NY: Berkley Books.

Michigan governor: Solve Flint water crisis instead of laying blame. (2016, February 5). *Reuters*.

Michigan governor's emails shine light on Flint water crisis. (2016, Feb. 7). *CNN.com*.

Milgram redux. (2008). *The Psychologist, 21*, 748–755.

Milgram, S. (1965). Some conditions of obedience and disobedience to authority. *Human Relations, 18*, 57–76.

Milkman, K. L., Chugh, D., & Bazerman, M. H. (2008). How can decision-making be improved? Harvard Business School Working Paper 08-102.

Minton-Eversol, T. (2012, July 19). Virtual teams used most by global organizations, survey says. *Society for Human Resource Management*.

Mirvis, P. H. (1997). "Soul work" in organizations. *Organization Science, 8*, 193–206.

Misra. T. (2015, April 9). Where minority populations have become the majority. *Citylab.*

Mitchell, M. S., & Palmer, N. F. (2010). The managerial relevance of ethical efficacy. In M. Schminke (Ed.), *Managerial ethics: Managing the psychology of morality* (pp. 9–108). New York, NY: Routledge.

Mitchell, S. (Trans.). (1988). *Tao te ching: A new English version.* New York, NY: Harper Perennial.

Mitroff, I. I. (2005). *Why some companies emerge stronger and better from a crisis.* New York, NY: AMACOM.

Mitroff, I. I., & Alpsaian, M. C. (2003, April). Preparing for evil. *Harvard Business Review,* 109–115.

Mitroff, I. I., & Anagnos, G. (2001). *Managing crises before they happen: What every executive and manager needs to know about crisis management.* New York, NY: American Management Association.

Mitroff, I. I., Pearson, C. M., & Harrington, L. K. (1996). *The essential guide to managing corporate crises: A step-by-step handbook for surviving major catastrophes.* New York, NY: Oxford University Press.

Moll, J., de Oliveira-Souza, R., Zahn, R., & Grafman, J. (2008). The cognitive neuroscience of moral emotions. In W. Sinnott-Armstrong (Ed.), *Moral psychology: Vol. 3. The neuroscience of morality: Emotion, brain disorders, and development* (pp. 1–17). Cambridge: MIT Press.

Monin, B., Pizarro, D. A., & Beer, J. S. (2007). Deciding versus reacting: Conceptions of moral judgment and the reason–affect debate. *Review of General Psychology, 11,* 99–111.

Monin, B., Pizarro, D. A., & Beer, J. S. (2007). Reason and emotion in moral judgment: Different prototypes lead to different theories. In K. D. Vohs, R. F. Baumeister, & G. Lowenstein (Eds.), *Do emotions help or hurt decision making? A hedgefoxian perspective* (pp. 219–244). New York, NY: Russell Sage Foundation.

Monks, R. G., & Minow, N. (2004). *Corporate governance* (3rd ed.). Malden, MA: Blackwell.

Moore, C., Detert, J. R., Trevino, L. K., Baker, V. L., & Mayer, D. M. (2012). Why employees do bad things: Moral disengagement and unethical organizational behavior. *Personnel Psychology, 65,* 1–48.

Moore, E. C. (1961). *American pragmatism: Peirce, James and Dewey.* Westport CT: Greenwood Press.

Moore, M. (2016). *10 things they won't tell you about the Flint water tragedy. But I will.* Retrieved from http://michaelmoore.com/10FactsOnFlint/

Moorhead, G., Neck, C. P., & West, M. S. (1998). The tendency toward defective decision making within self-managing teams: The relevance of groupthink for the 21st century. *Organizational Behavior and Human Decision Processes, 73,* 327–351.

Moorhead, J. (2007, May 15). Milking it. *The Guardian,* p. 8.

Mor Barak, M. E. (2011). *Managing diversity: Toward a globally inclusive workplace* (2nd ed.). Thousand Oaks, CA: SAGE.

Morrell, M., Capparell, S., & Shackleton, A. (2001). *Shackleton's way: Leadership lessons from the great Antarctic explorer.* New York, NY: Viking Press.

Morris, J. A., Brotheridge, C. M., & Urbanski, J. C. (2005). Bringing humility to leadership: Antecedents and consequences of leader humility. *Human Relations, 58,* 1323–1350.

Moscovici, S., Mucchi-Faina, A., & Maass, A. (Eds.). (1994). *Minority influence.* Chicago, IL: Nelson-Hall.

Moscovici, S., Mugny, G., & Van Avermaet, E. (Eds.). (1985). *Perspectives on minority influence.* Cambridge, England: Cambridge University Press.

Moses, A. (2012, December 23). Privacy concern as apps share data from kids left to their own devices. *Sunday Age* (Melbourne, Australia), News, p. 3.

Moutet, A. (2011, May 7). "I love women, et alors?" *The Daily Telegraph,* p. A3.

Moxley, R. S., & Pulley, M. L. (2004). Hardships. In C. D. McCauley & E. Van Velsor (Eds.), *The Center for Creative Leadership handbook of leadership development* (2nd ed., pp. 183–203). San Francisco, CA: Jossey-Bass.

Mumford, M. D., Gessner, T. L., Connelly, M. S., O'Conner, J. A., & Clifton, T. (1993). Leadership and destructive acts: Individual and situational influences. *Leadership Quarterly, 4,* 115–147.

Murphy, J. G. (2003). *Getting even: Forgiveness and its limits.* Oxford, England: Oxford University Press.

Murphy, K. (2014, November 9). The ethics of infection. *The New York Times*, p. SR5.

Musekura, C. (2010). *An assessment of contemporary models of forgiveness.* New York, NY: Peter Lang.

Mutsaka, F. (2015, September 7). Why would Zimbabwe step back from extraditing Cecil's hunter? *The Christian Science Monitor.*

Muzaffar, C. (2002). Conclusion. In P. F. Knitter & C. Muzaffar (Eds.), *Subverting greed: Religious perspectives on the global economy* (pp. 154–172). Maryknoll, NY: Orbis.

NAFDAC warns violators of BMS international code. (2007, August 7). *Africa News.*

Nagourney, A., & Goodnough, A. (2015, January 22). Measles cases linked to Disneyland, and debate over vaccinations intensifies. *The New York Times*, p. A13.

Nanus, B. (1992). *Visionary leadership.* San Francisco, CA: Jossey-Bass.

Narvaez, D. (2006). Integrative ethical education. In M. Killen & J. Smetana (Eds.), *Handbook of moral development* (pp. 717–728). Mahwah, NJ: Erlbaum.

Narvaez, D., & Lapsley, D. K. (2005). The psychological foundations of everyday morality and moral expertise. In D. K. Lapsley & F. C. Power (Eds.), *Character psychology and character education* (pp. 140–165). Notre Dame, IN: University of Notre Dame Press.

Nash, L. L. (1989). Ethics without the sermon. In K. R. Andrews (Ed.), *Ethics in practice: Managing the moral corporation* (pp. 243–257). Boston, MA: Harvard Business School Press.

Nash, L. L. (1990). *Good intentions aside: A manager's guide to resolving ethical problems.* Boston, MA: Harvard Business School Press.

Navarick, D. J. (2009). Reviving the Milgram obedience paradigm in the era of informed consent. *Psychological Record, 59,* 155–170.

Neck, C. P., & Manz, C. C. (2012). *Mastering self-leadership: Empowering yourself for personal excellence* (6th ed.). Upper Saddle River, NJ: Prentice Hall.

Neiman, S. (2002). *Evil in modern thought: An alternative history of philosophy.* Princeton, NJ: Princeton University Press.

Nemeth, C. (1994). The value of minority dissent. In S. Moscovici, A. Mucchi-Faina, & A. Maass (Eds.), *Minority influence* (pp. 3–15). Chicago, IL: Nelson-Hall.

Nemeth, C. (1995). Dissent, group process and creativity: The contribution of minority influence research. In E. Lawler (Ed.), *Advances in group processes* (Vol. 2, pp. 57–75). Greenwich, CT: JAI Press.

Nemeth, C., & Chiles, C. (1986). Modeling courage: The role of dissent in fostering independence. *European Journal of Social Psychology, 18,* 275–280.

Neubert, M. J., Carlson, D. S., Kacmar, K. M., Roberts, J. A., & Chonko, L. B. (2009). The virtuous influence of ethical leadership behavior: Evidence from the field. *Journal of Business Ethics, 90,* 157–170.

Ng, T. W. H., & Feldman, D. C. (2014). Ethical leadership: Meta-analytic evidence of criterion-related and incremental validity. *Journal of Applied Psychology, 100,* 948–965.

Nicholson, C. (2013). Education and the pragmatic temperament. In A. Malachowski (Ed.), *The Cambridge companion to pragmatism* (pp. 249–271). Cambridge, England: Cambridge University Press.

Nobles, M. (2008). *The politics of official apologies.* Cambridge, England: Cambridge University Press.

Nocera, J. (2015, August 21). Jeff Bezos and the Amazon way. *The New York Times*, Op-Ed.

Noddings, N. (2003). *Caring: A feminine approach to ethics and moral education.* Berkeley: University of California Press.

North Korea committed crimes against humanity, but not genocide: U.N. commission chief. (2015, February 18). *The Japan Times.*

Not so smart. (2015, November 28). *The Economist.*

Nye, J. S. (2008). *The powers to lead.* Oxford, England: Oxford University Press.

Nzou, G. (2015, August 5). In Zimbabwe, we don't cry for lions. *The New York Times*, p. A19.

Oatley, K. (2008). The mind's flight simulator. *Psychologist, 21,* 1030–1032.

Obermann, M. L. (2011). Moral disengagement among bystanders to school bullying. *Journal of School Violence, 10,* 239–257.

Obermann, M. L. (2011). Moral disengagement in self-reported and peer-nominated school bullying. *Aggressive Behavior, 37,* 133–134.

O'Boyle, E. H., Jr., Forsyth, D. R., Banks, G. C., & McDaniel, M. A. (2012). A meta-analysis of the dark triad and work behavior: A social exchange perspective. *Journal of Applied Psychology, 97,* 557–579.

O'Connor, A. (2015, August 9). Coca-Cola funds scientists who shift blame for obesity away from bad diets. *The New York Times,* p. A1.

O'Fallon, M. J., & Butterfield, K. D. (2005). A review of the empirical ethical decision-making literature: 1996–2003. *Journal of Business Ethics, 59,* 375–413.

Olinto, P., Beegle, K., Sobrado, C., & Uematsu, H. (2013, October). The state of the poor. *Economic Premise* (The World Bank).

Olmsted, K. S. (2009). *Real enemies: Conspiracy theories and American democracy, World War I to 9/11.* Oxford, England: Oxford University Press.

Onishi, N. (2014, August 20). Clashes erupt as Liberia sets an Ebola quarantine. *The New York Times,* p. A1.

Onishi, N. (2015, August 11). Best way to save Africa's lions? Hunt them, some experts say. *The New York Times,* p. A1.

Onorato, M., & Zhu, J. (2014, Winter). An empirical study on the relationships between authentic leadership and organizational trust by industry segment. *SAM Advanced Management Journal,* 26–39.

Opotow, S. (1990). Deterring moral exclusion. *Journal of Social Issues, 46*(1), 173–182.

Opotow, S. (1990). Moral exclusion and injustice: An introduction. *Journal of Social Issues, 46*(1), 1–20.

Opotow, S. (2007). Moral exclusion and torture: The ticking bomb scenario and the slippery ethical slope. *Peace and Conflict: Journal of Peace Psychology, 13,* 457–461.

Opotow, S., Gerson, J., & Woodside, S. (2005). From moral exclusion to moral inclusion: Theory for teaching peace. *Theory Into Practice, 44,* 303–318.

Opotow, S., & Weiss, L. (2000). Denial and the process of moral exclusion in environmental conflict. *Journal of Social Issues, 56,* 475–490.

Oppel, R. A. (2014, March 3). Military sex assault trial showcases 2 approaches to prosecution. *The New York Times,* p. A12.

O'Shea, J. (2015, August 21). The leak that could end your marriage. *Irish Independent,* pp. 34, 35.

Osswald, S., Greitemeyer, T., Fischer, P., & Frey, D. (2010). What is moral courage? Definition, explication, and classification of a complex construct. In C. L. S. Pury & S. J. Lopez (Eds.), *The psychology of courage: Modern research on an ancient virtue* (pp. 149–164). Washington, DC: American Psychological Association.

Oswick, C. (2009). Burgeoning workplace spirituality? A textual analysis of momentum and directions. *Journal of Management, Spirituality & Religion, 6,* 15–25.

Otken, A. B., & Cenkci, T. (2012). The impact of paternalistic

leadership on ethical climate: The moderating role of trust in leader. *Journal of Business Ethics, 108,* 525–536.

Oum, R., & Lieberman, D. (2007). Emotion is cognition: An information-processing view of the mind. In K. D. Vohs, R. F. Baumeister, & G. Lowenstein (Eds.), *Do emotions help or hurt decision making? A hedgefoxian perspective* (pp. 133–154). New York, NY: Russell Sage Foundation.

Pacanowsky, M. E., & O'Donnell-Trujillo, N. (1983). Organizational communication as cultural performance. *Communication Monographs, 5,* 126–147.

Padilla, A., Hogan, R., & Kaiser, R. B. (2007). The toxic triangle: Destructive leaders, susceptible followers, and conducive environments. *Leadership Quarterly, 18,* 176–194.

Pagan, N. O. (2008). Configuring the moral self: Aristotle and Dewey. *Foundations of Science, 13,* 239–250.

Pagliery, J. (2014). Apps aimed at children collect a shocking amount of data. *CNN.*

Paine, L. S. (1996, March–April). Managing for organizational integrity. *Harvard Business Review,* 106–117.

Paine, L. S., Deshpandé, R., Margolis, J. D., & Bettcher, K. E. (2005, December). Up to code: Does your company meet world-class standards? *Harvard Business Review,* 122–133.

Palanski, M. E., & Yammarino, F. J. (2007). Integrity and leadership: A multi-level conceptual framework. *Leadership Quarterly, 20,* 405–420.

Palmer, P. (1996). Leading from within. In L. C. Spears (Ed.), *Insights on leadership: Service, stewardship, spirit, and servant-leadership* (pp. 197–208). New York, NY: John Wiley.

The Panama Papers: Here's what we know. (2016, April 4). *The New York Times*.

Panchak, P. (2002). Time for a triple bottom line. *Industry Week*, p. 7.

Parbotheeah, K. P., Martin, K. D., & Cullen, J. B. (2014). An international perspective on ethical climate. In N. M. Ashkanasy, C. P. M. Wilderom, & M. F. Peterson (Eds.), *The handbook of organizational culture and climate* (2nd ed., pp. 600–617). Los Angeles, CA: SAGE.

Park, G., & DeShon, R. P. (2010). A multilevel model of minority opinion expression and team decision-making effectiveness. *Journal of Applied Psychology, 95*, 824–853.

Park, R. (2012, November 24). Genocide and crimes of humanity ongoing in North Korea. *Forbes*.

Park, R. (2013, July/August). The forgotten genocide: North Korea's prison state. *World Affairs Journal*.

Parker, C. F. (2011). The purpose, functions, and ethical dimensions of postcrisis investigations: The case of the 9/11 Commission. In L. Svedin (Ed.), *Ethics and crisis management* (pp. 183–198). Charlotte NC: Information Age.

Parker-Pope, T. (2015, January 6). In with the new mission statement. *The New York Times*, p. D4.

Parliamentary Commission on Banking Standards. (2013).

An accident waiting to happen: The failure of HBOS. House of Commons, London, England.

Pauchant, T. C., & Mitroff, I. I. (1992). *Transforming the crisis-prone organization: Preventing individual, organizational, and environmental tragedies.* San Francisco, CA: Jossey-Bass.

Paul, J., & Strbiak, C. A. (1997). The ethics of strategic ambiguity. *Journal of Business Communication, 34*, 149–159.

Paulus, D. L., & Williams, K. M. (2002). The dark triad of personality: Narcissism, Machiavellianism, and psychopathy. *Journal of Research in Personality, 36*, 556–563.

Pearce, M. (2014, September 27). Growing use of police body cameras raises privacy concerns. *Los Angeles Times*.

Pearson, C. M., & Judith, A. C. (1998). Reframing crisis management. *Academy of Management Review 23*, 59–71.

Pearson, C. M., & Porath, C. L. (2004). On incivility, its impact and directions for future research. In R. W. Griffin & A. M. O'Leary-Kelly (Eds.), *The dark side of organizational behavior* (pp. 131–158). San Francisco, CA: Jossey-Bass.

Pearson, C. M., & Porath, C. L. (2005). On the nature, consequences and remedies of workplace incivility: No time for "nice"? Think again. *Academy of Management Executive, 19*, 7–18.

Pearson, G. (1995). *Integrity in organizations: An alternative business ethic.* London, England: McGraw-Hill.

Peck, M. S. (1983). *People of the lie: The hope for healing human evil.* New York, NY: Touchstone.

Pedicini, S. (2015, October 6). Anti-immigration activists plan Disney protest, call for boycott. *Orlando Sentinel*.

Pellegrini, E. K., & Scandura, T. A. (2008). Paternalistic leadership: A review and agenda for future research. *Journal of Management, 34*, 566–593.

Perez, C. (2015, August 5). Lion-killing dentist hires ex-cops to protect vacation home. *New York Post*.

Perez, J. (2006, December 4). Yellow pad: What the milk companies don't want you to know. *BusinessWorld*, 1–5.

Perkins, D. N. T. (2000). *Leading at the edge.* New York, NY: AMACOM

Perkins, L. (2015, June 30). California governor signs school vaccination law. *NPR*.

Perlman, L. R., & Roberts, K. (2014). The ethics of state policies restricting access to infant formula and their impact on women's and children's health. In L. Boyd-Judson & P. James (Eds.), *Women's global health: Norms and state policies* (pp. 91–113). Lanham, MD: Lexington Books.

Perrone, M. (2015, November 4). Senate panel summons price-hiking CEO of Turing Pharma. *Associated Press*.

Perrow, C. (1999). *Normal accidents: Living with high-risk technologies.* Princeton, NJ: Princeton University Press.

Peters, T. (1992). *Liberation management.* New York, NY: Ballantine.

Peterson, C., & Seligman, M. E. P. (2004). *Character strengths and virtues: A handbook and classification.* Oxford, England: Oxford University Press.

Peterson, D. K. (2002). The relationship between unethical behavior and the dimensions of the Ethical Climate Questionnaire. *Journal of Business Ethics, 41,* 313–326.

Peterson, S. (2008, August 6). In K2 aftermath, lessons learned. *The Christian Science Monitor.*

Petesch, C. (2015, August 23). With many Ebola survivors ailing, doctors evaluate situation. *Associated Press.*

Petit, V., & Bollaert, H. (2012). Flying too close to the sun? Hubris among CEOS and how to prevent it. *Journal of Business Ethics, 108,* 265–283.

Petrick, J. A. (1998). Building organizational integrity and quality with the four Ps: Perspectives, paradigms, processes, and principles. In M. Schminke (Ed.), *Managerial ethics: Moral management of people and processes* (pp. 115–131). Mahwah, NJ: Erlbaum.

Petrick, J. A. (2008). Using the business integrity capacity model to advance business ethics education. In D. L. Swanson & D. G. Fisher (Eds.), *Advancing business ethics education* (pp. 103–124). Charlotte, NC: Information Age.

Peus, C., Wesche, J. S., Streicher, B., Braun, S., & Frey, D. (2012).

Authentic leadership: An empirical test of its antecedents, consequences, and mediating mechanisms. *Journal of Business Ethics, 107,* 331–348.

Pfaff, C. A., Reich, T., Redman, W., & Hurley, M. (2011). Ethics in dangerous situations. In P. Sweeney, M. D. Matthews, & P. B. Lester (Eds.), *Leadership in dangerous situations: A handbook for the armed forces, emergency, services, and first responders* (pp. 121–138). Annapolis, MD: Naval Institute Press.

Pfeffer, J. (1992, Winter). Understanding power in organizations. *California Management Review, 34,* 29–50.

Pfeffer, J. (2015). *Leadership BS: Fixing workplaces and careers one truth at a time.* New York, NY: HarperBusiness.

Phillip, A. (2015, May 21). Texas hunter who paid $350,000 to kill an endangered rhino has bagged his prey. *The Washington Post.*

Philips, R. (2003). *Stakeholder theory and organizational ethics.* San Francisco, CA: Berrett-Koehler.

Picchi, A. (2016, March 30). 'Woody breast' could bite the chicken business. *CBS News.*

Pierce, J. L., & Newstrom, J. W. (2011). *Leaders and the leadership process: Readings, self-assessments and applications* (6th ed.). New York, NY: McGraw-Hill.

Piliavin, J. A., & Chang, H. W. (1990). Altruism: A review of recent theory and research. *American Sociological Review, 16,* 27–65.

Pittinsky, T. L. (2010). A two-dimensional model of intergroup

leadership: The case of national diversity. *American Psychologist, 65,* 194–200.

Pittinsky, T. L., & Simon, S. (2007). Intergroup leadership. *Leadership Quarterly, 18,* 586–605.

Pless, N. M. (2007). Understanding responsible leadership: Role identity and motivational drivers. *Journal of Business Ethics, 74,* 437–456.

Pless, N. M., & Maak, T. (2009). Responsible leaders as agents of world benefit: Learnings from "Project Ulysses." *Journal of Business Ethics, 85,* 59–71.

Pless, N. M., & Maak, T. (2011). Responsible leadership: Pathways to the future. *Journal of Business Ethics, 98,* 3–13.

Plucinska, J. (2015, July 22). Twenty percent of the Canadian capital's residents are registered on Ashley Madison. *Time.com.*

Podsakoff, P. M., MacKenzie, S. B., Moorman, R. H., & Fetter, R. (1990). Transformational leader behaviors and their effects on followers' trust in leader, satisfaction, and organizational citizenship behavior. *Leadership Quarterly, 1,* 107–142.

Pogatchnik, S. (2010, March 14). Abuse scandals hit Catholic Church across Europe. *The Oregonian,* p. A11.

Pogge, T. (1992). Cosmopolitanism and sovereignty. *Ethics 103*(1), 48–75.

Politics, power and sex. (2011, May 21). *Belfast Telegraph,* p. 20.

Pollack, A. (2015, September 21). Once a neglected treatment, now an expensive specialty drug. *The New York Times*, p. B1.

Pollack, A. (2015, October 13). New York Attorney General examining if Turing restricted drug access. *The New York Times*, p. B4.

Pollack, A., & Creswell, J. (2015, September 23). The man behind the drug price increase. *The New York Times*, p. B1.

Pollack, A., & Tavernise, S. (2015, October 18). Big price hikes put spotlight on drugmakers. *The Oregonian*, pp. D1, D2.

Pollard, C. W. (1996). *The soul of the firm.* Grand Rapids, MI: HarperBusiness.

Polman, D. (2015, June 1). Dennis Hastert completes the hypocrisy trifecta. *NewsWorks*.

Pope, J. (2011, October 11). New caution for US universities overseas. *Associated Press*.

Porath, C. L., & Erez, A. (2007). Does rudeness really matter? The effects of rudeness on task performance and helpfulness. *Academy of Management Journal, 50*, 1181–1197.

Porubcansky, M. (2015, July 30). Cecil the lion had a better life than most people in Zimbabwe. *MinnPost*.

Power, M. (2008, November). K2: The killing peak. *Men's Journal.*

Powers, C. W., & Vogel, D. (1980). *Ethics in the education of business managers.* Hastings-on-Hudson, NY: Institute of Society, Ethics and the Life Sciences.

Pradhan, S., & Pradhan, R. K. (2015). An empirical investigation of relationship among transformational leadership, affective organizational commitment and contextual performance. *Vision, 19*, 227–235.

Prati, L. M., Douglas, C., Ferris, G. R., Ammeter, A. P., & Buckley, M. R. (2003). Emotional intelligence, leadership effectiveness, and team outcomes. *International Journal of Organizational Analysis, 11*, 21–40.

Pratkanis, A., & Aronson, E. (2001). *Age of propaganda: The everyday use and abuse of persuasion.* New York, NY: Holt.

Press Association. (2006, January 28). Ex-HBOS bosses face City bans as watchdogs launch bank failure probes. *Daily Mail.* Retrieved from http://www.bankofengland.co.uk/pra/documents/publications/reports/hbos.pdf

Preston, J. (2015, June 4). Pink slips at Disney. But first, training foreign replacements. *The New York Times*, p. A1.

Preston, J. (2015, June 12). Outsourcing companies under scrutiny over visas for technology workers. *The New York Times*, p. A17.

Preston, J. (2015, September 29). Toys 'R' Us brings temporary foreign workers to U.S. to move jobs overseas. *The New York Times*.

Price, T. L. (2006). *Understanding ethical failures in leadership.* Cambridge, England: Cambridge University Press.

Profile, C. (2015, April 26). Love 'em or hate 'em, sea lions raise concerns on the Columbia. *Oregon Public Broadcasting.*

Provis, C. (2010). Virtuous decision making for business ethics. *Journal of Business Ethics, 91*, 3–6.

Pruitt, D. G. (1983). Achieving integrative agreements. In M. H. Bazerman & R. J. Lewicki (Eds.), *Negotiating in organizations* (pp. 35–50). Beverly Hill, CA: SAGE

Puffer, S. M., & McCarthy, D. J. (2008). Ethical turnarounds and transformational leadership: A global imperative for corporate social responsibility. *Thunderbird International Business Review, 50*, 304–314.

Pulley, B. (2005, October 17). Last days of the lion king. *Forbes.*

Quenqua, D. (2012, October 21). Clinic raffles could make you a winner, and maybe a mother. *The New York Times*, p. A1.

Quigley, N. R., Sully de Luque, M., & House, R. J. (2005). Responsible leadership and governance in a global context: Insights from the GLOBE study. In J. P. Doh & S. A. Sumpf (Eds.), *Handbook on responsible leadership and governance in global business* (pp. 352–379). Cheltenham, England: Edward Elgar.

Rahimina, F., & Sharifirad, M. S. (2015). Authentic leadership and employee well-being: The mediating role of attachment insecurity. *Journal of Business Ethics, 132*, 363–377.

Rainey, M. (2012, April/May). Fired before you're hired. *INSIGHT into Diversity*, 18–21.

Rajah, R., & Arvey, R. D. (2013). Helping group members develop resilience. In A. J. DuBrin (Ed.), *Handbook of research on crisis* leadership in organizations (pp. 149–173). Cheltenham, England: Edward Elgar.

Ramesh, R. (2008, August 5). K2 tragedy: Death toll on world's most treacherous mountain reaches 11. *The Guardian,* Home Pages, p. 2.

Rampersad, A. (1997). *Jackie Robinson.* New York, NY: Alfred A. Knopf.

Ramzy, A. (2013, January 24). After successful missile launch, North Korea threatens new nuclear test. *Time.*

Rancer, A. S., & Avtgis, T. A. (2006). *Argumentative and aggressive communication: Theory, research, and application.* Thousand Oaks, CA: SAGE.

Ransley, C., & Spy, T. (Eds.). (2004). *Forgiveness and the healing process: A central therapeutic concern.* New York, NY: Brunner-Routledge.

Rapisarda, B. A. (2002). The impact of emotional intelligence on work team cohesiveness and performance. *International Journal of Organizational Analysis, 10,* 363–370.

Rasche, A., & Gilbert, D. U. (2012). Institutionalizing global governance: The role of the United Nations Global Compact. *Business Ethics: A European Review, 21,* 100–114.

Rawls, J. (1971). *A theory of justice.* Cambridge, MA: Belknap.

Rawls, J. (1993). Distributive justice. In T. Donaldson & P. H. Werhane (Eds.), *Ethical issues in business: A philosophical approach* (4th ed., pp. 274–285). Englewood Cliffs, NJ: Prentice Hall.

Rawls, J. (1993). *Political liberalism.* New York, NY: Columbia University Press.

Rawls, J. (2001). *Justice as fairness: A restatement* (E. Kelly, Ed.). Cambridge, MA: Belknap.

Reave, L. (2005). Spiritual values and practices related to leadership effectiveness. *Leadership Quarterly, 16,* 655–687.

Reb, J., Goldman, B. M., Kray, L. J., & Cropanzano, R. (2006). Different wrongs, different remedies? Reactions to organizational remedies after procedural and interactional injustice. *Personnel Psychology, 59,* 31–64.

Reed, L. L., Vidaver-Cohen, D., & Colwell, S. R. (2011). A new scale to measure executive servant leadership: Development, analysis, and implications for research. *Journal of Business Ethics, 101,* 415–434.

Regester, M., & Larkin, J. (2005). *Risk issues and crisis management: A casebook of best practice* (3rd ed.). London, England: Kogan Page.

Rego, A., & Pina e Cunha, M. (2008). Workplace spirituality and organizational commitment: An empirical study. *Journal of Organizational Change Management, 21,* 53–75.

Renati, R., Berrone, C., & Zaneti, M. A. (2012). Morally disengaged and unempathetic: Do cyberbullies fit these definitions? An exploratory study. *Cyberpsychology, Behavior, and Social Networking, 15,* 391–398.

Resick, C. J., Hanges, P. J., Dickson, M. W., & Mitchelson, J. K. (2006). A cross-cultural examination of the endorsement of ethical leadership.

Journal of Business Ethics, 63, 345–359.

Resick, C. J., Martin, G. S., Keating, M. A., Dickson, M. W., Kwan, H. K., & Peng, C. (2011). What ethical leadership means to me: Asian, American, and European perspectives. *Journal of Business Ethics, 101,* 435–457.

Rest, J. R. (1986). *Moral development: Advances in research and theory.* New York, NY: Praeger.

Rest, J. R. (1993). Research on moral judgment in college students. In A. Garrod (Ed.), *Approaches to moral development* (pp. 201–211). New York, NY: Teachers College Press.

Rest, J. R. (1994). Background: Theory and research. In J. R. Rest & D. Narvaez (Eds.), *Moral development in the professions: Psychology and applied ethics* (pp. 1–25). Hillsdale, NJ: Erlbaum.

Rest, J. R., & Narvaez, D. (1991). The college experience and moral development. In W. M. Kurtines & J. L. Gewirtz (Eds.), *Handbook of moral behavior and development: Vol. 2. Research* (pp. 229–245). Hillsdale, NJ: Erlbaum.

Rest, J. R., Narvaez, D., Bebeau, M. J., & Thoma, S. J. (1999). *Postconventional moral thinking: A neo-Kohlbergian approach.* Mahwah, NJ: Erlbaum.

Reynolds, S. J. (2006). A neurocognitive model of the ethical decision-making process: Implications for study and practice. *Journal of Applied Psychology, 91,* 737–748.

Reynolds, S. J. (2008). Moral attentiveness: Who pays attention to the moral aspects of life? *Journal of Applied Psychology, 93,* 1027–1041.

Reynolds, S. J., & Ceranic, T. L. (2007). The effects of moral judgment and moral identity on moral behavior: An empirical examination of the moral individual. *Journal of Applied Psychology, 92*(6), 1610–1624.

Rezaee, A. (2009). *Corporate governance and ethics.* Hoboken, NJ: Wiley.

Rhoads, K. V. L., & Cialdini, R. B. (2002). The business of influence: Principles that lead to success in commercial settings. In J. P. Dillard & M. Pfau (Eds.), *The persuasion handbook* (pp. 513–542). Thousand Oaks, CA: SAGE.

Rich, N. (2015, August 9). Hurricane's wake. *The New York Times,* p. BR11.

Richter, A. W., West, M. A., Van Dick, R., & Dawson, J. F. (2006). Boundary spanners' identification, intergroup contact, and effective intergroup relations. *Academy of Management Journal, 49,* 1252–1269.

Richter, J. (2001). *Holding corporations accountable: Corporate conduct, international codes and citizen action.* London, England: Zed.

Rid, A., & Emanuel, E. J. (2014, October 1). Why should high-income countries help combat Ebola? *Journal of the American Medical Association, 312*(13), 1297–1298.

Riggio, R. E., Zhu, W., Reina, C., & Maroosis, J. A. (2010). Virtue-based measurement of ethical leadership: The Leadership Virtues Questionnaire. *Consulting Psychology Journal: Practice and Research, 62*(4), 235–250.

The rise of workplace spying. (2015, July 5). *The Week.*

Ritzer, G. (2004). *The globalization of nothing.* Thousand Oaks, CA: Pine Forge.

Rivlin, G. (2015). *Katrina: After the flood.* New York, NY: Simon & Schuster.

Roberto, M. A. (2005). *Why great leaders don't take yes for an answer.* Upper Saddle River, NJ: Wharton School Publishing.

Roberts, K. H. (2006). Some characteristics of one type of high reliability organization. In D. Smith & D. Elliott (Eds.), *Key readings in crisis management: Systems and structures for prevention and recovery* (pp. 159–179). London, England: Routledge.

Roberts, P. F. (2015, August 20). The troubling ripple effect of the Ashley Madison data dump. *Christian Science Monitor.*

Roberts, T. P., & Zigarmi, D. (2014). The impact of dispositional cynicism on job-specific affect and work intentions. *International Journal of Psychology, 49,* 381–389.

Robertson, C. (2015, August 30). A decade after Katrina, New Orleans is partying again, and still rebuilding. *The New York Times,* p. A15.

Robins, F. (2006). The challenge of TBL: A responsibility to whom? *Business and Society Review, 111,* 1–14.

Robinson, R. J., Lewicki, R. J., & Donahue, E. M. (2000). Extending and testing a five factor model of ethical and unethical barging tactics: Introducing the SINS scale. *Journal of Organizational Behavior, 21,* 649–664.

Rochlin, G. I., LaPorte, T. R., & Roberts, K. H. (1987). The self-designing high-reliability organization: Aircraft carrier flight operations at sea. *Naval War College Review, 40*(4), 76–90.

Rockman, K. W., & Northcraft, G. B. (2006). The ethical implications of virtual interaction. In A. E. Tenbrunsel (Ed.), *Ethics in groups* (pp. 101–123). Oxford, England: Elsevier.

Rockness, H., & Rockness, J. (2005). Legislated ethics: From Enron to Sarbanes-Oxley, the impact on corporate America. *Journal of Business Ethics, 57,* 31–54.

Rogers, B. (2013, January 29). North Korea in the dark. *The New York Times,* Op-Ed.

Rogers, E. M., & Steinfatt, T. M. (1999). *Intercultural communication.* Prospect Heights, IL: Waveland.

Rogers, K. (2015, July 31). U.S. and U.N. respond to killing of lion in Zimbabwe. *The New York Times,* p. A6.

Rohman, J. (n.d.). *With an "employee-first" mentality, everyone wins.* Retrieved from http://www. greatplacetowork.com

Roig-Franzia, M. (2015, August 23). A bittersweet influx. *The Washington Post,* p. A01.

Roig-Franzia, M., Higham, S., Farhi, P., & Flaherty, M. P. (2014, November 24). Revealed: The case against Bill Cosby. *The Independent* (UK).

Roloff, M. E., & Paulson, G. D. (2001). Confronting organizational transgressions. In J. M. Darley, D. M. Messick, & T. R. Tyler (Eds.), *Social influences on ethical behavior in organizations* (pp. 53–68). Mahwah, NJ: Erlbaum.

Rosanas, J. M., & Velilla, M. (2003). Loyalty and trust as the ethical bases of organizations. *Journal of Business Ethics, 44,* 49–59.

Rosenberg, T. (2011, November 24). An electronic eye on hospital hand-washing. *The New York Times,* Opinionator blog.

Rosenfeld, P., Giacalone, R. A., & Riordan, C. A. (1995). *Impression management in organizations: Theory, measurement, practice.* London, England: Routledge.

Rosenthal, R. (1993). Interpersonal expectations: Some antecedents and some consequences. In P. D. Blank (Ed.), *Interpersonal expectations: Theory, research, and applications* (pp. 3–24). Cambridge, England: Cambridge University Press.

Ross, J., & Staw, B. M. (1993). Organizational escalation and exit: Lessons from the Shoreham Nuclear Plant. *Academy of Management Journal, 36,* 701–732.

Rossman, J. (2014). *The Amazon Way: 14 leadership principles behind the world's most disruptive company.* North Charleston, SC: CreateSpace Independent Publishing Platform.

Roth, B. (2015, April 22). After 60 years, a final lap for Al Buehler. *Duke Magazine*

Rowley, A. (2011, March 24). Fukushima fifty: Japan's new heroes. *The Business Times Singapore.*

Royce, J. (1920). *The philosophy of loyalty.* New York, NY: Macmillan.

Rubin, R. S., Dierdorff, E. C., & Brown, M. E. (2010). Do ethical leaders get ahead? Exploring ethical leadership and promotability. *Business Ethics Quarterly, 20,* 215–236.

Ruschman, N. L. (2002). Servant-leadership and the best companies to work for in America. In L. C. Spears & M. Lawrence (Eds.), *Focus on leadership: Servant-leadership for the twenty-first century* (pp. 123–139). New York, NY: John Wiley.

Rushton, J. P., Chrisjohn, R. D., & Fekken, G. C. (1981). The altruistic personality and the self-report altruism scale. *Personality and Individual Differences, 2,* 293–302.

Russell, R. F., & Stone, A. G. (2002). A review of servant leadership attributes: Developing a practical model. *Leadership & Organization Development Journal, 23*(3), 145–157.

Ryan, K. (2014, July 31). The bottom line: Patagonia, North Face, and the myth of green consumerism. *Groundswell.*

Rybacki, K. C., & Rybacki, D. J. (2004). *Advocacy and opposition: An introduction to argumentation.* Boston, MA: Pearson.

Sachs, J. (2015, August 27). Subway's silence over the Fogle fiasco leaves a bad taste. *The Guardian.*

Sack, K., Fink, S., Belluck, P., & Nossiter, A. (2014, December 29). How Ebola roared back. *The New York Times,* p. D1.

Salvador, R., & Folger, R. G. (2009). Business ethics and the brain. *Business Ethics Quarterly, 19,* 1–31.

Sanborn, J. (2016, February 3). The toxic tap. *Time,* 34–39.

Sandler, M. (2015, August 8). CEO pay soars at top not-for-profits. *Modern Health Care.*

Sanford, N., & Comstock, C. (Eds.). (1971). *Sanctions for evil.* San Francisco, CA: Jossey-Bass.

Sauser, W. I. (2011). Beyond the classroom: Business ethics training for professionals. In R. R. Sims & W. I. Sauser (Eds.), *Experiences in teaching business ethics* (pp. 247–261). Charlotte, NC: Information Age.

Savage, D. G. (2004, January 17). Trip with Cheney puts ethics spotlight on Scalia. *Los Angeles Times.*

Sawyer, K. (2003, August 24). Shuttle's "smoking gun" took time to register. *The Washington Post,* p. A1.

Scarre, G. (2010). *On courage.* London, England: Routledge.

Schaler, J. A. (Ed.). (2009). *Peter Singer under fire.* Chicago, IL: Open Court/Carus.

Schawbel, D. (2014, October 7). Kip Tindell: How he created an employee-first culture at The Container Store. *Forbes.*

Schlanger, Z. (2015, January 19). New York University: A case study in what not to do. *NYTimes.com.*

Schrag, B. (2001). The moral significance of employee loyalty. *Business Ethics Quarterly, 11,* 41–66.

Schriesheim, C. A., Castor, S. L., & Cogliser, C. C. (1999). Leader–member exchange (LMX) research: A comprehensive review of theory, measurement, and data-analytic practices. *Leadership Quarterly, 10*, 63–114.

Schubert, S., & Miller, T. C. (2008, December 21). Where bribery was just a line item. *The New York Times*, p. BU1.

Schulte, L. E. (2001). Graduate education faculty and student perceptions of the ethical climate and its importance in the retention of students. *College Student Retention, 3*, 119–136.

Schulte, L. E. (2002). A comparison of cohort and non-cohort graduate student perceptions of the ethical climate and its importance in retention. *Journal of College Student Retention, 4*, 29–38.

Schulte, L. E., & Carter, A. F. (2004). An assessment of a college of business administration's ethical climate. *The Delta Pi Epsilon Journal, XLVI*, 18–29.

Schulte, L. E., Thompson, F., Hayes, K., Noble, J., & Jacobs, E. (2001). Undergraduate faculty and student perceptions of the ethical climate and its importance in retention. *College Student Journal, 35*, 565–576.

Schultz, B. (1982). Argumentativeness: Its effect in group decision-making and its role in leadership perception. *Communication Quarterly, 3*, 368–375.

Schultz, H., & Gordon, J. (2011). *Onward: How Starbucks fought for its life without losing its soul*. New York, NY: Rodale.

Schultz, M. (2014). *Foxcatcher*. New York, NY: Dutton.

Schuman, S. (2010). *The handbook for working with difficult groups: How they are difficult, why they are difficult and what you can do about it*. Chichester, England: Wiley.

Schwartz, A. (2007, January 18). Expert ties ex-player's suicide to brain damage from football. *The New York Times*, p A1.

Schwartz, T. (2015, August 21). Why Jeff Bezos should care more for Amazon's employees. *The New York Times*.

Schweiger, D. M., Sandberg, W. R., & Rechner, P. (1989). Experiential effects of dialectical inquiry, devil's advocacy, and consensus approaches to strategic decision making. *Academy of Management Journal, 32*, 745–772.

Schwepker, D. H., & Schultz, R. J. (2015). Influence of the ethical servant leader and ethical climate on customer value enhancing sales performance. *Journal of Personal Selling & Sales Management, 35*, 93–107.

Schyns, B., & Schilling, J. (2013). How bad are the effects of bad leaders? A meta-analysis of destructive leadership and its outcomes. *Leadership Quarterly, 24*, 138–158.

Seattle Department of Construction and Inspections. (2015, January 9). *Seattle permits: Demolition and deconstruction*. Retrieved from http://www.seattle.gov/sdci

Seeger, M. W., Sellnow, T. L., & Ulmer, R. R. (2003). *Communication and organizational crisis*. Westport, CT: Praeger.

Sellnow, T. L., & Seeger, M. W. (2013). *Theorizing crisis communication*. Malden, MA: Wiley-Blackwell.

Sendjaya, S., Perketi, A., Hartel, C., Hirst, G., & Butarbutar, I. (2016). Are authentic leaders always moral? The role of Machiavellianism in the relationship between authentic leadership and morality. *Journal of Business Ethics, 133*, 125–139.

Sendjaya, S., & Sarros, J. C. (2002). Servant leadership: Its origin, development, and application in organizations. *Journal of Leadership & Organizational Studies, 9*(2), 57–64.

Sengupta, S. (2015, July 8). Panel calls W.H.O. unfit to handle a crisis like Ebola. *The New York Times*, p. A7.

Shackleton, E. (1998). *South: A memoir of the Endurance voyage*. New York, NY: Carroll & Graf.

Shamir, B. (2007). From passive recipients to active co-producers: Followers' roles in the leadership process. In B. Shamir, R. Pillai, M. C. Bligh, & M. Uhl-Bien (Eds.), *Follower-centered perspectives on leadership* (pp. ix–xxxix). Greenwich CT: Information Age.

Shao, R., Aquino, K., & Freeman, D. (2008). Beyond moral reasoning: A review of moral identity research and its implications for business ethics. *Business Ethics Quarterly, 18*, 513–540.

Shaw, J. B., Erickson, A., & Harvey, M. (2011). A method for measuring destructive leadership and identifying types of destructive leaders in organizations. *Leadership Quarterly, 22*, 575–590.

Shear, M. D., Perez-Pena, R., & Blinder, A. (2015, August 27). Gunman kills 2 on air and posts carnage online. *The New York Times*, p. A1.

Shen, H. (2011, July 26). Wealth gap between whites, minorities widens to greatest level in a quarter century. *Huffington Post*.

Shenton, Z. (2015, August 21). Who is Josh Duggar? All you need to know after shamed TV star is exposed in Ashley Madison hack. *Irish Mirror*, Showbiz News.

Shields, C. (2014). *Aristotle* (2nd ed.). New York, NY: Routledge.

Shin, L. (2014, January 23). The 85 richest people in the world have as much as the 3.5 billion poorest. *Forbes*. Retrieved from http://www.forbes.com

Shockley-Zalabak, P. S. (2006). *Fundamentals of organizational communication: Knowledge, sensitivity, skills, values* (6th ed.). Boston, MA: Pearson.

Shockley-Zalabak, P. S., Ellis, K., & Cesaria, R. (2000). *Measuring organizational trust: A diagnostic survey and international indicator*. San Francisco, CA: International Association of Business Communicators.

Shockley-Zalabak, P. S., Ellis, K., & Winograd, G. (2000). Organizational trust: What it means, why it matters. *Organization Development Journal, 18*(4), 35–48.

Shockley-Zalabak, P. S., Morreale, S. P., & Hackman, M. Z. (2010). *Building the high-trust organization: Strategies for supporting five key dimensions of trust*. San Francisco, CA: Jossey-Bass.

Shriver, D. W. (1995). *An ethic for enemies: Forgiveness in politics*. New York, NY: Oxford University Press.

Shriver, D. W. (2001). Forgiveness: A bridge across abysses of revenge. In R. G. Helmick & R. L. Peterson (Eds.), *Forgiveness and reconciliation: Religion, public policy, and conflict transformation* (pp. 151–167). Philadelphia, PA: Templeton Foundation Press.

Shu, L. L., Gino, F., & Bazerman, M. H. (2009). Dishonest deed, clear conscience: Self-preservation through moral disengagement and motivated forgetting. Harvard Business School Working Paper 09-078.

Silverman, D. (2013, August 16). *Demolition of dwelling units is strictly regulated by the San Francisco planning code*. Retrieved from http://www.reubenlaw.com/index.php/rj/singleUpdate/new_rules_on_residential_demolitions_and_merger

Silverman, R. E. (2012, February 4). Where's the boss? Trapped in a meeting. *The Wall Street Journal*.

Sim, M. (2007). *Remastering morals with Aristotle and Confucius*. Cambridge, England: Cambridge University Press.

Simola, S. (2003). Ethics of justice and care in corporate crisis management. *Journal of Business Ethics, 46*, 351–361.

Simola, S. (2005). Concepts of care in organizational crisis prevention. *Journal of Business Ethics, 62*, 341–353.

Simola, S. (2010). Anti-corporate anger as a form of care-based moral agency. *Journal of Business Ethics, 94*, 255–269.

Simons, T. L. (2002). Behavioral integrity: The perceived alignment between managers' words and deeds as a research focus. *Organization Science, 13*, 18–35.

Simonson, I., & Staw, B. M. (1992). De-escalation strategies: A comparison of techniques for reducing commitment to losing courses of action. *Journal of Applied Psychology, 77*, 419–426.

Sims, R. L., & Keon, T. L. (1997). Ethical work climate as a factor in the development of person–organization fit. *Journal of Business Ethics, 16*, 1095–1105.

Sims, R. R. (2003). *Ethics and corporate social responsibility: Why giants fall*. Westport, CT: Praeger.

Singer, P. (1972). Famine, affluence, and morality. *Philosophy and Public Affairs, 1*, 229–243.

Singer, P. (2009). *The life you can save: Acting now to end world poverty*. New York, NY: Random House.

Single dose Ebola vaccine is safe and effective in monkeys against outbreak strain. (2015, August 6). *NIH News*.

Situation summary. (2015, August 19). *World Health Organization*. Retrieved from http://apps.who.int/gho/data/view.ebola-sitrep.ebola-summary-20150813?lang=en

Sleesman, D. J., Conlon, D. E., McNamara G., & Miles, J. E. (2012). Cleaning up the big muddy: A meta-analytic review of the determinants of escalation of commitment. *Academy of Management Journal, 3*, 541–562.

Smit, A. (2013). Responsible leadership development through management education: A business ethics perspective. *African Journal of Business Ethics, 7*, 45–51.

Smith, A. E., & Jussim, L. (1999). Do self-fulfilling prophecies accumulate, dissipate, or remain stable over time? *Journal of Personality and Social Psychology, 77*, 548–565.

Smith, C. M., & Tindale, R. S. (2009). Direct and indirect minority influence in groups. In R. Martin & M. Hewstone (Eds.), *Minority influence and innovations: Antecedents, processes and consequences* (pp. 263–284). Hoboken, NJ: Psychology Press.

Smith, I. H., Aquino, K., Koleva, S., & Graham, J. (2014). The moral ties that bind . . . even to out-groups: The interactive effect of moral identity and the binding moral foundations. *Psychological Science, 25*, 1554–1562.

Smith, J. Y. (2009, August 12). The Olympian force behind a revolution. *The Washington Post*, p. A07.

Smith, P. K., Jostmann, N. B., Galinsky, A. D., & van Dijk, W. W. (2008). Lacking power impairs executive functions. *Psychological Science, 19*, 441–447.

Smith, T. (1999). Justice as a personal virtue. *Social Theory & Practice, 25*, 361–384.

Smith, W. (2007). Cosmopolitan citizenship: Virtue, irony and worldliness. *European Journal of Social Theory, 10*, 37–52.

Smithson, J., & Venette, S. (2013). Stonewalling as an image-defense strategy: A critical examination of BP's response to the Deepwater Horizon explosion. *Communication Studies, 64* (4), 395–410.

Snow, N. E. (1993). Self-forgiveness. *Journal of Value Inquiry, 27*, 75–80.

Snyder, C. R., & Lopez. S. J. (2005). *Handbook of positive psychology.* Oxford, England: Oxford University Press.

Snyder, P., Hall, M., Robertson, J., Jasinski, T., & Miller, J. S. (2006). Ethical rationality: A strategic approach to organizational crisis. *Journal of Business Ethics, 63*, 371–383.

Soble, J. (2015, July 22). Scandal upends Toshiba's lauded reputation. *The New York Times*, p. B3.

Sokoll, S. (2014). Servant leadership and employee commitment to a supervisor. *International Journal of Leadership Studies, 8*, 88–104.

Solomon, C. M. (2001). Put your ethics to a global test. In M. H. Albrecht (Ed.), *International HRM: Managing diversity in the workplace* (pp. 329–335). Oxford, England: Blackwell.

Solomon, R. C. (1990). *A passion for justice: Emotions and the origins of the social contract.* Reading, MA: Addison-Wesley.

Solomon, R. C. (1992). *Ethics and excellence: Cooperation and integrity in business.* New York, NY: Oxford University Press.

Sosik, J. J. (2006*). Leading with character: Stories of valor and virtue and the principles they teach.* Greenwich, CT: Information Age.

Spangle, M. L., & Isenhart, M. W. (2003). *Negotiation: Communication for diverse settings.* Thousand Oaks, CA: SAGE, p. 15.

Spangler, T. (2016, February 5). Second U.S. House panel to hold hearing on Flint water. *Detroit Free Press.*

Spears, L. C. (1998). Introduction: Tracing the growing impact of servant-leadership. In L. C. Spears (Ed.), *Insights on leadership* (pp. 1–12). New York, NY: John Wiley.

Spears, L. C. (2004). The understanding and practice of servant leadership. In L. C. Spears & M. Lawrence (Eds.), *Practicing servant leadership: Succeeding through trust, bravery, and forgiveness* (pp. 9–24). San Francisco, CA: Jossey-Bass.

Spencer-Hartle, B. (2015, October 7). The state of demolitions in Portland. *Restore Oregon.*

Squires, N. (2012, July 11). Costa Concordia captain: "I ***** up." *The Telegraph.*

Srivastva, S. (Ed.). (1988). *Executive integrity.* San Francisco, CA: Jossey-Bass.

Stanley, D. J., Meyer, J. P., & Topolnytsky, L. (2005). Employee cynicism and resistance to organizational change. *Journal of Business and Psychology, 19*, 429–459.

Stansbury, J. (2009). Reasoned moral agreement: Applying discourse ethics within organizations. *Business Ethics Quarterly, 19,* 33–56

Starmann, R. G. (1993). Tragedy at McDonald's. In J. A. Gottschalk (Ed.), *Crisis response: Inside stories on managing image under siege* (pp. 309–322). Detroit, MI: Gale Group.

Staw, B. M. (1981). The escalation of commitment to a course of action. *Academy of Management Review, 6,* 577–587.

Stein, Y., & Richter, E. D. (2010, Fall). Suspected mass killings—call them democide, politicide, or maybe genocide in North Korea. *Genocide Prevention Now*, no. 4. Retrieved from http://www .genocidepreventionnow.org

Sternberg, R. J. (2002). Smart people are not stupid, but they sure can be foolish. In R. J. Sternberg (Ed.), *Why smart people can be so stupid* (pp. 232–242). New Haven, CT: Yale University Press.

Stogdill, R. M., & Coons, A. E. (1957). *Leader behavior: Its description and measurement.* Columbus: Ohio State University, Bureau of Business Research.

Stone, B. (2013). *The everything store: Jeff Bezos and the age of Amazon.* New York, NY: Little, Brown,

Stott, B. R. (2001, January–February). The great divide in the global village. *Foreign Affairs,* 160–177.

Street, M. D. (1997). Groupthink: An examination of theoretical issues, implications, and future research suggestions. *Small Group Research, 28,* 72–93.

Streitfeld, D. (2011, September 19). Inside Amazon's very hot warehouse. *The New York Times Blogs.*

Subway planned to rebrand Jared Fogle as family man before FBI raid. (2015, July 9). *Thespec.com*

Sucher, S. J. (2008). *The moral leader: Challenges, tools, and insights.* London, England: Routledge.

Sun, W., Xu, A., & Shang, Y. (2014). Transformational leadership, team climate, and team performance within the NPD team: Evidence from China. *Asia Pacific Journal of Management, 31,* 127–147.

Tabuchi, H. (2011, April 11). Less pay, fewer benefits, more radiation; disaster in Japan. *The International Herald Tribune,* p. 6.

Talbot, M. (1999). Against relativism. In J. M. Halstead & T. H. McLaughlin (Eds.), *Education in morality* (pp. 206–217). London, England: Routledge.

Tangney, J. P. (2000). Humility: Theoretical perspectives, empirical findings and directions for future research. *Journal of Social and Clinical Psychology, 19,* 70–82.

Taras, V., Kirkman, B. L., & Steel, P. (2010). Examining the impact of *Culture's consequences*: A three-decade, multilevel, meta-analytic review of Hofstede's cultural value dimensions. *Journal of Applied Psychology, 95,* 405–439.

Tavis, T. (2000). The globalization phenomenon and multinational corporate developmental responsibility. In O. F. Williams (Ed.), *Global codes of conduct: An*

idea *whose time has come* (pp. 13–36). Notre Dame, IN: University of Notre Dame Press.

Taylor, J. (2008, August 5). What makes K2 the most perilous challenge a mountaineer can face? *The Independent,* Comment, p. 30.

Taylor, S. G., & Pattie, M. W. (2014). When does ethical leadership affect workplace incivility? The moderating role of follower personality. *Business Ethics Quarterly, 24,* 595–616.

Taylor S. S., & Elmes, M. B. (2011). Aesthetics and ethics: You can't have one without the other. *Tamara: Journal for Critical Organization Inquiry, 9,* 61–62.

Tenbrunsel, A. E., Diekman, K. A., Wade-Benzoni, K. A., & Bazerman, M. H. (2009). The ethical mirage: A temporal explanation as to why we aren't as ethical as we think we are. Harvard Business School Working Paper No. 08-012.

Tenbrunsel, A. E., & Messick, D. M. (2004). Ethical fading: The role of self-deception in unethical behavior. *Social Justice Research, 17,* 223–236.

Tepper, B. J. (2000). Consequences of abusive supervision. *Academy of Management Journal, 43,* 178–190.

Tepper, B. J. (2007). Abusive supervision in work organizations: Review, synthesis, and research agenda. *Journal of Management, 33,* 261–289.

Terez, T. (2001, December). You could just spit: Tales of bad bosses. *Workforce,* 24–25.

Tessman, L. (2014). Virtue ethics and moral failure: Lessons from neuroscientific moral psychology. In. M. W. Austin (Ed.), *Virtues in action: New essays in applied virtue ethics* (pp. 171–189). New York, NY: Palgrave Macmillan.

Thoma, S. J. (2006). Research on the Defining Issues Test. In M. Killen & J. G. Smetana (Eds.), *Handbook of moral development* (pp. 67–91). Mahwah, NJ: Erlbaum.

Thomas, G. (2000, January 10). The forgiveness factor. *Christianity Today*, 38–43.

Thomas, R. J. (2008). *Crucibles of leadership: How to learn from experience to become a great leader.* Boston, MA: Harvard Business Press.

Thoresen, C. E., Harris, H. S., & Luskin, F. (2000). Forgiveness and health: An unanswered question. In M. E. McCullough, K. I. Pargament, & C. E. Thoresen (Eds.), *Forgiveness: Theory, research, and practice* (pp. 254–280). New York, NY: Guilford.

Thoroughgood, C. N., & Padilla, A. (2013). Destructive leadership and the Penn State scandal: A toxic triangle perspective. *Industrial and Organizational Psychology, 6,* 144–149.

Thoroughgood, C. N., Padilla, A., Hunter, S. T., & Tate, B. W. (2012). The susceptible circle: A taxonomy of followers associated with destructive leadership. *Leadership Quarterly, 23,* 897–917.

Thoroughgood, C. N., Tate, B. W., Sawyer, K. B., & Jacobs, R. (2012). Bad to the bone: Empirically defining and measuring destructive leader behavior. *Journal of Leadership & Organizational Studies, 19,* 230–255.

Tileaga, C. (2006). Representing the "other": A discursive analysis of prejudice and moral exclusion in talk about Romanies. *Journal of Community & Applied Social Psychology, 16,* 19–41.

Timmons, M. (2002). *Moral theory: An introduction.* Lanham, MD: Rowman & Littlefield.

Tims, D. (2010, February 17). Bob gives Red Mill to workers. *The Oregonian*, pp. A1, A5.

Tindall, K. (2014). *Uncontainable: How passion, commitment and conscious capitalism built a business where everyone thrives.* New York, NY: Grand Central.

Tirrell, M. (2015, November 4). Turing CEO: Senate drug probe is "mountain out of molehill." *CNBC.*

Tivnan, E. (1995). *The moral imagination.* New York, NY: Routledge, Chapman, and Hall.

Toffler, B. L., & Reingold, J. (2003). *Final accounting: Ambition, greed, and the fall of Arthur Andersen.* New York, NY: Broadway.

Toh, M. (2015, July 21). Ashley Madison: 'Moral' hacking or old-fashioned stealing? *Christian Science Monitor.*

Toor, S. R., & Ofori, G. (2009). Ethical leadership: Examining the relationships with full range leadership model, employee outcomes, and organizational culture. *Journal of Business Ethics, 90,* 533–547.

Toppo, G. (2013, June 11). At-risk cities ramp up disaster-response planning. *USA Today.*

Toulmin, S. (1958/2003). *The uses of argument.* London, England: Cambridge University Press.

Tourish, D. (2008). Challenging the transformational agenda: Leadership theory in transition? *Management Communication Quarterly, 21,* 522–528.

Tourish, D. (2013). *The dark side of transformational leadership: A critical perspective.* New York, NY: Routledge.

Tourish, D., & Pinnington, A. (2002). Transformational leadership, corporate cultism, and the spirituality paradigm: An unholy trinity in the workplace? *Human Relations, 55,* 147–172.

Trevino, L. K., & Brown, M. E. (2005). The role of leaders in influencing unethical behavior in the workplace. In R. E. Kidwell & C. L. Martin (Eds.), *Managing organizational deviance* (pp. 69–87). Thousand Oaks, CA: SAGE.

Trevino, L. K., Brown, M. E., & Pincus, L. (2003). A qualitative investigation of perceived executive ethical leadership: Perceptions from inside and outside the executive suite. *Human Relations, 56,* 5–37.

Trevino, L. K., Butterfield, K. D., & McCabe, D. L. (1998). The ethical context in organizations: Influences on employee attitudes and behaviors. *Business Ethics Quarterly, 8,* 447–476.

Trevino, L. K., Hartman, L. P., & Brown, M. E. (2000). Moral person and moral manager: How executives develop a reputation for ethical leadership. *California Management Review, 42*(4), 128–133.

Trevino, L. K., & Nelson, K. A. (2004). *Managing business ethics: Straight talk about how to do it right* (3rd ed.). Hoboken, NJ: John Wiley.

Trevino, L. K., & Weaver, G. R. (2001). Organizational justice and ethics program "follow-through": Influences on employees' harmful and helpful behavior. *Business Ethics Quarterly, 11,* 651–671.

Trevino, L. K., & Weaver, G. R. (2003). *Managing ethics in business organizations: Social scientific perspectives.* Stanford, CA: Stanford University Press.

Triandis, H. C. (1995). *Individualism and collectivism.* Boulder, CO: Westview Press.

Tronto, J. C. (1993). *Moral boundaries: A political argument for an ethic of care.* New York, NY: Routledge.

Troyer, J. (2003). *The classical utilitarians: Bentham and Mill.* Indianapolis, IN: Hackett.

Turner, N., Barling, J., Epitropaki, O., Butcher, V., & Milner, C. (2002, April). Transformational leadership and moral reasoning. *Journal of Applied Psychology, 87,* 304–311.

Turning a blind eye to North Korea's "hidden gulag." (2012, April 12). *The Washington Post.*

Twenge, J. M., & Campbell, W. K. (2009). *The narcissism epidemic: Living in the age of entitlement.* New York, NY: Free Press

Twenge, J. M., & Foster, J. D. (2010). Birth cohort increase in narcissistic personality traits among American college students, 1982–2009. *Social Psychological and Personality Science, 1*(1), 99–106.

The twilight zone. (2011, November 15). *Economist,* 49–50.

Uhl-Bien, M., & Pillai, R. (2007). The romance of leadership and the social construction of followership. In B. Shamir, R. Pillai, M. C. Bligh, & M. Uhl-Bien (Eds.), *Follower-centered perspectives on leadership* (pp. 187–209). Greenwich CT: Information Age.

Ulmer, R. R., Seeger, M. W., & Sellnow, T. L. (2007). Post-crisis communication and renewal: Expanding the parameters of post-crisis discourse. *Public Relations Review, 33,* 130–134.

Ulmer, R. R., & Sellnow, T. L. (2000). Consistent questions of ambiguity in organizational crisis communication: Jack in the Box as a case study. *Journal of Business Ethics, 25,* 143–155.

Ulmer, R. R., Sellnow, T. L., & Seeger, M. W. (2008). Post-crisis communication and renewal: Understanding the potential for positive outcomes in crisis communication. In R. L. Heath & D. H. O'Hair (Eds.), *Handbook of risk and crisis communication* (pp. 302–322). Hoboken, NJ: Routledge.

Unell, A. E., & Unell, B. (2012). *Starting at the finish line: Coach Al Buehler's timeless wisdom.* New York, NY: Perigree/Penguin.

United Nations. (1948). *The Universal Declaration of Human Rights.* Retrieved from http://www.un.org/en/universal-declaration-human-rights/

Upper 1 percent of Americans are rolling in the dough. (December 12, 2012). *The Oregonian,* p. A2.

Useem, M. (1998). *The leadership moment: Nine stories of triumph and disaster and their lessons for us all.* New York, NY: Times Books.

Vaglanos, A. (2015, February 19). 1 in 3 women has been sexually harassed at work, according to survey. *Huffington Post.*

Valacich, J. S., & Schewenk, C. (1995). Devil's advocacy and dialectical inquiry effects on face-to-face and computer-mediated group decision making. *Organizational Behavior and Human Decision Processes, 63,* 158–173.

Valentine, S., & Barnett, T. (2003). Ethics code awareness, perceived ethical values, and organizational commitment. *Journal of Personal Selling & Sales Management, 23,* 359–367.

Van Hoot, S. (2009). *Cosmopolitanism: A philosophy for global ethics.* Montreal, Quebec, Canada: McGill-Queen's University Press

Van Slyke, J. A. (2014). Moral psychology, neuroscience, and virtue. In K. Timpe & C. A. Boyd (Eds.), *Virtues and their vices* (459–479). Oxford, England: Oxford University Press.

Van Vuuren, L. J., & Crous, F. (2005). Utilising appreciative inquiry (AI) in creating a shared meaning of ethics in organizations. *Journal of Business Ethics, 57,* 399–412.

Varachaver, N. (2004, November 15). Glamour! Fame! Org charts! *Fortune,* 76–85.

Vecchio, R. P. (1982). A further test of leadership effects due to between-group variation and in-group variation. *Journal of Applied Psychology, 67,* 200–208.

Vega, G., & Comer, D. R. (2005). Bullying and harassment in the workplace. In R. E. Kidwell, Jr., & C. L. Martin (Eds.), *Managing organizational deviance* (pp. 183–203). Thousand Oaks, CA: SAGE.

Velasquez, M. G. (1992). *Business ethics: Concepts and cases* (3rd ed.). Englewood Cliffs, NJ: Prentice Hall.

Vetelson, A. J. (2005). *Evil and human agency: Understanding collective evildoing.* Cambridge, England: Cambridge University Press.

Victor, B., & Cullen, J. B. (1988). The organizational bases of ethical work climates. *Administrative Science Quarterly, 33,* 101–125.

Victor, B., & Cullen, J. B. (1990). A theory and measure of ethical climate in organizations. In W. C. Frederic & L. E. Preston (Eds.), *Business ethics: Research issues and empirical studies* (pp. 77–97). Greenwich, CT: JAI Press.

Victor, D. (2014, August 19). The Ashley Madison data dump, explained. *The New York Times,* Technology.

Viesturs, E., & Roberts, D. (2009). *K2: Life and death on the world's most dangerous mountain.* New York, NY: Broadway.

Viswesvaran, C., & Ones, D. S. (2002). Examining the construct of organizational justice: A meta-analytic evaluation of relations with work attitudes and behaviors. *Journal of Business Ethics, 38,* 193–203.

Vitell, S. J., Nwachukwu, S. L., & Barnes, J. H. (1993). The effects of culture on ethical decision-making: An application of Hofstede's typology. *Journal of Business Ethics, 12,* 753–760.

Voegtlin, C., Patzer, M., & Scherer, A. G. (2012). Responsible leadership in global business: A new approach to leadership and its multi-level outcomes. *Journal of Business Ethics, 105,* 1–16.

Von Drehle, D. (2014, December 22). The ones who answered the call. *Time,* 74.

Vozza, S. (2014, February 25). Personal mission statement of 5 famous CEOS (and why you should write one too). *Fast Company.* Retrieved from http:// www.fastcompany.com

Waddock, S. (2014). Wisdom and responsible leadership: Aesthetic sensibility, moral imagination, and systems thinking. In D. Koehn & D. Elm (Eds.), *Aesthetics and business ethics* (pp. 129–147). New York, NY: Springer.

Wagner, D. (2014, June 9). VA scandal audit: 120,000 veterans experience long waits for care. *The Arizona Republic.*

Wahba, P. (2016, May 9). Why Container Store's founder is quitting CEO job. *Fortune.com.*

Waldman, D. A. (2011). Moving forward with the concept of responsible leadership: Three caveats to guide theory and research. *Journal of Business Ethics, 98,* 75–83.

Waldman, D. A., & Balven, R. M. (2015). Responsible leadership: Theoretical issues and research directions. *The Academy of Management Perspectives, 1,* 19–29.

Waldman, D. A., Bass, B. M., & Yammarino, F. J. (1990). Adding to contingent-reward behavior: The augmenting effect of charismatic leadership. *Group and Organizational Studies, 15,* 381–394.

Wallace, T. (2015, November 19). Up to 10 former HBOS executives could be banned over collapse, damning report finds. *The Telegraph.*

Waller, J. (2007). *Becoming evil: How ordinary people commit genocide and mass killing* (2nd ed.). Oxford, England: Oxford University Press.

Waltman, M. A., Russell, D. C., Coyle, C. T., Enright, R. D., Holter, A. C., & Swoboda, C. M. (2009). The effects of a forgiveness intervention on patients with coronary artery disease. *Psychology and Health, 24*(1), 11–27.

Walumbwa, F. O., Avolio, B. J., Gardner, W. L., Wernsing, T. S., & Peterson, S. J. (2008). Authentic leadership: Development and validation of a theory-based measure. *Journal of Management, 34,* 89–126.

Walumbwa, F. O., Hartnell, C. A., & Oke, A. (2010). Servant leadership, procedural justice climate, service climate, employee attitudes, and organizational citizenship behavior: A cross-level investigation. *Journal of Applied Psychology, 95,* 517–529.

Wang, H., Sui, Y., Luthans, F., Wang, D., & Wu, Y. (2014). Impact of authentic leadership on performance: Role of followers' positive psychological capital and relational processes. *Journal of Organizational Behavior, 35,* 5–12.

Wang, Y-D., & Hseih, J-H. (2012). Toward a better understanding of the link between ethical climate and job satisfaction: A multilevel analysis. *Journal of Business Ethics, 15,* 535–545.

Waples, E. P., Antes, A., Murphy, S. T., Connelly, S., & Mumford, M. D. (2009). A meta-analytic investigation of business ethics instruction. *Journal of Business Ethics, 87,* 133–151.

Warnke, G. (1993). *Justice and interpretation.* Cambridge, England: MIT Press.

Washington, R. R., Sutton, C. D., & Feild, H. S. (2006). Individual differences in servant leadership: The roles of values and personality. *Leadership & Organization Development Journal, 27,* 700–716.

Watts, J. (2014, January 13). Eleven cities to receive funds to increase resiliency. *Bond Buyer, 123,* 34–42.

Wayne, L. (2005, March 8). Boeing chief is ousted after admitting affair. *The New York Times,* p. A1.

Weaver, G. R. (2006). Virtue in organizations: Moral identity as a foundation for moral agency. *Organization Studies, 27,* 341–368.

Weaver, G. R., Trevino, L. K., & Cochran, P. L. (1999). Integrated and decoupled corporate social performance: Management commitments, external pressures, and corporate ethics practices. *Academy of Management Journal, 42,* 539–552.

Weber, E. T. (2011). What experimentalism means in ethics. *Journal of Speculative Philosophy, 25*(1), 98–115.

Weber, J., & Wasieleski, D. M. (2013). Corporate ethics and compliance programs: A report, analysis and critiques. *Journal of Business Ethics, 112,* 609–626.

Weber, J. A. (2007). Business ethics training: Insights from learning theory. *Journal of Business Ethics, 70,* 61–85.

Webley, K. (2013, January 21). The baby deficit. *Time,* 30–39.

Weick, K. E., & Roberts, K. H. (2006). Collective minds in organizations: Heedful interrelating on flight decks. In D. Smith & D. Elliott (Eds.), *Key readings in crisis management: Systems and structures for prevention and recovery* (pp. 343–368). London, England: Routledge.

Weick, K. E., & Sutcliffe, K. M. (2001). *Managing the unexpected: Assuring high performance in an age of complexity.* San Francisco, CA: Jossey-Bass.

Weinstein, S. (2015, August 26). Jared Fogle's childhood obesity charity is a sham. *TVGuide.com.*

Werhane, P. H. (1999). *Moral imagination and management decision-making.* New York, NY: Oxford University Press.

West, H. R. (2004). *An introduction to Mill's utilitarian ethics.* Cambridge, England: Cambridge University Press.

West, M. A. (2012). *Effective teamwork: Practical lessons from organizational research.* Hoboken, NJ: Wiley.

What we stand for. (2016). *The Container Store.* Retrieved from http://sstandfor.continerstore.com

Wheeler, D., Colbert, B., & Freeman, R. E. (2003). Focusing on values: Reconciling corporate social responsibility, sustainability, and a stakeholder approach in a network world. *Journal of General Management, 28,* 1–28.

Wheeler, M. (2004, March). Fair enough: An ethical fitness test quiz for negotiators. *Negotiation,* 3–5.

White, B. J., & Prywes, Y. (2007). *The nature of leadership: Reptiles, mammals, and the challenge of becoming a great leader.* New York, NY: AMACOM.

White, S. S., & Locke, E. A. (2000). Problems with the Pygmalion effect and some proposed solutions. *Leadership Quarterly, 11,* 389–415.

Whitney, D., & Trosten-Bloom, A. (2003). *The power of appreciative inquiry: A practical guide to positive change.* San Francisco, CA: Berrett-Koehler.

Whoriskey, P. (2010, March 19). Toyota resisted government safety findings; automaker followed "game plan," escaped a broad early recall. *The Washington Post,* p. A01.

Why your negotiating behavior may be ethically challenged—and how to fix it. (2008, April). *Negotiation, 11*(4), 1–5.

Will a humbled VW now adopt a leadership model of humility? (2015, October 1). *The Christian Science Monitor,* Commentary.

Williams, A. (2015, August 29). Trust me, I'm skinny. *National Post,* p. WP2.

Williams, G., & Zinkin, J. (2008). The effect of culture on consumers' willingness to punish irresponsible corporate behaviour: Applying Hofstede's typology to the punishment aspect of corporate social responsibility. *Business Ethics: A European Review, 17,* 210–226.

Williams, K. D., Harkins, S. G., & Karau, S. J. (2003). Social performance. In M. A. Hogg & J. Cooper (Eds.), *The SAGE handbook of social psychology* (pp. 327–346). London, England: SAGE.

Williams, M. E. (2015, October 20). Don't feed the Shkreli. *Salon .com.*

Wilmers, R. G. (2009, July 27). Where the crisis came from. *The Washington Post,* p. A19.

Wilmot, W. W., & Hocker, J. L. (2001). *Interpersonal conflict* (6th ed.). New York, NY: McGraw-Hill Higher Education.

Wilson, D. (2009, March 4). Senator asks Pfizer to detail pay to Harvard. *The New York Times,* p. B3.

Wilson, D. S. (2015). *Does altruism exist? Culture, genes, and the welfare of others.* New Haven, CT: Yale University Press.

Wilson, S. R. (2002). *Seeking and resisting compliance: Why people say what they do when trying to influence others.* Thousand Oaks, CA: SAGE.

Witt, J. L., & Morgan, J. (2002). *Stronger in the broken places: Nine lessons for turning crisis into triumph.* New York, NY: Times Books/ Henry Holt.

Wolff, L. (2012, October 17). Free to be a sexual predator? *The New York Times,* Op-Ed.

Wolvin, A. D., & Coakley, G. C. (1993). A listening taxonomy. In

A. D. Wolvin & C. G. Coakley (Eds.), *Perspectives in listening* (pp. 15–22). Norwood, NJ: Ablex.

Woods, J. (2015, July 30). Cecil the lion—has the reaction tipped dangerously into overreaction? *The Telegraph.*

Woodzicka, J. A., & LaFrance, M. (2001). Real versus imagined gender harassment. *Journal of Social Issues, 57*(1), 15–30.

Wooten, L. P., & James, E. H. (2008). Linking crisis management and leadership competencies: The role of human resource development. *Advances in Developing Human Resources, 10,* 352–379.

Worthington, E. L. Lavelonk, C., Van Tongeren, D. R., Jennings, D. J., Gartener, H. A. L., Davis, D. E., & Hook, J. N. (2014). Virtue in positive psychology. In K. Timpe & C. A. Boyd (Eds.), *Virtues & their vices* (pp. 433–458). Oxford, England: Oxford University Press.

Worthington, E. L., Jr. (2005). Initial questions about the art and science of forgiving. In E. L. Worthington (Ed.), *Handbook of forgiveness* (pp. 1–13). New York, NY: Routledge.

Wright, D. K. (1993). Enforcement dilemma: Voluntary nature of public relations codes. *Public Relations Review, 19,* 13–20.

Wright, M. (2011, November 7). Success means telling people to buy less. *The Guardian.*

Wu, L-Z., Kwan, H. K., Hong-kit, F., Chiu, R. K., & He, X. (2014). CEO ethical leadership and corporate social responsibility:

A moderated mediation model. *Journal of Business Ethics, 130,* 819–831.

Wyatt, E. (2012, March 20). Behind the blood money. *The New York Times,* p. B1.

Xi, Y. (2015, February 5). Union official links Foxconn deaths to excessive overtime. *LaborNotes.*

Xian, Z. (2015, February 3). Foxconn's long hours causing workers' deaths: Union. *ChinaDaily. com.cn.*

Yidong, T., & Xinxin, L. (2013). How ethical leadership influences employees' innovative work behavior: A perspective of intrinsic motivation. *Journal of Business Ethics, 116,* 441–455.

Yokota, T., & Yamada, T. (2012, March 12). Disposable heroes. *Newsweek* (International ed.).

Young, N. (2011, February 16). Apple's new chief visits Chinese factory to hang nets after workplace suicides. *DailyMail.com.*

Yousafzai, M., & Lamb, C. (2013). *I am Malala: The girl who stood up for education and was shot by the Taliban.* New York, NY: Back Bay Books.

Yukl, G. (2013). *Leadership in organizations* (8th ed.). Upper Saddle River, NJ: Prentice-Hall.

Yukl, G., Falbe, C. M., & Yount, J. (1993). Patterns of influence behaviors for managers. *Group and Organization Management, 18,* 5–28.

Yunus, M. (1998, October 31). Banker to the poor. *The Guardian.*

Yurtsever, G. (2006). Measuring moral imagination. *Social Behavior and Personality, 34,* 205–220.

Zack, N. (2009). *Ethics for disaster.* Lanham, MD: Rowman & Littlefield.

Zadek, S. (2004, December). The path to corporate responsibility. *Harvard Business Review,* 125–132.

Zhu, W., May, D. R., & Avolio, B. J. (2004). The impact of ethical leadership behavior on employee outcomes: The roles of psychological empowerment and authenticity. *Journal of Leadership & Organizational Studies, 11*(1), 16–26.

Zimbardo, P. G. (2005). A situationist perspective on the psychology of evil. In A. G. Miller (Ed.), *The social psychology of good and evil* (pp. 21–50). New York, NY: Guilford.

Zimbardo, P. G. (2007). *The Lucifer effect: Understanding how good people turn evil.* New York, NY: Random House.

Zinnbauer, B. J., & Pargament, K. I. (2005). Religiousness and spirituality. In R. F. Paloutzian & C. L. Park (Eds.), *Handbook of the psychology of religion and spirituality* (pp. 21–42). New York, NY: Guilford.

Zuckerman, P., & Padoan, A. (2012). *Buried in the sky: The extraordinary story of the Sherpa climbers on K2's deadliest day.* New York, NY: Norton.

Zyglidopoulos, S. C. (2002). The social and environmental responsibilities of multinationals: Evidence from the Brent Spar case. *Journal of Business Ethics, 36,* 141–151.

INDEX

ABOUT THE AUTHOR

Craig E. Johnson (PhD, University of Denver) is emeritus professor of leadership studies at George Fox University, Newberg, Oregon, where he taught undergraduate and graduate courses in leadership, ethics, management, and communication. During his time at the university, he served as director of the George Fox Doctor of Business Administration program and chair of the Department of Communication Arts. Though retired from full-time teaching, Johnson continues to serve as an adjunct professor. He is the author of *Organizational Ethics: A Practical Approach* (also published by SAGE) and coauthor, with Michael Z. Hackman, of *Leadership: A Communication Perspective.* His research findings, instructional ideas, and book reviews have been published in the *Journal of Leadership Studies,* the *Journal of Leadership and Organizational Studies,* the *Journal of Leadership Education, Academy of Management Learning and Education,* the *International Leadership Journal, Communication Quarterly, Communication Reports,* and other journals. In 2016, he received the George Fox University outstanding graduate faculty researcher award. Johnson has led and participated in service and educational trips to Honduras, Kenya, Rwanda, New Zealand, China, and Brazil and has held volunteer leadership positions in a variety of religious and nonprofit organizations. In addition to teaching and writing, he enjoys working out, reading, fly-fishing, watching sports, and spending time with family.